FIFTH EDITION

SOCIAL WELFARE

in Canadian Society

Rosalie Chappell, B.S.W., M.S.W.

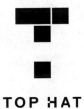

TOP HAT   NELSON

TOP HAT

Social Welfare in Canadian Society, Fifth Edition

by Rosalie Chappell

Vice President, Editorial Higher Education:
Anne Williams

Executive Editor:
Anne-Marie Taylor

Marketing Manager:
Ann Byford

Developmental Editor:
Liisa Kelly

Photo Researcher and Permissions Coordinator:
Carrie McGregor

Senior Content Production Manager:
Natalia Denesiuk Harris

Production Service:
Cenveo Publisher Services

Copy Editor:
Dawn Hunter

Proofreader:
Kavitha Ashok

Indexer:
BIM Publishing Services

Design Director:
Ken Phipps

Managing Designer:
Franca Amore

Interior Design:
Joanne Slouenwhite with modifications by Trinh Truong

Part Opener Image:
© ThomasVogel/iStockphoto

Cover Design:
Trinh Truong

Cover Image:
© ThomasVogel/iStockphoto

Compositor:
Cenveo Publisher Services

Library and Archives Canada Cataloguing in Publication Data

Chappell, Rosalie, 1955–, author

Social welfare in Canadian society / Rosalie Chappell. — Fifth edition.

Includes bibliographical references and index.
ISBN 978-0-17-651543-0 (pbk.)

1. Social service—Canada.
2. Public welfare—Canada.
3. Canada—Social conditions.
I. Title.

HV105.C48 2013   361.971
C2013-902785-8

ISBN-13: 978-0-17-651543-0
ISBN-10: 0-17-651543-7

To the memory of Jack Layton (1950–2011), federal leader of the New Democratic Party and a champion of social welfare for all Canadians.

BRIEF TABLE OF CONTENTS

TABLE OF CONTENTS

PREFACE

The structure of Canada's social welfare system continues to shift. Determined to "provincialize" social welfare, the federal government has relinquished many social welfare programs and services. Any plans to create national strategies related to child care, home support, poverty, or homelessness have been put to rest. The Social Union Framework Agreement—with its emphasis on federal and regional collaboration in social welfare development—is virtually dead. Even federal funding for social welfare initiatives is at issue: in their quest for more "innovative" ways of funding social welfare programs, the federal government is calling upon business to finance programs that offer a social benefit.

As the federal and regional governments clarify their roles in social welfare provision, many Canadians face ongoing challenges. The number of homeless and food-insecure Canadians continues to rise. Unemployed adults have fewer options and resources, and more working Canadians find themselves stuck in poor paying, insecure jobs with few or no benefits. Reports confirm that income inequality is on the rise while the standard of living is declining. As always, social agencies are struggling to meet the growing demand for social services.

But there is also good news. For example, most provinces and territories have developed comprehensive poverty-reduction plans, and Canada's ratification of the UN's Convention on the Rights of Persons with Disabilities ensures the full inclusion of Canadians with disabilities. The body of knowledge on social welfare issues and best practices keeps growing, while the launch of large-scale longitudinal studies promises new insights into the needs of specific populations. This fifth edition of *Social Welfare in Canadian Society* takes a critical look at these and other developments and their influence on the social well-being of Canadians.

TEXT OBJECTIVES

Specifically, this fifth edition aims to

- introduce the basic concepts and processes related to social welfare
- strike a balance between historical and current content
- explore a wide range of Canadian social welfare policies and programs
- provide real-life examples of social welfare initiatives from across the country
- consider the impact of social welfare restructuring on Canadians

- emphasize the uniquely Canadian approach to social provision and draw from Canadian research
- critically analyze social welfare issues, approaches, and initiatives
- discuss the role of social workers in the social welfare field

This fifth edition aims to meet these objectives and, in so doing, give students grounding in Canadian social welfare and an appreciation of the strengths and shortcomings of Canada's approach to social well-being.

ORGANIZATION

This edition retains the basic three-part structure of previous editions. Part 1 introduces readers to some of the fundamental aspects of Canada's social welfare system, including the nature of its programs and services and the social policy development process. Chapters in this section also focus on the ideological base and historical foundations of the social welfare system, and political and economic trends that affect social provision.

Part 2 is devoted to social welfare's service delivery system. Here, readers learn about the various service sectors and the principal activities of social agencies. This section also looks at the range of service providers in social welfare settings and the knowledge and skills they bring to the helping process. Concluding Part 2 is a chapter on planned change at the micro, mezzo, and macro levels of society.

Part 3 examines the social issues and achievements of selected populations: people living in poverty, families with children, seniors, Aboriginal peoples, recent immigrants, and people with disabilities. This section explores the social welfare programs and social work approaches related to each population.

Readers will be interested in the themes that weave through this new edition and reflect the major trends in Canada's social welfare system. For example, this edition emphasizes the role of empirical research and best practices in the development of social welfare theory and initiatives. A main theme is the influence of neoliberalism, globalization, and the business model on social welfare provision. This edition also sharpens its focus on issues related to poverty, income inequality, an aging population, and Aboriginal peoples in Canada. In terms of social work practice, more attention is given to anti-oppressive approaches.

Chapters that have undergone significant revisions include Chapter 4, which examines the effects of conservatism on social welfare policy and programs. A new Chapter 9 provides current material on poverty and its consequences, and on poverty-reduction strategies in Canada. Additional content in Appendix A expands the chronology of key events in Canadian history and in the evolution of social welfare initiatives. Appendix B aims to enhance readers' understanding of the impact of globalization on social welfare in Canada. Finally, this new edition updates social statistics and includes new content on social welfare policies, initiatives, and related issues.

PEDAGOGICAL FEATURES

Reviews of *Social Welfare in Canadian Society* suggest that certain features of previous editions enhance the reader's comprehension and enjoyment of the book. These tried-and-true features include

- chapter-opening quotes, which set the tone for the content and inspire reader interest and engagement
- a list of learning objectives at the beginning of each chapter to set the direction of the content
- boldfaced key terms in the text and at the end of each chapter, with their page references
- a variety of exhibits that expand on certain points and pull together complex concepts
- photographs to enhance visual appeal and bring the content alive
- discussion questions in each chapter to draw readers' attention to specific content and issues, to encourage critical thinking, and to provoke lively in-class discussions
- profiles and examples of Canadian social welfare programs, services, and organizations
- examples of social work practice in social welfare settings
- chapter summaries
- a glossary of key terms to familiarize readers with words and phrases specific to the social welfare field
- a thorough index to help the reader find information quickly and easily

Unique to this book is access to the *Social Welfare in Canadian Society* website at **retail.tophat.com**. At that website, students will find links to the most current information on issues related to social welfare.

ANCILLARY MATERIALS

About the Nelson Education Teaching Advantage

The **Nelson Education Teaching Advantage (NETA)** program delivers research-based instructor resources that promote student engagement and higher-order thinking to enable the success of Canadian students and educators.

Instructors today face many challenges. Resources are limited, time is scarce, and a new kind of student has emerged: one who is juggling school with work, has gaps in his or her basic knowledge, and is immersed in technology in a way that has led to a completely new style of learning. In response, Nelson Education has gathered a group of dedicated instructors to advise us on the creation of richer and more flexible ancillaries and online learning platforms that respond to the needs of today's teaching environments. Whether your course is offered in-class, online, or both, Nelson is pleased to provide pedagogically driven, research-based resources to support you.

In consultation with the editorial advisory board, Nelson Education has completely rethought the structure, approaches, and formats of our key textbook ancillaries and online learning platforms. We've also increased our investment in editorial support for our ancillary and digital authors. The result is the Nelson Education Teaching Advantage and its key components: *NETA Assessment*, *NETA Presentation*, and *NETA Digital*. Each component includes one or more ancillaries prepared according to our best practices and may also be accompanied by documentation explaining the theory behind the practices.

NETA Assessment relates to testing materials. Under *NETA Assessment*, Nelson's authors create multiple-choice questions that reflect research-based best practices for constructing effective questions and testing not just recall but also higher-order thinking. Our guidelines were developed by David DiBattista, a 3M National Teaching Fellow whose recent research as a professor of psychology at Brock University has focused on multiple-choice testing. All Test Bank authors receive training at workshops conducted by Prof. DiBattista, as do the copyeditors assigned to each Test Bank. A copy of *Multiple Choice Tests: Getting Beyond Remembering*, Prof. DiBattista's guide to writing effective tests, is included with every Nelson Test Bank/Computerized Test Bank package. (Information about the NETA Test Bank prepared for *Social Welfare in Canadian Society*, Fifth Edition, is included in the description of the online resources below.)

NETA Presentation has been developed to help instructors make the best use of PowerPoint® in their classrooms. With a clean and uncluttered design developed by Maureen Stone of StoneSoup Consulting, *NETA Presentation* features slides with improved readability, more multi-media and graphic materials, activities to use in class, and tips for instructors on the Notes page. A copy of *NETA Guidelines for Classroom Presentations* by Maureen Stone is included with each set of PowerPoint slides. (Information about the NETA PowerPoint® prepared for *Social Welfare in Canadian Society,* Fifth Edition, is included in the description of the online resources below.)

NETA Digital is a framework based on Arthur Chickering and Zelda Gamson's seminal work "Seven Principles of Good Practice in Undergraduate Education" (*AAHE Bulletin*, 1987) and the follow-up work by Chickering and Stephen C. Ehrmann, "Implementing the Seven Principles: Technology as Lever" (*AAHE Bulletin*, 1996). This aspect of the NETA program guides the writing and development of our digital products to ensure that they appropriately reflect the core goals of contact, collaboration, multimodal learning, time on task, prompt feedback, active learning, and high expectations. The resulting focus on pedagogical utility, rather than technological wizardry, ensures that all of our technology supports better outcomes for students.

Online Instructor Resources

Key instructor ancillaries are provided at **retail.tophat.com** , giving instructors the ultimate tools for customizing lectures and presentations.

- **NETA Assessment**: The Test Bank for *Social Welfare in Canadian Society*, Fifth Edition, includes multiple-choice questions written according to NETA guidelines for effective construction and development of higher-order questions. Also included is a selection of true/false and essay questions for each chapter. Test Bank files are provided in Word format for easy editing and in PDF format for convenient printing whatever your system.

- **NETA Presentation:** Microsoft® PowerPoint® lecture slides have been created for every chapter of *Social Welfare in Canadian Society*, Fifth Edition. NETA principles of clear design and engaging content have been incorporated throughout.

- **DayOne:** *DayOne—Prof InClass* is a PowerPoint presentation that you can customize to orient your students to the class and their text at the beginning of the course.

- **Instructor's Manual:** The instructor's manual to accompany *Social Welfare in Canadian Society*, Fifth Edition, contains sample lesson plans, learning objectives, and suggested classroom activities to give you the support you need to engage your students in the classroom.

ACKNOWLEDGMENTS

No one ever creates a book alone. Many thanks go to those who have supported me through the review, research, and development of this project. Sincere appreciation to

- Paul Wallin, for the many hours at the computer, researching, and giving feedback on my chapter drafts

- Margaret Leitner, for her insights into the workings of voluntary social agencies

- the many individuals who responded to my research questions, including Kevin Wilheim (Edleun Group Inc.), staff at the Canadian Association of the Deaf, Rosemary Spendlove and Leilani Farha (Canada Without Poverty), and staff at the Vancouver Island Regional Library

- the review panel participants for providing me with excellent suggestions on how to improve the fifth edition: Brian Dwyer, Sheridan College; Carol Halle-Bowering, Okanagan College; Mohamad Haniff, University of Guelph; Donna Hinds, Centennial College; and Luc Theriault, University of New Brunswick

- the reviewers of the previous editions for their feedback and direction. Reviewers of the fourth edition include Dan Andreae, University of Waterloo; Mike Devine, Memorial University; Mary Lou Karley, King's College University; Eleanor Wint, University of Northern B.C.; and Gail Zuk, University of Calgary. Reviewers of the third edition include Ken Barter, Memorial University of Newfoundland; Les Jerome, University of Calgary; Neil McMahon, Mohawk College; and Margaret Wright, University of British Columbia. Reviewers of the second edition include Brian Dwyer, Sheridan College; Luke Fusco, Wilfrid Laurier University; and Paul MacIsaac, Georgian College. Reviewers of the first edition include Mac Davis, Humber College; Phil Durrant, Niagara College; Arvey Hanowski, University of Regina; Cheryl Hebert, Memorial University; Emmett Hogan, Mount Royal College; and Rory Mahood, Cariboo College.

In 2013, I celebrated the twentieth anniversary of my working relationship with Nelson Education and the best publishing team in Canada! Thanks to sales representative Anthony Fast for making sure my original book proposal got into the right hands in 1993. Many sincere thanks go to the acquisitions editors, developmental editors, copy editors, production and permissions teams, marketing department, sales representatives, and others at Nelson who have supported this project and me over the years.

I hope that the revisions to this text meet the needs and expectations of students and instructors, and that these changes enhance the reader's understanding and appreciation of Canada's social welfare system.

—Rosalie Chappell

ABOUT THE AUTHOR

Rosalie Chappell received her Bachelor of Social Work and Master of Social Work degrees from the University of Calgary. She has taught social work and social service work in British Columbia and Alberta at the University-College of the Fraser Valley, Open Learning Agency, Malaspina University-College, North Island College, and Red Deer College. Besides teaching, Rosalie has worked as a clinical social worker, supervisor, trainer, consultant, and program evaluator in a diverse range of public- and private-sector organizations, including family counselling agencies, employment agencies, community corrections, alcohol and drug treatment centres, and extended care.

SOCIAL WELFARE IN CANADA

An Overview

1

The Nature of Canadian Social Welfare

OBJECTIVES

The social welfare of Canadians depends on the extent to which human needs are met. This chapter will

- define the term *social welfare*
- describe the scope and purpose of the social welfare system
- discuss social welfare programs and services
- examine three political ideologies and their influences on social welfare provision

INTRODUCTION

Undeniably, the "social safety net" we built over the past several decades helped make Canada one of the world's most successful countries, rich in prosperity and opportunity. Programs such as unemployment insurance, social assistance and social services, child benefits, universal pensions and a national network of widely accessible colleges and universities have made our nation a beacon of civilized values. (Human Resources Development Canada [HRDC], 1994a)

Social welfare is the cornerstone of a caring, benevolent, and democratic society. Moreover, social welfare is key to a nation's general quality of life and prosperity. Underlying social welfare are core Canadian values, such as compassion and collective responsibility, and a fundamental belief in the social equality of all people.

Despite its importance, social welfare is a highly abstract term with no single, exhaustive, or universally agreed on definition. The term gained popularity in Canada during the late nineteenth and early twentieth centuries, when industrialization, urbanization, and an influx of immigrants were transforming city life. With those transformations came "modern problems," such as poverty, unemployment, and family breakdown. People eventually realized that those problems were not specific to any one group; everyone was at risk. These realizations brought demands for the redefining of social values and the development of more effective ways of helping the poor and disadvantaged (Hareven, 1969). People began to treat the vulnerable members of society with more fairness, respect, and compassion, and to take responsibility for one another. The time was right for a new language to reflect the spirit of social reform: thus, the term "social welfare" replaced the old-fashioned word "charity" to mean a formal, organized, and governmental approach to ensuring a basic standard of living for all (Leiby, 1977).

Over time, **social welfare** has come to mean various things. As a *concept*, social welfare refers to a society's vision of well-being, health, happiness, and prosperity—in other words, a society that sees itself as faring well. Social welfare is also a *system* comprising policies and programs designed to help individuals, families, and communities meet their basic needs. From the perspective of a *field or discipline*, social welfare involves the study and implementation of strategies designed to alleviate human suffering, prevent social problems, and improve the quality of life of disadvantaged groups; social work is the professional occupation most closely associated with the field of social welfare. This chapter focuses on the concept of social welfare and on the social welfare system; subsequent chapters explore the field of social welfare in more depth.

 ## 1 THE SCOPE AND PURPOSE OF THE SOCIAL WELFARE SYSTEM

The scope of Canada's social welfare system is limited to the members of society who require some assistance in meeting their basic needs. To determine who is in need, governments must first measure social well-being and then identify which human needs the social welfare system will address and how those needs will be met.

MEASURING SOCIAL WELL-BEING

The abstract nature of social welfare makes it difficult to say with any certainty whether society is faring well or not. For example, is society doing well only if it has zero poverty? Is society still doing well if it has a moderate amount of poverty? What is "moderate"? For that matter, what is "poverty"? From a *subjective* view, how well a society is doing is open to interpretation and is shaped by people's values, cultural norms, and beliefs about wellness and such constructs as "healthy lifestyles." Various surveys—such as the Canadian Survey on Disability and the General Social Survey—collect data on people's assessment of their personal experiences.

While subjective assessments of well-being are useful, governments also require measures that are concrete or *objective* before they will direct precious resources, such as time, energy, and taxpayers' money, toward improving people's life situations. Dozens of statistical tools are available to gauge social well-being objectively. On a global scale, the United Nations uses the Human Development Index to rank countries, including Canada, in terms of life expectancy, literacy, education, and standards of living. Statistical tools are also available to assess the well-being of specific social groups. For example, the First Nations Community Well-Being Index reports on the social and economic conditions in Canada's First Nations communities; likewise, the Federation of Canadian Municipalities uses its Quality of Life Reporting System to assess the environmental, social, and economic trends in Canada's major cities and municipalities.

In 2007, the Government of Canada introduced the Indicators of Well-being in Canada (IWC), a measurement framework designed to provide a national and comprehensive picture of the well-being of Canadians. The IWC recognizes ten broad domains of individual and social well-being: learning, work, financial security, environment, security (safety), health, leisure, social participation, family life, and housing. Each domain uses three types of **indicators** to measure the characteristics of, or changes in, the well-being of Canadians:

- *Status* indicators focus on human conditions or progress in major life areas, such as employment.

- *Life events* indicators track the rates of significant life-course events, such as marriage and divorce.

- *Key influences* indicators report on individual and community resources required for well-being, as well as people's access to, the availability of, and the maintenance of those resources (Human Resources and Skills Development Canada [HRSDC], 2012a).

Exhibit 1.1 illustrates the five domains that the social welfare system is most likely to address—that is, work, financial security, social participation, family life, and housing. The remaining five domains are the primary focus of the environment, healthcare, education, recreation and leisure, and criminal justice systems.

EXHIBIT 1.1

SELECTED INDICATORS OF WELL-BEING IN CANADA

DOMAIN	STATUS	LIFE EVENTS	KEY INFLUENCES
WORK	• Employment rate • Weekly earnings • Weekly hours worked	• Strikes and lockouts • Unemployment duration • Unemployment rate • Work-related injuries	• Unionization rates
FINANCIAL SECURITY	• Standard of living • Family income • Retirement income • Low income incidence • Low income persistence • Net worth (wealth)	• Personal bankruptcies	• Income distribution
SOCIAL PARTICIPATION	• Participation in political activities • Participation in social activities • Charitable donations • Volunteering		• Sense of belonging • Social networks • Trust in others
FAMILY LIFE	• Infant mortality	• Marriage • Age of mother at childbirth • Divorce • Young adults living with their parent(s)	
HOUSING	• Housing need		• Housing starts • Rental vacancy rates • Homeless shelters and beds

Status: indicators of conditions or progress in important life areas

Life events: indicators related to significant transitions that a person might experience over the life course

Key influences: indicators that reflect individual and societal resources

Source: Author-generated table, information derived, excerpted, and adapted from Human Resources and Skills Development Canada. (2012). *Indicators of well-being in Canada.* Retrieved from http://www4.hrsdc.gc.ca/h.4m.2@-eng.jsp.

Researchers must update the tools used to measure well-being on a regular basis to capture society's changing perceptions of well-being. A variety of factors can influence people's perceptions over time. For example, as baby boomers retire, they are likely to adopt a different view on what constitutes the "good life" than they had when they were working or going to school (Policy Horizons Canada, 2011).

According to IWC reports, the well-being of Canadians is on the decline. From 1994 to 2010, Canada's economy grew by an impressive 29 percent, while the quality of life grew by a mere 5.7 percent. During that period, well-being experienced the greatest decline between 2008 and 2009, when the economy suffered a downturn; however, even with the economic recovery in 2010, the well-being of most Canadians continued to decline. These findings dispel the myth that economic prosperity guarantees social well-being (Canadian Index of Wellbeing, 2012).

THE PRIMARY FUNCTIONS OF THE SOCIAL WELFARE SYSTEM

For a society to fare well, its members must be physically, socially, psychologically, financially, and materially healthy. To achieve health in these life areas, people must adequately meet their needs. A human **need** is a necessary condition or requirement of human development that if not met will result in serious physical, psychological, or social harm. As its primary function, Canada's social welfare system attempts to identify and meet basic human needs.

Identifying Human Needs

The diversity of human beings is such that it is impossible to list all possible needs that arise for people over a lifetime. Several models nevertheless attempt to outline the range of human needs; Abraham Maslow's hierarchy of needs is one of the best known of these models. Originally, Maslow argued that a person must first meet basic survival and security needs before trying to meet higher-order needs related to social interaction, self-esteem, and self-actualization. In later works, Maslow acknowledged that the meeting of human needs does not necessarily follow a fixed order; thus, people may be motivated to meet higher-order needs before they have fully satisfied those lower down on the pyramid (Ashley, 2000). Exhibit 1.2 illustrates the different levels of human needs as identified by Maslow: basic needs appear at the bottom of the pyramid, with higher-order needs listed successively up

EXHIBIT 1.2

MASLOW'S HIERARCHY OF NEEDS

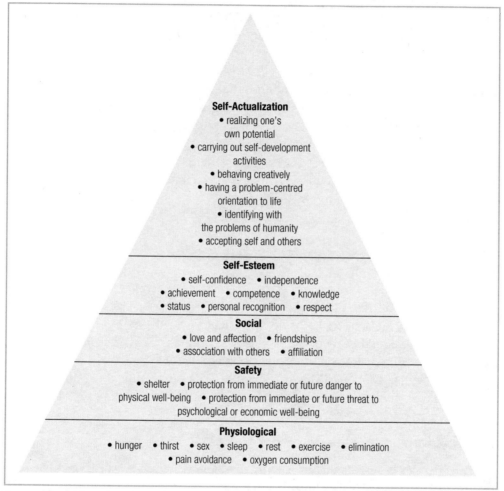

Self-Actualization
- realizing one's own potential
- carrying out self-development activities
- behaving creatively
- having a problem-centred orientation to life
- identifying with the problems of humanity
- accepting self and others

Self-Esteem
- self-confidence • independence
- achievement • competence • knowledge
- status • personal recognition • respect

Social
- love and affection • friendships
- association with others • affiliation

Safety
- shelter • protection from immediate or future danger to physical well-being • protection from immediate or future threat to psychological or economic well-being

Physiological
- hunger • thirst • sex • sleep • rest • exercise • elimination
- pain avoidance • oxygen consumption

Source: Adapted from A. Harber and R.P. Runyon, *Fundamentals of Psychology* McGraw Hill (1983), 304. Copyright 1983. Reproduced with permission of The McGraw-Hill Companies.

the hierarchy. Canada's social welfare system addresses many of the needs (to limited degrees) listed in Maslow's hierarchy.

Meeting Human Needs

While basic needs are common to all humans, how a particular culture chooses to satisfy those needs can vary. For the most part, Canadians are responsible for meeting their own needs, such as the need for food, shelter, safety, and affection. People meet those needs primarily through interactions with informal support systems, such as family and friends, and through formal institutions, such as the workplace and places of worship. When people are able to meet their needs, they are more likely to fully participate in and contribute to society; this social engagement is important for maintaining the social order, promoting the health and sustainability of communities, and ensuring a robust economy (Maxwell, 2006).

Canadian governments are reluctant to leave the meeting of social welfare needs entirely up to individuals. As a result, governments support a range of social welfare programs for people who fail to meet their needs adequately through traditional means. Those programs aim to

- provide the basic necessities to people who cannot sufficiently provide for themselves

- help isolated or **marginalized groups** to meet their social needs, such as the need to belong and participate in society

- assist people having trouble fulfilling important social roles, such as parent or income-earner

- ensure that people can access resources and opportunities to meet their needs and support their families

- address "special needs" related to substance abuse, mental disorders, and other conditions that inhibit human development

- protect vulnerable members of society, such as children and the elderly, from abuse or neglect (Dobelstein, 1978)

In their determination of how publically funded resources should be used, elected officials must act in the best interests of all citizens and target public assistance to those who really need it. As the Office of the Auditor General of Canada (2006, p. 5) notes: "Demands on government are unlimited, but the resources available to meet them are not. Governments must therefore . . . [decide] how much they can afford to spend, what to spend it on, and how to get the most for the money spent." To make these decisions, political leaders must determine which types of human needs and issues they will treat as *public* matters and which needs and issues they will consider *private*. Public issues refer to needs and conditions that government takes responsibility for and that affect (or have the potential to affect) a large segment of the population; included here are poverty, domestic violence, and racism. In contrast, private needs and issues are those that individuals are responsible for resolving on their own by using their own resources or purchasing the services they require. Canadians generally view marital disagreements, for example, as private matters left to the resources of individuals.

Canadian governments encourage people to be as self-sufficient as possible and to avoid relying on government for meeting their needs. To foster self-sufficiency, governments have introduced measures that help Canadians accumulate **capital**. Capital can take several forms, but human capital and social capital are particularly relevant to social welfare.

- *Human capital* includes the skills, capabilities, knowledge, and other personal assets that people use to earn a living, cope with life's problems and challenges, and achieve self-reliance. The Employment Insurance system, for example, focuses on building human capital in its provision of job skills training, career planning workshops, and other services to help people find work.

- *Social capital* refers to the social supports, networks, and contacts that people rely on for emotional support, access to resources, and general participation in society. Examples of programs focused on building social capital include early childhood education, parent support groups, and peer counselling for seniors.

DISCUSSION QUESTIONS

■ **The Scope and Purpose of the Social Welfare System**

1. Everyone has his or her own interpretation of social well-being. How do you define social well-being? Do you find that your perception of well-being changes over time? If so, how?

2. In your opinion, what conditions, resources, or activities are fundamental to a person's (or society's) well-being? How would you rate your community in the provision of the elements you have identified: poor, average, or excellent?

3. Why is it important (or not) for our politicians and governments to be concerned with people's well-being?

2 SOCIAL WELFARE PROGRAMS AND SERVICES

A wide range of government-sponsored programs makes up Canada's social welfare system. A **social welfare program** is a set of projects or activities that aim to meet a public need. Many programs provide tangible goods, such as cash, food, and shelter, to people in need. Other programs have a service component; services typically involve direct, face-to-face assistance in the form of counselling, peer support, information giving, or advocacy. Rather than offering direct **client** services, a number of social welfare programs focus on social research, policy analysis, program development, or another activity that enhances social welfare provision. (Appendix A provides a historical timeline of key events in the development of Canada's social welfare programs and services.)

Along with healthcare and postsecondary education, social welfare is an essential **social program**. These systems often work closely together on behalf of people in need; this is particularly true of social welfare and healthcare, which have integrated their services on various levels. For example, it is common for social welfare and health agencies to provide services under the same roof or to share the same administration, as in the case of the Yukon government's Department of Health and Social Services. It is also common for front-line workers in social welfare and healthcare agencies to coordinate their services with departments in the justice system; for instance, social workers and community health nurses often team up to help older adults access health and psychosocial supports. Despite these points of overlap, the social welfare system has its own distinct mandate, goals, and objectives. Social welfare programs and services can be classified into two broad categories: (1) income security programs and (2) social services. Each category is described below.

INCOME SECURITY PROGRAMS

Income security programs provide financial aid to replace or supplement a person's income during times of unemployment caused by, for instance, pregnancy, old age, sickness, or disability. These programs attempt to ensure that all Canadians enjoy a reasonable standard of living, otherwise known as a **social minimum**. The four main types of income security programs are as follows:

- **Targeted cash transfers:** These are benefits that government transfers to individuals whose income or assets fall below a certain level. Targeted cash transfers include the Guaranteed Income Supplement, social assistance, and disability pensions for people with severe disabilities.

- **Universal cash transfers:** Government gives these benefits to all persons, regardless of financial status or need, who meet a basic requirement, such as age or residency. The Universal Child Care Benefit, for example, gives a monthly payment of $100 to all parents and guardians for each child under the age of six, irrespective of the family's financial circumstances.

- **Contributory programs:** Also known as "social insurance," these benefits are forced savings plans that require working individuals to contribute to a program that then compensates them when they are not working. These programs base the amount of benefits on the claimant's contributions and limit benefits to those who maintain a strong connection to the labour force. Employment Insurance, Workers' Compensation, and the Canada and Québec Pension Plans are examples of contributory programs.

- **Tax relief measures:** Various programs and incentives reduce the amount of tax owed by individuals; government bases the amount of tax savings on income earned and reported on an individual's tax returns. Tax relief measures include tax credits (such as the Canada Child Tax Benefit and the Disability Tax Credit) and tax deductions (such as child care expenses and registered retirement savings plan contributions). Canada's progressive tax system allows individuals with low and modest incomes to pay proportionately less income tax. Governments have come to prefer using the tax system, rather than cash transfers, for assisting low-income Canadians.

SOCIAL SERVICES

Canada's **social services** are non-income benefits funded in part or in full by government. Designed to improve the living conditions of individuals, families, and communities, these direct services fulfill several important functions:

- They provide goods and services aimed at meeting basic social, material, and emotional needs.

- They support and help people resolve problems of daily living related to, for example, disability or family breakdown.

- They protect vulnerable members of society, such as children and the elderly.

- They aim to prevent or minimize the negative effects of social problems, including poverty, domestic violence, and drug abuse.

Demand for social services is increasing in Canada, fuelled in part by an aging population, which drives the need for home support and other seniors' programs. Changes in family composition—including a rise in lone-mother families and families with two working parents—are also creating more demand for family-oriented services, such as child care.

Because the provinces and territories are primarily responsible for developing their own social services, the type and range of services across jurisdictions will vary. However, most provinces and territories offer social services for specific populations, such as children and youth, parents, seniors, and people with disabilities. In many cases, these services complement or replace the support and care that family or other informal support system might normally provide.

Political leaders often disagree on whether an identified need would be best met by a social service or a cash benefit. For example, between 2004 and 2006, federal politicians debated the merits of services versus cash benefits for meeting the child-care needs of Canadian families. Liberal politicians wanted to establish an extensive system of government-regulated child-care spaces; in contrast, Conservative politicians preferred that families receive cash to purchase the type of child care best suited to their needs. Each type of provision has pros and cons. People tend to use child-care services when they are available in a community; thus, the identified need is likely to be met. Public child-care services are nevertheless restrictive in some ways: for example, government is likely to subsidize the costs of placing a child in a government-approved setting but not the costs of employing a babysitter in the home. The provision of cash, on the other hand, allows people to choose the type of service they want; however, a potential problem with giving cash is that recipients may spend the money on something other than its intended purpose, and the need may go unmet.

PROGRAM ELIGIBILITY

The federal, provincial and territorial, and municipal levels of government have developed specific criteria to determine who may participate in, or potentially benefit from, a publicly sponsored program. In Canada, the issue of **program eligibility** is largely resolved through two broad classifications of programs: targeted and universal.

Targeted Programs

Targeted programs are limited to narrowly defined segments of the population that a government deems to be vulnerable or at risk for a certain social or economic hardship; these groups include children living in poverty, Aboriginal peoples, seniors, the unemployed, people with disabilities, and recent immigrants. Social assistance, child tax credits, and rental subsidies are some of the programs that target specific groups.

Canadian governments use three types of financial tests to determine eligibility for targeted income security programs:

- **Income tests** determine eligibility based on the applicant's annual income and generally ignore individual needs or other assets (such as property or investments).

- **Needs tests** assess an applicant's needs or necessary expenses and determine whether his or her income and assets are sufficient to meet those needs.

- **Asset tests** analyze an applicant's assets (such as savings and investments); assets above a certain value may disqualify a person from benefits.

Since the late 1980s, income tests have become a common method for ensuring that only low- or modest-income earners receive benefits; these tests rely on income tax returns to assess an individual's eligibility. Old Age Security is an example of an income-tested program; in 2012, recipients earning more than $69 562 a year received a reduced benefit rate, and those with annual incomes of more than $112 772 were ineligible (Service Canada, n.d.). Provincial social assistance programs commonly use needs tests and asset tests. In those programs, financial assistance workers consider an applicant's income, needs, and assets by identifying all sources of household income, taking an inventory of the applicant's fixed and liquid assets, and determining the total needs of the household. If the household's assessed needs are greater than its resources, the worker deems the applicant as being eligible for assistance (National Council of Welfare, 2010).

In recent decades, government cutbacks to social spending have led to tighter restrictions on who can use social welfare programs, making government assistance available to fewer people (see Exhibit 1.3). For example, Employment Insurance is an income security program that is becoming increasingly difficult to qualify for; legislative changes in the 1990s led to a sharp drop in the proportion of unemployed Canadian workers eligible for benefits—from 74 percent in 1990 to just over 31 percent in 2010 (Mendelson & Battle, 2011). Social services are also becoming less accessible. To deal with reduced funding and greater demands, social service agencies must restrict their services to those in the greatest of need. Requiring clients to meet many criteria is one method of restricting services; for instance, the federally funded Nobody's Perfect program targets parents with children five years of age or younger and gives priority to "parents who are young, single, socially or geographically

THAT AWKWARD AGE

Len Norris, "That Awkward Age" (1990). Reprinted by permission.

"He's at that awkward age . . . too young for old age security, too old for Opportunities for Youth, too late for family allowance, too conventional for Canada Council or local initiative programs, too poor for tax loopholes, too rich for subsidized housing . . ."

isolated or who have low income or limited formal education" (Public Health Agency of Canada, 2011).

Universal Programs

Universal programs are comprehensive in the sense that they are available to broad segments of the population, such as all children under the age of six, or all adults over the age of sixty-five. The notion of universality supports the belief that benefits should be available as a matter of a citizen's rights rather than economic need or risk. Since need or risk are not factors of eligibility, applicants for these programs are not required to undergo a needs, income, or asset test; however, they must meet basic criteria, often related to age or residency. Canada's first universal program, Family Allowances, was introduced in 1945 and provided a monthly cash benefit to all Canadian families—rich or poor—that had children. (see Exhibit 1.4)

Every beneficiary of a universal program receives the same quality of service or amount of money (a flat rate); as a result, this type of program does not identify anyone in the population as being "in need." Findlay (1983, p. 18) sees certain advantages to this approach: "universality avoids divisions among those who are entitled and those who are not: it eliminates a two-tier system that results in 'second-class' citizens and 'second-class' services for the less influential." Thus, universality might minimize the labelling, stigmatization, or segregation of disadvantaged individuals or groups in society (Jewell, 2005). On a more practical level, universal programs may be more cost-effective than targeted programs, since they do not require an assessment of individual needs and are therefore relatively simple to administer.

Library and Archives Canada. Richard Harrington/Richard Harrington fonds/ PA-129879. © Library and Archives Canada. Reproduced with permission of Library and Archives Canada.

EXHIBIT 1.4

An Inuit mother with her children signs for a family allowance cheque at the Royal Canadian Mounted Police headquarters in Coppermine, Northwest Territories (circa 1949–1950).

While Canadians generally support universality in public healthcare and public education, universality in income security programs has lost its popularity. The critics of universality argue that giving financial assistance to people who do not need it is a waste of taxpayer's money (Canadian Economy Online, 2007). The gradual elimination of universal income security programs began in the late 1980s when the federal government introduced a "clawback" to Family Allowances and Old Age Security benefits. Clawbacks required high-income earners receiving payments from those programs to repay some or all of their benefits.

Canadian governments favour a contemporary and largely European version of universality called **progressive universalism**. The priority of this approach is to reduce poverty rather than benefit all citizens; thus, all persons who meet the basic criteria receive a benefit, with a larger proportion of benefit given to those who need it most. Québec's early childhood education and child-care program is an example of a progressive universalism approach. In that province, parents with children under five years of age pay a daily fee of $7 for child-care services. Families on social assistance with young children may receive the same quality of services free (Doré & Le Hénaff, 2013).

Some programs are touted as universal, but because of their structural design, they end up benefiting some recipients more than others. The federally funded Universal Child Care Benefit (UCCB) is one of these "in name only" universal programs. Although the program gives $1200 per year for each Canadian child under six, the benefit is taxable, which means that parents may have to pay back a portion of it in tax. A study by policy analyst Ken Battle (2006) found that, depending on the household's income tax bracket and whether the family received other cash transfers or tax credits, the amount per child might be anywhere from $460 to $1200 per year after taxes. The "universal" structure of the UCCB is in sharp contrast to that of Family Allowances, which, from 1945 to 1973, provided tax-free benefits to families with children.

DISCUSSION QUESTIONS

■ **Social Welfare Programs and Services**

1. While some politicians think that providing government-regulated child-care services is the right way to meet families' child-care needs, others believe that families should receive cash to purchase their own child-care services. What is your position on this issue? Why might one approach be more or less effective than the other?

2. In general, Canadian governments provide social welfare programs on either a targeted or a universal basis. What are the pros and cons of each approach?

3 SOCIAL WELFARE PROVISION: IDEOLOGY AND APPROACHES

Along with a nation's values, priorities, goals, and resources, political ideologies influence the degree to which a government intervenes in social welfare matters. In turn, those ideologies play an important role in the approach taken by government to ensure the social well-being of citizens. This section looks at three political ideologies and their related approaches to social welfare.

POLITICAL IDEOLOGY

A **political ideology** is a set of beliefs that shape people's views of society, their ideas on how society should function, and their opinions about how they might achieve social well-being. Canada's social welfare system is not the product of any one political ideology; rather, the system reflects various ideologies that have evolved over time in response to social, economic, and political developments. However, three classic political ideologies—conservatism, social democracy, and liberalism—have predominated in the shaping of people's views of "need" and the extent to which they think government should help people meet their needs (see Exhibit 1.5 for a comparative view of the ideologies).

What follows are brief descriptions of each political ideology within a social welfare context. Note that the ideologies discussed here are reflected in the platforms of three main political parties in Canada: the Conservative Party, the New Democratic Party, and the Liberal Party; however, these parties are unlikely to adopt all the concepts and practices of any one ideological stance.

CONSERVATISM

While not entirely opposed to change, **conservatism** supports traditional values and social roles, and moral (religious) standards. Individualism is important in terms of economic advancement—that is, people are encouraged to compete, work hard, and accumulate wealth and property. In addition to gainful employment, conservatives believe that a person's own skills and fortitude, the family, the place of worship, and other nongovernment social supports should be a person's main defence against want and need. Self-sufficiency is highly regarded.

Conservatives tend to believe that many people are poor because they made poor choices, they lack initiative, or they simply do not want to work

EXHIBIT 1.5

POLITICAL IDEOLOGIES: A COMPARATIVE VIEW

	CONSERVATISM	SOCIAL DEMOCRACY	LIBERALISM
BASIC VALUES	• Moralism • Family, church, tradition • Class, privilege • Competition	• Collectivism • Fellowship • Equality • Cooperation	• Individualism • Self-interest • Self-reliance • Competition
KEY TO PROSPERITY AND WELL-BEING	• Saving • Investing • Working ("any job is a good job")	• Working together • Pooling society's resources and sharing the wealth	• Knowledge, education, training • Having a "good" job to ensure self-reliance
ROLE OF GOVERNMENT	• Maintain social order • Strengthen family • Defend role of church and charities • Protect interests of business	• Regulate the means of production • Create equal conditions • Ensure social welfare • Protect rights of workers and unions	• Enable economic progress • Create equal opportunity through legislation • Defend individual rights and freedoms • Protect private property
TAXATION AND REDISTRIBUTION	• No or low taxation • Whoever earns the money should enjoy it • User pays	• Heavy taxation • Redistribute the wealth from rich to poor	• Moderate taxation • Give "reasonable" support to selected disadvantaged groups
CAUSE OF POVERTY	• Personal failure, bad choices; unfortunate circumstances	• Unequal distribution of wealth and power in capitalist system	• Structural flaws in capitalist system
VIEW OF PEOPLE WHO ARE POOR	• "Deserving" (justifiably in need) or "undeserving" (lazy, immoral, lacking in resourcefulness)	• "Trapped" (in a subordinate position to the wealthy and powerful)	• "Unskilled" or "disadvantaged" (limited in ability to compete)
INDIVIDUAL RESPONSIBILITY	• Obey laws, work hard, fulfill duties	• Share, cooperate, avoid excess	• Take initiative, be self-reliant, participate in society
APPROACH TO SOCIAL WELFARE	• Residual (government help is a last resort)	• Institutional (government help is a citizen's right)	• Social investment (government help is a long-term investment)

Source: Adapted from Pollard, J. (1993). Ideology, social policy and home-based child care [table 1]. In I. Kyle et al. (Eds.), *Proceedings from the Child Care Policy and Research Symposium* (pp. 101–112). Toronto, Canada: Childcare Resource and Research Unit, Centre for Urban and Community Studies, University of Toronto. Retrieved from http://www.childcarecanada.org/sites/default/files/op2.pdf.

(Morel, 2002). Conservatives nevertheless recognize that some people are victims of circumstance; for example, they may view children who are poor not as being responsible for their circumstances but as "innocent victims" of wasteful or inept parents (Ismael, 2006).

For conservatives, the most desirable government is the one that regulates, controls, or intervenes in people's lives the least. For this reason, conservative governments are sometimes described as being laissez faire (a French term meaning "leave alone"). Laissez faire governments expect the market, private enterprise, and the law of supply and demand to provide people with the income and other resources to meet all human needs. Conservatives see government as having a primarily protective role: to secure the country by maintaining the military and to uphold law and order by strengthening police services. With so few responsibilities, governments are expected to keep their administrations as small and as non-bureaucratic as possible.

According to conservative thought, people's problems are largely personal and private and best resolved by individual effort rather than government intervention (Wharf, 2007). Conservatives generally view state intrusion in people's private lives as being detrimental because it restricts individual freedoms and undermines people's inherent sense of initiative and responsibility (International Federation of Social Workers, 2012b). Social welfare programs, in particular, are believed to foster a dependency on the state and to "weaken moral fibre" (Galper, 1975, p. 3).

Neoliberalism is a contemporary form of conservatism closely related to globalization. (What makes neoliberalism new or "neo" is its global rather than national perspective; the use of the word "liberal" is in reference to liberation from government.) At the heart of neoliberalism is the support for capitalism, free trade, and market expansion. According to neoliberals, government intervention and regulation hinder a country's ability to compete successfully in international markets: in a global economy, capital or wealth must flow freely across boundaries, and transnational corporations expect to set up shop anywhere in the world with little government interference (Teeple, 2000). Neoliberals argue that if government would stop interfering in the market by, for example, taxing the rich and giving to the poor, then the market would be able to function properly, economic growth and prosperity would follow, and wealth would naturally "trickle down" to all members of society.

SOCIAL DEMOCRACY

Since the coining of the term *socialism* in the early nineteenth century, two main camps have evolved: (1) the revolutionary or communist camp, which advocates a primarily government-owned and -operated economy; and (2) the evolutionary or social democratic camp, which supports an economy that has a mix of public and private enterprise. **Social democracy**, which tends to oppose the extreme of communism, gained more support in Canada than its communist counterpart did. This section therefore discusses socialism from a social democratic point of view.

According to Canadian economist Tom Kent (2011, p. 1), social democracy "is a society where the enterprise of productive employment in a market economy is joined with active government to secure the public interest in equality of opportunities and fairness of outcomes." Traditionally, social democracy rejects the competitive values of capitalism, individualism, and private enterprise. Instead of personal competition, social democrats advocate fellowship and cooperation among citizens. Solidarity is important to social democrats, who prefer to work toward collective rather than individual goals and who frequently use collective action, such as labour strikes, to do so. Egalitarianism—that is, equal power and advantage among citizens—is also considered a worthy goal (Spicker, 2012).

Social democrats challenge the conservative notion that poverty is the result of an individual's shortcomings; instead, they see poverty as a consequence of capitalism and the unequal distribution of wealth and power. From a social democratic viewpoint, the rich inherit wealth while the poor inherit poverty, which traps the poor in a subordinate position (George & Wilding, 1985).

While conservatives view government intervention as a threat to individual freedom, social democrats are willing to give up some freedom if it means that everyone—not just the rich—can benefit from a country's wealth. Thus, social democrats encourage government to use its taxation and other powers to equalize social and economic conditions and opportunities. Social democrats believe that government can achieve this goal through an extensive system of universal health, education, and social welfare programs available to all citizens.

LIBERALISM

In many respects, **liberalism** is similar to conservatism in terms of supporting individualism and competitive private enterprise. However, Canada traditionally links its brand of liberalism to efforts to "humanize" capitalist values and thus strike a balance between economic goals and human development. Accordingly, while liberals expect governments to promote capitalism and economic growth, they also want governments to ensure individual rights, social justice, and equal opportunity. Unlike conservatives, who tend to cling to tradition, liberals support people's rights to individuality, freedom of self-expression, and choice of lifestyle.

Liberals tend to view poverty and other social problems as resulting not from individual shortcomings but from flaws in the capitalist system. Although liberals promote economic progress, they also see this type of progress as a potential source of hardship. Liberals therefore question the ability of the market alone to meet the full range of human needs in modern society and see a role for government in helping citizens reach their full potential.

According to liberals, if the market fails to meet people's needs, government should then provide a **social safety net**—that is, a limited range of targeted, publically funded programs. Liberals tend to favour programs that help people develop the skills and knowledge they need to become self-sufficient; many of those programs focus on creating jobs, building skills, and helping people find well-paying and secure jobs.

APPROACHES TO SOCIAL WELFARE PROVISION

A study of the social welfare system is likely to reveal what Jacqueline Ismael (1985, p. i) refers to as a "maze of programs" and a "hodge-podge pattern of service provision"—in other words, the provision of social welfare in Canada is highly fragmented, uncoordinated, and inconsistent. Gerald Boychuk (2004) explains that when developing Canada's social welfare system, governments have introduced new approaches to helping people while keeping many of the existing approaches. The result is a mix of old and new approaches, many of which contradict one another in their design, philosophy, and delivery. Despite the variation, there are three main approaches to social welfare provision: the residual approach, the institutional approach, and the social investment approach.

The main political parties in Canada tend to favour different approaches to social welfare. While conservatives generally support the residual approach, social democrats have traditionally leaned toward an institutional approach. In general, liberals take a social investment approach. Despite these tendencies, it is common for political parties to choose elements from all three approaches, depending on the presenting social issue or problem, party priorities, political climate, and public pressure.

Residual Approach to Social Welfare

The word residual refers to "remains" or something "left over." Thus, a **residual approach** to social welfare assumes that although economic, social, and other systems meet people's needs most of the time, some outstanding human needs will be left that government must address (Dobelstein, 2003). Residualists see government assistance as a last resort for those who have exhausted all possible help from family, place of worship, and other private resources, and can demonstrate true need. Assuming that the demand for government aid will always exceed supply, the residual approach uses certain strategies either to deter people who are not truly needy from seeking public assistance or to make the conditions of receiving benefits so adverse that people seek alternative, non-government forms of assistance. Thus, this approach ensures that any help given is *targeted* (available to a select few), *meagre* (to discourage people from preferring government benefits to gainful employment), and *short term* (terminated as soon as the individual being helped can once again be self-reliant).

Stigmatization is one of the strategies used by residualists to limit the use of government assistance to those who really need it. The stigmatization of the poor dates back to Canada's early settlement period, when settlers classified the poor as being either deserving or undeserving of public aid. The **deserving poor** were sick or aged, had a disability, or otherwise were incapable of supporting themselves through work and therefore worthy of public aid. In contrast, the **undeserving poo**r were able-bodied, unemployed adults who were capable of working and paying their own way; this group received either inferior services or no services at all. Today's stereotypes of the poor reflect these residual attitudes (see Exhibit 1.6). People on social assistance, for example, are often assumed to be "lazy, unwilling to work, and lacking in self-discipline" (Handel, 1982, p. 4). The comments made by some of the country's top political leaders reflect those derogatory sentiments. Former prime minister Jean Chrétien, for example, once suggested that people on welfare sit at home, drinking beer ("Chrétien Says," 1994). Former Calgary mayor and Alberta premier Ralph Klein once referred to unemployed migrants as "Eastern bums and creeps." It may be difficult to see how stigmatization can be helpful to people who are struggling to make ends meet. However, the original intent of this strategy was to discourage dependency on government, a condition that residualists consider a hindrance to proper human development.

Institutional Approach to Social Welfare

The **institutional approach** maintains that social welfare is a primary institution of society (similar to religion, government, and education) and therefore has a normal, legitimate, and necessary function in a civilized, modern society (Wilensky & Lebeaux, 1965). Governments that adopt an institutional

EXHIBIT 1.6

© Denis Pepin/Shutterstock

A residual approach to social welfare does not recognize able-bodied men as "vulnerable" members of society or as a high priority for government assistance.

approach to social welfare do not require people to pay full market prices for goods and services that are essential for well-being (see Exhibit 1.7). This rights-based view—which is closely aligned with a social democratic ideology—assumes that every citizen, not just people in need, is entitled to a minimum level of food, shelter, clothing, and security (Davies, McMullin, Avison, & Cassidy, 2001). Because citizens have a right to social welfare programs, no stigma is attached to receiving government assistance.

Welfare states (sometimes called "social welfare states") embody the values and principles of an institutional approach. A welfare state refers to an industrial capitalist nation whose government uses its power to intervene in the workings of the market to correct **income inequality**, a problem represented as a gap between the incomes of the very rich and the very poor. To equalize incomes, governments use the tax system to take a portion of income from high- and moderate-income earners and give it to low-income

EXHIBIT 1.7

Both the institutional and social investment approaches to social welfare support the notion of government-subsidized child-care services.

earners. This **income redistribution** enables low-income individuals and families to spend more, which, in turn, can stimulate the economy. Welfare states also aim to

- ensure a minimum income to all citizens
- protect people from economic insecurity arising from old age, unemployment, sickness, and other contingencies
- provide all citizens with a range of social services (Briggs, 1961)

Following the Second World War, Canadian governments assumed many responsibilities for social welfare that private charitable organizations had long taken on. The greatest expansion of social welfare programs occurred from 1963 to 1973; by the early 1980s, these programs represented close to 14 percent of Canada's gross domestic product (Drover, 1983). With the introduction of universal healthcare, Unemployment Insurance, the Old Age Security pension, and the Canada and Québec Pension Plans, Canada was well on its way to becoming a welfare state. However, unlike some European nations, Canada did not fully support the establishment (or expense) of an extensive range of income security programs and social services required to reach welfare state status. Thus, Canada became not so much a welfare state as a country that offers minimum protection by government, through a limited range of programs, for designated "at-risk" segments of the population.

Social Investment Approach to Social Welfare

Canadian governments see the market as the primary source of well-being. However, governments also recognize the need for innovative strategies to address the challenges associated with globalization and other socioeconomic shifts. Since the mid-1990s, Canadian governments have considered the **social investment approach** to social welfare as a viable alternative to residual and institutional approaches and well suited to addressing modern problems (Dobrowolsky, 2003).

While the institutional approach tends to help people after a problem has occurred, the social investment approach takes a proactive stance, before problems arise. The **social inclusion** of all citizens is particularly important for preventing social problems. Thus, social investment initiatives aim to foster social inclusion by removing barriers to participation in society and allowing visible minorities, Aboriginal peoples, people with disabilities, and other marginalized groups to access jobs, resources, and opportunities.

Governments that take a social investment approach favour programs that promise to yield long-term benefits. Preschool-age children—who are the country's future—are a primary focus (see Exhibit 1.7 for an example). Social welfare programs that invest in young Canadians include the National Child Benefit and a wide range of early childhood development, early learning, and child-care programs. Young working-age adults are another focus of social investment initiatives. Instead of providing cash benefits to the able-bodied unemployed, the social investment approach attempts to help adults form a long-term attachment to the workforce. Programs designed to achieve this objective include welfare-to-work initiatives, employment counselling, and work incentives, such as government wage subsidies. According to the social investment approach, employment is the best protection against poverty.

To foster self-sufficiency, social investment strategies also try to help individuals, families, and communities build various types of capital. In terms of human capital, governments may provide incentives to people to set aside a portion of their income for the future. Saving for retirement, for example, is made possible through the Canada Pension Plan and registered retirement savings plans (RRSPs). Other human capital programs encourage the development of employable skills; included here are federal government subsidies for post-secondary training and education, and the Canada Learning Bond that helps low-income Canadians save for educational purposes. Some programs—such as the federal tax-free savings account—aim to help Canadians save money to cover the costs of any need that arises.

Social investors also believe that social capital is central to economic self-sufficiency. A wide range of programs and services can help people build social capital. For instance, family resource centres aim to foster healthy relationships among families, neighbours, and friends. To help children and youth strengthen their attachments to family, community, and the larger society, early learning programs and youth engagement programs are available. Finally, many programs promote multiculturalism, address racism, and help immigrants integrate into society—all efforts to foster harmony, understanding, and cooperation among groups.

DISCUSSION QUESTIONS

■ **Social Welfare Provision: Ideology and Approaches**

1. In your opinion, which political ideology—conservatism, social democracy, or liberalism—is most dominant in today's social welfare programs and services? Give examples to support your views.

2. Which approach to social welfare provision—the residual, institutional, or social investment—might be the most effective for reducing poverty in Canada? Give reasons for your answer.

SUMMARY

Introduction

Despite its abstract nature, social welfare implies a formal, organized, and governmental approach to ensuring a basic standard of living. Social welfare can refer to a concept, a field, or a system. The primary function of the social welfare system is to help individuals, families, and communities meet their basic needs.

1 **The Scope and Purpose of the Social Welfare System**

A variety of surveys and statistical tools can be used to measure individual and social well-being. To achieve well-being, it is important to identify and meet human needs; Maslow's hierarchy lists many of those needs. The social welfare system intervenes when traditional support systems break down; however, that system tends to limit help to the most vulnerable members of society. Canadian governments encourage self-sufficiency and provide incentives to help people accumulate capital.

2 Social Welfare Programs and Services

Income security programs provide targeted cash transfers, universal cash transfers, contributory programs, and tax credits. Social services offer goods, services, support, and opportunities; some services protect vulnerable members of society, while others address broader social problems. Social welfare programs may be either targeted or universal, but all require some type of test to determine program eligibility. While universalism has potential benefits, it is no longer popular in a social welfare context. Overall, most programs are becoming more targeted and less accessible.

3 Social Welfare Provision: Ideology and Approaches

Conservatism, social democracy, and liberalism are political ideologies that influence people's perception of "need" and determine which human issues government should treat as private troubles or public issues. The level of responsibility that governments assume for social welfare shifts over time. Canada has three main approaches to social welfare provision: the residual approach, the institutional approach, and the social investment approach.

KEY TERMS

For definitions of the key terms, consult the Glossary on page 453 at the end of the book.

CHAPTER 2

Social Welfare Policy

OBJECTIVES

Policy provides the direction and structure to social welfare programs and services. This chapter will

- introduce the concept of *social welfare policy* and related terms
- identify the ways in which social policymakers learn about social issues and problems
- explain how social policymakers come to understand social issues and problems
- introduce the policy community and the consulting and reviewing process
- describe how policymakers formalize social welfare policies
- briefly explain how social welfare policies are implemented
- summarize the process of evaluating social welfare policies

INTRODUCTION

Social policies are never neutral or value-free. By looking at social policies, we see the expression of Canada, the value choices made, the attitudes and beliefs expressed, the judgements made by countless people. In doing so, in making social policies and implementing them every day, and through the years, we establish certain boundaries of care, assistance and community. (Prince, 2008, p. 7)

Policies provide structure to almost every aspect of our lives. Personal policies are typically unwritten rules that we set for ourselves, such as "I don't eat after 8 p.m.," or "I don't participate in gossip." Many parents have rules (or policies) for their children, such as "No TV after 9 p.m." or "Brush after every meal." Policies also guide people's behaviours in formal institutions, including schools ("No talking in class") and the workplace ("Internet access is for job-related activities only"). Policies are also central to government decision making and intervention. There are many types of government or **public policies**, including economic policy, domestic policy, and defence policy. **Social policy** is most concerned with the development and implementation of social programs—that is, social welfare, healthcare, and postsecondary education. These policies affect all Canadians since they "determine who pays for and who benefits from government spending, how well or poorly people live, the nature of their relationships to each other, the overall quality of life, and the nation's commitment to social justice" (Abramovitz, 2004, p. 19).

Social welfare policy is a subset of social policy that provides the structure of most income security programs and social services. Tightly integrated with economic policy, social welfare policy aims to

- strengthen job security and labour market supports, such as employment insurance and pension contributions

- provide opportunities for training and skill development

- motivate adults to work and to save for the future

- redistribute income to minimize the number of people living in poverty

- create acceptable living and work standards to attract foreign investment

- enhance the quality of life for individuals, families, and communities (Conference Board of Canada, 2000)

To understand social welfare programs, we must be familiar with their related policies and the process by which they are created. Canada has no official or preferred method of policy development; however, the stages model is commonly used. Any number of stages may take place during policy development; Exhibit 2.1 summarizes six generic stages and their respective tasks. Note that certain activities, such as decision making and consultation, take place throughout the policy development process.

EXHIBIT 2.1

STAGES OF SOCIAL WELFARE POLICY DEVELOPMENT

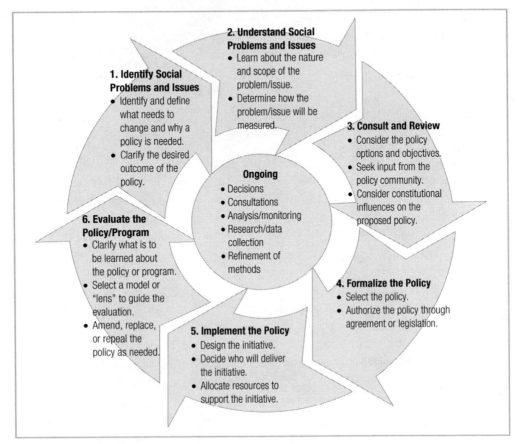

Source: Rosalie Chappell

1 STAGE 1: IDENTIFYING SOCIAL PROBLEMS AND ISSUES

An important role of elected government officials is to make the laws, legislation, and policies related to social programs. In stage 1, these **social policymakers** have to identify the issue or problem for which a policy is needed. Policymakers must also clarify which conditions need to change to address the issue or problem and what they hope to accomplish by creating a policy. This section looks at these tasks.

FROM SOCIAL CONDITIONS TO SOCIAL ISSUES AND PROBLEMS

A number of circumstances—such as living arrangements, relationships, and work or learning environment—can affect people's ability to meet their needs. These circumstances may be desirable or undesirable. For example, some adults may find working in chaotic or noisy conditions to be stimulating, while others may find the same experience to be stressful. Thus, living and working conditions are not problematic until people label them as such. **Social conditions** may be understood in a similar way. Unemployment, substandard housing, and divorce are social conditions that exist for large segments of the Canadian population but are not problematic in and of themselves. Over time, however, people may perceive a social condition as a threat to society and something that should be treated as either a *social issue* or a *social problem*.

A **social issue** is a widespread condition that is not problematic but has the potential to become so if not addressed promptly. One social issue facing Canadians is an **population aging**. Older people undoubtedly can benefit Canadian society in many ways. However, concerns arise when considering the increasing number of elderly people, their needs, and the dwindling resources to meet those needs. In general, policymakers agree that policies and programs related to health promotion, housing, social support, employment, and other life areas must be introduced now to head off problems for future generations of elderly people, their families, and society.

For society to consider a social condition to be a **social problem**, it must meet certain criteria. First, a large segment of the population must recognize the condition to be undesirable in some way. Second, the condition must create a measurable degree of economic or social hardship, psychological or physical injury, or other negative consequence that people want changed. Finally, the undesirable condition must spark some kind of collective response aimed at correcting the situation (Henslin, 2003; Thompson, Howard, & Jin, 2001).

Certain social conditions are generally accepted as social problems, while others are not. In Canada, the general consensus is that crime, child poverty, racism, violence against women, drug addiction, and homelessness (see Exhibit 2.2) are serious social problems. Policymakers recognize these problems as public issues that government should address and pay for. Other social conditions, such as bisexuality and divorce, are seen as social problems by fewer Canadians and are subsequently lower priorities for social policymakers.

EXHIBIT 2.2

Homelessness is a major social problem in Canada, especially in large urban centres.

CHANGING PERCEPTIONS OF SOCIAL PROBLEMS

What Canadians currently view as a social problem might have been socially acceptable in the past. A case in point is racism. During the first half of the twentieth century, the Government of Canada enacted racist immigration laws to limit the numbers of so-called undesirables—including people of Chinese origin, Jewish people, and Black people—from entering the country. Today, racism and discrimination are not tolerated in Canada, as evidenced by the number of anti-discrimination and anti-hate laws, and policies that promote multiculturalism, diversity, and social inclusion. As Canadian culture continues to evolve, people's views of social conditions and problems change as well. With those changes come different expectations of government intervention. Thus, social welfare policy tends to reflect the values of the nation at any given time.

It is not unusual for changing economic or social conditions to create new social problems or exacerbate existing ones. In recent decades, globalization and a shift from an industrial to a postindustrial era have been associated with a wide range of social problems, including **social exclusion**. Socially excluded people feel left out of society and often fail to enjoy the full social, economic, political, and other benefits that society has to offer. Many experts point to shifts in the labour market, the subsequent rise in low-paid, part-time, and insecure jobs, and the resulting strain on people's ability to support themselves and their families as the primary causes of social exclusion. A lack of sufficient income naturally puts individuals and families at a high risk of **poverty**. Living in poverty can raise the risk of additional challenges, such as health problems, poor housing, and welfare dependency—all conditions that can create further barriers to inclusion in society (Galabuzi & Labonte, 2002). People living in poverty are at such a high risk of social exclusion that some policymakers treat "social exclusion" and "poverty" as synonymous since each condition can cause the other, and both conditions relate to deprivation (Voyer, 2005).

DISCUSSION QUESTIONS

■ **Stage 1: Identifying Social Problems and Issues**

1. Identify five social conditions. For each condition, decide whether it meets the criteria for a social issue, a social problem, or neither.

2. What types of programs or services are available in your community (or other locale) to address the issues or problems identified in question 1?

2   STAGE 2: UNDERSTANDING SOCIAL ISSUES AND PROBLEMS

In Stage 2, policymakers must learn about the nature and prevalence of issues and problems that affect society. Policymakers also search for ways to define and measure the existence of social problems.

SOCIAL KNOWLEDGE

Social knowledge is a type of empirical research that helps policymakers learn about society's conditions, issues, and problems. Social knowledge comes from many sources. For example, at the government level, Policy Horizons Canada studies a wide range of social issues to inform and structure policy decisions in federal departments. In the private sector, the studies undertaken by research institutes and think tanks provide invaluable insight into social trends, conditions, and risks. Professionals in the helping fields, such as social workers, psychologists, and psychiatrists, contribute to social knowledge in various ways; one way is by sharing the knowledge derived from observing and working with clients, such as what appears to help or hinder human development. A number of academic disciplines, including sociology, economics, and anthropology, also enrich the body of social knowledge available to policymakers. Each discipline applies its own theoretical frame of reference to the study of society's problems and their impact on people's health and well-being.

Depending on the nature of the information needed, social scientists use various **data collection tools** to gather information on social conditions and problems. Those tools include surveys, interviews, and focus groups, with **longitudinal surveys** being one of the most useful in the social welfare field. This type of survey follows the progress of the same group of people over time. The survey's focus may be on one or more aspects of a condition or problem, such as the negative events people experience (for instance, job loss or divorce), the time it takes people to make transitions through life (for example, from losing a job to finding new employment), and the influences (such as the economy) on those events and transitions. In short, longitudinal surveys identify how changes and emerging patterns in the general population might create either social well-being or problems. Initiated in 2001, the Canadian Longitudinal Study on Aging (CLSA) is one of the most comprehensive longitudinal studies in the world. This national study aims to track about 50 000 Canadian adults for at least twenty years. Researchers expect the CLSA to provide invaluable information on factors related to health, disease, and disability as people age—information that policymakers can use to make informed decisions in social welfare, health, and other policy areas.

Ironically, the more we learn about social problems, the less we might understand them. As Denis Saint-Martin (2004, p. 7) explains, "Nowadays, social problems are viewed as wicked not necessarily because they are, in themselves, more complex but because we, as societies, have accumulated more knowledge about such problems." Social knowledge has called attention not only to the complex, multidimensional aspects of social problems but also to how those problems can compound and exacerbate each other. For example, thirty years ago, people viewed poverty simply as a lack of money. In 2001, the United Nations (2001, p. 2) called attention to the complicated nature of poverty when it redefined poverty as "a human condition characterized by sustained or chronic deprivation of the resources, capabilities, choices, security and power necessary for the enjoyment of an adequate standard of living and other civil, cultural, economic, political and social rights."

Much of Canada's body of social knowledge has come from the census, which Statistics Canada conducts every five years. Since 1971, the census has included both a short form (with questions on basic demographic topics, such as age, gender, and marital status) and a long form (with questions on people's socioeconomic conditions, such as housing, income, and education). In 2010, the federal government scrapped the mandatory long-form census questionnaire in favour of a voluntary household survey. Researchers, academics, and others who rely on the long-form data criticized the government's decision. Among those groups is the Canadian Association of Social Workers, which believes that the loss of the mandatory form will have a long-range negative impact on Canada's most vulnerable citizens (see Exhibit 2.3).

EXHIBIT 2.3

CASW: MAINTAIN THE LONG-FORM CENSUS

CASW CANADIAN ASSOCIATION OF SOCIAL WORKERS

The Right Honourable Stephen Harper   August 5, 2010
Prime Minister of Canada

Open Letter to Prime Minister Stephen Harper: Maintain the Long Form Census

Dear Mr. Prime Minister:

The Canadian Association of Social Workers (CASW) is deeply concerned with the recent decision of the Government of Canada to cancel the 2011 long form Census and replace it with a less reliable voluntary survey.

An unfortunate consequence of replacing the Census with a voluntary survey will be that the most vulnerable in society will not be accurately accounted for in the data collected since they are among those that are less likely to complete a voluntary survey. It is our understanding that the current Census information collected, analyzed and disseminated by Statistics Canada is considered world class. The lack of reliable data in the future could well undermine the delivery of social and community services by all levels of government and service agencies.

This letter is being sent on behalf of the over 17,800 social workers that CASW represent through our provincial and territorial member organizations. We urge you to reconsider your decision and allow the 2011 long form Census to proceed unchanged. Social workers are delivering vital services from coast to coast to coast in Canada and we depend on the data collected by the Census to provide the best practices for every community served.

Sincerely,

Darlene MacDonald
President, CASW

Source: *Open Letter to Prime Minister Stephen Harper: Maintain the Long Form Census*, dated August 5, 2010 is reprinted here with the permission of the Canadian Association of Social Workers (CASW).

DEFINING AND MEASURING SOCIAL PROBLEMS

Once a social problem has been identified, it must be defined and measured. The definition and measurement of social problems is a highly complex process, largely because everyone involved in the process has his or her own perception of the problem and its cause, impact, and solution. Nevertheless, a general consensus on definitions and measurements must be reached before policymakers can design effective policies.

One of the first tasks in defining a social problem is labelling it; for example, the terms, "child abuse," "racism," "poverty," and "social exclusion," are all labels assigned to various and widespread problems in society. Naming a social problem is relatively easy compared with identifying its essential qualities or meaning—in other words, describing how people might perceive or recognize the problem when it is occurring. It is common for definitions of a social problem to vary between countries and between regions within a country, depending on such things as the values and culture of those observing the problem and on the objectives of the researchers studying the problem. However, sometimes a consensus on definitions can be reached. For example, in 1993, the international community (including Canada) signed the United Nations Declaration on the Elimination of Violence against Women. The member countries agreed that "the term 'violence against women' means any act of gender-based violence that results in, or is likely to result in, physical, sexual or psychological harm or suffering to women, including threats of such acts, coercion or arbitrary deprivation of liberty, whether occurring in public or in private life" (United Nations, 1993).

Over time, research may reveal more information about a social problem, resulting in the need for a more accurate label. Some departments of the Government of Canada, for instance, have begun to use the more inclusive term of "woman abuse" over the traditional one of "violence against women"; woman abuse includes violence against women, as well as other forms of maltreatment, such as the neglect of women by caregivers (Public Health Agency of Canada, 2009).

Social and economic **indicators** help researchers to measure the existence of social problems. Indicators are data or statistical measures that represent the various aspects of a social problem and therefore frame problems in concrete, observable, and objective ways. Some indicators serve to *quantify* such things as how many or how often people are affected by a problem; other indicators *qualify* by reporting on how people perceive or experience a social problem. The following indicators (with examples) can be used to paint a picture of what woman abuse "looks like" to observers or "feels like" to those who experience it:

- emotional or psychological indicators (women are afraid or angry, feel isolated, have suicidal or homicidal thoughts)

- physical indicators (women have visible or internal injuries, or make excuses for how they received their injuries)

- sexual indicators (women experience non-consensual sex, recurring genital pain, or unwanted touching)

- financial indicators (abusers control women's finances, or women seek permission from the abusers before spending money)

- stalking or harassment indicators (women are followed or watched or receive unwanted telephone calls or gifts) (York Region Violence Against Women Coordinating Committee, 2006)

Not only can indicators illustrate how a problem manifests itself in society, but they can also report on how problems change over time. Indicators are particularly useful for identifying emerging trends. For instance, by tracking various indicators of violence against women, social scientists have discovered that some women are at a higher risk of abuse than others; the high-risk groups include women who are young, poor, or Aboriginal, have a disability, and are dating, in a common-law relationship, or recently out of a relationship (Baker & Cunningham, 2005). Clearly, the type of information derived from indicators can help policymakers target their policies and programs to certain populations in potentially harmful circumstances.

At times, policymakers fail to agree on what a social problem looks like, how it manifests in people's lives, and how it should be defined or measured. Poverty is a case in point. While some regional governments and private sector groups have proposed their own definitions of poverty, no nationally agreed on definition of poverty exists in Canada. Furthermore, unlike the United States, Canada has no single official set of indicators to measure poverty. The lack of consensus on what poverty is, and how to measure it, has made it difficult to determine the prevalence of poverty in Canada and to find effective solutions to the problem.

DISCUSSION QUESTIONS

■ **Stage 2: Understanding Social Issues and Problems**

1. Racism and child abuse are two serious social problems in Canada. What are some of the indicators you might use to measure the existence of these two problems?

2. A number of definitions for "poverty" exist; however, the federal and provincial and territorial governments have failed to reach a consensus on what poverty is or how governments should address it across the nation. Why do you think it is so difficult to reach such a consensus?

3 STAGE 3: CONSULTING AND REVIEWING

At Stage 3 of the policy development process, policymakers consult with the other members of the **policy community**; that community consists of a broad mix of individuals, organizations, and groups from both inside and outside government. These **stakeholders** represent varying interests and have their own political agendas; while some stakeholders might advocate for a particular policy, others might vehemently oppose it. Thus, the consultation phase is likely to be "a spicy endeavour," fraught with dynamic and unpredictable tensions (Watson-Wright, 2001).

Cabinets are ultimately responsible for setting policy at the federal, provincial, and territorial levels. A number of groups also influence the nature and content of social policy decisions, including civil servants, the voting public, opposition political parties, and interest or lobby groups. While the media, foreign governments, the judiciary, and others tend to have less power and influence over policy decisions, they play an important role in the clarification, interpretation, and shaping of the public's understanding of policy. Each participant in the policy community interacts with and influences the others, yet no single entity dominates the policymaking process (Pross, 1995).

During the consultation and review phase of policymaking, the various members of the policy community must come together to

- define the desired **outcomes** or benefits of the proposed policy (for example, the outcomes of a youth-oriented policy may be that youth are happy, healthy, and socially engaged)
- determine which type of policy would most likely achieve the desired outcomes (for example, a social service may be more effective than a cash benefit)
- debate the pros and cons of policy choices

This section introduces some of the key stakeholders in the policymaking process and examines selected issues influencing their policy decisions on social welfare matters.

GOVERNMENT PARTICIPANTS

When setting social welfare policies, government policymakers enter into a variety of cost-sharing arrangements, address regional differences, and, at times, seek intergovernmental cooperation. This section looks at some of the challenges and opportunities related to these activities.

Federalism and Cost-Sharing Arrangements

To appreciate how the different levels of government work together on policy matters, it is important to consider the role of Canada's constitution, and the division of governmental power. Canada is a federal state—that is, a country that divides legislative power between a central or federal government and regional (provincial and territorial) governments. Each level of government has its own sources of revenue and the authority to pass certain laws. This arrangement allows the federal government to look at overall Canadian values and objectives while regional governments deal with local needs unique to their area.

At the time of confederation in 1867, social welfare matters seemed insignificant and potentially inexpensive, since Canada had a relatively small, rural, and self-sufficient population, and people in need turned to family, neighbours, or religious charities. With a few exceptions, government intervention in social welfare matters seemed unnecessary; therefore, the provinces and territories—rather than the federal government—took on this relatively minor responsibility. Things changed in the early twentieth century, when the social and economic problems created by industrialization, urbanization, and immigration created the need for an expanded social welfare system. Before long, social programs grew so costly that the provinces and territories could not afford them. The federal government, on the other hand, had broad taxation powers and the ability to redistribute resources across the nation.

Over time, the federal government not only assumed a greater responsibility for social policy and programs but also took on more of the related costs. Various cost-sharing arrangements between the federal and provincial and territorial governments have attempted to reduce the fiscal disparities between the two levels of government. An early example of cost sharing occurred during the Great Depression of the 1930s. At the time, the provinces were constitutionally responsible for employment matters; however, as the costs of assisting a growing number of unemployed workers skyrocketed, the federal government bore more of the expense and responsibility for unemployment. A more modern cost-sharing arrangement for social welfare is the Canada Social Transfer (CST). Under the CST, each province and territory receives an equal per capita payment. About 75 percent of the CST finances social assistance, child-care services, and social services across Canada, while the remaining 25 percent supports postsecondary education (Canada, Department of Finance, 2011a). In 2014, the legislation governing the CST expires, calling for the federal, provincial, and territorial governments to re-negotiate a new funding arrangement.

Regional Differences

Although the regional governments welcome financial support from the federal government, they have always asserted their constitutional right to design and deliver social programs as they see fit. In asserting those rights, the provinces and territories have traditionally resisted any attempts by the federal government to impose "national" values on regional policies and programs. Rather, the regional governments prefer to retain their own values and identities, which their locally developed social welfare policies and programs tend to reflect. A number of factors shape regional identity and create differences in how each region sets its priorities and implements its policies. Some of these differences are described below.

Heritage

Many regional differences are rooted in the traditions brought to Canada by the early European settlers. Ontario, for example, originally based its approach to social welfare policy on English civil law, which favoured the delivery of social services by private charities or places of worship. In contrast, British Columbia's colonial government (followed by the provincial government) played a dominant role in developing that region and assigned government workers to deliver many social welfare programs. Québec relied on the Catholic Church to provide the bulk of social welfare support, while Newfoundland and Labrador expected its residents to seek help from friends, family, and charities. Nova Scotia and New Brunswick both adopted the English Poor Laws, which required parishes to use local tax revenue to "manage" the poor. The way in which a region has responded to social problems in the past is likely to influence its current approach to social welfare policy today.

Economic Capacity

Simply put, some provinces and territories are richer than others, mainly because some jurisdictions have more resources or a larger tax base to generate greater revenues. To help correct the regional disparities in wealth, the federal government created the Equalization program and Territorial Formula

Financing (TFF). Under the Equalization program, the federal government gives additional funding to the less prosperous provinces so that they can implement social programs of similar quality to those in wealthier provinces. In 2012–2013, the federal government transferred more than $15 billion in equalization payments to six provinces: Québec, Manitoba, Prince Edward Island, Nova Scotia, New Brunswick, and Ontario. The TFF transfers extra funding to the three territorial governments in recognition of the higher costs of providing public services in the North. In 2012–2013, the three territories received payments totalling more than $3 billion (Canada, Department of Finance, 2011b, 2011c).

Despite attempts to distribute the nation's wealth fairly across the regions, disparities in wealth still exist. Moreover, the various jurisdictions cannot seem to agree on how equalization payments should be calculated to ensure fairness. Meanwhile, some poorer areas of the country struggle to provide the same range and quality of social welfare programs as those found in wealthier jurisdictions.

Ideological Views

Social policies across Canada reflect the social problems in each region, local attitudes toward people in need, and the various strategies for helping at-risk populations. In Québec, for instance, social welfare has traditionally played an important role in preserving the province's unique culture and identity. Even in tough economic times, Québec has been a staunch supporter of social welfare programs, resulting in one of the most highly developed social welfare systems in the country (Beland & Lecours, 2008). In contrast, Alberta's approach to social welfare is more residual. Alberta's wealth allows for a wide range of public programs, yet since 1995, that province's spending on social services has been well below the average of other provinces (Taft, 2010). A survey by Ornstein and Stevenson (2003) suggest that the degree of regional difference depends largely on the type of social issue. In that survey, respondents in Québec and Atlantic Canada gave the most support to the notion of government assisting the poor or unemployed, while the Western provinces gave the least support.

Intergovernmental Cooperation

As a federal state, Canada disperses its political power across the country and among different levels of government; while this sharing of power has its advantages, a consensus on policy decisions can be difficult. Over time, the federal and regional governments have made concessions to achieve common social objectives. During the 1990s, Canada began moving toward **collaborative governance**, a new approach to leadership in which the various levels of government enjoy an equal status in policy decisions and agree to put their differences aside to address issues and problems in the interest of all Canadians. The Social Union Framework Agreement is an example of collaborative governance (see Exhibit 2.4). Signed in 1999 by representatives

HIGHLIGHTS FROM CANADA'S SOCIAL UNION FRAMEWORK AGREEMENT (1999)

Under Canada's Social Union Framework Agreement (SUFA), and within their respective constitutional jurisdictions and powers, the federal, provincial, and territorial governments agree to the following principles and actions.

PRINCIPLES
- Treat Canadians fairly, equitably, and with dignity.
- Ensure equal opportunity and respect rights.
- Ensure access to social programs and help people in need.
- Respect the principles of medicare.
- Promote participation in social and economic life.
- Seek Canadians' input on social policy matters.
- Ensure adequate, affordable, stable, and sustainable funding for social programs.
- Ensure that this agreement is in accord with Aboriginal treaties or other rights.

ACTIONS
- Ensure the MOBILITY of Canadians by removing any barriers to economic opportunities or social programs across the country.
- Be ACCOUNTABLE to Canadians for social programs, and operate in an open and TRANSPARENT manner.
- WORK TOGETHER when developing, improving, and evaluating Canada's social programs; and work with Aboriginal peoples to find practical ways to meet their needs.
- AVOID DISPUTES by working collaboratively, and RESOLVE DISPUTES in a fair and expedient fashion.
- The federal government will consult with the regional governments before exercising its SPENDING POWER to change funding arrangements or introduce new national social initiatives. The federal government agrees to share the cost of regional social programs as long as the provinces/territories are accountable and respect mutual agreements.

Source: "Agreement—A Framework to Improve the Social Union for Canadians." © Privy Council Office. Reproduced and revised with the permission of the Minister of Public Works and Government Services, 2013.

of the federal, provincial (except Québec), and territorial governments, this intergovernmental agreement outlines the mutually agreed-on principles and commitments for pan-Canadian social welfare developments.

Collaborative governance—like any working relationship—has its challenges. In a roundtable sponsored by the Public Policy Forum and the Policy Research Initiative, many of the participants saw the federal government as presenting the greatest obstacles to collaborative efforts because of that government's tendency to

- be inflexible, overly dependent on procedures, and adverse to risk-taking and therefore unlikely to support innovative ideas and strategies to goal achievement

- use a dictatorial or top-down approach to decision-making rather than an approach that emphasizes cooperation and equal status among all levels of government

- be reluctant to share accountability, resources, information, and decision-making powers with others

- bog down the collaborative process by imposing many terms and conditions on projects and initiatives (Gravelle, Baird, & Green, 2008)

In recent years, the federal government has also cancelled or reduced funding to institutions that focus on consensus building (for example, the Status of Women Canada) and virtually ignored agreements (including the Social Union Framework Agreement) that are designed to improve intergovernmental cooperation (Hay, 2009). Don Lenihan (2012) of Canada's Public Policy Forum in Ottawa urges governments to work collaboratively with one another and with non-government stakeholders and, in the process, create better public policies. The alternative, Lenihan suggests, is that the public will lose confidence in the government to resolve important issues and problems.

NON-GOVERNMENT PARTICIPANTS

Since 1968 and Prime Minister Trudeau's call for "participatory democracy," governments have encouraged the Canadian public to speak out about social concerns, voice their opinions about policy decisions that affect them, and take responsibility for social and economic changes in their communities. Citizens and interest groups are two significant non-government participants in the policymaking process. International bodies also play an important role in social welfare policy.

Citizens

The involvement of citizens in the policymaking process is an essential element of a democratic and equitable society. In recent decades, policymaking models have emphasized **citizen participation** and an interactive dialogue between citizens and government decision makers. Citizens can consult with government officials in a variety of ways. For example, in 2012, the Alberta government encouraged Albertans to give their input on the development of a new social policy framework through public meetings, surveys, and social media. Governments commonly use "roundtables"—a group of people exchanging views on selected topics—to seek input from citizens on policy issues. An example of this occurred at the federal level in 2012, when the Minister of Labour called on labour-related experts and organizations to share their views on how to improve conditions for working women.

Ideally, public forums give both citizens and government officials the opportunity to engage in dialogue that is meaningful, deliberative, and interactive. However, as Susan Phillips (2001, pp. 10–11) observes, the consultation process is flawed because "government usually determines who is invited, there are few opportunities for a real exchange of views and genuine dialogue, and participants receive limited information on how the results are used." Despite potential flaws, the consultation process is something that Canadians generally support. A study by researcher Mary Pat MacKinnon (2004, p. 10) found that, in general, Canadians want to be more involved in the democratic process (beyond voting) and seek "more meaningful opportunities to connect with decision-makers on issues that affect their collective quality of life."

Interest Groups

Over the years, the efforts of **interest groups** (also called pressure or lobby groups) have shaped many of Canada's social policies. Interest groups are organized collectives that form to support specific causes and try to influence government policies for the benefit of their own members or on behalf of the public. Canada has five broad categories of interest groups (with examples):

- business associations (Canadian Manufacturers and Exporters)
- labour groups (Canadian Labour Congress)
- professional associations (Canadian Association of Social Workers)
- research institutes (Caledon Institute of Social Policy)
- advocacy groups (Ontario Coalition Against Poverty) or advisory councils (National Seniors Council)

In the early 1990s, a panel created by the Conference Board of Canada concluded that interest groups are vital to a democratic society: "The only legitimate way for government to develop policy is by accepting, even seeking, information and views from those affected and the public at large. Lobbyists present competing views, supply otherwise unavailable information, propose solutions, provide unique insight and counsel so government can assess the implications of proposed policy" (cited in Overton, 1991, p. 18).

In the political arena, interest groups compete with one another for public recognition and government dollars to support their causes. Typically, interest groups that successfully influence social policy decisions are those with abundant and secure financial resources, and a cohesive and stable membership. Politically successful groups also tend to have former politicians as leaders and represent causes that are favourable to politicians and civil servants (Thorburn, 2012). Success also hinges on an interest group's ability to gain access to Cabinet ministers at the federal and provincial or territorial levels.

Interest groups use a variety of strategies to pressure governments to change existing policies, create new policies, or lend more support to specific causes. Some groups use *traditional strategies* to achieve their objectives, including collective bargaining, polling, holding public information sessions, directly contacting policymakers, participating in government consultation processes, financing elections, and publicizing issues and concerns through various media. Other groups try to influence government decisions through *radical strategies*, such as hunger or work strikes, protest marches, boycotts, sit-ins, and public rallies (see Exhibit 2.5). It is common for government committees to invite representatives of an interest group to give an opinion or provide information on a particular issue. An example of this occurred in 2008, when a parliamentary committee invited some of Canada's most prominent interest groups, including the National Council of Welfare, the Canadian Council on Social Development, and the Canadian Association of Social Workers, to give their input on a proposed national poverty-reduction plan (Canadian CED Network, 2008).

International Bodies

Such terms as the *global economy* and *global village* reflect the interdependence of nations around the world in political, economic, social, and cultural matters. While all nations set their own domestic policies, these policies are open to scrutiny by the global community and, at times, must be modified to conform to international standards and practices. Canada is an active member of several international organizations, including the United Nations,

EXHIBIT 2.5

Ontario Coalition Against Poverty

An Ontario Coalition Against Poverty poster promotes a public march to raise aware-ness of poverty in Ontario.

the Organisation for Economic Co-operation and Development (OECD), the World Trade Organization (WTO), and the North Atlantic Treaty Organization (NATO). Many of Canada's partners in the global community (such as the OECD) promote the economic integration of nations through international trade and relations, while others (such as the United Nations) focus more on social development and human rights.

One of Canada's most significant social welfare reforms involved a shift from passive to active public policies—a direct result of the OECD's influence. Traditionally, Canada supported **passive labour market policies**, whereby recipients of government assistance were not required to work or train in exchange for benefits. Beginning in the early 1990s, the OECD pressured Canada and other member countries to "activate" their income-security policies; as a result, Canadian governments now require people drawing benefits from Employment Insurance or social assistance to participate in work experience or training programs. The idea behind **active labour market policies** is to strengthen people's attachment to the paid labour force, to help unemployed workers gain the knowledge and skills they need to quickly enter or re-enter the workforce, and to discourage dependency on the state.

Canada's commitment to human rights is reflected in a number of United Nations' treaties, most of which Canada has ratified and implemented to varying degrees. These treaties influence the direction of Canada's social policies because they require conformity to international standards and conditions. In recent years, Canada has been criticized for failing to comply with certain obligations under international human rights law, specifically the United Nations' International Covenant on Economic, Cultural and Social Rights (ICECSR). The ICECSR outlines fifteen socioeconomic rights, including the right to quality healthcare, income security, and factors related to an adequate standard of living, such as food and housing. Some policy analysts attribute Canada's social problems—such as growing rates of poverty and homelessness—to the country's failure to incorporate many of the ICECSR rights into domestic legislation, policies, and practices (Canada Without Poverty, 2012a). The international community, along with many Canadians, continue to pressure the federal government to meet its international human rights obligations through social policies.

DISCUSSION QUESTIONS

■ **Stage 3: Consulting and Reviewing**

1. Which unique features in your community (or province or territory) should policymakers consider when developing social welfare policies for your area? Those features may include local politics, the economy, heritage/ethnic diversity, or certain social conditions.

2. In what types of activities (for example, voting or a protest march) have you participated to influence government policy? Do you feel those efforts were effective? Why or why not?

4 STAGE 4: FORMALIZING POLICY

In the fourth stage, policymakers must choose one type of policy over another. Once the policy is selected, government must authorize it through either legislation or mutual agreement. A transition period follows, during which government officials consider the merits and potential weaknesses of a policy. The following section looks briefly at the tasks and processes required at this stage.

DECIDING ON THE MIX OF POLICIES

Even after extensive consultation on policy options, it is common for policy-makers to disagree on which type or mix of policies is likely to achieve the desired outcomes. Some policymakers favour policies that give tax breaks rather than social services to people in need. Other policymakers may opt for policies that provide a mix of cash benefits and services; for example, a policy to assist unemployed workers may have an income security component (such as Employment Insurance benefits) and a social service component (such as the provision of employment counselling).

The wrangling among politicians as to which type of policy is best has delayed the eradication of many social problems in Canada, including home-lessness and child poverty (see Exhibit 2.6). However, most policymakers, regardless of their political stripe, are likely to agree that the most desirable policy is the one that benefits the most people, negatively affects the fewest people, produces the most benefits in the shortest time, and costs the least (Torjman, 2005).

EXHIBIT 2.6

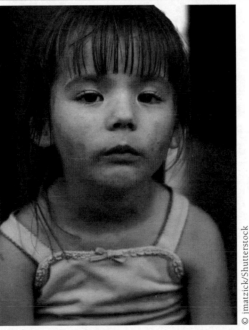

© jmatzick/Shutterstock

Historically, politicians have disagreed on what policies are likely to eliminate child poverty. Meanwhile, many Canadian children go without adequate food, shelter, and other necessities of life.

CHOOSING AN APPROACH

Traditionally, Canadian policymakers have taken a *piecemeal* rather than a *holistic* approach to policymaking. In so doing, policymakers have taken large complex social issues, broken them down into smaller discrete parts, and then created individual policies to address each part. Poverty is a case in point: over the years, policymakers have created several individual policies to reduce poverty; those policies focus on such things as low-cost housing, tax benefits for low-income families, and subsidized child care. Although these individual poverty-related policies and programs may ease the financial burden of people living in poverty, they do little to address the complexities of poverty in a comprehensive way.

Evidence suggests that the piecemeal approach to policymaking is gradually losing ground in Canada. This is particularly true at the regional level, where governments have (or are in the process of developing) long-range, comprehensive, and integrated strategies to reduce poverty in their jurisdictions. Those strategies recognize the multidimensions of poverty in one policy package and support a coordinated system of programs and services to improve the quality of life of all citizens.

AUTHORIZING SOCIAL POLICY

The process that Canadian policymakers use to authorize social policies depends on such considerations as the perceived importance of the policy, how committed policymakers are to the policy, and how urgently the policy is needed. Decision makers may designate a social policy as either a "hard law" (a policy that has undergone the legislative process and been passed into law) or a "soft law" (a policy that is not legally binding or enforceable).

Legislated Policies

Many social policies—such as the federal Canada Pension Plan and provincial child welfare acts—are the product of enacting laws or legislation. In its initial state, a social policy is introduced as a proposal or **bill**, of which there are two types: (1) public bills, which involve matters of law and have a broad application over a large area, such as the nation or a province; and (2) private bills, which grant powers, privileges, or exemptions to individuals, groups, or corporations. At the federal level, both the House of Commons and the Senate give the bill three readings; if the bill passes in both houses, the governor general approves the bill, which then becomes law in the form of an act or a statute. At the provincial and territorial level, the legislative assembly approves the bill; the lieutenant governor of the province or territory then gives "royal consent" to the bill before it becomes an act or a statute.

The legislative process involves a great deal of debate and review among governmental departments, committees, and legislators to ensure that bills receive proper scrutiny before being either rejected or passed into law. Exhibit 2.7 illustrates the number of channels through which a bill passes at the federal level.

EXHIBIT 2.7

THE FEDERAL LEGISLATIVE PROCESS

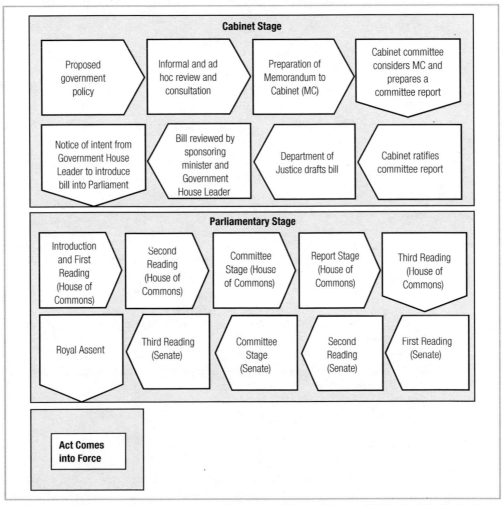

Source: Adapted from Barnes, A., Parliamentary Information and Research Service. (2012, May 17). *The legislative process: From government policy to proclamation:* Appendix. Retrieved from http://www.parl.gc.ca/Content/LOP/ResearchPublications/prb0864-e.pdf.

It is common for several months or years to pass between the proposal of a bill and its enactment. Several factors may slow a bill's progress through the legislative process. For instance, Canadian law provides for several "Opposition Days" to allow the official Opposition to criticize and debate the details of a proposed bill. Sometimes the government deliberately delays a bill's enactment so the public has adequate time to consider the content and the direction of the proposed policy. At the federal level, the Senate may find a flaw in a bill and return it to the House of Commons to amend. These types of delays can potentially delay the implementation of new social policies, making them outdated by the time they reach the program stage.

Non-Binding Policies

Non-binding social policies include mutual agreements, declarations, codes of practice, and resolutions. These types of policies may be preferred over legislated policies because they are relatively inexpensive to create and can be more flexible in the way they are developed, modified, or applied. In many cases, non-binding policies promote compromise among those trying to reach an agreement; on the other hand, these policies tend to be more difficult to monitor and less enforceable if members do not follow the agreed-on conditions. One of the most significant non-binding social-welfare policies in Canada is the Social Union Framework Agreement.

DISCUSSION QUESTIONS

■ **Stage 4: Formalizing Policy**

1. Many provincial and territorial governments are recognizing that a holistic rather than piecemeal approach to poverty is likely to reduce the problem. Identify other complex social problems that you believe governments should tackle by using a holistic approach.

2. What are the potential pros and cons of a policy that is either (a) legislated, or (b) non-binding?

5 STAGE 5: IMPLEMENTING POLICY

In stage 5, policymakers take the necessary steps to put policies into action. In a social welfare context, the implementation stage involves the development of an income security program, a social service, or other type of initiative aimed at enhancing social well-being. It is imperative that policymakers adhere to certain core principles when developing social welfare initiatives. For example, initiatives must be

- sustainable (capable of surviving over time, using a reasonable number of resources)
- inclusive (foster participation in society)
- responsive (adapt to changing times and circumstances)
- accessible (capable of being reached and used by Canadians) (Stewart, 2002)

Once a government transforms an initiative from a policy to a program or service, it must decide who will deliver the initiative to those who need it; government must also determine the money, staffing, equipment, and other types of resources the initiative needs to meet its goals. Governments tend to deliver **mandated services**—such as provincial social assistance and child protection services—that derive from an act or a statute. Non-governmental agencies are more likely to deliver non-mandated services, such as family counselling and child-care services.

The primary focus of this book is policy implementation. Each chapter gives examples of "policy in action"—programs and services that have as their primary goal the enhancement of social welfare.

DISCUSSION QUESTIONS

■ **Stage 5: Implementing Policy**

1. Social welfare programs and services are policies "in action." Identify three social welfare programs and services in your community. For each initiative, determine what its underlying policy is trying to achieve (for example, some policies aim to increase employment, while others try to reduce homelessness).

6   STAGE 6: EVALUATING POLICIES

Stage 6 of the policy development process focuses on analyzing policies to determine whether they are being carried out the way that they were intended or whether they are achieving what they set out to achieve. Analysts must first decide what they hope to learn from this type of review and then select a model or framework to guide their investigation. Periodically, such an analysis reveals flaws in the policy that make it necessary to amend or replace the policy or, in extreme cases, repeal the policy altogether.

MODELS OF ANALYSIS

Whether conducted during or at the end of the development process, a formal review can help to identify which areas of the policy or program are doing well and which areas might need improvement. Many models exist either to analyze policies or to evaluate programs; these models provide structure and focus to the formal review. Among these models are a cost-benefit evaluation (looks at the relationship between a policy's or program's results and its costs), a needs assessment (determines whether an existing or a new policy or program is needed), and an outcome measurement (assesses whether the policy or program has achieved the desired outcomes or results). Two generic models—a logic model and a process model—are briefly described below.

A Logic Model

A **logic model** identifies the connections between the activities of a policy or program and the achievement of its goals. This model assumes that successful policies and programs are the result of a series of "if-then" relationships: if we invest *inputs*, then certain *activities* can take place; if these activities are carried out successfully, then we can expect specific *outputs* and *outcomes* (Innovation Network, 2005). These components are summarized below:

- Inputs are the resources that are invested in an initiative and include money, staff, equipment, time, expertise, and physical facilities.

- Activities (or processes) refer to how inputs are used; for example, resources may be used to provide staff training, improve service delivery, recruit volunteers, or promote services.

- Outputs are the goods or services produced by the policy or program, such as information pamphlets for clients, counselling sessions, and the distribution of food baskets to people in need.

- Outcomes are the ultimate effects or benefits of the policy or program in relation to the goals set; for instance, at the end of a program, clients may report improved health or higher day-to-day functioning (Canada, Treasury Board Secretariat, 2010).

Analyzing the content of a policy or program has many advantages. For instance, the study of discrete parts can help to reveal what happens at each stage of policy development or implementation and how those parts relate to each other. This type of review can also be useful for identifying gaps or inefficiencies in program resources or activities.

A Process Model

While a logic model focuses on the content of a policy, a **process model** emphasizes the process by which policy is created and implemented. Process models assume that policies and their related programs evolve from sequential stages or steps, such as planning, setting goals and objectives, and designing. One or more of these steps may be the subject of analysis.

A process model can help to explain what a policy or program does, how it does it, and how those processes relate to the final results. An explanatory approach may seek answers to the following questions:

- How do people understand, interpret, or define the presenting issue or problem?
- What are the political processes that shaped the policy?
- Who are the main stakeholders of the policy—that is, who is most interested in, or affected by, the policy?
- Who has influence on the types of solutions that are considered? For example, have policymakers sought the public's input or consulted with experts?
- Which type of organization—such as a government agency or a nonprofit organization—is responsible for delivering and managing the program?
- Is the program achieving its goals, objectives, and intended outcomes?

Researchers can use any number of methods—such as focus groups and surveys—to gather information about a policy's or program's process. Because creating and implementing policies and programs is so complex, a mix of data collection tools is usually preferred over a single method (Westhues, 2002).

ANALYSIS THROUGH LENSES

One way to analyze a policy or program is through a particular filter or lens. These tools allow analysts to study a policy or program from a specific frame of reference to see if it adheres to certain principles, standards, or values. Two examples of Canadian-based analysis frameworks are provided below.

An Inclusion Lens

Many Canadian governments, non-government organizations, and community groups use an **inclusion lens** when analyzing their policies. Exhibit 2.8 depicts the inclusion lens introduced by Malcolm Shookner in 2002. Shookner's

EXHIBIT 2.8

AN INCLUSION LENS

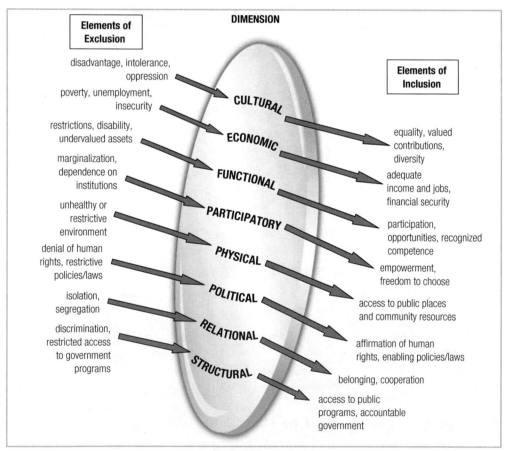

Source: *An Inclusion Lens: A Workbook for Looking at Social and Economic Exclusion and Inclusion.* Malcolm Shookner and Health Canada, 2002. Adapted with permission from both Malcolm Shookner and the Minister of Health, 2013.

framework includes eight dimensions in which analysts can observe inclusion or exclusion; for each dimension, analysts can assess to what degree a policy, program, or practice either includes or excludes people from the social and economic benefits of Canadian life. Among the key questions analysts might ask when using this inclusion lens are the following:

- Who is being excluded (or included) and from what?
- How are people being excluded (or included)?
- Who benefits from the exclusion (or inclusion)?

Since 2002, a number of Canadian governments have developed their own version of an inclusion lens to assess the extent to which their communities are inclusive and equitable. For instance, the City of Ottawa (2010) uses an *equity and inclusion lens* to ensure that its programs, services, and workplaces are accessible to all persons; the lens is particularly valuable for ensuring the inclusion of at-risk populations, such as Aboriginal peoples, immigrants, people with disabilities, francophones, people living in poverty, seniors, women, youth, members of visible minority groups, rural residents, and LGBT (lesbian, gay, bisexual, and transgendered) people.

A Life-Course Lens

Traditionally, policymakers have based social welfare policy on the life-cycle model, which focuses on the standard stages of life, such as infancy, childhood, youth, adulthood, and old age. Those life stages, however, do not reflect reality as closely as they once did. Today, most people engage in activities independent of their age or stage of life; for example, it is common for people to attend university, college, or trade school at any time in their life, not just in early adulthood, which used to be the norm (Voyer, 2005).

The Government of Canada uses a life-course approach to better understand how people transition from one life phase to another (for instance, from work to retirement), what types of choices they make during these transitions (which impact later life experiences), and what types of resources they need to successfully make life transitions. Policy analysts study policies with a **life-course lens** to ensure that policies respond to people's experiences over the lifespan and that they focus on individuals rather than predetermined or stereotyped groups of people, such as "youth" or "the elderly." In recent years, researchers have used the life-course lens to study and report on various aspects of Canadian life, including social participation, housing insecurity, Aboriginal health, trends in earnings, and late-life transitions (McDaniel & Bernard, 2011).

AMENDING, REPLACING, OR REPEALING POLICY

No policy is immune to change or abolition. Indeed, Canada's political history is rich with examples of policies that Parliament or provincial legislatures introduced, then later declared as inadequate, and subsequently amended, repealed, or replaced. One example is the Unemployment Insurance (UI) Act. A review of that Act in 1971 prompted a series of *amendments* that introduced more restrictive eligibility criteria, shorter benefit periods, and higher premium rates. After it underwent another major review in 1994, the UI Act was seen as being so inefficient that Parliament *repealed* it and then *replaced* it with the Employment Insurance Act of 1996.

Sometimes policies are introduced, and even legislated, and then later declared illegal or "unconstitutional." Many Canadians have had the courage to challenge public policies in the courts, claiming that such policies violate their rights under the Canadian Charter of Rights and Freedoms. Alleged Charter violations often relate to the interpretation of sections 7 and 15 of the Charter:

- Section 7. "Everyone has the right to life, liberty and security of the person and the right not to be deprived thereof except in accordance with the principles of fundamental justice."

- Section 15. "Every individual is equal before and under the law and has the right to the equal protection and equal benefit of the law without discrimination and, in particular, without discrimination based on race, national or ethnic origin, colour, religion, sex, age or mental or physical disability."

Citizens whose claims relate to section 15 of the Charter have had a number of victories. Many of those success stories have involved violations of disability rights and discrimination based on race, sex, or poverty status.

Since the Charter was enacted in 1982, the courts have struggled with the interpretation of the word "security" in section 7. Specifically, the courts have considered whether certain social problems, such as poverty, could be interpreted as a threat to an individual's security. The courts have also raised the possibility that "security" might include economic security and therefore guarantee a person's right to adequate food, housing, clothing, and income security benefits. In general, Canadian courts have concluded that while security is a worthy social goal, government is not responsible for ensuring it (Buckley, 2005). In 2008, the Supreme Court of British Columbia went one step further on the security issue. In the *City of Victoria v. Adams et al.*, the Supreme Court ruled that while government may not be responsible for a person's security, it must not impede a person's right to seek his or her own security (security in this case referred to shelter). Exhibit 2.9 provides

EXHIBIT 2.9

VICTORIA'S ANTI-CAMPING BYLAWS RULED UNCONSTITUTIONAL

In 2005, about seventy homeless people could not find beds in local shelters so they set up tents in Cridge Park, a public park in Victoria, British Columbia. Law officials ordered the campers to remove their tents because they violated the city's anti-camping bylaws, which prohibited "temporary abodes" in public parks.

When the campers refused to leave, the city took legal action to evict them. In response, nine homeless people challenged the constitutionality of the anti-camping bylaws.

In her 2008 ruling on the case, B.C. Supreme Court Justice Carol Ross concluded that because of the insufficient capacity of local shelters, "a significant number of people in the City of Victoria have no choice but to sleep outside in the City's parks or streets." Expert witnesses in the case noted that tents were more likely than blankets or sleeping bags to provide sufficient protection from the elements.

The B.C. Supreme Court ruled that the City of Victoria's bylaws that prohibited the erection of temporary shelters on public property violated "[section] 7 of the Canadian Charter of Rights and Freedoms in that they deprive homeless people of life, liberty and security of the person in a manner not in accordance with the principles of fundamental justice."

The Court added that Victoria's anti-camping bylaws "impose upon those homeless persons, who are among the most vulnerable and marginalized of the City's residents, significant and potentially severe additional health risks. In addition, sleep and shelter are necessary preconditions to any kind of security, liberty or human flourishing."

The City of Victoria appealed the court's decision but lost their case in 2009. The city then changed its bylaws in 2010 to comply with the Charter, limiting the erection of temporary shelters to homeless people, in certain areas, and during specific times.

Sources: *Victoria (City) v. Adams*, 2008 BCSC 1363. Retrieved from CanLII website: http://www.canlii.org/en/bc/bcsc/doc/2008/2008bcsc1363/2008bcsc1363.html; *Victoria (City) v. Adams*, 2009 BCCA 563. Retrieved from CanLII website: http://www.canlii.org/en/bc/bcca/doc/2009/2009bcca563/2009bcca563.html.

more details on this landmark case. Since the *Adams* decision, Canadians have been scrutinizing the "anti-homeless" bylaws in other cities. In 2012, Pivot Legal Society challenged the constitutionality of the City of Vancouver's bylaws that allow officials to ticket homeless people who are sleeping outdoors (Bennett, 2012).

DISCUSSION QUESTIONS

■ Stage 6: Evaluating Policies

1. Identify a social welfare policy that you are interested in learning more about. If you were to conduct a process evaluation of that policy, what types of things would you want to learn about? What are some of the basic steps you would take to evaluate the policy?

2. Identify an income security program or a social service program in your community. What do you think the program is trying to achieve? Do you believe that it is achieving its objectives? Why or why not?

3. Do you think that social policies should ensure that people have access to the basic necessities of life, such as food and shelter? Give a rationale for your answer.

SUMMARY

Introduction

Social welfare policy is a type of public policy and a subset of social policy. Closely linked to economic policy, social welfare policy provides the structure for most income security programs and social services. Policymakers often use the stages model to guide the development of policy.

1 Stage 1: Identifying Social Problems and Issues

Social policymakers must decide which social conditions are social issues and which are social problems. Social problems create a negative consequence for a large segment of the population. The perception of social problems changes over time, as do the types of social risks that confront people. Globalization and the shift to a postindustrial era have created or exacerbated social problems in Canada. Some social problems—such as social exclusion and poverty—are so closely linked that policymakers address them as one complex problem.

2 **Stage 2: Understanding Social Issues and Problems**

Government, private research institutes, academic disciplines, and professionals are some of the groups that contribute to social knowledge. Researchers use various data collection tools to gather information on social conditions and problems. Social and economic indicators describe social problems in concrete terms. A single social problem, such as poverty, may have multiple sets of indicators.

3 **Stage 3: Consulting and Reviewing**

Government and non-government stakeholders make up Canada's policy community. Government participants are influenced by federalism and the division of powers between levels of government. Although the provinces and territories are constitutionally responsible for social policy and programs, the federal government has assumed some responsibility as well—this situation has created tension between those two levels of government. Non-government participants try to influence Canada's policies through citizen participation, interest group activities, and international agreements.

4 **Stage 4: Formalizing Policy**

Policymakers often disagree as to which type of policy is likely to achieve the desired results. Once a policy is selected, it may be authorized either through legislation or as a non-binding set of guidelines. The legislative process is complex and can delay the enactment of social welfare policies.

5 **Stage 5: Implementing Policy**

Governments implement social welfare policies through income security programs or social services. Policymakers must adhere to certain principles when designing programs and allocate resources to the service delivery organization.

6 **Stage 6: Evaluating Policies**

The logic model and the process model are two of the many models available to guide the review of policies and their related programs. Policy analysts sometimes use a lens or frame of reference to evaluate social welfare policies. It is common for analysts to review a policy and find it flawed in some way; in this case, policymakers may amend, repeal, or replace the policy. Occasionally, citizens have challenged public policies in courts of law on the basis that they violate people's constitutional rights.

KEY TERMS

For definitions of the key terms, consult the Glossary on page 453 at the end of the book.

public policies, p. 30

social policy, p. 30

social welfare policy, p. 30

social policymakers, p. 31

social conditions, p. 32

social issue, p. 32

population aging, p. 32

social problem, p. 32

social exclusion, p. 33

poverty, p. 34

social knowledge, p. 34

data collection tools, p. 35

longitudinal surveys, p. 35

indicators, p. 37

policy community, p. 39

stakeholders, p. 39

outcomes, p. 39

collaborative governance, p. 43

citizen participation, p. 45

interest groups, p. 45

passive labour market policies, p. 47

active labour market policies, p. 47

bill, p. 50

mandated services, p. 53

logic model, p. 54

process model, p. 55

inclusion lens, p. 56

life-course lens, p. 57

Historical Foundations

OBJECTIVES

Canada's social welfare system expanded over several decades until the mid-1970s. This chapter will

- introduce this period in the history of social welfare

- consider the early governmental attempts to ensure social well-being from colonial times to Confederation

- explore the rapidly changing social welfare needs during the transitional phase, from Confederation to the Second World War

- examine the major social welfare achievements of the interventionist phase, from the Second World War to the mid-1970s

INTRODUCTION

Histories of welfare states are much more than collections of facts and chronologies of programs. They are also compilations of human memories and myths, of political conflict and struggle, of compassion and sharing, and of aspirations and achievements. They are the stories of community members coming together to protect themselves or organizing and encouraging their governments to create security against unforeseen misfortune. And they can teach us so much. (James Rice and Michael Prince, 2000, p. 34)

Canada's social welfare system is not the product of any one period or circumstance in history. Rather, social welfare policies and programs have been introduced and revised at different times and in response to various human needs and social problems. For the most part, the level of social provision at any time in history has depended on public demand, the political and economic climate of the day, and government priorities.

While compassion and generosity have long been cherished Canadian values, a residual approach to social welfare predominated in the early settlement years. Early settlers expected to either support themselves through work or, if in need, turn to family, neighbours, the church, or charitable organizations. It was not until the aftermath of the Great Depression and the social and economic disruption it caused that Canadians seriously considered a more institutional approach to social welfare.

This chapter looks at the evolving role of government in the development of Canada's social welfare system from the early settlement period to the mid-1970s.

1 THE EARLY PHASE (COLONIAL TIMES TO CONFEDERATION)

The early phase was characterized by self-sufficiency and minimal government involvement in people's lives and well-being. Many of the first immigrants to Canada received food, clothing, work tools, and land grants from government and private sources; however, for the most part, Canadians took responsibility for themselves and their dependants. People met their basic needs primarily through self-employment (mostly farming). Asking for charity—even from the churches—was generally discouraged, and recipients of "handouts" were often made to feel like personal failures. With few exceptions (mainly in New France), Canada's early European settlers took a residual approach to social welfare (Guest, 2012).

SOCIAL WELFARE IN NEW FRANCE

Although the French settlers valued work and self-sufficiency, they also welcomed various forms of support. Guided by the belief that government is responsible for its citizens, the Government of France funded a range of educational, health, and other services for those who settled in New France (now Québec). Many private **charities** were available as well, which gave housing and education to poor children, care to sick and elderly people, and refuge to the so-called lunatic. Charitable organizations also helped the able-bodied poor, albeit on the condition that they would work hard to become productive members of society. Some organizations, such as Québec City's Hôpital-Général (general hospital) and the Congregation of Notre Dame, offered skills training to settlers who had trouble finding or creating work.

In general, the French had little tolerance for begging. As early as 1674, France passed a royal decree prohibiting begging by able-bodied persons in Montréal; by 1676, Montréal had banned vagrants and beggars from the city unless they had special permission from a parish priest to stay (Meinhard & Foster, 2002; Olasky, 1992). Those banished from Montréal could often find solace and help from the nuns living in outlying settlements (see Exhibit 3.1).

EXHIBIT 3.1

Painted by Father Chauchetière between 1682–1693.

From 1677 to her death in 1680, Kateri Tekakwitha tended to the poor and sick in Sault Saint-Louis, near Montréal. In 2012, Kateri became North America's first Aboriginal saint.

Soon after the British conquered New France in 1759, the social welfare supports established by the French government disintegrated, causing great hardship (Martin, 1985). However, after Britain passed the Québec Act in 1774, the Roman Catholic Church assumed a prominent role in the provision of social welfare. The Church saw the giving of charity as a moral responsibility and as a good deed leading to salvation; the Church was also well suited to the role of charity provider. As Donald Bellamy (1965, p. 36) points out: "Long experience in ministering to the weak and suffering, backed by a strong administrative organization, dedicated personnel and wealthy patrons, and its own abundant material resources fitted the Church well for meeting the temporal needs of the people no less than the spiritual needs."

The number of French charities, largely staffed by volunteers, grew during the nineteenth century. These volunteers ran soup kitchens and clothing depots, delivered food and fuel, collected and distributed donations of furniture, visited the sick and infirm, and helped unemployed people find jobs. In the larger centres of Québec City and Montréal, religious societies—such as the Society of Saint Vincent de Paul—provided basic goods and services to people in need, regardless of religious affiliation, and advocated for improvements in living conditions for disadvantaged people (Lautenschlager, 1992).

THE PROTESTANT WORK ETHIC

The Protestant Reformation in sixteenth-century Europe brought the belief that success at work, in the form of profits and wealth, was evidence of godly living, virtue, and God's grace. This new understanding of salvation and work—indeed, the creation of a "work ethic"—accompanied an emerging view of poverty as a sign of a sinful life and divine retribution. While many British Protestant settlers helped to relieve the poor from hardship, they did so in the belief that people must work in this world to be saved in the next. Thus, help for the poor "was often accompanied by unsolicited and often irrelevant advice on how the poor might regain God's grace through the exercise of . . . thrift, hard work, self-help, and self-discipline" (Guest, 1997, p. 18).

Over time, the religious references in programs for the poor gradually diminished in Canada. However, the **Protestant work ethic** became a core value underlying many later social welfare programs, such as work camps during the Great Depression and, more recently, welfare-to-work programs.

POOR LAW PRINCIPLES AND PUBLIC RELIEF

Many of the principles underlying Canada's current social welfare system have their origins in a series of British parliamentary acts collectively called the **English Poor Laws**, the first of which was passed in 1601. Although the poor laws were meant to deal with poverty in England, they influenced how the British colonies viewed and treated the poor. Nova Scotia and New Brunswick enacted poor laws in 1763 and 1786, respectively. In those areas, the colonial governments (or parishes) assumed a public responsibility for social welfare by collecting taxes to assist destitute settlers. Newfoundland and Prince Edward Island never endorsed poor law practices to any real extent; rather, they encouraged their poor to rely on family, friends, and charities. Since work was plentiful in Upper Canada (now Ontario), that colony rejected the notion of government intervention to help the poor, including poor law legislation (Guest, 2012).

While the adoption of poor law *practices* varied across colonial settlements, many parishes developed their systems of **public relief** according to poor law *principles*. Those principles include the following:

- Public relief should be residual. Only after all private sources of help (friends, family, neighbours, and charities) were exhausted did people have the right to seek help from the government.

- Public relief should be **categorical**. Governments categorized people in need as being either "deserving" or "undeserving" of public assistance. The deserving poor (or "impotent poor") included elderly or sick adults, those with disabilities, orphaned children, and others who could not support themselves through paid employment. The undeserving poor included able-bodied adults who could not find work, as well as vagrants or beggars who were capable of, yet unwilling, to work.

- Public relief should be conditional. Recipients of public relief were expected to compensate society for any benefits they received. For example, poverty-stricken parents were given public relief on the condition that they not abandon their children.

- Public relief amounts should be calculated according to the **principle of less eligibility**. To discourage people from seeking or becoming dependent on government, benefits were to be minimal and less than the wage of the lowest-paid workers in a settlement (Rice & Prince, 2000).

When doling out public relief (an early form of social assistance or welfare), parish officials gave either outdoor or indoor relief, depending on whether the person lived at home or in an institution. People who lived at home, were, incapable of working, and were deserving of assistance, received **outdoor relief**, which consisted of cash and other direct assistance. But that relief was typically sporadic and meagre. Historical documents reveal that many deserving seniors had to resort to begging to supplement what little relief they received from local government (Canadian Museum of Civilization Corporation [CMCC], 2008).

The parish officials provided **indoor relief** in institutions, such as **workhouses** and **poorhouses**. The workhouses (or houses of industry) were for able-bodied, unemployed adults to learn good work habits and pay for their keep through labour. Exhibit 3.2 profiles Ontario's houses of industry and refuge. The parishes established separate poorhouses to confine various groups of poor people, such as elderly people and orphaned children. However, to keep poor law taxes down, parish authorities sometimes herded all poor people into the same facility; thus, poorhouses became catchall institutions for anyone who was destitute (Guest, 1980). In general, poorhouses and workhouses were unappealing even to the most desperate individuals. Dennis Guest (2012) notes that, in the larger towns, the reputation of these establishments "was so fearsome that only those facing starvation would seek such help."

The parishes dealt with poverty and other social problems in their own unique ways. In some of the smaller towns, poorhouses or workhouses were too expensive to build or maintain. As an alternative, settlement officials (such as those in New Brunswick) auctioned off the poor to work for local families. Some of the larger settlements built a variety of institutions to manage certain "problem" populations; for example, the populated areas had orphanages and what were then called insane asylums, and asylums for the care of immigrant women and children who had become widows or orphans during the voyage from Europe (Guest, 1997; Taylor, 1969).

Despite the laws that enabled colonial governments to provide some relief to the needy, a residual approach to social welfare predominated, and parish officials offered benefits only in cases of extreme emergency. In English settlements, the Protestant work ethic legitimated this approach and reinforced the notion that work was preferable to public assistance. Governments expected families to care for their own members and, in the eighteenth century, some governments began imposing fines on those who failed to do so (Morel, 2002).

EXHIBIT 3.2

HOUSES OF INDUSTRY AND REFUGE IN ONTARIO

© Waterloo Region Museum, Regional Municipality of Waterloo, Kitchener, Ontario

The House of Industry and Refuge in Berlin (later Kitchener), Ontario, opened in 1869.

Beginning in the mid-nineteenth century, counties in Ontario followed the British lead and established institutions for the poor and needy. Municipal law regulated these institutions, which they called Houses of Industry and Refuge. Officers of the law had the authority to commit individuals to the institutions, where they were "diligently employed" either indoors or on adjoining farmlands.

In 1868, Norfolk County became the first county in Ontario to establish a house of refuge for the "elderly, orphaned, indigent and lunatic." Provincial legislation soon followed that required all Ontario counties to establish similar institutions. The Toronto Home for Incurables was one such institution.

New ideas about poverty and the treatment of poor people, and the financial security provided by Mothers' Allowances (1920), Old Age Pensions (1927), and Family Allowances (1944) acts, caused the demand for large institutions to dwindle. Many of the houses of refuge and industry were either demolished or sold and converted into other operations.

Sources: Hardin, E. (2004). *Regional History: Peace & Prosperity: Waterloo County 1853–1972*. Retrieved from www.region.waterloo.on.ca/web/region.nsf/0/63C468981ACA86E385256E0500504073?OpenDocument; and Cottonwood Mansion Preservation Foundation. (April 22, 2008). Newsletter, p. 4. From http://linetap.com/cottonwoodmansion/May-08.pdf.

CONFEDERATION

The passage of the British North America (BNA) Act in 1867 united New Brunswick, Nova Scotia, Ontario, and Québec into the Dominion of Canada and divided legislative responsibilities between the federal and regional governments. The provinces accepted responsibility for "hospitals, asylums, charities and eleemosynary [alms-giving] institutions," which, for the most part, summed up the extent of social programs in populated areas. Since governments generally considered social welfare to be a private and local matter, many provinces in central and eastern Canada delegated their social welfare functions to municipal governments (Guest, 2012). The BNA Act gave the federal government a minor role in the health and welfare of Canadians and did little to increase the amount of federal revenue flowing to social welfare causes.

DISCUSSION QUESTIONS

■ **The Early Phase (Colonial Times to Confederation)**

1. Canada's pioneers took a predominantly residual approach to social welfare. Putting yourself in the shoes of a person living in this early period, give reasons why a residual approach may have seemed to be appropriate (and even helpful) for the times.

2. Identify the possible pros and cons of making public relief residual, conditional, categorical, and according to the principle of less eligibility.

2 | THE TRANSITIONAL PHASE (CONFEDERATION TO SECOND WORLD WAR)

The transitional phase was characterized by Canadians' rapidly changing social welfare needs. Industrialization was drawing many rural dwellers into urban centres and, at the same time, the traditional, family-based economy (especially family farming) was giving way to an economy based on wage labour. As a result of these changes, family roles shifted: men became the primary wage earners, while women and children became their dependants. If the head of the household fell ill, was injured at work, lost his job, or died, the entire family's financial security was jeopardized (Bellemare, 1993). Urbanization and related problems, such as poverty, crime, and social fragmentation, threatened the stability of growing cities. Despite these pressing social problems, governments staunchly defended residualism and continued to restrict assistance to the poor or those at immediate risk of becoming poor (Guest, 1997). By the end of the transitional phase, however, Canadian governments had assumed more responsibility for social welfare provision, a move that signalled the beginning of a philosophical shift from private troubles to collective responsibility (Meinhard & Foster, 2002).

SOCIAL MOVEMENTS AND CHANGING ATTITUDES

Industrialization and its associated problems prompted an increase in social consciousness and a feeling of mutual responsibility for fellow human beings. As they learned about the underlying causes of social problems, Canadians began questioning the prevailing belief that poverty and other social ills were the result of individual shortcomings. A number of **social movements**—such as those related to labour reform, child welfare, and women's rights—took firm root during this period. Social reformers (or activists) called attention to the inability of families, charities, churches, and local governments to adequately meet the needs of a modern industrial society. Those reformers also pressured governments to take a more active role in the social and economic lives of citizens (Bellemare, 1993). During this period, a growing interest in social democracy and the rise of such political parties as the Cooperative Commonwealth Federation (CCF) advanced the notion of **social citizenship**—that is, a right to minimum levels of health and well-being and equitable access to services. Some of the highlights of the major social movements of this era are reviewed below.

The Labour Movement and Workers' Compensation

Industrialization required labourers in the mining, fishing, construction, and manufacturing sectors to put in long hours for low pay, often in unpleasant or dangerous conditions. Mounting dissatisfaction among workers resulted in sporadic protests and the formation of unions as a means to demand higher standards of living, income security programs, and better wages with paid overtime. By the 1870s, trade unions were gaining collective bargaining power and becoming a powerful political force (Carniol, 1990).

During the early years of industrialization, primitive and dangerous machines caused frequent work-related accidents and injuries. Neither workers nor employers had financial protection when accidents occurred. For instance, in the late nineteenth and early twentieth centuries, a worker could sue an employer over a workplace injury. If the company lost, the court made it pay the injured worker. If the damages awarded were considerable, the company was often forced to declare bankruptcy and shut down, which hardly benefited the injured worker (McGilly, 1998).

Many trade unions drew public attention to the increasing number of industrial accidents and the shortcomings of the compensation system, and they pressured governments to improve the situation for workers. Although Québec had a form of workers' compensation by 1908, Canada's first comprehensive and compulsory plan was the Ontario Workmen's Compensation Act of 1914. Under this act, all major Ontario employers contributed to the compensation fund; in the event of a work-related accident, a worker could apply for compensation from the fund. The Ontario act was Canada's first **social insurance** program and became known across North America as one of the most advanced pieces of legislation for its time. The act also started a national workers' compensation movement; by 1920, every province except Prince Edward Island had similar legislation (Guest, 1997).

Improving Conditions for Women and Children

As the pace of industrialization accelerated, families grew more economically insecure. Dependent women and children often had to care for themselves if a male breadwinner failed, for whatever reason, to provide for his family. Divorce was becoming more common, and many women who needed to work had to leave their children unattended. These types of events and conditions triggered a change in attitude toward women, children, and the role of government in family life, and added fuel to the fire of social change (Strong-Boag, 1979).

The Child Welfare Movement

Canada's child welfare movement gained momentum in the late nineteenth century when John Joseph Kelso, a reporter for the *Toronto Globe*, wrote a series of articles about the neglect and abuse of children in Toronto. These articles spurred a public outcry that led to the passage of the 1888 Act for the Protection and Reformation of Neglected Children in Ontario. Later, Ontario's legislature passed the 1893 Act for the Prevention of Cruelty to and Better Protection of Children. Considered the first comprehensive piece of legislation in North America to protect children, the new act placed Canada at the forefront of child welfare legislation. The act promoted nonprofit children's aid societies in Ontario and the placement of neglected, abused, and dependent children in foster homes rather than institutions. Appointed superintendents monitored the foster homes to ensure an adequate level of care for the children (Guest, 1997). Ontario's act also prompted other jurisdictions across Canada to introduce and enforce child welfare legislation.

The First Wave of the Women's Rights Movement

During the late nineteenth and early twentieth centuries, the women's rights movement focused primarily on improving social and economic conditions for women and children. At that time, society took a woman's issues seriously only if she raised them within a religious context. Christie and Gauvreau (1996, p. 108) observe: "Under the impress of Christian thought, even the most 'radical social teachings,' which in any other venue would have been perceived as a threat to the social order, were deemed legitimate forms of social amelioration because they were conducted within the respectable avenues of church reform." Women's church associations led to the establishment of national organizations, such as the Young Women's Christian Association (YWCA) and the Woman's Christian Temperance Union.

Women also advocated for extended legal and political rights, such as the right to vote and to run for political office. Although women were under-represented in political parties, they exerted considerable influence on social change through pressure groups, such as the National Council of Women of Canada (see Exhibit 3.3). By the 1920s, women's groups and early feminists like Emily Murphy and Nellie McClung were making headway in a number of social causes, such as mother's pensions, the minimum wage, prison reform, and medical care for women and children (Christie & Gauvreau, 1996).

THE FIRST WORLD WAR, PENSIONS, AND ALLOWANCES

The First World War reminded Canadians of the vulnerability of the family unit. The considerable loss of life on the battlefields led to concerns about the growing number of fatherless families. At the same time, a high infant-mortality rate made it difficult for families to replenish "the stock of healthy males" (Moscovitch & Drover, 1987, p. 24).

The federal government established a variety of charities to aid Canadian soldiers overseas and to provide relief to soldiers' families. A more organized system of relief was established when the government introduced two schemes for veterans' pensions: the Soldier Settlement, which provided unemployed soldiers with financial assistance and a parcel of farm land; and the Employment Service of Canada, which helped veterans to find jobs. The federal government also made financial assistance available to the families of soldiers who had been lost or killed in combat. These systems marked a new direction in social policy, as government accepted greater responsibility for social welfare needs (Struthers, 1983).

The war's social and political impact stimulated an interest in legislated income security for mothers and their children. In Canada, the traditional

THE NATIONAL COUNCIL OF WOMEN OF CANADA

The National Council of Women of Canada (NCWC) was founded in 1893, during a time when women were beginning to organize themselves for community action. Many women, looking beyond the charitable societies, garden clubs, cultural clubs, and missionary societies to which they belonged, saw the need for societal reform, better education for women, and women's suffrage (the right to vote). These women realized that they would be much more effective if they spoke with a united voice.

Members of the NCWC can be proud of many achievements, including the following:

- In the late nineteenth century, the NCWC focused on improving the conditions for female prisoners, female factory workers, and female immigrants. Through its efforts, for example, the NCWC helped to bring about the appointment of female prison officers.

- The NCWC was instrumental in the federal government's enactment of the Act to Confer the Electoral Franchise upon Women in 1918, legislation that gave Caucasian Canadian women the right to vote in federal elections.

- The Persons Case was taken to Canada's highest court of appeal, and resulted in the 1929 declaration that women were indeed "persons" and therefore eligible to be appointed to the Senate of Canada. Three of the five women involved in this famous case were active participants in the NCWC.

- The NCWC has played an active role in promoting child welfare, including the prevention of child abuse, the education of children, the provision of quality child care, and the formation of Children's Aid Societies in Ontario.

- The NCWC has consulted with governments on a variety of work-related issues. These efforts have contributed to legislation aimed at improving women's working conditions, pay equity, and access to health insurance and pension plans.

As one of Canada's oldest women's organizations, the NCWC continues to work toward its vision of "a vibrant, pro-active, credible Council of Women reflecting the diversity of society, encouraging informed political decision making and public attitudes for the well being of society, through research, education, consultation and cooperation."

Sources: National Council of Women of Canada. (2002). *History, achievements, and about us.* Retrieved from http://www.ncwc.ca/aboutUs_history.html, http://www.ncwc.ca/aboutUs_achievements.html, and http://www.ncwc.ca/aboutUs.html.

practice of placing abandoned or poor children in institutions or foster homes was giving way to a more enlightened approach, under which children were kept in the home whenever possible. This change meant that mothers required additional support to raise healthy children. In 1916, the Government of Manitoba passed the first mothers' allowance act in Canada. This provided a small but certain income to all women with dependants and established the government's role as the provider of income security and protector of minimum social standards. Soon after Manitoba took the lead, mothers' allowances were established in Saskatchewan (1917), Alberta (1919), and Ontario and British Columbia (1920) (Guest, 1997, 2012).

INCOME SECURITY FOR ELDERLY CANADIANS

During the early twentieth century, many Canadians expressed concerns about the ability of the elderly to provide for themselves and about the capacity of poor families to care for their aging parents. Many older Canadians applied for public relief, but it was not until several provinces complained about the rising costs of relief that the federal government seriously considered an old-age pension scheme (McGilly, 1998).

The Old Age Pensions Act of 1927 established pensions as a right for all seniors, the first federal long-term commitment to social welfare. At that time, the pension was highly restrictive; to collect pension benefits, Canadians had to be seventy or older—a remarkably high age requirement compared with that in other advanced countries. Moreover, the **means test** for assessing eligibility was strict and humiliating; clearly, policymakers were reluctant to abandon their poor law attitudes (Guest, 2012).

RISING UNEMPLOYMENT IN THE "DIRTY THIRTIES"

Various factors triggered the Great Depression in Canada, including the 1929 stock market crash in the United States and Europe's slow postwar economic recovery. Severe economic problems in these countries drastically reduced the demand for Canada's primary products. This hurt Canada's entire economy, which relied heavily on the exporting of raw materials and semi-processed goods. Unemployment rates soared from 3 percent in 1929 to 27 percent in 1933, especially among unskilled labourers and workers in the export industries (Horn, 1984).

High unemployment created a number of social and health problems. For example, by the time the Depression ended in 1939, almost one-third of

Canadians were too poor to buy adequate amounts of nutritious food. On top of this, slum conditions had developed in the larger cities. In 1934, the lieutenant-governor's Committee on Housing Conditions in Toronto reported that "there are thousands of families living in houses which are unsanitary, verminous and grossly overcrowded" (Cassidy, 1943, pp. 57–58). Similar concerns were raised in Montréal, Vancouver, Winnipeg, and other Canadian cities.

Unlike the United States and Britain, Canada was unprepared for the widespread needs created by the Depression. With no unemployment insurance system, those who lost their jobs sought help wherever they could find it. Private charitable organizations, such as the Canadian Welfare Council and the Federation of Jewish Philanthropies, launched various fundraising campaigns to help the unemployed, but their efforts had little impact on the problem of mass unemployment and widespread need (Bellamy, 1965).

Many provinces assigned the municipalities to provide some form of public relief to the poor and unemployed. Two forms of relief were available; **direct relief** consisted of cash, vouchers, or tangible goods like food, fuel, and clothing; **indirect relief** was provided through government-funded work projects intended to get the unemployed back to work (these public work projects were nevertheless poorly planned and expensive). The number of Canadians depending on public relief continued to grow, reaching 1.5 million people in 1933 and 2 million in 1934 (Horn, 1984). Many municipal governments soon found it impossible to cover the growing costs of public relief and other social services. The economic strain was particularly hard on the poorer municipal governments, which struggled to meet their financial obligations and maintain the public's confidence (McGilly, 1998).

As the economic depression wore on, the federal government became concerned about the growing number of unemployed, transient, and homeless able-bodied men. To quell the simmering threat of social anarchy and widespread revolt, the government set up work camps in remote regions of the country where these men could work building railway lines, clearing forests, or constructing bridges. By many accounts, these camps resembled nineteenth-century workhouses (McGilly, 1998).

While government struggled with the financial strain of relief programs, tension continued to rise among the unemployed. Before long, vast numbers of unemployed men organized protests against the government and the unemployment crisis. The On to Ottawa Trek of 1935 was possibly the largest and most famous protest of the Depression years. About 4000 men from work camps across the country boarded trains and headed to Ottawa to protest unemployment, poor wages, and unacceptable conditions in the work camps (Carniol, 2005). Exhibit 3.4 profiles that famous trek.

EXHIBIT 3.4

ON TO OTTAWA

Courtesy On to Ottawa Historical Society.

Boarding the trains for Ottawa, 1935.

During the Great Depression (1929–1939), thousands of young, unemployed, single men found employment in the work camps set up in British Columbia. However, by April 1935, they were fed up with labouring six-and-a-half days a week for twenty cents a day. The workers abandoned the camps and congregated in Vancouver, where they went on strike for two months. During that time, the men tried to achieve union wages but were unsuccessful. They decided to take their case to Ottawa; this journey became known as the On to Ottawa Trek.

Leaving Vancouver on June 3, the workers "rode the rods" (on and in railway freight cars) as far as Regina, where they were stopped by the RCMP. On July 1, the police broke the strike and arrested the strike leaders.

In a federal election a few months later, the Liberals defeated Prime Minister R. B. "Iron Heel" Bennett's Conservative government and abolished the work camps.

Source: On to Ottawa Historical Society. (2002). *On to Ottawa Trek*. Retrieved October 19, 2008, from http://www.ontoottawa.ca/index1.html. Used by permission.

UNEMPLOYMENT INSURANCE

Although the provinces were responsible for the costs of public relief, the federal government began sharing those costs during the Great Depression. With its broad taxation powers and greater capacity to borrow, the federal government had richer sources of revenue and the ability to equalize economic conditions across the provinces, some of which neared bankruptcy (McGilly, 1998). The federal involvement in public relief was intended to be temporary. Nonetheless, by the time the cost-sharing program ended in 1941, the federal government had assumed 40 percent of the total costs of public relief (Bellamy, 1965).

By the end of the Great Depression, unemployment rates were so high that Canadians could no longer attribute joblessness to a personal failure of individuals. As Armine Yalnizyan (1994, p. 31) points out: "The shiver of universal risk had swept over everyone, and people started demanding protections by pooling that risk across society, and not just at the traditional levels of municipalities and provinces." Canadians began to place greater pressure on governments to provide a minimum of assistance with respect to income, nutrition, health, housing, and education.

Although the Second World War had created jobs, government officials worried that unemployment would be a problem with the mass reintegration of soldiers at war's end. To minimize the threat, Prime Minister Mackenzie King introduced a comprehensive unemployment insurance scheme. Since unemployment was a provincial responsibility, King had to seek a constitutional amendment from the British government; Britain granted that request and, in 1940, Canada passed the Unemployment Insurance Act. Except for veterans' pensions during the First World War, unemployment insurance was Canada's first large-scale income security program. During the plan's first year, almost 4.6 million Canadians—including dependants—benefited from unemployment insurance (Guest, 1997).

DISCUSSION QUESTIONS

■ **The Transitional Phase (Confederation to Second World War)**

1. This phase is marked by social unrest, social movements, and citizens demanding more from government in terms of quality of life and social well-being. Compare that era with today, in terms of how you see citizens trying to make their voices heard and government's response to public demands.

2. Many of the public programs introduced during this phase were focused on improving the income security of Canadians. Identify the main income security programs developed during this era. What historical events warranted the establishment of these programs?

3 THE INTERVENTIONIST PHASE (SECOND WORLD WAR TO MID-1970s)

From the beginning of the Second World War until the mid-1970s, Canadians urged governments to respond to "modern problems" by intervening during hard economic times and raising living standards through an extensive system of public programs. New social attitudes also prompted a growing interest in social equality, human rights, social citizenship, and the social stability that a welfare state promised. This era of strong economic growth, high employment, and rising government revenues allowed governments to spend more on social programs and to assume much of the responsibility that private charities had long held. During this period, Canada established a range of universal social and healthcare programs designed to protect its citizens from the insecurities of an industrial economy and to help them to participate in modern society (Banting, 1987). In other words, governments developed programs to ensure a certain level of **social security**. The building of a publicly sanctioned system of support represented a shift from a residual to a more institutional approach to well-being and established government as "the predominant force of social welfare" (Meinhard & Foster, 2002, p. 3).

THE MARSH REPORT ON SOCIAL SECURITY

The end of the Second World War marked an economic turning point for Canada. The social and economic damage incurred by the Great Depression made it clear that capitalism alone could not meet everyone's needs. Politicians generally agreed that only through ongoing state intervention in the economy could all Canadians enjoy the benefits of capitalism. Without that intervention, politicians believed, "inequality would deepen and instability would result" (Broadbent, 2001, p. 6). To determine what interventions were needed, the federal government set up several committees to assess the postwar needs of Canadians.

The committees produced a flurry of reports outlining potential postwar programs. Perhaps the best known among the documents concerned with social policy was the *Report on Social Security for Canada* (commonly known as the Marsh Report). Released in 1943, the Marsh Report was influenced by, and contained many principles from, the famous Beveridge Report that came out of Great Britain in 1942. Leonard Marsh, a prominent social researcher and professor, outlined a comprehensive social security plan for postwar Canada. According to Marsh, this plan was long overdue, considering the progress that had already been made in other countries (see Exhibit 3.5).

EXHIBIT 3.5

MARSH SAYS CANADA'S SOCIAL SERVICES LAG

Winnipeg, May 16 (CP)—Dr. Leonard Marsh, of Ottawa, research advisor of the advisory committee on reconstruction, in an interview today named Great Britain, New Zealand and Russia as the countries with the most complete social legislation.

Dr. Marsh, author of the Marsh Report on Social Security, said Russia had the most comprehensive training and educational services of any country today.

"As far as English-speaking countries are concerned, Canada seems to be lagging behind. We lack health insurance, widows' and orphans' pensions, and sickness benefits. Our one redeeming quality is our excellent unemployment insurance."

A delegate to the Canadian Conference on Social Work here, Dr. Marsh emphasized the need for a national health insurance scheme and children's allowances.

Source: "Marsh Says Canada's Social Services Lag," *Victoria Daily Colonist*, 17 May 1944, 7. Reprinted by kind permission of The Canadian Press.

The Marsh Report underscored the notion that economic and social risks were part of modern industrial life and that governments could minimize those risks through publicly supported benefits from cradle to grave (Maioni, 2004). Central to Marsh's vision of social security for Canadians was full employment at a living wage, supplemented by employment skills training and job placement services. Marsh proposed that social insurance programs could replace earnings lost because of unemployment, retirement, accident, maternity, disability, illness, or death and therefore minimize employment risks. Social assistance would serve as a program of last resort for the small segment of the population who were in need, unable to work, and had no income. Marsh (1975) believed that three main programs could meet social security and human welfare needs: (1) children's allowances to help with the additional costs of raising a child, (2) national health insurance to provide health services, and (3) a contributory old-age pension scheme.

A primary principle underpinning Marsh's social security proposal was the **social minimum**, which Marsh (1950, p. 35) defined as "the realization that in a civilized society, there is a certain minimum of conditions without which health, decency, happiness, and a 'chance in life' are impossible."

According to Marsh, social security programs were the means to establish a social minimum.

Historian Michael Bliss (1975, p. ix) hailed the Marsh Report as the "most important single document in the history of the development of the welfare state in Canada." However, despite its apparent significance, Marsh's plan for a comprehensive and coordinated social security system only got as far as being reviewed by the Parliamentary Committee on Social Security in 1943. Some members of that committee feared that the economy could not support Marsh's plan; others maintained that poverty was the responsibility of individuals and families, not government. Committee members also criticized the plan's recommendations for a greater federal role in providing social security to Canadians, a role that the provinces were constitutionally entitled to. Marsh's report was therefore never tabled in the House of Commons. Even so, the document provided the structural framework for many of Canada's future health and social welfare programs (CMCC, 2002; Guest, 1997).

FAMILY ALLOWANCES ACT OF 1944

According to Marsh, the purpose of family allowance legislation was to ensure a minimum income level for families and, in so doing, reduce poverty, especially among large families living on low incomes. The supporters of family allowances also saw the plan as a solution to the growing problems of poor nutrition and the high rates of infant mortality revealed by Depression-era and wartime studies.

Even though its enactment required a constitutional amendment, the Family Allowances Act passed in 1944. Noted for being Canada's first universal social welfare program, this federally administered allowance went to all Canadian families with dependants under sixteen. In its first year of operation, the program cost taxpayers about $250 million, which was until then the most spent on any social program in Canada (Blake, 2009).

SOLIDIFYING CANADA'S RETIREMENT INCOME SYSTEM

The Old Age Pensions Act of 1927 had been criticized for many years because of its stigmatizing means test and inadequate benefits. In 1951, that act was replaced by two new pension plans: Old Age Security (OAS), which provided universal benefits and was fully funded and administered by the federal government, and Old Age Assistance, a means-tested scheme that was cost-shared by the provincial and federal governments and administered by the provinces (Guest, 1997).

In 1965, the Canada Pension Plan (CPP) and its counterpart, the Québec Pension Plan (QPP), were introduced. These plans provided a first line of defence for paid workers and their families who suffered a loss of income because of retirement, disability, or death; the plans were especially important to workers without employer-sponsored pension schemes. The CPP and QPP shared some similarities: for example, both had comparable eligibility criteria and benefit levels, and both were compulsory social insurance schemes that required all workers between eighteen and seventy to contribute as long as they were working. Initially, the CPP/QPP were available to 92 percent of the paid labour force.

Although the CPP/QPP have many unique features, their historical significance lies in the fact that they were the first income security programs to be subject to **indexation**—in other words, benefits increase automatically as the cost of living rises. Before the CPP/QPP, Parliament had to authorize any increases in benefits for federal income security programs (such as Old Age Security).

The introduction of Old Age Security, Old Age Assistance, and the CPP/QPP underscored the federal government's newfound responsibility for the security of elderly Canadians. These plans also took the retirement income system a step closer to ensuring a social minimum for seniors (Oderkirk, 1996).

CANADA ASSISTANCE PLAN OF 1966

Before 1966, the funding arrangement for provincial and territorial social welfare programs was highly problematic. For one thing, the federal funds to the provinces and territories were categorical—that is, the funds could be used only for specific purposes. Old Age Assistance, for example, was limited to people aged 65 to 69; Blind Persons' Allowances were restricted to those deemed legally blind; and only people who had total or permanent disabilities were eligible for Disabled Persons' Allowances. Many people in need, such as abused women, did not fit into any specific category or meet a program's criteria and therefore lacked adequate support. John Osborne (1986), a policy adviser to the federal government, suggests that governments used "tight and inflexible" eligibility criteria for many programs to assure Canadians that benefits would go only to truly needy and "deserving" people. However, many equally needy people were denied help if they did not meet the eligibility criteria. To prevent people from falling through the cracks of the system, the federal government introduced the Canada Assistance Plan (CAP) in 1966.

Under CAP, the provinces and territories could design and administer their own social welfare programs as long as they met certain national standards. Meanwhile, the federal government paid half the costs. Social assistance recipients received financial aid to meet basic living needs, including food, clothing, and shelter; in some cases, assistance was also available for transportation, child care, and uninsured health needs, such as dental and eye care. Also under CAP was a wide range of social services (originally called welfare services), which included protection services for children, rehabilitation programs for people with disabilities, home support for seniors, and employment programs. Ideally, welfare services would not only reduce the negative effects of poverty, child neglect, and dependence on social assistance but also eradicate the causes of those problems (Human Resources Development Canada [HRDC], 1994b).

The introduction of CAP resulted in an increase in federal funding to the provinces and territories; that funding allowed each jurisdiction to expand, integrate, and improve its own social welfare programs. Thus, CAP was instrumental in the development of Canada's social safety net and the assurance of a minimum standard of living for low-income groups, regardless of why they needed help (HRDC, 1994b).

POVERTY AND THE NOTION OF GUARANTEED INCOME

Several events during the early 1960s motivated Prime Minister Lester B. Pearson to introduce a plan to eliminate poverty in Canada. These events included an increasing awareness of poverty, the American government's declaration of a war on poverty in the United States, and the development of new methods for measuring poverty. The prime minister's announcement paved the way for several studies on poverty. One study, by the Economic Council of Canada (1968, p. 1), concluded

> Poverty in Canada is real. Its numbers are not in the thousands, but the millions. There is more of it than our society can tolerate, more than the economy can afford, and far more than existing measures and efforts can cope with. Its persistence, at a time when the bulk of Canadians enjoy one of the highest standards of living in the world, is a disgrace.

Also in 1968, the Senate Committee on Poverty was appointed to look at the extent of poverty in Canada and to recommend policy changes. Two findings of the inquiry were of particular concern to the committee: the high number of children who were growing up in poverty and the approximately two million **working poor**, defined as people who maintain regular employment but remain poor. The committee's report called attention to poverty as a growing social problem, provided insight into the causes of poverty, and suggested the establishment of a social minimum.

Policy experts agreed that to establish a social minimum, the entire income security system would have to be overhauled; this would involve scrapping a number of existing poverty-oriented programs and introducing a federally funded and administered **guaranteed annual income** (GAI). A GAI suggests that all citizens have the right to a minimum income as the result of either paid work or government subsidies. Under a federal GAI scheme, the government would assure Canadians a minimum income based on marital status, number of children, financial resources, age, and geographic location (Guest, 1997).

The Canadian government flirted with the idea of a GAI, but a nationwide plan never materialized. However, several provinces implemented variations of a GAI for seniors who were already receiving the federally funded Old Age Security and Guaranteed Income Supplement. For example, in 1974, Ontario introduced the Guaranteed Annual Income System (GAINS) to ensure a basic income for residents 65 and older whose annual income fell below a certain threshold.

SOCIAL MOVEMENTS: SHAKING ESTABLISHED FOUNDATIONS

The counterculture of the 1960s and 1970s significantly challenged the status quo in Canada and other Western countries. Among the most prominent social movements at the time were the second wave of the women's movement, the environmental movement, the gay rights movement, and the peace movement. Although concerned with changing conservative public policies and practices, these social movements were perhaps most intent on changing those social values that ultimately oppressed, demoralized, or marginalized people (Howlett, 1992; Smith, 2004).

Among the many social movements of the time, the women's liberation (or feminist) movement was especially effective in influencing social policy. Declaring, "the personal is political," women politicized a variety of issues, such as family violence, that were traditionally regarded as private matters rather than public issues (Smith, 2004). Two primary objectives of the women's movement were (1) to achieve social justice for women in all areas of human endeavour, including the media, law, education, religion, and science; and (2) to break down established patriarchal power structures that oppressed and controlled women (Armitage, 2003; Eichler & Lavigne, 2012).

The Royal Commission on the Status of Women (RCSW), federally appointed in 1967, was one of the driving forces behind Canada's women's movement. Not only did the commission establish an agenda of issues and strategies for improving conditions for women, but it also identified government as the most suitable system for addressing equality and equity concerns. The RCSW's efforts led to the establishment of several groups devoted to improving women's conditions in Canada, including the Canadian Advisory Council on the Status of Women.

By the early 1970s, social activism had found its way into provincial politics. Colourful political figures—some of whom would become provincial premiers—asserted new ideas and reforms to social welfare policies and programs. Those social trailblazers included British Columbia's premier, Dave Barrett, a staunch supporter of welfare state ideals, and Premier Allan Blakeney of Saskatchewan, who improved a wide range of health and social programs during his eleven years in office.

THE EARLY 1970s: A TIME FOR REVIEW

By the 1970s, Canada's growing economy encouraged a public endorsement of social programs, particularly those that would reduce poverty. At the same time, Canadians expressed concern over the rising costs of social welfare programs. These and other developments sparked a renewed interest in reviewing Canada's income security programs.

The Income Security Review of 1970

In 1970, the federal government published *Income Security for Canadians*, which outlined a strategy to retarget income-security benefits so that low-income Canadians could receive a greater share of available resources (Canada, Department of National Health and Welfare, 1970). The report also called for the elimination of universality as it applied to Family Allowances and Old Age Security. This proposal drew a mixed reaction in the House of Commons.

Owing to the lengthy debates on the proposed reforms and an impending federal election in 1972, the federal government decided to postpone its proposed revisions to income security programs.

The Social Security Review (1973–1976)

In 1973, the federal government under Prime Minister Trudeau (see Exhibit 3.6) launched a joint federal/provincial/territorial review of Canada's social welfare system. A few months later, the federal government issued its report, *Working*

EXHIBIT 3.6

Library and Archives Canada/National Archives of Canada fonds/C-46600. © Library and Archives Canada. Reproduced with the permission of Library and Archives Canada.

As prime minister of Canada (1968–1979, 1980–1984), Pierre Elliott Trudeau was committed to creating a more humane, caring, and "just society"—a society free of poverty and one in which all Canadians could enjoy equal opportunity.

Paper on Social Security in Canada (Lalonde, 1973), which outlined some of the broad policy areas to consider when planning for a more effective social welfare system. By this time, however, globalization and a revolution in information technology were reshaping the way that people lived and worked. Machines were rapidly replacing workers, and the emerging service industry and computer fields were demanding skills that many workers lacked. As Canada struggled to adjust to a new economic order, unemployment and inflation rates skyrocketed, and a general economic decline severely strained government revenues.

By the end of 1975, the federal and regional governments either cancelled or severely cut back many reforms initiated by the social security review in an attempt to control public spending. Despite these curtailments, the review paved the way for income security programs at the provincial and federal levels; these programs included Saskatchewan's Family Income Plan (1974), the federal Refundable Child Tax Credit (1978), and Manitoba's Income Support Program (1980). In addition, the review prompted the federal government to triple Family Allowances benefits (from an average of $7.21 to $20 a month per child) and to index those benefits to the consumer price index.

Shifting of the Tide

In a climate of rising inflation and unemployment rates, Canadians focused on the costs of the social welfare system. Many Canadians were also criticizing social welfare programs for being of poor quality and for doing little to solve social problems. Furthermore, people had concerns about the growing number of Canadians relying on social assistance (Heclo, 1981; Rice & Prince, 2000).

In the years following the social security review, Canada's social welfare system underwent considerable downsizing as governments reduced, eliminated, or froze funding for many programs and services. Any ambition that Canada may have had in becoming a full-fledged welfare state vanished. By the mid-1970s, at the peak of social welfare development, Canada had a network of programs that provided partial income security to working people and more extensive support to non-working Canadians, such as seniors and children (Ross, 1987). Despite this limited protection, the social welfare system had managed to redistribute resources so that no Canadian had to do without and, in so doing, created a more equitable nation. Social democrat Edward Broadbent (2001) believes that the redistribution of resources not only increased the freedom of Canadians to the highest level ever but also eased the nation's internal conflict to the lowest level in a century.

DISCUSSION QUESTIONS

■ **The Interventionist Phase (Second World War to Mid-1970s)**

1. Many modern-day social welfare programs were established during this era. Why do you think the decades from the end of the Second World War to the mid-1970s were particularly receptive to greater government responsibility for social welfare? (Consider the political, social, economic, and cultural events of the time, and their possible influence on the development of social welfare programs.)

2. The 1960s and 1970s were a particularly important time for social movements to advance social democratic views. How might have these groups influenced the expansion of Canada's social welfare system?

SUMMARY

Introduction

Canada's social welfare system has evolved over several decades in response to public demand, politics, and government priorities. A residual approach dominated early social welfare provision until after the Great Depression, when Canadians recognized a social role for government.

1 The Early Phase (Colonial Times to Confederation)

French and British immigrants had their own methods of caring for the poor, the sick, and the needy. The Roman Catholic Church and secular charities helped the early French settlers. In the British settlements, the Protestant work ethic and the English Poor Laws guided the provision of public relief. Although the British North America Act assigned responsibility for social welfare to the provinces, they had little interest in or need for a social welfare system.

2 The Transitional Phase (Confederation to Second World War)

Urbanization and its related problems threatened the stability of growing Canadian cities. Industrialization sparked labour reform and workers' compensation legislation. Conditions for women, children, and seniors improved as a result of mothers' allowances, child welfare legislation, and old-age pensions. The introduction of veterans' pensions indicated a greater government intervention in social welfare matters. During the Great Depression, severe economic and social problems, along with ineffective public programs, spurred the federal government to introduce unemployment insurance in 1940, Canada's first large-scale income security program.

3 The Interventionist Phase (Second World War to Mid-1970s)

By the end of the Second World War, Canadians wanted a higher standard of living. The Marsh Report outlined a comprehensive social security plan, and promoted the concepts of a social minimum and family allowances. Income security for seniors improved with the passage of various pension plans. During the 1960s, an expansion of social welfare programs became possible under CAP, and the war on poverty brought a renewed interest in a guaranteed annual income. The rise of social movements signalled a greater acceptance of collective responsibility. By the early 1970s, Canadians were concerned about the economy and the growing costs of social welfare. The federal government tried to review those programs, but politics and economic problems were greater priorities. Any notion of Canada becoming a full-fledged welfare state was discarded.

KEY TERMS

For definitions of the key terms, consult the Glossary on page 453 at the end of the book.

charities, p. 64
Protestant work ethic, p. 66
English Poor Laws, p. 67
public relief, p. 67
categorical, p. 67
principle of less eligibility, p. 67

outdoor relief, p. 68
indoor relief, p. 68
workhouses, p. 68
poorhouses, p. 68
social movements, p. 71
social citizenship, p. 71
social insurance, p. 72

means test, p. 75
direct relief, p. 76
indirect relief, p. 76
social security, p. 79
social minimum, p. 80
indexation, p. 82
working poor, p. 84
guaranteed annual income, p. 84

4 CHAPTER

Social Welfare in the Globalization Era

OBJECTIVES

The globalization era is characterized by a new economic order, welfare state retrenchment, the rise of neoliberalism, and a general uncertainty for the direction of social welfare in Canada. This chapter will

- introduce the economic challenges faced by Canadians in the 1970s

- examine the neoliberal approach to social welfare during the Mulroney and Chrétien years

- discuss the dynamics of welfare state retrenchment and reinvestment in the 1990s and early 2000s

- explore the Conservative approach to social welfare

- take stock of current social conditions and trends in social welfare

INTRODUCTION

The social welfare structure so laboriously and painstakingly erected in Canada over the past forty years has clearly outlived its usefulness. The social scientists who have studied it, the bureaucrats who have administered it, and the poor who have experienced it are of one mind that in today's swiftly changing world the [social] welfare system is a hopeless failure. The matter is not even controversial. But what is to take its place? (Special Senate Committee on Poverty, 1971, p. vii)

Economists sometimes refer to the period from 1945 (the end of the Second World War) to the early 1970s as the "golden era" of capitalism. During this period, most Canadians had well-paying jobs, and many workers belonged to strong unions, which pushed for job security and workplace benefits. At the same time, governments assumed responsibility for the welfare of those who could not fully meet their needs. Canadians generally supported the notion of income redistribution, especially if it meant preventing a repeat of conditions in the Great Depression, including large-scale poverty, unemployment, and social unrest. Thus, governments used their powers to distribute both income and opportunities more equally across the population. British economist John Maynard Keynes (see Exhibit 4.1) influenced the

EXHIBIT 4.1

© ClassicStock/Alamy

British economist John Maynard Keynes (1883–1946) believed that giving money to citizens through income security programs, tax breaks, and other government initiatives encourages spending, which in turn, stimulates the economy.

use of redistributive mechanisms, such as income security programs and a **progressive tax system**. Keynes believed that if government directed more money to low-income earners, then they would be more likely to spend money, which would, in turn, help to stimulate the economy. **Keynesian economics** worked well for Canada during the economic boom after the Second World War, when most people saw steady growth in their income, and government was flush with tax revenues.

Canada's economy—along with that of other advanced nations—began to slow in the early 1970s. As the economy worsened, unemployment, inflation, and interest rates inched their way upward, and government revenues and household incomes started a downward slide. At first, Western nations believed that the economic downturn was temporary, so rather than raise taxes or cut public programs, they chose to borrow money. Reduced government revenues, plus interest payments on the borrowed money, made it increasingly difficult for governments to balance their annual budgets. As a result, countries began incurring yearly **budget deficits** (spending exceeded their income); over the years, those deficits accumulated, creating a huge **public debt** (the total sum of all unpaid deficits). Eventually, the Western world realized that the economic decline that began in the 1970s was not temporary; rather, it was part of a long-term trend associated with **globalization** and a shift from an industrial to a postindustrial era. (See Appendix B for a primer on globalization.)

The globalization era of capitalism began in the mid-1970s and continues today. This period supports a new form of conservatism called **neoliberalism** and a rejection of Keynesian economics in favour of **monetarism**, an economic philosophy that calls for debt reduction, reduced public spending, and minimal government intervention in the market. Neoliberals believe that monetarism can solve the economic problems created by a burgeoning public debt, and eventually restore the economy. In Canada, governments continue to shift their priorities away from social development to putting their respective fiscal houses in order; this has resulted in drastic cuts in public spending, relaxed regulations governing business, and the devolution of many public programs and responsibilities to the private sector. Neoliberals expect these and other measures to free the market from all political and social restraints and, in so doing, allow capitalism to work the way it was intended.

What began as a gradual reduction in social expenditures in the 1970s transformed into a steady erosion of social programs in the 1980s, and escalated into a dismantling of Canada's social welfare system from the 1990s on. Thus, **welfare state retrenchment** has characterized the course of social welfare in Canada for almost four decades. Chapter 3 looked at the building of the social welfare system from colonial times to the mid-1970s. This chapter continues that historical review by chronicling the main events of the globalization era—a period that reflects what Rice and Prince (2000, p. 84) aptly refer to as a "crisis of the welfare state."

1 A NEOLIBERAL APPROACH TO SOCIAL WELFARE

Since the early 1980s, the federal and regional governments have taken a more neoliberal approach to social welfare provision. This neoliberal trend has not been unique to Canada: other advanced countries, such as the United States and Britain, have also adopted a less generous and more business-oriented approach to meeting social welfare needs. This section explores some of the effects of neoliberalism on social well-being in Canada from 1984 to 1995.

PROGRESSIVE CONSERVATIVES AND THE END OF UNIVERSALISM

When Brian Mulroney and the Progressive Conservatives (PCs) formed a federal government in 1984, Canada was still recovering from the global recession of 1981 to 1983. Unemployment was widespread, inflation was soaring, and the federal deficit exceeded $32 billion. After years of deficit spending under the Trudeau government, Canadians were hoping that the PCs would reverse the rise in public debt and annual deficits, and restore the economy.

Cuts to Programs

In 1985, the Royal Commission on the Economic Union and Development Prospects for Canada (commonly known as the Macdonald Commission) criticized Canada's income security system for being ineffective and unsustainable and for creating disincentives to work. The commission made several recommendations for change, including the introduction of a guaranteed annual income (GAI) scheme to strengthen the income security system. The PC government nevertheless dismissed the notion of a GAI and either scrapped or reduced social welfare programs, resulting in a weakening of the income security system.

A significant change came in 1989, when the PCs introduced the concept of **clawbacks**, and put an end to universal social welfare programs. Those most affected were seniors with high annual incomes, who had to repay part or all of their Old Age Security benefits, and high-income-earning families who had to pay back a portion of their family allowances cheques. In 1993, the federal government scrapped family allowances altogether and replaced it with the Child Tax Benefit, which was restricted to low- and moderate-income families.

The PCs targeted other well-established programs as well. In 1990, the federal government stopped financing Unemployment Insurance (UI), leaving it up to employers and workers to fund UI through their own contributions. Other UI amendments resulted in more restrictive eligibility criteria, shortened benefit periods, and harsher penalties for those who quit their jobs. One year later, an act of Parliament (Bill C-69) put a "cap" on the Canada Assistance Plan (CAP) by requiring the wealthiest provinces (at that time Alberta, Ontario, and British Columbia) to pay for any CAP programs whose costs increased by 5 percent or more. This change served as a disincentive to provinces to develop social welfare programs beyond a certain level.

When the economic recession hit Canada in the early 1990s, the PCs decided that rising unemployment, high inflation, and skyrocketing deficits could be partially contained by further cuts to what they saw as a costly and overgenerous social welfare system.

Legacy of the Progressive Conservatives

Throughout their years in power (1984–1993), the PCs steadily chipped away at the social safety net. However, the PCs were careful not to slash social expenditures too blatantly; instead, they adopted what Grattan Gray (1990, p. 17) describes as "social policy by stealth," whereby social programs were cut incrementally—in fact, almost invisibly—through clawbacks, reduced transfers to the provinces, and other cost-saving measures. Because individual cuts were hard to identify, it was difficult to track the changes in social program funding from year to year.

Although the PCs reduced many long-established social welfare programs, they also contributed to the development of others; for example, they enriched the refundable Child Tax Credit and Spouses' Allowance, increased assistance to people with disabilities, and launched the Family Violence Initiative. Battle and Torjman (2001, p. 22) observe that despite these advances, the drastic changes made by the PCs to Canada's social welfare system "built a momentum that prepared the way for even more radical changes by the

Liberals in the 1990s and into the new century. The Conservatives proved that the universalist welfare state was no longer a 'sacred trust,' if it ever had been."

A NEW LIBERAL DIRECTION

The Liberals won the federal election in 1993 and returned to power with a history of generally supporting welfare state principles. Indeed, former Liberal governments had introduced some of Canada's key social policies, including the Old Age Pension (in 1927), Unemployment Insurance (in 1940), and CAP (in 1966). In 1993, however, the Liberals recognized the need for new strategies to confront the challenges of a much different economic and political climate from when they last held office in the early 1980s. For one thing, Canadians were beginning to feel the effects of globalization, including the disappearance of permanent, full-time positions with benefits, and a rise in the number of low-paying, part-time, and temporary positions.

Taking a Business Approach

Although Liberal politicians had traditionally been *social* liberals who supported social program spending and Keynesian economics, the Liberals under Jean Chrétien promoted themselves as *business* Liberals. These rebranded Liberals still strived toward traditional Liberal goals, such as the pursuit of individual freedom and self-development; however, their primary goal was to create a fiscally responsible government and a strong market economy that would provide social security in the form of good jobs (Human Resources Development Canada [HRDC], 1994c). As a first step toward achieving its financial goals, the new federal government set out to reduce the federal deficit (which stood at over $40 billion in 1993), and to curb a growing national debt (which by 1993 had reached about $510 billion) (see Exhibit 4.2).

The 1995 Budget

Following an extensive review of all federal programs and services, the federal government introduced the 1995 budget, which set out a plan for downsizing its departments and cutting spending to programs and services. The plan included a reduction of $7 billion over two years in transfer payments to the provinces for health, postsecondary education, and social welfare. In addition to direct spending cuts, the federal government began to decentralize many of its operations. **Decentralization** involves one level of government transfer-

EXHIBIT 4.2

THE NATIONAL DEFICIT

ring or *devolving* some or all of its functions, decision-making authority, and assets to a lower level of government or to the private sector. By transferring a portion of or the entire program or function, the federal government also transfers many related costs.

Many Canadians expressed concern over the potentially negative impact of the government's plan on social programs and people's well-being. The National Council of Welfare (NCW, 1995, p. 1), for example, maintained that the proposed changes "marked a giant step backward in Canadian social policy. Followed through to its most likely conclusion, it would dismantle a nation-wide system of welfare and social services that took a generation to build." The federal government defended the proposed **austerity measures** as necessary steps towards Canada's economic recovery and to ensuring that important social programs, such as healthcare and pensions, would be sustainable for future generations. Finance Minister Paul Martin—the architect of the 1995 budget—summed up his position by stating that "there are times in the progress of a people when fundamental challenges must be faced, fundamental choices made—a new course charted. For Canada, this is one of those times" (Canada, Department of Finance, 1995, preface).

DISCUSSION QUESTIONS

■ A Neoliberal Approach to Social Welfare

1. Based on what you know about globalization and political ideologies, explain why Canadian governments might have seen no other choice but to severely restrain public spending during the 1980s and 1990s.

2. Both the Progressive Conservatives (1984–1993) and the Liberals (1993–2006) managed the country's affairs by using neoliberal strategies. One strategy was to reduce funding to government programs. Identify other neoliberal strategies used by these governments. (Note: neoliberalism is also discussed in Chapter 1 and Appendix B.)

2   FROM RETRENCHMENT TO REINVESTMENT

Much evidence suggests that Canada's poor economic performance from the 1970s to late 1990s was more to blame for the fiscal crisis than was social spending. Social programs nevertheless bore the brunt of fiscal restraint during Canada's deficit-fighting years (from 1995 to 1998). Both the federal and regional governments rationalized their drastic cuts as being necessary to eliminating deficits and getting their fiscal houses in order. However, some critics blamed governments for exploiting the fiscal crisis to achieve their largely neoliberal objectives, including dismantling Canada's so-called "overly generous social welfare system" (McQuaig, 1995, p. 9).

This section reviews the social welfare reforms of the deficit-fighting years, the impact of those reforms, and the efforts by some governments to eventually reinvest in social welfare programs.

FEDERAL REFORMS

The 1995 budget identified Canada's labour market as a major target of reform. Government and the business community had long argued that, to lower unemployment, the labour market had to become more flexible—that is, free of any laws, regulations, or programs that interfered with work, productivity, and economic activity (Canadian Auto Workers, 2007). At the federal level, dramatic reforms significantly altered the Unemployment Insurance program and the Canada Assistance Plan.

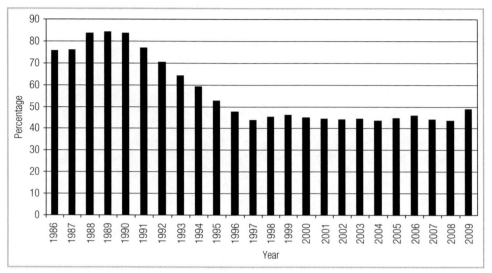

EXHIBIT 4.3

PERCENTAGE OF UNEMPLOYED CANADIANS ELIGIBLE
FOR EI BENEFITS, 1986 TO 2009

Source: "EI and Individuals," from http://www.hrsdc.gc.ca/eng/employment/ei/reports/eimar_2010/Chapter5_1_1.shtml. Human Resources and Skills Development Canada, 2010. Reproduced with the permission of the Minister of Public Works and Government Services Canada, 2013.

Changes to Unemployment Insurance

One of the main criticisms of the Unemployment Insurance (UI) system was that it provided overly generous benefits, which offered little incentive for recipients to get back to work. Another problem was the soaring costs of the UI program, which had doubled from $8 billion in 1982 to almost $16 billion in 1995 (HRDC, 1995). To address these problems, the federal government under the Liberals scrapped the UI system in 1996 and introduced the Employment Insurance (EI) Act. (The name change reflects the emphasis on employment.) The EI Act tightened the criteria for determining eligibility and shortened the period during which workers could draw benefits. All of this led to a sharp drop in the proportion of unemployed Canadians eligible for EI benefits (see Exhibit 4.3).

Out with CAP, In with the CHST

For many years, CAP had been the vehicle by which the federal government transferred funds to the provinces and territories for social welfare programs. However, in an effort to cut direct program costs, the federal government eliminated CAP in 1996 and combined all transfers for health, postsecondary education, and social welfare into one funding arrangement called the Canada Health and Social Transfer (CHST).[1]

Under CAP, the federal government had paid half the costs of social welfare programs, whatever those costs were. In contrast, the CHST allowed the federal government to give the regional governments an equal amount of federal dollars on a per capita basis, without considering the actual program costs. For provinces and territories that had built extensive or costly programs, the shift to the CHST meant they had substantially less money to maintain those programs. Exhibit 4.4 illustrates the funding changes for social welfare, health, and postsecondary education programs from 1993 to 2001.

The CHST also set up a competition for funds among the three main provincial and territorial social programs: healthcare, postsecondary education, and social welfare. Under the CHST, the regional governments received a lump sum or **block fund**, which they could divide among the social programs in whatever way they saw fit. Most provinces and territories responded to their funding shortfall by reducing their social welfare and postsecondary education budgets in order to enrich the more popular health-care programs. This move severely undermined the capacity of social welfare programs to meet human needs.

Although CAP had required the provinces and territories to adhere to certain national standards for social assistance, the CHST eliminated all but one of those standards.[2] Thus, the CHST gave the provinces and territories free rein to set their own eligibility criteria and benefit rates for social welfare programs. The regional governments generally welcomed the elimination of CAP's national standards: they had long wanted more autonomy in social programming, and the conditional nature of CAP was contrary to their constitutional right to deliver those programs.

Some social analysts saw the loss of CAP as a sign that Canada had given up on the notion of the federal government providing leadership and cohesion to the social welfare system. The new trend was toward **provincialized social policy** and the creation of thirteen independent social welfare systems. In the absence of CAP's standards, there was no longer any pan-Canadian protection against poverty; for instance, the varying provincial and territorial eligibility criteria for social assistance meant that a person could be eligible for welfare in

---

[1] In 2003–2004, the federal government split the CHST into two separate funding streams: the Canada Health Transfer (CHT) to support healthcare and the Canada Social Transfer (CST) to finance postsecondary education and social welfare programs. As with the CHST, the CST left it up to the regional governments to decide how to divide the funds between postsecondary education and social welfare programs.

[2] The one national standard that remained under the CHST was the residency requirement, which forbids welfare authorities to deny social assistance to anyone on the basis of how long the person has lived in a province or territory.

EXHIBIT 4.4

CHANGES IN FEDERAL TRANSFERS, 1993 TO 2001

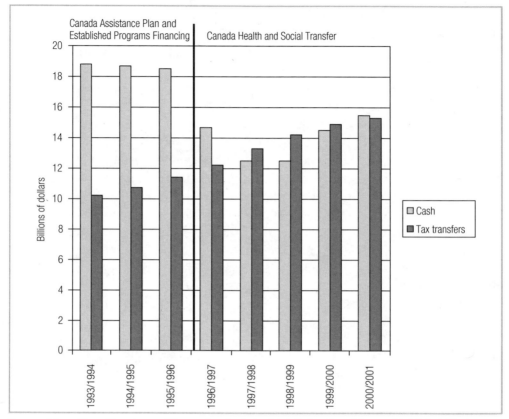

Source: Adapted from *Department of Finance Canada, Budget 2000: Budget Plan*, February 28, 2000, Table 6.2. Retrieved from http://www.fin.gc.ca/budget00/bp/bpch6_1-eng.asp. Reproduced with the permission of the Minister of Public Works and Government Services, 2013.

one province but not in another. Moreover, without CAP's requirements, the federal government could no longer withhold transfer payments to governments that adopted inferior standards (Ross, 1995).

The shift from CAP to the CHST meant a significant loss of support for disadvantaged Canadians. Exhibit 4.5 details the impact on women of the shift to the CHST.

REFORMS AT THE REGIONAL LEVEL

Although social welfare reform had been an ongoing process at the regional level, the dramatic changes of the mid-1990s presented an entirely new set

EXHIBIT 4.5

FROM CAP TO THE CHST: WHAT IT MEANS FOR WOMEN

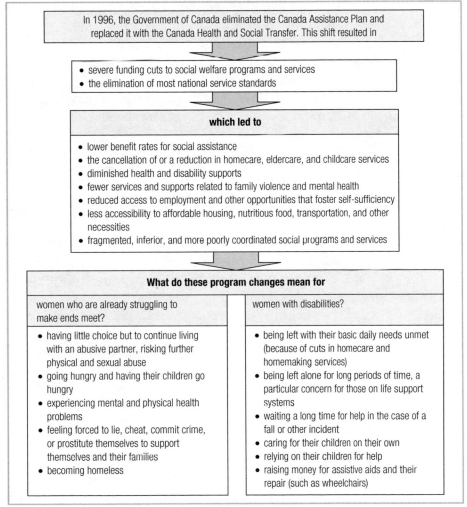

In 1996, the Government of Canada eliminated the Canada Assistance Plan and replaced it with the Canada Health and Social Transfer. This shift resulted in

- severe funding cuts to social welfare programs and services
- the elimination of most national service standards

which led to

- lower benefit rates for social assistance
- the cancellation of or a reduction in homecare, eldercare, and childcare services
- diminished health and disability supports
- fewer services and supports related to family violence and mental health
- reduced access to employment and other opportunities that foster self-sufficiency
- less accessibility to affordable housing, nutritious food, transportation, and other necessities
- fragmented, inferior, and more poorly coordinated social programs and services

What do these program changes mean for

women who are already struggling to make ends meet?	women with disabilities?
• having little choice but to continue living with an abusive partner, risking further physical and sexual abuse • going hungry and having their children go hungry • experiencing mental and physical health problems • feeling forced to lie, cheat, commit crime, or prostitute themselves to support themselves and their families • becoming homeless	• being left with their basic daily needs unmet (because of cuts in homecare and homemaking services) • being left alone for long periods of time, a particular concern for those on life support systems • waiting a long time for help in the case of a fall or other incident • caring for their children on their own • relying on their children for help • raising money for assistive aids and their repair (such as wheelchairs)

Sources: M. Morris et al. (2007, August). Integrating the voices of low-income women into policy discussions on the Canada Social Transfer. Retrieved November 22, 2008, from Canadian Research Institute for the Advancement of Women, www.criaw-icref.ca; and S. Masuda. (1998, March). *The impact of block funding on women with disabilities.* Retrieved from http://publications.gc.ca.

of challenges. Many provinces and territories found themselves struggling to deal with

- their own deficits and rising debt
- the impact of the federal government's cap on CAP in 1991

- the dramatic reductions in transfer payments under the new CHST
- the federal government's decision to offload the responsibility for, and costs related to, many social welfare programs

These issues forced the regional governments to take a hard look at their programs and budgets, and to determine how they could manage to meet a growing need for social programs with significantly fewer resources. Like the federal government, the provinces and territories decided to devolve many of their program responsibilities and costs to the private sector or to lower (in this case, municipal) governments, albeit with reduced funding. Certain mandated programs, such as social assistance, became prime targets for extensive reform.

Social Assistance under Attack

Although social assistance programs were singled out for many reasons, the attack was fuelled by neoliberal beliefs that welfare trapped people in long-term dependence on government; welfare was therefore seen as a problem, not a solution, for needy Canadians (Greenwood, 2005). Since the CHST allowed the provinces and territories to develop most of their own standards for social assistance, the regions could take whatever steps they deemed necessary to control their social spending. The phrase "race to the bottom" refers to the successive cuts most jurisdictions made to their social assistance programs: one province slashed its welfare benefits to motivate welfare recipients to seek more generous benefits elsewhere; this put pressure on other provinces to cut their own welfare benefit rates to discourage an influx of welfare seekers (LeRoy & Clemens, 2003). Reductions to welfare benefits continued through the 1990s; by 2002, rates were so low that anyone relying solely on social assistance could expect to live in poverty.

Fiscal pressures prompted some provinces to restrict welfare eligibility in an attempt to contain the costs of social assistance. For instance, in 1996, British Columbia started refusing welfare to anyone under the age of 25, preferring instead to offer a means-tested living allowance to young adults who participated in employment programs. Later, in 2002, BC became the first province in Canada to announce its plan to put a time limit on welfare eligibility, a move that would prevent employable recipients from collecting welfare for more than 24 out of every 60 months. Because of a public outcry, the BC government cancelled its plan to impose welfare time limits, but it did manage to implement other rules to restrict welfare eligibility, including the requirement that welfare applicants had to have two years of financial independence before they could collect welfare (Wallace & Richards, 2008).

EXHIBIT 4.6

FALLING NUMBERS OF PEOPLE ON WELFARE: 1995 TO 2000

	1995	2000	% CHANGE
ALBERTA	113 200	64 800	−43
ONTARIO	1 344 600	802 000	−40
YUKON	2 100	1 400	−33
PRINCE EDWARD ISLAND	12 400	8 400	−32
BRITISH COLUMBIA	374 300	262 400	−30
NOVA SCOTIA	104 000	73 700	−29
MANITOBA	85 200	63 300	−26
QUÉBEC	802 200	618 900	−23
SASKATCHEWAN	82 200	63 800	−22
NEWFOUNDLAND AND LABRADOR	71 300	59 400	−17
NEW BRUNSWICK	67 400	56 300	−16
NORTHWEST TERRITORIES AND NUNAVUT	12 000	10 700	−11

Source: National Council of Welfare Reports: Welfare Incomes 2005, http://publications.gc.ca/collections/Collection/SD25-2-2005E.pdf, National Council of Welfare 2006. Reproduced with the permission of the Minister of Public Works and Government Services Canada, 2013.

The various strategies used by the provinces proved to be successful in reducing the number of people on welfare. However, not all provinces tracked the people who left welfare to know what happened to them. Moreover, studies have indicated that, while many people who left welfare eventually found work, they did not find work that paid well enough to lift them or their families out of poverty (Canadian CED Network, 2003). See Exhibit 4.6 for an illustration of the falling numbers of welfare recipients between 1995 and 2000.

FROM PASSIVE TO ACTIVE PROGRAMS

By the mid-1990s, governments had decided that social assistance (SA) and Employment Insurance (EI) not only fostered dependency on the state but also were ineffective in terms of moving people off public assistance into the workforce. The ineffectiveness of SA and EI was largely attributed to their **passive labour market policies**, which supported giving unconditional benefits to jobless Canadians and generally leaving it up to employable recipients to find their way into—or back into—the workforce. Beginning in the mid-1990s, Canadian governments introduced **active labour market policies** to SA and EI by requiring beneficiaries of those programs to work, volunteer, retrain, or otherwise engage in work-related activity in exchange for benefits. The underlying assumption of active policies is that if workers had more training or work experience, they would be able to find good jobs.

Welfare-to-Work Programs

Canada's adoption of active policies allowed the provinces and territories to require welfare recipients to work or train in exchange for benefits. Governments touted these work programs as a way to foster self-sufficiency; reinforce the intrinsic values of work, discipline, and productivity; and help people gain the confidence and skills they needed to compete and succeed in the workforce. According to this school of thought, any job—regardless of pay or conditions—was better than government assistance and had the potential to lift people out of poverty (Social Research and Demonstration Corporation, 2005). Beginning in 1996 with Ontario, government-sponsored **welfare-to-work programs** (or "workfare") sprang up across Canada, all aimed at getting employable welfare recipients off SA and into jobs.

Activating the Unemployed

The federal Liberal government began to invest in active employment programs to not only get unemployed Canadians quickly back to work but also to ensure they had the skills they needed to work in a rapidly changing labour market. Those investments included

- job creation programs, targeted wage subsidies, skills development, and self-employment opportunities

- employment assistance programs, which offer job search workshops, employment counselling, or work experience opportunities

- various federal initiatives—such as the Opportunities Fund for Persons with Disabilities, and the Youth Employment Strategy—to help groups facing specific barriers in the labour market

Beginning in 1996, the federal government entered into a variety of labour market agreements with the provinces and territories to give the regional governments more control over their employment development programs. Those agreements enabled each province and territory to develop its own local and regional labour markets, remove barriers to employment, make training more accessible, and create job opportunities for unemployed workers.

BALANCED BUDGETS

By 2000, Canada had reached many of its economic goals: not only had the federal Liberal government delivered its third consecutive balanced budget, but strong economic growth had also created 1.5 million (mostly full time) jobs over four years. The national unemployment rate had fallen below 7 percent (its lowest level in 24 years), and, for the third straight year, Canada was leading the Group of Seven (G7) countries in job creation (Canada, Department of Finance, 2000). There was every indication that Canada's fiscal prudence in the 1990s had paid off.

The regional governments also had good news. The combined provincial and territorial deficit in 2001–2002 was a more "manageable" $22 billion, down from almost $59 billion in 1993–1994. Some provinces, including Saskatchewan and Alberta, had been operating on balanced budgets since 1994–1995 (Canada, Department of Finance, 2003).

THE SOCIAL DEFICIT

By 2003, the restructuring of the social welfare system had undermined Canada's ability to ensure the well-being of vulnerable citizens. In their zeal to eradicate deficits, not only had Canadian governments slashed funding to programs for low-income groups, but most national standards for social assistance had vanished, enabling the provinces and territories to refuse welfare to people in need. Cuts to social welfare programs had marginalized large segments of the population, and denied the already poor and disadvantaged any chance of participating in society.

Although the fiscal crisis appeared to be over, many Canadians were asking whether the economic victory was worth the social cost. According to the National Anti-Poverty Organization (2003), the country's economic and fiscal success had failed to provide a reasonable standard of living, let alone prosperity, for almost five million Canadians. Statistics reflect the hardship and unmet human potential—otherwise known as a **social deficit**—experienced by Canadians during the 1990s:

- From 1990 to 2000, the number of Canadians living in poverty rose from 4.39 million to 4.72 million (or 16.2 percent of Canadians).

- In 1999, 18.7 percent of children (1.1 million) lived in poverty, compared with 15.2 percent in 1989.

- Between 1989 and 2000, the number of food bank visits doubled (NCW, 2003; National Anti-Poverty Organization, 2003).

Canada's drastic social spending cuts were noticed by the international community. In 1998, a submission to the United Nations (UN) by the Charter Committee on Poverty Issues reprimanded Canada for its rising poverty rates, especially among children, lone-parent families, and Aboriginal peoples, and for the growing number of food banks and homeless people. Between 1993 and 2003, Canada fell from first to eighth place on the UN's list of the most desirable places to live in the world.

BUDGET SURPLUSES

In the mid-1990s, the federal government promised that, once it restored fiscal balance, it would eventually reinvest in high-priority programs. That day came in 1998, when the federal government began directing money into programs that had been neglected during the deficit-fighting years. Between 1999 and 2005, federal program expenditures grew steadily from $162 billion to $210 billion (Office of the Auditor General of Canada, 2006).

The Liberal government's 2005 budget committed more than $75 billion over ten years to "strengthen and secure Canada's social foundations." The government earmarked significant investments for early learning and child care, seniors' programs, Aboriginal communities, and tax relief for people with disabilities. The promise of increased funding met favour with the regional governments, especially since some of them were still struggling with deficits. Before it could implement many of these plans, the Liberal government lost the 2006 federal election to the Conservative Party of Canada.

DISCUSSION QUESTIONS

■ From Retrenchment to Reinvestment

1. Why might the provinces and territories positively view the elimination of national standards for social assistance?

2. In the 1990s, politicians regularly lowered social assistance benefit rates to discourage people from choosing welfare over work. Do you believe that was the right thing to do? Give reasons for your answer.

3. Did the social welfare reforms from 1995 to 2006 reflect a residual, institutional, or social investment approach to social welfare? Give evidence to support your answer.

3 A CONSERVATIVE APPROACH TO SOCIAL WELFARE

The Conservative government under Prime Minister Stephen Harper encourages self-reliance and frequently reminds Canadians that government is not the solver of social problems. In 2012, Human Resources and Skills Development Canada announced, "Social and economic challenges, such as homelessness, youth crime, chronic poverty, skills shortages, and persistent unemployment, continue to exist in Canada despite the various initiatives all levels of government, community organizations and foundations have taken to address them. *New* thinking, *new* methods, *new* partnerships and *new* approaches are needed if we are to continue to make progress" (Human Resources and Skills Development Canada, 2013a, italics added). Although many of those "new" ways have yet to be fully explored, developments in recent years suggest a unique approach to social welfare. This section takes a critical look at some of those developments.

LOWER TAXES

Conservative governments generally hold a negative view of heavy taxation and blame high taxes for discouraging foreign investment and reducing the country's ability to compete for business in the global market. According to conservative thought, high taxes also represent a "burden," or a form of "punishment" against hard-working Canadians. Soon after taking office in 2006, the Conservative government declared that taxes in Canada were too high. To lighten the tax burden on Canadians, the Conservatives set out to reduce all taxes (including personal taxes, consumption taxes, and corporate taxes) by $220 billion between 2006 and 2014.[3] This plan would bring federal tax revenue to its lowest level in fifty years and give corporations some of the biggest tax breaks anywhere in the Western world (Canada, Department of Finance, 2009; Conservative Party of Canada, 2012).

Many social and economic analysts argue that taxes in Canada are not too high and are in fact relatively low when compared with those of the Nordic countries. Studies suggest that, contrary to popular belief, high taxation does not automatically inhibit economic progress, nor do low taxes naturally attract foreign investment. Lower taxes nevertheless reduce government revenues and the capacity of governments to fund health, social welfare, and educational

---

[3] These tax cuts followed on the heels of the former Liberal government's regime, which reduced taxes by $152 billion between 1997 and 2004.

programs. Having less money to work with can be an advantage for governments focused on reducing public spending. The term "starving the beast" refers to a strategy used by neoliberal governments to cut off the source of funding (in this case, tax revenue) for "undesirable" (usually social) programs. With less funding, programs will likely struggle to meet their objectives. Government can then declare those programs as ineffective and justifiably cancel them.

Many people who value social progress take exception to the Conservatives' penchant for tax reduction. According to social policy expert Marvyn Novick (2007, p. 7), "If communities of inclusion and opportunity are what Canadians want, then we have to be willing to create a better balance between money in our pockets and money we pool together for what we value in common." Brooks and Hwong (2006, p. 7) caution against Canada's falling taxation rates by noting, "Tax cuts are disastrous for the well-being of a nation's citizens."

FISCALIZATION

In general, conservative governments do not support the practice of taking tax money from working Canadians and then using those public funds to create programs and services. Rather, conservatives prefer to achieve social goals through **fiscalization**, which lowers the amount of tax owed by low-income Canadians. While the social welfare system has traditionally based eligibility for benefits on need or disadvantage, fiscalization uses a person's tax return to assess whether he or she is deserving of benefits. By 2013, an average family of four received more than $3100 in tax savings as a direct result of the federal government's tax cuts and tax benefits (Canada, 2013).

Fiscalization has its advantages and disadvantages. Proponents of fiscalization maintain that the use of the tax system is an effective and efficient way to identify and aid low-income earners. Fiscalization also rewards labour market participation since tax benefits are only possible if taxable income is earned. The practice also avoids stigmatizing the poor, since recipients receive benefits privately through the tax system (Brodie & Bakker, 2007).

One potential problem with fiscalization is that tax benefit recipients might not always use the benefit in the way that government intended; for example, the Canada Child Tax Benefit aims to improve conditions for Canada's poorest children, but there is no way of knowing whether parents use the benefit to help their children. Moreover, on the surface, tax relief schemes may sound generous when they really offer little help to the poorest of Canadians. About one-third of Canadians who file tax forms earn so little they do not pay taxes and therefore do not benefit from tax relief schemes (see Exhibit 4.7).

EXHIBIT 4.7

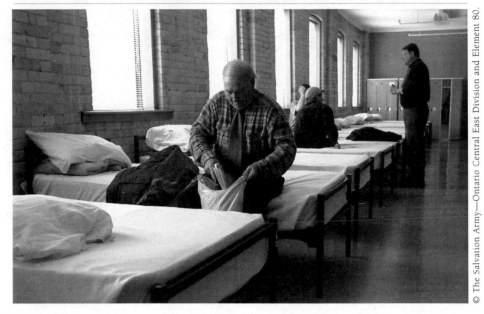

Many Canadians who visit homeless shelters pay little or no tax and therefore do not benefit from tax credits or deductions.

Some so-called social benefits may actually penalize low-income families. The Universal Child Care Benefit (UCCB), for example, pays $100 per month for each child under the age of six. Not only are those payments taxable, but they can also push a family into a higher tax bracket. For many low-income families, being in a higher tax bracket means losing their eligibility for other tax breaks. Social policy analysts Battle, Torjman, and Mendelson (2006, p. 1) found that the UCCB's tax structure allows many middle-income families to keep a greater proportion of the benefit than lower-income families do, making the UCCB "deeply flawed . . ., paying net payments that are unfair and irrational."

PROVINCIALIZATION

Throughout Canada's history, the federal government has used its spending power to intervene in social welfare matters—such as unemployment and poverty-related issues—that are constitutionally the responsibility of the provinces. Some social analysts have a positive view of federal intervention, suggesting that such involvement has contributed to nation building, a sense of national unity, and a general feeling of citizenship. Others have criticized the increasingly blurry lines separating federal and regional powers for creating a highly confusing, uncoordinated, and fragmented social welfare system.

Shortly after winning the 2006 election, Prime Minister Harper declared a "renewed respect" for the constitutional division of powers between federal and regional levels of government. In practice, that "respect" means putting an end to the federal government's involvement in matters—such as social welfare—that are constitutionally the responsibility of the provinces and territories. The federal government's decision to pull out of regional affairs put an end to the long-running conflict between the two levels of government over social welfare issues; it also quashed any hope of the federal government taking a leadership role in national initiatives related to child care, homelessness, or poverty.

It is unclear how the provinces and territories will fund social welfare programs in the future, now that the federal government has relinquished its political grip on the regional governments. The legislation governing the funding of social welfare programs expires in 2014. Although the provinces and territories seek a renewal of federal financial support under the CST, the extent of that support is yet to be determined; however, the Conservatives will likely limit federal spending in social welfare and other matters that fall within provincial jurisdiction.

PRIVATIZATION

In recent decades, Canadians have witnessed a dramatic reduction in government's role as the provider or funder of social welfare programs. At the same time, governments have found innovative ways to engage the private sector in meeting social welfare needs. For example, various levels of government in Canada

- have devolved service delivery responsibilities to charities and nonprofit organizations, and now require those agencies to seek part of their revenue from non-government sources
- have contracted with profit-making organizations to deliver employment support services
- offer tax incentives to private-sector housing developers to build or modify affordable rental units for low-income earners

- give tax credits to employers to create child-care spaces in the workplace
- have introduced more generous tax breaks to encourage individuals and corporations to donate to charitable causes

Canadian governments continue to seek innovative ways to offload social welfare matters to the private sector. In 2011, Diane Finley, the federal minister for Human Resources and Skills Development travelled to England to learn about that country's "Big Society" experiment. Under the Big Society, governments are shifting social welfare responsibilities to local authorities and citizens and calling on volunteers and the private sector to provide the human and financial resources needed for programs and services. According to Finley, Canada is ready to test some of the Big Society's ideas: "It's time for us to unleash individual initiative so that those who are motivated can help others, and those who need help are given the opportunity to take more responsibility for themselves" (Canada, 2012a). As a first step, Finley launched a "Call for Concepts for Social Finance" in late 2012 and invited individuals and organizations from across Canada to submit their ideas on how communities might use private funds to achieve social welfare goals. The federal government plans to use those ideas to reshape social policy in Canada.

THE 2008–2009 ECONOMIC RECESSION

In 2008, Canada—along with other advanced nations—slid into the worst global economic recession since the Great Depression. Contrary to neoliberal values, the Harper government bowed to public and international pressure and applied Keynesian principles to kick-start a rapidly deteriorating economy. In January 2009, the federal government introduced its Economic Action Plan, a multibillion dollar economic stimulus package consisting of tax cuts and a wide range of publically funded "make work" projects. The plan targeted most of the available benefits to middle-class Canadians, which the federal government heavily relied on to continue working and paying income tax. Although the action plan focused largely on job-creating infrastructure projects, it also directed modest provisions to unemployed and low-income Canadians. In creating jobs and putting cash in the pockets of Canadians, the government hoped that people would spend, rather than save, their money, and subsequently stimulate the sluggish economy.

The recession took a financial toll on governments at all levels. At the federal level, the combination of high unemployment and falling government revenues (largely due to shrinking tax revenues) prompted the government to cut low-priority programs and return to deficit spending. At the regional level, all provinces and territories experienced some degree of economic slowdown. The number of unemployed workers on EI rose sharply in late 2008 and continued to climb well into 2009, especially in Ontario, British Columbia, Alberta, Saskatchewan, Nunavut, and Yukon. (The chart in Exhibit 4.8 illustrates the upward trend in unemployment during this period.) Municipal governments struggled with a fiscal squeeze related to higher unemployment, lower government revenues, and an increasing demand for social welfare programs; that demand nevertheless outpaced the capacity of municipalities to respond effectively (Federation of Canadian Municipalities, 2010).

Canada's economic recession raised concerns for the many nonprofit organizations that provided social services, such as emergency shelters, food banks, and outreach for low-income seniors. These organizations experienced an economic squeeze of their own because of cutbacks in government funding and declines in charitable donations ("Financial Crisis Creating," 2008).

EXHIBIT 4.8

CANADA'S UNEMPLOYMENT RATE, 2007 TO 2012

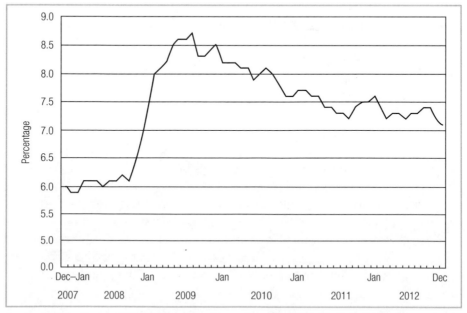

Source: Statistics Canada. (2013). Labour Force Survey, December 2012. *The Daily*, Friday, January 4, 2013, Chart 2: Unemployment rate. Retrieved from http://www.statcan.gc.ca/daily-quotidien/130104/dq130104a-eng.pdf.

DISCUSSION QUESTIONS

■ **A Conservative Approach to Social Welfare**

1. The Conservatives planned to reduce federal taxes by $220 billion between 2006 and 2014. What are the pros and cons of lower taxes?

2. There is much debate on the merits of using the tax system to meet people's social welfare needs. Identify the potential advantages and disadvantages of such an approach.

3. The Conservatives under Prime Minister Stephen Harper believe that the provinces and territories should manage most social welfare matters. Explain why the Conservatives might take this position.

4 TAKING STOCK

Studies show that while some Canadians are benefiting from neoliberal policies, many others are falling behind socially and economically. Two trends in Canada are particularly disturbing: (1) a declining quality of life and (2) increasing income inequality.

DECLINING QUALITY OF LIFE

The term "quality of life" relates to how satisfied (or dissatisfied) a person is with his or her living conditions. A number of reports suggest that the quality of life for Canadians is generally on the decline. For example, the Canadian Index of Wellbeing (CIW) shows that over the seventeen years from 1994 to 2010, Canada's gross domestic product (GDP) grew by almost 29 percent, while living standards improved by less than 6 percent. (Exhibit 4.9 illustrates the divergent paths of GDP and living standards.) The CIW also finds that although poverty and unemployment rates have decreased since 1994, the quality of the jobs has also deteriorated; for example, many full-time jobs have disappeared and been replaced by unstable, low-paying, temporary or part-time positions with few benefits. Another finding of the CIW was that housing affordability in Canada has significantly declined (Canadian Index of Wellbeing, 2011).

In its *Report Card on Canada*, the Conference Board of Canada (2013a, 2013b) compares the quality of life in Canada with that of other advanced countries. Overall, Canada ranks seventh out of seventeen countries in terms of its social performance. However, Canada gets low marks for its relatively high levels of child poverty and gender inequity. In terms of its poverty rate

EXHIBIT 4.9

FALLING LIVING STANDARDS

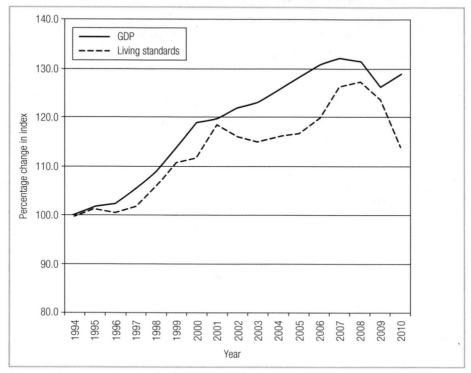

Source: Author-generated graph; data from Canadian Index of Wellbeing. (2012). Standardised data tables from the Canadian Index of Wellbeing: Composite index: National report 2012, CIW and GDP 1994 to 2010 Standardised Data tables. Retrieved from https://uwaterloo.ca.

among working-age adults, Canada ranks as the third-worst country. Not only is this form of poverty a waste of opportunity and human resources, but it is also likely to inhibit Canada's ability to sustain economic growth in the coming years (Organisation for Economic Co-operation and Development [OECD], 2005).

INCOME INEQUALITY

Although Canada has become a wealthier country in the last two decades, it has also seen a steady rise in **income inequality**—that is, an increasingly uneven distribution of income across the population. In 2012, the richest 1 percent of

Canadians received 14 percent of all available income, while 99 percent of the population had to share the remaining 86 percent of total wealth (Broadbent Institute, 2012a). The Occupy Movement has popularized the slogan "We are the 99 percent," to draw the world's attention to the fact that the very rich have a much greater share of the world's wealth (see Exhibit 4.10).

Rising income inequality is a problem in most advanced countries; however, in its *Report Card on Canada*, the Conference Board of Canada (2013c) ranks Canada's level of income inequality the twelve worst out of seventeen countries. The main drivers of income inequality in this country include an increased number of low-paying, part-time and temporary jobs; changes in policies and tax breaks that favour the rich; and a reduced level of income redistribution through tax and benefit systems to low-income Canadians (OECD, 2011)

Income inequality has serious implications for the economic and social well-being of a nation. When a large segment of the population has relatively

EXHIBIT 4.10

© REUTERS/Andrew Burton

Occupy Movement protesters use the slogan "We are the 99 percent" to refer to the income inequality between the wealthiest 1 percent of the population and everyone else.

little disposable income, they stop buying goods and services, which can lead to business closures, job layoffs, unemployment, and underemployment. When people are not working or paying taxes, the country's economic growth slows, and governments have less money to fund important social programs. Erosion in social programs can lead to social instability and higher incidences of mental illness, violence, and other social problems (Wilkinson & Pickett, 2010). Research suggests that income inequality can also transfer from generation to generation: children from poor families grow up to be poor adults, and children from rich families grow up to be rich (Corak, 2013). Some regions in Canada are more unequal than others are. A report by the Ontario Common Front found that Ontarians are currently experiencing the greatest income inequality in Canada; in that province, the gap between the rich and poor has reached a proportion not seen since the Great Depression (Mehra, 2012).

To date, Canadian governments have been generally indifferent to the rise in income inequality. A number of social advocates, academics, and others are nevertheless taking steps to raise the profile of income inequality issues. For instance, the left-leaning Broadbent Institute has released a report on the growing income gap, with the intent to stimulate debate among political leaders on this important topic (Broadbent Institute, 2012b).

DISCUSSION QUESTIONS

■ Taking Stock

1. According to various reports, economic progress has not improved the quality of life for many Canadians. Why do you think this is so?
2. Canada has become a more unequal society in recent decades. What should governments or the private sector do (if anything) to equalize income and opportunities for all Canadians?

SUMMARY

Introduction

As the economy slowed during the early 1970s, the federal and regional governments began to borrow money rather than cut programs or raise taxes. As a result, governments incurred annual budget deficits and ran up huge public debts. Realizing that deficit spending was unsustainable, governments drastically cut public spending in an attempt to balance their budgets.

1 A Neoliberal Approach to Social Welfare

The Progressive Conservatives overhauled Old Age Security, Unemployment Insurance, CAP, and Family Allowances; many other funding cuts were gradual and subtle. A new Liberal government in 1993 recommended strategies to confront the challenges of a new global economy. In 1995, the Liberals announced major spending cuts, rationalizing that if Canadians cut back then, they could make social programs sustainable in the future.

2 From Retrenchment to Reinvestment

To reduce expenses, the federal government replaced UI with a new EI Act and replaced CAP with the CHST. The CHST was less generous than CAP but gave the provinces and territories more discretion in how they designed and delivered social welfare programs. To deal with fewer funds, the regional governments slashed SA benefit rates and devolved many programs to municipalities and the private sector. Governments shifted SA and EI programming from a passive to an active model, requiring recipients to work or train in exchange for benefits. Although balanced budgets and economic growth in the 2000s led to an economic boom, Canada had to deal with a serious social deficit.

3 A Conservative Approach to Social Welfare

Since 2006, the Conservatives have reduced tax revenues and cut social programs. Fiscalization is a preferred method of distributing social welfare benefits, but this system does little to help Canadians who pay little or no tax. Social welfare responsibilities are increasingly provincialized, and the Conservative government continues to seek new ways to privatize social welfare programs and services. The 2008–2009 recession forced the federal government to return to deficit budgets and adopt Keynesian principles to stimulate the economy.

4 Taking Stock

Although the incomes of some disadvantaged groups have improved over the last few decades, many Canadians continue to struggle to meet basic needs. Studies show that Canada's quality of life is on the decline, despite economic growth. Income inequality is a particularly worrisome problem in Canada; however, political leaders have been slow to address inequality issues.

KEY TERMS

For definitions of the key terms, consult the Glossary on page 453 at the end of the book.

progressive tax system, p. 92

Keynesian economics, p. 92

budget deficits, p. 92

public debt, p. 92

globalization, p. 92

neoliberalism, p. 92

monetarism, p. 92

welfare state retrenchment, p. 92

clawbacks, p. 94

decentralization, p. 95

austerity measures, p. 96

block fund, p. 99

provincialized social policy, p. 99

passive labour market policies, p. 103

active labour market policies, p. 104

welfare-to-work programs, p. 104

social deficit, p. 105

fiscalization, p. 108

income inequality, p. 114

PART 2

THE SERVICE DELIVERY SYSTEM

CHAPTER 5

Service Sectors

OBJECTIVES

Three service sectors are responsible for delivering social welfare programs to Canadians. This chapter will

- introduce the notion of a mixed economy of welfare

- review the main characteristics of the public, commercial, and voluntary sectors in a social welfare context

- examine the alternative service delivery model and its implications

- describe the expanded service delivery role of the voluntary sector

- consider the social economy as an emerging fourth service sector

INTRODUCTION

There is now an increasingly common awareness that a healthy Canada depends on the best possible collaboration between all three sectors of society. We need all sectors to be vibrant, strong and effective: [t]o share their views; [t]o be more and more involved in contributing to the decision-making processes; [t]o address the major challenges facing all Canadians and that can help to ensure that Canada's values are reflected in world affairs. (Mel Cappe, Former Clerk of the Privy Council, February 6, 2002)

From the Second World War to the mid-1970s, Canadians generally supported liberal governments that provided a balance between the interests of individuals and the interests of society (Jenson, 2004). To strike that balance, these governments assumed a certain level of responsibility for the delivery of social welfare programs. Canadian governments have nevertheless been reluctant to monopolize the delivery of those programs, preferring instead that businesses and nonprofit organizations play a primary role in that respect. What has evolved in Canada, then, is a variety of service delivery systems—or what Rice and Prince (2000) refer to as a **mixed economy of welfare**. The mixed economy reflects a loosely defined division of labour between the public and private sectors. The **private sector** can be further broken down into the commercial and voluntary sectors. Thus, the mixed economy really has three broad service sectors: the **public sector**, the **commercial sector**, and the **voluntary sector**. All three systems focus on the enhancement of well-being but are organized, funded, and managed in their own distinct ways.

The Liberal Party of Canada (1997) dubbed the public, commercial, and voluntary sectors the "three pillars" of Canadian society and economy because of their many valuable contributions to Canada's development. However, a fourth sector—called the **social economy**—is emerging as a legitimate service provider in Canada's social welfare system. The Government of Canada defines the social economy as a community-based (or grassroots) sector that is entrepreneurial and yet nonprofit in nature. With strong ties to the voluntary sector, the social economy aims to strengthen communities through entrepreneurial activities and, at the same time, improve conditions for disadvantaged groups (Human Resources and Social Development Canada [HRSDC], 2005). See Exhibit 5.1 for a graphic illustration of the four service sectors and their distinguishing features.

Although many people might view the service sectors as discrete entities, considerable overlap exists between them. Katherine Scott (2003a, p. 8) describes the boundaries of the sectors as "'fuzzy'—if not downright porous." These boundaries lack clear definition for the following main reasons:

- Government and private sector agencies often work together on, or share the costs of, joint projects.

- The activities, functions, and roles of private and public organizations are often similar, making it difficult to discern which sector does what.

- While governments tend to participate at some level in the provision of social welfare—whether through regulation, planning, or funding—they are constantly adjusting their degree of involvement in service delivery, which affects the scope of programs delivered by the private sector.

EXHIBIT 5.1

CANADA'S SERVICE SECTORS, AGENCIES, AND PROGRAMS

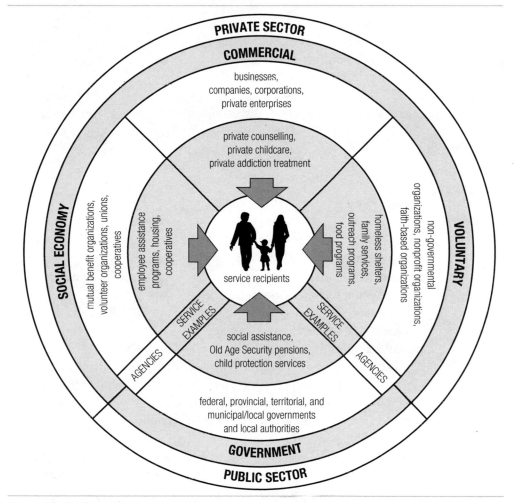

Source: Rosalie Chappell

Since the mid-1990s, the boundaries of the service sectors have been undergoing significant realignment, creating what Hrab (2004, p. 3) refers to as "a new era with respect to the delivery of public services." This chapter explores the impact of that realignment on social welfare organizations in Canada and on their capacity to serve. First, however, is a brief introduction to the public, commercial, and voluntary sectors within a social welfare context. (The social economy is discussed later in the chapter.)

1 SERVICE SECTORS: PUBLIC, COMMERCIAL, AND VOLUNTARY DOMAINS

Although each service sector has its own goals and functions, they all play an important role in social provision. The *public sector* includes the federal, provincial and territorial, and municipal governments, which use tax or other public revenues to develop, monitor, administer, and deliver programs and services. Companies in the *commercial sector* are profit motivated and sell services to consumers for full market price. Also called the charitable, independent, or third sector, the *voluntary sector* includes non-governmental agencies and organizations that fulfill a social purpose and deliver programs on a nonprofit basis.

THE PUBLIC SECTOR

Over the decades, Canadians have come to expect governments to protect them from poverty, unemployment, disability, illness, and other risks inherent in modern society. Indeed, in Canada's postwar era, many Canadians came to view government as having the resources and knowledge to cure society's ills. Today's broad range of social welfare programs is government's attempt to meet the public's social security needs.

Constitutionally, the responsibility for social welfare lies with the provincial and territorial governments. However, over time, social welfare has become a shared responsibility among the federal, provincial and territorial, and municipal levels of government. Income security programs and social services are referred to as **public programs** because they "belong" to the public: that is, the public pays for these programs mainly through taxes, and the public expects elected government officials to be accountable for how those programs are developed, managed, and delivered. Government controls most aspects of income security programs, from policy development to implementation. Although many social services today are delivered by organizations in the private sector, certain social services are fully controlled by government and delivered directly by government workers (or civil servants). The following section provides examples of social welfare services delivered at each level of government.

Federal Government

Among the few social services that the federal level of government directly delivers are mental health services for identified "client groups," including

First Nations and Inuit peoples, federal offenders, the Canadian forces, veterans, members of the Royal Canadian Mounted Police, recent immigrants and refugees, and federal public service employees. In addition, the federal government directly delivers several national income security programs, including Old Age Security, the Canada Pension Plan, and the Canada Child Tax Benefit. Although many departments at the federal level deliver programs related to social welfare, Human Resources and Skills Development Canada is considered the main social welfare department.

Provincial and Territorial Governments

Regional governments directly deliver mandated (as opposed to discretionary) social welfare programs that need to be delivered in a consistent manner across communities or that require a certain level of enforcement (August, 2006). **Mandated services** include social assistance; each provincial and territorial government has its own social assistance program in which government workers deliver the bulk of services. Many regional governments also directly deliver child welfare, adult protection, and mental health services. Most regional governments have ministries devoted to the delivery or funding of social services, such as Nova Scotia's Department of Community Services and Saskatchewan's Ministry of Social Services. In some jurisdictions—such as the Northwest Territories—the ministry of social services provides the funding, structure, and leadership to social services, while leaving the delivery of services to local social service authorities.

Municipal Government

Canada has never had an established pattern for the delivery of social welfare services at the municipal (or local) level. However, since the 1970s, provincial and territorial governments have been devolving more responsibilities to municipalities. Today, many municipalities directly deliver programs that relate to, for example, social housing, social assistance, child care, or community development. In many cases, those programs are a segment of a larger provincial or territorial program; for instance, the City of Toronto delivers a significant portion of Ontario's social assistance and employment services programs.

Reports show that many cities are struggling to meet their growing responsibilities and provide adequate social services with their limited resources. Specific challenges in cities across Canada relate to poverty, rising numbers of working poor families, growing income inequality, and high unemployment (Federation of Canadian Municipalities, 2010).

THE COMMERCIAL SECTOR

The concept of social welfare implies a collective, public responsibility for social well-being and is therefore associated with government intervention that is not profit motivated. Thus, the commercial sector is not considered part of the social welfare system. Businesses nevertheless offer a wide range of services aimed at enhancing personal well-being. These services include private child care, addiction treatment, and personal counselling, all of which are available for a fee.

Commercial services can be paid for in various ways. In many cases, a business may charge the consumer a flat rate for services rendered. Other businesses may offer their services according to a sliding fee scale and adjust the fee according to the client's financial means; this practice is most common when government subsidizes the costs of services for low-income clients. (See Exhibit 5.2 for an example of a company that allows government subsidies to cover the costs of child-care services.) People who pay out of pocket for services—for example, at a private addiction treatment centre—may be reimbursed for service costs if they are covered under an extended health insurance program or other compensatory program, such as workers' compensation.

EXHIBIT 5.2

COMPANY PROFILE: EDLEUN GROUP INC.

Edleun is the leading provider of high quality, community-based early learning and child-care centres in Canada. The centres offer early education and child-care services to children ages six weeks to thirteen years. Edleun is committed to preparing children for the next step in their education and life, offering families and employers access to, and choice of quality in, early childhood education programs.

Edleun is publicly traded on the Toronto Stock Exchange (TSX-V:EDU). The company's objectives include the acquisition and subsequent improvement of existing child-care centres and the development of new state-of-the-art early learning and child-care centres in under-served Canadian communities.

The company currently has fifty operating centres in Alberta, British Columbia, and Ontario, and is in the process of acquiring, developing, or redeveloping three additional centres. In all, Edleun will be able to provide approximately 5400 licensed child-care spaces.

Source: Excerpted and adapted from Edleun Group. (2012, November 5). *Growth in Ontario continues with acquisition of Ottawa Montessori centres* [News release]. Retrieved from http://www.edleungroup.com/upload/file/Growth_in_Ontario_with_Acquisition_Ottawa_Montessori.pdf.

It has never been easier for businesses to sell helping services to Canadian markets, thanks to an expansion of government-issued licences and privatization policies that encourage free enterprise. Private helping services are also legitimated by a growing number of Canadians who welcome the innovative ideas associated with business, can afford to purchase services (or are insured for such services), and do not want government involved in their personal affairs. Moreover, the many trade agreements, such as NAFTA, struck between Canada and its international neighbours make it relatively easy for private enterprises to cross borders and offer specialized services for a profit.

More and more businesses are leaning toward **corporate social responsibility**, a concept whereby a company engages in activities that are important not only for the good of the company but also for the good of society. Donating a portion of company profits to a children's charity, for example, may not only benefit children in need but also attract shareholders and customers, boost staff morale, raise the company's image, and ultimately increase profits.

THE VOLUNTARY SECTOR

The voluntary sector comprises a broad spectrum of organizations, otherwise known as voluntary agencies, charitable or nonprofit societies, or non-governmental organizations (NGOs). These organizations are highly diverse, covering the spectrum in sizes, causes, and activities. While many voluntary organizations support such areas as sports or the arts, 12 percent of all voluntary organizations focus on meeting human need through the provision of social services (Imagine Canada, 2006). Among these **voluntary social agencies** are relatively small, community-based groups, such as family service societies (see Exhibit 5.3), and large, national organizations, such as the National Action Committee on the Status of Women. Despite their diversity, most voluntary social agencies are

- organized (they have some internal organizational structure)
- non-governmental (they are structurally separate from government institutions)
- nonprofit (they use any profits to improve the agency, not to benefit the agency owners or directors)
- self-governing (they are independent from other institutions and regulate their own operations)
- volunteer friendly (they involve volunteers to some degree in agency activities or management) (Saunders, 2004)

© Kristiina Paul

Catholic Family Services is one of the many voluntary social agencies across Canada that aims to meet human need through the provision of social services.

More than 19 000 voluntary social agencies exist in Canada, and they employ almost 130 000 people. In addition to paid staff, almost two million Canadians (mostly women) volunteer their time for these agencies (Imagine Canada, 2006).

In general, voluntary social agencies perform three main functions:

1. They *do good works*, which may be understood in terms of delivering tangibles, such as food, clothing, or shelter, or intangibles, like counselling or support services to families with children.

2. They *advocate* by, for instance, educating the public about an issue or a social problem, or lobbying for change in laws or policies to improve the living conditions of a particular client group.

3. They *mediate*, often by bringing together individuals or groups in a community to find solutions or compromises to common problems (Evans & Shields, 2006).

In many respects, voluntary social agencies complement the work performed by government: while government responds to national or regional concerns, such as child poverty and homelessness, agencies in the voluntary sector apply their knowledge and expertise at the community level (Voluntary Sector Steering Group, 2002). In 1999, the Government of Canada formally recognized the voluntary sector as playing "an increasingly critical and complex role in helping to achieve the goals important to Canadians and ensure a high quality of life. It has become a vital third pillar in Canadian society, working alongside the public and [commercial] . . . sectors to make Canada a more humane, caring and prosperous nation" (Privy Council Office, 1999, p. 1).

Most voluntary social agencies rely on diverse funding sources. However, government provides the bulk of funding (about 66 percent of all agency revenue), with most of those funds coming from a provincial or territorial government. The second-largest source of income (about 20 percent) is agency-generated earnings derived from, for example, bake sales or raffles (Hall et al., 2005).

DISCUSSION QUESTIONS

■ **Service Sectors: Public, Commercial, and Voluntary Domains**

1. Identify the social welfare or "helping" programs in your community. In which service sector (public, commercial, or voluntary) does each program best fit? What criteria did you use to categorize each program?

2. What might be the pros and cons of the public, commercial, and voluntary sectors, in terms of how each might manage or deliver social welfare programs?

2 NEW DIRECTIONS IN SERVICE DELIVERY

By the 1980s, government departments had evolved into large, bureaucratic systems that were criticized for being expensive, wasteful, rigid, remote, impersonal, and unresponsive to the public's needs (see Exhibit 5.4). Governments were also blamed for failing to control their spending and balance their budgets. In the 1990s, it became clear that most governments could not effectively address the social and economic problems (such as massive job losses) created by globalization and the shift from a manufacturing to a knowledge-based economy (Richmond & Shields, 2003). Neoliberals saw these and other developments as proof that traditional government approaches in general, and Keynesian economics in particular, were no

EXHIBIT 5.4
GOVERNMENT ASSISTANCE

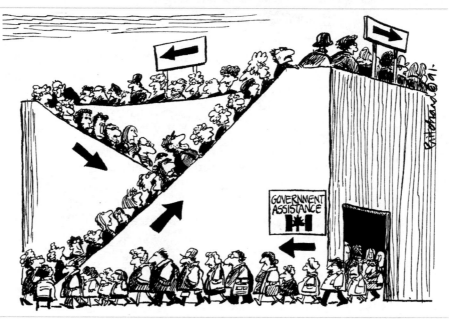

Reprinted courtesy of the estate of the artist, Denny Pritchard.

longer effective. Neoliberals argued that monetarism—with its emphasis on controlled public spending, low taxes, and smaller yet more efficient government systems—was a more suitable approach in a global economy (Shields, 2003). For neoliberals, smaller governments delivering fewer programs made sense.

Fewer social welfare programs, however, was not what Canadians wanted in the 1990s. The demand for social services, in fact, increased because of an aging population, changing family structure and roles, growing poverty and homelessness, and widespread unemployment (Cooper & Bartlett, 2008). Canadian governments found themselves in a dilemma: How could they meet the social welfare needs of Canadians while at the same time reduce public spending and taxes? To address this problem, the federal government began looking into new methods of governance and the innovative ways that services might be delivered. The federal government concluded that it had to "reinvent" its roles and shift from a "rowing" to a "steering" capacity: government rows when it delivers public programs directly and steers when it sets policy and oversees the services that a non-government organization delivers (Hrab, 2004).

ALTERNATIVE SERVICE DELIVERY

To shift to a steering capacity, the federal government had to convince private sector agencies of the benefits of assuming more service delivery responsibilities. The government promoted the notion of **collaborative governance** as an effective way to address what Rittel and Webber (1973) refer to as "wicked problems"—that is, complex social problems that are best solved by multiple actors across all service sectors. Through collaboration, agencies could pool their resources, share expertise and knowledge, and work toward common goals. To foster collaboration and provide guidance in the transition, the federal government chose an **alternative service delivery** (ASD) framework.

Although the ASD was not a new framework, the federal government began to apply the ASD's business-oriented principles more extensively in the 1990s. The ASD provides direction on such things as how to reduce the size and costs of government programs, reorganize government departments and agencies, coordinate efforts within a government or among different levels of government, and form effective working relationships with private sector organizations to meet service delivery objectives (Treasury Board of Canada Secretariat, 2002). Before long, the ASD caught on at the provincial and territorial and municipal levels of government.

ASD includes a wide variety of strategies; however, the main strategy used by Canadian governments to deliver social programs is **contracting-out**. In a social welfare context, a government agency pays a non-government individual or organization to provide specific services for a limited period while remaining accountable for the quality of service delivery. As a rule, Canadian governments continue to deliver income security programs while leaving it up to contracted non-government agencies to deliver the bulk of social services.

The value of competition is central to the notion of contracting-out. Competition is an integral part of government's business model and is seen as a way to keep the costs of services down, keep service quality up, and generally make service delivery more efficient (Antony et al., 2007). Thus, any individual or organization in the private sector wanting to deliver a service that uses public funds must compete for those funds. The competitive bidding process typically begins with a government agency inviting members of the private sector to submit a proposal that outlines the applicant's plan for meeting service delivery requirements. The government agency then evaluates the proposals to determine which contractor might deliver the best quality of service for the lowest cost.

The introduction of ASD in general and contracting-out in particular is significant for the delivery of Canadian social services in three main ways:

1. It represents a shift in government's priorities from an emphasis on *equity* to a focus on *efficiency* in the delivery of public services and distribution of resources (Evans, Richmond, & Shields, 2005).

2. It reflects government's preference for a *business* (or market) model over a *welfare state* model (Ilcan & Basok, 2004).

3. It promotes the privatization or "marketization" of social welfare programs, and a shift from a *public* to a *private* responsibility for social well-being.

PRIVATIZATION: ISSUES AND CONCERNS

Since the 1990s, when governments were eagerly pursuing ASD strategies, Canadians have voiced their concerns about the offloading of public programs onto the private sector. Many of those concerns relate to the potential impact of **privatization** on Canada's cherished social programs. The fear is that private organizations generally have lower service standards than government (White, 2003). Issues have also been raised about **accountability** and which sector—the public or voluntary—will answer to the public for the delivery of services. By nature, private organizations are free agents, operating at arm's length from government and without any electoral responsibility or accountability. The issue here is that while government can be made accountable to the public for its expenditures and practices, private operations may not be to the same extent (Ilcan & Basok, 2004).

Canadians have also raised concerns about the privatization of social welfare if it means that businesses (as opposed to nonprofit organizations) are able to compete for and win social service contracts. As Sauber (1983, p. 26) points out, the idea of large companies using public funds to profit from people's problems runs counter to the core values of the welfare state, such as compassion and "the alleviation of human suffering." Another issue revolves around the goals of for-profit operations: business pursues profit, not the public good. As long as the service makes a profit, the company will provide it; however, once a better rate of return is found elsewhere, the owners will likely drop the program and move, leaving communities without needed services (Quarter, 1992). There is also the worry that businesses may fall short when serving the most vulnerable and marginalized members of society. According to Israt Ahmed (2006, p. 19), "When for-profit corporate entities win a contract, the tendency is for them to seek out the easiest-to-serve clients for quick and favourable results, and ignore the most vulnerable or hard-to-serve clients, who require more staff time and face greater challenges."

Corporate-owned child-care services in Canada have been at the centre of controversy in recent years. Exhibit 5.5 reflects a common sentiment toward this type of profit-making service.

When the federal government replaced the Canada Assistance Plan with the Canada Health and Social Transfer in the mid-1990s, it gave the provinces and territories more flexibility in the delivery of social services. More flexibility meant having the option of contracting out social service programs in part or in whole. Until recently, businesses have not been that attracted to government contracts to deliver social services, since those contracts rarely offered much potential for profit making. Governments are now changing policies and legislation to encourage businesses to become more involved in social service delivery. For example, some regional governments are offering lucrative contracts to large (often non-Canadian) corporations. This happened in Ontario from 2005 to 2007, when the government contracted the American-based WCG

EXHIBIT 5.5

CHILDREN AREN'T WIDGETS

The expansion of big box, commercial daycare centres in British Columbia is not a good thing. Children aren't widgets. Their care should not be entrusted to a corporate entity. I mean, would you trust your three-year-old to WalMart?

Private daycare operator Edleun recently announced it was taking over five daycare centers in BC, including three in the Lower Mainland. The focus of a corporation is to deliver a return to its shareholders, which has no place in our child-care system.

The only way private daycare centers make a profit is by charging higher fees, paying staff less, and by gambling on real estate. None of these prospects is good for working families. Average families probably can't afford private daycare—and certainly not if you have more than one child.

We need an alternate vision: a publicly funded, accessible, community-based early childcare system. And we need it yesterday. We needed it five years ago. This type of care brings out the best in children, is affordable for BC families, and encourages the development of a skilled and committed workforce.

We are being let down. Big box daycare is not a solution. BC families deserve better.

Source: Walker, D. (2011). *Children aren't widgets*. Retrieved from B.C. Government and Service Employees' Union website: http://m.bcgeu.ca/children_are_not_widgets_110811?device=mobile.

International to run JobsNow, a pilot project aimed at helping welfare recipients move off welfare into permanent jobs (Goss Gilroy, 2008).

Despite the commercialization of certain social services, Canadians have expressed more confidence in voluntary organizations than in businesses to deliver social services. Studies conducted over the years suggest that Canadians perceive the voluntary sector

- as meeting special needs that governments do not offer or businesses fail to satisfy and therefore filling service gaps in communities (Evans & Shields, 2006)

- being more trustworthy than government and less opportunistic than business (Hrab, 2004)

- being dedicated to their communities, understanding local needs, and personalizing the provision of services more than government

- being less bureaucratic and more flexible and responsive to local needs than either government or large businesses (Eakin, 2007)

Traditionally, it has been the voluntary sector—not commercial enterprise—that has predominated in the provision of social welfare programs in Canada. That honour is largely due to the unique role that voluntary agencies play in Canadian community life. As the federal government points out, "By its very nature and particularly because of its connection to communities, the voluntary sector brings a special perspective and considerable value to its activities" (Voluntary Sector Initiative, 2002, p. 6). Although profit-making organizations are making inroads into the delivery of certain social services, the public and voluntary sectors are likely to continue delivering the bulk of those services. The values and motivations underlying public and nonprofit social services are more suitable than those of business for meeting the complex needs of individuals and families. Moreover, the inherent competitive nature of business is incompatible with the degree of interagency cooperation needed to serve clients effectively (Dean, 2011).

DISCUSSION QUESTIONS

■ New Directions in Service Delivery

1. What is your opinion about government's decision to steer, not row, the delivery of social services? Do you think that government should be more or less involved in the direct delivery of social services? Give reasons for your answers.

2. What are your personal concerns (if any) about the privatization of social services? In what ways might privatization benefit social service provision in Canada?

3 FORGING A NEW PUBLIC–VOLUNTARY RELATIONSHIP

In the early 1990s, Canadian governments devolved an unprecedented number of social service programs to the voluntary sector; those programs included foster care, women's shelters, substance abuse treatment, homeless and emergency shelters, employment assistance programs, and emergency food programs. The heavier workload came with considerably fewer government dollars than in the past; as a result, the struggle to meet the diverse expectations of funders, clients, and communities strained the capacity of many voluntary agencies.

In 1995, members of various national organizations and coalitions formed the Voluntary Sector Roundtable to lobby the federal government to improve the voluntary sector's capacity to deliver services and to strengthen the federal–voluntary working relationship. The federal government responded favourably by supporting the creation of three major initiatives: the Panel on Accountability and Governance in the Voluntary Sector (1997–1998), the Working Together: A Government of Canada/Voluntary Sector Joint Initiative (1999), and the Voluntary Sector Initiative (VSI) (2000–2005). These initiatives generated a great deal of research, reports, guidelines, and new projects, including the development of an *Accord Between the Government of Canada and the Voluntary Sector* and the *Code of Good Practice on Policy Dialogue*. The federal government also gave extra funding to the provinces and territories to help them strengthen the capacity of their voluntary sectors to serve communities. In 2002, for example, funding from the VSI supported the launch of the Manitoba Voluntary Sector Initiative and the Premier's Voluntary Sector Initiative in Saskatchewan.

A number of research studies under the VSI found that, despite government support, conditions in voluntary social agencies were deteriorating. One report by Eakin and Richmond (2004, p. 265) concluded, "By every measure, in every study, community-based service providers are faring poorly. They have serious financing problems, reduced organizational capacity, and staff and volunteer recruitment and retention problems. They struggle to meet reporting requirements, juggle short-term contracts, and improvise essential services in the face of the continual decline of necessary resources." While front-line workers, managers, and volunteers tried to deal with these adverse conditions, the demand for social services kept growing.

Some analysts argue that not only has government's new business approach degraded the public–voluntary relationship, but it has actually

EXHIBIT 5.6

THE TRANSFORMATION OF VOLUNTARY SOCIAL AGENCIES

VOLUNTARY SOCIAL AGENCIES USED TO	VOLUNTARY SOCIAL AGENCIES MUST NOW
focus primarily on the organization and its clients	focus primarily on the needs of the market
be largely accountable to service users (clients)	be largely accountable to the taxpayer (through government)
be autonomous and independent	collaborate (and even merge) with other agencies to share resources
receive most of their funding from government	diversify their funding sources or match government contributions with non-government funding
rely on government to provide core funding	be satisfied with project-based funding from government
expect government grants	compete for government contracts
fundraise for special projects	fundraise to survive
run programs on long-term and stable government funding	run programs on short-term and unpredictable government funding
freely adapt their programs to meet client and community needs	deliver programs according to government specifications
fill gaps in government services	replace government as primary service provider
freely advocate on behalf of clients and society	limit advocacy according to strict government rules
strive to achieve philanthropic goals	strive to become more businesslike, entrepreneurial, and market oriented

Source: Rosalie Chappell

transformed voluntary social agencies (see Exhibit 5.6). The following section identifies some of these transformations and their effect on the capacity of voluntary social agencies to serve.

NEW FUNDING MECHANISMS

In the past, Canadian governments primarily gave grants to voluntary agencies. Agencies could apply these lump sums to any aspect of their operations, without having to account for how they spent the money. Voluntary agencies generally appreciated the flexibility of grants, since the money could be used for ongoing expenses, such as rent, utilities, and retaining staff, or for whatever priority the agency had at any given time.

Neoliberal governments generally consider grants a form of "government charity," that opposes the competitive spirit of a business approach (Brock, Brook, Elliott, & LaForest, 2003, p. 21). Beginning in the early 1990s, Canadian governments began to phase out the regular use of grants in favour of contracts; that meant a shift away from core funding to project-based funding.

- **Core funding** is money that an agency can apply to its core activities, such as administration (for instance, bookkeeping and reception), operational costs (including rent and building maintenance), agency promotion, and ongoing programs.

- **Project funding** is money earmarked for a specific project or program. It is often short term, lasting only as long as the initiative, and cannot be used to cover costs that are not directly related to the initiative (Calgary Chamber of Voluntary Organizations, 2006).

Since grants were typically long term and stable, voluntary agencies were able to build infrastructures that could support ongoing activities in the community. The shift to project funding has changed all that. For one thing, the short-term nature of project funding has forced some agencies to constantly develop and disassemble programs. Project funding has also proven to be unpredictable; for example, government funders are notoriously slow to approve or reject contracts and can subsequently delay program startup until funding is confirmed (Eakin & Richmond, 2004; Evans, Richmond, & Shields, 2005). Project funding does not always cover the full costs of service delivery, either. In her study of community service organizations in Ontario, Eakin (2007) found that agencies delivered an average of $1.14 worth of service for every $1 of government funding.

Project-based funding usually comes with funding conditions. One condition requires contracted agencies to diversify their funding sources, that is, to seek funding not just from government but from private sources as well. In some cases, government will fund a project only if the recipient agency can match the government's contribution with funding from a private source. The new funding requirements have forced voluntary agencies to become more creative in raising funds. For example, some agencies have stepped up their fundraising events, such as bake sales, rummage sales, raffles, and bingos. Other agencies have turned to corporations for donations or to private foundations for financial backing. In some cases, voluntary agencies have introduced user fees; this practice is nevertheless controversial because it bases a client's access to goods and services on an ability to pay rather than on need, which runs counter to welfare state principles (Jiwani, 2000).

Unfortunately, voluntary social agencies have not been very successful at raising funds from non-government sources. In fact, only 1 percent of voluntary agency funding in Canada comes from corporate donations and only 3 percent from individual donations (Hall et al., 2005). Economic slowdowns can add additional strain on already cash-strapped organizations. According to one survey, 48 percent of charitable organizations had trouble fulfilling their mandates during the 2008–2009 economic downturn; at the same time, 45 percent of charities experienced an increased demand for their products or services. To cope with the effects of the slowing economy, many of those organizations had to take such actions as reducing spending on training and staff development and relying more on volunteers (Lasby & Barr, 2010).

In 2010, the Government of Canada (2010) announced that it would "look to innovative charities and forward-thinking private sector companies to partner on new approaches to many social challenges." One of those "new approaches" is **social financing**—a method of money management that relies on the private rather than the public sector to fund social welfare programs and other "public benefit" initiatives. For example, one strategy may be to create a public–private partnership called a **social impact bond**—in this case, an investor (or business) would provide the upfront money, the nonprofit organization would deliver the service, and, if they met specific agreed-on goals, then the government would pay a bonus to the investor. The federal government is currently testing the feasibility of social impact bonds through various pilot projects.

ADMINISTRATIVE OVERLOAD

To ease the public's concerns over privatization, the federal and regional governments have kept a tight grip on how contracted agencies spend public funds. For the most part, government control is exercised through contracts that specify how funding should be spent, how the service is to be delivered and monitored, what the service results and performance requirements should be, and how agencies are expected to report on progress and outcomes. Contracted agencies are also obliged to participate in regular government audits and program evaluations to demonstrate that they are using public funds properly and efficiently. These types of demands by government funders have drastically altered the nature of activities in voluntary agencies, which, in the past, focused more on service delivery than on tasks related to accountability, funding, or administration (Evans, Richmond, & Shields, 2005).

Many voluntary social agencies have found that administrative staff workloads are increasing because of the disproportionate amount of time devoted to finding, securing, and maintaining funds. Completing applications for government contracts is especially time-consuming, since it often requires agency staff to write long and detailed proposals, outlining how they would deliver the service on behalf of government (see Exhibit 5.7). Obtaining private funds to match government contributions can be another onerous task, increasing the existing administrative burden (Scott, 2003a).

EXHIBIT 5.7

ADMINISTRATIVE OVERLOAD

© Paul Wallin

In many contracted social agencies, the administrators are overloaded with paperwork related to government contracts, funding, and accountability.

In addition to funding-related tasks, voluntary agencies are required to complete detailed accountability reports; these reports are particularly time-consuming for agencies with multiple funders, since every funder has its own reporting system, forms, timelines, and audits (Scott, 2003b). A study of community service agencies found that many senior managers had to drop important responsibilities, such as staff development and program management, to free up time to meet the varied reporting demands of funders (Eakin, 2007).

ADVOCACY "CHILL"

Traditionally, an important role of voluntary social agencies has been **advocacy**. The type of advocacy an agency performs depends largely on the presenting issue and the organization's purpose. Many agencies advocate on behalf of individual clients when, for example, the individual has been denied service or been discriminated against. Other agencies advocate on behalf of society in general, raising public awareness of conditions that foster injustice and inequality. Regardless of the form of advocacy taken, all advocacy efforts have the potential to enhance social welfare to some degree.

Following the Second World War, it was common for Canadian governments to fund the advocacy efforts of a wide range of voluntary organizations that represented minority groups; this public support, write Evans and Shields (2006, p. 13), helped to foster social inclusion and broaden "the democratic experience." Over the years, government has withdrawn much of its support for advocacy and has stopped funding many advocacy groups. In 2002, the federal government introduced the "10 percent rule" under the Income Tax Act to prohibit registered charities from devoting any more than 10 percent of their resources to advocacy. In addition, registered charities were told to refrain from engaging in certain "political activities," such as supporting (or opposing) a political party or a candidate running for public office.

The new rules around advocacy and political activity have made it difficult for some voluntary agencies to fulfill their advocacy role. These rules have also increased anxiety among voluntary sector staff and volunteers. Reports suggest that some organizations are afraid of inadvertently devoting more than 10 percent of their resources to advocacy and subsequently contravening the Income Tax Act; others fear that their advocacy activities may be construed by government as "political activities" or as criticism of the government. In any case, they are concerned that advocacy activities may somehow jeopardize their government funding or charitable status. Voluntary agencies are dealing with these fears in various ways: some are choosing not to advocate on any issue, while others err on the side of caution and speak out less than they are legally entitled to (Rektor, 2002). The general reluctance by voluntary agencies to negotiate on behalf of their clients has created what Katherine Scott (2003b, p. 117) refers to as "advocacy chill." Regrettably, these barriers to advocacy dull the political sword that voluntary agencies have long wielded when representing vulnerable groups and pushing for political and social change (Richmond & Shields, 2003).

In its 2012 budget, the federal government raised concerns that some charities may be exceeding the allowable limit of political activity and that charities in general are not as transparent as they should be in terms of how they use taxpayer's money or public donations. To correct the situation, the federal government tightened the advocacy rules even further by requiring charitable and government-funded nonprofit organizations to give more details on their political activities. The federal government also proposed changes to the Income Tax Act to impose stricter sanctions—such as fines and loss of charitable status—on charities that exceed their limits on political activities (Canada, 2012b).

LOSS OF AUTONOMY AND IDENTITY

A number of social researchers write about the transformation in the character of voluntary agencies; for the most part, that transformation is attributed to the new public–voluntary relationship and the pressure on agencies to become more businesslike. Evans, Richmond, and Shields (2005, p. 93) believe that the emphasis on business practices and entrepreneurism may be pushing voluntary agencies away from their original philanthropic goals toward a "new market-based managerialism" in which agencies are "servants to contracts controlled by state funders." To survive financially, voluntary agencies may find themselves catering more to the needs of the market than the people they are supposed to serve. The move to a more businesslike or "bottom line" approach may ultimately create more efficient service delivery; however, as Jiwani (2000) points out, efficiency is no guarantee of empathy, a caring approach, or a high-quality service.

Another threat to agency autonomy and identity relates to agency mission. Voluntary social agencies are often referred to as "mission-based organizations," because they are motivated by a certain social cause. However, since the new contracting system came into effect, many nonprofit organizations have struggled to fulfill their missions. With government cutbacks and the shift to contract funding, some agencies find themselves competing not only for fewer government contracts but also for contracts that narrowly define the services the agency can offer. Those contract conditions may not be compatible with an agency's mission; consequently, agencies run the risk of drifting away from their original mission in the pursuit of badly needed funds (Eakin & Richmond, 2004). The sacrifice of an agency's mission for government dollars can create a number of potential problems, such as increased stress among staff and the loss of the agency's autonomy. Agencies that lose sight of their mission may not only lose touch with local needs but also sacrifice their legitimacy and credibility in the community (Scott, 2003a).

Governments and voluntary organizations formed their working relationship in the spirit of a "collaborative partnership," which implies an equal sharing of decision-making, risk, responsibility, and resources (Evans & Shields, 2006). Critics of public–voluntary agreements suggest that while government appears content to share some things, it is unwilling to share decision-making power. The more government takes control over voluntary agencies—through such mechanisms as contract funding and strict accountability procedures—the less autonomous those agencies may be. It is commonly believed that as the voluntary sector replaces government as a primary provider of social welfare programs, the voluntary sector will morph into a "shadow state" with no real identity of its own.

DISCUSSION QUESTIONS

■ Forging a New Public–Voluntary Relationship

1. Pretend that you have been hired as a consultant to review the problems facing the voluntary sector and to consider how the voluntary–public relationship might be strengthened. What would you recommend to improve the relationship? What might voluntary agencies do to improve things? What changes should government make?

2. Identify the potential pros and cons of the shift to *contract funding* for (a) government, (b) voluntary social agencies, and (c) service users (clients). What might be the pros and cons of *social financing* for (a) government, (b) voluntary social agencies, and (c) profit-making groups?

3. Traditionally, voluntary agencies have been free to operate as they see fit and advocate on behalf of clients. However, the federal government has recently taken steps to curb that freedom. What is your opinion on this topic? To what degree should government control the activities of funded agencies?

4 THE SOCIAL ECONOMY

Although the social economy has traditionally served a vital role in Québec's social and economic arenas, it was not until the Throne Speech of 2004 that the social economy appeared on the federal policy agenda. Since then, the social economy has been growing steadily across Canada. Little consensus exists on the definition of social economy or what constitutes this alternative service sector. However, in their study of the social economy in Canada, Smith and McKitrick (2010) found some agreement on the underlying principles of the social economy. In short, this sector

- puts people before profits
- encourages citizen participation, collective responsibility, and a democratic decision-making process
- seeks to empower individuals and communities, and encourage self-sufficiency
- fosters innovative approaches to solving social and economic problems

This section takes a brief look at the relationship between the social economy and the voluntary sector, and describes the various types of social economy enterprises in Canada.

RELATIONSHIP TO THE VOLUNTARY SECTOR

Some theorists see the social economy and the voluntary sector as the same, mainly because these two sectors share many of the same values and principles. However, these two sectors tend to differ in terms of the degree to which they rely on the market economy. Using this criterion as a distinguishing feature, voluntary social agencies that depend largely on government for their income would not be part of the social economy. In contrast, voluntary social agencies that generate some or all of their income from the sale of goods or services, and do so to achieve their social and economic goals, would have a place under the social economy banner. As time goes on, Canadians can expect that more voluntary social agencies will reposition themselves within the social economy, especially as governments continue to cut funding to the voluntary sector. Moreover, as governments require contracted agencies to seek non-governmental sources of income and to achieve the social goals that government once did, voluntary social agencies are likely to take a more entrepreneurial approach (B.C.–Alberta Social Economy Research Alliance, n.d.).

SOCIAL ECONOMY ENTERPRISES

Organizations in the social economy are generically called **social economy enterprises** (SEEs). SEEs operate like businesses and use market-oriented strategies to generate their own revenue, usually through the sale of goods or services. Although this economic activity is important, the central mission of SEEs is the achievement of a social or public goal, such as reducing poverty or ending violence against women. It is common for SEEs to recruit a combination of volunteers and paid staff (who are often former recipients of service). Organizations that make profits from their operation either invest them back into the organization or use them to meet other identified social needs in the community (HRSDC, 2005). Among the wide variety of SEEs are *market-based associations*, such as housing cooperatives and the YWCA; these associations generate the bulk of their income from membership fees and community donations. *Civil society organizations* also qualify as SEEs; these organizations include nonprofit mutual-benefit organizations (such as church-based retirement homes) and volunteer organizations (such as Habitat for Humanity), which generate income from their own operations and do not rely on government funding (Mook, Quarter, & Richmond, 2007).

Most SEEs devise innovative ways to use their resources. A SEE food program, for example, might receive food donations from local supermarkets, use that food to make meals, and then sell those meals at a low cost to people in need (Policy Research Initiative, 2005). Some SEEs run second-hand stores to fund their social service programs; others manage housing and consumer cooperatives. Many types of entrepreneurial possibilities exist. Exhibit 5.8 profiles the Women in Need Society, a SEE in Calgary that finds innovative ways to raise money, provide employment to people in the community, and help women in low-income situations.

The federal government envisions SEEs as playing a prominent role in the future provision of social welfare services. To encourage existing voluntary social agencies to become SEEs, the federal government is taking steps to change the tax rules so that charities can raise money through side businesses without losing their charitable status. The provinces and territories are also supporting the development of SEEs; for example, in 2012, the Government of Nova Scotia promised to remove all barriers to social enterprise in provincial policies and legislation. As time goes on—especially in view of shrinking government funds and a shift to social financing—Canadians can expect more voluntary social agencies to reposition themselves within the social economy.

EXHIBIT 5.8

AGENCY PROFILE: WOMEN IN NEED SOCIETY (WINS)

WINS
women in need society

The Women in Need Society (WINS) is a charitable, nonprofit, Calgary-based organization. Since 1992, WINS has helped women gain the resources, knowledge, skills, and confidence they need for self-sufficiency and to support their families. WINS' services focus primarily on women with low-income, including

- women coming in or out of shelters;
- single mothers and their children;
- women in transition;
- recent immigrants;
- the working poor; and
- those on income assistance.

Family Resource Centres

WINS operates five Family Resource Centres (FRCs) which are located in subsidized housing complexes.

The FRCs help low-income families connect with community resources, including the local food bank and low-cost recreation activities. The FRCs also offer programs for children and youth, and adult lifeskills workshops (for example, budgeting, stress management, and healthy eating on a budget).

Programs include:
- *The Girl Talk program*, which allows pre-teen girls to discuss topics important to them in a positive, respectful environment.
- *Regular social events* such as monthly potlucks, which help women and families experiencing social isolation.
- *Compassionate listening*, which provides a safe, supportive place for women and their families to come to.

Free Goods Referral

This program is for women coming out of crisis situations or in transition.
After consultation, WINS provides a voucher that entitles the client to access goods from any one of the four WINS Thrift Stores at no cost.

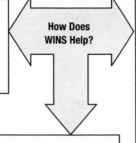

How Does WINS Help?

WINS Thrift Stores

WINS four stores:
- provide entry-level employment opportunities for those with little or no employment skills, those returning to the workforce, and those needing Canadian work experience;
- sell donated clothing and household goods at affordable prices; and
- generate revenue to partially support WINS' community programs.

Source: Excerpted and adapted from Women in Need Society (WINS). (2012). *Website*, Retrieved from http://www.womeninneed.net.

DISCUSSION QUESTIONS

■ The Social Economy

1. In what ways is the social economy similar to the public, commercial, and voluntary sectors? What makes the social economy distinctly different from the other three sectors?

2. The federal government envisions social economy enterprises as having a prominent role in the future provision of social welfare services. What is your

opinion on this? Do you believe that these enterprises would provide quality services to populations at risk?

3. Do you think that voluntary social agencies should become SEEs? Why or why not? What might be the advantages or disadvantages of becoming SEEs?

SUMMARY

Introduction

The public, commercial, and voluntary sectors make up Canada's mixed economy of welfare. Considerable overlap exists between the service sectors, making it difficult to see which sector is responsible for the various aspects of service delivery. In recent years, the boundaries between the sectors have been shifting to create new ways to deliver services. A fourth service sector—the social economy—is emerging as a viable service provider.

1 Service Sectors: Public, Commercial, and Voluntary Domains

Each level of government delivers its own mix of programs and services. The federal government is responsible for certain client groups and for pan-Canadian programs; regional governments are likely to deliver mandated social services; and the municipalities tend to deliver components of larger provincial programs. The commercial sector is not part of the social welfare system; this sector sells private helping services for a fee. The voluntary sector delivers the bulk of social services; in general, agencies in this sector "do good works," advocate, and mediate.

2 New Directions in Service Delivery

During the 1980s, public criticism and the rise of neoliberalism fostered efforts to shrink the size and power of government. To meet the demand for services, governments devolved many service-delivery responsibilities to the private sector; the alternative service delivery framework provided options for new working relationships. Contracting-out to the private sector has become the main strategy for delivering social services. Overall, Canadians prefer voluntary agencies rather than businesses to deliver social services.

3 Forging a New Public–Voluntary Relationship

Government's new business approach has transformed voluntary social agencies in various ways. Financial instability has increased, and the federal government is currently pursuing social financing as a funding strategy. Many voluntary agencies are experiencing administrative overload, have been stifled in their advocacy role, and risk losing their identity. Although governments and voluntary organizations formed their new relationship in a spirit of collaboration, governments tend to retain decision-making power and restrict the autonomy of voluntary agencies.

4 The Social Economy

The social economy is a rapidly growing service sector in Canada. Social economy enterprises are entrepreneurial yet nonprofit in nature, are run like businesses, draw from a variety of funding sources, and rely on both paid staff and volunteers. The Government of Canada envisions social economy enterprises as having an increasingly prominent role in the delivery of social services.

KEY TERMS

For definitions of the key terms, consult the Glossary on page 453 at the end of the book.

mixed economy of welfare, p. 122
private sector, p. 122
public sector, p. 122
commercial sector, p. 122
voluntary sector, p. 122
social economy, p. 122
public programs, p. 124
mandated services, p. 125

corporate social responsibility, p. 127
voluntary social agencies, p. 127
collaborative governance, p. 131
alternative service delivery, p. 131
contracting-out, p. 131

privatization, p. 132
accountability, p. 132
core funding, p. 137
project funding, p. 137
social financing, p. 138
social impact bond, p. 138
advocacy, p. 140
social economy enterprises, p. 144

6

CHAPTER

Social Agencies

OBJECTIVES

Social agencies are responsible for delivering a wide range of social welfare resources to people in need. This chapter will

- introduce the concept of *social agency* and the main characteristics of social agencies

- describe community-based residential and non-residential organizations, and the community system of care

- explore the internal structures and functions of social agencies in terms of strategic and operational frameworks

- examine the primary features of organic organizational structures

INTRODUCTION

> Organisations are of two kinds, those which aim at getting something done, and those which aim at preventing something from being done. (Bertrand Russell, British philosopher and advocate for social reform, 1952, p. 51)

Social agencies are formally structured organizations that fulfill a variety of functions: they provide goods, services, and financial assistance to people in need; engage local community members in local projects; and mobilize resources to address community problems (Jaco & Pierce, 2005). All social agencies operate on a nonprofit basis in either the public or the voluntary sector. **Public social agencies** are government departments and divisions, and include social assistance offices and, in most jurisdictions, child protection units. **Voluntary social agencies** are nonprofit social service organizations in the private sector; examples include family service bureaus, immigrant settlement agencies, and women's shelters. These agencies may be either sectarian (religious) or secular (non-religious).

Although social agencies vary in their tasks, administration, organizational structure, goals, and mandate, most agencies share the following basic functions (with examples):

- service delivery (assessing client needs and providing goods or services to clients)

- administration (guiding agency activities by developing and revising policies and procedures)

- funding (securing funding and following budgets)

- accountability (ensuring the quality of service and evaluating the effectiveness of programs)

- recruitment (hiring and supervising staff and volunteers)

- public relations (fostering and maintaining positive relationships with the community)

The way an agency carries out its responsibilities depends largely on whom it serves, what it intends to accomplish, and how its programs are designed. An agency's activities are usually targeted toward a certain population, such as families with children or people with disabilities. Those activities are planned with a specific goal; for example, a program that teaches parents how to discipline their child by using nonviolent methods (the activity) aims to prevent child abuse (the goal).

The identified needs of people living in a community usually determine the types of goods or services a social agency delivers (see Exhibit 6.1). An area that has a high rate of teen moms, for instance, is likely to need child-care or young parent programs, preferably located near the high school. How well an agency meets local needs depends on several external factors, including community and political support and funding availability. Moreover, the effectiveness of programs and services is often a function of various internal factors, such as the setting in which services are delivered, the agency's strategic and operational plans, and the agency's organizational structure. This chapter looks at some of these factors.

EXHIBIT 6.1

Soup kitchens and other emergency food programs are designed to meet the specific needs of a community.

1 COMMUNITY-BASED SOCIAL AGENCIES

Most social agencies in Canada plan and deliver their programs according to a **community-based model**. Agencies that adopt this type of model try to respond to changing community needs and be flexible when matching services to people's needs and preferences. Community-based agencies also focus on clients' strengths rather than their limitations. Clients are encouraged to make decisions about their own well-being and to foster positive relationships with family, friends, and other support systems. It is common for community-based agencies to offer a comprehensive range of services from a variety of service providers and, if feasible, to provide outreach services to reach a broader segment of the community. A great deal of local support and collaboration often goes into developing community-based services, which tend to be integrated with other local organizations and groups. Features of the community-based model are found in public, commercial, and voluntary agencies, and in both residential and non-residential settings (Standing Senate Committee on Social Affairs, Science and Technology, 2006a).

RESIDENTIAL CENTRES

The majority of **residential centres** provide living quarters, meals, and other services for people who require round-the-clock care. Depending on local needs and resources, every community will have various types of residential centres, which may include

- long-term-care facilities or nursing homes for seniors
- shelters for homeless or transient people
- assessment or treatment centres for children or youth with emotional or behavioural disorders
- group homes for people with developmental delays
- rehabilitation centres for children and youth with physical disabilities
- care centres for people with psychiatric disabilities
- inpatient addiction treatment centres
- transition houses for abused women and their children

Provincial and territorial governments fund, license, or approve more than 4600 residential centres across Canada. More than 247 000 Canadians live in residential centres; the majority of those residents are elderly persons or people with a mental health disorder (Statistics Canada, 2011a).

Although residential centres are sometimes called "institutions," they are nothing like the poorhouses, workhouses, or insane asylums of the nineteenth and early twentieth centuries (see Exhibit 6.2). Those institutions placed more importance on rules and procedures than on residents' needs, and residents were usually discouraged from accessing alternative services if they disagreed with what the institution had to offer. In contrast, modern residential centres try to integrate the principles of community-based practice into their services and help their residents retain ties to supports and other resources in the community. Moreover, the residential centres of today try to avoid appearing institutional. Many centres, for example, locate themselves in residential neighbourhoods and strive to make the building, residents' rooms, and gathering places (such as dining rooms) as natural and homey as possible.

Obviously, not everyone who is in need or experiences a problem requires residential care. This type of service is most appropriate when a professional needs to complete a psychiatric or other type of assessment in a more structured environment than a client's home. People who exhibit violent or inappropriate behaviour, or need supervision or stabilization beyond what family or a non-residential service provider can give, may also be suited to residential care.

EXHIBIT 6.2

What were then called lunatic asylums, such as this one in Toronto in 1867, were some of Canada's first residential centres.

Residential services are also appropriate for those who need specialized treatment, such as intensive drug rehabilitation. Whatever the reason for the placement, individuals living in residential settings must have regularly scheduled reviews to adjust the level of care as needed and to ensure that the services are meeting the client's needs and goals (Conceptual Framework Subcommittee of the Residential Services Advisory Committee, 2002).

Many concerns have been raised about the current and future use of residential services in Canada, particularly when it comes to the care of seniors. Because the population is both growing and aging, the demand for residential services is increasing. To manage that demand, many residential-care facilities are finding ways to ration their services; for instance, some long-term-care centres create longer wait lists or limit their admission criteria to exclude people with complex care needs who require more resources. These restrictions may mean that people who need residential care do not get it when they need it or must move to another community to find it.

A growing body of evidence suggests that the demand for residential care would lessen if better systems of home- and community-care services were available; those services include meal programs (such as Meals on Wheels), homemaking services, in-home personal care, occupational therapy, and care-giver support (Williams et al., 2009). Other strategies—many of which promote the principle of **aging in place**—aim to reduce unnecessary admissions to residential care. For example, a variety of innovative housing adaptations and options allow elderly persons to live at home longer and either delay or avoid institutionalization.

NON-RESIDENTIAL CENTRES

Non-residential centres normally provide services on a drop-in, appointment, or outreach basis. These centres cater to those who can look after many of their own needs, who require only short-term help, and who do not pose a threat to themselves or to the rest of society. It is common to find a continuum of services in non-residential centres; this is the case with **multiservice centres**. These one-stop centres offer people a variety of social services under one roof. It is common for multiservice centres to offer services to a variety of populations, such as people with disabilities, victims of abuse, or immigrants. On the other hand, many multiservice centres restrict their services to a particular population (such as women) or age group (such as teens).

One Toronto study suggests that social agencies that are actively expanding their range of services and becoming multiservice centres may be doing so in response to a greater demand for services and more complex needs among their clientele. It is also possible that, by stretching their mandates and offering a wider range of services, agencies will tap into a greater number of funding sources (Toronto Community and Neighbourhood Services, 2004).

Non-residential centres try to deliver their services in a flexible and user-friendly manner and provide options in the ways people can participate. *Drop-in centres*, for example, usually offer loosely scheduled programs that people can access at any time during service hours. *Telephone services* offer support and anonymity and—in the case of crisis lines—are available around the clock. Agencies provide *outreach services* in environments outside the office setting; services such as *home support* and *street outreach* enable front-line workers to connect with people who may be reluctant or physically unable to seek services in a formal setting. A growing number of agencies offer *online support* via the Internet; those in need of help or information can connect with professional or peer counsellors through chat rooms, discussion forums, email, and proprietary systems, such as Skype.

COMMUNITY SYSTEM OF CARE

In general, residential and non-residential centres differ in the range and intensity of services they offer, and in the ways they deliver those services; that said, neither type is inherently more effective than the other. Each type of centre has something to offer the community and, working in tandem, these centres can form a solid base of community support and care. The term **community system of care** refers to the mix of public and private services in a community

EXHIBIT 6.3

COMMUNITY SYSTEM OF CARE FOR CHILDREN AND YOUTH

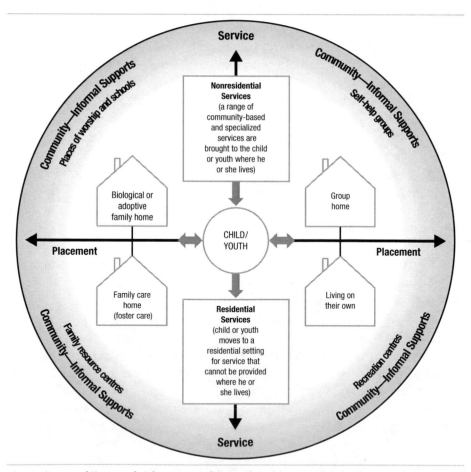

Source: Conceptual Framework Subcommittee of the Residential Services Advisory Committee (January 2000). *Working with Community to Support Children, Youth and Families*: Page 9. Copyright © Province of British Columbia. All rights reserved. Reprinted with permission of the Province of British Columbia. www.ipp.gov.bc.ca.

that, when offered in a coordinated and integrated fashion, is responsive to the varying levels and changing needs of specific populations (Board of Trustees of Michigan State University, 2000). Exhibit 6.3 offers a conceptualization of a community system of care for children and youth; this system includes both residential and non-residential services, as well as informal support systems, such as families and self-help groups. The arrows in the exhibit indicate the route the child or youth might take from one type of service to another to meet his or her needs or circumstances at any given time.

DISCUSSION QUESTIONS

■ **Community-Based Social Agencies**

1. Identify the potential advantages and disadvantages of services provided in (a) residential centres and (b) non-residential centres. How might communities combine or integrate both types of services to benefit clients?

2. Many Canadians are concerned that there will not be enough residential centres available for a growing number of old people. What types of strategies or resources might reduce the need for residential care among older Canadians?

2 AGENCY SYSTEMS: INTERNAL STRUCTURES AND FUNCTIONS

Before a social agency can deliver services, it must develop a solid internal structure on which to base its work. Strategic and operational frameworks provide this structure. A **strategic framework** identifies the agency's priorities and how the agency intends to achieve its goals, mission, and vision. In contrast, an agency's **operational framework** is a practical plan for two main levels of internal activities: **direct services** involve face-to-face interactions between front-line workers and clients, and **indirect services** are conducted off the front line and include administration, program planning and evaluation, and the development of policies and procedures. This section explores some of the components of strategic and operational frameworks and their implications for service delivery.

A STRATEGIC FRAMEWORK

To develop a sound strategic framework, a social agency must have a good understanding of the community in which it functions, realize its potential for sustainability, and clarify its direction as a service provider.

Understanding Community Conditions and Needs

Many social agencies conduct an **environmental scan** to learn about local social and economic conditions that may influence the community's needs. For example, a study of a community's demographics, welfare and crime rates, educational opportunities, housing affordability, economic outlooks, and life cycles may reveal characteristics and patterns that can help in the development of programs and services.

A **community needs assessment** is one tool that social agencies may use to gather information and paint a picture of local needs. Various sources may provide that information, including direct observation, interviews, and focus groups; documents, such as community profiles or census data can also be useful. Members of the community and professionals who work in health and social service agencies are often excellent sources of information on perceived community needs.

Through community needs assessments, social agencies may be able to clarify the social, emotional, physiological, and other needs of a specific population and the type of program that might benefit that group. A community needs assessment might also identify the resources required to run a program. Some social agencies rely on community needs assessments to determine whether the **target population** will likely use a proposed program. For example, an assessment may reveal that local elderly people are in need of companionship and emotional support and would use a peer-counselling program run by trained volunteers.

Many social agencies are able to accurately assess a community's needs and offer services that are well used by local residents. The offering of services, however, does not guarantee their use. Exhibit 6.4 points out potential barriers to men who may need help, but are reluctant to seek it. Whenever possible, social agencies should try to mitigate barriers to help-seeking when planning new programs.

Assessing an Agency's Sustainability

When developing a strategic framework, a social agency must determine its own sustainability—in other words, its ability to meet local needs over the long term. To be sustainable, an agency must

- have adequate opportunities to do its work
- be able to attract and retain competent staff
- obtain sufficient funding and other resources

EXHIBIT 6.4

BARRIERS TO MEN WHO ARE SEEKING HELP

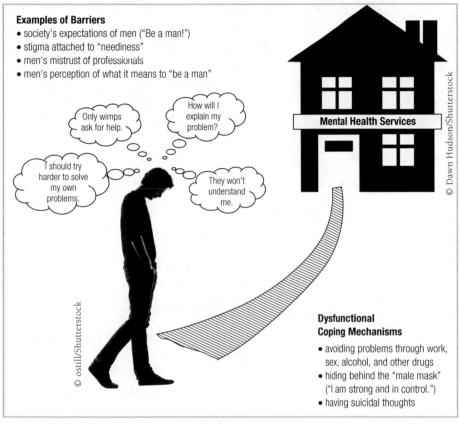

Examples of Barriers
- society's expectations of men ("Be a man!")
- stigma attached to "neediness"
- men's mistrust of professionals
- men's perception of what it means to "be a man"

Only wimps ask for help.

How will I explain my problem?

I should try harder to solve my own problems.

They won't understand me.

Mental Health Services

© Dawn Hudson/Shutterstock

© ostill/Shutterstock

Dysfunctional Coping Mechanisms
- avoiding problems through work, sex, alcohol, and other drugs
- hiding behind the "male mask" ("I am strong and in control.")
- having suicidal thoughts

Source: Author-generated diagram using content from Hoy, S. (2012). Beyond men behaving badly: Meta-ethnography of men's perspectives on psychological distress and help seeking. *International Journal of Men's Health, 11*(3), 202 -226. doi:10.3149/jmh.1103.202.

- demonstrate its achievements to attract future funding
- gain support from the community (Shapiro, 2003)

One way to assess an agency's potential sustainability is through a **SWOT analysis**—that is, an in-depth look at an agency's internal strengths and weaknesses, and its external opportunities and threats. As an example, an agency may have well-trained staff (strength), lack a good communication system (weakness), enjoy good relations with other organizations in the community (opportunity), and struggle with budget restrictions and high staff turnover (threat). A SWOT analysis can help an agency take advantage of the strengths and opportunities, and minimize the weaknesses and threats.

Establishing the Agency's Direction

A strategic framework typically describes what the agency hopes to achieve and how. Most social agencies develop a **vision statement** that articulates the agency's image of an ideal community. For example, Winnipeg's Fort Garry Women's Resource Centre (2012) envisions "a community where women and children are safe, healthy, valued and empowered."

While an agency's vision gives it something to strive for, its mission clarifies what it intends to achieve. Every social agency has a **mission statement** that describes what the organization does, and to whom the programs are targeted. Family Services of Greater Vancouver (2013), for instance, has the following mission: "We work to inspire and support those in our community who need help to reach their full potential: children are nurtured, youth find optimism, adults feel empowered, and parents make choices that build strong families."

An **agency goal** states in realistic terms what the organization plans to do in the long-term to achieve its vision and mission. For example, if the agency's mission is to alleviate homelessness, the overall goal might be to provide housing options for homeless people in the community. Well-written goals are compatible with the organization's vision and mission, and are consistent with information from the environmental scan. Goals must also be appropriate to community needs, provide a clear direction and scope for the agency's programs, and be relevant over the long term (Treasury Board of Canada Secretariat, 2008).

Underlying an agency's vision, mission, and goals is a set of values or acceptable standards that govern an agency's conduct with those it serves. When articulated, **value statements** reflect the social agency's core ideology. For example, the Family Services of Greater Vancouver (2013) has a clearly defined set of values: *quality* in programs and services, *respect* for all individuals, belief in the *possibility* that people can overcome their challenges, recognition of and response to *diversity* in the community, and *accountability* for responsibly managing resources. Organizational values are reflected in every aspect of an agency's operations, including its programs and administration.

AN OPERATIONAL FRAMEWORK: DIRECT SERVICES

An operational framework outlines the types of services that an agency will deliver. Most social agencies offer direct services that are preventive in nature—that is, they try either to prevent the emergence of human problems or to lessen the negative effects of problems once they have arisen. Typically, agency services operate at one or more of the following three levels:

- **Primary prevention** activities aim to prevent the development of personal and social problems by educating people, providing information, or promoting certain practices. They are usually targeted at large segments of healthy populations to maintain or enhance well-being. Alcohol and drug education for preteens is a well-known primary prevention initiative.

- **Secondary prevention** activities (also called "early intervention") address problems in the early stages of development before they have become serious or chronic. This level of prevention involves controlling or changing the conditions that are creating the problem. Respite services, for example, can help family caregivers to reduce stress related to caregiving and subsequently prevent burnout.

- **Tertiary prevention** activities (also called "treatment") aim to reduce the negative effects of problems—such as disability and dependence—that have become chronic or complex. Social welfare programs in this category include child protection services, family therapy, and residential care for youth with emotional disorders. Some tertiary prevention programs are mandatory and sanctioned by law; for example, if a child protection worker suspects that child abuse or neglect has occurred in the home, that worker has the legal authority to intervene in a family's affairs.

Tertiary prevention has long been the focus of direct services. In recent years, however, social programmers have shown a greater interest in primary prevention because it is easier, less expensive, and more humane than treating problems after they develop. Furthermore, program evaluators tend to have difficulties identifying and measuring the direct benefits of treatment, whereas a growing number of studies point to the effectiveness of primary prevention programs. Such findings as these have prompted many Canadian municipalities to funnel their resources into building healthy communities. By being proactive and responsive to local needs, municipalities hope to curb crime, homelessness, and other social problems before they occur.

AN OPERATIONAL FRAMEWORK: INDIRECT SERVICES

An operational framework also outlines the types of indirect services that will help an agency deliver its direct services. Indirect services include administration, program planning, program evaluation, and the setting of policies and procedures. In this section, we look at each of these aspects and their relation to client services

Administration

An agency's **administration** is primarily concerned with the exercise of authority and decision making. Two main levels of the organization perform administrative duties: the governance level and the management level.

The governance level of an agency is responsible and accountable for both the organization and the work it does in the community. In the voluntary sector, a board of directors or trustees usually governs social agencies (see Exhibit 6.5). In the public sector, governance is the responsibility of a first minister (such as the federal minister of human resources and skills development) and his or her senior staff. Among other things, the governance level of administration must carve out a niche in the community for the agency, develop a positive public image, and ensure that the agency is accountable to its staff, volunteers, funders, locals, and other stakeholders who have an interest in the agency's activities and achievements.

At the management level, agency managers and supervisors perform such duties as obtaining and allocating resources, designing programs, and recruiting staff. A primary activity at this level is finding effective ways to achieve the agency's goals. This usually involves providing training and professional development opportunities for staff and monitoring the effectiveness of programs. Management is also responsible for ensuring that programs are responsive to the changing needs of the community (Institute on Governance, 2011).

In theory, the governance and management levels in voluntary agencies are separate entities, requiring different types of knowledge and skills. In reality, it is common for the roles and responsibilities of the two levels to overlap to achieve mutual goals. The degree of overlap depends on the agency's particular type of organizational structure. For example, some voluntary agencies with a collective model of organization encourage their members to participate in a wide range of activities related to the running of the organization. This type of organization might have a working board of directors that requires its members to perform day-to-day duties (such as answering phones or sorting files) in addition to their governing responsibilities (such as setting policy). The Institute on Governance (2008) cautions against letting the lines between levels become too blurred or confused: "The real danger is not the mixing of these roles, but unclear definition of responsibilities and lost lines of accountability."

EXHIBIT 6.5

© 2009 Jupiterimages Corporation

Most voluntary agencies are governed by a volunteer board of directors or trustees that is accountable to various stakeholders and the local community.

Program Planning

Program planning involves deciding how the agency will design, run, and deliver its programs to clients. Various program-planning models are available to social agencies, each with a different focus and set of procedures. However, a generic program-planning process involves six key steps:

1. Determine how people in the planning process will work together, make decisions, and move through the planning stages.

2. Confirm whether the program development plan should be carried out and, if so, in what manner.

3. Set goals and objectives, and define the target population.

4. Design program strategies and activities.

5. Identify indicators of success—that is, signs that the program is achieving its objectives.

6. Review the viability of the proposed program and determine whether it can be easily evaluated.

These steps do not always progress in chronological order. As new information comes in and fresh challenges arise, the activities for one step may have to be undertaken earlier or later in the process.

To assess the feasibility of a program plan before making a long-term investment, some agencies run new programs on a pilot basis. During this trial period, an agency can monitor a program's expenditures and activities to ensure that the program is achieving its goals and objectives. Program developers can modify any shortcomings in the program during this pilot phase.

Program Evaluation

Social agencies use various tools to evaluate their programs and services. **Program evaluation** can be understood "as the process in which services and programs are examined to determine whether they are needed and used, how well they are run, whether they meet their stated objectives, and whether they are worth the costs" (McDonald, 2009, p. 418). Although various types of program evaluations are available, most social welfare programs today undergo an **outcome evaluation**, which focuses on the impact or results of a program. More specifically, outcome evaluations seek to identify how a program has changed participants in terms of behaviours, attitudes, skills or knowledge. For example, in 2009, an outcome evaluation of British Columbia's settlement programs found that immigrant participants had improved their English skills, formed connections to people and services in their host community, and had a better understanding of Canadian systems and customs (Ference Weicker & Company, 2009).

Program funders like outcome evaluations since they are likely to tell them whether their dollars are producing expected results. In a national survey of the evaluation practices of Canada's voluntary sector, 89 percent of funders that required program evaluation in funded agencies wanted information about client outcomes (Hall, Phillips, Meillat, & Pickering, 2003). Outcomes are not only important to funders but can also be useful to agencies: knowing how (or if) programs benefit clients is critical for improving existing programs or developing new ones. In the case of voluntary agencies, the ability to demonstrate positive outcomes may lend credibility and increase an agency's chances of continued funding.

Evaluating programs is not always an easy task. One challenge for many voluntary agencies is that outcome evaluation is an expensive, complicated, and time-consuming process that requires expertise that is not always available in-house (Hall, Andrukow, et al., 2003). In addition, evaluators often have a difficult time proving that the enhanced well-being of program participants is the result of the program and not some other influence in participants' lives. This is a particular challenge when evaluating large-scale, ongoing government programs, such as child protection and seniors' pensions. To report on the public good of these universal programs, government agencies must use randomized control trials or other non-traditional evaluation models.

Policies and Procedures

All social agencies—whether large government bureaucracies or small voluntary agencies—operate according to fixed rules, otherwise known as **policies and procedures**. Typically, an agency has policies that outline how it intends to reach its long- and short-term goals. Procedures naturally flow from policy and describe the activities and resources that will be applied to meet policy requirements (Huebner, 1999).

Social agencies that provide direct client services usually have policies and procedures that outline the structure and process of programs and how clients are expected to enter, participate in, and exit from programs. Agency staff often refer to the rules that govern the stages of programs as intake, participation, and termination policies.

- An *intake policy* outlines the criteria a person has to meet to enter a program. A program, for example, may require participants to be within a certain age range or have an income below a specified limit.

- A *participation policy* clarifies what a participant has to do to continue in a program. For instance, participants may be required to attend regularly or follow specific rules of conduct.

- A *termination policy* identifies when a program participant can expect to leave a program. Agency staff may use various markers to indicate the end of service, including a point in time or when the participant has reached a goal.

Program policies and procedures fulfill a number of functions: they can help agency staff organize their work; they can prevent chaos and confusion;

and they can ensure that, with the limited resources available, only people who qualify for services use them. Despite their usefulness, agency policies and procedures can create a number of challenges for clients and workers alike. In extreme cases, the rules and regulations governing so-called helping services can contribute to tragic outcomes (see Exhibit 6.6).

Case Study: Intake Screening Process, Ontario Works

"User-friendly" is hardly the term most people would use to describe the policies and procedures of Canada's social assistance programs. A number of studies have examined welfare systems and their impact on service users; overall, researchers have concluded that the complex rules and requirements of those systems can cause considerable anxiety and stress for clients, and even discourage people who are in legitimate need from seeking help. The intake screening process for Ontario's social assistance program—called Ontario Works—is no exception.

Backgrounder: Ontario Works

In response to concerns about rising caseloads and the costs of social assistance, the Government of Ontario overhauled its social assistance system in 1997; the result was Ontario Works and a new service delivery model (SDM). The SDM promised to improve the methods used to verify people's eligibility for welfare by screening out ineligible applicants sooner in the intake process. The government expected this approach to save money for taxpayers and to direct welfare resources more quickly to people who qualified for benefits.

A Two-Step Application Process

The SDM requires people applying for welfare to participate in a two-step application process.

Step one is a preliminary telephone assessment. Welfare applicants are required to phone one of the province's intake screening units; during that call, applicants are given information about social assistance and application procedures, and are asked about their employment and financial situation.

Step two is a face-to-face verification interview. Applicants who pass the initial telephone assessment are referred to a local Ontario Works office for the in-person interview and further processing. During this stage, a caseworker verifies an applicant's eligibility for welfare; this process may involve multiple appointments, participation in an employment information session, and the completion and signing of forms. Applicants are required to provide a variety of documents to verify their financial circumstances, including pay stubs,

EXHIBIT 6.6

WHEN RULES MATTER MORE THAN PEOPLE: THE CASE OF KIMBERLY ROGERS

In April 2001, Kimberly Rogers was convicted of welfare fraud for collecting both social assistance and student loans while attending community college in Ontario. The penalty for the fraud conviction was severe:

- a six-month sentence of house arrest (allowing her to leave her apartment for a maximum of three hours a week);
- a requirement to repay over $13000 in welfare benefits to Ontario Works;
- eighteen months probation;
- loss of the right to have part of her student loan forgiven; and
- suspension of welfare benefits for three months.

Rogers was pregnant at the time of her conviction and, without welfare, had no source of income to pay for rent, food, and other basics.

In May 2001, Rogers launched a case under Canada's Charter of Rights and Freedoms, challenging Ontario's right to suspend her welfare benefits. Specifically, Rogers argued that

- cutting her off welfare (leaving her with no income) violated the Charter's guarantees to life, liberty and security of the person;
- disqualifying her from welfare benefits after already punishing her with house arrest constituted "cruel and unusual punishment;" and
- depriving a pregnant and disabled woman from welfare benefits violated the Charter's guarantee of equality.

The Ontario Superior Court of Justice temporarily reinstated Rogers' welfare benefits; however, those benefits totalled just $468 a month—an inadequate income to cover the necessities of life. Just weeks after the court's ruling, Kimberly Rogers—eight months pregnant and confined to her apartment under house arrest—died in her apartment.

Following an inquest into Rogers' death, the Coroner's Jury recommended several changes to the policies and procedures governing welfare provision under Ontario Works.

Source: Keck, Jennifer (2002). Remembering Kimberly Rogers, *Perception*, Vol. 25, #3/4, Winter/Spring, http://www.ccsd.ca/perception/2534/kimberly.htm.

income tax slips, bank records, student loan assessments, rent receipts, and divorce papers (Herd, Mitchell, & Lightman, 2005).

Program Reviews

Various studies and reviews have identified a wide range of problems with Ontario Works' intake screening policies and procedures. For example, in her 2004 report to Ontario's minister of community and social services, Deb Matthews (2004) found that front-line workers had to apply approximately 800 rules and regulations before the SDM system could determine an applicant's eligibility. Those administrative requirements demanded about 80 percent of the worker's time with the client, leaving little time to address the client's needs.

In another study of Ontario Works systems, Herd, Mitchell, and Lightman (2005) found the following:

- The telephone assessment process posed potential barriers to welfare, especially for those who did not have a telephone, or had weak English skills, a physical or mental disability, or little education.

- The system's emphasis on paperwork and documentation had the potential to discourage people in legitimate need from applying or cause them to drop out before the application could be completed.

As part of its 2008 Poverty Reduction Strategy, the Ontario government appointed a commission to conduct a comprehensive review of its social assistance program, including its intake screening process. In their final report, Commissioners Lankin and Sheikh (2012, p. 20) recommended several changes to Ontario's social assistance program; one recommendation was to eliminate "at least half of the rules and directives in the existing system."

DISCUSSION QUESTIONS

■ Agency Systems: Internal Structures and Functions

1. If a community needs assessment were being conducted in your community and you were asked to give your opinion on what new services might be needed, how would you respond? What makes you think your community needs those particular services?

2. List some of the social services or income security programs in your community. Which level of prevention (primary, secondary, or tertiary) does each service or program provide? What do you think each program is trying to prevent?

3. Complex policies and procedures govern many social welfare programs (including social assistance) and can frustrate clients or discourage them from seeking help. Why might some social agencies be reluctant to eliminate or simplify these complex rules?

3 ORGANIC MODELS OF ORGANIZATION

For much of the twentieth century, the **bureaucratic model of organization** was praised for its reliability and predictability. People came to know bureaucracies as "well-oiled machines" that were characterized by

- specialization (clear divisions of labour)
- formalization (work roles defined by set job descriptions)
- departmentalization (activities grouped according to function)
- a clear chain of command (directives flowing vertically from upper management to front line)
- centralization (decision making concentrated at a single point in the organization)
- a pyramidal, hierarchical structure (a relatively small group of upper managers at the top of the organization, one or more levels of management in the middle, and several front-line workers at the lower level)

All organizations are bureaucratic to some extent. However, governments, hospitals, public school systems, universities, and many large corporations are common examples of large bureaucracies.

Support for the bureaucratic model began to wane in the late 1970s, when a faltering economy made it difficult for governments to cover their high operating costs. People began to see big bureaucracies as being too slow, inflexible, and inefficient, and having too many complex procedures, otherwise known as "bureaucratic red tape." Canadians also criticized government bureaucracies for their **service silos**—that is, the various ministries and departments, all working in isolation from one another, with their own mandates, resources, objectives, and little regard for consumers' needs (Morley, 2005).

By the 1990s, large organizations were struggling with expanding workloads and trying to meet the rapidly changing needs of service users, funders, and governing bodies. The time was ripe for new structures—specifically, **organic models of organization**—that allowed workers to respond quickly to change. The term "organic" implies that organizations are like living organisms, capable of adapting to an ever-changing environment.

Although many variations of organic models exist, most emphasize "flat" hierarchical structures, flexibility, diversity, innovation, and cooperative ways of working; the following section reviews these features.

HIERARCHICAL STRUCTURES

Large bureaucracies tend to have tall, pyramid-shaped organizational structures with several vertical layers or departments. Those with the most decision-making powers in the organization are at the top of the hierarchy; that individual or group oversees and sets policies for the agency's general operations. Below the top level are various levels of subordinates. Middle management makes up one or more tiers; at this level, the executives, department heads, supervisors, and other middle managers are responsible for the various departments and for the day-to-day operations of programs and services. At the lowest level of the hierarchy are the front-line workers and support staff, who carry out the program activities, tasks, and services. Each department in an organization tends to have a narrow range of control—that is, a small number of subordinates per manager.

Governments are notorious for their tall hierarchical structures. In contrast, voluntary social agencies tend to have relatively **flat hierarchical structures**, with fewer layers of middle management. Exhibit 6.7 gives a comparative view of these two types of organizational structures.

During the 1980s and 1990s, Canadian governments tried to reduce the costs of the public service by reducing middle management, amalgamating departments, and otherwise flattening the hierarchy. With a reduction in the number of supervisors, governments expected their front-line workers to develop more general skills, take on more varied tasks, and assume a broader range of responsibilities At the same time, governments assigned the remaining managers larger numbers of staff to supervise.

Flatter organizational structures have advantages and disadvantages. With few or no levels of middle management, there may be opportunities for a greater degree of contact, communication, and even shared decision making between front-line workers and upper management. Moreover, managers in flat organizations can usually approve changes more quickly because decisions do not have to travel through so many departments. One possible disadvantage is the difficulty in recruiting workers who are skilled in several areas of expertise. Furthermore, a small number of managers may find it difficult to supervise a relatively large group of staff.

EXHIBIT 6.7

EXAMPLES OF TALL AND FLAT HIERARCHIES

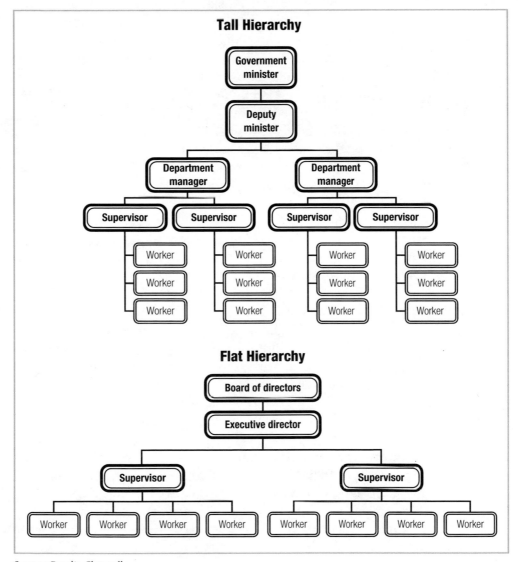

Source: Rosalie Chappell

FLEXIBILITY

Flexibility is central to a social agency's ability to adapt to changes in funding, workload, or community needs. Organic organizations are well suited to change because of their relatively informal and decentralized structures. These types of organizations tend to recruit workers who have broad or generic skill sets and can perform a wide variety of duties. Staff is usually expected to multitask, multiskill, and wear multiple hats (for example, counsellors may double as supervisors). A team with a diverse skill base is particularly useful in agencies that carry several service contracts or have a broad client base. Even workers whose duties lie on the front line are likely to need a wide range of helping skills, including counselling, teaching, mediation, group work, and crisis intervention (Hiscott, 2002). The demand for flexibility may increase job satisfaction by encouraging workers to upgrade their skills and participate in varied decision-making processes. On the other hand, the push for flexibility might create more job stress "by increasing workloads, intensifying the work pace, producing conflicting demands and multiplying workers' responsibilities" (Kashefi, 2009, pp. 810–811).

While agencies have to be flexible to the demands of the work environment, they also have to be willing to respond to the needs of workers. Because of shifts in government policy and funding arrangements, many social agencies now operate on short-term contracts and cannot offer workers more than temporary, part-time, or contract positions. As a result, many people in the social welfare field have to take on several different jobs or contracts or work for more than one employer to earn a decent income. Other workers may not want full-time permanent employment and seek only temporary work. In either case, organizations must be open to negotiating creative schedules and work conditions that meet the needs of both staff and employers.

Flexible social agencies tend to recognize the importance of a healthy work–life balance—that is, a balance between personal, family, and work responsibilities—and try to help staff achieve a balance. There are potential benefits of a work–life balance for both employers and employees, including improved staff morale, decreased stress and burnout, increased productivity, and fewer sick days. Exhibit 6.8 outlines some of the employment policies, programs, and practices that a flexible and family-friendly organization might offer.

DIVERSITY

One of the effects of globalization and other socioeconomic changes taking place is increasing **diversity** in the workforce. Workplace diversity refers to the varied characteristics of workers with regard to ethnicity, age, gender, values, ability, physical appearance, skill and experience, economic status,

EXHIBIT 6.8

STRIKING A WORK-LIFE BALANCE

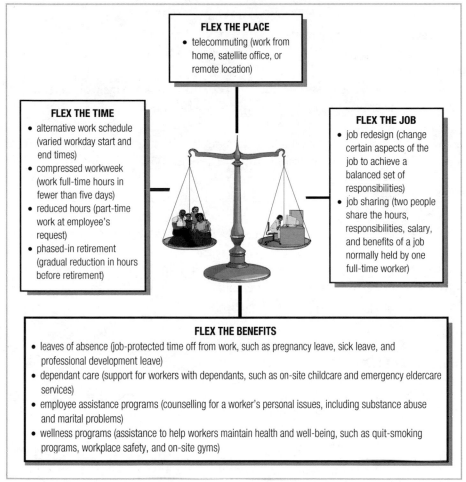

FLEX THE PLACE
- telecommuting (work from home, satellite office, or remote location)

FLEX THE TIME
- alternative work schedule (varied workday start and end times)
- compressed workweek (work full-time hours in fewer than five days)
- reduced hours (part-time work at employee's request)
- phased-in retirement (gradual reduction in hours before retirement)

FLEX THE JOB
- job redesign (change certain aspects of the job to achieve a balanced set of responsibilities)
- job sharing (two people share the hours, responsibilities, salary, and benefits of a job normally held by one full-time worker)

FLEX THE BENEFITS
- leaves of absence (job-protected time off from work, such as pregnancy leave, sick leave, and professional development leave)
- dependant care (support for workers with dependants, such as on-site childcare and emergency eldercare services)
- employee assistance programs (counselling for a worker's personal issues, including substance abuse and marital problems)
- wellness programs (assistance to help workers maintain health and well-being, such as quit-smoking programs, workplace safety, and on-site gyms)

Source: Author-generated graphic. Information derived from Alberta Human Resources and Employment. (2004). *Better balance, better business.* Retrieved from http://alis.alberta.ca/pdf/cshop/betterbalance.pdf.

and sexual orientation. Diversity in age is one of the most obvious dynamics in social agencies and other organizations. In today's workplace, it is common to find four generations—the Second World War generation, the baby boomers, and Generations X and Y—working together in programs and services, with their distinct expectations, attitudes, and work ethics.

While some people may view diversity as a source of conflict, most organizations recognize its potential benefits. A diverse team in a social agency, for instance, is likely to be representative of a local community;

subsequently, people in need may find it easier to approach an agency where all the staff don't look, act, or think the same way (Bredin Institute, 2006). Moreover, an ethnically diverse staff can assist in the development of culturally appropriate programs and services for their equally diverse client base. At the management level, a diverse board of directors is likely to view issues and problems from various perspectives and draw from a broad range of possible solutions.

Studies suggest that, despite the potential advantages of diversity in the workplace and the increasing diversity of Canadian communities, many voluntary agencies are far from diverse. For example, one study found that, with the exception of organizations that provided immigrant services, voluntary and nonprofit organizations did not reflect the ethnic diversity of their communities, especially in health and social service agencies in large cities (HR Council for the Voluntary and Non-profit Sector, 2008). Another study looked at the diversity of boards of directors in the Greater Toronto Area (GTA) and found that although visible minorities represent 40 percent of the GTA's population, less than 16 percent of the total board positions in nonprofit agencies are filled by members of visible minorities. On a more promising note, the majority (78 percent) of those agencies have at least one visible minority board member (Fredette, 2012).

INNOVATION

A rapidly changing society requires innovative strategies for dealing with those changes. In a social welfare context, **social innovation** refers to the development and implementation of new ideas and strategies to solve pressing social problems. Innovation is particularly important to the delivery of social welfare programs. Social agencies are forever seeking more creative and effective ways to help people and to connect people with the resources that they need.

Innovative ideas at the agency level are often referred to as **best practices**— simply put, these are strategies or approaches that people perceive as working well and would recommend to others. Best practices are sometimes identified during program evaluations, but often they are discovered by trial and error. Each level of a social agency is likely to have its own collection of best practices; for example, front-line workers might have preferred methods of assessing client needs; supervisors might use proven team-building techniques; and boards of directors might rely on fundraising strategies that have worked in the past.

COOPERATION

Since the late 1970s, organizations have been de-emphasizing masculine values that encourage competition and an authoritarian way of working, and emphasizing feminine values, such as power sharing, group consensus, and a democratic approach to decision making. Cooperative working relationships can occur within a social agency (*intra*-agency) and among social agencies (*inter*-agency).

Cooperation within Organizations

Intra-agency cooperation focuses on empowering workers and the people who use services, and on fostering an environment of inclusion and participation in the workplace. For voluntary social agencies, intra-agency cooperation means the inclusion of stakeholders in various aspects of the organization's operations. For example, an agency's planning or advisory committee might invite staff to participate in meetings, and former clients might serve on a board of directors.

In recent years, Canadian governments have promoted the notion that pervasive and complex social problems are best addressed when people unite, identify and interpret the issues, share their expertise and views, and work together toward solutions (Canada, 2004a). Thus, for governments, intra-agency cooperation means breaking down hierarchical structures, integrating various ministries and departments, and eliminating service silos. The main objective of these efforts is to allow information and resources to flow more easily across departmental boundaries and, in the process, streamline services for people who use them.

Cooperation among Organizations

Inter-agency cooperation involves two or more organizations working together. A collective approach to community initiatives often involves a pooling of money and other resources, making team efforts more efficient than individual ones. Inter-agency cooperation may also foster coordination, leading to, for example, simplified client referral systems, shared locations, improved communication and information sharing, and integrated service delivery (Thomas & Skage, 1998). Increasingly, inter-agency cooperation is a key factor in community-based projects across Canada.

While cooperative efforts have their advantages, they can also be challenging. For instance, it takes time to establish good working relationships and to

EXHIBIT 6.9

LEVELS OF MUTUAL RELATIONSHIPS

LEVELS	PURPOSE	STRUCTURE	PROCESS
NETWORKING (E.G., NEWFOUNDLAND AND LABRADOR HOUSING AND HOMELESSNESS NETWORK)	• To foster dialogue and a common understanding • To provide a clearinghouse for information • To create a base of support	• Non-hierarchical • Informal or flexible links among members • Loosely defined roles • Community action is primary link among members	• Low-key leadership • Minimal decision making • Little conflict • Informal communication
ALLIANCE (E.G., NATIONAL CHILDREN'S ALLIANCE)	• To match needs and coordinate activities • To limit the duplication of services • To ensure tasks are completed	• Core group acts as communication hub • Semiformal links • Roles somewhat defined • Members act in advisory capacity • Group raises funds	• Facilitative leaders • Complex decision making • Little conflict • Formal communication within core group
PARTNERSHIP (E.G., CANADA-NOVA SCOTIA AFFORDABLE HOUSING AGREEMENT)	• To share resources to address common issues • To pool resources to create something new	• Clearly defined roles • Formal links among members • Group generates new resources and a joint budget	• Autonomous leadership • Focus on issue • Group decision making among core members • Frequent and clear communication
COALITION (E.G., COALITION AGAINST FAMILY VIOLENCE IN NORTHWEST TERRITORIES)	• To share ideas • To draw resources from existing systems • To commit to projects for a minimum period	• Roles, time, and commitment are defined • Formal links • Group generates new resources and a joint budget	• Shared leadership • Formal and group decision making • Frequent and prioritized communication
COLLABORATION (E.G., AN ACCORD BETWEEN THE GOVERNMENT OF CANADA AND THE VOLUNTARY SECTOR)	• To achieve a shared vision • To build an interdependent system to address issues and opportunities	• Formal roles, time commitment, and evaluation • Formal links among members • Written work assignments	• Strong leadership • Consensus model of decision making • High level of trust and productivity • Well-developed communication systems

Source: Adapted from Hogue, T. (1994). *Community Based Collaboration: Community Wellness Multiplied.* Retrieved from University of Vermont, http://www.uvm.edu/extension/community/nnco/collab/wellness.html.

make decisions through consensus—time that is often in short supply in the helping fields. Moreover, inter-agency work often requires well-developed organizational and coordination skills—skills that not all workers bring to the job (Community Social Planning Council of Toronto and Family Service Association of Toronto, 2006).

A variety of terms—such as strategic alliances, collaborations, and partnerships—describe types of inter-agency relationships; each type has a slightly different purpose, structure, and process, as outlined in Exhibit 6.9.

DISCUSSION QUESTIONS

■ **Organic Models of Organization**

1. Identify a social agency in your community that has a tall organizational structure and one that has a flat structure. How might the organizational structure of each agency affect the way it serves the public?

2 Many social agencies are striving to become more flexible, diverse, innovative, and cooperative. Identify how these agency characteristics might benefit (a) people living in poverty and (b) persons with disabilities.

3. Although the trend is toward greater intra- and inter-agency cooperation, not all workers are comfortable working as part of a team. What characteristics should a social worker (or other professional helper) have to succeed in a cooperative-oriented environment?

SUMMARY

Introduction

Social agencies include voluntary agencies and government departments. The way an agency carries out its functions and activities depends on whom it serves, what it intends to accomplish, and how its programs are designed. Local needs tend to determine the type of goods or services an agency offers.

1 Community-Based Social Agencies

Most residential and non-residential organizations deliver services according to a community-based model. Residential centres provide round-the-clock care, while non-residential centres offer services on a drop-in, appointment, or outreach basis. Many non-residential centres (such as multiservice centres) offer a continuum of service. A community system of care, when well coordinated, can respond to the varied and changing needs of clients.

2 Agency Systems: Internal Structures and Functions

Social agencies need a solid internal structure on which to base their work. An understanding of the community forms the basis of a strategic framework, which clarifies an agency's direction through vision, mission, goals, and value statements. An operational framework provides a plan for the provision of direct services (primary, secondary, and tertiary prevention) and indirect services (administration, program planning, and program evaluation). Policies and procedures can help agencies organize their work; however, those rules are not always conducive to meeting the needs of clients or staff.

3 Organic Models of Organization

Organic organizational models provide an alternative to the bureaucratic model. Organic models are known for their adaptability to changes in the environment, their emphasis on flat hierarchical structures, and their promotion of flexibility, diversity, innovation, and cooperative ways of working.

KEY TERMS

For definitions of the key terms, consult the Glossary on page 453 at the end of the book.

social agencies, p. 148

public social agencies, p. 149

voluntary social agencies, p. 149

community-based model, p. 150

residential centres, p. 151

aging in place, p. 153

non-residential centres, p. 153

multiservice centres, p. 153

community system of care, p. 154

strategic framework, p. 155

operational framework, p. 155

direct services, p. 155

indirect services, p. 155

environmental scan, p. 156

community needs assessment, p. 156

target population, p. 156

SWOT analysis, p. 157

vision statement, p. 158

mission statement, p. 158

agency goal, p. 158

value statements, p. 158

primary prevention, p. 159

secondary prevention, p. 159

tertiary prevention, p. 159

administration, p. 160

program planning, p. 161

program evaluation, p. 162

outcome evaluation, p. 162

policies and procedures, p. 163

bureaucratic model of organization, p. 167

service silos, p. 167

organic models of organization, p. 167

flat hierarchical structures, p. 168

diversity, p. 170

social innovation, p. 172

best practices, p. 172

intra-agency cooperation, p. 173

inter-agency cooperation, p. 173

CHAPTER

Service Providers

OBJECTIVES

Professional and non-professional helpers share the responsibility for social welfare provision. This chapter will

- introduce the role of professional and non-professional helpers in a social welfare context

- explore aspects of the social work profession and the role and responsibilities of social service workers

- consider the contributions of volunteers in social agencies

- discuss the role of peer helpers in social provision

- examine selected issues and challenges facing unpaid caregivers

INTRODUCTION

At the center of the universe is a loving heart that continues to beat and that wants the best for every person. Anything we can do to help foster the intellect and spirit and emotional growth of our fellow human beings, that is our job. Those of us who have this particular vision must continue against all odds. Life is for service. (Fred Rogers, host of TV's *Mister Rogers' Neighborhood*, 2001)

Before the expansion of the social welfare system, volunteers provided the bulk of help to people in need. In fact, volunteers established some of Canada's first social welfare institutions, including orphanages and homes for the aged. During the 1950s and 1960s, the growth of the welfare state encouraged the establishment of formal programs and services and the hiring of professional helpers, such as social workers and psychologists. By the 1970s, formally trained helpers had largely displaced volunteers "who, by implication, could not provide adequate service" (Chappell, 1999). This view of volunteers began to change in the 1980s when governments started cutting back on social welfare spending. Governments assumed that volunteers would fill any service gaps that resulted from the cuts and that families would take more responsibility for the care of their members (Jiwani, 2000).

Today, professional helpers are still in demand; however, non-professionals provide a considerable share of support to people in need. Thus, social welfare provision has become the responsibility of two broad helper groups:

- **Professional helpers** are paid to provide services and bring a recognized knowledge base, training, and relevant experience to the helping process. Social workers, social service workers, and other professional helpers use planned, systematic, measurable, and otherwise scientific methods and processes when working with clients. Often, practice is guided by a code of ethics specific to a profession.

- **Non-professional helpers** include lay helpers, volunteers, self-help groups, family caregivers, peer counsellors, friends, and other informal helpers, all of whom help others without expecting a payment in return. Although many non-professional helpers have received training in basic helping techniques, this group is recognized for its use of natural helping skills.

A mix of professional and non-professional help can offer a wide range of service options. For example, a parent in conflict with a teen may seek assistance from a social worker, attend a self-help group for parents, and learn about other community resources through a volunteer information line. At first glance, different types of helpers seem to naturally complement each other. Historically, however, tension has existed between professional and non-professional groups. Some of that tension relates to the issue of expertise. Professional helpers, for instance, may see themselves as experts with more credible and scientific solutions to human problems. At the same time, unpaid helpers may consider themselves experts because of their own struggles in life and having "been there." In recent years, as the demand for help has increased, and government funding to social services has decreased, professional and non-professional helpers have shown a greater willingness

EXHIBIT 7.1

LINKS AMONG PROFESSIONAL AND NON-PROFESSIONAL HELPERS

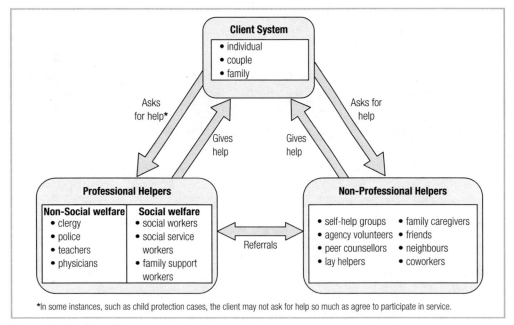

*In some instances, such as child protection cases, the client may not ask for help so much as agree to participate in service.

Source: Rosalie Chappell

to put their differences aside and work more closely together on behalf of people in need.

Professionals, volunteers, peer helpers, and unpaid caregivers might work together at various points. One point of contact is **care team** meetings, which agency workers often form to coordinate services for clients who have a variety of needs or receive service from multiple agencies in the community. It is common for clients to invite a volunteer (such as a sponsor from a twelve-step self-help program), a family member, or a friend to care team meetings for moral support or practical assistance (such as help with language translation). Exhibit 7.1 illustrates possible linkages, points of contact, and the give and take between professional and non-professional helping systems.

1 PROFESSIONAL HELPERS

Of the professional helpers, social workers are the most closely associated with the social welfare system. Social service workers also play an important role in service delivery. This section looks at the contributions of these occupational groups to social welfare, and explores the issues, rewards, and challenges of working in the helping field.

SOCIAL WORKERS

During the nineteenth century, **social workers** began taking a compassionate and empathic approach to the problem of poverty, as opposed to the punitive approach associated with the poor laws. Through social reform movements, social workers educated the public about poverty and its related problems, and lobbied for legislation to improve living standards for people in need. Social workers also worked directly with people who were disadvantaged, providing material aid and counselling that aimed not only to meet their basic physical needs but also to empower them. These efforts established a long-standing association between social workers and the social welfare system. Social workers practise alongside a wide range of other occupational groups, including psychologists, child-care workers, and guidance counsellors; however, social workers make up the largest single occupational group in Canada's social welfare system and have considerable input into the development and delivery of income security programs and social services.

Social workers are employed in many different settings, including hospitals, voluntary agencies, religious organizations, employee assistance offices, Aboriginal band councils, and private practice. More than three-quarters of social workers in Canada work in healthcare and social service agencies. Certain trends—such as an aging population and a growing need for child protection services—are likely to increase the future demand for social workers (Service Canada, 2012a).

Social Work Values and Knowledge

The **social work** profession is based on altruistic, humanitarian, and egalitarian ideals, all of which shape its philosophy and its service goals and interventions. Underlying social work's philosophy are a number of core values, including respect for persons, social justice, and service to humanity. A fundamental belief in confidentiality, integrity, and competence guides professional practice (Canadian Association of Social Workers [CASW], 2005).

Social work's theoretical knowledge base is the product of activities within the social work profession and in other disciplines. Knowledge produced within the profession draws from the shared experience of workers, individual professional experiences, and applied research. Knowledge is also derived from other such disciplines as psychology, psychiatry, education, and public health, and from many academic fields, including sociology, philosophy, economics, and law. This "cross-pollination" of various fields gives social work a highly **interdisciplinary knowledge base** (Johnson, McClelland, & Austin, 2000).

Social Work Practice

Social work's **scope of practice** defines the types of activities that a qualified social worker may practise. The relationship between individuals and their environment, otherwise known as **person-in-environment**, is central to social work's domain of practice. According to the person-in-environment perspective, external factors in a person's life, such as family and formal organizations, can either help or hinder individual well-being (CASW, 2008). To work from a person-in-environment perspective, social workers must learn about (1) a client's personal level of functioning; (2) how that functioning may be affected by external forces, such as work or the economy; and (3) how a client interacts with her or his environment (McMahon, 1994). This approach acknowledges the complexity of interactions between people and the world around them, and recognizes that people both shape and are shaped by their environment (International Federation of Social Workers, 2012a). In 2008, the CASW published its national scope of practice statement to promote a better understanding of social work practice.

The person-in-environment perspective requires social workers to take a **multilevel approach to practice**. At the *micro* level, social workers aim to help individuals, families, and small groups enhance their social well-being; this goal may be achieved through a variety of methods, including one-to-one, family, or group counselling (see Exhibit 7.2). At the *mezzo* level, social workers seek to improve conditions within and among social welfare organizations; this approach may involve engaging in activities to strengthen inter-agency relations or advocating for new programs. The *macro* level of practice addresses broader social problems and political issues and may require social workers to advocate for change in social legislation or policy. What social workers actually do at each level depends largely on the setting in which they work and on what they are trying to achieve. Most social work activities, however, require some degree of skill in assessment, intervention, and evaluation.

Social Work Education

In most provinces and territories, a minimum of a bachelor of social work (B.S.W.) degree is required for entry into the social work profession.

At the micro level, many social workers work one on one with their clients.

People who have completed a B.S.W. may continue their education to obtain a graduate degree (master of social work) or a postgraduate degree (doctor of social work or Ph.D.). It is normally at the graduate and post-graduate education levels that students specialize in a particular field of practice. Since 1967, the Canadian Association for Social Work Education has worked to advance the quality and relevance of social work training in Canada.

Ideally, the context in which practice takes place shapes the structure and content of social work education. In reality, social work programs struggle to keep up with rapid changes in political, economic, and social environments, and the ongoing restructuring of service delivery systems. One challenge involves keeping social work courses and programs relevant to changing human needs and problems. In particular, social workers must learn how to

- address client needs that are becoming increasingly complex as a result of persistent poverty and chronic unemployment

- meet rising demands for services in a climate of shrinking social welfare resources

- provide effective service in an environment in which social problems, such as family violence and substance abuse, are becoming more pervasive
- take the kind of social action that can change current political and economic systems (Rondeau, 2001)

An ongoing challenge for educators is to raise social work students' awareness of the diverse social issues and problems in Canadian society. In her review of social work literature, Anne Westhues (2005) found that issues related to gender and, to a lesser extent, racism, have received the most coverage during the last twenty years. More recently, the topics of sexual orientation, Aboriginal issues, and the experiences of older adults have been gaining more attention in social work classrooms.

In response to an increasingly culturally diverse society, social work education programs are becoming more reflective of the communities that the graduates will serve. For instance, these programs are making progress in attracting more visible-minority and Aboriginal social workers to the profession. Furthermore, changes to the education and accreditation policies of the Canadian Association for Social Work Education, and to the CASW's code of ethics, aim to strengthen social work students' skills in working with a culturally and racially diverse clientele (Yan & Chan, 2010).

Regulation of Social Work

The practice of social work is regulated at various levels. Each province and territory has a professional association to govern social work practice; the associations in nine of those provinces and the territories form a federation under the Canadian Association of Social Workers (CASW). The CASW plays a leadership role in advancing the social work profession in Canada and sets national standards and guidelines for social work practice. These standards include a social work code of ethics, which guides professional conduct and practice (CASW, 2005).

In addition to professional associations, Ontario, Québec, British Columbia, and Alberta each have a college of social work; other provinces are in the process of establishing colleges as well. (In this context, colleges are governing bodies, not educational institutions.) While social work associations and colleges share many of the same values and principles, each regulatory body has its own mission: professional associations tend to represent the interests of the social work profession, while colleges aim to protect the public from unqualified or incompetent practitioners.

Legislation and regulation in each province and territory define the limits of what social workers can and cannot do. These limitations are articulated in various sources, such as social work acts, scope of practice statements, and documents that specify the qualifications (such as educational achievement) that social workers must have to practise the profession. Depending on the jurisdiction, social workers who join a regulatory body in their region become registered, certified, or licensed; the public expects these social workers to practise in accordance with the standards set by their profession and to be accountable to their clients, their profession, and society. Legislation in each jurisdiction protects the use of the titles "social worker" and "registered social worker"; only those who meet certain professional standards can use these designations.

Professional Identity

Social work is similar to other helping **professions** (such as nursing and policing) in that it possesses a code of ethics, it has the means to regulate and enforce standards of behaviour among its members, and it has developed a theoretical body of knowledge that guides practice (Cross, 1985). (See Exhibit 7.3 for some of the commonalities and distinctions between social work and two other helping professions.)

For much of the twentieth century, social work distinguished itself from other helping professions by "a distinct set of professional skills, based on an identified knowledge base, provided through formal education, and refined through years of practice with others in the profession" (Stephenson, Rondeau, Michaud, & Fiddler, 2000, p. 5). Since the early 1980s, however, it has become more difficult to discern what is or is not social work. Changes in social and economic policies—largely enforced by neoliberal governments—have contributed to social work's loss of professional identity. Those policies have affected the definition of social work in a variety of ways, including the following:

- To save money, primary healthcare centres, such as hospitals, have grouped workers from various disciplines under generic titles, such as "healthcare professionals." In these types of settings, social workers may be supervised by non-social-workers who may not recognize or encourage the use of social work skills (Fildes & Cooper, 2003).

- In an attempt to keep costs down and meet service demands, social agencies are hiring greater numbers of helpers with fewer credentials or with little or no social work training. Although non-social-workers may meet the demands of the job, their predominance can weaken social work's presence in the social welfare field.

EXHIBIT 7.3

A COMPARISON OF THREE HELPING PROFESSIONS

	SOCIAL WORK	PSYCHOLOGY	PSYCHIATRY
PRIMARY FOCUS OF HELP	Interactions between people and their social environment	Individual thoughts, feelings, and behaviour	Thought processes and brain functioning
GENERAL AIM OF PRACTICE	To help people develop and use personal and community resources to solve problems	To help people understand, explain, and change their behaviour	To help people prevent or manage mental illness or behavioural disorders
ASSESSMENT/ DIAGNOSTIC TOOLS	Psychosocial history-taking; client interviews; observation	Diagnostic tests (IQ, personality, etc.); interviews; observation	Medical exam; *Diagnostic and Statistical Manual of Mental Disorders*; interviews; observation
EXAMPLES OF PRACTICE METHODS	Individual counselling; marital/family therapy; group work; advocacy; community practice	Individual counselling; marital/family therapy; group work; consultation	Psychotropic medication; biological treatments; psychotherapy
EXAMPLES OF SPECIALIZATIONS	Clinical (counselling); child welfare; gerontology; school; family services	Clinical; counselling; developmental; school; forensic; sports	Child and adolescent; geriatric; forensic; liaison; addictions
EDUCATION LEVELS	B.S.W., M.S.W., D.S.W., Ph.D.	B.A. or B.Sc., M.A., Ph.D.	Medical degree plus minimum five years psychiatric training
PROFESSIONAL ASSOCIATIONS AND REGULATORY BODIES	Canadian Association of Social Workers; college of social workers (in some provinces)	Canadian Psychological Association; Association of Canadian Psychology Regulatory Organizations	Canadian Psychiatric Association; Royal College of Physicians and Surgeons of Canada

Source: Rosalie Chappell

Social work's identity has been redefined over the past few years in part because of the regulation of **restricted practice activities**—that is, practices that only certain occupational groups or designated professionals within those groups can carry out. Provincial legislation sets out the restricted practices for social workers. For example, under Ontario's Psychotherapy Act, only social workers with certain qualifications and membership in the Ontario College of Social Workers and Social Service Workers can legally practise psychotherapy in that province.

SOCIAL SERVICE WORKERS

The expansion of the social welfare system in the 1950s and 1960s led to an increased demand for service providers and, subsequently, to the development of college-level social work programs. Today, over sixty certificate or diploma programs across Canada offer basic social work training; these college-level programs combine classroom work with practical experience and tend to tailor their curriculums to the needs of the job market (Lecomte, 2005). Typically, students train as generalist social workers and learn basic social work methods, values, and ethics. Graduates of these programs are most commonly known as **social service workers** or human service workers, but other titles—such as community support worker or family support worker—may apply. Since people in this group have a lower level of social work education than a bachelor's degree, they are sometimes referred to as **paraprofessionals** (Stephenson, Rondeau, Michaud, & Fiddler, 2000).

Many of the same types of agencies that employ social workers also hire social service workers. Healthcare organizations and social assistance offices provide the majority of social service workers (about 70 percent) with employment. Supervisors assign these workers a variety of duties, including

- preparing intake reports
- referring clients to community resources
- providing crisis intervention
- leading client groups, such as life skills workshops
- coordinating and supervising volunteers
- participating in the admission of clients to appropriate programs (Human Resources and Skills Development Canada, 2012b)

Although social service workers perform similar tasks as social workers, they tend to have fewer responsibilities and less discretionary power. It is common for a social service worker to serve as a caseworker under the supervision of a social worker.

Industry sources suggest that certain trends will drive the need for social service workers; those trends include the community integration of people with disabilities, the increasing rates of social problems (such as child poverty), and the retirement of older workers in social welfare occupations. An expansion of social services for First Nations peoples is also opening up new job prospects for social service workers, especially in the areas of outreach and community development (British Columbia, Work Futures, 2011).

There is no uniform regulation of social service workers in Canada. Alberta and Ontario are the only provinces that have a regulatory process to oversee social service practice. The Ontario College of Social Workers and Social Service Workers (OCSWSSW) has developed various documents to guide social service practice; one of those documents is a scope of practice for

EXHIBIT 7.4

SCOPE OF PRACTICE FOR SOCIAL SERVICE WORK

The scope of practice of the profession of social service work means the assessment, treatment and evaluation of individual, interpersonal and societal problems through the use of social service work knowledge, skills, interventions and strategies, to assist individuals, dyads, families, groups, organizations and communities to achieve optimum social functioning and includes, without limiting the generality of the foregoing, the following:

SSW1—The provision of assessment, treatment and evaluation services within a relationship between a social service worker and a client;

SSW2—The provision of supervision and/or consultation to a social service worker or social service work student or other supervisee;

SSW3—The provision of social support to individuals and/or groups including relationship-building, life skills instruction, employment support, tangible support including food and financial assistance, and information and referral services;

SSW4—The provision of educational services to social service worker students;

SSW5—The development, promotion, management, administration, delivery and evaluation of human service programs, including that done in collaboration with other professionals;

SSW6—The provision of services in organizing and/or mobilizing community members and/or other professionals in the promotion of social change;

SSW7—The provision of contractual consultation services to other social service workers, or professionals; or organizations;

SSW8—The development, promotion, implementation and evaluation of social policies aimed at improving social conditions and equality;

SSW9—The conduct of research regarding the practice of social service work, as defined in paragraphs (1) to (8) above; and

SSW10—Any other activities approved by the College.

The Principles and Interpretations set out in the *Standards of Practice Handbook* are to be applied in the context of the scope of practice of each profession.

Source: From Ontario College of Social Workers and Social Service Workers. (2008). *Code of ethics and standards of practice handbook*, 2nd ed., p. 8. Retrieved from http://www.ocswssw.org/docs/codeofethicsstandardsofpractice.pdf. Used with permission.

social service workers who are members of the OCSWSSW (see Exhibit 7.4 for a summary of that scope of practice).

REWARDS AND CHALLENGES FOR PROFESSIONAL AND PARAPROFESSIONAL HELPERS

Some Canadian studies have found that social workers and social service workers generally experience work overload, job insecurity, lower pay and fewer benefits than other occupations; stress and burnout, work–life conflict, and a general dissatisfaction with work are also common complaints (CASW, 2004; Evans, Richmond, & Shields, 2005). Other studies emphasize the rewards of social work and related service. For example, many people enter the social welfare field because they are committed to a cause, and they see social service as an important and meaningful endeavour; these workers report being generally satisfied with their jobs (Saunders, 2004). Others are attracted to the field because of the flexible work schedules, a culture that promotes teamwork, and a highly dynamic work environment that provides stimulating challenges and opportunities (Ahmed, 2006).

Some analysts question whether the rewards of social service are enough to compensate for low wages and poor working conditions or to keep qualified helpers committed to the field over the long term. Ron Saunders (2004, p. 48) predicts a looming crisis within the social welfare field: The "dissatisfaction with earnings in the non-profit sector rises with age, suggesting that employees in the sector eventually reach a point where the gap between the intrinsic rewards of working in the sector (fulfilling a valued mission) and the extrinsic rewards (pay, job security) becomes a problem for them. Since the paid workforce in the sector is older, on average, than that of the for-profit sector, this issue may become more acute in the coming years." Reports suggest that social agencies, especially in the voluntary sector, are having a harder time retaining staff. A migration of qualified workers out of social service to higher-paying jobs in other fields—such as Alberta's booming oil and gas sector—is already under way ("Social Service Staff," 2007).

A Labour Force Study of paid employment in Canada's voluntary and nonprofit organizations suggests that a new generation of workers may be attracted to the social welfare field because of its challenging and rewarding work. On the other hand, the field's overemphasis on paperwork and other administrative duties may not appeal to many young people (Human Resources Council for the Voluntary & Non-Profit Sector, 2008).

In any case, growing numbers of social workers and social service workers are completing their training and seeking work in social and health services. There are also indications that some provinces and territories are increasing funding to social services and thereby creating new positions. Those funding increases are in response to various developments, such as a need to fulfill service obligations under provincial and territorial poverty-reduction plans, and mounting public pressure to address persistent social problems with concrete interventions (Service Canada, 2012a).

DISCUSSION QUESTIONS

■ Professional Helpers

1. Social work educators face the challenge of trying to keep social work courses relevant to the changing political, economic, and cultural climate. What can educators do to ensure that students are well prepared to enter the social work field? What can students do to ensure that they are getting the best training available?

2. As a profession, social work has been experiencing an "identity crisis." Do you think that social workers should have a clearly defined role and title or simply blend into the larger (and more generic) group of "healthcare professionals"? Give reasons for your answer.

3. If applicable, identify what attracts you to a career in the social welfare field. How do you think you can make a difference in this field?

2 AGENCY VOLUNTEERS

Approximately 12 percent of Canadian adults donate their time to social agencies, primarily in the voluntary sector. These **agency volunteers** may perform any number of duties, including fundraising; mentoring, teaching, or giving information; delivering or serving food; driving people to appointments and community activities; and supporting people in distress (Vézina & Crompton, 2012).

The integration of volunteers in social agencies is becoming more common in Canada. Professionals and volunteers work side by side in many types of organizations and on behalf of various groups, including recent immigrants, children and families, and victims of crime. In these days of government cutbacks and growing demand for services, many social agencies have become so reliant on volunteers that they could not survive without them (see Exhibit 7.5).

EXHIBIT 7.5

The financial survival of many food banks and other social agencies depends heavily on volunteer labour.

BENEFITS OF VOLUNTEERING

Among other things, social agency volunteers are valued for their interest in and concern for others, their innate understanding of the human condition, and their use of **natural helping skills**. To provide support to agency clients, volunteers are likely to use facilitating skills (such as listening, encouraging, and empathizing) and perform tasks (such as giving advice and information, and shopping for food and other basics) (Stahl & Hill, 2008).

A study by Patterson, Memmott, Brennan, and Germain (1992) found that the most helpful volunteers are the ones who provide humour, exchange personal experiences, share material resources, reach out to others, and follow up after problems are resolved. Helpful people are also those who assist others to clarify needs and problem solve, and who provide suggestions and information. In their study of a parent support group, Parrott, Buchanan, and Williams (2006) found that at-risk parents appreciate that volunteers are more flexible than professional helpers who, for the most part, are available only during regular office hours and have more restrictions on the type of help they can give.

Social service agencies generally recognize volunteers for the wide range of benefits they bring to the organization. For example, because volunteers choose to serve an agency for no material gain, they lend credibility to the agency. Volunteers also bring vitality to their work, as well as knowledge, focus, objectivity, and specialized skills. Agencies often rely on volunteers for their objective views on agency operations and for their constructive feedback and ideas on how to improve existing programs or procedures (Muegge & Ross, 1996). Specific volunteer groups can benefit organizations in different ways. For example, immigrant volunteers are recognized for increasing diversity, sharing new perspectives, and expanding the range of linguistic and other skills within organizations (Volunteer Canada, 2010). As well as bringing enthusiasm, fresh ideas, and creativity to organizations, youth volunteers are valued for making services more accessible to younger populations (Community Sector Council Newfoundland and Labrador, 2010).

MANDATORY VOLUNTEERS

Volunteer Canada (2006a, p. 22) defines volunteering as "the offering of time, energy and skills of *one's own free will*" (italics added). Thus, forcing someone to volunteer runs contrary to the definition and spirit of volunteering. Since the late 1990s, however, it has become more common for people to volunteer because they are required to. These **mandatory volunteers**—known in some circles as *voluntolds*—account for 7 percent of Canadian volunteers. Mandatory volunteers may include high school students who must volunteer in order to graduate and people sentenced by the courts to complete community service (Vézina & Crompton, 2012).

Many organizations promote the potential benefits of mandatory community service. Government social assistance programs, for example, see volunteering as a way for social assistance recipients "to contribute to their communities, learn basic work and life skills, gain experience and make contacts for future employment" (District of Nipissing Social Services Administration Board, 2012). Opponents of mandatory volunteering suggest that forced volunteerism may pose problems for sponsoring agencies. By trying to accommodate mandatory volunteers, voluntary agencies may use up precious resources that could go to supporting volunteers who really want to be there. Agency supervisors may also need to devote extra time to reporting on the participant's progress to probation officers, welfare workers, or other authorities. Agencies that accept young offenders in community service placements may have to address issues related to the safety and security of their clients and staff. Moreover, agency staff may find it particularly challenging to work with mandatory volunteers who are less willing or motivated to serve than are regular volunteers (Volunteer Canada, 2006b).

GOVERNMENT SUPPORT OF VOLUNTEERISM

Since 1977, the Government of Canada has promoted volunteerism through Volunteer Canada. It was nevertheless the United Nations' proclamation of the International Year of Volunteers in 2001 that made government recognize the invaluable role that volunteers play in society.

In 2002, the Government of Canada introduced the Canada Volunteerism Initiative (CVI) to promote the participation of Canadians in society. Under this initiative, federal funding supported the establishment of volunteer centres across the country, the promotion of volunteerism, and the development of how-to documents to help voluntary agencies learn the science of managing volunteers. Evaluation reports suggest that the strategies developed under the CVI were highly successful in terms of helping organizations recruit, manage, and recognize volunteers more effectively (Volunteer Canada, 2008).

For governments, volunteerism has a tremendous economic value: estimates show that the approximately two billion hours of volunteer work annually performed by Canadians is the equivalent of over one million full-time jobs (Statistics Canada, 2012a). Governments are increasingly seeing volunteers as possible solutions to the rising demand for and costs of social welfare provision.

Clearly, organizations that use volunteers require some level of funding to recruit, train, supervise, and adequately recognize volunteers; since 2002, much of that funding had been available through the CVI. However, in 2006, the newly elected federal government cancelled the CVI (and the $9.7 million going to that program) on the basis that the initiative did not "meet the priorities of the federal government or Canadians" (Treasury Board of Canada Secretariat, 2006). The government's move surprised many Canadians, especially since governments usually want nonprofit organizations to cut costs by using more volunteers. To compensate for the federal government's withdrawal of funding, many provinces and the territories stepped in to support voluntary agencies and volunteerism. The

Government of Nova Scotia (2006), for example, appointed a minister of volunteerism and, in so doing, made a commitment to work with the voluntary sector to increase the number of volunteers needed to ensure the quality of nonprofit service.

BARRIERS TO VOLUNTEERISM

Despite provincial and territorial support of volunteerism, Canadians face a number of barriers to volunteering. In the 2010 Canada Survey of Giving, Volunteering and Participating (Vézina & Crompton, 2012), most respondents cited a lack of time as the main reason for not volunteering, and more than half of respondents said they were unable to make a long-term commitment to volunteering. A study by Volunteer Canada (2010) found that, even when volunteers were committed to their cause, they had less than ideal volunteer experiences. Some of those volunteers reported a frustration with agency politics and disorganization, while others felt that they were not making a difference or believed that their skills were under-used. Researchers in the study suggested that voluntary agencies could do more to improve their volunteer recruitment and retention practices. For example, agencies might make a greater effort to learn about volunteers' motivations and interests and the types of experiences they are seeking. In addition, agencies could try to be more flexible and accommodating to the schedules and time restraints of volunteers; be more sensitive to volunteers' needs in terms of age, culture, ability, language, and gender; and be more willing to tailor volunteer experiences to match the interests of participants.

Canadian studies on volunteering show that smaller numbers of volunteers are doing a greater portion of the work; specifically, 25 percent of all volunteers contribute 77 percent of all volunteer hours (Vézina & Crompton, 2012). Those who donate the bulk of volunteer hours are at a high risk of burnout—women are particularly vulnerable because they tend to be already overextended yet feel obligated to contribute even more (Mailloux, Horak, & Godin, 2002). Social agencies may find themselves in a bind: they need volunteers to meet increasing service demands and yet are reluctant to overwork existing volunteers. A possible solution is to limit the range of services that volunteers provide; this prospect is nevertheless an undesirable one for those social agencies struggling to meet community needs.

DISCUSSION QUESTIONS

■ **Agency Volunteers**

1. Do you think that it is a good idea for social agencies to use volunteers in the provision of service? What are the potential pros and cons of relying on volunteer labour from the perspective of (a) clients and (b) social agency staff?

2. In your opinion, what are the top three things that a nonprofit organization should do to show its volunteers that they are valued and needed?

3. In what situations (if any) might a client benefit more from the services provided by a volunteer than those provided by a professional helper? Give reasons for your answer.

3 PEER HELPERS

While **peer support** normally takes place between friends on an informal, ad-hoc basis, this type of help can also develop into more organized and structured arrangements. Such is the case with self-help groups and peer counselling. In these situations, people form relationships with others who share a common concern or experience for the purpose of providing mutual support, information, or physical assistance.

THE ROLE OF PEER SUPPORT

Research suggests a strong link between peer support and improvements in well-being, including physical health benefits, reduced reliance on hospital and mental health services, and improved quality of life (Peters, 2010). By connecting with peers, people can also make more friends and therefore reduce feelings of isolation or loneliness. Peer support programs for adults—such as those for parents of children with disabilities—can help participants feel better able to accept and cope with the challenges they face (British Columbia Schizophrenia Society, 2005). Children and adolescents might benefit from peer helping in terms of learning effective problem-solving skills or dealing with peer pressure or bullying. Peer support might also be an option for youth needing to make tough decisions around drugs, sex, and other high-risk behaviours.

Those receiving help are not the only ones that benefit. Through the process of sharing knowledge, skills, and resources with others, peer helpers can become empowered to solve their own problems. In turn, personal empowerment is likely to foster physical and mental energy, personal understanding, and motivation. Another benefit relates to the helper therapy principle. According to self-help expert Frank Riessman, a person who is simultaneously a helper and a recipient of help "acquires the enhanced self-esteem and feeling of worth that comes with being important to others. The experiential knowledge, gained from coping with a common problem, is valued, just as credentials and technical expertise are valued in a professional helping situation" (cited in Pape, 1990, p. 5).

The first peer support service in Canada was the Mental Patients Society, established in Vancouver in 1971. Since then, the peer support, self-help, and paraprofessional movements have promoted the many benefits of peer-delivered services. Today, peer support is an important adjunct to professional health services, especially in light of an aging population and an overburdened healthcare system. Shrinking social welfare budgets are making it more difficult for professional helpers to meet service demands; as a result, professionals are enlisting the help of peer-based programs to help their clients meet their social and emotional needs. Certain social trends—such as an overall increase in family instability and a growing number of people seeking helping services—are also driving the demand for peer support.

Peer intervention programs exist in many settings, such as schools, hospitals, workplaces, and community centres. Although many peer-based programs function with little or no government funding, this situation is gradually changing as governments recognize the economic, health, and social benefits of peer intervention. Québec, Ontario, New Brunswick, and British Columbia are ahead of other Canadian jurisdictions when it comes to developing and funding peer programs (Peters, 2010).

SELF-HELP GROUPS

Self-help groups are non-professional networks of individuals with a common experience or concern. These groups typically meet to pool resources, exchange information, and provide mutual support to its members. Participants in self-help groups connect on the basis "that all members are equal—all are experts on their own lives, no one knows more than anyone else and no one has all the answers" (Standing Senate Committee on Social Affairs, Science and Technology, 2006a, p. 234). In general, self-help groups are voluntary and any help given is free of charge. These groups are essentially egalitarian and do not include professionals in the helping process. Although self-help groups have much in common with other types of groups, they are unique in many ways; Exhibit 7.6 compares self-help, peer support, and therapy groups.

EXHIBIT 7.6

MAKING DISTINCTIONS: SELF-HELP, PEER SUPPORT, AND THERAPY GROUPS

	SELF-HELP GROUP	PEER SUPPORT GROUP	THERAPY GROUP
PRIMARY GOAL	Personal change through helper-therapy principle	Personal change through information and support	Personal change through evidence-based therapeutic models and strategies
GROUP MODEL	Peer participatory	Peer participatory	Professional expert
GROUP PROCESS	Identification and interactions with peers	Identification and interactions with peers	Interactions with members and therapist
GROUP ACTIVITIES	Personal storytelling, listening to others, giving emotional and practical support	Discussion, skill-building exercises, information exchange	Discussion or other form of self-expression (such as dance or art)
OUTCOMES OF GROUP	Encouragement, sense of belonging, empowerment, recovery	New skills, understanding, comfort, ability to cope	Improved communication and behavioural functioning, trust, personal insight
MEMBERSHIP	Open to new members (sometimes restricted on basis of gender)	Often closed groups; members must meet eligibility criteria	Closed group; members must meet eligibility criteria
LEADERSHIP	No leader, or leader shares same issue as group members	Professional or trained volunteer, usually has first-hand experience with the group's issue	Professional leader, usually trained in a discipline (such as psychotherapy)
MEETING STRUCTURE	Meetings are structured and task oriented	Meetings may or may not be structured	Structure depends on therapist's therapeutic approach
MEETING PLACE	Donated space (e.g., room in church); Internet	Social agency or private agency; Internet	Social agency, institution, or private agency
COST OF MEMBERSHIP	Free (possible donation to cover cost of refreshments, etc.)	Free, subsidized by agency, or minimal fee	Free, subsidized by agency, or fee-for-service
SIZE OF GROUP	Flexible (limited only by physical space)	Depends on purpose of group and needs of members	Usually small (about 6 to 8 participants)

Source: Self-Help Resource Association of B.C. (2004). *Self-help mutual aid and professionals: A practical alliance*, p. 2. Self-Help/Mutual Aid Workshop Series Manuals: Vancouver.

A self-help group exists for practically every human issue imaginable, including bereavement, disability, parenting, and relationships. Self-help groups are particularly powerful sources of support for persons with a mental health disorder or an addiction. Depending on its purpose, a self-help group may focus on problem solving (such as Al-Anon), self-development (for example, Parents Supporting Parents Society in Nova Scotia), or consciousness raising (including Senior Power of Regina).

At one time, the only way that members of self-help groups could connect with each other was in person. However, in the Internet era, more and more people are able to participate in cyber self-help groups. Online groups have many advantages over face-to-face groups; for instance, members do not have to arrange for meeting space, transportation, or child care; also, schedules for group meetings are flexible. Online self-help groups are especially appealing to people who are concerned about anonymity or who live in rural or isolated areas where groups are limited or non-existent. There are a number of possible online venues for self-help groups, including newsgroups, email discussion groups, chat rooms, and discussion forums.

PEER COUNSELLORS

Peer counsellors are volunteers who use natural helping skills and basic counselling skills to help others deal with challenges in their personal or professional lives. Depending on the situation, peer counsellors can be helpful in a number of ways, including helping others develop self-esteem and confidence, learn effective coping strategies, and deal with difficult feelings, such as anxiety, grief, and anger. Perhaps most importantly, peer counsellors offer what a friend might normally provide: a listening ear, understanding, and encouragement (Hunte, 2009).

It is critical that peer counsellors can identify with those they are trying to help. Typically, peer counsellors have similar backgrounds, or have experienced similar challenges, as those they are trying to help. For example, the Ontario Provincial Police's employee assistance program offers peer counselling to "employees and their families to discuss emotional issues with someone they trust and who can understand their struggles, particularly as they are shaped by the policing profession" (OPP Human Resources Bureau, 2006). A wide range of organizations—such as those for families, seniors, and people with disabilities—rely on peer counsellors to provide various types of support to their clientele.

Like other types of helpers, peer counsellors have a well-defined role in the helping process. For example, it would be reasonable for peer counsellors to offer suggestions, point out the potential consequences of actions, or share their own experiences with those they are assisting. On the other hand, it would be inappropriate for these non-professional counsellors to give advice or make decisions for someone else. Moreover, peer counsellors do not provide therapy or replace professional helpers; however, they can be instrumental in referring people to social workers, psychologists, or other certified professional if more intensive counselling is needed (Carr, 1996).

All peer counsellors receive some level of formal training. Ideally, a qualified adult instructor with experience in peer counselling facilitates the training sessions. Successful training sessions are usually based on a reliable curriculum, offer a balance of counselling theory and experiential learning, and encourage and engage participants in the learning process. It is important that the training meet the needs of the sponsoring organization and the community, and that relevant groups, organizations, and caregivers in the community legitimate the training program. In addition to training, peer counsellors should receive ongoing supervision and regular opportunities to upgrade their skills (Carr, 1996).

DISCUSSION QUESTIONS

■ **Peer Helpers**

1. List some of the peer support groups or programs in your community. For each group or program, identify its target population and its main function. How might the participants of these groups or programs benefit from peer interactions? Do you think that professional helpers could produce those same benefits? Why or why not?

2. Some provincial and territorial governments are starting to show a greater interest in supporting peer support programs. What are some of the possible reasons for this interest? (Consider some of the social, economic, political, and cultural changes taking place in Canada.)

4 UNPAID CAREGIVERS

As governments cut back on social welfare funding informal support systems find themselves assuming a greater responsibility for the care of dependent adult children, aging parents, and others who cannot care for themselves. **Unpaid caregivers**—who may be a spouse, relative, friend, or neighbour—provide 70 to 80 percent of necessary care to older Canadians and those with a chronic illness or disability. Caregivers provide a wide range of assistance, including helping with the tasks of daily living, giving emotional or social support, and providing personal care; that care may take place in a private home or an institution. Most caregivers are women (see Exhibit 7.7). It is also women who tend to perform the most intensive caregiving tasks, such as cooking, cleaning, bathing, and dressing (Special Senate Committee on Aging, 2009).

People may become caregivers at any point in their lifespan. However, many caregivers belong to what is known as the **sandwich generation**—a group of middle-aged adults who care for both dependent children and older relatives. According to one Canadian study, one in five (2.3 million) members of the sandwich generation juggle the dual responsibilities of caregiving and paid work (Research on Aging, Policies, and Practice, 2011).

EXHIBIT 7.7

© Orange Line Media/Shutterstock

Caring for aging relatives, friends, and neighbours is a growing trend in Canada. Women are more likely than men to be primary caregivers.

THE PERSONAL IMPACT OF FAMILY CAREGIVING

Most caregivers recognize the benefits of helping; however, nearly 20 000 unpaid caregivers (16 percent) report distress related to their caregiving role (Canadian Institute for Health Information, 2010). The term **caregiver strain** refers to the potential negative emotional, physical, financial, or other negative consequence of caring for another person for an extended period. According to Robert Dobie of the National Advisory Council of Aging, caregiver strain not only can affect those who give care but also those who receive it:

> The added responsibility of informal caregiving can lead to physical and mental exhaustion and have a detrimental effect on the health of caregivers. Lack of formal supports can lead to burn out, causing caregivers to withdraw from caregiving. This, in turn, can lead to higher rates of institutionalization for seniors [who need care]." (Robert Dobie, cited in Special Senate Committee on Aging, 2009, p. 118)

Caregiver strain can manifest itself in a variety of ways. In one Canadian study on caring for seniors, researchers found that both genders of caregivers experienced employment difficulties related to caregiving responsibilities. However, the female caregivers in the study were affected the most: 30 percent missed at least a full day of work a week; more than 6 percent took early retirement, quit, or lost their job because of caregiving responsibilities; and another 5 percent turned down a job offer or promotion to care for a friend or family member (Research on Aging, Policies, and Practice, 2011). Another Canadian study found that, although middle-aged and older caregivers reaped many rewards from caregiving, they also experienced difficulties in several life areas (see Exhibit 7.8).

SERVICES FOR CAREGIVERS

For unpaid caregivers to care effectively for someone over the long term, they must also care for themselves. Many caregivers turn to informal sources of help. For instance, caregivers might rely on children to help with household chores, a spouse to share employment responsibilities, or neighbours to provide social support to the one requiring care. About one in ten caregivers seek help from a health or social welfare program (Cranswick & Dosman, 2008).

EXHIBIT 7.8

THE IMPACTS OF CAREGIVING

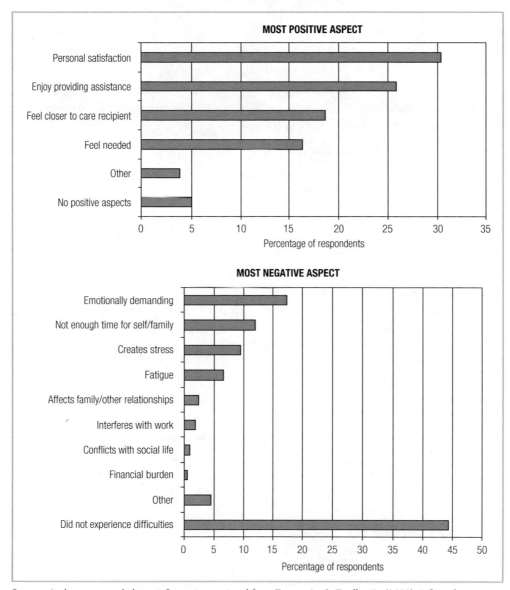

Source: Author-generated chart, information retrieved from Turner, A., & Findlay, L. (2012). Informal caregiving for seniors. *Health Reports* 23(3), table 3, p. 4. Retrieved from Statistics Canada website: http://www.statcan.gc.ca/pub/82-003-x/2012003/article/11694/tbl/tbl3-eng.htm.

Many health and social service organizations offer a range of programs and services to support the work that unpaid caregivers do. For example, the provincially funded Vancouver Coastal Health (2012) sponsors the following:

- education programs (to help caregivers define and adjust to the emotional and practical demands of caregiving)

- support groups (to give caregivers a chance to share experiences, provide mutual support, find solutions to common problems, and exchange information about community resources)

- telephone support (to provide peer counselling to caregivers)

- information and referral services (to help caregivers access community programs or find information on specific illnesses or disabilities)

- caregiver forums (to provide an opportunity for caregivers to come together, to meet and network, and to advance their skills and knowledge on caregiving issues)

Respite services are a particularly important resource for unpaid caregivers. These services give caregivers a break from the demands of caregiving by leaving the care recipient in the temporary care of someone else. Various types of respite care are available in Canada, including day programs for elderly people, summer camps for children with special needs, and the assignment of home support workers to help with housework, meal preparation, and other household tasks. While respite care has many potential benefits for caregivers, the Canadian Healthcare Association (2012) points out that respite can also be beneficial to care recipients. For example, by spending time with a different caregiver or in a new environment, care recipients may have an opportunity to meet a range of therapeutic needs or to develop life, social, or recreational skills.

GOVERNMENT SUPPORT OF CAREGIVERS

By the end of the 1990s, it was clear that, despite various supports in place for caregivers, Canada's system of community care with its overreliance on informal caregiving was unsustainable. A number of reports identified the need for a more organized, coordinated, and comprehensive caregiving strategy—one that would involve various levels of government, the private sector, families, and community groups, and that would meet the caregiving needs of a growing number of old people. From time to time, a federal government has considered a national, comprehensive system of care; however, economic, political, or other events have always interfered with those plans.

In 2006, the Special Senate Committee on Aging set out to review government programs and services for seniors. Three years later, the committee reached a dismal conclusion: "The current supports for caregivers are insufficient, and Canadians are forced to choose between keeping their jobs and caring for the ones they love" (Special Senate Committee on Aging, 2009, p. 8). The federal government responded to the committee's criticism by introducing the Family Caregiver Tax Credit to lighten the financial load of working individuals caring for an infirm, dependent relative. Canadians were quick to point out the shortcomings of the tax credit—specifically, the tax credit offers little financial compensation (less than a dollar a day), and, because it favours high-income-earning caregivers, the majority of unpaid caregivers are not eligible for the credit (Goar, 2011).

Clearly, unpaid caregivers play a valuable role in the lives of Canadians. In terms of economic value, informal caregivers provide the equivalent of $26 billion of eldercare services a year (Hollander, Liu, & Chappell, 2009). According to the Victorian Order of Nurses (2011, p. 6), "without the unpaid labour that [informal caregivers] provide, the health care system would be unable to cope with the increasing demands for care." Those demands show no sign of letting up for unpaid caregivers. In 2002, more than 19 percent (almost 2.3 million) of Canadians aged 45 or older spent unpaid time caring for a relative, friend, or neighbour with a chronic health problem or physical disability; by 2007, that percentage had reached almost 29 percent (3.8 million) (Research on Aging, Policies, and Practice, 2010). Forecasters expect that over the next thirty years, as the baby boomers age, the demand for professional and unpaid caregivers will double. In the future, a greater number of younger adults will be taking care of older relatives (Keefe, 2011).

DISCUSSION QUESTIONS

■ **Unpaid Caregivers**

1. Envision the type of care you would like to receive when you are elderly. What role, if any, would you want your family, friends, or other informal supports to play in your caregiving scheme?

2. Unpaid caregivers are at a high risk of health, economic, and other problems. How might unpaid caregivers minimize the risks of long-term caregiving?

3. Many experts believe that government has a role to play in the care of elderly or otherwise dependent adults. Do you agree with this? If so, what should government do to ensure the proper care of dependent adults?

SUMMARY

Introduction

Over the years, professional and non-professional helpers have come to share the responsibility for social welfare provision. Sometimes, the various types of helpers work together, as in the case of care teams.

1 Professional Helpers

Social work is the predominant occupation in the social welfare field. Social work practice focuses on the person-in-environment, takes a multilevel approach to practice, and bases practice on humanitarian ideals, a set of core values and beliefs, and an interdisciplinary knowledge base. Schools of social work offer training at the undergraduate, graduate, and post-graduate levels, and try to keep their curriculums relevant to changing human needs. Legislation and regulation define the social work profession. Social service workers perform basic social work duties and are subject to regulation in some provinces. There are both benefits and challenges to working in the social welfare field.

2 Agency Volunteers

About 12 percent of adults volunteer in social agencies, where they use their natural helping skills with clients and benefit the agencies in various ways. Mandatory volunteers are required to perform community service; there are pros and cons of this type of volunteering. Many governments recognize the economic value of volunteering and promote volunteerism in their jurisdictions. A declining number of volunteers, and the risk of volunteer burnout, are among the issues facing agencies that rely on volunteers.

3 Peer Helpers

Peer support can be given informally or through structured situations. Research confirms a link between peer support and many aspects of well-being. Self-help groups exist for a variety of needs or issues; members of these groups may connect in person or online and focus on problem solving, self-development, or consciousness raising. After completing a structured peer-counselling program, peer counsellors use basic counselling and natural helping skills to assist those with similar backgrounds or issues as they have; these counsellors are non-professional helpers who provide help on a volunteer basis.

4 Unpaid Caregivers

Government cutbacks, an aging population, and other factors are increasing the demand for unpaid caregivers. Most caregivers recognize the benefits of helping; a small percentage experience caregiver strain.

Caregivers receive help from family and friends, and may be eligible for tax breaks from government; many health and social welfare programs offer support services (such as respite services) to caregivers. Unpaid caregivers play a valuable economic and social role in Canadian society; this role will continue to grow as the baby boomers age.

KEY TERMS

For definitions of the key terms, consult the Glossary on page 453 at the end of the book.

professional helpers, p. 178

non-professional helpers, p. 178

care team, p. 179

social workers, p. 180

social work, p. 180

interdisciplinary knowledge base, p. 181

scope of practice, p. 181

person-in-environment, p. 181

multilevel approach to practice, p. 181

professions, p. 184

restricted practice activities, p. 185

social service workers, p. 186

paraprofessionals, p. 186

agency volunteers, p. 189

natural helping skills, p. 190

mandatory volunteers, p. 191

peer support, p. 194

self-help groups, p. 195

peer counsellors, p. 197

unpaid caregivers, p. 198

sandwich generation, p. 199

caregiver strain, p. 200

respite services, p. 202

CHAPTER

Planned Change in Micro, Mezzo, and Macro Systems

OBJECTIVES

Every social welfare initiative involves some degree of planned change. This chapter will

- introduce the planned change process

- explore the strategies used to promote change in individuals, families, and small groups (micro level of society)

- consider change strategies within organizations (mezzo level of society)

- examine three models of community change (macro level of society)

INTRODUCTION

> Change is inevitable in a progressive country. Change is constant. (Benjamin Disraeli, British Prime Minister, October 29, 1867)

In the social welfare field, it is common to find front-line workers, clients, policymakers, and others either responding to, or creating, change. Change can be either spontaneous or planned. *Spontaneous change* can occur quickly and is often unpredictable; such is the case when people face an unexpected death in the family or must flee from a natural disaster. It is also common for spontaneous change to take place slowly over a long period—for instance, when a community's economic base shifts over several decades. Unlike spontaneous change, *planned change* is predictable, controllable, and carried out with a conscious intent.

In a social welfare context, planned change applies a scientific method with a specific set of procedures to modify a situation, condition, or state of being so that people can meet their needs more effectively. For the **planned change process** to be successful, five elements must exist. First, there must be a *target of change*—that is, a person, an organization, a system, or some other entity that is slated for change. Second, planned change requires a *change agent*, who is a person or team that is responsible for carrying out the plan. A third element—the *method of change*—comprises specific interventions, strategies, or approaches, and a clear plan of action for creating the change. Fourth, planned change involves a *beneficiary of change*, an identifiable individual or group who is expected to benefit from the change effort. Many social welfare policies and programs identify the most vulnerable members of society—such as children living in poverty or seniors living alone—as the intended beneficiaries of change efforts.[1] Fifth, change agents must identify the setting in which the planned change effort will take place; this *context of change* may be found at the micro, mezzo, or macro levels of society.

- At the **micro level**, social welfare programs target individuals, families, and small groups to help them develop their *capacity* for self-sufficiency.

- At the **mezzo level**, organizations take steps to change themselves to increase their *capacity* for serving clients more effectively.

- At the **macro level**, change is directed at large segments of the population (such as communities) so they may have a greater *capacity* for meeting local needs.

The word **capacity** is emphasized above to highlight the importance of this concept in the planned change process. There is a general consensus in the social welfare field that well-being is largely a function of a system's capacity or capability to perform certain roles (such as the role of parent) or produce something worthwhile (such as a sufficient income). Thus, a primary aim of the planned change process is to help individuals, families, small groups, organizations, or communities build capacity by developing skills, building knowledge, making social connections, and creating or accessing opportunities and resources (Frank & Smith, 1999).

---

[1] It is common for the target and beneficiary of change to be the same. For example, job readiness programs for youth target young people by helping them develop job search skills; those youth are also likely to benefit in terms of future employment. Some programs target one group to benefit another. For instance, in family violence initiatives, the target may be men who abuse women; although these men may benefit from the program, the main beneficiary is women.

EXHIBIT 8.1

ELEMENTS OF PLANNED CHANGE

	MICRO LEVEL	MEZZO LEVEL	MACRO LEVEL
EXAMPLES OF TARGETS OF CHANGE	Small groups, individuals, families	Social agencies, places of worship, workplaces, businesses, schools	Social values and attitudes, political systems, community, economy, laws and legislation
EXAMPLES OF METHODS OF CHANGE	Individual counselling, family services, social group work	Staff training, team building, structural social work	Community development, social planning, social action
EXAMPLES OF AGENTS OF CHANGE	Social workers, social service workers	Management, workers and staff, steering committees	Grassroots organizations, social activists, community developers, social planners
EXAMPLES OF BENEFICIARIES OF CHANGE	Individuals, families	Service users, service providers, community	Community, general society

Source: Rosalie Chappell

Exhibit 8.1 illustrates the main elements of planned change at the three levels of society, and gives examples of possible targets and beneficiaries of change, change agents, and methods of change at each level.

1 CHANGE AT THE MICRO LEVEL: INDIVIDUALS, FAMILIES, AND SMALL GROUPS

Social welfare programs that focus on micro-level change aim to help individuals, families, or small groups obtain the basic necessities for proper human development, social functioning, and self-sufficiency. One advantage of such programs is that they target relatively small systems, which makes it more likely that identified needs will be met. A disadvantage of such a narrow focus is that even after a person's needs are met, the social or environmental conditions that created those needs may remain. For example, a food bank may provide visitors with food, but food banks can hardly be expected to change a society that allows its members to go hungry. In this case, the environment needs to include certain elements—such as new legislation that raises minimum wage or welfare rates—to enable people to purchase food. Despite their limitations, programs that attempt to change micro-level systems are necessary, and they are the main focus of many social agencies.

PROGRAMS FOR INDIVIDUALS

Most social agencies that offer client services have programs for individuals. Examples include mental health counselling, employment services, and settlement programs for recent immigrants. These programs and services are justified by the belief that communities suffer—as does society as a whole—when individual needs are not met. Social workers and other professional helpers also recognize that providing services on a one-on-one basis is an effective way to help people change their behaviour, learn new coping strategies, and either change or adapt to their environment (Fischer, 1978).

Each individual who seeks help from a social agency has a unique set of needs, issues, and concerns. That said, most requests for service by individuals relate to one or more of the following areas:

- *Interpersonal conflict* involves disagreement between two or more people who recognize that a problem exists. Examples include marital discord and parent–teen conflict.

- *Dissatisfaction in social relations* refers to a lack or an excess of something that a person perceives as being damaging to a relationship. Examples include loss of sexual desire in a marriage and spending too much time surfing the Internet.

- *Problems with formal organizations* relates to a discrepancy between the desires of an individual and the actions of an organization. Examples include getting arrested and getting fired.

- *Role performance difficulties* have to do with trouble fulfilling a particular social role. Examples include a parent's neglect of a child and a student failing courses.

- *Decision problems* reflect uncertainty around taking a particular course of action. Examples include deciding to leave a spouse and choosing a new career.

- *Reactive emotional distress* refers to challenges in dealing with difficult feelings. Examples include coping with grief and loss and learning to manage anger.

- *Inadequate resources* indicate a lack of a minimum standard of food, shelter, and other necessities. Examples include living in poverty and homelessness (Epstein, 1980).

Programs that are designed for individuals are rooted in the **social casework** approach, which evolved in the late nineteenth century as an outgrowth of the organized charity movement. That movement recognized the shortcomings of providing haphazard and inconsistent help to the poor and called for a more coordinated approach to helping. Originally, "friendly visitors" used the casework method; these individuals were volunteer social workers who visited the poor and provided friendship and support rather than financial relief. After the First World War, a growing body of research paved the way for more professional, systematic, and scientific approaches to change. It was no longer enough for social workers to simply mean well; they were required to have formal training in the social sciences, to draw from recognized bodies of practice models when helping others, and to conduct a thorough and systematic exploration of the individual's social environment by using formal interviewing skills and assessment procedures (Johnson, McClelland, & Austin, 2000).

Depending on their particular discipline, service providers in the social welfare field may draw from a variety of casework models to help individuals achieve their goals. The recent popularity of **brief therapies** is compatible with a rapidly changing political and economic environment that values efficiency and results. Brief therapies are solution-focused, which means that they try to help clients achieve their goals rather than address the underlying causes of their problems. Unlike psychoanalysis and other traditional therapies, brief therapies prefer client goals that are specific, measurable, and short term. Moreover, brief therapies encourage clients to build on their strengths rather than dwell on their personal deficits.

FAMILY SERVICES

The family is the basic unit of social organization and plays an indispensable role in the economic, physical, and emotional lives of individuals and society. Canadian governments recognize the autonomy and privacy of families; thus, with the exception of child protection laws (and adult protection laws in some provinces), governments are reluctant to intervene in the private realm of the family. Governments nevertheless provide a wide range of support to help families carry out their basic roles and functions.

Modern-day family needs and challenges are diverse and often complex. However, most families approach social agencies in the wake of one or more of the following events:

- an addition to the family, be it through marriage, remarriage, birth, adoption, fostering, an adult child moving back home, or an elderly relative being taken in

- the separation or loss of a family member through divorce, marital separation, death (including suicide), incarceration, institutionalization, or a child leaving home

- dysfunctional behaviour, such as addiction, delinquency, domestic violence, or child abuse

- a change in status or role, which can be the result of job loss, retirement, children growing up and leaving home, a mid-life crisis, or other transition (Janzen & Harris, 1997)

In the 1920s and 1930s, **family casework** emerged as a scientific approach to helping families. The "science" included a thorough assessment (or investigation) of a family's problems and a detailed plan for how the family would go about adjusting to their social environment (Scott, 2004). When providing services, early family caseworkers chose interventions that were likely "to reinforce and strengthen the endangered family, by drawing in the community's resources, not only in material relief, but in character and spiritual strength as well" (McGill University, 1931). Family services quickly gained acceptance as a form of support from which all families—not just those living in poverty—might benefit from time to time.

Today, a number of non-residential programs are available to support and strengthen families. These programs each take their own unique approach to helping and are provided by practitioners from various disciplines, including social work and psychology. Below are some of the types of family services offered in Canada:

- *Family support and resource programs* generally focus on helping families access resources and learn problem-solving skills so that members can fulfill their respective social roles, such as parent or provider. Examples include the Nobody's Perfect Parenting Program, Family Place, and Families in Transition.

- *Family therapy* aims to restructure family dynamics and communication patterns or to alter dysfunctional behaviour patterns. There are many models of family therapy, including structural, systemic, strategic, solution-focused, and narrative (see Exhibit 8.2).

- *Family preservation* provides an alternative to removing at-risk children from the home. Intensive interventions take place in the family home or another setting familiar to the family and aim to improve family functioning, especially in terms of caring for children. Facilitators tailor interventions to the needs of the family and may include anger management, communication skills training, and household management.

- *Family reunification* helps separated families reunite. There are various reunification programs, depending on the circumstances surrounding the separation. Some programs focus on helping a child or youth transition from foster care back into the family. Other programs help immigrants or refugees reunite with a spouse or children living overseas, or help legal offenders reunite with family following incarceration.

- *Family group conferencing* (also known as *family group decision making*) usually takes place in a child protection context. The process involves

EXHIBIT 8.2

© Bruce Ayres/Stone/Getty Images

Family therapy often includes all members of a family and provides a safe, supportive, and non-judgmental environment for individuals to address their issues.

the family, its closest supports, and a professional facilitator, who collaborate on developing a plan to meet the safety and well-being needs of the child.

Not all families seek services voluntarily. In the case of child protection matters, for example, families can be compelled to accept services or risk having their children legally apprehended and placed in alternative care.

SOCIAL GROUP WORK

Some social agencies provide group programs as a more affordable and less time-consuming alternative to individual services. In addition to these practical advantages, **social group work** can often help clients meet certain goals more effectively than one-on-one sessions. For example, the face-to-face interactions inherent in small groups can increase the emotional maturity of members. Some people find that relationships formed within the group can complement outside relationships. Group experience can also help members try out new relationship skills in a relatively safe and controlled environment, and receive feedback from fellow members before applying those skills in the real world (Coyle, 1959). Social groups typically have three to ten members who share common goals, needs, or lifestyles. These groups include the following:

- socialization groups (such as anger management groups for adolescent boys)
- peer support groups (such as parent groups that focus on parent–teen interactions)
- personal growth groups (such as marriage enrichment groups)
- educational skill-enhancement groups (such as life skills groups for people with severe disabilities)
- therapy groups (such as those focused on issues related to schizophrenia, manic depression, or other psychiatric disorders)

Group facilitators play an important role in the functioning and success of social groups. Facilitators must be able to attend to a wide range of emotional, physical, learning, and social needs that arise during group sessions. In terms of preparedness, facilitators must have expertise related to group processes and dynamics, and a solid understanding of the stages of group development. Effective facilitators will also have training in group facilitation, leadership, and dealing with client resistance.

It is common for clients to attend a group in conjunction with individual counselling: groups can offer opportunities to address interpersonal difficulties, while one-to-one counselling sessions may provide an appropriate venue for exploring personal issues.

THE ROLE OF SOCIAL WORKERS IN MICRO-LEVEL CHANGE

Social casework, family casework, and social group work are three approaches that social workers use to encourage **empowerment** in their clients—that is, to help people "identify and use their own problem solving skills in order to improve their life situations" (Canadian Association of Social Workers [CASW], 2008, p. 4). Choosing which approach to apply depends on a variety of factors, including the presenting need or problem, and the social worker's role in the planned change process. Although the approach taken may vary, social workers usually follow certain generic steps when working with micro systems:

1. Identify the need for change.
2. Establish a working relationship.
3. Clarify (assess) the client's needs or concerns.
4. Set goals for change, and identify indicators of success.
5. Develop an action plan, which specifies who will do what, when, where, and how.
6. Implement the plan.
7. Monitor the effectiveness of the plan, and modify strategies as necessary to achieve the goal.
8. Evaluate the intervention to determine its effectiveness.
9. Terminate the working relationship.

The planned change process does not always evolve in a linear fashion; as client needs or goals arise, steps may be repeated or deferred. Similarly, at some point in the helping process, it may seem reasonable to shift direction, which may mean modifying, or even reworking, the plan. In any case, the planned change process must be a cooperative team effort, with the change agent and client working together toward a goal and each fulfilling her or his role in the various stages of change.

DISCUSSION QUESTIONS

■ **Change at the Micro Level: Individuals, Families, and Small Groups**

1. By its very nature, the planned change process is manipulative because it systematically moves individuals, families, or groups toward a different way of being or behaving. Do you think that this type of manipulation is acceptable or not? Give reasons for your answer.

2. Identify the organizations in your community that offer services for individuals, families, or groups. Based on what you know about your community's needs, are there any gaps in these services? For example, if a large number of teen moms live in your area, are there adequate programs to meet their needs?

2 CHANGE AT THE MEZZO LEVEL: ORGANIZATIONS

Most social agencies run smoothly, and when problems or issues arise, they make the necessary adjustments and move on. Some situations may nevertheless threaten the stability or even survival of the organization; to deal with these situations, the organization may need to undergo a significant restructuring of one or more aspects of its operation. Major changes that occur within social agencies take place at the mezzo level of society and are generically referred to as **organizational change**.

IDENTIFYING THE NEED FOR CHANGE

Organizational change begins with someone recognizing the signs that something in the agency is not working as well as it could. Any stakeholder may call attention to an agency's "symptoms" and initiate a call for change. Clients are a rich source of insight into the strengths and weaknesses of an agency's services; social agencies often obtain this information through client satisfaction questionnaires. Stakeholders external to an agency may also notice when something in the organization needs improvement. Funders, for example, may detect inefficiencies in an agency's financial reporting system; similarly, professionals in the community may find that an agency's intake or referral system is not as streamlined as it should be. Management is likely to notice when the agency's resources are not used the way they were intended. An agency's staff tend to speak out on issues directly affecting clients, such as program facilities that are too noisy or do not offer adequate space. In any case, for social agencies to remain viable and relevant, they must be willing to seek out, listen to, and respond to stakeholders' feedback.

PREPARING FOR CHANGE

For organizational change to succeed, front-line workers, administrators, supervisors, board members, and other stakeholders must prepare for the changes to come. Preparing for change involves developing a vision of success, building knowledge about the agency, and committing to change.

Developing a Vision

In addition to identifying what needs to change, it is important to clarify the organization's vision of success—that is, what the result of change will look or feel like (Ontario Healthy Communities Coalition [OHCC], 2004). According to Genither Dujon (2010, p. 46), "Visions are the ultimate goal that people rally around and that inspire them to be successful. They represent the future; they reflect the highest standard of what is being strived for, and what is not yet accomplished." For some organizations, that vision may involve becoming more gender equitable or family friendly; other organizations may envision themselves as being more inclusive or culturally diverse (see Exhibit 8.3). Whatever vision the agency creates for itself will eventually need to be translated into concrete goals. Goals that are SMART—specific, measurable, attainable, realistic, and time-lined—are likely to provide clear markers of success.

Building Knowledge

An important step in the preparatory stage of change is building knowledge about the agency's own organization to clarify what is working (and should be kept) and what is not working (and needs to change). This process often involves an assessment of the strengths and weaknesses of an agency's major systems, including its strategic and operational plans, financial performance and costs, policies and procedures, human resource management, and programming (Rogers & Fong, 2000). A wide range of tools and strategies, such as program evaluations and internal audits, can give an agency this type of information. Many organizations find it helpful to apply a certain "lens" when scrutinizing their operations. For example, an agency that wants to become more inclusive might use an inclusion lens (discussed in Chapter 2).

Preparing for organizational change requires a sound knowledge of not only the workplace but also of the environment in which the organization

EXHIBIT 8.3

AGENCY PROFILE: ORGANIZATIONAL CHANGE AT THE CHILDREN'S AID SOCIETY OF HAMILTON

In 2001, the Children's Aid Society of Hamilton (CAS) embarked on an Anti-Racism Multicultural Organizational Change Initiative to respond more effectively to the ethnic, racial, religious, and cultural diversity of the Hamilton, Ontario, area. The initiative aimed to identify and remove barriers to CAS services and to enhance the quality of those services.

Before developing a change plan, the CAS surveyed more than seven hundred staff, volunteers, and other agency stakeholders, and conducted a community needs assessment. The findings from those surveys formed the basis of a change plan. Five areas of CAS were targeted for change: data collection and information systems; human resources; training; services and programs; and communications and community linkages. An action plan was developed for each area.

Over the next few years, the CAS achieved several goals. For example, the CAS

- provided cultural competency and anti-racism training to staff, managers, and foster parents
- shared the Implementation Plan and lessons learned about the change process with other organizations
- introduced outreach strategies to build bridges with community members and to educate the community about child protection legislation and CAS programs
- approved a Diversity and Inclusion Policy to guide board members, managers, supervisors, and agency staff in the creation of a workplace that is free from discrimination, prejudice, racism, and harassment

The CAS acknowledges that the anti-racism organizational change is a learning process that takes time, commitment, patience, dedication, and long-term vision. The process also requires ongoing support from agency staff and the community.

Source: Excerpted and adapted from the Children's Aid Society of Hamilton. (2008). *Anti-racism organizational change initiative* and (2011) Human Resources Policies and Procedures Manual: Diversity and inclusion policy, http://www.hamiltoncas.com/images/_PDFs/Diversity%20Policy.pdf.

functions. Before restructuring, an agency will want to know whether its changes are likely to reflect the community it serves. An agency can obtain this information through an environmental scan, community needs assessment, or other data collection tool.

Committing to Change

For organizational change to be successful, the individuals at all levels of the organization—such as the board, management, staff, and volunteers—must commit to the change. Successful change also requires change agents who can guide the organization and its members through the process. These change agents should have credibility in the organization and be able to make sound decisions, effectively problem solve, and appropriately plan the change process.

The change agents—who are often agency managers—may form a steering committee to plan and implement the change process. Ideally, a steering committee is representative of the entire agency and therefore includes a mix of staff, volunteers, and managers. The committee may also include other stakeholders, such as service users and local residents (OHCC, 2004).

One of the first tasks of the steering committee is to develop an action plan, which serves as a guide to the organizational change process. A good action plan reflects the vision of change and the change goals, and describes specific steps and activities of the change process. The plan also identifies who is responsible for which task, the expected completion date of each task, and what resources (such as money and equipment) are needed to successfully carry out the plan.

IMPLEMENTING CHANGE

Changes in the external environment often serve as catalysts to organizational change. Social agencies are particularly sensitive to funding cuts, changes in government policies, competition from other agencies, and demographic shifts in the community; to survive these types of changes, social agencies may need to make significant adjustments in their internal operations. Once an agency establishes the need for organizational change, the change process must occur simultaneously at two levels. At the *individual level*, staff, volunteers, and others in the agency learn new skills, attitudes, and behaviours; at the *systemic level*, various operational systems are improved. Each level of change requires help from the other: for individuals to change, the system must provide a supportive environment; for a system to change, the staff and others must be willing to embrace the agency's new policies, procedures, and practices (Brewster, Buckley, Cox, & Griep, 2002).

Individual Change

Training is a key strategy for facilitating individual change (see Exhibit 8.4). A variety of training kits exist in Canada to increase awareness, improve skills, or change behaviour in the workplace. For example, the Prince Edward Island Public Service Commission has developed a training series for public service managers and employees to increase their awareness of diversity in the

EXHIBIT 8.4

Staff training is a key component of organizational change

workplace. Similarly, the Manitoba Civil Service Commission uses a number of training modules to help government workers understand workplace discrimination and harassment, and to suggest what they can do to develop a healthy work environment.

All training packages vary, depending on their content, design, length of training, size of group, and other factors. However, an effective training program will have the following elements:

- a thorough *needs assessment*, to ensure that training is relevant to the needs, abilities, and expectations of the participants

- clear *goals and objectives*, to guide the training and to articulate what the training aims to achieve

- training *information*, which describes the rationale for training, the training schedule, the content and methods of training sessions, and the expectations of the trainers and management

- an *evaluation plan*, to measure the outcomes of training and to identify what is required to improve future training sessions (Brewster, Buckley, Cox, & Griep, 2002)

Training can be a useful way to help staff, volunteers, and others learn about, adjust to, and eventually accept workplace change; training nevertheless has its limitations. In addition to training, the change agents must provide a safe forum for stakeholders to ask questions about the proposed changes and address any concerns they might have. Change agents should also encourage workers to discuss their needs, wants, and expectations about the proposed changes, and to explore the options they have for adapting to the changes (Block, 1996).

When an organization decides it needs to undergo major change, it is normal for stakeholders to support the proposed changes on one level and yet feel some resistance as well. Fuchs (2004) writes: "Change, by nature, intrudes on people's 'comfort zones,' so many equate it with pain, whether or not they think it will result in improvements." To prevent or reduce resistance, staff must be encouraged to engage in, take ownership for, and shape the change efforts; for example, staff might be asked to design a segment of the change plan or lead a training session.

Systemic Change

Normally, **systemic change** involves the modification of an agency's policies, procedures, and practices. This type of change occurred during the 1990s and early 2000s when voluntary social agencies underwent significant changes in response to new funding arrangements with governments (Chapter 5 reviews these changes). In her study of more than 100 voluntary and nonprofit organizations across Canada, Katherine Scott (2003b) found that two-thirds of respondents changed their programs and services, modified or adopted new methods of program evaluation and accountability reporting, or changed their organizational structure and processes to pursue new funding opportunities. Funding shortages led to major restructuring, especially at the program level. Some agencies had to narrow their eligibility criteria, or shift their priorities, to serve only those who needed help the most (Reed & Howe, 2000). To successfully complete these types of structural changes, an agency needs to have a clear vision of success, a good grasp of what needs to change, and a staff that is committed, cooperative, and engaged in the change process.

EVALUATING CHANGE

An agency that invests in major organizational change will want to know if its efforts have paid off—in other words, did the agency achieve its goals and vision of success? An agency may apply two types of evaluation to determine the effectiveness of change: (1) **formative evaluation** usually occurs during the change process and is mainly concerned with whether the action plan is working and what, if anything, in the plan needs modification; and (2) **summative evaluation** measures the end results of the change effort.

A formative evaluation involves monitoring the change process and introducing tests at certain points. Suppose, for example, an agency wants to improve its reporting procedures, and the staff takes a series of training sessions to learn the new system. In this case, the trainer might give staff a questionnaire immediately after each training session to assess how well they understand the new reporting procedures. Then, a few months after training, the trainer might conduct a follow-up assessment to determine whether staffers are applying the new procedures correctly. Finally, staff might be required to attend an annual refresher course to reinforce the new reporting system (Canadian International Development Agency, 2006).

Summative evaluation occurs at the end of an initiative and measures whether the organization has reached its goals. Some organizations find it useful to assess the results of change by applying qualitative and quantitative measures. **Qualitative measures**, such as job satisfaction questionnaires, provide information about individuals' subjective experiences with the changes. **Quantitative measures** focus on aspects that researchers can count or quantify in some way, such as staff turnover rates or service utilization statistics (OHCC, 2004). Research designs that include both qualitative and quantitative measures tend to provide a more comprehensive picture of the results.

A SOCIAL WORK APPROACH TO ORGANIZATIONAL CHANGE

While many casework, group work, or other traditional social work approaches focus on changing the client, a number of approaches target social agencies to try to make them more responsive to people's needs. **Structural social work** is one among many of the **anti-oppressive approaches** taken by social workers to change the organizations that employ them. A proponent of the structural model, Robert Mullaly (1997) contends that to change a social agency from within, social workers have to radicalize and democratize the agency. *Radicalizing* an agency involves confronting agency policies and procedures that negatively affect clients and working to ensure that clients can access the full range of available services. Workers in a homeless shelter, for example, might speak up against a discriminatory policy that requires the segregation of residents with HIV. *Democratizing* the agency involves taking steps to make the organization less bureaucratic and hierarchical, and more democratic and inclusive. This process may involve inviting former clients to serve on the agency's board of directors and share in the organization's decision-making process. Democratizing might also mean replacing boss–subordinate relationships with ones that are more equitable; in this case, staff might *consult with* instead of *report to* supervisors.

DISCUSSION QUESTIONS

■ **Change at the Mezzo Level: Organizations**

1. What are some of the environmental forces (such as politics or economics) that might affect a social agency's ability to function properly, and ultimately create a need for organizational change?

2. The section on training gives an example of how staff might be engaged in the organization's change process. How else might staff be engaged in, shape, or take ownership of the change process?

3 CHANGE AT THE MACRO LEVEL: COMMUNITIES

While social welfare programs and agencies do what they can to help people meet individual needs, their success often depends upon the functioning of systems at the macro level of society. Macro systems may be understood as the largest structures and systems of society, and include communities, a society's norms and values, a culture's traditions and customs, government policies and practices, and economic processes. These structures tend to be complex, well established, and supported by the status quo. Even so, these structures are not immune to change: Canada has a rich history of challenging and changing structures to make them more responsive to people's needs and expectations.

THE NATURE OF COMMUNITY CHANGE

Perhaps more than any other macro system, communities are prime candidates for change. Rather than focusing on changing individuals, community change seeks to modify neighbourhoods, social or economic conditions, institutions, or another aspect of a community that threatens well-being. One trend in Canadian communities is to be more *inclusive*, that is, to value diversity and the engagement of all citizens, and to eliminate potential physical, attitudinal, cultural, and other barriers to resources, services, and opportunities. A related trend focuses on creating *age-friendly* urban communities that are supportive and accessible to older people.

The ability of a community to not only survive but also thrive depends largely on its capacity to prepare for and respond to social and economic trends. Policymakers expect that, over the next decade, the following trends will force many Canadian communities to change in significant ways:

- The *knowledge-based and global economy* will continue to dictate the types of jobs and industries that a community must offer to remain viable, and pressure communities to improve access to postsecondary education, especially for at-risk populations, such as older workers, high-school dropouts, recent immigrants, and Aboriginal youth.

- As governments continue to practice *fiscal restraint*, communities will need to address social and economic problems with fewer resources.

- *Demographic changes*—such as an aging population and a shrinking workforce—will require community health, social welfare, and other organizations to care for a growing number of old people.

- Canada's growing ethnocultural, religious, and linguistic *diversity* will motivate communities to become more inclusive, equitable, and cohesive.

- A widening *income gap* between the rich and the poor will mean more people living in poverty and a greater urgency to address the negative consequences of persistent poverty.

- With increasing *urbanization*, rural communities will struggle to remain viable with fewer human and other resources. At the same time, rapidly growing urban centres will face several challenges, including a rise in crime, and the concentration of social problems in disadvantaged neighbourhoods (Canada Co-operatives Secretariat, 2010).

MODELS OF COMMUNITY CHANGE

A number of models are available to guide change at the community level. Many of those models are based on the principles and practices of three classic approaches to community change: community (or locality) development,

EXHIBIT 8.5

THREE APPROACHES TO COMMUNITY CHANGE

CHARACTERISTIC	COMMUNITY DEVELOPMENT MODEL	SOCIAL PLANNING MODEL	SOCIAL ACTION MODEL
GOALS	Self-help; improve community living; emphasis on process goals	Using problem-solving approach to resolve community problems; emphasis on task goals	Shifting of power relationships and resources to an oppressed group; basic institutional change; emphasis on task and process goals
ASSUMPTIONS CONCERNING COMMUNITY	Everyone wants community living to improve and is willing to contribute to the improvement.	Social problems in the community can be resolved through the efforts of planning experts.	The community has a power structure and one or more oppressed groups; social injustice is a major problem.
BASIC CHANGE STRATEGY	Broad cross-section of people involved in identifying and solving their problems	Experts using fact gathering and the problem-solving approach	Members of oppressed groups organizing to take action against the power structure, which is the enemy
CHARACTERISTIC CHANGE TACTICS AND TECHNIQUES	Consensus: communication among community groups and interests; group discussion	Consensus or conflict	Conflict or contest: confrontation, direct action, negotiation
PRACTITIONER ROLES	Catalyst; facilitator; coordinator; teacher of problem-solving skills	Expert planner; fact gatherer; analyst; program developer and implementer	Activist; advocate; agitator; broker; negotiator; partisan
VIEWS ABOUT POWER STRUCTURE	Members of power structure as collaborators in a common venture	Power structure as employers and sponsors	Power structure as external target of action, oppressors to be coerced or overturned
VIEWS ABOUT CLIENT POPULATION	Citizens	Consumers	Victims
VIEWS ABOUT CLIENT ROLE	Participants in a problem-solving process	Consumers or recipients	Employers, constituents

Source: From Zastrow, *Introduction to Social Work and Social Welfare*, 10E. © 2010 Wadsworth, a part of Cengage Learning, Inc. Reproduced by permission. www.cengage.com/permissions.

social planning, and social action. Exhibit 8.5 compares these three models, while the following section introduces some of the goals, assumptions, strategies, and other characteristics of each model.

In the following discussion, *community* may be a geographic location—such as a town, city, neighbourhood, or region—or a group of people who support and identify with each other.

Community Development

Community development involves planned change efforts that have a specific goal, focuses on improving community well-being, and calls on individuals and groups to work together to address local concerns.

Approaches to Change

While there is no typical strategy to community change, most projects are likely to target economic functions (such as small business and the workforce) in conjunction with social functions (such as safety and social supports). In Canada, various approaches come under the broad umbrella of community development, including the following:

- *Community economic development* aims to stimulate local business and employment while enhancing a community's social and environmental conditions.

- *Community capacity building* concentrates on the development of local skills, resources, and abilities to prepare a community for future challenges and opportunities.

- *Neighbourhood action* attempts to revitalize troubled neighbourhoods and create more positive, safer, and healthier places to live.

During the expansionary years of Canada's welfare state, governments took over many community development responsibilities and, with a bureaucratic top-down approach, decided what communities needed and how they would meet those needs. As voluntary sector agencies became more prominent, communities began to favour a bottom-up or **grassroots approach**, in which residents identify and articulate their goals, design their own methods of change, and pool their resources in the problem-solving process (Halseth & Booth, 1998).

Today, a more cooperative working relationship exists between government and communities, leading to the creation of such projects as Canada's Rural Partnership and Vibrant Communities. As with all community development initiatives, these projects aim not to challenge or reform established social structures but to work with existing structures to improve community conditions. Much of the focus of that work is on "building from within"—that is, finding ways for communities to strengthen their local assets, be they workforce skills, businesses, or social services (Bradford, 2003).

Comprehensive Community Initiatives

As a relatively new form of community development, **comprehensive community initiatives** (CCIs) reject the idea that individual, isolated, or unrelated programs can solve such complex social problems as poverty, homelessness, and crime. Instead, CCIs assume that all problems affecting neighbourhoods are interrelated and therefore require coordinated and integrated approaches that simultaneously target the social, economic, educational, health, and environmental aspects of a community. While every CCI is unique in terms of size, purpose, and process, they are all

- comprehensive (focus on multiple issues and relationships between organizations and other systems)
- multisectoral (encourage the participation of a wide range of individuals, organizations, and service sectors)
- community based (build on the interests and needs of local residents)
- asset based (identify and build on the community's strengths and resources)
- long term (recognize that resolving complex social issues can take a long time)
- collaborative (develop effective multisectoral and multi-partner working relationships)
- adaptive (recognize and respond to changing circumstances and opportunities)
- innovative (find new and effective methods of providing services, taking action, and working together)
- analytical and intentional (develop a "theory of change" that explains how the initiative is expected to solve the target of change) (Gardner, 2011)

CCIs may address a variety of social problems; however, in Canada, CCIs are usually associated with efforts to reduce poverty (see Exhibit 8.6 for Calgary's CCI to reduce poverty in that city).

EXHIBIT 8.6

VIBRANT COMMUNITIES: CALGARY'S VISION OF CHANGE

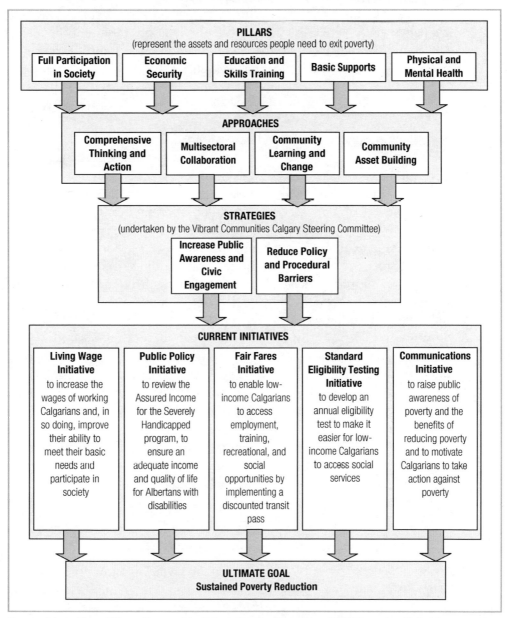

PILLARS
(represent the assets and resources people need to exit poverty)

Full Participation in Society	Economic Security	Education and Skills Training	Basic Supports	Physical and Mental Health

APPROACHES

Comprehensive Thinking and Action	Multisectoral Collaboration	Community Learning and Change	Community Asset Building

STRATEGIES
(undertaken by the Vibrant Communities Calgary Steering Committee)

Increase Public Awareness and Civic Engagement	Reduce Policy and Procedural Barriers

CURRENT INITIATIVES

Living Wage Initiative	**Public Policy Initiative**	**Fair Fares Initiative**	**Standard Eligibility Testing Initiative**	**Communications Initiative**
to increase the wages of working Calgarians and, in so doing, improve their ability to meet their basic needs and participate in society	to review the Assured Income for the Severely Handicapped program, to ensure an adequate income and quality of life for Albertans with disabilities	to enable low-income Calgarians to access employment, training, recreational, and social opportunities by implementing a discounted transit pass	to develop an annual eligibility test to make it easier for low-income Calgarians to access social services	to raise public awareness of poverty and the benefits of reducing poverty and to motivate Calgarians to take action against poverty

ULTIMATE GOAL
Sustained Poverty Reduction

Source: Adapted from Vibrant Communities Calgary Steering Committee. (2004, December 1). *Igniting community action through collaboration, education, and mutual problem-solving* (p. 45, Appendix B). Retrieved from http://tamarackcommunity.ca/downloads/vc/Cal_Community_Plan_dec04.pdf.

Social Planning

Social planning tackles community change through a rational, formal, and technical problem-solving procedure led by professional social planners. Although social planners often seek the opinions of community members about proposed initiatives, they depend heavily on facts, statistics, and other objective data to guide community change efforts.

Approach and Evolution

Social planning councils emerged across Canada during the 1950s, 1960s, and early 1970s in response to rapid economic growth and the expansion of social programs. These councils performed a variety of community planning activities, including identifying social issues, needs, and resources, and helping organizations set up new services. Today, an informal network of nonprofit social planning organizations exists in Canada, including such groups as the Social Planning Coalition of the Northwest Territories. In some communities, local government takes responsibility for social planning. The City of Toronto, for example, supports social planning initiatives through its Community Partnership and Investment Program, the Community Safety Secretariat, and Youth Employment programs.

While social planning activities may vary across communities, they all focus on enhancing community well-being. A key objective of social planning initiatives is to improve the general functioning of residents by meeting a comprehensive set of needs through the provision of goods and services. This is the case in British Columbia, where the City of Dawson Creek's Social Plan outlines a strategy for improving a wide range of services related to children and youth, community development, crime and public safety, education and skills training, food security, housing and homelessness, and health and addiction (Social Planning and Research Council of BC, 2008).

A Step-by-Step Process

The social planning process often begins with a formal community assessment strategy to identify local social trends, the community's capacity to change (its strengths), as well as the community's needs, issues, gaps in services, or risks (its weaknesses). Social planners consider the alternatives for meeting the identified needs and then set objectives for new programs, services, or facilities. At this stage, it is common for social planners to educate the community on issues that affect specific groups or the community's quality of life; planners may also take a political role by, for example, submitting research-based proposals for change to government policymakers or advocating for services on behalf of disadvantaged members of the community. The next steps involve developing an action plan and implementing that plan. This stage may involve helping local residents and organizations to take action through community-based coalitions, networks, or partnerships. Evaluating the outcomes of the plan—that is, how effective the plan was in meeting its objectives—is the final stage of the process.

The Edmonton Social Planning Council (ESPC) used a version of this systematic process to address the city's affordable-housing shortage. The Council held two public forums to assess the impact of rent increases and low vacancy rates in Edmonton. After reviewing the information generated from the forums, the Council produced a final report that outlined their recommendations. The Alberta government responded to the report by targeting funds to help renters find or keep their housing. In 2008, the ESPC launched a survey (evaluation) to find out if the housing situation had indeed changed for renters. The survey results showed that many renters continued to have difficulties finding affordable accommodation; this information prompted another series of actions to remedy the problem.

Social Action

Social action assumes that the achievement of social justice for disadvantaged or oppressed groups is only possible through large-scale organization and activism. Social activists may choose to either join forces with disadvantaged groups or act on their behalf in pursuit of a cause. In either case, social action is a collective effort that attempts to convince those holding power (such as politicians) to reform unjust policies, practices, or systems.

Approaches and Strategies

Like community development and social planning, social action often involves the use of *campaign strategies*—such as lobbying, submitting signed petitions, and collective bargaining—to influence the decisions of government officials or other powerful organization. However, unlike community development, social action does not require a consensus for change within the community; indeed, social action may take place even when a majority of the community denies that a problem exists. Social action also tends to emphasize *contest and confrontation strategies*—such as demonstrations, protest marches, and sit-ins—to promote a cause, gain public support, and influence change. In contrast, community development and social planning both emphasize *collaborative strategies*—such as group problem solving, cooperative working relationships and partnerships—to reach community change goals.

Many contemporary social activists rely on the collective efforts of citizens to achieve their goals. This grassroots approach is obvious when members of a community come together because of a common concern and go on to establish an organization or a group committed to addressing that concern. The members of these organizations often advocate on their own or another group's behalf. An example of such an organization is Canada Without Poverty (CWP). Founded in 1971 under the name of National Anti-Poverty Organization, CWP works to raise awareness of poverty in Canada and to influence government policies related to the prevention and elimination of poverty (Canada Without Poverty, 2012b).

Catalysts and Social Movements

A specific issue often serves as a catalyst for social action. Labour-related problems, for example, have fuelled many labour strikes in Canada, including the famous Winnipeg General Strike of 1919, when almost 30 000 workers left their jobs in protest of poor wages and deplorable work conditions. Aboriginal peoples' issues regularly spark **political protests**; some of these protests have occurred on the annual Aboriginal Day of Action, when Aboriginal peoples have used various strategies to call attention to poverty and other disadvantages facing Indigenous peoples. Seniors' issues increasingly serve as catalysts for change; for instance, in 1997, seniors came together to protest the federal government's proposed changes to prescription drug legislation (see Exhibit 8.7). Social action has become a legitimate means for citizens to call attention to circumstances that threaten their well-being and to influence the decisions of those in power.

In some cases, a series of protests related to a common theme can spark a social movement. During the late nineteenth and early twentieth centuries, a general increase in social consciousness and collective responsibility for fellow human beings gave rise to a wave of social movements, including the labour reform, women's rights, and child welfare movements. Later, from the early 1960s on, Canada and other Western countries witnessed a flurry of social movements related to the environment, women's and gay rights, and other issues, that significantly challenged the status quo. More recently, a string of protests and flash mobs under the Idle No More banner have quickly exploded into a nationwide social movement aimed at educating the public on

EXHIBIT 8.7

About 150 senior citizens took social action in 1997 when they marched on Parliament Hill to protest against the Federal Drug Patent Bill—a piece of legislation that would substantially drive up the cost of prescription drugs. The federal government was pressured to amend the bill.

Aboriginal peoples' issues and revitalizing Indigenous peoples through awareness and empowerment (Meekis, 2013).

One of the most publicized international social movements has been the Occupy movement. Initiated in 2011 by the Canadian activist group Adbusters, the Occupy Movement caught on around the globe, motivating thousands of people to voice their anger at corporate greed, government cutbacks, and social, political, and income inequality. Such social movements as this one not only have the potential to shape social values and attitudes toward social problems but can also pressure governments to bow to public demands.

COMMUNITY PRACTICE

By virtue of their training and knowledge base, social workers can make effective community organizers (CASW, 1998). For example, they tend to have good listening and communication skills, understand how systems work, and be comfortable working with both individuals and groups. Social workers who engage in **community practice** do so with the "belief that people acting together have a great capacity to improve their own circumstances, as they have first-hand knowledge of the situation and what needs to happen to change things for the better" (Hall, 2007). The process of community practice involves organizing citizens around certain issues or unmet needs, developing strategies for change, and providing relevant information to community groups to assist the change process.

Depending on the type of community organization they work with, social workers fulfill various roles:

- *Community development.* As *brokers*, social workers help individuals and groups connect with needed programs and services in the community. Since a focus of community development is problem solving, social workers may also act as *enablers* by teaching community members effective problem-solving skills.

- *Social planning.* In a social planning capacity, social workers may develop action plans, collect and analyze data on local issues and concerns, and share research findings with social planning councils, government departments, and others. Social workers may also be instrumental in connecting with, generating interest among, and motivating local groups to participate in the planning process.

- *Social action.* Until the professionalization of social work in the early twentieth century, all social workers were social activists: "Whether through visits to the poor and homeless, demonstrations in the streets, or surveys to expose shocking conditions, the first social workers were crusaders whose full-time occupation was social action" (Thursz, 1977, p. 1274). Today's social workers may assume the role of *activist* who seeks change in social or political power structures to improve conditions for a disadvantaged group. Social workers may also act as *advocates*, speaking or acting on behalf of clients to achieve certain goals, or as *initiators*, calling attention to problems or injustices that need correction (Zastrow, 2010).

DISCUSSION QUESTIONS

■ **Change at the Macro Level: Communities**

1. Have you ever lived in a community in which community development, social planning, or social action took place? If so, describe the sequence of events, the types of actions people took to create change, and the outcomes of that change process. In your opinion, what have been the positive and negative impacts of the change?

2. Which of the three community change approaches (or strategies from one or more approaches) might be most effective for reducing poverty? Give reasons for your answer.

SUMMARY

Introduction

Planned change refers to a scientific method of changing conditions so that people can meet their needs. Central to the planned change process is a target of change, one or more change agents, a method of change, and an identified beneficiary of change. In terms of context, planned change can take place at the micro, mezzo, or macro levels of society. Capacity building is a key element of planned change.

1 ### Change at the Micro Level: Individuals, Families, and Small Groups

Micro-level change focuses on helping individuals, families, or small groups. Social casework models (such as brief therapies) aim to help individuals. Family services are available to support and strengthen the family unit. In some instances, social group work may be more effective than one-on-one sessions. A social worker's choice of approach to empowerment depends on such factors as the presenting need or problem.

2 ### Change at the Mezzo Level: Organizations

Organizational change begins with recognizing the need for change. To change, agencies must have a vision of success, prepare for change by learning about the organization and the community, and be committed to change. Change agents, and a steering committee, can guide the organization through the change process. The actual change occurs at an individual level and a systemic level. Formative and summative evaluations determine the effectiveness of change. Structural social work is an approach taken by social workers to improve the organizations that employ them.

3 **Change at the Macro Level: Communities**

Many Canadian communities are facing conditions that will force significant change. Most community change reflects the principles and practices of community development, social planning, and social action. Community development focuses on working with existing structures to improve community conditions; social planning seeks community change through a rational, formal procedure led by professional planners; and social action aims to shift the power structures in society that oppress certain groups. Community practice is a field of social work that involves organizing citizens, developing strategies for change, and providing information to community groups.

KEY TERMS

For definitions of the key terms, consult the Glossary on page 453 at the end of the book.

planned change process, p. 207
micro level (of society), p. 207
mezzo level (of society), p. 207
macro level (of society), p. 207
capacity, p. 207
social casework, p. 210
brief therapies, p. 210
family casework, p. 211
social group work, p. 213

empowerment, p. 214
organizational change, p. 215
systemic change, p. 220
formative evaluation, p. 221
summative evaluation, p. 221
qualitative measures, p. 221
quantitative measures, p. 221
structural social work, p. 221

anti-oppressive approaches, p. 221
community development, p. 225
grassroots approach, p. 225
comprehensive community initiatives, p. 226
social planning, p. 228
social action, p. 229
political protests, p. 230
community practice, p. 232

3 PART

MEETING THE NEEDS OF CANADIANS THROUGH PROGRAMS AND SERVICES

9

The Social Welfare of Canadians Living in Poverty

OBJECTIVES

Poverty, unemployment, and their associated challenges inhibit the well-being of individuals, families, and society as a whole. This chapter will

- introduce the concept of poverty

- explore definitions and measurements of poverty, and identify at-risk groups

- discuss the effects of poverty

- examine the programmatic and systemic approaches to poverty

- summarize a social work approach to working with low-income and marginalized groups

INTRODUCTION

Poverty is to be without sufficient money, but it is also to have little hope for better things. It is a feeling that one is unable to control one's destiny, that one is powerless in a society that respects power. The poor have very limited access to means of making known their situation and their needs. To be poor is to feel apathy, alienation from society, entrapment, hopelessness and to believe that whatever you do will not turn out successfully. (Royal Commission on the Status of Women of Canada, 1977, p. 311)

Canada is often praised for its healthy and stable economy, and for having one of the world's highest per capita levels of economic productivity. Despite this, the nation's wealth fails to trickle down to all Canadians, many of whom can barely make ends meet. Poverty affects more than just unemployed people; indeed, a growing number of Canadians work full time yet do not earn enough to support themselves and their families. A disturbingly high number of individuals—many of them with children—visit food banks daily and rely on the good will of charities for clothing, shelter, and other basics.

Canadian governments spend billions of dollars annually to enhance the financial security of citizens. Those funds reach individuals and families through various means, including tax credits, cash transfers (including social assistance and Old Age Security), and government-subsidized social services, such as child care. Although these programs provide some level of economic security, many Canadians continue to fall into poverty, while others already living in poverty see little hope of ever climbing out. A troubling and persistent aspect of poverty is the rate of child poverty: while Canada has always had both the financial means and the social knowledge to eradicate child poverty, it has failed to do so.[1] On a positive note, many provincial and territorial governments are beginning to recognize poverty reduction as a necessary condition for social stability and economic well-being. By 2012, all but two regional governments had made a long-term commitment to reducing poverty in their jurisdictions.

It is difficult to give due consideration to the complexities of poverty in one chapter. Thus, this chapter serves as a primer on basic poverty-related concepts, issues, and interventions in Canada.

1 POVERTY IN CANADA

To prevent or reduce poverty, we must first understand what poverty is (or what it looks like) and how it affects people. This section looks at definitions of poverty, measurements of low income and other dimensions of poverty, and the populations at risk of poverty in Canada.

---

[1] In 2012, UNICEF ranked Canada as having the twenty-fourth-worst child poverty rate among thirty-five industrialized countries (UNICEF, 2012).

WHAT IS POVERTY?

Poverty has no single official or universally accepted definition; every country has a different view of poverty and, even within the same country, people's views of poverty change over time. In Canada, various definitions exist. Most definitions relate poverty to a certain level of income or financial security; in this case, poverty may be framed as "a subsistence standard of living with an income that is not sufficient to purchase the bare necessities" (Michaud, Cotton, & Bishop, 2004, p. 6).

Over time, poverty definitions have become multidimensional, relating poverty not only to a certain level of income but also to the experience of being poor or deprived. For example, many people equate poverty with **social exclusion**—that is, poverty exists when a person is unable, or is denied the opportunity, to fully engage in the economic, cultural, social, and political realms of society, or meet society's expectations in terms of roles, relationships, and participation (Townsend, 1993). Other definitions emphasize the powerlessness of being poor, being voiceless and dependent on others for resources. This chapter uses the term *poverty* in reference to low income and its associated conditions and challenges.

MEASUREMENTS OF POVERTY

Economists, social workers, and other professional groups are likely to define poverty in statistical terms. To calculate which Canadians are living in low income, the Government of Canada uses three statistical measuring devices: the low-income measure (LIM), the market basket measure (MBM), and the low-income cut-offs (LICOs). Both the LIM and LICOs provide a *relative* measure of poverty by estimating which Canadians are worse off than others. In contrast, the MBM defines poverty in *absolute* terms by estimating whether a person's income is adequate to purchase basic goods and services (Collin, 2008). International studies have shown that using a variety of low-income measures, and assessing both the relative and absolute levels of poverty, can provide a comprehensive snapshot of poverty. Below is a brief description of the three measuring devices; note that the term *family* refers to one or more persons.

Low-Income Measure (LIM)

The LIM estimates the proportion of a selected geographic area that has substantially less income than that in the rest of the area. Low-income families are defined as those whose incomes are less than half the median family income in the area (income is adjusted according to family size). The LIM is often used at the international level to compare family income between countries.

Market Basket Measure (MBM)

The MBM estimates the costs of necessities, such as food, shelter, and transportation, and then compares those costs with a family's disposable income. Low-income households are those with a lower level of income than what is needed to purchase a specified basket of goods and services. Often used in conjunction with the LICOs and the LIM, the MBM is useful for identifying regional variations in the cost of living and people's purchasing power across Canada.

Low-Income Cut-Offs (LICOs)

The **LICOs** identify a minimum level of income required for a family to purchase food, shelter, and other basics; that minimum varies with the family's size and place of residence. Exhibit 9.1 illustrates the 35 low-income cut-offs or thresholds in Canada. According to the LICOs, a family that spends 20 percent or more of its after-tax income than the average household on basic goods and services is living with low income. The government adjusts the LICOs periodically to reflect changes in the economy, the types of things people consider basic necessities, and the amount of money required to enjoy a reasonable standard of living in Canada.

The LICOs have become the most widely used measures of poverty in Canada. Although the Government of Canada originally designed the LICOs to measure *low income*, as opposed to *poverty*, many analysts refer to them collectively as Canada's "poverty line."

Other Dimensions of Poverty

One of the functions of the LICOs is to report on the percentage of Canadians living with low income, otherwise known as the **poverty rate**. According to the after-tax LICOs, 9.4 percent of Canadians (or three million people) lived in poverty in 2010; this is a dramatic decrease since 1996, when the rate reached more than 15 percent (Human Resources and Skills Development Canada [HRSDC], 2012c).

While poverty rates are useful for reporting on how many Canadians live in low-income, they offer little information on how poor people are, or how long

EXHIBIT 9.1

LOW-INCOME CUT-OFFS (LICOS), AFTER TAX, 2011

FAMILY SIZE	RURAL (FARM AND NON-FARM)	POPULATION OF COMMUNITY			
		UNDER 30 000	30 000 TO 99 999	100 000 TO 499 999	500 000 OR MORE
1	12 629	14 454	16 124	16 328	19 307
2	15 371	17 592	19 625	19 872	23 498
3	19 141	21 905	24 437	24 745	29 260
4	23 879	27 329	30 487	30 871	36 504
5	27 192	31 120	34 717	35 154	41 567
6	30 156	34 513	38 502	38 986	46 099
7	33 121	37 906	42 286	42 819	50 631

Source: Adapted from Statistics Canada. (2012, November). *Low income lines, 2010–2011* (table 1). Retrieved from http://www.statcan.gc.ca/pub/75f0002m/2012002/tbl/tbl01-eng.htm.

they remain poor. Thus, the LICOs are also used to measure the depth and persistence of poverty.

- The **depth of poverty** refers to how far a person's income dips below the poverty line; for instance, in 2010, low-income families needed, on average, to earn an additional 50 percent of their income to rise above the poverty line (Statistics Canada, 2012b).

- The **persistence of poverty** refers to the percentage of people living in low-income every year over a six-year period. From 2005 to 2010, more than 17 percent of low-income Canadians were poor for at least one year; 4 percent lived in poverty for at least four of the six years; and 1.5 percent were poor for most of the six-year period (HRSDC, 2012d).

POPULATIONS AT RISK OF POVERTY

Anyone can fall into poverty; however, certain people are more likely to experience poverty than others are. In 2010, the groups experiencing the highest rates of poverty in Canada were

- single adults ages 45 to 65 (one in three lived in poverty)
- people with disabilities (more than one in five lived in poverty)

- lone-parent families (one in five lived in poverty, the majority of which were headed by females)

- immigrants who arrived in Canada after 2000 (one in six lived in poverty)

- Aboriginal people living off-reserve (one in six lived in poverty) (HRSDC, 2012c)

Risk Factors

Risk factors of poverty are conditions or circumstances that make some social groups more susceptible to poverty than others. Geographic location is one risk factor: a person living in British Columbia, for instance, has a greater chance of living in poverty than someone living in Alberta. Age makes a difference: younger people are more likely than senior citizens to live in poverty. Similarly, members of visible minorities are at a higher risk of poverty than Caucasians.

Women

The term **feminization of poverty** calls attention to the fact that women are more likely than men to be poor, regardless of the woman's age, family status, ethnicity, or other characteristic (Mayo, 2010). Those at a particularly high risk of poverty include women who are Aboriginal, have a disability, belong to a visible minority group, or are single parents or unattached seniors. Statistics show that the poverty rates among women are gradually falling: in 1976, 15 percent of Canadian women were poor, but by 2008, that rate had dropped to 10 percent. Poverty rates among lone mothers fell from 54 percent in 1976 to 21 percent in 2009 (Williams, 2010).

While the falling poverty rates among women are encouraging, a number of public policies and social norms continue to put women at a distinct disadvantage in society. For example, women provide the bulk of housework, child care, and, in many cases, eldercare; while those activities are valuable to the well-being of families and the functioning of society they largely go unpaid. Women are also at a disadvantage in the workplace. Among women who work, one in four holds a temporary or part-time position (Ferrao, 2010). Many of these workers do not qualify for Employment Insurance or employer benefits, such as medical or dental insurance. Most employed women (more than 60 percent) earn minimum wage, and fewer than half contribute to an employer pension plan (Statistics Canada, 2010b; Williams, 2010). Although a postsecondary education can open the door to better-paying jobs, women with a university education who work full time earn 30 percent less than their male coworkers doing similar work (Statistics Canada, 2010c).

Seniors

Thanks to improvements in the Old Age Security pension and other government benefits, seniors have seen a dramatic decrease in their rate of poverty over the years. According to the LICOs, the poverty rate for seniors has steadily fallen in the last four decades (see Exhibit 9.2). However, when using the LIM, there appears to be a significant increase in senior's poverty, (from more than 7 percent in 2000 to 12 percent in 2010). These findings suggest that while seniors' incomes have generally increased, they have not increased enough to cover the costs of basic goods and services. This is especially true for seniors living in large urban centres, such as Toronto, Vancouver, and Montréal (Vital Signs, 2013a).

The economic recession from 2007 to 2009 was especially hard on low-income seniors. According to the MBM, twice as many seniors had trouble

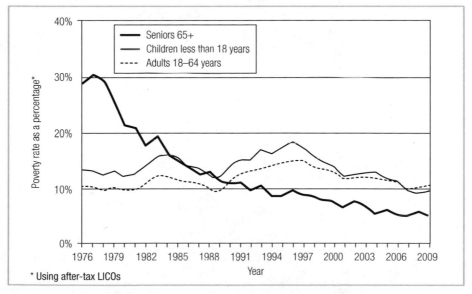

EXHIBIT 9.2

POVERTY RATES BY AGE GROUP, 1976–2009

Source: National Council of Welfare Reports: The Dollars and Sense of Solving Poverty, http://publications. gc.ca/collections/collection_2011/cnb-ncw/HS54-2-2011-eng.pdf. National Council of Welfare, 2011. Reproduced with the permission of the Minister of Public Works and Government Services Canada, 2013.

buying essential goods and services during the recession than in previous years. Statisticians conclude that economic downturns are more likely to create financial hardship for low-income seniors living on fixed incomes—most of whom are women—than for other age groups (HRSDC, 2012c).

Children

In 1989, Canada decided to eliminate child poverty by the year 2000. Although child poverty rates did fall from a high of 16 percent in the mid-1980s to 13 percent in the mid-1990s, those rates have been climbing ever since (Conference Board of Canada, 2013d). According to the LICOs, more than 14 percent of Canadian children lived in poverty in 2010. Some provinces have rates much higher than the national average, including Prince Edward Island (22 percent) and Manitoba (21 percent).

The type of family a child lives in raises the chances of experiencing poverty; for example, living in a lone-parent, female-led family raises the risk, as does living in a visible minority family (Campaign 2000, 2011). Aboriginal children are particularly vulnerable to poverty; for instance, half of all status First Nations children are poor (Macdonald & Wilson, 2013). Exhibit 9.3

EXHIBIT 9.3

POVERTY RATES FOR CHILDREN: SELECTED GROUPS, 0–14 YEARS, 1996–2006

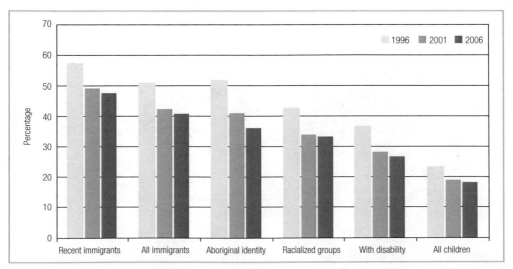

Source: Family Service Toronto. (2012). *Needed: An action plan to eradicate child and family poverty in Canada* (chart 7, p. 11). Retrieved from http://www.campaign2000.ca/reportCards/national/C2000ReportCardNov2012.pdf.

compares the poverty rates among selected groups of children, based on statistics from 1996, 2001, and 2006.

Children are poor because their parents are poor. Parents living in poverty tend to be young and unemployed, with little formal education, and, in some cases, are grappling with physical or mental health problems. Many parents work full time but do not earn enough to support their families adequately. More than 30 percent of children living in poverty have a parent who works full time (Campaign 2000, 2010).

A growing number of children live in middle-class families that have high levels of personal debt and few savings. Two-parent families owe $1.70 for every dollar earned; lone-parent families have the highest debt load, owing $2.27 for every dollar they earn (Statistics Canada, 2012c). While these families may not currently live in poverty, they may be on the brink of falling into poverty should they experience a sudden job loss, the death of a family breadwinner, or other unexpected change in financial status. Parents in manufacturing and service jobs are particularly vulnerable to job loss during economic restructuring or downturns.

DISCUSSION QUESTIONS

■ **Poverty in Canada**

1. What are the advantages of Canada using three measures of poverty (the LIM, the MBM, and the LICOs) rather than relying on just one measure?

2. Many definitions of poverty exist. How would you define poverty? What signs, symptoms, or indicators provide evidence that poverty exists in your community?

3. Certain groups are at a higher risk of poverty than others. What social, economic, or other factors might make those groups vulnerable to poverty?

2   THE EFFECTS OF POVERTY

Following the Second World War, Canada created a social welfare system to prevent large segments of the population from falling into extreme poverty. However, in recent decades, Canadian governments have steadily chipped away at the social welfare system to the point that many people in need do not have a basic level of support. Thus, poverty has become a more visible social problem in this country. Food insecurity and homelessness are two of the most obvious signs of poverty.

FOOD INSECURITY

At one time, the notion that anyone in Canada might go hungry was beyond comprehension. But in the 1980s, with the emergence of food banks and children's meal programs in schools, food insecurity became recognized as a social problem. The term **food insecurity** refers to "the inability to obtain sufficient, nutritious, personally acceptable food through normal food channels or the uncertainty that one will be able to do so" (Davis & Tarasuk, 1994, p. 51). A variety of factors may contribute to food insecurity, but most often it is associated with low income and the unaffordability of a healthy diet (National Food Security Assembly, 2006). According to the Canadian Community Health Survey, almost 8 percent of households (or 956 000 people) are food insecure (Statistics Canada, 2010a).

One yardstick for measuring food insecurity is the number of people using emergency food programs, of which food banks are the most common type. Edmonton opened the country's first food bank in 1981 as a temporary response to the hardships created by the economic recession at the time. Since then, the demand for food banks has steadily grown; by 2012, more than 450 food banks across Canada were serving almost 900 000 people. More than half of Canadians relying on food banks are welfare recipients, and almost four in ten people helped by food banks are children (see Exhibit 9.4) (Food Banks Canada, 2012).

HOMELESSNESS

Canadians have witnessed a dramatic rise in the cost of housing in recent years. As a result, many people cannot afford **acceptable housing**—that is, housing that is adequate (in good repair), suitable (uncrowded), and affordable (costs less than 30 percent of a household's before-tax income). Families living in housing that does not meet these criteria are said to be in **core housing need**—a reality for about 1.5 million Canadian households (Canada Mortgage and Housing Corporation [CMHC], 2013).

Rising rents—especially in large urban centres—are making it increasingly difficult for low-income Canadians to afford decent housing. According to one Canadian study, four out of ten renter households spend more than 30 percent of their income on shelter and have little money left to purchase other basics, such as food and clothing (Vital Signs, 2013b). This situation is known as **shelter poverty** because the household is left in poverty once the rent is paid (Hulchanski, 2005). In addition to high rents, fewer rental units are available; for example, in Regina and Winnipeg, only 1 percent of apartments were vacant in 2010 (Federation of Canadian Municipalities, 2012).

EXHIBIT 9.4

An unacceptable number of visitors to Canada's food banks are children.

The unavailability of acceptable housing contributes to the problem of **homelessness** (see Exhibit 9.5). In Canada, a person is homeless if he or she is

- *unsheltered* (has no home and sleeps in the street or other place not intended for human habitation)

- *emergency sheltered* (has temporary accommodation, provided by the emergency shelter system, such as homeless shelters and shelters for abused women and their children)

- *provisionally sheltered* (has temporary shelter in an institution, immigrant reception centre, hostel, friend's house, or other time-limited housing arrangement)

- *at-risk of homelessness* (has permanent yet unaffordable, unsafe, or otherwise unstable housing that is at risk of being lost) (Canadian Homelessness Research Network, 2012)*

For some Canadians, homelessness is *temporary* and relatively brief, as is the case when people must evacuate their homes because of a flood

*Canadian Homelessness Research Network. (2012). Canadian definition of homelessness. Retrieved from the Homeless Hub, http://www.homelesshub.ca/ResourceFiles/CHRNhomelessdefinition-1pager.pdf.

EXHIBIT 9.5

Homelessness is becoming an increasingly visible social problem in Canada.

or fire. For others, homelessness may be *cyclical* (interspersed with short-term shelter) or *chronic* (long term or repeated over time) (Echenberg & Jensen, 2008). Estimates suggest that approximately 80 000 Canadians are homeless on any given day; this figure includes the "visible" homeless (people who use emergency shelters) and the "hidden" homeless (people who are provisionally sheltered or do not access any emergency shelters). More than 47 percent of homeless people are single men aged 25 to 55, and another 20 percent are youth aged 16 to 24. Many of these individuals have a mental illness, an addiction, or a disability, and a large proportion of them are of Aboriginal descent. A growing number of homeless Canadians are families with children, most often headed by a single mom (Gaetz, Donaldson, Richter, & Gulliver, 2013).

THE CYCLE OF POVERTY

Poverty-related problems—such as neighbourhood decay, an eroding sense of community, and crime—impact the quality of life for everyone, not just those who are poor. As a concept, the **cycle of poverty** is a useful tool for

EXHIBIT 9.6

THE CYCLE OF POVERTY

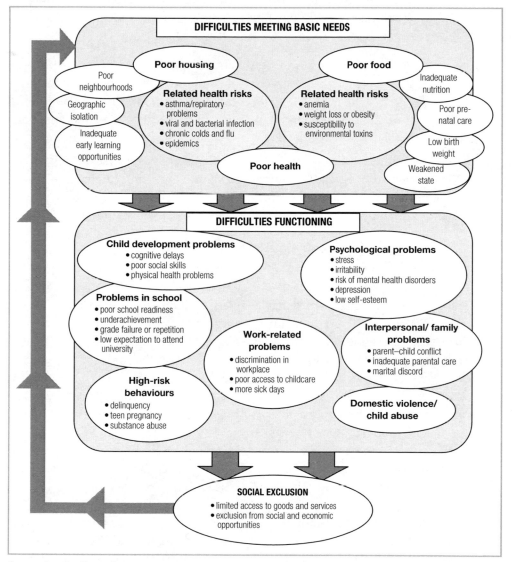

DIFFICULTIES MEETING BASIC NEEDS

Poor neighbourhoods

Geographic isolation

Inadequate early learning opportunities

Poor housing

Related health risks
- asthma/repiratory problems
- viral and bacterial infection
- chronic colds and flu
- epidemics

Poor food

Related health risks
- anemia
- weight loss or obesity
- susceptibility to environmental toxins

Inadequate nutrition

Poor pre-natal care

Low birth weight

Weakened state

Poor health

DIFFICULTIES FUNCTIONING

Child development problems
- cognitive delays
- poor social skills
- physical health problems

Psychological problems
- stress
- irritability
- risk of mental health disorders
- depression
- low self-esteem

Problems in school
- poor school readiness
- underachievement
- grade failure or repetition
- low expectation to attend university

Work-related problems
- discrimination in workplace
- poor access to childcare
- more sick days

Interpersonal/ family problems
- parent–child conflict
- inadequate parental care
- marital discord

High-risk behaviours
- delinquency
- teen pregnancy
- substance abuse

Domestic violence/ child abuse

SOCIAL EXCLUSION
- limited access to goods and services
- exclusion from social and economic opportunities

Source: Rosalie Chappell

understanding poverty's negative effects on individuals and families, and on society as a whole. Exhibit 9.6 highlights some of the factors and events that can trap people in a vicious circle of poverty.

At the top of the chart in Exhibit 9.6 are two main features of poverty: poor housing and poor food. Each feature has its own health risks.

- The negative consequences of inferior housing conditions on physical health are well documented; for example, one Canadian study found that, among 1200 people living in poor housing conditions, 33 percent had arthritis, 30 percent had hepatitis B or C, and 23 percent had asthma (Research Alliance for Canadian Homelessness, Housing and Health, 2010).

- People who live in poverty often lack the means to buy fresh, nutritious, or adequate amounts of food. A growing body of scientific research confirms the relationship between poor nutrition and health problems. Those problems include inadequate prenatal and postnatal care, low birth weight, obesity, diabetes, and anemia.

The middle section of Exhibit 9.6 highlights the potential effects that inadequate housing and food, and their related health problems, can have on human functioning. For children, difficulties in functioning may manifest themselves as delays in cognitive, social, and physical development, which in turn may lead to learning problems and involvement in high-risk behaviours. Adults may have trouble meeting the demands of postsecondary education or training programs, or be unable to find or keep a job. Poverty conditions are also associated with psychological problems, such as stress and mental illness; these factors, in turn, may create interpersonal or family conflicts, including family violence.

Difficulties in personal functioning and the fulfillment of important responsibilities and social roles—be it in school, work, or other life areas—may lead to social exclusion. People who are not socially included are typically denied their rights and often have difficulties accessing opportunities in the community, such as basic services and employment. In turn, social exclusion puts people at an even greater risk of poverty and related problems.

The disadvantages of persistent poverty often repeat themselves, sometimes over several generations. Eventually, the health, social, and other problems created by poverty can compound and converge to create even greater hardship and deprivation. Thus, poverty can become both the *cause* and the *effect* of social ills. The upward arrow in Exhibit 9.6 suggests the circular nature of poverty.

One of the most concerning aspects of poverty is its potentially negative effect on children. Growing up poor usually means living in inadequate housing in rundown or unsafe neighbourhoods with limited access to recreation centres, libraries, and other community resources. Material deprivation can have a negative effect on a child's development; studies show that children living in poverty are at a higher risk of physical health problems, emotional and behavioural disorders, and learning disabilities when compared with their wealthier peers (Lipman & Offord, 1994). The harmful effects of growing up in poverty can carry into adulthood and compromise a person's ability to get a proper education, find and hold down a job, earn a sufficient income, and be an active member of society.

THE ECONOMIC COSTS OF POVERTY

Society as a whole bears the costs of poverty. In its study on poverty in Canada, the National Council of Welfare (2011) identified three types of economic costs created by poverty:

- *Direct costs* are from poverty-related income security programs (such as social assistance and low-income tax benefits) and social services (such as subsidized child care and homeless shelters).

- *Indirect costs* include those related to the overuse of expensive services (such as hospital emergency wards, remedial education, and police services) by low-income groups.

- *Societal costs* are from lost opportunities for disadvantaged children, decreased work productivity, and lower levels of community engagement among adults.

In terms of actual dollars, one study estimates that poverty consumes about $13 billion a year in federal and provincial or territorial income tax revenue (Laurie, 2008). Child poverty has a particularly high economic cost; in Ontario, for example, child poverty costs up to $6 billion annually (Ivanova, 2011). Whichever way researchers crunch the numbers, the result is the same: Canadians pay far too much for poverty in terms of diminished social and economic participation and well-being. By all accounts, poverty is unsustainable.

DISCUSSION QUESTIONS

■ **The Effects of Poverty**

1. Poverty has immediate and long-term consequences for children. What are some of those consequences, and how might they affect a child's future functioning as an adult?

2. Explain how poverty can be both a cause and an effect of human hardship.

3 ORGANIZED RESPONSES TO POVERTY

Canada has tackled the problem of poverty in a variety of ways, including improving the economy, creating jobs, and introducing policies and programs to help adults meet their basic needs. Before making these types of efforts, policymakers have to identify the root causes of poverty. This section reviews two predominant theories on the causes of poverty, and examines Canada's two-pronged approach to poverty reduction.

UNDERSTANDING THE CAUSES OF POVERTY

Unfortunately, the complex and multidimensional nature of poverty makes it difficult, if not impossible, for policymakers to agree on underlying causes. Even when policymakers can agree on the causes of poverty, their views may shift as new information about the determinants of poverty emerges. Despite these types of challenges, policymakers tend to agree that poverty is the result of deficiencies in either people or systems or both:

- *Poverty is the result of deficiencies in individuals, families, or other micro system.* Historically, society has blamed poverty on the poor, claiming that poverty is the result of foolish choices, moral failings, or a lack of character and ambition. Today's more politically correct policymakers are likely to refer to an individual's deficiencies in terms of a lack of skills, opportunities, support, or other factors needed to compete successfully in the labour market.

- *Poverty is the result of flaws in social, political, economic, or other macro system.* The term **structural poverty** refers to the failure of society (or government) to meet the social and economic needs of individuals and families. According to the structural poverty theory, certain entities in our culture systematically exclude relatively powerless or under-valued groups in society (for example, visible minorities) from good jobs, wealth, material resources, and opportunities (Raphael, 2011). Today, structural poverty is most often associated with globalization, growing income inequality, and neoliberal policies that favour the rich.

TAKING A TWO-PRONGED APPROACH

Traditionally, social policies and programs have focused on helping individuals change some aspect of themselves so they become more employable and, subsequently, more productive members of society. However, in recent years, policymakers have taken a greater interest in correcting the flaws in larger systems and, in so doing, eliminating the barriers that prevent disadvantaged groups from accessing good jobs and fully participating in society. Today, Canadian governments take a two-pronged approach to poverty issues: (1) they aim to support individuals through a wide range of *programs*; and (2) they employ various *systemic interventions* to change existing policies or practices, social attitudes, or other macro system to make them more responsive to people's needs. Through this mix of interventions, governments attempt to meet the diverse needs of low-income Canadians (Loewen, 2009).

The following are examples of the many programs and systemic interventions aimed at reducing or preventing poverty in Canada.

Social Assistance

Social assistance is the income program of last resort for people who have exhausted all other avenues of financial support and can prove (through needs, asset, or income testing) that they are in need. Each province and territory has its own welfare system and its own criteria for eligibility, benefit rates, appeal procedures, and monitoring. However, all social assistance programs provide some level of financial assistance to help individuals and families purchase food, shelter, and other basics. Additional benefits may also cover costs related to age, disability, education, employment, or other special circumstance. Further assistance is available under the National Child Benefit (NCB) to support children living in families on social assistance.[2]

Canadian governments are always looking for ways to motivate people on welfare to become more self-sufficient. During the 1990s, the provinces and territories regularly lowered their welfare benefit rates to pressure people to leave welfare and find a job. Before long, government officials realized that punishing or blaming the poor for their circumstances drove welfare recipients not into jobs but more deeply into poverty. Program reviews helped to identify the specific ways in which welfare systems actually discourage people from leaving welfare. For instance, many families found that when they left welfare for a job (especially a job that did not come with benefits), they lost access to certain subsidized welfare services, as well as medical, dental, and prescription drug benefits. At the same time, employment brought work-related expenses, such as transportation, work clothes, child care, and income taxes. Individuals and families in this situation hit what is called the **welfare wall**, because they became financially worse off employed than they were on welfare.

To break down the welfare wall and to ensure that people choose work over welfare, most provincial governments have reformed their social assistance systems. One reform allows families to receive the NCB tax benefit and supplement, as well as many welfare benefits and services, even after the parents leave social assistance for paid employment. Another reform allows welfare recipients to work and keep some of their earnings and some of their social assistance. For instance, in Alberta, employable individuals can keep up

---

[2] The National Child Benefit offers support to families in two ways: (1) the Canada Child Tax Benefit (CCTB) is an income-tested monthly payment available to low- and middle-income families with children under eighteen; and (2) the National Child Benefit Supplement tops up the monthly CCTB payments for Canada's lowest-income families with children.

to $230/month in earnings and 25 percent of any additional earnings, on top of their regular welfare benefits (Alberta Ministry of Human Services, 2011). These earnings exemptions not only increase the amount of money that welfare recipients can live on but also encourage employable individuals to form a long-term attachment to the labour force.

Employment Insurance

Employment Insurance (EI) is an income security program that offers temporary financial support to Canadians who have lost their job and are looking for other work or upgrading their skills. Because it is a contributory insurance program, people must have paid into the EI program in the past to be eligible for benefits when unemployed. Many types of benefits are available under the EI system, including regular benefits (for those who have been laid off work through no fault of their own) and benefits related to maternity, parental duties, sickness, compassionate care, and training.

Since the passage of the EI Act in 1996, Canadian governments have expected EI recipients to engage in some type of work-related activity in exchange for benefits. Underlying this active labour market policy is the assumption that if workers had more training or better job search skills, they would be able to find good jobs. Thus, various intergovernmental agreements allow insured unemployed workers not only to receive regular EI benefits but also to tap into financial assistance while attending a training program, or to access a skills development program (such as a career planning workshop) to aid in the job search process.

Canadian governments tout EI's training supplements and skills development programs as a way to reinforce the intrinsic values of work, discipline, and productivity, and to help people gain the confidence and skills they need to compete and succeed in the workforce (Social Research and Demonstration Corporation, 2005). However, these supports do little to prevent unemployment or to eliminate the systemic barriers that limit labour force participation among marginalized groups. Those barriers are beyond the control of individuals and include the following:

- The structure of Canada's labour market ensures that there are always more people looking for work than there are jobs, especially jobs that pay a living wage. Canada's **unemployment rate** hovers around 7 percent, meaning that at any given time, seven of every 100 adults are actively looking for work. An ongoing competition for jobs puts employers in the position of being able to choose who gets work and allows them to offer less competitive wages and benefits.

- A segment of the workforce is chronically **underemployed**, meaning that people are not working as much as they could or want to, or are overqualified for the job they have. Many Canadians seek full-time work but can find only part-time or non-standard jobs (temporary, contract, or seasonal jobs). Underemployed workers often have to either juggle several part-time jobs or seek financial help from welfare departments to make ends meet. Recent immigrants are among the most underemployed groups in Canada, even though they are, on average, more educated than Canada-born workers.

- Minimum wage legislation has not kept up with inflation and the rising costs of food, rent, and other staples. As a result, many minimum wage workers do not earn enough to stay out of poverty. Among the **working poor**[3] are young adults, people with a disability, recent immigrants, and First Nations people living off-reserve (Collin & Jensen, 2009). An estimated 400 000 Canadians are in full-time jobs that pay less than ten dollars an hour (Campaign 2000, 2010).

Government policies and labour laws play an important role in preventing or eliminating systemic barriers to employment. Canadian governments have begun to identify and break down those barriers and open up the labour market to all working-age Canadians. The likely targets for reform are

- employment standards (the minimum provisions of work that protect workers from exploitation by employers, related to minimum wage levels,[4] hours of work, and workplace health and safety)

- employment equity (people have equal access to jobs—regardless of race, gender, or other personal attribute—as long as they are able and qualified to do the job)

- pay equity (equal pay for work of equal value in terms of duties, responsibilities, and qualifications)

- work supports (resources, such as affordable child care or wheel-chair accessible workplaces, that allow workers to maintain employment once they get it)

---

[3] This definition of *working poor* includes working-age adults but does not include adult students or young adults still living with their parents.

[4] As an example, Ontario has made incremental increases to minimum wages, from $6.85 in 2003, to $8.75 by 2008, and to $10.25 in 2010, giving the province one of the highest minimum wage rates in Canada.

- training (ensuring that postsecondary education and job training is accessible)
- job creation (creating job opportunities for unemployed workers) (Goss Gilroy, 2004)

Asset Building

Savings, investments, and other financial assets can enable people to start a business, buy a home, or provide a cushion to soften the blow of job loss or other interruption of income. In short, financial assets give a person a sense of control over his or her life and future (Jackson, 2004). Unfortunately, many low-income earners can barely afford to buy the basics, let alone save for the future. They live hand to mouth, with few reserves for emergencies and little prospect of ever improving their economic situation. To address this situation, the federal government has introduced a number of **asset-based social policies**—such as **individual development accounts** (IDAs)—to help low-income individuals and families build assets and essentially "save their way out of poverty" (Social and Enterprise Development Innovations, 2003, p. 1).

Individuals who participate in an IDA program save whatever they can from their earnings; in turn, the government matches that amount. For example, in one IDA program in Winnipeg, Manitoba, eligible participants receive $3 for every $1 they save (SEED Winnipeg, n.d.). Through these types of government programs, low-income earners can gradually accumulate savings toward long-term goals. The Canada Learning Bond and projects under *learn*$ave are specific types of IDAs designed to help low-income Canadians pay for postsecondary education.

Traditionally, social assistance programs have required welfare applicants to exhaust all their assets before they could receive benefits. However, that requirement lessened people's chances of ever becoming self-sufficient. In recent years, provincial and territorial governments have reformed their welfare rules around assets. For example, the Government of Ontario (Ontario Ministry of Community and Social Services, 2013) now allows welfare recipients to keep up to $5000 (couples can keep up to $7500) in cash or other liquid assets. Moreover, when calculating the assets of welfare applicants, welfare workers can now exempt up to $60 000 in savings in a registered retirement savings plan, a registered education savings plan, or an IDA.

In addition to promoting self-sufficiency, asset-based policies encourage habits of saving and try to help people gain an understanding of finances. Increasingly, governments are seeing asset building as a more progressive solution to poverty than traditional income security programs (such as welfare), which focus on meeting immediate rather than long-term needs.

Housing Security

Although the vast majority of Canadians obtain their housing from the private housing market, Canadian governments intervene in that market to ensure that low-income Canadians have equal access to affordable, adequate, and permanent housing. In recent decades, that intervention has occurred primarily through bilateral agreements between the federal and provincial or territorial governments, including the Affordable Housing Initiative (2001–2011) and the Investment in Affordable Housing (2011–2014).

All **government-assisted housing** is government-subsidized or **rent-geared-to-income**, meaning that a government pays a proportion of rent based on a tenant's total income. For instance, a senior living in a social housing unit and relying on Old Age Security and Guaranteed Income Supplement cheques would pay about 30 percent of their income on rent. There are four main types of government-assisted housing programs in Canada:

- public or social housing (rental apartments or houses that are built, owned, and managed by a government housing authority or corporation) (see Exhibit 9.7)

- nonprofit housing (rental units that are built and managed by a non-profit group, such as a church or ethnic association)

- co-operative (or co-op) housing (homes that are owned and managed by the people living in them)

- rent-supplement units (houses or apartments that are owned and managed by private landlords) (CMHC, 2012a)*

Since the early 1990s, the federal government has regularly cut funding to subsidized housing, stopped funding long-term housing projects, and devolved many of its responsibilities for housing programs to lower levels of government. At the same time, most provinces and territories have relaxed their rent controls and subsequently allowed landlords to increase rent at any time, resulting in dramatic jumps in rent. When individuals and families can no longer afford to pay the rent, they have few options left but to become "unhoused."

The federally funded Homelessness Partnering Strategy supports the majority of homeless shelters, most of which offer temporary, short-term, emergency accommodation, as well as clothing, food, and counselling. Although shelters provide some degree of protection from the elements, they offer little in terms of long-term solutions to homelessness. Emergency shelters, in particular, are a poor substitute for proper housing. It is common for the demand

---

* Canada Mortgage and Housing Corporation (CMHC). All rights reserved. Reproduced with the consent of CMHC. All other uses of this material are expressly prohibited.

EXHIBIT 9.7

Canada's oldest and largest social housing project is Regent Park in Toronto, Ontario. Built in the late 1940s, this housing project covers 28 hectares (69 acres). It is currently undergoing revitalization.

for shelters to exceed the available beds (especially in winter) and, in some parts of Canada, shelter staff must turn away homeless people seeking shelter because of a lack of beds (Crossroads Christian Communications, 2013). The demand for homeless shelters in Canada continues to grow: in 2006, there were 859 shelters providing almost 22 000 beds; by 2011, there were 1086 shelters with more than 28 000 beds (HRSDC, 2013b).

Over the last two decades, ongoing funding cuts, the lifting of rent regulations, and the general deterioration of social housing policies have created an affordable housing and homelessness crisis in Canada. It will take more than sporadic, short-term investments in housing programs to resolve this crisis. Indeed, the solution may lie in correcting the many structural problems that systematically prevent low-income Canadians from accessing affordable, permanent housing (Hulchanski, 2005). Those structural flaws include

- chronically low vacancy rates and rising rents, especially in large urban centres
- a shrinking supply of low cost rental units and rooming houses

- a decreasing number of new social housing units
- falling incomes among the poor and those at risk of poverty
- landlord discrimination against marginalized groups
- social assistance programs that offer insufficient payment for adequate housing
- chronic unemployment, underemployment, and low-paying jobs for a growing number of Canadians (Buckland, Jackson, Roberts, & Smith, 2001).

Food Security

Traditionally, food security initiatives in Canada have been short term or emergency based, with a primarily local rather than national focus. Those initiatives include

- the provision of free or subsidized food (for example, school-based meal programs, food banks, and soup kitchens)
- educational programs to improve food preparation and grocery shopping skills (for example, community kitchens and targeted nutrition education programs)
- the promotion of alternative methods of obtaining food (for example, farmers' markets, community gardens, and food box programs) (McIntyre, 2003)

Food banks and related programs are generally inadequate methods of addressing the growing problem of food insecurity in Canada: they are not reliable sources of nutritious food, and they rarely have enough food to meet the demand. These programs also rely heavily on the public to donate food and on volunteers to manage and distribute food to those in need. Many food banks are not geographically accessible to everyone who needs them, and the stigma attached to food banks may stop some people from using them.

In 1998, the Government of Canada introduced a comprehensive national Action Plan for Food Security to guide governments, communities, and individuals in their efforts to improve food security. (Exhibit 9.8 illustrates Canada's perspective of the essential elements of food security.) Since then, many communities have introduced measures to improve access to local nutritious food and to enhance community capacity to address food security issues. Some communities have adopted a food security charter. Most charters outline a

EXHIBIT 9.8

CANADIAN PERSPECTIVE ON FOOD SECURITY

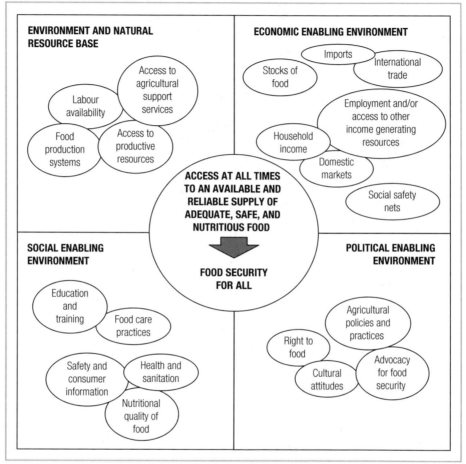

Source: Adapted and excerpted from Canada. (1998). *Canada's action plan for food security.* Retrieved from Agriculture and Agri-Food Canada website: http://www.agr.gc.ca/misb/fsec-seca/pdf/action_e.pdf.

community's vision for a sustainable food system and possible strategies to ensure that food producers and processors make a fair living. Perhaps most importantly, food charters recommend actions to ensure an ongoing stable supply of nutritious, sufficient, and ethically produced food for local residents (Thompson, 2010).

In recognizing that there is power in numbers, some individuals and organizations have formed food security networks or policy councils. One of the main activities of these collectives is to influence government policies on food security issues. To do this, a network or council might use a food security lens to assess the impact of existing policies and laws on food security, and to recommend policy changes at the federal, provincial or territorial, and municipal levels.

Poverty-Reduction Plans

The term **poverty reduction** refers to a process that addresses both the symptoms and the root causes of poverty (Tamarack, 2012). Unlike many European countries, Canada has no national poverty-reduction plan. Nevertheless, progress is being made at the provincial and territorial levels. In 2002, Québec became the first province to introduce a poverty-reduction plan, and is the only province to enforce its plan through legislation. Since Québec has taken the lead, the other provinces and the territories either have put poverty-reduction strategies in place or are in the process of doing so.

Although the details of each poverty-reduction plan are unique, all the provincial plans make poverty a government responsibility and a focal point of economic development. These plans also provide a balance between helping employable people find jobs and ensuring that those who cannot work, or have specific needs, receive adequate financial assistance and other supports. Moreover, all the current plans are long term, receive ongoing human and financial resources, and have built-in mechanisms to measure progress, report to the public, and coordinate efforts among partners (Collin, 2007). Exhibit 9.9 illustrates Newfoundland and Labrador's vision, goals, and strategies to reduce poverty in that province.

Poverty-reduction plans usually call for a multisectoral response to poverty. This means that no one sector or group in society—be it government, business, voluntary agencies, or families—is expected to resolve poverty on its own. Rather, every sector and segment of society has a role to play in poverty reduction. A multisectoral approach also assumes that people working together have the best chance of alleviating poverty and other complex social problems (Hay, 2009).

A common feature of poverty-reduction plans in Canada is their comprehensive approach. These plans typically support a wide range of programs and services, including child-care services, healthcare, affordable housing, income security, education and training, and the development of jobs that pay a living wage. The degree to which a plan is comprehensive varies across communities and depends on many factors, including available resources and the level of community engagement in the plan.

Some communities are choosing to reduce poverty through a **comprehensive community initiative** (CCI). Vibrant Communities is a type

EXHIBIT 9.9

NEWFOUNDLAND AND LABRADOR'S POVERTY REDUCTION STRATEGY

Newfoundland and Labrador's Poverty Reduction Strategy aims to prevent, reduce, and alleviate poverty. The strategy's goals and objectives for the 2006–2010 period were as follows:

Goal 1: Improved access and coordination of services to people with low incomes

- increase the provincial government's capacity to take an integrated and coordinated approach
- enhance access to existing programs and services for those with low income
- find ways to analyze the combined impact of programs
- work with Aboriginal peoples to improve their quality of life

Goal 2: A stronger social safety net

- help people with disabilities to participate fully in society by increasing disability supports
- improve the justice system for vulnerable people
- increase the availability of affordable housing
- improve access to basic necessities for those most vulnerable to poverty
- increase Income Support* rates

Goal 3: Improved earned incomes

- reduce barriers to work
- provide more support for low-income workers
- improve supports for employment skills development, labour force participation, and earnings from employment
- give youth an alternative to Income Support* to better meet their needs
- develop and expand employment skills programs for vulnerable groups whose needs are not currently being met

Goal 4: Increased emphasis on early childhood development

- strengthen the regulated early learning and childcare system
- promote healthy child development
- strengthen early intervention services and programs

Goal 5: A better-educated population

- increase high school completion rates
- increase responsiveness of the K to 12 system
- improve access to post-secondary education, literacy, and adult basic education

VISION

The province is a place where poverty has been eliminated. This will be a prosperous, diverse province in which all individuals are valued, can develop to their full potential, and have access to the supports they need to participate fully in the social and economic benefits of Newfoundland and Labrador.

*Income Support benefits include basic and non-basic financial supports.

- *Basic benefits* include family and individual benefits (to assist with such expenses as food, clothing, personal care, household maintenance, and utilities) and shelter (including rent and mortgage).

- *Non-basic benefits* include municipal tax payments, eye exams and prescription glasses, medical transportation, private childcare (related to employment or training), and expenses for burials. The eligibility for non-basic benefits may vary according to personal circumstances.

Source: Adapted from Newfoundland and Labrador. (2006). *Reducing poverty: An action plan for Newfoundland and Labrador*. Retrieved from Department of Advanced Education and Skills website: http://www.aes.gov.nl.ca/poverty/consultations/2008/poverty-reduction-strategy.pdf.

of CCI that adapts a variety of poverty-reduction strategies to the specific needs of communities. Despite being unique to each community, all Vibrant Communities initiatives tend to focus on identifying and building on local economic and social assets; engaging local residents, government, and the private sector; and promoting change, learning, and the sharing of experiences (Loewen, 2009).

DISCUSSION QUESTIONS

■ **Organized Responses to Poverty**

1. Historically, Canada has tried to prevent or reduce poverty by either changing individuals or reforming some aspect of the social, economic, political, or other system. Identify the advantages and disadvantages of this two-pronged approach.

2. How realistic are asset-based social policies for low-income earners? Identify some of the pros and cons of asset-based policies and programs in the fight against poverty.

3. Describe the ideal poverty-reduction plan. To what degree, if any, should government be involved in the plan? What might be the role for the voluntary or commercial sectors? How might individuals help to reduce poverty?

4 WORKING WITH LOW-INCOME AND MARGINALIZED GROUPS

Traditionally, social workers have focused on helping people cope with the effects of poverty and improve their life circumstances. They have also rallied to many poverty-related causes and advocated on behalf of low-income individuals and groups. Social workers, more than any other professional group, have the training and education to help individuals become self-sufficient. Moreover, social workers assume a professional obligation to advocate for the most vulnerable members of society and to urge governments to move poverty to the top of their political agendas (Canadian Association of Social Workers & National Association of Social Workers, 2008).

Many social workers use an **anti-oppressive approach** when working with clients living in poverty. Although there is a variety of anti-oppressive approaches—including structural, feminist, and radical frameworks—they all share similar values and principles. For example, they all value egalitarianism, social inclusion, and empowerment. These frameworks also assume that an unequal distribution of power and resources in capitalist societies leads to social exclusion and poverty among certain social groups. Anti-oppressive approaches link individual difficulties—such as a lack of income and social isolation—not to individual shortcomings but to structural flaws in larger systems. Although social workers taking this type of approach help individuals, they also critically analyze and challenge oppressive rules, procedures, laws, and institutions that contribute to poverty and other social problems. It is common for these social workers to participate in social movements designed to change some aspect of the system and in so doing, help their disadvantaged clients become empowered (Campbell, 2003).

One of the challenges in working with disadvantaged groups is learning to appreciate the complexities of living in hardship. Jones and colleagues (2002, p. 3) suggest that some of these hardships may be exacerbated by well-meaning social workers and other professionals; for example, welfare workers may feel pressured by employers to move their clients into work or training and, in so doing, create "a complex juggling of work and domestic responsibilities for those with children." In turn, clients may experience stress, marital discord, and difficulties in parenting. Through careful observation and active listening and by maintaining a person-in-environment perspective, practitioners may help families identify, describe, and effectively deal with the various pressures they feel.

DISCUSSION QUESTIONS

■ **Working with Low-Income and Marginalized Groups**

1. In what ways might an anti-oppressive approach be more (or less) effective than helping individuals, families, and small groups resolve their issues or problems?

2. Social workers are often required to move their clients toward self-sufficiency without creating more stress for their clients in the process. How might social workers successfully achieve both objectives?

SUMMARY

Introduction

Canada has one of the most robust economies in the world, and yet many citizens do not share in the nation's wealth. Despite government spending to improve the financial security of citizens, low income remains a problem. Historically, policymakers have treated poverty as a low priority; however, in recent years, regional governments and communities have been taking more aggressive steps to reduce poverty in Canada.

1   Poverty in Canada

Several definitions and measurements of poverty exist, but most relate poverty to a certain level of income. The federal government uses the low income measure, market basket measure, and low-income cut-offs to measure poverty. Populations at the highest risk of poverty include single adults, people with disabilities, lone-parent families (mostly women), recent immigrants, and Aboriginal peoples. Canada has unacceptable levels of child poverty.

2   The Effects of Poverty

Ongoing cuts to social welfare programs and services have made poverty more visible. Food insecurity is a potential consequence of poverty, as is evidenced by the emergence of food banks and other emergency food programs. Housing is becoming more unaffordable; Canadians are spending a greater proportion of their income on shelter; and homelessness is a growing social problem. Poverty can be both the cause and the effect of social problems, and trap people in a cycle of poverty. There are many economic costs of poverty, making poverty unsustainable.

3   Organized Responses to Poverty

Canadian policymakers tend to see poverty as the result of deficiencies in individuals or flaws in society's macro systems. Canada attempts to reduce poverty through a variety of programs and systemic interventions. Social assistance offers cash benefits and social services; welfare systems are trying to lower the welfare wall by providing incentives to work. EI offers financial assistance, training, and skills development programs; systemic interventions focus on eliminating barriers to labour market participation. Governments offer asset-building programs to help people save for the future; welfare system reforms allow welfare recipients to keep a higher level of liquid assets. Canada is experiencing an affordable housing and homelessness crisis, which can be resolved only by correcting structural problems that prevent low-income Canadians from earning an adequate income and accessing government-assisted housing. Food banks and other emergency food programs do little to enhance food security; systemic interventions aim to improve access to nutritious food and help communities improve the supply of food. Most provinces and territories have developed poverty-reduction plans.

4   Working with Low-Income and Marginalized Groups

Traditionally, social workers have focused on helping people cope with poverty conditions. Many social workers use an anti-oppressive approach when working with disadvantaged clients. To be effective, practitioners must try to understand people's experiences of poverty and the complexities of living in hardship. An important task for social workers is to help welfare recipients deal effectively with any pressures they might feel when moving from social assistance to independence.

KEY TERMS

For definitions of the key terms, consult the Glossary on page 453 at the end of the book.

poverty, p. 239
social exclusion, p. 239
LICOs, p. 240
poverty rate, p. 240
depth of poverty, p. 241
persistence of poverty,
   p. 241
risk factors of poverty,
   p. 242
feminization of poverty,
   p. 242
food insecurity, p. 246
acceptable housing,
   p. 246

core housing need,
   p. 246
shelter poverty, p. 246
homelessness, p. 247
cycle of poverty, p. 248
structural poverty,
   p. 252
social assistance,
   p. 253
welfare wall, p. 253
unemployment rate,
   p. 254
underemployed, p. 255
working poor, p. 255

asset-based social
   policies, p. 256
individual development
   accounts, p. 256
government-assisted
   housing, p. 257
rent-geared-to-income,
   p. 257
poverty reduction, p. 261
comprehensive
   community initiative,
   p. 261
anti-oppressive
   approach, p. 263

CHAPTER 10

The Social Welfare of Children and Their Families

OBJECTIVES

The social welfare of children and their families is central to the well-being of society. This chapter will

- introduce the roles of parents and the state in the care of children

- describe the developmental needs of children and youth

- consider the influence of parenting style and family type on child development

- discuss the issues and programs related to family violence

- summarize social work approaches to working with families with children

INTRODUCTION

> The true measure of a nation's standing is how well it attends to its children—their health and safety, their material security, their education and socialization, and their sense of being loved, valued, and included in the families and societies into which they are born. (UNICEF, 2007, p. 1)

In proclaiming 1994 the International Year of the Family, the United Nations was calling attention to the importance of the **family** in society. Families are not only essential to individual and social well-being but are also a primary source of support and stability, and the foundation of communities. Families are also a fundamental unit of production and consumption, and therefore make valuable contributions to a country's economy (Bibby, 2004–2005). Families with children play a particularly important role by supplying the nation's future adults, workers, and parents. Researcher Katherine Scott (2008, p. 1) reminds us that "what happens to children affects us all. If our children do not thrive, our societies will not thrive."

Parents are the primary caregivers and are ultimately responsible for their children's well-being. Canadian governments nevertheless assume a collective responsibility for the welfare of children. The Government of Canada (2004b, p. 5) articulates its obligation to children this way: "The role of government and society with respect to children is to provide the legislative and policy framework, the institutional and organizational structures, the fiscal and other supports and services to enable families to ensure their children's healthy development. However, if families are unable to care for their children, then governments and society have a responsibility to provide support and ensure that they are cared for and protected." Universal healthcare, public education, city recreation programs, and other publically funded programs reflect government's commitment to young Canadians and a collective effort to help children reach their full potential.

Studies confirm that, in general, young Canadians are doing well: most children are born healthy and live in caring families and supportive communities. However, many young people grow up in poverty or other disadvantaged circumstances that threaten their development. For families that need extra support, a wide range of social welfare programs and services are available. Many of the federal government's commitments to children and youth are the result of agreements made at the international level. For instance, in 2002, Canada made several commitments to young people at the United Nations General Assembly Special Session on Children and subsequently incorporated those commitments into a national plan to improve the lives of children and youth. Exhibit 10.1 outlines that plan's main goals, related priorities, and national initiatives.

Despite Canada's official commitment to children, many child advocates argue that Canadian governments are not doing enough for families raising children. Part of the problem may be what Omidvar and Richmond (2003) see as an inconsistent approach to children's needs, especially when other issues—such as budget deficits or terrorism—become a higher priority on government agendas. Canada's lack of attention to children's material needs, in particular, has been noticed by certain international groups. For example,

EXHIBIT 10.1

A CANADA FIT FOR CHILDREN

VISION (2004)			
Children have the opportunity to be fully prepared to live a responsible life in a free society, in a spirit of understanding, peace, dignity, tolerance, equality and solidarity.			
GOALS (2004)			
To support families and strengthen communities	To promote healthy lives	To protect from harm	To promote education and learning
PRIORITIES FOR ACTION (2004)			
1. Child- and family-friendly policies 2. Early learning and child care 3. Poverty 4. Separation and divorce 5. Social inclusion and diversity 6. Aboriginal children 7. Inclusion and support of children with disabilities 8. Poverty and sustainable development (international level)	1. Healthy active living 2. Effective parenting 3. Mental health 4. Immunization 5. Physical environment and prevention of injuries 6. Sexual/reproductive health 7. Tobacco, alcohol, drug abuse and addictions 8. Aboriginal children's health 9. Paediatric health care and research 10. Health services in official language minority communities	1. Child maltreatment 2. Out-of-home care and adoption 3. Violence, bullying and other forms of intimidation 4. Youth justice 5. Violent and harmful content in the media 6. Immigrant, refugee and asylum seeking children 7. Sexual exploitation and trafficking	1. Quality learning 2. Arts and culture 3. Human rights education and global citizenship 4. Canadian culture and national identity 5. Environment learning and sustainability 6. Literacy 7. Trained and professional educators 8. Education for all children
NATIONAL INITIATIVES TO MEET GOALS (EXAMPLES IN 2012)			
• Universal Child Care Benefit • Canada Child Tax Benefit • Employment Insurance (maternity and parental benefits)	• Registered Disability Savings Plan • National Mental Health Strategy • Children's Fitness Tax Credit	• Youth Justice Initiative • Family Violence Initiative • National Clearinghouse on Family Violence • Family Violence Prevention Program (First Nations)	• Canada Education Savings Program • Children's Arts Tax Credit • Special Education Program (First Nations)

Source: Created with information from Canada. (2004). A Canada fit for children: Canada's plan of action in response to the May 2002 United Nations Special Session on Children. Retrieved from http://publications.gc.ca/collections/Collection/SD13-4-2004E. pdf; and Canada. (2012). Website. Retrieved from http://www.canada.gc.ca/home.html.

in its comparison of child poverty in thirty-five developed countries, UNICEF placed Canada in the bottom third of the countries studied, behind such nations as Estonia and Slovakia (Adamson, 2012). When measuring material well-being, the Organisation for Economic Co-operation and Development (OECD, 2009) found that poverty rates among young Canadians are, on average, higher than in other member countries.

Although many provinces and territories offer considerable support to children, youth, and families, Québec is the only jurisdiction in Canada—in fact, in all of North America—where a comprehensive **family policy** and related programs and services aim to meet the full range of needs of families with children. Initiatives under Québec's family policy include programs to help families balance the obligations of work and family, and financial support to cover the extra costs of raising children. In 2009, the Government of Québec (2009) announced that its generous family policy was beginning to show positive results in three key areas: a growing birth rate, a higher employment rate among women, and lower child poverty rates compared with the rest of Canada.

1 MEETING THE DEVELOPMENTAL NEEDS OF CHILDREN AND YOUTH

In the early 1990s, policymakers began to look more closely at the demographic shift that was taking place in Canada. With the large baby boom generation beginning to retire and the country's low birth rates, Canada would soon have considerably fewer workers to share the costs of caring for a comparatively large group of seniors and dependent children. To offset this demographic shift, policymakers decided to introduce measures aimed at improving the health—and therefore, the potential level of productivity—of future workers.

A FOCUS ON YOUNG CHILDREN

Research confirms that the first five years of a child's life are critical to how well he or she does in school, copes with life's challenges, and wards off chronic disease in his or her adult years (Canada, 1999). Thus, to ensure that future workers are healthy, well functioning, and productive, policymakers began shifting their attention to the needs of young children (Exhibit 10.2 outlines some of those needs). The result has been the introduction of policies and programs aimed at helping children get a good start in life, including the National Children's Agenda and child-care services.

National Children's Agenda

In 1999, Canada launched the National Children's Agenda (NCA), a comprehensive and long-term plan that articulates a shared vision for Canadian children. Initiatives under the NCA aim to enhance children's lives

---

EXHIBIT 10.2

KEY ELEMENTS AND INFLUENCES ON CHILD AND YOUTH DEVELOPMENT (CITY OF OTTAWA)

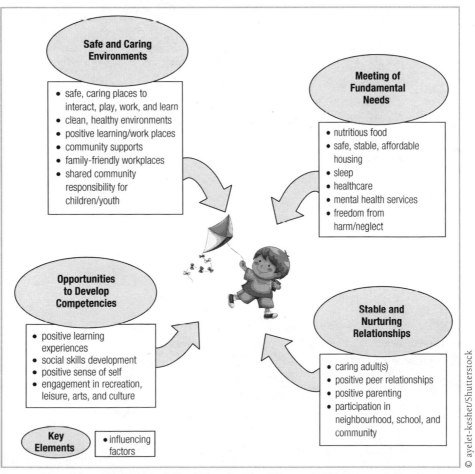

Source: Adapted from The Children & Youth Agenda, City of Ottawa. (2008). *Framework for promoting healthy child and youth development.* Retrieved from http://app06.ottawa.ca/calendar/ottawa/citycouncil/occ/2008/11-12/cpsc/ACS2008-CPS-DCM-0009%20Doc%201.pdf.

by improving physical and emotional health, personal safety and security, learning, and social engagement and responsibility. (Although Québec agrees with the objectives of the NCA, it has opted out of the agreement, choosing instead to develop its own programs for families with children.)

The NCA supports a number of child-focused research projects. For example, the National Longitudinal Survey of Children and Youth studies the influential factors on child development from birth to early adulthood. The NCA also supports the development of various health and social welfare programs, including the National Child Benefit (NCB), and the Early Childhood Development (ECD) Initiative:

- The NCB has three objectives: to prevent and reduce child poverty; to support parents as they move off welfare into the workforce; and to integrate the child benefits offered by various levels of government into a single, more efficient system. Under the NCB, low-income families with children receive monthly financial benefits and access to community-based programs and services (Canada, 2011). A program evaluation in 2005 found that the NCB had prevented about 171 100 children from falling into poverty that year (Federal, Provincial, and Territorial Ministers Responsible for Social Services, 2010).

- The ECD enables the provinces, territories, and First Nations to develop their own early childhood development programs. ECD programs aim to help children reach their full potential by ensuring that they are healthy, safe, prepared for school, and socially engaged (Human Resources and Social Development Canada, 2007a). Each jurisdiction determines its own mix of early childhood development programs, in accordance with the region's identified needs and priorities.

Child-Care Services

Studies have long confirmed the potential of quality **child care** to enhance child development; to prepare children for school and adulthood; and to enable parents, especially those with lower incomes, to go to work or school. Canadian families rely on various sources to meet their child-care needs, including private daycare centres, family, and paid sitters. In Canada, private, nonprofit organizations provide the bulk of all centre-based child-care services; however, the number of private, profit-making child-care centres continues to grow. All centre-based services are required to meet provincial or territorial regulations.

Many reports suggest that Canada is in the midst of a child-care crisis. UNICEF, for example, compared the child-care services in twenty-five developed countries and ranked Canada last for failing to address its child-care needs adequately (Adamson, 2008). The main problem facing Canadian families is the lack of child-care spaces in most provinces and territories (see Exhibit 10.3). Experts expect the demand for child-care spaces to grow in the coming years, in large part because of a mini baby boom between 2006 and 2011. During those years, the number of children age four and under jumped 11 percent, the highest growth rate for this age group since the baby boom years between 1956 and 1961 (Statistics Canada, 2012d).

A number of international organizations—including UNICEF and the OECD—have criticized Canada for neglecting to establish a national child-care plan that would give priority to disadvantaged children. Studies show that Canadians are generally in favour of a national child-care program; one national poll found that 66 percent of Canadians support the idea of a

EXHIBIT 10.3

REGULATED CHILD-CARE SPACES IN CANADA FOR CHILDREN AGES ZERO TO TWELVE

	TOTAL REGULATED CHILD-CARE SPACES	PERCENTAGE OF CHILDREN FOR WHOM THERE IS A REGULATED CHILD-CARE SPACE
NEWFOUNDLAND AND LABRADOR	6 200	9.6
PRINCE EDWARD ISLAND	5 084	25.9
NOVA SCOTIA	15 295	13.0
NEW BRUNSWICK	18 785	19.6
QUÉBEC	379 386	37.4
ONTARIO	276 410	14.9
MANITOBA	29 382	16.8
SASKATCHEWAN	10 848	7.2
ALBERTA	82 050	14.7
BRITISH COLUMBIA	97 170	17.0
NORTHWEST TERRITORIES	1 785	21.7
NUNAVUT	1 015	11.3
YUKON	1 431	29.5
CANADA	921 841	19.9

Source: Adapted from Public Investments in Early Childhood Education and Care in Canada 2010, http://www .ecd-elcc.ca/eng/ecd/ececc/early_childhood_education-eng.pdf, Human Resources and Skills Development Canada 2012. Reproduced with the permission of the Minister of Public Works and Government Services Canada, 2013.

government-subsidized $10 per day child-care program (University of British Columbia, 2012a). Nevertheless, the development of a national child-care program is unlikely under a conservative federal government, which tends to devolve family-related matters to the regional governments (Amoroso, 2010). In lieu of a national child-care program, the federal government offers the Universal Child Care Benefit (UCCB)—a taxable payment of $1200 per year for every Canadian child under six. Shortly after the government introduced the UCCB in 2006, a national poll found that most Canadians preferred a national child-care system to monthly UCCB cheques (Environics Research Group, 2006).

Québec is the only jurisdiction in Canada that has an affordable, widely accessible, and regulated child-care system. Other provinces are nevertheless making strides in their support for child care. For example, in their 2012 budgets, Saskatchewan created five hundred more child-care spaces; Alberta increased child-care subsidies by $21 million; and New Brunswick invested more than $3 million into creating more child-care spaces and enriching child-care subsidies.

THE NEEDS OF OLDER CHILDREN AND YOUTH

Although the needs of young children currently dominate policy agendas, governments recognize that older children also need support. Children in middle childhood (age six to twelve) face challenges related to entering the school system, choosing friends, and becoming more independent (Hanvey, 2002). As children enter adolescence (age thirteen to eighteen), they must deal with issues related to rapid growth and development while learning the life skills they will need as adults. Today's youth must also make decisions about drug and alcohol use, sexual relations, and other activities that have implications for their health and welfare and may have long-term consequences. This section looks at two topics related to the needs of older children and youth: mental health and youth policy.

Mental Health

A young person's state of mental health influences the way he or she will meet the challenges of growing up. The term **mental health** refers to a person's capacity to think, feel, and behave in ways that enhance the quality and enjoyment of life, and to an ability to effectively deal with life's challenges (Public Health Agency of Canada, 2012). Research suggests that, in general, Canadian youth enjoy positive mental health. However, one in every five young persons struggles with a **mental health disorder**. A number of conditions raise the risk of mental health disorders among children and youth. For example, young people who live in poverty are three times as likely to suffer from a mental health disorder as those in affluent families (Lipman & Boyle, 2008). In recent years, various studies have called attention to the mental health effects of bullying. According to Freeman, King, and Pickett (2011), young people who either bully or are the victims of bullying are at a particularly high risk of emotional and behavioural problems.

Mental health disorders in young people can manifest in various ways, including learning disabilities, substance abuse, eating disorders, and attention deficit hyperactivity disorder (ADHD). Many more young people suffer from milder but significant forms of mental distress (Canadian Paediatric Society, 2012). Depression and anxiety are the most common mental health disorders among Canadian youth. A disturbing outcome of mental distress is suicide, which is the second-leading cause of death among Canadian youth; First Nations youth are at the greatest risk, with a suicide rate that is five to seven times as high as that among non-Aboriginal youth (Centre for Suicide Prevention, 2011; Health Canada, 2006).

If left untreated, mental health disorders can have substantial negative consequences, such as interfering with a young person's ability to succeed in school, make friends, and solve problems. As an adult, the individual may be prone to physical illnesses or find it difficult to work or form meaningful relationships. Not only can mental health disorders take a personal toll, but they also represent a loss for society in terms of social participation and future economic productivity (Kutcher & McLuckie, 2010).

A wide range of programs and services exist in Canada to prevent or reduce the debilitating effects of mental health disorders among young people. Non-residential programs include

- preventive and early intervention programs (to increase awareness of mental health issues, reduce the risk factors associated with mental disorders, and promote healthy lifestyles and choices)
- assessment services (to diagnose developmental disorders or delays, learning disabilities, attention deficit disorders, and other functional difficulties)
- individual and family counselling (to address psychological issues)
- support and educational groups (to give opportunities for young people to interact with their peers with similar issues and to learn effective coping strategies)
- creative therapy (to help young people deal with traumatic experiences through art, play, dance, or other expression)

- crisis intervention (to respond to children and youth in distress or emergency situations)

Residential programs exist for children and youth who are experiencing severe emotional, social, or behavioural difficulties. One such program is the Woodlands Residential Treatment Program in Waterloo, Ontario; this centre offers a wide range of services for twelve- to sixteen-year-olds, including emotional management, life skills training, and peer relationship building (Lutherwood, 2012).

Despite the availability of mental health resources, less than half of all youth will get the help they need. Barriers to help seeking are largely due to inadequate provincial and territorial policies; for example, many jurisdictions lack a mental health plan that specifically addresses the needs of young people. Moreover, mental health programs for youth tend to be fragmented, uncoordinated, and incomprehensive (Canadian Association of Paediatric Health Centres, National Infant, Child, and Youth Mental Health Consortium Advisory, and Provincial Centre of Excellence for Child and Youth Mental Health at CHEO, 2010). In 2007, in an effort to improve mental health services for all Canadians, the federal government appointed the Mental Health Commission of Canada. After extensive consultations with Canadians, members of the Commission proposed a national child and youth mental health framework to help governments, organizations, and other institutions develop effective child- and youth-oriented policies and programs. Exhibit 10.4 illustrates the main components of that framework.

Youth Policy

In declaring 1985 the International Youth Year, and 2010–2011 as the International Year of Youth, the United Nations affirmed the importance of youth around the world. The international community recognizes that a globalized world not only creates new opportunities for youth but also increases the pressure on youth to prepare for a competitive and rapidly changing labour market. This new reality has prompted governments around the world to rethink their perspectives on youth and to develop policies and programs—often with input from youth—to give this population adequate support, guidance, and opportunities (Hay, 2008).

Unlike many countries around the world, Canada lacks a comprehensive national **youth policy**. However, many regional governments have a policy framework to help policymakers and service providers understand and respond appropriately to the needs of youth. Some municipalities—such as the City of Ottawa—also have a youth policy framework in place.

EXHIBIT 10.4

EVERGREEN PROJECT FRAMEWORK FOR CHILD AND YOUTH MENTAL HEALTH

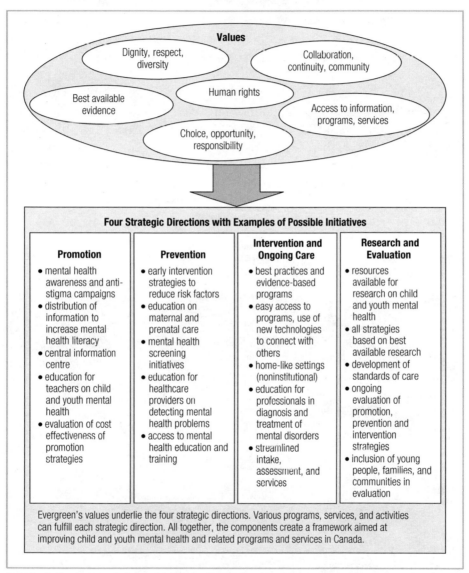

Values

Dignity, respect, diversity

Collaboration, continuity, community

Best available evidence

Human rights

Access to information, programs, services

Choice, opportunity, responsibility

Four Strategic Directions with Examples of Possible Initiatives

Promotion	Prevention	Intervention and Ongoing Care	Research and Evaluation
• mental health awareness and anti-stigma campaigns • distribution of information to increase mental health literacy • central information centre • education for teachers on child and youth mental health • evaluation of cost effectiveness of promotion strategies	• early intervention strategies to reduce risk factors • education on maternal and prenatal care • mental health screening initiatives • education for healthcare providers on detecting mental health problems • access to mental health education and training	• best practices and evidence-based programs • easy access to programs, use of new technologies to connect with others • home-like settings (noninstitutional) • education for professionals in diagnosis and treatment of mental disorders • streamlined intake, assessment, and services	• resources available for research on child and youth mental health • all strategies based on best available research • development of standards of care • ongoing evaluation of promotion, prevention and intervention strategies • inclusion of young people, families, and communities in evaluation

Evergreen's values underlie the four strategic directions. Various programs, services, and activities can fulfill each strategic direction. All together, the components create a framework aimed at improving child and youth mental health and related programs and services in Canada.

Source: Author-generated diagram, based on content from Kutcher, S. & McLuckie, A. (2010). *Evergreen: A child and youth mental health framework for Canada. Retrieved from Mental Health Commission of Canada,* http://www.mentalhealthcommission.ca/SiteCollectionDocuments/family/Evergreen_Framework_English_July2010_final.pdf.

Every youth policy framework has a slightly different focus. For instance, some policies focus on helping youth develop skills or *assets*, while other policies emphasize strategies to help youth become more *resilient* to change or stress (Jeffrey, 2008). Many youth policies and programs in Canada take a **youth engagement approach**, which asserts that youth benefit from participating in meaningful activities, having a voice in matters that affect them, and sharing power with adults. This type of approach can enhance the lives of youth in a variety of ways. For example, as the Centre of Excellence for Youth Engagement (2012) notes, "Through engagement, youth gain a sense of empowerment as individuals and make healthy connections with others, which is associated with reduction of risk behaviours and increased participation in positive activities." Many youth-engagement programs exist across Canada and each offers a unique opportunity for youth (see Exhibit 10.5). Some of those programs are available at HeartWood (2012), a centre for community youth development in Nova Scotia; here, youth can develop leadership skills through outdoor adventures, community service, teamwork, and peer support.

EXHIBIT 10.5

© Lespalenik/Dreamstime.com

Youth-engagement programs that offer wilderness adventures can help youth learn new skills, interact positively with others, and gain a sense of empowerment.

DISCUSSION QUESTIONS

■ **Meeting the Developmental Needs of Children and Youth**

1. Although Canada offers programs and services for children and youth, governments do not always make child and youth development a priority when it comes to investing money and other resources. Why do you think this is?

2. Based on your observations or experience, what are some of the pressures on parents today that make it tough to raise healthy and well-adjusted children?

3. Child advocates continue to push for the establishment of a national child-care program. Do you think that Canadians might benefit from such a program, or is the provision of cash (through the Universal Childcare Benefit) a better way to meet the child-care needs of families? Give reasons for your answers.

2 PARENTAL AND FAMILY INFLUENCES ON CHILD DEVELOPMENT

Both parenting style and family type are key influences on the way a child develops physically, socially, and cognitively. This section considers these two factors and their effect on child development.

PARENTING STYLE

A parent's style of caregiving can have a profound impact on a child's social, emotional, intellectual, and moral development. Researchers have found that severe parenting approaches, such as harsh discipline or over-controlling or coercive behaviour, can lead to the development of aggressive or antisocial tendencies in children. Those behaviours, in turn, can put children at a higher risk of substance abuse, mental health disorders, learning difficulties, and other problems (Offord Centre for Child Studies, 2012).

Child development experts generally agree that a **parenting style** characterized as *authoritative*—that is, an approach that is warm and fair yet firm—is most conducive to healthy developmental growth in children (Bornstein & Bornstein, 2009).[1] Information is gradually emerging on the link between parenting styles and socioeconomic status. Contrary to popular belief, non-positive parenting is not limited to poor families. One Canadian

---

[1] The researchers point out that their findings are based on the parenting practices of Caucasian, middle-class parents and their children. More research is needed to determine the effectiveness of parenting styles across a broader range of socioeconomic, racial, and cultural groups.

study found that while 37 percent of at-risk children live in the poorest families, more than 24 percent are from wealthy families (Willms, 2007).

Most parent support and training programs focus on helping parents learn the skills, obtain the information, and access the resources they need to raise happy and healthy children. Among the widely known parenting programs is Health Canada's Nobody's Perfect Parenting Program, which provides education and support to parents of preschool children. Another popular program is COPE (Community Parent Education), which teaches parents techniques to respond to children who have challenging behaviours. Many parent support programs are the result of grassroots efforts; Parents Together, for example, is a self-help group started by parents in British Columbia who were experiencing conflict with their teens. Despite much anecdotal evidence on the positive results of parenting programs, few programs in Canada have been formally studied or evaluated. Thus, it is difficult to determine which parenting programs might be the most effective (Cleveland et al., 2006).

FAMILY TYPE

Some experts suggest that the traditional family headed by married, biological, and heterosexual parents offer children the most material advantages and the most stable environment, and therefore provides the best environment for children (Rosenfeld, 2009). Other experts argue that there is no ideal **family type**—each family has its own strengths and weaknesses, opportunities, and challenges. The following is a review of three non-traditional family types:[2] lone-parent families, stepfamilies, and families of divorce.

Lone-Parent Families

Increases in marital separation and out-of-union births are driving up the proportion of Canadian families headed by a lone parent. In 2011, **lone-parent families** accounted for almost 10 percent of all families with children. Female lone-parent families outnumber male lone-parent families four to one (Milan & Bohnert, 2012).

The family's income level is a main determinant of a child's experience in a lone-parent family. In 2009, the median annual household income

---

[2] Same-sex-couple families are another non-traditional family type. While some studies have found that children of same-sex parents fare no worse than children of straight parents, other studies have cited a wide range of negative outcomes for children in terms of mental health, academic achievement, and social relationships. Further research is needed on how this family type might influence child development.

for lone-parent families in Canada was $36 000, compared with more than $75 000 for two-parent families (Statistics Canada, 2012e). Among lone-parent families, young mothers are especially vulnerable to economic challenges. These women often lack the education, job skills, or financial supports necessary to keep themselves and their families out of poverty (Milan, 2000). According to Lipman and Boyle (2008), children who live with a lone female parent tend to experience more mental and physical health problems than children who live in poor two-parent families.

Even if poverty is not an issue, children living in lone-parent families are at a higher risk of behavioural and academic problems than their peers in two-parent families. Children of lone parents, for example, are more likely to be aggressive or hyperactive, to fail grades, or to drop out of high school. When older, individuals from lone-parent families are at a greater risk of teen pregnancy, unemployment, criminal activity, and marital problems (Ambert, 2006).

Although studies tend to highlight the deficits rather than the assets of lone-parent families, the majority of children growing up in these families are healthy (Ross, Roberts, & Scott, 1998). The differences in child outcomes in lone- and two-parent families may be a function not so much of family type as of a cluster of factors—such as low income, depression, and lack of social support—that are commonly experienced by lone (mostly female) parents (Human Resources Development Canada, 1999a). Child and family experts also remind us that raising a child is simply a greater challenge for one parent than two. Two parents are able to share the parenting duties, and children with two parents are more likely to get emotional support and parental attention when needed. Two parents also have the potential for two incomes and a pooling of resources, which lessens the chances of poverty (Ambert, 2006).

The growing number of lone-parent families is creating a demand for specialized services. For example, the Single Parent Association of Newfoundland (2012) operates a resource centre where lone parents can obtain information and referrals specific to lone-parenthood and access support services, food, and clothing. This organization also receives provincial government grants to help lone parents on welfare re-enter the workforce through employment programs.

Families of Divorce

With more relaxed divorce laws and less stigma placed on failed marriages, divorce has become an acceptable option for people in unhappy marriages.

Since it peaked in 1987, Canada's divorce rate has been falling. Even so, four out of ten married couples in Canada can expect to divorce within the first thirty years of marriage (Kelly, 2012). Nearly half of all divorces in Canada involve dependent children (Statistics Canada, 2005).

In general, children from divorced families show higher levels of antisocial behaviour—such as aggression and criminal behaviour—than children from intact families (Statistics Canada, 2005). As adults, children of divorce tend to have lower rates of education, higher divorce rates, and more conflicted relationships (Jolivet, 2011).

The effects of divorce on children depend largely on the way in which the parents handle the break up. Most children do not suffer severe developmental problems as a result of divorce. However, the loss of emotional support, contact with one or both parents, or financial resources can make divorce harder on children. Parental conflict related to a relationship breakdown puts children at the highest risk of adjustment problems, especially if that conflict relates to such things as custody or child support payments. Children exposed to chronic parental conflict often experience stress, anxiety, guilt, fear, helplessness, or a general lack of interest in their own well-being.

Various programs aim to help children and their parents cope with the challenges of separation and divorce. Most of these programs tend to fit within one or more of the following categories:

- *Child-focused programs* are typically education or therapy groups that try to help children understand and cope with divorce.

- *Parent-focused programs* try to help children by helping their parents deal with divorce issues.

- *Counselling programs* provide one-to-one, couples, and family support to parents and children affected by divorce.

Most group programs for children of divorce are available through family courts, government, family service agencies in the voluntary sector, or organizations related to places of worship. The negative effects of divorce on children are often noticeable in the school setting in terms of academic problems—thus, many schools in Canada have established programs to help children cope with their parents' divorce.

Stepfamilies

It is common for divorced individuals to bring a child from a previous union into a new relationship or to have another child with a new partner (see Exhibit 10.6). These situations create what Statistics Canada defines as a

EXHIBIT 10.6

© Andi Berger/Shutterstock

Since the 1970s, higher rates of divorce and remarriage have led to an increase in the number of stepfamilies in Canada.

stepfamily.[3] According to the 2011 census, almost 11 percent of families with children are stepfamilies (Vézina, 2012).

The beginning stages of forming a stepfamily can be a particularly stressful time for family members, especially if both parents have one or more children from a previous union. One challenge for couples may be trying to simultaneously bond with each other and a stepchild. Unresolved conflicts between the divorced parents and their former partners may also complicate stepfamily life. For many stepfamilies, the greatest challenge is dealing with the conflicts

---

[3] Although the literature refers to stepfamilies by other terms (such as blended families, recombined families, and reconstituted families), subtle differences exist between these family types.

that arise between its members—for instance, between two stepsiblings, or between a stepparent and stepchild. It is common for marital problems to stem from conflict with a stepchild or from disagreement on parenting styles in dealing with that conflict (Preece, 2003). Unfortunately, most stepfamilies are unable to meet the various challenges they face and rarely survive past five years (Gosselin as cited in Laucius, 2011).

Children in stepfamilies tend to have more adjustment problems than do children in stable, intact families, although the reasons for those findings are not entirely clear (Kerr & Michalski, 2007). Young adolescents, for example, tend to have difficulties adjusting to changes in the family structure at a time when they are trying to form their own self-identity (American Psychological Association, 2012). Girls who have held important roles and responsibilities in their previous family may find it difficult to give up control to a new stepparent (Gosselin as cited in Laucius, 2011). Adjustment problems may relate to insufficient bonding. While most parents and their children are able to bond early in the child's life, that early childhood bonding experience is usually lacking in stepfamilies, which may partially explain why stepparent–stepchild relationships tend to be susceptible to stress within the family (Preece, 2003). Studies show that the best-adjusted children in stepfamilies have parents that are warm, supportive, and consistent; keep punishment to a minimum; and get along with each other and their former spouses (Step Families Canada, 2012).

In response to the unique situation of stepfamilies, a number of social agencies offer information and support that is specific to stepfamily issues and needs; for example, the booklet *Building Your Stepfamily: A Blueprint for Success* from the BC Council for Families offers tips for how to make stepfamilies work. A number of voluntary agencies across Canada provide information and support services specifically for stepfamilies, including the Stepfamily Foundation of Alberta. Some organizations, such as the University of Ottawa's Stepfamily Research Laboratory, devote their efforts to learning more about the needs and challenges facing stepfamilies.

DISCUSSION QUESTIONS

■ **Parental and Family Influences on Child Development**

1. What do you think is the ideal family type (if any) for children? Give reasons for your answer.

2. Every family type has potential strengths and weaknesses. Identify what you believe may be the strengths of (a) lone-parent families, (b) stepfamilies, and (c) divorced families.

3 FAMILY VIOLENCE

Family violence is a social problem that has far-reaching social, economic, justice, and health consequences. The Government of Canada defines family violence as the abuse of power within relationships based on intimacy, trust, kinship, or dependency. Family violence includes a wide range of behaviours, including physical assault, emotional abuse, neglect, sexual assault, financial exploitation, stalking, and witnessing violence within the family (Jamieson & Gomes, 2010). In 2010, about 99 000 Canadians were victims of family violence (Sinha, 2012).

Every child exposed to family violence will respond differently, depending on his or her age, the severity and frequency of the conflict, and other factors. However, family violence tends to create some level of emotional, social, or behavioural difficulty for most children. Two types of family violence— spousal abuse and child abuse—may be particularly detrimental to a child's well-being.

SPOUSAL ABUSE

Spouses are the victims in almost half of all family violence acts (Sinha, 2012). **Spousal abuse** (also called intimate partner abuse) occurs when one marital, common-law, separated, divorced, or same-sex partner abuses the other. Six percent of Canadians suffer spousal abuse, which may be physical (the most common), emotional, financial, or sexual (Statistics Canada, 2011b). When compared with male victims, female victims of spousal abuse are more likely to incur physical injuries, require medical attention, and suffer emotional consequences, such as depression or anxiety attacks (Mihorean, 2005).

Spousal abuse is a complex social problem with no single, definitive cause; however, certain factors put some people at a higher risk of abuse than others. Just being a woman increases the risk of spousal abuse because of the power imbalances between men and women in society; more than eight out of every ten victims of spousal abuse are female. Age is another risk factor: younger women (ages twenty-five to thirty-four) are particularly vulnerable to abuse by their partners (Sinha, 2012). Women who are Aboriginal, poor, living in a common-law relationship, or in the process of ending a relationship are also at a higher risk of abuse (Cunningham & Baker, 2007). Women in some provinces experience a higher incidence of spousal abuse than others (see Exhibit 10.7).

EXHIBIT 10.7

SELF-REPORTED SPOUSAL ABUSE, BY PROVINCE

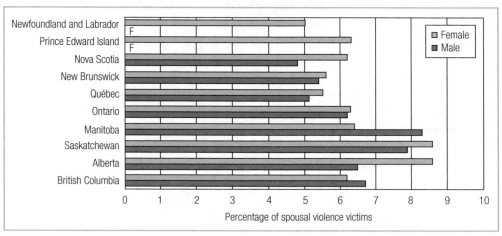

Notes: Includes legally married, common-law, same-sex, separated, and divorced spouses who reported having experienced spousal violence within the five years preceding the 2009 General Social Survey. Not included are data for the proportion of males who experienced spousal violence in Newfoundland and Labrador and Prince Edward Island (data are too small to produce reliable estimates).

Source: Brennan, S. (2011). Self-reported spousal violence 2009 (chart 1.1, p. 9). In Statistics Canada, *Family violence in Canada* (pp. 3–19). Retrieved from http://www.statcan.gc.ca/pub/85-224-x/85-224-x2010000-eng.pdf.

Abuse can potentially create problems in all aspects of an abused person's life; many victims, for example, experience physical or mental health problems or difficulties working or parenting. One of the greatest concerns about spousal abuse is its potential to harm children. Studies show that children who see or hear violence in the home can experience the same negative effects as children who are directly abused. Those effects include short- and long-term emotional, behavioural, and developmental disorders (Royal Canadian Mounted Police, 2012a). Boys who witness their father's abuse of a woman are three times as likely as their peers to grow up and abuse their own partner (AuCoin, 2005). Moreover, girls who witness family violence or suffer abuse as a child are more likely to grow up to be victims of spousal abuse (Hart & Jamieson, 2001). Spousal abuse is more visible than it used to be: in 2009, children witnessed 52 percent of all reported cases of spousal abuse, up from 43 percent in 2004. Children who are exposed to family violence typically witness assaults against their mother rather than their father (Statistics Canada, 2012f).

Canada's Family Violence Initiative supports the development and provision of many services for abused women and their children.[4] Among these resources, shelters are a primary source of help. Shelters include

- transition houses (short- or moderate-stay housing)
- second-stage housing (longer-term housing in conjunction with support and referral services)
- emergency shelters (short-term respite)
- safe homes (short-term emergency housing in private homes)

A number of programs exist across Canada to assist children who have witnessed violence by one parent against the other. For example, the Children Exposed to Violence in Families Program in Saskatchewan offers support and information to young people to help them cope with the effects of domestic violence and to prevent them from becoming victims or perpetrators of violence in the future.

CHILD ABUSE AND NEGLECT

Exposure to family violence is the most common form of **child abuse**; children may also endure physical, emotional, or sexual abuse (Public Health Agency of Canada, 2010a). The term, **child neglect**, refers to a specific type of abuse in which a caregiver fails to provide appropriate care, supervision, or protection to a child (see Exhibit 10.8). Some child welfare experts use the term *child maltreatment* when referring to child abuse and neglect.

Child welfare statistics (2008 figures) reveal that more than 85 000 Canadian children suffer some form of maltreatment (Public Health Agency of Canada, 2010a). Child welfare experts suggest that the actual number of child abuse incidences is much higher than the number of reported cases (Dudding, 2011). While every Canadian has a legal responsibility to report suspected incidences of child abuse, many incidences do not come to the attention of the police or other child protection authority. Thus, because of the hidden nature and underreporting of this type of abuse, it is difficult to estimate how many children, or the proportion of all children, experience maltreatment.

---

[4] Studies suggest that men are almost as likely as women to be victims of spousal abuse; however, men are less likely to report those incidents to police. Without the statistics to confirm the prevalence of male victimization, governments are reluctant to fund services specifically for male victims.

EXHIBIT 10.8

John Joseph Kelso fonds/Library and Archives Canada/PA-118221

Historically, child neglect has been the most common form of child abuse in Canada and can affect physical, emotional, and cognitive development.

Child maltreatment usually occurs while a child is in the care of someone he or she trusts and depends on, such as a parent, caregiver, or teacher. Any child is vulnerable to abuse or neglect to some extent; however, children at the highest risk are those who have a disability, live in poverty, are Aboriginal, or belong to a racial or ethnic minority family (Canada Department of Justice, 2006). Various signs may indicate that a child may be suffering abuse or neglect:

- developmental delays in speech, language, motor, or social skills
- regressive behaviours, such as bedwetting or thumb sucking
- difficulties meeting expected standards of growth (a failure to thrive)

- unusual parent–child interactions, such as a parent showing little interest in the child or the child taking on the role of parent

- mental health issues, including depression, anxiety, low self-esteem, and suicidal tendencies

- academic decline

- inappropriate or problem behaviours, including unexplained fears and aggressive or sexual acting out (MyHealthAlberta, 2011)

The effects of abuse or neglect on children depends on many factors, including the severity and frequency of the abuse, the child's age and his or her ability to cope, and the relationship between the child and the abuser (Victims of Violence, 2011). For some people, the negative effects of maltreatment during childhood can have long-term consequences. In adulthood, victims of abuse are more likely to have health problems, such as asthma or chronic pain; they are also at a higher risk of addictions, aggressive or criminal behaviour, and abuse of their own children (Canadian Resource Centre for Victims of Crime, 2006). Child maltreatment also has its social and economic costs. For example, some adult survivors of abuse experience difficulty working, earning a sufficient income, and participating fully in society. One study estimates that child abuse in Canada costs $15 billion a year for healthcare, social welfare services, and lost productivity by parents (Johnson, 2006).

CHILD PROTECTION SERVICES

Before Confederation, people considered children—along with farm animals—as important family assets that were "owned" by the head of the household (usually the father). However, beginning in the late nineteenth century, society began to see children less as property and more as individuals in need of protection. During this period, the state introduced a number of child-saving policies to protect young people from harm; at the same time, the courts began to apply the principle of **parens patriae** in decisions related to children. Under *parens patriae*—a Latin term meaning "father of the nation"—the state can use its authority in special circumstances to override parental rights and intervene on behalf of a child (Volpe, Cox, Goddard, & Tilleczek, 1997). Canada's child welfare systems, and the wide range of services designed to protect children and youth, reflect this country's *parens patriae* jurisdiction.

This section explores the ways in which Canada aims to protect its young people from maltreatment; the focus here is on three levels of prevention; child welfare systems; out-of-home care; and children's rights. Concluding this section is a brief look at some of the criticisms and reforms of child welfare services.

Three Levels of Prevention

Canada addresses the problem of child maltreatment at three levels of prevention. *Primary prevention* activities target the general population in an effort to prevent the incidence of child abuse or neglect. These initiatives aim to raise public awareness about child maltreatment, promote healthy living, and generally prevent the risk factors that may contribute to child mistreatment. *Secondary prevention* activities focus on families at risk of child maltreatment, and try to reduce any negative factors that may result in child abuse or neglect. Those risk factors include poverty, parental substance abuse or mental health issues, and the disability of a family member. If child maltreatment has already occurred, *tertiary prevention* activities attempt to reduce the negative effects of the maltreatment, and to prevent further incidences of abuse or neglect (Shangreaux & Blackstock, 2004). Exhibit 10.9 provides a graphical illustration of the three interrelated levels of prevention and gives examples of strategies or interventions at each level.

Child advocates generally agree that primary prevention strategies are a wise investment in the future of children and society in general. Nevertheless, tertiary prevention programs have traditionally dominated the focus of child protection services. In practice, this has meant that child welfare agencies give priority to families in which a child has suffered neglect or abuse; meanwhile, families under stress but in which maltreatment has not yet occurred go without services. This situation has been changing in recent years as child welfare authorities recognize the value of secondary prevention programs in reducing the risk of child maltreatment. Today, many regional governments fund both protective services (when there is substantiated child maltreatment) and supportive services (when there is no immediate risk of harm to a child). Family services in the voluntary sector usually deliver supportive services, which include parenting skills groups, addiction services, and family support programs (National Aboriginal Health Organization, 2011).

Child Welfare Systems

The Canadian Constitution allows each province and territory to develop its own **child welfare system** for abused or neglected children and their families.

EXHIBIT 10.9

CHILD MALTREATMENT: THREE LEVELS OF PREVENTION

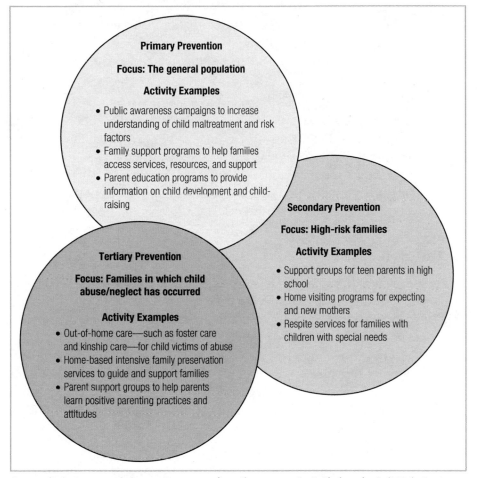

Primary Prevention

Focus: The general population

Activity Examples

- Public awareness campaigns to increase understanding of child maltreatment and risk factors
- Family support programs to help families access services, resources, and support
- Parent education programs to provide information on child development and child-raising

Secondary Prevention

Focus: High-risk families

Activity Examples

- Support groups for teen parents in high school
- Home visiting programs for expecting and new mothers
- Respite services for families with children with special needs

Tertiary Prevention

Focus: Families in which child abuse/neglect has occurred

Activity Examples

- Out-of-home care—such as foster care and kinship care—for child victims of abuse
- Home-based intensive family preservation services to guide and support families
- Parent support groups to help parents learn positive parenting practices and attitudes

Source: Author-generated chart, using content from Shangreaux, C., & Blackstock, C. (2004). *Staying at home: Examining the implications of least disruptive measures in First Nations child and family service agencies* (pp. 25–26). Retrieved from First Nations Child and Family Caring Society of Canada website: http://www.fncfcs.com/sites/default/files/docs/Staying_at_Home.pdf.

As a result, approaches to child protection vary across jurisdictional boundaries in terms of legislation, investigative procedures, and child welfare services.

- *Legislation.* Each province and territory has its own definition of child abuse and neglect, its own ideas about the state's role in family life, and its own concept of what factors constitute risk to children. There is also disparity as to the age limit of children who can receive protection services; for example, British Columbia's age of protection is nineteen years and under, whereas in Ontario, the age is sixteen years and under.

- *Investigative procedures.* Each province and territory has its own guidelines as to the types of abuse that child welfare workers must investigate, the kind of investigative procedures to use, and the criteria they must apply when deciding whether to remove a child from the home.

- *Services.* While each jurisdiction provides similar types of services— such as the investigation of reported child maltreatment and the provision of foster care—they differ in the way they deliver those services. For instance, in the territories and most provinces, government workers deliver child welfare services. In contrast, the Government of Ontario contracts out the delivery of its child protection services to fifty-three voluntary agencies called Children's Aid Societies.

Out-of-Home Care

Studies show that children who remain in their own homes tend to fare better psychologically and academically than children who are placed in alternative care (Fowler, 2008). Thus, child welfare authorities prefer to keep children in the home if it is in the child's best interests to do so; in these cases, a family is likely to receive extra support, such as a referral to addictions counselling or a parent support program.

In cases of abuse or extreme neglect, child welfare authorities are justified in removing the child from the home and placing him or her in **out-of-home care**. Three placement options are used most by child welfare workers:

- kinship care (a home of someone with whom the child has a relationship, such as grandparents, another relative, or a family friend)

- foster care (an approved family home that provides temporary care, specialized care for a child or youth with complex needs, or an environment in which the needs of a child or youth can be properly assessed)

- residential care (a private or government community-based facility that is run by professional staff; facilities include group homes, therapeutic treatment centres, and secure/custody facilities)

Today, most child welfare workers prefer to place children in kinship and foster care, and rarely use residential care as a placement option (Smith, Van Wert, Ma, & Fallon, 2012).

When a child is placed in out-of-home care, the child welfare worker and the parent or caregiver develop a temporary care plan based on the needs of the child and the family circumstances. The plan is a written agreement that outlines what the parent must do (for example, take a parenting course) to regain custody of the child. In 2007, approximately 67 000 young Canadians were living in out-of-home care (Mulcahy & Trocmé, 2010).

Aboriginal children are overrepresented in Canada's child welfare system, and the rate of overreprésentation increases each year. Although Aboriginal children compose less than 6 percent of all Canadian children, they represent almost 80 percent of the **children in care** in some provinces and territories (Centre of Excellence for Child Welfare, 2011). The Assembly of First Nations (2007a) estimates that one in ten First Nations children can expect to be involved in the child welfare system, compared with one in two hundred non-First-Nations children.

Although most children living in out-of-home care will return to their family within a year of their being placed, reunification with family is not always a viable option. In these cases, the child welfare agency must consider other placements for the permanent care of a child or youth (Trocméi et al., 2009). The term **public adoption** refers to the process of adopting a child or youth who is in the care of a provincial or territorial child welfare agency. There are never enough adoptive families to meet the need. According to the Adoption Council of Canada (2012), approximately 30 000 Canadian children and youth in care are waiting for permanent adoptive homes.

Children's Rights and Child Welfare Services

Canada's child welfare systems share similar principles concerning children and families. For instance, each system respects the autonomy of the family and the parent's responsibility for raising children, and recognizes the importance of cultural heritage and the continuity of care for children (Gough, Shlonsky, & Dudding, 2009). Many of those principles stem from the United Nations Convention on the Rights of the Child (CRC). Under the CRC, children have three main rights:

- the right to protection (from abuse, neglect, and exploitation)
- the right to participation (as full citizens in family, social, and community life)
- the right to provision (of food, shelter, adequate care, and other basics) (Standing Senate Committee on Human Rights, 2007)

While all the CRC principles have influenced child-related policies and programs to some extent, two principles have had a particular influence on Canada's child welfare legislation. The *principle of the right to participation* requires child welfare authorities to consider the age-appropriate views of children on matters that concern them, including their placement in out-of-home care. The *principle of the best interests of the child* requires anyone making decisions on behalf of a child—such as child welfare workers and the courts—to take into account what is best for the child rather than what may be preferred by parents or the state.

The provinces and territories have made some headway into incorporating CRC principles into child welfare laws. However, according to the United Nation's Committee on the Rights of the Child (2012, p. 8), Canada is not doing enough. For instance, in 2012, the Committee found that Canada had failed to facilitate "meaningful and empowered child participation" in issues and processes that affect children. Moreover, the principle of the best interests of the child is poorly understood in Canada, and has not been integrated or applied across child-related laws, policies, or programs.

Criticisms and Reforms

Historically, Canada's child welfare systems have been criticized for either intruding into the lives of families too much (the large-scale removal of Aboriginal children from their homes illustrates this point), or for failing to intervene promptly enough (resulting in several tragic deaths of children in care). Critics have also charged child welfare agencies for lacking cultural sensitivity, particularly when serving Aboriginal children; for relying too heavily on out-of-home placements; and for ignoring social conditions that contribute to child maltreatment, including poverty, isolation, and substandard housing. In response to these criticisms, child welfare systems have undergone considerable reform in recent years. Many of those reforms have come about through the sharing of best practices in child welfare and the expansion of research-based institutions, such as Canada's Centre of Excellence for Child Welfare.

DISCUSSION QUESTIONS

■ **Family Violence**

1. It is often difficult for victims of family violence to talk about their abusive experiences. Identify some of the personal qualities that professional helpers should have when working with victims of abuse.

2. Although men are at risk of spousal abuse, society is more likely to cast them in the role of victimizer rather than victim. What needs to change for society to respond more effectively to the needs of male victims?

3. Everyone plays a role in protecting children from harm. What are some important things a community might do to prevent the incidence of child abuse or neglect?

4 SOCIAL WORK WITH FAMILIES WITH CHILDREN

Working with families is an important activity in social welfare programs and a primary focus for many social workers. There are a number of rewards associated with helping families meet their basic needs, effectively problem-solve, and reach their goals. There are also challenges to working with families; social workers, for example, have to regularly upgrade their assessment and intervention skills to help families deal with the rapidly changing social, economic, and political environment.

Many social workers take a **strengths-based approach** to family service, in which they help families to identify and build on their strengths as a means to solving problems and overcoming obstacles. **Empowerment** plays an important role in a strengths-based approach. When social workers engage in empowering activities with families, they are essentially helping family members help themselves. A family may be empowered when it can (1) identify its needs and know how to meet those needs; (2) advocate on its own behalf to obtain necessary resources; and (3) provide input on programs and policies that directly affect them.

Empowered families are knowledgeable about the services available to them. Social workers can provide these services directly, or they can help families learn about and access community resources. As cuts to social welfare programs make services less available, unaffordable, or unsuitable, many families may need to do more on their own, such as minding children in the home rather than taking them to a child-care centre. This will require front-line workers to help families discover their own *internal* strategies for meeting needs and resolving problems, as opposed to relying on *external*, government-sponsored supports.

Another way social workers might help families is by providing information on what parents can do to support their child's development. In the role of coach, social workers can encourage parents to listen to and talk with their children; to show love, support, and affection; and to help their children or teens make decisions and solve problems. Social workers can provide practical support as well; for example, they might help parents plan for spending time with their children or give tips on how to budget for purchasing goods or services, such as music lessons or hockey equipment. Finally, social workers can help parents recognize their own strengths, intuitive abilities, and successes as caregivers.

DISCUSSION QUESTIONS

■ **Social Work with Families with Children**

1. Identify some of the potential rewards and challenges of working with families with children, given the rapidly changing economic, social, and political environment.

2. To become empowered, families might benefit from discovering their own internal strategies for meeting needs and resolving problems. How might social workers help families with this task?

SUMMARY

Introduction

Families with children supply the nation's future adults, workers, and parents. Most Canadian children are doing well, yet many live in disadvantaged circumstances. Parents are the primary caregivers; however, government also assumes responsibility for children's well-being. Although Canada has many social welfare programs for children and families, governments have been inconsistent in their approach to family policy.

1 Meeting the Developmental Needs of Children and Youth

Such policies as the National Children's Agenda aim to help children get a good start in life. Canada is not meeting current child-care demands, which are likely to increase in the coming years. Mental health plays an important role in how young people deal with challenges. Various residential and non-residential centres provide mental health services for youth. Despite these supports, mental health disorders among young people are increasing, and only half of Canadian youth get the help they need.

2 Parental and Family Influences on Child Development

There is no ideal family type, but all have an influence on a child's well-being. Although most children growing up in lone-parent families are healthy, children in these families are at a higher risk of behavioural and academic problems; this family type is also at risk of poverty, especially if headed by a female. Developmental or adjustment problems among children in divorced families are often related to conflict between the parents.

The greatest challenge for many stepfamilies is dealing with conflicts between their members. Children in stepfamilies tend to suffer adjustment problems; however, the reason for this is unknown. A range of specialized services is available for lone-parent families, divorced families, and stepfamilies.

3 Family Violence

Family violence is a wide-spread social problem in Canada. Spousal abuse has many potential negative consequences for the victims, including children who witness it. Support services (such as shelters) are available for abused women and their children. Various forms of child abuse exist, all of which can have far-reaching effects on children. Although statistics are collected on reported cases of child abuse, many incidences of child maltreatment are unreported. Child welfare systems vary across the country and offer a range of care options for children at risk.

4 Social Work with Families with Children

Family practice is the focus for many social agencies and workers. It is important for workers to continually refine their skills to help families deal with a rapidly changing environment. Empowerment is a central theme in family services. To help families cope with cuts to services, social workers engage families in activities that promote internal and empowering solutions. Social workers may provide information about child development and assist parents in activities that support their child's development.

KEY TERMS

For definitions of the key terms, consult the Glossary on page 453 at the end of the book.

11

CHAPTER

Social Welfare and Older Canadians

OBJECTIVES

The social welfare of older Canadians is becoming an increasingly critical issue in the context of an aging population. This chapter will

- introduce concepts and issues related to population aging

- examine organized approaches to meeting seniors' needs

- explore programs and services aimed at improving the physical, mental, financial, and social well-being of seniors

- discuss seniors' housing options and supports for independence

- describe work and participation among seniors

- summarize social work practice with elderly populations

INTRODUCTION

[Seniors are] a rich and vibrant part of our country. As we increasingly draw on seniors to meet labour force requirements strained by decades of low fertility, our society has new motivation to value seniors as contributing members of society, and not as burdens to be problematized. At the same time, it is necessary to provide the services and supports which will allow seniors to live with dignity. (Special Senate Committee on Aging, 2007, p. 1)

The United Nations declared 1999 as the International Year of Older Persons to raise awareness of a global aging trend. The term **population aging** refers to the rising proportion of aging or older people in the general population. Population aging is a worldwide phenomenon, affecting the vast majority of countries. Canada's aging population is largely attributable to the following three main factors:

1. *Aging baby boom generation.* The baby boomers—born between 1946 and 1965—represent the largest generational group in Canada's history. In 2011, the baby boomers represented 29 percent of the population (Martel & Ménard, 2012). As the **baby boom generation** moves into its senior years, the aging of Canada's population will accelerate. (In Exhibit 11.1, the bulge in the population pyramid reflects the dominance of the baby boomers.)

2. *Increased life expectancy.* Canadians are living longer because of new medical technologies, improvements in healthcare and nutrition, better methods of controlling infectious diseases, and healthier lifestyle choices. Today, the average woman can expect to live to eighty-three years and the average man to seventy-nine years (Statistics Canada, 2012g).

3. *Declining birth rate.* In 1959, Canadian women had an average of almost four children. Since that time, families have been getting smaller; on

EXHIBIT 11.1

CANADA'S AGING POPULATION

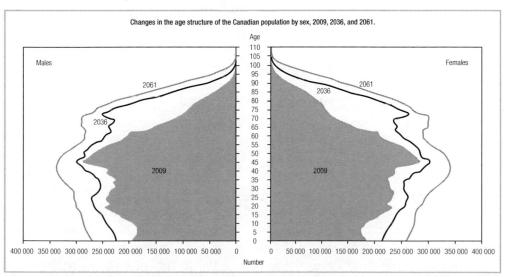

Source: Statistics Canada. (2010). *Population projections for Canada, provinces and territories: 2009 to 2036* (chart 3.5, p. 45). Retrieved from http://www.statcan.gc.ca/pub/91-520-x/91-520-x2010001-eng.pdf.

average, women now have 1.7 children (Human Resources and Skills Development Canada [HRSDC], 2012f). A falling birth rate means that fewer young people are entering the population, which, in turn, increases the average age of the population.

In 1971, just more than 8 percent of Canada's population was over sixty-five; that figure rose to about 11 percent in 1991 and to 15 percent in 2011, and is predicted to be about 25 percent by 2051 (HRSDC, 2012g). Although the life expectancy of men is rising, most seniors are women, especially among those aged eighty and over; this trend will likely continue for several years (Statistics Canada, 2010d).

The implications of an aging population have been widely debated over the past few decades. Many who see this demographic shift as a potential problem refer to the **population dependency ratio**, which measures the number of working-age adults relative to those who are either too young or too old to work. Statistics show that the dependency ratio is increasing. For example, in 2006, there were approximately 60 dependent people per 100 working-age people; demographers predict that by 2056, that rate will reach 84 dependants per 100 workers (Statistics Canada, 2010e). The shifting dependant-to-worker ratio raises several concerns. One is that a growing number of retired or non-contributing members of society will consume a greater share of resources (such as healthcare, social services, public pensions, and housing). Another concern is that a relatively small workforce will have to support a rather large group of dependants—a burden that is both unreasonable and unsustainable.

Although population aging will undoubtedly create challenges, not everyone accepts the doom-and-gloom predictions of an "age quake." After studying population aging from various angles, the Special Senate Committee on Aging (2007) concluded that while the retirement of the baby boomers is likely to impact the labour market, it will not necessarily erode Canada's standard of living or collapse its public programs. Indeed, Canada has made considerable progress in developing measures to counteract the negative impacts of population aging. Many Canadian governments do this by promoting **active aging**—that is, by offering opportunities that ensure an active and engaged life from birth to death. By creating a generally healthy population, governments expect to reduce the demand for health, social services, and other limited resources by a large number of old people. There is also the hope that healthy older people will continue to contribute to society through work or volunteering (Special Senate Committee on Aging, 2009).

This chapter provides an overview of some of the challenges and opportunities related to aging in Canada. In the following discussion, the terms *senior, older person*, and *elderly person* are used interchangeably to refer to persons aged sixty-five or over.

1 ORGANIZED APPROACHES TO MEETING SENIORS' NEEDS

Canada supports a wide range of programs, services, and initiatives to address the needs of older citizens. These organized approaches include *gerontological research*, which provides important information on aging, and *government initiatives* aimed at enhancing seniors' quality of life. *Senior's groups* play an important role in improving the lives of older people, as do grassroots initiatives that create *age-friendly communities*. Various aspects of these organized approaches are explored below.

GERONTOLOGICAL RESEARCH

In 1944, the Gerontologic Research Unit was founded at McGill University and Canada's first step was taken in the formal study of aging, otherwise known as **gerontology**. Since that time, Canada has been building a solid body of knowledge on gerontological issues. Gerontological research is either sponsored or carried out by

- universities (for example, the Gerontology Research Centre at Simon Fraser University)
- voluntary organizations (for example, the Canadian Association on Gerontology)
- federally funded institutions (for example, the Institute of Aging)
- provincial and territorial government departments (for example, Newfoundland and Labrador Healthy Aging and Research Program)
- municipalities across Canada (for example, the Older Adult Perception Study by the City of Greater Sudbury, Ontario)

One of the most comprehensive studies on aging in the world is the Canadian Longitudinal Study on Aging (CLSA). This national study is tracking the biological, psychological, social, economic, and other aspects of life among 50 000 older men and women over twenty years. Part of the CLSA's mandate is to identify the components of "successful aging" and determine which factors contribute to disease or disability as people age. The CLSA began recruiting subjects in 2009.

Ageism

Gerontological research not only can lead to a better understanding of the aging process but can also help to dispel certain stereotypes and myths about old age (see Exhibit 11.2). The term **ageism** refers to the discrimination of individuals and groups (usually older people) because of their age. In Western cultures, where youth tends to be more valued than old age, ageist social attitudes typically portray older people as being useless, stupid, or a burden on family and society (World Health Organization [WHO], 2007). These attitudes

EXHIBIT 11.2

MYTHS AND FACTS ABOUT OLDER CANADIANS

MYTH	FACT
Intellectual functioning decreases as we age.	Current research does not support the notion that intellectual functioning declines after middle age.
Most older people lose interest in or a capacity for sexual relations.	Research suggests that the normal aging process alone does not directly affect sexuality.
Age affects older adults' ability to drive safely.	Statistically, healthy older adults are the safest of all age groups on the road.
Most older adults live in institutions.	Only about 7 percent of seniors live in institutions.
Older people have little interest in using the Internet.	Seniors are the fastest-growing group of Internet users in Canada.
Developing dementia is a normal part of aging.	While age raises the risk for dementia, most people do not develop dementia as they age.
It is becoming less likely for older people to be employed.	Over the last decade, the number of employed older adults has increased.
Older adults are more likely to be victims of crime than younger people.	According to the 2009 General Social Survey, young people (ages fifteen to twenty-four) are fifteen times as likely as seniors to be victims of crime.
Older people are more likely to commit suicide than younger people.	As a group, seniors are less likely than teenagers or middle-aged adults to commit suicide.
Older people have little influence on our government.	Seniors are more likely than young adults to vote in elections.
Most older adults live alone.	Most older adults live with a spouse, with children or grandchildren, or in a collective dwelling.
Most older adults are preoccupied with death.	In general, older adults are not overly anxious about death.
The majority of older adults are poor.	Most seniors live above the poverty line.

Source: Adapted from Ontario Seniors' Secretariat. (2011). Aging quiz. Retrieved from http://www.seniors.gov. on.ca/en/agingquiz/quiz.php. © Queen's Printer for Ontario, 2007. Reproduced with permission.

can lead to the discriminatory treatment of older people in the workplace, health settings, and other areas.

In an effort to reduce ageism, Canadian governments sometimes use a discrimination lens when analyzing public policies related to seniors. This type of analysis has revealed that basing eligibility for some health and social benefits on a person's age is both discriminatory and unrealistic. For instance, studies show that the health and social conditions of an average fifty-five-year-old First Nations person is equivalent to that of a sixty-five-year-old non-Aboriginal senior; thus, the use of the chronological marker of age sixty-five to determine eligibility for long-term care makes little sense (Special Senate Committee on Aging, 2007). The fact that age-related issues may arise at various ages and stages of life—not just at age sixty-five or beyond—has implications for who receives care and support. Since recognizing the ageist beliefs in certain social policies, service providers are more likely these days to consider a person's *level of need or functioning* than *age* when determining that person's eligibility for health or social welfare programs (Katz, 2012).

Diversity

Gerontolgical research is revealing the diverse nature of the senior population. As Dobie (2006, p. 44) points out, the seniors of today hardly fit the stereotype of "a monolithic group of poor, frail, sick or dependent persons." Rather, seniors represent a highly diverse group, with different interests, backgrounds, levels of participation, sexual orientations, and living arrangements. The experience of being older is also changing: in general, today's seniors are wealthier, better educated, and more active than previous generations (Canada Mortgage and Housing Corporation, 2012b).

Old age used to encompass a relatively short period of a person's life: for example, a male born in 1945, could expect to be a senior from the age of sixty-five (when he retired) to sixty-eight (when he died) (Bothwell, Drummond, & English, 1989). Today, a person's senior years encompass a longer period. Thus, some researchers recognize three stages of late adulthood:

- The "young old" (aged sixty-five to seventy-five) are likely to be financially well-off, healthy, and fit (see Exhibit 11.3), and can function on their own with no or minimal assistance; many people in this group still work, go to school, and travel.

- The "middle old" (aged seventy-five to eighty-five) tend to have less money, fewer resources, and a diminished desire to work or travel. By this stage, individuals are likely to experience widowhood, health problems, and a loss of mobility.

EXHIBIT 11.3

© iStockphoto.com/McIninch

In general, today's seniors are healthier and more physically active than those of previous generations.

- The "frail old" (aged eighty-five and older) are the most likely of the three subgroups to have health problems and cognitive impairment. This group needs the greatest degree of support, which, in some cases, is provided in long-term-care facilities (Special Senate Committee on Aging, 2008).

The diversity of the senior population and the different needs among the three subgroups of seniors have implications for how social welfare, health, and other public systems design and deliver programs to older Canadians.

GOVERNMENT INITIATIVES

Canada participates in both international and domestic efforts to meet the needs of aging citizens. This section reviews international action plans on aging and looks at how Canadian governments share the responsibilities for seniors.

International Action Plans

In 1982, the United Nations introduced its first International Plan of Action on Ageing to guide governments in the development of policies and programs related to aging. Twenty years later, the UN revised the plan to promote aging more as a "milestone of human progress" than a "challenge" (Zelenev, 2008). While the international plan recognizes key principles and priorities, each country is free to adapt the priorities to its own circumstances.

Canada's rendition of the UN's International Plan of Action on Ageing focuses on the enhancement of health and well-being over the life course, the promotion of independent living, and the expansion of opportunities for older persons to participate in society (Edwards & Mawani, 2006). Although the initiatives under Canada's plan are highly varied, most are based on one or more of the following concepts:

- *Inclusivity* targets all seniors, including those at risk and those who are healthy and active.

- *Healthy aging* promotes behaviours, habits, and choices that enhance the well-being of people of any age over the entire life course.

- *Population health* recognizes that such factors as income, housing, social support, education, and transportation are powerful determinants of overall health.

- **Aging in place** ensures that older people can access the resources they need to continue living in their own homes for as long as possible.

- *Social justice* promotes the belief that every person, regardless of age, is entitled to security, autonomy, and dignity, protection from discrimination and abuse, and appropriate care and services (McLachlin, 2008).

Over the years, Canada has incorporated these concepts into programs for seniors. In 2005, the Organisation for Economic Co-operation and Development (OECD) praised Canada for being well prepared to meet the challenges of an aging population, especially in terms of having sustainable public pensions and job opportunities for older workers (Tobin, 2005). Nevertheless, Canada has more work to do in terms of, for example, addressing mental health issues among seniors and expanding services for the frail elderly, a group with particularly complex needs (Public Health Agency of Canada, 2010b; University of British Columbia [UBC], 2011).

Shared Responsibility for Seniors

In Canada, governments at all levels share a responsibility for the health and social welfare of older Canadians. The federal government develops and manages programs that have a national scope (such as the Old Age Security pension), while departments in provincial and territorial governments focus on providing programs and services to improve the quality of life for seniors in each region. Over the years, municipal governments have assumed more responsibility for the well-being of seniors. The trend in many municipalities across Canada is to improve local recreational, cultural, transit, and other services to enable seniors to live healthy, fulfilling, and active lives (Federation of Canadian Municipalities, 2010).

Some of Canada's most important policies and programs for older Canadians are the result of collaborative efforts by the Federal-Provincial-Territorial Ministers Responsible for Seniors. In 1996, the ministers agreed on a National Framework on Aging (NFA), which outlines an overall vision for policies and programs for seniors in Canada. Also identified within the NFA are five principles—dignity, independence, participation, fairness, and security—that policymakers should follow when developing initiatives for seniors. Exhibit 11.4 outlines the various components of the NFA and its current priorities.

SENIORS' GROUPS

Voluntary organizations—often in the form of councils, charities, associations, or societies—play a particularly important role in the lives of seniors. Organizations that provide direct services to seniors sometimes focus on a specific aspect of senior life, such as housing or continuing education. However, in many communities, senior's centres offer a variety of programs—such as peer support, information and referral, and social events—in a convenient, "one-stop-shop" location.

Seniors councils perform a political function. In general, these councils of older adults consult with seniors and seniors' organizations, and then give feedback to government. Policymakers can then use that information to

EXHIBIT 11.4

HEALTHY AGING IN CANADA: A FRAMEWORK FOR ACTION

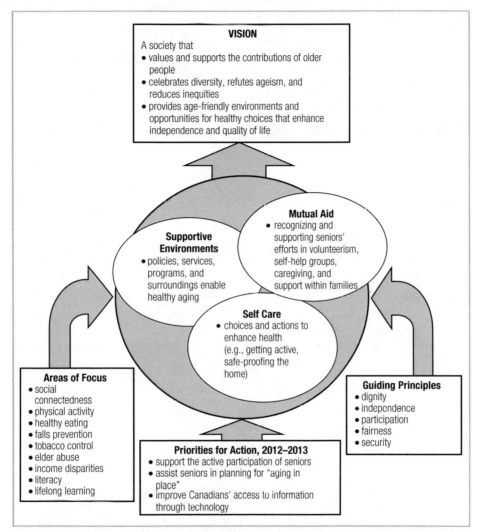

VISION
A society that
- values and supports the contributions of older people
- celebrates diversity, refutes ageism, and reduces inequities
- provides age-friendly environments and opportunities for healthy choices that enhance independence and quality of life

Mutual Aid
- recognizing and supporting seniors' efforts in volunteerism, self-help groups, caregiving, and support within families

Supportive Environments
- policies, services, programs, and surroundings enable healthy aging

Self Care
- choices and actions to enhance health (e.g., getting active, safe-proofing the home)

Areas of Focus
- social connectedness
- physical activity
- healthy eating
- falls prevention
- tobacco control
- elder abuse
- income disparities
- literacy
- lifelong learning

Guiding Principles
- dignity
- independence
- participation
- fairness
- security

Priorities for Action, 2012–2013
- support the active participation of seniors
- assist seniors in planning for "aging in place"
- improve Canadians' access to information through technology

Sources: Adapted from P. Edwards & A. Mawani. (2006 September). Healthy aging in Canada (p. 45). Retrieved from http://www.phac-aspc.gc.ca/seniors-aines/alt-formats/pdf/publications/public/healthy-sante/vision/vision-eng.pdf, and Canada News Centre. (2012, November 16). 14th Meeting of Federal, Provincial and Territorial (F/P/T) Ministers Responsible for Seniors. Retrieved from http://news.gc.ca/web/article-eng.do?nid=707459.

develop senior-related policies and programs. The National Seniors Council performs this function at the federal level. Councils also exist in many communities across Canada to inform municipal and provincial or territorial governments on local seniors' issues.

Seniors' centres are some of the busiest and well-used organizations in Canadian communities. It is common for older people to manage these centres, which offer social, educational, recreational, and other activities of interest to local seniors. Although the mandates of these voluntary groups may vary, most of them support seniors in their efforts to live independently, to carry out daily activities in a normal community context, and to make decisions about their own lives.

AGE-FRIENDLY COMMUNITIES

Following the launch of the World Health Organization's (WHO) Global Age-Friendly Cities Project in 2006, countries around the world have been transforming their towns, cities, or villages to make them more age friendly. The first city in Canada that WHO officially accepted as a Global Age-Friendly Community was the City of London, Ontario, in 2010; since then, other cities have earned that honour, including Welland (Ontario), Saanich (British Columbia), and Edmonton (Alberta).

An **age-friendly community** is one that has policies, services, physical spaces, and structures in place to help older persons live well, remain active, and age in place. In most cases, the creation of age-friendly communities are collaborative efforts, involving various levels of government, businesses, voluntary organizations, and community groups and individuals. While each locality will be age-friendly in its own unique way, they are all likely to

- recognize seniors for their capabilities and resources
- be responsive to the needs and preferences of seniors
- respect seniors' decisions and lifestyle choices
- protect the vulnerable members of the senior population
- promote the inclusion of and contributions by seniors in community life by, for example, including seniors in the planning, development, and evaluation of aging-related policies, programs, and practices (WHO, 2007)

An age-friendly community benefits more than older people. Indeed, environments supportive of seniors tend to be good for everyone's quality of life and ensure active and healthy aging. Exhibit 11.5 identifies some of the features of an age-friendly community, in terms of health, security and independence, and participation.

EXHIBIT 11.5

FEATURES OF AN AGE-FRIENDLY COMMUNITY

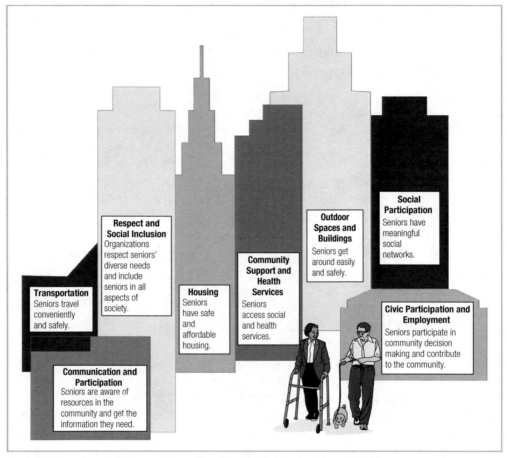

Respect and Social Inclusion
Organizations respect seniors' diverse needs and include seniors in all aspects of society.

Transportation
Seniors travel conveniently and safely.

Communication and Participation
Seniors are aware of resources in the community and get the information they need.

Housing
Seniors have safe and affordable housing.

Community Support and Health Services
Seniors access social and health services.

Outdoor Spaces and Buildings
Seniors get around easily and safely.

Social Participation
Seniors have meaningful social networks.

Civic Participation and Employment
Seniors participate in community decision making and contribute to the community.

Source: Author-generated diagram, content based on British Columbia, Seniors' Healthy Living Secretariat. (2011). *Age-friendly communities: Features.* Retrieved from http://www2.gov.bc.ca/gov/topic.page?id= 48EE80FD 4DC4421F91125E15F6CE66D5&title=Feature. Copyright © Province of British Columbia. All rights reserved. Reprinted with permission of the Province of British Columbia.

DISCUSSION QUESTIONS

■ **Organized Approaches to Meeting Seniors' Needs**

1. Many people believe that when the baby boomers are seniors, they will have a significant influence on policies, programs, and attitudes related to old people. What influence (if any) might baby boomer seniors have on the problem of ageism in our society?

2. The consensus in Canada is that society should respect and care for its older people; thus, a wide range of government initiatives aims to improve conditions for seniors. What might be the benefits for a society if governments support the well-being of seniors?

2 ENSURING THE WELL-BEING OF SENIORS

Seniors are valued members of society. It is therefore important to support seniors in their efforts to stay healthy, happy, and active in their communities. This section explores some of the issues and programs related to seniors' well-being: health, disability and activity, mental health, social connectedness, income security, and elder abuse.

HEALTH ISSUES

According to the 2009 Canadian Community Health Survey, most seniors enjoy good health. In terms of functional capacity—that is, the ability to carry out activities of daily living—most seniors under age eighty-five report having similar limitations as adults aged forty-five to sixty-four. Nevertheless, as people age, they are more likely to experience chronic or multiple health conditions. About three-quarters of all seniors have at least one chronic health condition, including high blood pressure, arthritis, or back problems (Canadian Institute for Health Information, 2011).

It is questionable whether Canada's healthcare system can continue providing adequate care, given the growing numbers of older people. Hospital use by seniors is a particular concern; for example, in 2009–2010, seniors made up only 15 percent of the Canadian population, but they accounted for 40 percent of acute hospital stays. Seniors are also heavy users of residential care, home care, prescription drugs, and doctor visits. The OECD estimates that between 2010 and 2025, Canada will need an extra $31 billion to pay for aging-related health and long-term care (Canadian Institute for Health Information, 2011).

Canadian governments continue to work together to meet the health needs of an aging population. In 2012, the provincial and territorial health ministers formed the Health Care Innovation Working Group, a collaborative effort to transform the healthcare system to ensure its sustainability in the future. By focusing on sharing best practices and innovative health strategies, the working group aims to find solutions to address the health needs of seniors (Council of the Federation, 2012).

DISABILITY AND ACTIVITY

Among the most common types of disability among seniors are those related to mobility (such as difficulty walking or standing for long periods), agility (such as getting in or out of bed), and pain (that restricts activity). The chance of developing a disability increases with age: 24 percent of seniors aged sixty-five to seventy-four have a mobility disability; that rate jumps to 61 percent of seniors aged eighty-five and over (HRSDC, 2012e). Disabilities can threaten an older person's ability to remain independent and active. Fortunately, a wide variety of assistance is available to Canadian seniors to ensure their full participation in community life; that assistance includes home care, technical aids (such as walkers and wheelchairs), housing adaptations, and modified transportation systems.

Exercise is an important determinant of health; however, only half of all seniors without a disability, and less than one-third of seniors with a disability, report being at least moderately active (HRSDC, 2012e). To address this issue, a number of voluntary seniors' groups, extended-care centres, and other organizations offer exercise classes, walking programs, and other activities to keep seniors physically active. A growing number of programs—such as the senior fitness instructors certification—are designed to train fitness leaders to help seniors meet their physical activity needs.

MENTAL HEALTH

Most seniors (70 percent) say they enjoy good mental health (Public Health Agency of Canada, 2010b). Nevertheless, about one in four seniors lives with a mental health issue, such as anxiety, dementia, or depression (the most common). Depression is associated with the challenges that come with aging, including physical ailments, cognitive and sensory impairments, and a sense of loss related to such things as forced retirement or the death of loved ones. Suicide is a possible outcome of severe depression: men aged eighty and over have the highest suicide rates in Canada (Mood Disorders Society of Canada, 2009).

Alzheimer's disease and related dementias (ADRD) are conditions that involve memory loss and cognitive impairments, such as having difficulty thinking, making decisions, understanding, and communicating. The most common form of dementia is Alzheimer's disease. At least one out of every eleven Canadian seniors (mostly women) suffers from some form of ADRD (Alzheimer Society of Canada, 2012a, 2012b). Currently, dementia has no cure. However, by helping older people to improve their coping skills and social support systems, mental health programs aim to prevent or at least delay the onset of dementia and placement in long-term care.

Many mental health programs take a **psychosocial approach** to the prevention and treatment of dementia and other mental health disorders. This approach focuses simultaneously on enhancing older people's psychological and spiritual life, while strengthening external supports, such as those related to income security, health care, and housing (Dudgeon, 2010; UBC, 2012b). Exhibit 11.6 illustrates some of the common determinants of mental health among seniors and the four main program areas (with service examples) that are available to older Canadians.

EXHIBIT 11.6

SENIORS' MENTAL HEALTH: DETERMINANTS AND SERVICES

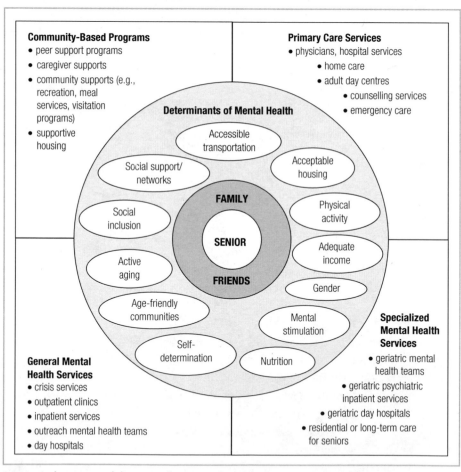

Source: Author-generated diagram, information adapted from MacCourt, P., Wilson, K., & Tourigny-Rivard, M. (2011). *Guidelines for comprehensive mental health services for older adults in Canada (executive summary).* Retrieved from Mental Health Commission of Canada website: http://www. mentalhealthcommission.ca/English/system/files/private/Seniors_MHCC_Seniors_Guidelines_Executive Summary_ENG_0.pdf

SOCIAL CONNECTEDNESS

The ability to connect with others is essential to good physical and mental health in the senior years. In contrast, **social isolation** is associated with a number of potential physical and mental health problems. Various factors may contribute to social isolation among older people; for example, isolation may be the result of having a relatively small social circle or losing connections to other people because of retirement, disability, or the death of a spouse. Women aged seventy-five and over—especially those who live alone—are at a particularly high risk of loneliness and social isolation (Milan & Vézina, 2011).

Social connectedness has four dimensions: social support, social networks, social engagement, and supportive social environments. Below is a brief description of each dimension, and an example of a related program.

- People who offer *social support* can help seniors feel valued, appreciated, and encouraged to live a good life. Seniors who live alone or have few friends or no family can use friendly visiting programs, which match volunteers with isolated seniors.

- Being socially connected also means having a well-developed *social network*. Many volunteer programs and seniors' centres try to help older people maintain old relationships and form new ones so they have more people to call on when needed.

- *Social engagement* refers to participation in the community and the relationships formed because of that involvement. To engage socially, a senior may attend a religious service, volunteer, or participate in an intergenerational program (see Exhibit 11.7).

- Finally, seniors are most likely to feel socially connected when they live in *supportive social environments*, such as age-friendly communities, where a wide range of resources and opportunities exist for seniors (Edwards & Mawani, 2006).

INCOME SECURITY

Canada designed its **retirement income system** to ensure that seniors have an income that provides a quality of life comparable to that enjoyed during their working years. Most Canadians rely to some extent on the retirement income system, which is based on three pillars:

- *Pillar 1: Old Age Security (OAS) and Guaranteed Income Supplement (GIS)*. These universal programs provide a basic guaranteed minimum income.

EXHIBIT 11.7

AGENCY PROFILE: AN INTERGENERATIONAL PROGRAM

LINKages Society of Alberta is a community-based registered charity that provides intergenerational programs in Calgary. LINKages matches youth with older Calgarians living alone or in local retirement facilities and lodges.

LINKages recognizes the value of creating caring relationships between youth and seniors, especially in light of an aging population, and a society that sometimes isolates older and younger generations from each other.

LINKages' intergenerational programs aim to

- build bridges between the generations
- reduce negative attitudes and dispel myths about seniors
- promote a greater understanding of and respect for generations
- enhance the personal benefits of volunteering

PROGRAMS

Junior High Program Junior high students visit seniors twice a week during the lunch hour. The visits take place in a central area and are supervised by LINKages staff. Many of the visits involve planned activities, such as games, crafts, reading, storytelling, and helping seniors write their autobiographies.

Senior High Program High-school students are usually more experienced and require less supervision. However, LINKages staff is available to provide support and advice to students as needed. Activities during the visits aim to enhance student–senior interactions, and students are encouraged to be true companions for their senior.

Calgary After-School Programs LINKages and the City of Calgary have teamed up to create four after-school programs for youth (ages twelve to sixteen). These programs connect seniors and youth during critical or high-risk hours (3 to 6 p.m.), giving youth an opportunity to use their time positively and constructively.

Source: Excerpted and adapted from LINKages Society of Alberta. (2009). *Website*. Retrieved from http://www.linkages.ca/schoolPrograms.html and http://www.link-ages.ca/aboutUs.html. Courtesy of LINKages Society of Alberta.

The OAS is a monthly retirement pension available to seniors who meet a basic residency requirement and have incomes under a set threshold. The GIS is a provincial or territorial benefit available to low-income seniors; many regional governments provide additional benefits and services to those who are eligible for the GIS.

- *Pillar 2: The Canada Pension Plan (CPP).* This mandatory contributory program requires workers and employers to make regular contributions to the plan during their working years. The plan aims to replace about one-quarter of a worker's employment income on retirement at age sixty-five. (Québec residents draw from their own plan, the Québec Pension Plan.)

- *Pillar 3: Private pension plans and savings.* These options include both self-administered and employer-sponsored registered pension plans (RPPs), registered retirement savings plans (RRSPs), and other private pension plans and investments.

The economic situation of Canadian seniors has been steadily improving over the last few decades: between 1980 and 2006, the proportion of seniors living in poverty fell from more than 21 percent to 5 percent. Despite these gains, many Canadian seniors are at a high risk of poverty; this is especially true for unattached seniors, most of whom are women. Aboriginal seniors, older recent immigrants, and people who have worked less than ten years—and therefore have limited retirement savings or pensions—are also at risk of poverty in old age (National Seniors Council, 2009). The incidence of poverty among seniors living in large cities is relatively high. For example, 27 percent of seniors living in Vancouver are poor, compared with only 8 percent of seniors living in the smaller city of Waterloo, Ontario (Federation of Canadian Municipalities, 2010).

In general, Canada's retirement income system is criticized for its failure to provide a sufficient income to vulnerable seniors, its complicated application process, and its lack of coordination between federal benefits (OAS and CPP) and provincial or territorial benefits (GIS) (Special Senate Committee on Aging, 2009). Since 2006, the federal government has taken actions to strengthen Canada's retirement income system, including reforming the CPP to provide better protection for pension members and easing the tax burden on older Canadians by relaxing the rules for RRSPS, RPPs, and other tax-sheltered savings plans. Moreover, the federal and provincial or territorial governments have established a joint working group to analyze and improve the retirement income system (Canada, Department of Finance, 2010).

In 2012, Parliament passed a highly controversial piece of legislation that will raise the eligibility age for OAS and GIS from sixty-five to sixty-seven, beginning in 2023. The federal government rationalized that change by noting the expected drain on pension funds and taxes created by an aging population (Service Canada, 2012b).

ELDER ABUSE

Elder abuse is a disturbing reality in Canada. The World Health Organization (2012) defines **elder abuse** as "a single, or repeated act, or lack of appropriate action, occurring within any relationship where there is an expectation of trust, which causes harm or distress to an older person." Abuse against an elderly person may be physical, emotional or psychological, spiritual, or financial (the most common). Elder abuse can also be systemic—that is, such systems as governments and long-term-care facilities may inadvertently perpetrate abuse through ageist policies or practices. The neglect by a caregiver to meet the basic needs of an older person is another form of elder abuse. Seniors at the highest risk of abuse are those who are very old, frail, or isolated, have a cognitive impairment or physical disability, or who depend heavily on others for care (National Seniors Council, 2007; Special Senate Committee on Aging, 2009).

Elder abuse is a largely "hidden crime," since most abuse incidents go unreported to police and therefore are neither investigated or prosecuted (Canadian Association for Retired Persons [CARP], 2012). However, some experts suggest that the number of seniors who suffer abuse or neglect may be as high as one out of six (Canadian Centre for Elder Law, 2010). Victimization can take its toll on older people in terms of chronic physical problems (such as heart attacks or high blood pressure) and psychological problems (such as depression or panic attacks) (Royal Canadian Mounted Police, 2012b).

At the international level, the United Nations recognizes elder abuse not just as a legal and human rights concern but also as a reflection of a lack of opportunities for older people to remain active, independent, and productive members of society (Zelenev, 2008). In response to this insight, countries around the world have introduced measures to prevent and address elder abuse. Canada's initiatives include

- World Elder Abuse Awareness Day (held June 15 each year) to raise awareness of elder abuse and explore solutions to the problem
- Elder Abuse Awareness Campaign (federal initiative) to improve the safety and security of older Canadians

- National Survey on the Mistreatment of Older Canadians (launched in 2012) to collect data on the prevalence, risk factors, and causes of elder abuse and neglect

- provincial elder abuse strategies (such as the Nova Scotia Elder Abuse Strategy) to raise awareness of, and prevent or reduce incidences of elder abuse

Many communities use an interdisciplinary approach to coordinate the efforts of a wide range of professionals in healthcare, social work, legal, and other fields on behalf of at-risk seniors. Some communities have also established specific elder abuse teams, such as the Elder Abuse Consultation Team in Toronto and the Elder Abuse Response Team in Calgary.

DISCUSSION QUESTIONS

■ **Ensuring the Well-Being of Seniors**

1. Research tells us that various types of activities may help to ward off mental health problems in late adulthood. What kinds of activities do you do now that may help you to prevent mental health problems in your old age? What else might you do?

2. In Canada, relying entirely on government pensions (such as OAS, CPP/QPP, and GIS) means living in poverty. Do you believe that government should enrich these pension funds, or should individuals and families do more to ensure the income security of seniors? Give reasons for your answer.

3. Elder abuse is a disturbing issue in our society. How might individuals, organizations, and communities prevent this particular social problem?

3 SENIORS' HOUSING AND SUPPORTS FOR INDEPENDENCE

Stereotypes would have us believe that to be old is to be institutionalized. However, while many seniors live in residential care, the vast majority live in their own homes (see Exhibit 11.8). Understandably, most seniors want to keep living in their own home for as long as they can. To age in place, and in the dwelling of their choice, requires a wide range of supports, services, and housing options. Moreover, seniors need a continuum of care to help them move to greater levels of assistance while remaining as active and independent as possible. This section looks briefly at housing options and the varying levels of assistance available to older Canadians.

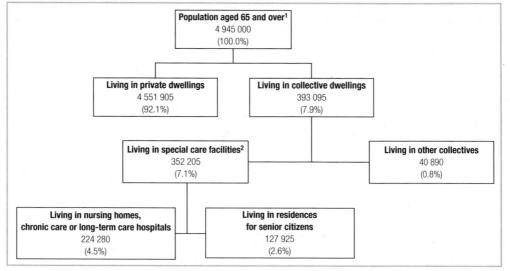

EXHIBIT 11.8

LIVING ARRANGEMENTS OF SENIORS, 2009

Notes: [1] Includes all individuals living in private or collective dwellings in Canada. Persons outside Canada on government, military, or diplomatic postings are not included.
[2] Nursing homes, chronic care or long-term hospitals, and residences for senior citizens.
Source: Milan, M., Bohnert, N., LeVasseur, S., & Pagé, F. (2012). *Living arrangements of seniors* (p. 7). Retrieved from Statistics Canada website: http://www12.statcan.gc.ca/census-recensement/2011/as-sa/ 98-312-x/ 98-312-x2011003_4-eng.pdf.

INDEPENDENT AND SUPPORTIVE HOUSING

Good housing is central to everyone's quality of life, but as Montgomery (1977, p. 253) states: "The quality of the housing environment becomes increasingly significant in the lives of many aged families and individuals. And the quality of this [environment] largely determines the extent to which they will retain their independence." For those who want to live independently in a private household, a variety of housing options are available; those options include retirement villages (small communities of seniors living in single-family or semi-detached homes, apartments, or townhouses) and granny flats (a self-contained unit located on a relative's property or a self-contained suite in a house).

Over the years, Canada has attempted to address the shelter needs of low-income seniors through the provision of **social housing**, which offers subsidized rental housing. One of the more recent initiatives of the federal government began in 2009 as part of Canada's Economic Action Plan. That plan dedicated $400 million to the construction of new housing units for low-income seniors across Canada; the provincial and territorial governments agreed to match the federal investment, as well as design and deliver the housing units. Despite these types of housing initiatives, more than 22 percent of Canadian seniors live in housing that is unaffordable, inadequate, or unsuitable in some way (Will Dunning, 2009). Finding affordable housing is especially difficult for seniors on fixed incomes living in large, expensive, urban centres, like Toronto and Vancouver. A lack of affordable housing contributes to homelessness among seniors; an estimated six thousand seniors are homeless in Canada (Regional Geriatric Program of Toronto, 2012).

Supportive housing is available to help seniors balance independence with specific support. Offering the least amount of support is **congregate housing**. In this living arrangement, a group of unrelated people live in the same house and pay a monthly fee. Each person has his or her own bedroom and shares the common areas of the house. In some cases, a house coordinator cooks meals and maintains the house. **Assisted living facilities** provide the most support to seniors. These facilities usually offer a private living space and meals, as well as other services, such as personal care, laundry, and housekeeping. In Canada, either government or private-sector organizations may provide supportive housing.

Many seniors are able to live in their own homes—and thereby delay or avoid institutionalization—if their living space can be adapted to meet their changing needs. Various government programs provide financial assistance to seniors to repair or modify their houses to enable daily living activities; these programs include the federally funded Residential Rehabilitation Assistance Program and the Home Adaptations for Seniors' Independence Program. Home adaptations may include installing a shower seat or grab bars in the bathroom, or building wheelchair ramps or lifts (see Exhibit 11.9).

Increasingly, seniors with special needs are turning to **gerontechnology** to help them age in place safely and comfortably. Gerontechnology combines knowledge from the fields of gerontology and technology to create a variety of innovative tools; for example, sensors can be installed around the house to automatically turn off appliances. A number of projects are underway to create robotic assistants for the elderly that, among other things, can remind a senior when to take medications or guide a senior from one room to another.

HOME AND COMMUNITY SUPPORT

Although help from friends and family can enable seniors to continue living in their own homes, many unpaid caregivers are unable to provide long-term

EXHIBIT 11.9

© Susan H. Smith/Getty

Many seniors are able to live in their own homes—and thereby delay or avoid institutionalization—if their living space can be adapted to meet their changing needs.

care for someone with complex needs. An alternative to informal caregiving is **home and community care** (HCC), which allow seniors to receive the care they need in their own homes. HCC programs can help seniors meet a variety of personal care needs (such as bathing, grooming, and toileting) and, in some cases, provide homemaking services (such as housecleaning and meal preparation). About eight out of ten Canadians using HCC services are seniors (Canadian Institute for Health Information, 2011).

In 2002, the Romanow Commission's study of the future of healthcare in Canada found HCC to be far more cost-effective than the institutional care of seniors. However, affordable and high-quality HCC services are becoming increasingly difficult to access in Canada. One study found that between 2001 and 2010, the number of seniors over the age of seventy-five in British Columbia increased by 28 percent, while access to HCC decreased by 14 percent (Cohen, 2012). One reason for the lack of accessibility to HCC is the increasing demand on this type of care. To manage that demand, many home support agencies are tightening their eligibility rules; unfortunately, reduced access to programs tends to limit services to only the neediest of seniors, leaving other seniors without adequate support.

A number of reports on Canada's healthcare system have stressed the need for a national home and community care system. Experts argue that such a system would standardize the quality of services that people receive and establish a minimum level of care across Canada. Although federal governments in the past have come close to introducing a national HCC system, the current government is not pursuing such an initiative.

RESIDENTIAL CARE

Provincial and territorial health authorities designate residential care for people who can no longer manage in their own homes because of one or more physical or cognitive limitations. About 7 percent of Canadian seniors—mostly women—live in residential care centres (McGregor & Ronald, 2011).[1] Each province and territory is responsible for its own provision of residential care; thus, the type, range, and quality of services vary across jurisdictions. However, residential care for seniors often consists of a shared or private living space, round-the-clock nursing services, assistance with daily living activities, meal services, administration of medications, rehabilitative services, and organized recreational or social activities. All residential care facilities must be approved by a provincial or territorial health or social service authority. Residential care for the elderly is largely government subsidized and delivered by a mix of public, commercial, and voluntary facilities (Statistics Canada, 2011c). A growing number of residential care centres specialize in serving Aboriginal, Chinese, Indo-Canadian, and other cultural minority populations.

Few people would argue that Canada's residential care system needs an overhaul. Some of the main criticisms levelled against this system include the following:

- There are never enough beds to meet the growing demand, and, with an aging population, the demand will only increase.

- The system lacks consistent standards and funding.

---

[1] Depending on the jurisdiction, residential care centres may also be called residential care facilities, long-term-care homes, nursing homes, continuing care centres, and similar terms.

- Residential care in Canada is two tiered—that is, richer residents can afford to purchase high-quality private care, leaving the government-subsidized care, and a more limited package of goods and services, for poorer residents (Jansen & Murphy, 2009).

To address the shortcomings in the system and to reduce the cost of government-run care centres, many provinces are contracting out residential care to for-profit organizations. While contracting out may prove to be cost effective for governments, it does not guarantee a high quality of service. In their study of residential care for seniors, McGregor and Ronald (2011, p. 2), concluded, "While the causal link between for-profit ownership and inferior quality of care does not imply that all for-profit facilities provide poor care, the evidence suggests that, as a group, such facilities are less likely to provide good care than nonprofit or public facilities."

DISCUSSION QUESTIONS

■ Seniors' Housing and Supports for Independence

1. The demands for home and community care are growing. What might be some of the trends driving this need?
2. One criticism against residential care is that it is two tiered. Do you think that Canada should allow a two-tiered system in which rich seniors have access to better care? Give reasons for your answer.

4 WORK AND PARTICIPATION

Many seniors continue to be active members of the workforce, while those who have retired spend time volunteering or participating in political activism and consultation. This section explores some of the ways in which seniors contribute to the economic and political health of their communities.

SENIORS IN THE WORKFORCE

Most Canadian seniors are retired; however, a growing number are employed or actively looking for employment. Older Canadians continue working past the traditional retirement age of sixty-five for many reasons. For example, many older people prefer work to retirement, enjoy working, and are physically and mentally capable of working. In some cases, older Canadians may need to keep working because they have inadequate retirement savings or are ineligible for CPP or private pension benefits. Studies show that it is becoming more common for retirees to return to work, largely because they want to remain active (Park, 2011).

Even though many older Canadians plan to work into their senior years, Canada is bracing for a labour shortage when the baby boomers retire. To offset that shortage, Canadian governments and many businesses offer incentives to either keep older Canadians working past the traditional retirement age of sixty-five or encourage retired workers to re-enter the work force. In 2010, the federal government assigned the National Seniors Council to examine the labour force participation among seniors and those nearing retirement age. The Council concluded that older workers need three main supports:

- *employment programs* to help them find work that is both meaningful and matched to their skill sets

- *retraining* that is accessible and affordable, especially for those who are not physically able to continue their current employment.

- *age-friendly work environments* that offer more flexible work arrangements (such as part-time employment or compressed workweeks), more accessible and adaptable workspaces, and the elimination of discrimination and stereotypes of older workers (National Seniors Council, 2011)

VOLUNTEERING

In addition to helping to improve the lives of others, volunteering can benefit the volunteers themselves. Some older people find that volunteering eases the transition from work to retirement by providing a sense of purpose, self-worth, and identity, as well as opportunities to use their skills. A number of studies have associated volunteering with good physical and mental health. Almost four out of ten seniors volunteer their time for worthy causes; as a group, seniors contribute 18 percent of the total number of volunteer hours in Canada (Statistics Canada, 2012h).

Shrinking government funding and the increasing demand for services are leading some social agencies to recruit more volunteer service providers. Those agencies see older people in general and baby boomers in particular as prime candidates for providing many of the services once delivered by professional helpers. Some organizations consider seniors' volunteer efforts to be vital to the survival of their community and are subsequently trying to engage this population, and meet their diverse needs and interests (Special Senate Committee on Aging, 2007). Canadian governments provide some assistance to organizations in that endeavour. For example, the federally funded New Horizons for Seniors Program funds projects across Canada that promote volunteerism among older people.

POLITICAL ACTIVISM AND CONSULTATION

For many senior citizens, active participation in society means taking political action. One Canadian study found that 87 percent of older Canadians believe that seniors are a significant political force in this country (CARP, 2011). As Turcotte and Schellenberg (2007, p. 178) note: "By taking part in the political debate, seniors can bring to the attention of public officials issues important to their well-being and to their communities. By exercising their right to vote, they may induce political parties to consider their needs in the formulation of social programs." Voting is the most common means that seniors use to assert their political will. Indeed, as a group, seniors pack a considerable punch at the ballot box. In 2011, 82 percent of Canadians aged sixty-five to seventy-four voted in the federal election, compared with about 50 percent of adults aged eighteen to thirty-four (Uppal & LaRochelle-Côté, 2012). Because seniors are more likely than any other age group to vote, political parties tend to pay attention to seniors' issues and concerns. A national poll by Nanos Research ("NDP Seen as Most in Touch," 2012) found that 28 percent of seniors chose the New Democratic Party of Canada as being most sensitive to seniors' needs, compared with 17 percent who chose the Conservatives.

Regardless of the means they use to assert their influence, seniors rarely hesitate to voice their dissatisfaction with government policy, especially when it relates to pensions and health care. In 1985, the largest seniors' protest in Canadian history took place in response to the federal government's proposal to de-index pension payments. The collective action of seniors forced the government to scrap the de-indexation plan. Since that incident, the seniors' movement in Canada—dubbed Grey Power—has been gaining momentum. A recent example occurred in 2012, when Prime Minister Harper announced his plan to change the eligibility age of Old Age Security (OAS) from sixty-five to sixty-seven. To express their anger, seniors staged protest rallies, marches, and other forms of collective action across Canada; in Ontario, seniors teamed up with labour activists and others to occupy Conservative MP offices (see Exhibit 11.10). Although they were unable to persuade the Harper government to cancel its changes

EXHIBIT 11.10

© Ontario Federation of Labour

Poster used by the United Food and Commercial Workers union in 2012, when they took social action against Prime Minister Harper's plan to raise the eligibility age for OAS from sixty-five to sixty-seven.

to OAS, the protesters reminded government leaders that seniors are a political force to be reckoned with.

Many seniors exercise their political clout from within organizations that are established by seniors and run by seniors for seniors. The Manitoba Society of Seniors and the Saskatchewan Seniors Mechanism are two examples of voluntary groups that represent and advocate on behalf of seniors in their respective provinces. Not only do these groups advise local and provincial governments on matters that concern seniors, but they also work to enhance the image of seniors and their quality of life.

Seniors have made it clear that they want to be consulted on matters that affect them and future generations; in turn, Canadian governments recognize the benefits of including seniors in public consultations and policymaking processes. Governments draw from seniors' knowledge and experience in various ways. For example, in 2003, the Liberal Task Force on Seniors included seniors in their study of social and economic issues related to aging. Two years later, the prime minister's appointment of a Seniors' Secretariat was, among other things, an attempt to give Canadian seniors a stronger voice in the issues, decisions, and policies that affect them. A number of provinces (notably Ontario, Manitoba, and Prince Edward Island) have also appointed seniors secretariats to help seniors advance their causes.

DISCUSSION QUESTIONS

■ Work and Participation

1. It is becoming more common for people to work into their senior years. Identify some of the benefits (and possible challenges) of having greater numbers of older people in the workplace.

2. The likelihood of volunteering decreases with age, yet nonprofit organizations need volunteers more than ever. What might organizations do to attract and retain senior volunteers?

3. Increasingly, seniors are becoming more comfortable with asserting their political will. Do you think that the baby boomers will be more or less involved in political activism when they are seniors? Give reasons for your answer.

5 GERONTOLOGICAL SOCIAL WORK

In many ways, social work practice is the same with elderly clients as with other populations, although this population has its own, unique issues related to healthcare, poverty, mental health, and housing. It is therefore necessary for gerontological social workers to understand the specific areas of concern among their senior clients and demonstrate a sound knowledge of the aging process. Moreover, since the majority of seniors are female, social workers need to tailor many of their responses to the needs of older women (Hick, 2004). Professionals with expertise in both social welfare and health services can assist in specialized areas, such as elder abuse, substance abuse, and mental health.

Gerontological social workers require a wide range of skills to help their older clients. For example, social workers who serve older populations should be well versed in how to plan, implement, and evaluate programs for elderly people, work with the families of elderly clients, and participate in multidisciplinary or inter-agency teams. Gerontological social workers may use these and other skills in one or more of the following service areas:

- *individual and family counselling*—assessing the needs and strengths of elderly clients and their families, and linking clients with resources to meet those needs

- *adult day programs*—providing outreach, supportive services, group work, and care-planning services in structured day program settings

- *adult protective services*—assessing factors that may put elderly clients at risk of abuse or neglect, and developing, implementing, and monitoring plans to ensure clients' safety and security

- *respite services*—recruiting and training respite care workers and identifying families in need of this service

- *hospital or nursing home care*—assessing social needs, providing counselling and support services, advocating on behalf of elderly clients and their families, and participating in program, care, and discharge planning (Zastrow, 2010)

The demand for gerontological social work and social services is growing as the population ages and as people live longer with a serious health problem or disability. Canada lacks trained gerontological social workers and other professionals who can provide the specialized services that older adults need; subsequently, many practitioners currently serving seniors do not have the appropriate training or experience in working with elderly populations. There is also a gap between what is known (through research) about aging and geriatrics, and the application of that knowledge in practice (McDonald, 2010). The National Initiative for the Care of the Elderly addressed many of these issues in a project aimed at attracting students to the field of gerontology and promoting the benefits of working with older people. A number of postsecondary institutions offer gerontology programs in Canada, including the Social Service Worker–Gerontology diploma program at Seneca College of Applied Arts and Technology, Ontario.

DISCUSSION QUESTIONS

■ Gerontological Social Work

1. Aging is sometimes called a "woman's issue" because most people living into advanced years are women. How might the needs of older women be different from those of older men? How might gerontological social workers best respond to the needs of elderly women?

2. What are some of the possible challenges and rewards of working in the field of gerontological social work?

SUMMARY

Introduction

Canada, like other Western industrialized countries, has an aging population. While some social analysts focus on the potential problems of an aging population, others emphasize the potential benefits. To prepare the nation for an older population, Canadian governments have introduced policies and programs that promote active aging.

1 Organized Approaches to Meeting Seniors' Needs

Canada's social knowledge on aging and late adulthood is expanding. Research is helping to expose the impact of ageism and recognize the diversity of seniors. Canada's policies on aging focus on health and well-being over the life course, independent living, and opportunities for older persons. While the responsibility for the well-being of older Canadians is shared by the different levels of government, a National Framework on Aging guides aging-related initiatives. Resources, opportunities, and organizations for seniors exist at the local level, where voluntary agencies, governments, and others work together to create age-friendly communities.

2 Ensuring the Well-Being of Seniors

Most seniors live with a chronic health problem and are at a high risk of disability. Depression and dementia are the most common mental health problems faced by seniors. The ability to connect with others is essential to good physical and mental health. Thanks in part to Canada's retirement income system, the economic situation of seniors has improved over the years; however, many Canadian seniors continue to live in poverty. Elder abuse is a serious social problem that is addressed through laws, adult protection legislation, and policies and programs that expand opportunities for older people.

3 Seniors' Housing and Supports for Independence

Seniors who want to live independently have various options, including supportive living arrangements and home-modification programs. Along with a growing senior population are greater demands for home and community care. Residential care is available for people with a physical or cognitive limitation. Although the provinces contract out residential care to private business, this approach does not guarantee quality service.

4 Work and Participation

For a variety of reasons, a growing number of seniors keep working after the traditional retirement age of sixty-five. Governments and businesses offer incentives to offset a labour shortage caused by baby boomers retiring. Many seniors volunteer for organizations, which are now targeting baby-boomer retirees as potential service providers. Seniors are politically active in various ways: some seniors belong to organizations that advocate on behalf of seniors; others engage in public policy consultations and policymaking processes.

5 Gerontological Social Work

Gerontological social work requires advanced assessment and intervention skills, as well as specialized knowledge of seniors' issues. Social workers must also be able to plan, implement, and evaluate programs for seniors, work with families, and participate in multidisciplinary teams. Seniors may be supported through a variety of services, including adult day programs. The demand for gerontological social work is growing as the population ages and as healthcare resources shrink. Some initiatives encourage students to enter the field of gerontology; training in this field is possible through a number of gerontological programs across Canada.

KEY TERMS

For definitions of the key terms, consult the Glossary on page 453 at the end of the book.

population aging, p. 299

baby boom generation, p. 299

population dependency ratio, p. 300

active aging, p. 300

gerontology, p. 301

ageism, p. 302

aging in place, p. 305

age-friendly community, p. 308

psychosocial approach, p. 311

social isolation, p. 313

social connectedness, p. 313

retirement income system, p. 313

elder abuse, p. 316

social housing, p. 318

supportive housing, p. 319

congregate housing, p. 319

assisted living facilities, p. 319

gerontechnology, p. 319

home and community care, p. 320

12 CHAPTER

The Social Welfare of Aboriginal Canadians

OBJECTIVES

The Aboriginal peoples of Canada are finding their identity and forging new ground in social, economic, and political arenas. This chapter will

- introduce concepts and issues related to Aboriginal peoples

- explore the historical roots of Canada's "Indian policy"

- describe attempts to "bridge the divide" between government and Indigenous peoples

- examine Aboriginal approaches to helping, healing, and wellness

- identify issues and achievements of selected Aboriginal groups

- review topics and programs related to Aboriginal children and youth

- summarize the role of social work in the lives of Aboriginal peoples

INTRODUCTION

We owe the Aboriginal peoples a debt that is four centuries old. It is their turn to become full partners in developing an even greater Canada. And the reconciliation required may be less a matter of legal texts than of attitudes of the heart. (Romeo LeBlanc, Governor-General of Canada, 1996)

Long before the arrival of European settlers, **Aboriginal peoples** lived across North America in several separate nations, each with its own culture, language, and system of government. Today, Canada's Aboriginal population consists of three distinct groups:

- **First Nations people** include Status and non-Status **Indians**.[1]

- **Métis** are people of mixed First Nations and European ancestry, and identify themselves as distinct from Inuit and First Nations people.

- **Inuit** inhabit the northern regions of Canada, principally Nunavut, the Northwest Territories, and the northern parts of Labrador and Québec.

According to the 2011 census, 4 percent of Canadians identify themselves as an Aboriginal person. The majority of Aboriginal peoples are First Nations (850 000), followed by Métis (450 000), and Inuit (60 000). In terms of demographics, Aboriginals are the youngest and fastest-growing population in Canada; more than 46 percent are under the age of twenty-five. In comparison, non-Aboriginal youth account for 29 percent of the non-Aboriginal population (Turner, Crompton, & Langlois, 2013).

In recent decades, Aboriginal peoples have seen progress in their overall health, economic development, and educational attainment. Although government interventions have contributed to these advances, many people attribute the progress made by Aboriginal peoples to their own strength, courage, and determination. These qualities have created what Esquimaux and Smolewski (2004, p. 1) refer to as a "renaissance of traditional Aboriginal values and mores," as Aboriginal peoples reclaim their traditional languages and practices and find effective ways to work on long-standing issues.

Despite their achievements, Aboriginal peoples are more disadvantaged than non-Aboriginal Canadians in terms of social, health, and economic well-being. These disadvantages—reflected in the following statistics—create barriers to the full inclusion of Aboriginal peoples in Canadian society:

- Half of status First Nations children live in poverty.

- Aboriginal peoples are three times as likely as non-Aboriginal Canadians to live in substandard housing.

---

[1] There are three categories of "Indian": (1) a Status Indian is entitled to have his or her name included on the Indian Register, is recognized as an Indian under the Indian Act, and is entitled to certain rights and benefits under Canadian law; (2) a non-Status Indian is neither recognized as an Indian under the Indian Act nor registered and is therefore not entitled to the same rights and benefits enjoyed by Status Indians; and (3) a Treaty Indian belongs to a First Nation that has signed a treaty with the Crown. The definition of "Indian" continues to evolve. In 1939, the Supreme Court of Canada ruled that the term *Indian* in the Constitution Act includes Inuit. In 2012, the Federal Court of Canada expanded the definition of Indian to include Métis and non-Status Indians.

- More than half of First Nations people are unemployed.

- One in eight Aboriginal children has a disability (twice the national rate).

- First Nations youth are half as likely as other Canadian youth to graduate from high school.

- When compared with non-Aboriginal women, Aboriginal women die younger and are more than twice as likely to be unemployed single parents (Macdonald & Wilson, 2013; O'Donnell & Wallace, 2011; Public Service Alliance of Canada, 2008).

According to the Community Well-Being (CWB) Index, the living conditions of First Nations and Inuit communities improved from 1981 to 1996; however, since then, the level of education, income, housing, and employment in those communities has slipped well below that of other Canadian communities. By 2006, only one First Nations community rated in the top 100 Canadian communities, while 96 placed in the 100 worst (Indian and Northern Affairs Canada [INAC], 2010). The graph in Exhibit 12.1 illustrates

EXHIBIT 12.1

COMMUNITY WELL-BEING INDEX

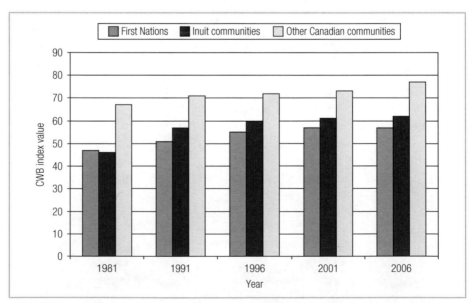

Note: The CWB Index assigns a numerical value to the community's level of education, employment, income, and housing: the higher the value, the higher the level of well-being.

Source: Indian and Northern Affairs Canada. (2010). *First Nation and Inuit community well-being*, p. 11. Retrieved from Aboriginal Affairs and Northern Development Canada website: http://www.aadnc-aandc. gc.ca/DAM/DAM-INTER-HQ/STAGING/texte-text/cwbdck_1100100016601_eng.pdf.

the rate of progress in First Nations and Inuit communities compared with the rest of Canada.

This chapter provides an overview of some of the historical events, successes, and challenges that have influenced the progress of Aboriginal peoples in their journey toward justice and social and economic well-being.

1 HISTORICAL ROOTS OF CANADA'S "INDIAN POLICY"

In 1763, King George III of England signed a Royal Proclamation to protect Aboriginal groups from exploitation by the European settlers and colonial officials in Canada. The proclamation recognized Aboriginal peoples as autonomous and self-governing groups within the colonial system, and deserving of their own lands separate from the colonial settlements (Rice & Snyder, 2008). Before long, however, the colonial government had plans to assimilate Aboriginal peoples into the dominant Caucasian society and to strip them of their rights and lands. This section reviews that assimilation process and related historical events that have shaped Canada's Aboriginal policies.

AN EARLY ASSIMILATION PLAN

In 1844, the British government transferred the management of Aboriginal affairs to the Province of Canada, which assigned Caucasian Indian Department superintendents to supervise the "Indians" (now called First Nations) living on land **reserves**. At that time, the colonial governments no longer saw Aboriginal groups as autonomous nations but as British subjects who, when compared with Caucasians, were inferior, uncivilized, and incompetent. The colonial governments decided that becoming members of the dominant British society would be the Aboriginal peoples' best chance at survival. Thus, government officials prepared the Indians for **assimilation**—a process that would "remake the Indian people in the image of European manners and values, to move them into the mainstream of Canadian life" (Federation of Saskatchewan Indian Nations, 1975, p. 6).

The assimilation process required Indians to learn English and convert to Christianity—tasks facilitated by the schools and churches established on the reserves. To become "civilized" and "normalized," the colonial governments taught the Indians farming techniques and other European occupations, as well as Euro-Canadian values and customs. Colonial officials aided assimilation by systematically weakening **band**[2] leadership, destroying trading patterns, and banning religious ceremonies and other traditional practices. Once the Indians acquired European habits of self-reliance, the colonial governments planned to wipe out the Aboriginal way of life, dismantle the reserves, and strip the people of their Indian status. Government officials expected that, before long, the Aboriginal peoples would abandon their traditional ways, join the dominant society, and pass along their new values and customs to their children (Federation of Saskatchewan Indian Nations, 1978).

ENFRANCHISEMENT

The passage of the Gradual Civilization Act in 1857 marked Canada's formal commitment to the process of assimilation. This statute introduced the concept of **enfranchisement**—a legal process whereby the Indians would surrender their special Indian status and lands in exchange for full citizenship in the British colony. Citizenship came with the right to vote, an honour that government officials believed would appeal to Aboriginal peoples.

The passage of the British North America Act in 1867 transferred the responsibility for Aboriginal peoples from Britain to the Dominion of Canada. Two levels of government shared that responsibility: the federal government oversaw Status Indians and reserves, while the provinces took responsibility for all non-Status Indians. One challenge facing the new Dominion government was the fact that few Aboriginal people were voluntarily choosing enfranchisement. Determined to assimilate the Indians into the Christian and Eurocentric society, the Government of Canada passed a compulsory enfranchisement law in 1869. Under this new act, Status Indian women who married non-Status men would lose their status; the act also denied Indian Status to any child born into the marriage (Makarenko, 2008).

The passage of the first Indian Act in 1876 reinforced the government's goal of assimilation. Through the Indian Act, the Government of Canada planned to free the so-called "red man" from a life of dependence, educate him, and "prepare him for a higher civilization by encouraging him to assume the privileges and responsibilities of full citizenship" (Royal Commission on Aboriginal Peoples, 1996, p. 3). Under the Indian Act, Status Indians became legal wards of the Crown. The Act also allowed the federal government to regulate the activities of Aboriginal peoples living on-reserve and fully control the education of their children.

---

[2] Today, many bands prefer to be called First Nations.

THE ROLE OF RESIDENTIAL SCHOOLS

Although Aboriginal children had been attending Christian residential schools since the 1600s, the Government of Canada needed a more comprehensive approach to assimilate children fully into the Euro-Canadian culture. In 1879, Prime Minister John A. Macdonald introduced a federal system of **residential schools** for Aboriginal children. Modelled after reformatories and jails for poor, urban children, these industrial schools were located on reserves (See Exhibit 12.2), or in remote regions of the country. Government officials removed Aboriginal children from the "uncivilizing influences" of their families and communities, and placed them in the boarding schools, which were run by Roman Catholic, United, Anglican, and Presbyterian churches (Chansonneuve, 2005).

One Aboriginal group describes the "civilizing" strategies used at the schools: "Students were discouraged from speaking their first language or practising native traditions. If they were caught, they would experience severe punishment. . . . All correspondence from the children was written in English, which many parents couldn't read. Brothers and sisters at the same school rarely saw each other, as all activities were segregated by gender" ("Residential Schools," 2010). The Euro-Canadian teachers taught the Aboriginal children to be ashamed of their heritage and to reject everything "Indian," including their families and spiritual beliefs.

Attendance at residential schools was mandatory, with government agents enforcing the rule. At the peak of the residential school system in 1931, close to eighty residential schools operated across Canada. Between 1883 and 1996 when the last school closed, almost 150 000 First Nations, Métis, and Inuit children had attended the schools ("Residential Schools," 2010).

DISCUSSION QUESTIONS

■ **Historical Roots of Canada's "Indian Policy"**

1. Identify the ways in which Canada's colonial government demonstrated racism in its treatment of Aboriginal peoples. Do you recognize racist practices by current governments toward Aboriginal peoples? Share your observations.

2. Describe how the concepts and practices of assimilation and enfranchisement are related.

3. Colonial governments maintained that Aboriginal peoples could only survive if they joined the mainstream society. Do you think that those governments had Aboriginal people's best interests at heart? What other reasons might colonial governments have had for pressuring Aboriginal peoples to abandon their cultures and integrate into the dominant society?

EXHIBIT 12.2

Children in class at the residential school on Stoney Reserve, Morley, Alberta (circa 1949–1950).

2 BRIDGING THE DIVIDE BETWEEN GOVERNMENT AND INDIGENOUS PEOPLES

By the Second World War, the federal government controlled most aspects of life on-reserve. However, isolationist policies—such as the residential schools and the system of reserves—had worked at cross-purposes to the goal of assimilation. The Indian Act had also served to disempower Indians and keep them in a state of dependency. The Aboriginal peoples nevertheless defended their original status as a distinct nation with a legal right to land, culture, and self-government.

A SHIFTING BALANCE OF POWER

As poverty, addiction, violence, and social disorganization worsened among Indigenous peoples, Aboriginal leaders emerged to demand change and to advocate for their people's rights. In particular, Aboriginal peoples wanted the federal government to end its enfranchisement policies, relax its grip on Aboriginal affairs, and honour its own **treaties**. In 1951, amendments to the Indian Act lifted the ban on potlatches, powwows, and other traditional ceremonies. However, the clauses in the Act relating to enfranchisement and Indian status remained intact.

In 1969, the Statement of the Government of Canada on Indian Policy (also known as the White Paper) formally recognized that having separate status had only hindered First Nations people and prevented them from fully participating in Canadian society. To correct injustices made in the past, the federal government proposed to abolish the Indian Act, relinquish its responsibility for Status Indians, and give First Nation communities more control over their lands. In exchange, Status Indians would give up their special status and achieve equal footing with non-Aboriginal Canadians (INAC, 1990). Although First Nations peoples generally viewed the Indian Act as being discriminatory, colonial, and out-dated, they also recognized the value of the Act in affirming the legal rights of First Nations and holding the Government of Canada to honour those rights (Hanson, 2009). Thus, most First Nations rejected the proposal as another attempt by the federal government to assimilate them into the dominant society and strip them of their rights under the Indian Act. That rejection left the federal government little choice but to abandon its scheme.

The 1969 White Paper created dialogue and protest among all Aboriginal peoples across Canada and sparked a nationwide Aboriginal rights movement. Canada's Aboriginal peoples began to organize themselves formally in an effort to protect their common interests and rights, promote their cause, and reclaim their rights. Many Aboriginal groups formed during that time (and since); however, five specific groups became collectively known as Canada's **National Aboriginal Organizations** (NAOs). Those five groups are known today as

- the Assembly of First Nations (representing First Nations)
- the Congress of Aboriginal Peoples (representing Aboriginal people across Canada who are Status or non-Status living off-reserve, Métis, and Inuit)
- the Métis National Council (representing the Métis Nation)
- the Inuit Tapiriit Kanatami (representing the four Inuit regions of Nunatsiavut in Labrador, Nunavik in northern Québec, Nunavut, and the Inuvialuit Settlement Region in the Northwest Territories)
- the Native Women's Association of Canada (representing Aboriginal women, particularly First Nations and Métis women)

These groups have been instrumental in raising awareness of Aboriginal issues, working with government on policies that affect Aboriginal peoples, and developing culturally appropriate programs and services across Canada. In short, the achievements of Aboriginal organizations on behalf of First Nations, Métis, and Inuit peoples have been nothing short of remarkable (Abele, 2004).

CONSTITUTIONAL RECOGNITION

A major step forward involved the entrenchment of Aboriginal rights in the Constitution Act of 1982. The legal recognition of Aboriginal rights has helped to advance Aboriginal causes and bring Aboriginal rights to the forefront of Canadian political agendas. With the Constitution backing their rights, Aboriginal peoples have also pushed for further reforms in Aboriginal policy and programs.

The Constitution Act—along with the Charter of Rights and Freedoms— led to a number of reforms in Aboriginal–government relations. For example, the Constitution Act reduced the federal government's power to arbitrarily cancel Aboriginal land claims and treaties. The Constitution Act also prompted amendments to the Indian Act to guarantee the equal treatment of Aboriginal men and women, to restore Status and band membership rights to First Nations, and to abolish enfranchisement policies.

THE 1990s

During the 1990s, governments mainly focused on eliminating budget deficits; however, they could hardly ignore the growing influence of Aboriginal peoples in Canada. The United Nations bolstered that influence by proclaiming 1993 as the International Year of the World's Indigenous People and the period 1995 to 2004 as the International Decade of the World's Indigenous People.[3] This international recognition highlighted the challenges faced by Aboriginal peoples and drew attention to the value of traditional cultures and the role of Indigenous people in society. The international spotlight also pressured governments around the world to address the deplorable conditions in which many Aboriginal people lived and to forge new mutual relationships to improve those conditions.

---

[3] A Second International Decade of the World's Indigenous People began in 2005.

Aboriginal peoples achieved several milestones during the 1990s, advancing them in their political and social aspirations. One milestone occurred in 1991, when the Government of Canada appointed a Royal Commission on Aboriginal Peoples (RCAP) to review Aboriginal–government relations and the role of Indian, Inuit, and Métis people in society. In 1996, the Commission released its final report, making 440 recommendations for resolving a broad range of Aboriginal issues.

In 1995, the Government of Canada released its Inherent Rights Policy, which recognizes Aboriginal peoples' right to **self-government**. In general, self-government agreements give First Nation, Inuit, and Métis communities and groups a greater responsibility for and control over the design, administration, and delivery of their programs and services (for example, policing, healthcare, and child and family services). Individuals from self-governed populations remain citizens of Canada, have the same rights and legal responsibilities as other Canadians, and work within the existing political and parliamentary structures.[4]

During the 1990s, the Government of Canada made a commitment to work with Aboriginal peoples, other levels of government, and the private sector to improve the living conditions of Aboriginal peoples in Canada. To formalize this commitment, the government launched Gathering Strength: Canada's Aboriginal Action Plan in 1998. To begin the reform process, the Government of Canada issued a Statement of Reconciliation, a formal apology that acknowledged government's unjust treatment of Aboriginal peoples in the past.

THE KELOWNA ACCORD

By the turn of the twenty-first century, Aboriginal peoples had regained control over many of their own affairs, including the design and delivery of various programs:

- A full range of social and health programs had become available to all Aboriginal groups (First Nations, Métis, and Inuit peoples), not just to those with Indian status.

---

[4] Aboriginal peoples who do not have a land-base—such as Métis and Status Indians living off-reserve—may enter self-government agreements with the federal government. Those agreements may include the option to control and influence certain programs and services, and to develop organizations to deliver culturally appropriate services. Not all Aboriginal peoples have sought self-government; however, by 2010, Canada had completed eighteen self-government agreements involving thirty-two First Nations, Inuit, and Métis communities and groups (Aboriginal Affairs and Northern Development Canada [AANDC], 2012a).

- Most First Nation councils and self-governments had taken administrative control over on-reserve health, education, and social welfare programs.

- Aboriginal organizations had begun to manage most social services, education, and other programs for Aboriginal people living off-reserve.

- NAOs were advising governments on policies related to Aboriginal child welfare, health, mental health, and women's issues (Abele, 2004).

Despite these achievements, the Indian Act and other complex government policies continued to limit the provision of Aboriginal programs and had little impact on the overall socioeconomic conditions of Aboriginal peoples. In its 2004 Speech from the Throne, the Government of Canada (2004c) recognized that "Aboriginal Canadians have not fully shared in our nation's good fortune. While some progress has been made, the conditions in far too many Aboriginal communities can only be described as shameful." To rectify this situation, Prime Minister Paul Martin initiated a process to raise the standard of living for Aboriginal peoples to that of non-Aboriginal Canadians within ten years. That process culminated in the Kelowna Accord, a comprehensive agreement between Aboriginal, provincial, territorial, and federal leaders. The agreement promised to guide a new Aboriginal–government relationship and lead to the development of a full range of economic, health, education, and housing initiatives. The Government of Canada pledged more than $5 billion over five years to support the initiatives, which Aboriginal groups would implement on reserves and in urban centres. However, in the 2006 federal election, the Liberal government fell and the Conservatives formed a minority government. Although the Conservatives promised to meet the targets of the Kelowna deal, they allocated just over $1 billion over four years, an amount far below that proposed by the former Liberal government and, according to many analysts, grossly inadequate to reach the Accord's goals.

FEDERAL–ABORIGINAL RELATIONS UNDER THE CONSERVATIVES

Although Aboriginal peoples participate in policy development and decision-making activities, the federal government controls most of the funding and administration of Aboriginal programs. Some observers interpret this control as a continuation of colonial attitudes, which disempower and exploit Aboriginal peoples (Rice & Snyder, 2008). Federal control has continued—and some say, *intensified*—since the Conservatives took office in 2006. Since then, Aboriginal Canadians have criticized the federal government for failing to consult with

Aboriginal leaders on matters that concern them and for making a series of unilateral changes to the Indian Act, the treaty negotiation process, and laws protecting Aboriginal land and resources. In 2012, these grievances came to a head with the passage of Bill C-45 in the House of Commons and the launch of the Idle No More social movement (see Exhibit 12.3). Both Aboriginal and non-Aboriginal groups across Canada support this ongoing grassroots movement. Idle No More activities—such as rallies, blockades, and flash mobs—aim to empower Indigenous peoples and to educate Canadians on treaty rights and other pressing issues affecting Aboriginal peoples.

In 2009, Canada's Economic Action Plan allocated $400 million to build or repair housing in First Nations communities. While that investment improved housing conditions in some communities, it made little difference for the Cree community of Attawapiskat in northern Ontario. In late 2011, the media showed images of residents of Attawapiskat living in overcrowded conditions and in makeshift shacks or tents, many of which lacked electricity, plumbing, and heat. In his court ruling on the federal government's handling of Attawapiskat's crisis, Justice Michael Phelan (2012, p. 4) referred to housing

EXHIBIT 12.3

© REUTERS/Dan Riedlhuber

The social movement Idle No More began in 2012 in protest of Bill C-45 (new federal legislation that Aboriginal peoples claim violates their rights and control over traditional lands). The movement quickly gained support among Canadians and Indigenous people around the world.

conditions in that community "as an embarrassment to a country as rich, strong and generous as Canada."

The federal budget of 2012 drove another wedge between the Government of Canada and Aboriginal peoples. Determined to reduce the federal deficit, the federal government cut funding to several Aboriginal organizations and slashed the departmental budget of Aboriginal Affairs and Northern Development Canada (the primary federal department serving Aboriginal peoples). Although the 2012 federal budget did increase funding to Aboriginal mental health, family violence, employment, education, and other programs, it is questionable whether those funds were enough to meet the growing needs of Aboriginal populations.

DISCUSSION QUESTIONS

■ **Bridging the Divide between Government and Indigenous Peoples**

1. Most people would agree that the Indian Act has hindered progress among First Nations; however, First Nations peoples are reluctant to lose the legal protection the Act provides. Do you believe that this act should remain or be amended or repealed? Give reasons for your answer.

2. What are some of the social and political events that have supported an Aboriginal human rights movement? What current conditions are likely to support the Idle No More social movement?

3. Although First Nations receive millions of dollars from the federal government each year, many continue to struggle socially and economically. What resources—other than money—do you believe First Nations people need to improve their quality of life? Where would those resources come from?

3 HEALING AND WELLNESS IN ABORIGINAL COMMUNITIES

McKenzie and Morrissette (2003) observe that "colonization is the source of historical trauma and unresolved grief among many Aboriginal people: it resulted in personal and collective losses including family connections, and a way of life." In their efforts to cope with the impact of loss, many Aboriginal peoples have turned to social welfare programs and services. But mainstream Euro-Canadian programs are not always sensitive to Aboriginal values, culture, or needs. Over the past two decades, a number of Aboriginal healing programs have emerged across Canada that are developed, delivered, and managed by Aboriginal groups. This section examines some of the affects of colonization on the well-being of Aboriginal peoples and the traditional healing strategies used to achieve health and wellness.

COLONIZATION AND THE RESIDENTIAL SCHOOL SYSTEM

The Indian Act, enfranchisement laws, residential schools, and other policies intended not only to "civilize" Aboriginal peoples but also to colonize them. Emma LaRocque (1994, p. 73), a Métis professor at the University of Manitoba, defines **colonization** as a "process of encroachment and subsequent subjugation of Aboriginal peoples since the arrival of Europeans. From the Aboriginal perspective, it refers to loss of lands, resources, and self-direction and to the severe disturbance of cultural ways and values." Colonization reflects a sense of racial superiority, whereby a dominant group (in this case, Euro-Canadians) portrays an allegedly "weaker" group as having "something wrong with them" (Foucault, 1965, p. 7). Myths about the incompetence and racial inferiority of Indigenous peoples have persisted through the years; today, those myths continue to reinforce negative and potentially harmful stereotypes (Rice & Snyder, 2008).

One of the key mechanisms used to colonize Aboriginal peoples was the residential school system, which taught students to reject their traditional ways and to feel ashamed of their Aboriginal heritage. Some school officials also physically and sexually abused students, many of whom are still dealing with the traumatic effects of that mistreatment. An estimated eighty thousand Aboriginal people alive today attended a residential school (Health Canada, 2012).

Psychiatrist Charles R. Brasfield (2001) suggests that although the effects of residential schools may resemble post-traumatic stress disorder, they also have a distinct cultural component. For this reason, the term **residential school syndrome** has been coined to describe the cluster of symptoms specific to the problems created by Indian residential schools. These symptoms include distressing memories or dreams of life at the school; sleeping disorders; anger management problems; and avoidance of people, places, and events that trigger memories of the school. A number of former students also encounter difficulties expressing love to or communicating with their children, resulting in an intergenerational impact from the school system (Truth and Reconciliation Commission of Canada, 2012).

A generally accepted view is that many current social and economic problems facing Aboriginal peoples are the symptoms of unresolved grief and historical trauma caused by long-term colonization processes (Chansonneuve, 2005). The legacy of residential schools, in particular, lives on in the form of mental health disorders, suicide, addictions, family violence, and chronic unemployment. These symptoms are interconnected, since they tend to share common causes and consequences. Moreover, the impact of these symptoms typically goes well beyond the individual. Addiction, for instance, can take a heavy toll on an individual's health, as well as on his or her family's well-being; addiction can also lead to such problems as accidents, violence, and criminal activity, and therefore puts the safety and resources of whole communities at risk (Standing Senate Committee on Social Affairs, Science and Technology, 2006b).

TRADITIONAL VERSUS MAINSTREAM APPROACHES TO HELPING

For many Aboriginal people, social welfare and other mainstream programs have failed to help them deal effectively with grief and trauma. Some theorists see mainstream interventions as being generally incompatible with Aboriginal cultural values and beliefs and insensitive to the realities and needs of Aboriginal peoples (Kirmayer, Brass, & Tait, 2000). In one study, Aboriginal people reported that they avoided using mainstream services because they perceived those services to be racist, culturally irrelevant, and fragmented; some respondents also noted a fear of not being understood, or even re-victimized, by the system (Chartrand & McKay, 2006).

Many **mainstream approaches** to helping are based on the medical model and tend to view human disorders as discrete entities that can be fixed or treated through medication, psychotherapy, or other conventional interventions. These approaches typically focus more on the individual client than the client's environment or the interaction between the two. Mainstream services tend to focus on a specific problem (such as addiction or family violence) while ignoring other complaints. Moreover, these services often function independently in isolated "service silos," making it necessary for people with multiple problems and needs to seek help from multiple service providers.

Over the years, a number of traditional Aboriginal approaches to helping and healing have emerged in Canada. **Traditional approaches** are likely to view a person's "problems in living" as an imbalance in need of adjustment or **healing**. A **holistic view** is central to most traditional approaches. This view recognizes the interconnectedness between the individual, the family, nature, and the community, and the relationship between the physical, psychological, social, and spiritual aspects of the individual. A holistic perspective also highlights the overlapping causes and effects of a wide range of human problems, such as addictions, poverty, and family violence. Thus, traditional approaches to healing are likely to address several problems simultaneously and go beyond the restoration of balance in an individual's life to include the recovery of whole communities (Hylton, 2002).

Recent literature on Aboriginal issues focuses on how First Nations communities are approaching the process of healing and, in turn, breaking free from their oppressive past. Exhibit 12.4 illustrates how some First Nations peoples might view the past before European contact, how they experience the consequences of contact, and how they look to the present and future as an opportunity for learning and healing.

Although Aboriginal people usually access traditional approaches outside the mainstream social welfare system, they also have the option of using

EXHIBIT 12.4

CYCLE OF HEALING

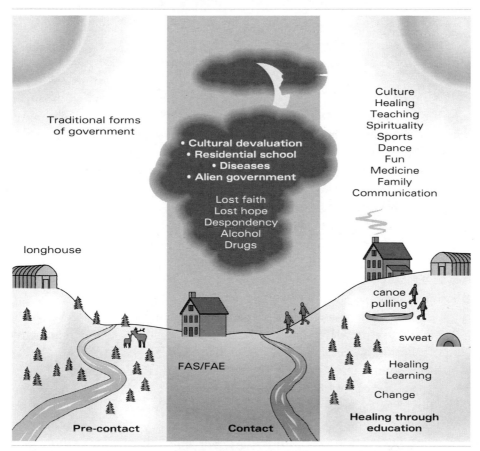

Source: Assembly of First Nations. (2003). *Investing in the future: First Nations education in Canada*, p. 58 (An illustration of healing that many First Nation communities face). Retrieved from http://www.afn.ca/uploads/files/education/13._2003_afn_investing_in_the_future_fn_education_in_canada_-_report.pdf.

mainstream services. Thus, Aboriginal peoples can choose between a broad range of mainstream modalities (such as psychotherapy) and traditional practices (such as the Medicine Wheel) or use both as needed.

HEALING STRATEGIES AND INITIATIVES

During the 1980s, government-funded healing initiatives focused on the pervasive problems of alcoholism and drug abuse in First Nations communities. However, people soon recognized that other social problems—such as those relating to residential schools, family relationships, and mental health—were serious and widespread in First Nations communities, and soon became priorities for healing initiatives.

To help Aboriginal peoples deal with the adverse effects of the residential school system, the federal government introduced the Aboriginal Healing Strategy in 1997. Part of this strategy involved the establishment of the Aboriginal Healing Foundation (AHF), a nonprofit, non-governmental corporation funded by the federal government and run by an Aboriginal board of directors. Since it began operating in 1998, the AHF has funded community-based traditional healing projects that address the historic trauma of abuse suffered in residential schools (Aboriginal Healing Foundation [AHF], 2012).

Native groups and organizations develop, deliver, and manage all AHF healing projects. These projects—which include healing circles and leadership training for healers—are based on traditional Aboriginal values, principles, and practices, and take place in culturally relevant settings. Although individuals are active in their own healing, well-respected Elders, skilled healers, and others guide the healing process. To reduce self-blame and denial, the healing process places an individual's personal problems within a social and historical context. Healing also employs cultural interventions, such as traditional ceremonies, to promote collective healing and a sense of belonging (AHF, 2008). A review in 2009 found that the AHF projects had resulted in healing at the individual level and that healing at the family and community levels had begun (INAC, 2009).

Many traditional healing programs exist across Canada. One of the more established programs is in the Ojibway community of Hollow Water, Manitoba. There, the Community Holistic Circle Healing (CHCH) program uses a thirteen-step process to address sexual abuse and related issues, such as addiction. The steps focus on educating people about the seriousness of abuse, changing people's attitudes toward abuse, preventing further incidents of abuse in the community, and helping people to heal. A variety of people can take part in the process, including the survivor of the offence, the offender, family members, and provincial justice system workers. A program evaluation conducted by the Public Safety and Emergency Preparedness Canada (2003, p. 2) found that CHCH had reduced the community's reliance on mainstream resources and could prove to "be a cost-effective alternative to the [mainstream] criminal justice process."

Systems and strategies continue to be developed in response to Aboriginal concerns. Exhibit 12.5 depicts a generic model—with nine interrelated interventions—that Aboriginal communities might use to prevent and reduce incidents of domestic violence in Aboriginal communities.

EXHIBIT 12.5

A COMMUNITY RESPONSE TO ABORIGINAL DOMESTIC VIOLENCE

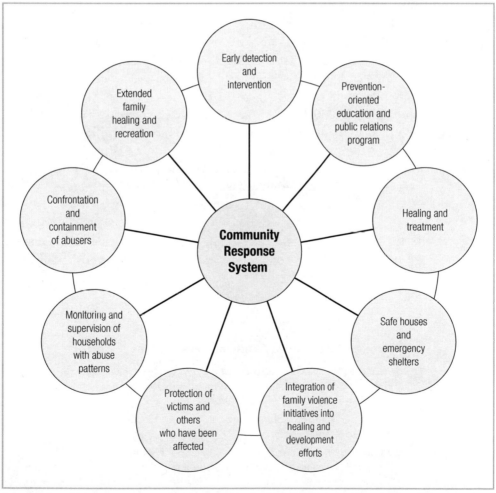

Source: Adapted from M. Bopp, J. Bopp, and P. Lane. (2003). *Aboriginal domestic violence in Canada* (fig. 3, p. 87). Retrieved from Aboriginal Healing Foundation website, http://www.ahf.ca/downloads/domestic-violence.pdf.

INDIAN RESIDENTIAL SCHOOLS SETTLEMENT AGREEMENT

While healing programs address the therapeutic needs of residential school survivors, compensation fulfills a legal responsibility. In 2006, the Government of Canada agreed to compensate Aboriginal peoples for their loss of culture and language at residential schools; in 2007, the Indian Residential Schools Settlement Agreement (IRSSA) came into effect. In anticipation of the IRSSA, Chief Phil Fontaine (2005) of the Assembly of First Nations stated: "While no amount of money will ever heal the emotional scars, this settlement package will contribute to the journey on the path to healing—not only for all residential school survivors, but for their children and grandchildren."

The IRSSA included a lump sum, one-time Common Experience Payment to all former residential school students—a gesture to formally recognize the experience of living at a residential school and its impacts. By 2012, almost all former students still living had received their Common Experience Payment, consisting of $10 000 for the first year at residential school plus $3000 for each subsequent school year. The IRSSA also provided a system through which former students could seek further compensation for the abuse they suffered. Additional funds were made available under the IRSSA to commemorate the legacy of the schools, support projects under the Aboriginal Healing Foundation, and create a Truth and Reconciliation Commission to educate the public on the impact of residential schools.

In addition to the IRSSA, Prime Minister Harper made a statement of apology to former students of Indian Residential Schools, on behalf of the Government of Canada (see Exhibit 12.6).

DISCUSSION QUESTIONS

■ **Healing and Wellness in Aboriginal Communities**

1. Identify the possible consequences of the residential school system for former students, Aboriginal families, and communities. How might those consequences have an intergenerational effect?

2. What are some of the potential advantages and disadvantages of a holistic approach to helping and healing?

3. The Government of Canada has given financial compensation to Aboriginal peoples for their loss of culture and language at residential schools. How might (or might not) financial compensation be an appropriate way to make amends for past wrongs?

EXHIBIT 12.6

STATEMENT OF APOLOGY BY PRIME MINISTER STEPHEN HARPER

Mr. Speaker, I stand before you today to offer an apology to former students of Indian residential schools.

The treatment of children in Indian residential schools is a sad chapter in our history. In the 1870s, the federal government, partly in order to meet its obligations to educate Aboriginal children, began to play a role in the development and administration of these schools.

Two primary objectives of the residential schools system were to remove and isolate children from the influence of their home, families, traditions and cultures, and to assimilate them into the dominant culture. These objectives were based on the assumption that Aboriginal cultures and spiritual beliefs were inferior and unequal. Indeed, some sought, as it was infamously said, "to kill the Indian in the child." Today, we recognize that this policy of assimilation was wrong, has caused great harm, and has no place in our country.

Most schools were operated as "joint ventures" with Anglican, Catholic, Presbyterian and United churches. The Government of Canada built an educational system in which very young children were often forcibly removed from their homes, often taken far from their communities. Many were inadequately fed, clothed and housed. All were deprived of the care and nurturing of their parents, grandparents and communities. First Nations, Inuit and Métis languages and cultural practices were prohibited in these schools. Tragically, some of these children died while attending residential schools and others never returned home.

The government now recognizes that the consequences of the Indian residential schools policy were profoundly negative and that this policy has had a lasting and damaging impact on Aboriginal culture, heritage and language. While some former students have spoken positively about their experiences at residential schools, these stories are far overshadowed by tragic accounts of the emotional, physical and sexual abuse and neglect of helpless children, and their separation from powerless families and communities.

The legacy of Indian residential schools has contributed to social problems that continue to exist in many communities today. It has taken extraordinary courage for the thousands of survivors that have come forward to speak publicly about the abuse they suffered. It is a testament to their resilience as individuals and to the strength of their cultures.

Regrettably, many former students are not with us today and died never having received a full apology from the Government of Canada. The government recognizes that the absence of an apology has been an impediment to healing and reconciliation. Therefore, on behalf of the Government of Canada and all Canadians, I stand

Continued

before you, in this chamber, so vital, so central to our life as a country, to apologize to Aboriginal Peoples for the role that Canada played in the Indian residential schools system.

To the approximately 80,000 living former students, and all family members and communities, the Government of Canada now recognizes that it was wrong to forcibly remove children from their homes and we apologize for having done this. We now recognize that it was wrong to separate children from rich and vibrant cultures and traditions, that it created a void in many lives and communities, and we apologize for having done this. We now recognize that, in separating children from their families, we undermined the ability of many to adequately parent their own children and sowed the seeds for generations to follow, and we apologize for having done this. We now recognize that, far too often, these institutions gave rise to abuse or neglect and were inadequately controlled, and we apologize for failing to protect you.

Not only did you suffer these abuses as children, but as you became parents, you were powerless to protect your own children from suffering the same experience, and for this we are sorry. The burden of this experience has been on your shoulders for far too long. The burden is properly ours as a government, and as a country. There is no place in Canada for the attitudes that inspired the Indian residential schools system to ever prevail again.

You have been working on recovering from this experience for a long time and in a very real sense, we are now joining you on this journey. The Government of Canada sincerely apologizes and asks the forgiveness of the Aboriginal Peoples of this country for failing them so profoundly.

We are sorry.

In moving towards healing, reconciliation and resolution of the sad legacy of Indian residential schools, the implementation of the Indian Residential Schools Settlement agreement began on September 19, 2007. Years of work by survivors, communities, and Aboriginal organizations culminated in an agreement that gives us a new beginning and an opportunity to move forward together in partnership. A cornerstone of the settlement agreement is the Indian Residential Schools Truth and Reconciliation Commission.

This commission represents a unique opportunity to educate all Canadians on the Indian residential schools system. It will be a positive step in forging a new relationship between Aboriginal Peoples and other Canadians, a relationship based on the knowledge of our shared history, a respect for each other and a desire to move forward with a renewed understanding that strong families, strong communities, and vibrant cultures and traditions will contribute to a stronger Canada for all of us.

Source: Video—Indian Residential Schools Statement of Apology—Prime Minister Stephen Harper—2008, http://www.aadnc-aandc.gc.ca/eng/1100100015677/1100100015680. Reproduced with the permission of the House of Commons Canada, 2013.

4 ISSUES AND ACHIEVEMENTS OF SELECTED GROUPS

Canada's Aboriginal population is diverse, with a wide range of ages, needs, and experiences. This section looks at some of the issues and achievements unique to three selected groups of Aboriginal peoples: First Nations people living on-reserve, Aboriginal peoples living in cities, and Aboriginal women.

FIRST NATIONS LIVING ON-RESERVE

Traditionally, a number of discriminatory laws and government policies have prevented Aboriginal peoples from participating in the mainstream economy and labour market. As a result, poverty has become the norm for many Aboriginal communities. About 34 percent of First Nations peoples living on-reserve receive social assistance (compared with 5 percent of non-Aboriginal Canadians) (AANDC, 2012b). Many of these individuals live on welfare their entire lives; it is also common for several generations of one family to depend on welfare. While welfare does not provide enough to live on, it has become a primary resource for First Nations people who lack job skills and education or struggle with mental health or substance abuse issues (INAC, 2007).

Politicians generally agree that improved education, access to jobs, and economic development are the way out of poverty for First Nations living on-reserve. Since 2007, the federal government has taken a more active approach to social assistance to help First Nations people get off (or avoid) welfare. That approach includes welfare-to-work programs, improved access to postsecondary education and skills training, and incentives to keep First Nations youth in school. A number of government programs—such as the Aboriginal Skills and Employment Training Strategy—aim to increase employability and self-sufficiency among First Nations peoples.

Through a wide range of projects and programs, First Nations communities are now strengthening their economies and, in turn, enhancing their quality of life. Much of this progress is due to First Nations gaining control over their land and resources through treaties, self-government settlements, and other agreements with government. A number of federal resources are available to help First Nations develop their economies; for example, the Community Economic Development Program gives First Nations access to funds to start businesses. First Nations peoples are also forming partnerships with the private sector; for instance, the Capital for Aboriginal Prosperity and Entrepreneurship is a social economy enterprise aimed at providing both a financial return for its investors and employment for Aboriginal peoples.

Some First Nation communities use the First Nations holistic policy and planning model (see Exhibit 12.7) to guide the development and delivery of economic and social initiatives. Developed by the Assembly of First Nations,

EXHIBIT 12.7

FIRST NATIONS HOLISTIC POLICY AND PLANNING MODEL

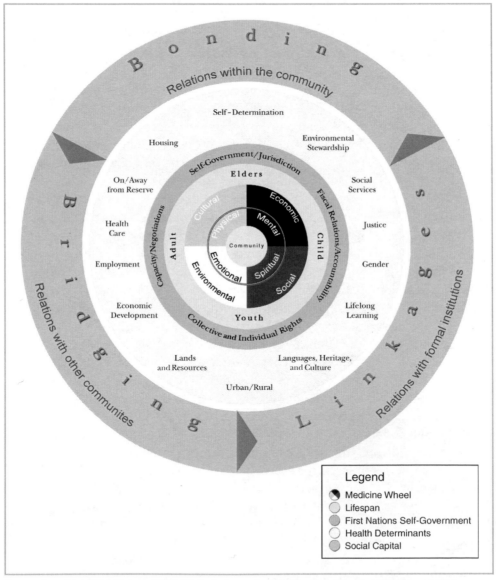

Source: Assembly of First Nations. (2007, May). *Sustaining the Caregiving Cycle: First Nations People and Aging: A Report from the Assembly of First Nations to the Special Senate Committee on Aging* (Figure 1, p. 8). Retrieved November 10, 2008, from http://www.afn.ca/misc/SCC.pdf.

the framework identifies the community as the core domain and the context of all initiatives. Moving out from the centre, each ring represents a domain that is central to policy and planning processes. Those domains are the individual (represented in the Medicine Wheel), the four cycles of the lifespan, key components of governance, fourteen determinants of health, and the three elements of social capital (relations within and outside the community).

ABORIGINAL PEOPLES LIVING IN CITIES

Over the years, the urban population of Aboriginal peoples has steadily grown; by 2006, more than half of Aboriginal Canadians lived in cities (Statistics Canada, 2008a). Urban life offers different things to different people; however, most Aboriginal males go to cities for work, and the majority of Aboriginal women move to urban centres for educational or family reasons. The Urban Aboriginal Peoples Study found that 65 percent of urban Aboriginal people like city life for the variety and convenience of amenities and overall quality of life (Environics Institute, 2010).

Although the development of programs for urban Aboriginal peoples has been inconsistent and largely uncoordinated, there have been concerted efforts to provide supports for this population. One of the most significant initiatives is the federally funded Urban Aboriginal Strategy (UAS), launched in 1998 to improve the coordination of Aboriginal policies and programs in urban centres, and make programs more responsive to local Aboriginal needs and priorities. A primary objective of the UAS is to increase the self-reliance of Aboriginal women, children, and families living in cities. Since 2003, the Government of Canada has invested in programs aimed at increasing job opportunities and improving access to family services, health and wellness, and learning programs, for Aboriginal city dwellers.

Aboriginal friendship centres are some of the most popular, well-organized, multipurpose facilities for Aboriginal people living in cities. These centres offer an alternative to mainstream social agencies by providing a wide range of programs aimed at improving quality of life. Since friendship centres tailor their programs to local needs, their programs vary across communities; however, it is common for those centres to offer family services, employment counselling, advocacy, and cultural events. In 2012, a network of 119 friendship centres across Canada operated under the umbrella of the National Association of Friendship Centres (NAFC, 2012).

Over the last few decades, studies on the urban experiences of Aboriginal peoples have undergone a distinct shift in focus. While studies in the 1980s and 1990s concentrated on the problems experienced by Aboriginal city dwellers—such as chronic poverty, alcohol abuse, and discrimination—recent studies have emphasized the achievements of this population. For example, the Toronto Aboriginal Research Project not only revealed the issues faced by urban Aboriginal peoples but also recognized the thriving middle class of well-educated, economically successful Aboriginal individuals living in the Greater Toronto Area (McCaskill, Fitzmaurice, & Cidro, 2011). Perhaps the most comprehensive study ever conducted on Aboriginal urbanites in Canada is the Urban Aboriginal Peoples Study; reports from this study chronicle many of the success stories of Aboriginal city-dwellers and, in so doing, aim to dispel some of the stereotyped images of Aboriginal Canadians (Environics Institute, 2010).

ABORIGINAL WOMEN

Before colonization, Aboriginal women held positions of social, political, and economic power in their traditional communities. Although women had different roles and responsibilities than men did, community members respected women and valued their contributions to the well-being of the family and community. In contrast, European men perceived women as being not only inferior to men but also the *property* of men, making them unworthy of any rights other than those allowed by their fathers or husbands (Manitoba Aboriginal Justice Implementation Commission, 1999).

Aboriginal women's status changed dramatically with the arrival of the European settlers. Intent on unseating Aboriginal women from their tribal positions of power, the colonists introduced laws that excluded Aboriginal women from participating in economic activities. The Indian Act of 1876 denied First Nations women any decision-making powers in their local governments or band councils and stripped them of all rights to Indian status or property if they married a non-Status man. To weaken Aboriginal women's influence on future generations, the federal government removed their children and placed them in remote residential schools (Boyer, 2006).

The early European settlers propagated the myth that Aboriginal women were inherently more promiscuous than European women. In recent decades, the media has reinforced this negative stereotype, resulting in serious repercussions. Emma LaRocque (cited in Manitoba Aboriginal Justice Implementation Commission, 1999) argues that the dehumanizing portrayal of Aboriginal women as "lustful, immoral, unfeeling and dirty" has put all Aboriginal women and girls at risk of "gross physical, psychological and sexual violence."

As a group, Aboriginal women continue to be among the most victimized Canadians (see Exhibit 12.8). While Aboriginal women represent only 3 percent of the total female population in Canada, they account for about 10 percent of all female homicides (Canadian Feminist Alliance for International Action, 2012). By 2010, more than 580 Aboriginal women and girls had either gone missing or been murdered in Canada (primarily in the Western provinces) (Native Women's Association of Canada, 2010). Several factors contribute to the incidence of violence against Aboriginal women, including poverty, racism, colonialism, child welfare practices, and justice system failures (Standing Committee on the Status of Women, 2011a).

The discriminatory nature of the Indian Act has served as a powerful catalyst to the Native Women's Movement, which began in Canada in the late 1960s. A major achievement for the movement came in 1985, when the Government of Canada amended the Indian Act and restored Status to First Nations women who married non-Status men. Since then, Aboriginal women have achieved considerable success: for example, Aboriginal women are completing high school and obtaining postsecondary degrees at a higher rate than Aboriginal men; moreover, the median income of Aboriginal women

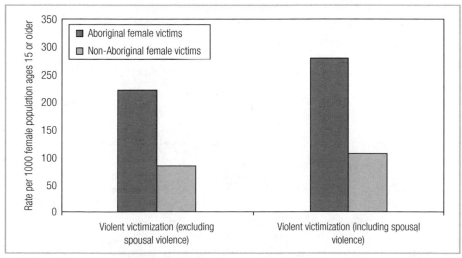

EXHIBIT 12.8

SELF-REPORTED INCIDENTS OF VIOLENCE AGAINST ABORIGINAL WOMEN, 2009

Note: Spousal violence includes incidents of physical or sexual assault.

Source: Brennan, S. (2011, May 17). *Violent victimization of Aboriginal women in the Canadian provinces, 2009* (p. 7, Catalogue no. 85-002-X). Retrieved from Statistics Canada website: http://www.statcan.gc.ca/pub/85-002-x/2011001/article/11439-eng.pdf.

with one or more university degrees is higher than that of non-Aboriginal women with equivalent education (Wilson & Macdonald, 2010).

Despite their achievements, Aboriginal women continue to be some of the most underprivileged people in Canada: for example, four out of ten women living off-reserve and almost half of women living on-reserve live in poverty (Morris & Gonsalves, 2012). Governments support various initiatives that aim to improve conditions for Aboriginal women and to support their full economic and political inclusion in communities and the larger society. The Department of Canadian Heritage funds many of those initiatives, addressing such issues as family relations and domestic violence. Nevertheless, Aboriginal women tend to underuse services, even when they are culturally appropriate. In recent years, professionals in victim services, violence reduction programs, and other programs for Aboriginal women have begun to share best practices in an effort to reach and serve Aboriginal women more effectively.

DISCUSSION QUESTIONS

■ **Issues and Achievements of Selected Groups**

1. Some people question whether reserves offer the optimal environment for First Nations people. What might be some of the pros and cons of reserves for the social and economic advancement of First Nations people?

2. Recent studies have focused more on the success stories of urban Aboriginal peoples than on their problems. How might this shift in focus help to challenge some of the stereotyped views of Aboriginal city dwellers?

3. Aboriginal women continue to be some of the most underprivileged people in Canada. What needs to happen—in terms of social, political, and cultural change—before Aboriginal women can become full participants in Canadian society?

5 ABORIGINAL CHILDREN AND YOUTH

Aboriginal young people represent the fastest-growing demographic in Canada, growing at twice the rate of other populations. These new generations of youth will have the opportunity to shape Canada's social and cultural future. Governments also look at young Aboriginal peoples as future workers who will ease an anticipated labour shortage. To succeed in school, compete in the labour market, and earn sufficient incomes, young people need a good start in life. Thus, important programs for Aboriginal peoples are those that help children in their early years. This section explores the particular needs of Aboriginal children and youth and the programs designed to meet those needs.

AREAS OF CONCERN

Despite some progress in recent years, Aboriginal children continue to lag behind other young Canadians in some important life areas. A growing body of evidence confirms that being an Aboriginal child in Canada means living in substandard housing and lacking quality education. Being Aboriginal also raises the likelihood of being poor: 27 percent of Métis, Inuit, and non-status First Nations children, and 50 percent of status First Nations children, live in poverty (Macdonald & Wilson, 2013). When compared with non-Aboriginal children, young Aboriginal children experience higher rates of substance abuse, physical and mental health problems, and disability. In some First Nation and Inuit communities, the suicide rate among youth is five to seven times as high as that of non-Aboriginal youth (Centre for Suicide Prevention, 2011).

A number of theories try to explain the inequities experienced by young Aboriginal Canadians; however, most analysts agree that "issues facing youth are rooted in a history of colonization, dislocation from their traditional territories, communities and cultural traditions, and the inter-generational impacts of the residential school system" (Urban Native Youth Association, 2003, p. 2). The formation of a self-identity is particularly challenging for Aboriginal youth living in communities where only remnants of their original culture remain. According to Chandler and Lalonde (2008, p. 70), "the predictable consequence of such personal and cultural losses is often disillusionment, lassitude, substance abuse, self-injury and, most dramatically, self-appointed death at an early age." Given the historical context of the problems facing young Aboriginal peoples, any programs developed for this population must also help the parents and other caregivers deal effectively with their own unresolved issues related to colonialization, including substance abuse, depression, and violence (Mussell, Cardiff, & White, 2004).

INITIATIVES UNDER THE NATIONAL CHILDREN'S AGENDA

In 1997, representatives of the NAOs and the federal, provincial, and territorial governments began developing a long-term action plan known as the National Children's Agenda (NCA). Under the NCA is the Federal Strategy on Early Childhood Development for First Nations and Other Aboriginal Children, an initiative that aims to meet the specific needs of preschool Aboriginal children who live on- and off-reserve (see Exhibit 12.9). The Strategy supports a wide range of programs, including the following:

- Aboriginal Head Start, which prepares First Nations, Inuit, and Métis children for school through activities that promote Aboriginal cultures and languages, health and nutrition, and parental involvement

- First Nations and Inuit Child Care Initiative, which offers First Nations and Inuit communities culturally relevant and affordable child care so that parents can work or attend school

- First Nations' National Child Benefit Reinvestment (NCBR) program, which allows First Nations communities to redirect unused funds from social assistance to culturally relevant projects (for example, hot lunch programs) that aim to reduce child poverty

- Brighter Futures (for First Nations on-reserve and Inuit communities) and the Community Action Plan for Children (for Métis, Inuit, and off-reserve First Nations families), which promote healthy living

EXHIBIT 12.9

© Paul Austring Photography/First Light/Getty Images

A wide range of federally funded programs focus on improving the quality of life and future prospects for Aboriginal children.

ABORIGINAL CHILDREN IN CARE

Before Europeans settled in Canada, Aboriginal communities successfully used traditional methods to care for and protect their children. However, with the establishment of mainstream child welfare systems in the late nineteenth century, social workers began to impose their own strategies of child protection on Aboriginal peoples. To facilitate the assimilation of Aboriginal people, social workers routinely apprehended Aboriginal children and placed them in non-Aboriginal foster care. This practice culminated in what is known as the "sixties scoop"—a massive apprehension of Aboriginal children that began in the 1960s and, before long, resulted in an overrepresentation of Aboriginal children in the child welfare system (Johnston, 1983).

Despite attempts to reduce the number of Aboriginal children coming into care, Canada's child welfare systems continue to remove Aboriginal children from their families at disproportionate rates (see Exhibit 12.10). By 2010, approximately twenty-seven thousand Aboriginal children were in

EXHIBIT 12.10

CHILDREN IN CARE IN SELECTED PROVINCES

	% OF CHILDREN IN CARE		% OF TOTAL CHILD POPULATION		NUMBER OF ABORIGINAL CHILDREN IN CARE FOR EACH NON-ABORIGINAL CHILD
	ABORIGINAL CHILDREN	NON-ABORIGINAL CHILDREN	ABORIGINAL CHILDREN	NON-ABORIGINAL CHILDREN	
BRITISH COLUMBIA	52	48	8	92	13
ALBERTA	59	41	9	91	15
SASKATCHEWAN	80	20	25	75	12
MANITOBA	85	15	23	77	19
ONTARIO	21	79	3	97	9
QUÉBEC	10	90	2	98	5
NOVA SCOTIA	16	84	6	94	3

Source: Sinha, V., Trocmé, N., Fallon, B., MacLaurin, B., Fast, E., Prokop, S.T., et al. (2011). *Kiskisik Awasisak: Remember the children, Understanding the Overrepresentation of First Nations Children in the Child Welfare System*, table 1.1, p. 5. Ontario: Assembly of First Nations. Retrieved from http://cwrp.ca/sites/default/files/publications/en/FNCIS-2008_March2012_RevisedFinal.pdf.

foster or other types of out-of-home care across Canada (AANDC, 2012c). In some jurisdictions, almost eight out of ten children in care are Aboriginal. One study found that, in 2010, the number of Aboriginal children in care was three times as high as those in residential schools during the 1940s (Canadian Child Welfare Research Portal, 2009; Standing Committee on the Status of Women, 2011b).

Historically, child welfare authorities have apprehended and placed Aboriginal children in alternative care outside of their communities—a practice that is associated with widespread family breakdown and a general lack of cohesion in Aboriginal communities. Being in the care of a child welfare agency also puts Aboriginal children at risk of losing their language, culture, and sense of Aboriginal identity and belonging. Moreover, Aboriginal children in care are susceptible to becoming street kids and sex-trade workers. In its study of street-involved and marginalized Aboriginal youth in British Columbia, the McCreary Centre Society found that four out of ten youth had been in foster care (Saewyc et al., 2008). Not surprisingly, many Aboriginal communities view mainstream child welfare systems more as colonization devices than as methods to protect children (Blackstock et al., 2006).

ABORIGINAL CHILD WELFARE SERVICES

Until recently, mainstream child welfare approaches have failed to recognize the value of Aboriginal beliefs and practices or to include Aboriginal peoples in decisions about the welfare of their children. One of the earliest attempts to correct these injustices came in 1990, when the federal government introduced the First Nations Child and Family Services program to help First Nations develop their own culturally appropriate child welfare services. Another boon to Aboriginal child welfare came in 2007, with the introduction of the Enhanced Prevention Focused Approach; this program allows First Nations child and family agencies to provide support to families to prevent child maltreatment or family breakdown. By 2012, Canada had more than 100 First Nations child and family service agencies across Canada, serving 75 percent of First Nation communities (mainstream provincial and territorial child welfare agencies provided the remaining 25 percent) (AANDC, 2012d).

Depending on the jurisdiction, Aboriginal family service agencies may provide some or all child welfare services. Some provinces and territories have *partially delegated* child welfare services to Aboriginal family service agencies; these agencies offer a limited range of support services (such as child abuse prevention, family support, and guardianship) but are not authorized to investigate reports of child abuse or neglect. Other provinces and territories have *fully delegated* child welfare services to Aboriginal agencies, giving those agencies the authority to provide any available child and family service, including those concerning child protection (National Collaborating Centre for Aboriginal Health, 2009–2010).

Manitoba has a unique system that gives control over the delivery of child protection services to four family service authorities: one of those authorities is Métis, two are First Nations, and one is a mainstream child welfare authority. Under that system, children and families in Manitoba can receive culturally appropriate services if they so choose, and First Nations authorities can serve First Nations families living either on- or off-reserve (Gough, 2006).

Efforts to identify and improve shortcomings in Aboriginal child welfare systems are ongoing. According to recent evaluations, the funding structures, service delivery, accountability, and service management in many Aboriginal child welfare agencies are seriously lacking. More work is also needed to address the overarching issues facing Aboriginal peoples—that is, the intergenerational impacts of colonialization and the legacy of the residential school system—which continue to affect the ability of parents to properly care for their children (Commission to Promote Sustainable Child Welfare, 2011).

DISCUSSION QUESTIONS

■ **Aboriginal Children and Youth**

1. How might the effects of colonization affect the ability of Aboriginal parents to raise and care for their children?

2. In your opinion, what factors have led to an overrepresentation of Aboriginal children in child welfare systems?

3. What are some advantages of Aboriginal groups providing child welfare services to Aboriginal children and youth? What are possible disadvantages?

6 SOCIAL WORK WITH ABORIGINAL PEOPLES

Aboriginal peoples often associate mainstream social workers with the operation of residential schools and the mass apprehension of Aboriginal children during the "sixties scoop." These associations have not only eroded the relationship between mainstream social workers and Aboriginal people but have also fuelled the demand for Aboriginal social workers. That demand has led to an expansion of Aboriginal-focused social work education programs. Many of these programs specifically prepare social workers for service in Aboriginal communities. The Blue Quills First Nations College in Alberta and the School of Indian Social Work at Saskatchewan's First Nations University of Canada are two examples of social work programs that offer courses on Aboriginal culture, philosophy, and values, and prepare students for working in various areas of practice, including child protection, addictions, and family services.

Today, trained Aboriginal social workers and other types of helpers have a wide range of opportunities in Aboriginal-controlled programs and systems, including self-governed communities. One of those opportunities is community development. In this field, social workers may be able to support Aboriginal peoples in their progress toward self-determination, self-government, and social justice—goals that are compatible with social work's values and principles.

Some experts believe that non-Aboriginal workers may be effective helpers if they first receive **Aboriginal cultural awareness training**. In general, this type of training focuses on

- terminology related to First Nations, Métis, and Inuit peoples
- the diversity of Aboriginal peoples in Canada
- awareness of the colonization process and its impact on Aboriginal peoples
- the history of Aboriginal peoples in Canada
- patterns of social inequalities and their determinants
- culture, racism, and stereotyping
- strategies for effective communication and social interaction (British Columbia Provincial Health Services Authority, 2012)

DISCUSSION QUESTIONS

■ Social Work with Aboriginal Peoples

1. What qualities or training should a non-Aboriginal social worker have to be able to relate to Aboriginal peoples' needs and issues?

2. Given what you know about community development (discussed in Chapter 8), how might Aboriginal social workers help First Nation communities to achieve self-determination, self-government, and social justice?

SUMMARY

Introduction

Canada's Aboriginal population consists of three distinct groups; First Nations, Métis, and Inuit. Four percent of Canadians are Aboriginal peoples. In recent decades, Aboriginal peoples have made great strides in many life areas, including health, economic development, and education. Despite this progress, Aboriginal peoples are generally more disadvantaged than other Canadians, and most First Nations communities experience some of the worst living conditions in Canada.

1 Historical Roots of Canada's "Indian Policy"

Colonial governments set out to assimilate Aboriginal peoples into mainstream society through enfranchisement policies, which included the first Indian Act of 1876. A more aggressive approach to assimilation came in the form of residential schools, where Aboriginal children were taught to reject their heritage, families, and communities.

2 Bridging the Divide between Government and Indigenous Peoples

Efforts to assimilate and enfranchise Aboriginal peoples generally failed. As conditions worsened for Aboriginal peoples, they demanded change; that assertion resulted in an Aboriginal rights movement and the formation of several National Aboriginal Organizations. Aboriginal peoples made significant political advances during the 1990s; however, in recent years, government–Aboriginal relations have deteriorated and subsequently fueled the Idle No More social movement.

3 Healing and Wellness in Aboriginal Communities

Many of the social and economic problems facing Aboriginal peoples are attributed to colonization and the residential school system. Mainstream social welfare programs are available to Aboriginal peoples; however, those programs are not always responsive to Aboriginal circumstances. The Aboriginal Healing Strategy funds various healing projects, many of which are delivered by Aboriginal organizations. In an attempt to compensate individuals for their losses incurred at residential schools, the federal government has issued a statement of apology and made financial restitution to former students.

4 Issues and Achievements of Selected Groups

Although many First Nation communities continue to struggle economically, other First Nations are gaining control over their resources and activities; the federal government offers a variety of economic development initiatives to bolster communities. While some Aboriginal peoples struggle to make ends meet in the city, others are thriving. Aboriginal friendship centres and initiatives, such as the Urban Aboriginal Strategy, provide support to Aboriginal urbanites. Many Aboriginal women are making significant progress socially and economically; however, as a group, they are at a high risk of violence, poverty, and other social problems.

5 Aboriginal Children and Youth

Conditions for Aboriginal children are improving overall, yet many children live in disadvantaged circumstances. The National Children's Agenda and other initiatives support young Aboriginal children and their families. Many Aboriginal communities are developing their own child welfare systems that are more responsive to Aboriginal needs. Nevertheless, Aboriginal children remain overrepresented in those systems, and more work is needed to address the overarching challenges (such as the effects of colonization) facing Aboriginal families.

6 Social Work with Aboriginal Peoples

Social workers' association with residential schools and the "sixties scoop" has eroded the relationship between mainstream social workers and Aboriginal peoples. However, demand for Aboriginal social workers is growing and, in turn, so are the numbers of Aboriginal-focused social work programs. At the community development level, social work's philosophy is compatible with the Aboriginal goals of self-government, self-determination, and social justice. To be more effective, non-Aboriginal service providers are encouraged to take Aboriginal cultural awareness training.

KEY TERMS

For definitions of the key terms, consult the Glossary on page 453 at the end of the book.

Aboriginal peoples, p. 331
First Nations people, p. 331
Indians, p. 331
Métis, p. 331
Inuit, p. 331
reserves, p. 333
assimilation, p. 333
band, p. 334

enfranchisement, p. 334
residential schools, p. 335
treaties, p. 337
National Aboriginal Organizations, p. 337
self-government, p. 339
colonization, p. 343
residential school syndrome, p. 343

mainstream approaches (to helping), p. 344
traditional approaches (to helping), p. 344
healing, p. 344
holistic view, p. 344
Aboriginal cultural awareness training, p. 362

13

The Social Welfare of Recent Immigrants

OBJECTIVES

The social well-being of recent immigrants depends largely on how well they integrate into Canadian society. This chapter will

- introduce immigrant populations and current views of immigration
- review the historical highlights of Canada's immigration policy
- explore the settlement process and related programs
- examine settlement patterns and issues
- discuss the challenges facing selected immigrant populations
- summarize the role of social workers in settlement practice

INTRODUCTION

Canada's history is replete with stories of people seeking a new life for themselves and their families. As a country populated to a very large extent by immigrants and their descendants, that experience is deeply rooted in our national consciousness. Canadian values have been influenced by the need to welcome and integrate people from many cultures, religions, languages and national experiences. (Citizenship and Immigration Canada, 1998, p. 1)

About one in five Canadians is born in a country other than Canada (Chui, Tran, & Maheux, 2007). Before 1967, most **immigrants** were from Europe; however, today, most newcomers to Canada come from Asia and the Philippines (see Exhibit 13.1). Most of those immigrants are **visible minorities**—that is, individuals, other than Aboriginal persons, who are not Caucasian. Statistics Canada (2010f) predicts that, by 2031, almost one in three Canadians will belong to a visible-minority group.

Polls suggest that most Canadians are generally supportive of immigrants and the immigration process; unlike Americans and Western Europeans, Canadians tend to "view immigration as an opportunity, not a problem" (Challinor, 2011). For many Canadians, immigration means interesting ethnic foods, art, music, and literature—all factors that enrich the country's social and cultural life. In economic terms, Canadians recognize immigrants for their investment of capital and expertise in the labour force. Immigrants are also helping to offset Canada's declining birth rate and aging population; over the

EXHIBIT 13.1

TOP TEN COUNTRIES OF ORIGIN: PERMANENT RESIDENTS TO CANADA, 2002 TO 2011

ORDER	2002	2005	2008	2011
1	People's Republic of China (33 304)*	People's Republic of China (42 292)	People's Republic of China (29 337)	Philippines (34 991)
2	India	India	India	People's Republic of China
3	Pakistan	Philippines	Philippines	India
4	Philippines	Pakistan	United States	United States
5	Iran	United States	United Kingdom	Iran
6	Republic of Korea	Columbia	Pakistan	United Kingdom
7	Romania	United Kingdom	Republic of Korea	Haiti
8	United States	Republic of Korea	France	Pakistan
9	Sri Lanka	Iran	Iran	France
10	United Kingdom (4 724)	France (5 430)	Columbia (4 995)	United Arab Emirates (5 223)

* Figures in brackets represent the number of permanent residents admitted that year.

Note: A permanent resident is someone who has lived in Canada for at least two years within a five-year period, has been granted permanent resident status, but is not yet a Canadian citizen.

Source: Author-generated chart, based on Citizenship and Immigration Canada. (2012). *Facts and Figures 2011*, p. 27. Retrieved from http://www.cic.gc.ca/english/pdf/research-stats/facts2011.pdf.

coming years, Canada will need to admit greater numbers of immigrants to fill the labour shortages created by the retiring baby boomers. Perhaps most importantly, the contributions made by immigrant workers—through labour and taxation—will help to support healthcare, social welfare, and other vital services that Canadians have come to value.

Overall, **recent immigrants** report that they feel positive about living in Canada and are adapting well to their new home. However, many recent immigrants arrive in Canada thinking that settling will be relatively easy, only to face a number of challenges. Some immigrants discover that they have inadequate language or life skills, or have trouble finding appropriate housing or making friends. Finding work is particularly difficult for recent immigrants: even those who have lived in Canada for a few years face a 14 percent unemployment rate (twice the rate of Canada-born adults) (Statistics Canada, 2012i).

This chapter provides an overview of the issues, challenges, and programs related to the social welfare of recent immigrants. First is some background information on Canada's immigration policies.

1 BACKGROUNDER: CANADA'S IMMIGRATION POLICY

Although Canada has always allowed immigrants and refugees from around the world, its immigration policies have clearly stated which individuals are "deserving" of entry. These same policies also reflect the country's attitudes toward people of various nationalities, races, and colours. This section chronicles the evolution of Canada's immigration policy since the late nineteenth century.

RACIST BEGINNINGS

During the settlement of the Canadian West, Canada welcomed newcomers who would develop the vast and sparsely populated land and help build the national railways. By relaxing immigration restrictions and offering free land, the federal government was able to attract large numbers of immigrants to Canada. In those early years, Canada's immigration policy stated a preference for Caucasian people from Britain, Europe, and the United States. The Canadian Immigration Acts of 1906 and 1910 restricted entry even more by banning poor, sick, or "immoral" applicants. Asian immigrants in particular were unwelcome in Canada (see Exhibit 13.2). To ensure Anglo-Saxon supremacy and to deter "undesirables" from entering the country, the Canadian government required immigrants of Chinese origin to pay a **head tax** (up to $500 a person) and placed strict limitations on the entry of Japanese and East Indian immigrants (Citizenship and Immigration Canada [CIC], 1995).

Library and Archives Canada. (2013). The Heathen Chinese in British Columbia. Retrieved from http://www.nlc-bnc.ca/pam_archives/public_mikan/index.php?fuseaction=genitem. displayitem&lang=eng&rec_nbr=2914880&rec_nbr_list=2914880.

EXHIBIT 13.2
THE "HEATHEN" CHINESE IN BRITISH COLUMBIA

"The Heathen Chinese in British Columbia": a cartoon from the *Canadian Illustrated News* in 1879, depicting Amor de Cosmos (Premier of British Columbia, 1872–1874) telling a Chinese immigrant to leave British Columbia because he refuses to assimilate with the rest of the province.

CANADA'S OPEN DOOR POLICY

Immigration peaked between 1904 and 1913, when two-and-a-half million people moved to Canada. Immigration then cooled during the First World War (1915 to 1918) and again in the Great Depression (1929 to 1939). By the end of the Second World War, Canada had become more interested in accepting greater numbers of immigrants, including those from non-Caucasian countries. Canada rationalized its more open-door policy on the following bases:

- Canada's economic needs had changed—the country needed skilled, well-educated immigrants who could work with new technologies.

- Jobs were plentiful and Canadians no longer perceived immigrants as competitors for jobs.

- Canadians were better educated, worldlier, less prejudiced, and more open to other cultures.

- Canadians were generally interested in challenging racism and pursuing human rights and the humane treatment of others.

- Minority groups were becoming more organized and gaining political power.

- An anti-communist sentiment motivated Canadians to give asylum to people fleeing communist countries.

- A declining birth rate and labour shortages forced Canada to consider increasing its numbers from well-populated regions of the world (Bélanger, 2006).

Despite more enlightened postwar attitudes toward immigration, Prime Minister Mackenzie King stressed that immigration policies would still be used as a tool to maintain a predominantly Caucasian society. King's position reflected a general assumption among Canadians that people who were not Caucasian had trouble fitting into a predominantly Euro-Canadian society and were therefore unsuitable candidates for immigration (Stasiulis & Abu-Laban, 2004). The new Immigration Act of 1953 reflected these views by making it more difficult for people from less-favoured nations to become Canadian citizens.

HUMAN RIGHTS AND MULTICULTURALISM

The recognition of universal human rights and more inclusive legislation characterized the 1960s. The Canadian Bill of Rights, proclaimed in 1960, prohibited the federal government from discriminating because of race, colour, gender, or ethnic origin. In 1967, the federal government amended Canada's Immigration Act to bring it in line with the Bill of Rights—no longer could government accept immigrants based on discriminatory criteria, such as ethnic origin or race. From then on, immigration authorities assessed applicants according to a **points system**, which awarded points for education, occupation, age, knowledge of English or French, employment opportunities in Canada, and other objective criteria.

When the government lifted its discriminatory immigration criteria, Canada's ethnic profile changed dramatically. Before the points system, people from Asia represented just 3 percent of all immigrants; by the 1970s, 33 percent of immigrants were from Asia (Statistics Canada, 2003). The points system had the effect of slowing Canada's **immigration rate**: for example, in 1967, eleven immigrants per thousand Canadians moved to Canada; by the mid-1980s, that number had dropped to less than eight per thousand (Milan, 2011).

A growing acceptance of cultural diversity, and the passage of Canada's new Multicultural Policy of 1971, paved the way for a new Immigration Act in 1976. This act favoured newcomers who were entrepreneurs or investors, and others who could contribute to Canada's economy. The Act made new demands on the federal government. For one thing, the government had to do more to help newcomers adapt to Canadian life, to reunite families, and to assist in the resettlement of refugees. In addition, the new Act required the federal government to project desired immigration quotas for one- to three-year periods. Initially, the quotas were used to anticipate the number of workers needed to fill Canadian jobs; later, the quotas became a tool for increasing the population, which was declining because of low birth rates (Chinook Multimedia, 2000).

Exhibit 13.3 illustrates the annual number of immigrants given **permanent resident** status in Canada from 1860 to 2010.

REFORMING THE IMMIGRATION ACT

During the 1980s, cracks in the Immigration Act began to emerge. One problem was that the immigration quotas were being filled by too many unskilled extended family members and not enough skilled and educated workers (Statistics Canada, 2008b). Immigration was also becoming a burden on social programs: although new immigrants were supposed to support the family members they sponsored, many of them reneged on their support agreements, costing taxpayers millions of dollars in welfare benefits (CIC, 1995). Overly complicated immigration procedures and their inconsistent application across the country created more problems.

NUMBER OF PERMANENT RESIDENTS TO CANADA, 1860 TO 2010

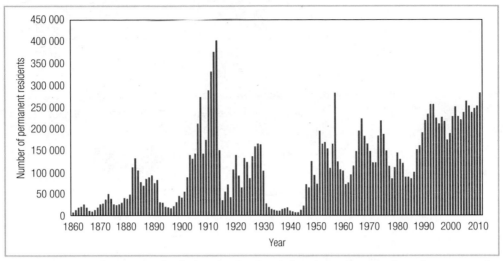

Note: Permanent residents are people who have lived in Canada for at least two years within a five-year period and have been granted permanent resident status.

Source: Immigration overview: Permanent and temporary residents, http://www.cic.gc.ca/english/pdf/research-stats/facts2010.pdf. Citizenship and Immigration Canada, 2010. Reproduced with the permission of the Minister of Public Works and Government Services Canada, 2013.

At the same time, the existing legislation failed to deal with a growing number of illegal aliens entering Canada. By 1985, public opinion of the immigration process had dropped to a new low.

Economic Priorities

In an attempt to correct some of the flaws in the immigration system, the federal government amended the Immigration Act in 1997. The reforms created three classes of immigrant applications: (1) an economic class (which included skilled workers and business immigrants), (2) a family class, and (3) a refugee class. Under the revised Act, Canada favoured immigrants who could meet the demands of a global economy and bring skills, education, experience, and other assets to Canada's changing labour market.

The immigration rules changed again in 2001 with the passage of the new Immigration and Refugee Protection Act. This Act put less emphasis on uniting immigrant families and a higher priority on **economic immigrants** who had the appropriate educational, language, and work skills to help them succeed in Canada's economy.

In 2008, the federal government amended the Immigration and Refugee Protection Act to make it more responsive to the needs of the labour market and to reduce the backlog and wait times for those wanting to move here. Although the Act still allowed for the sponsorship of family members under the family class, it expanded the immigration options for economic immigrants. By 2010, close to seven out of ten immigrants were entering Canada under the expanded economic class (CIC, 2011a). Economic immigrants are admitted by way of the following categories:

- Canadian experience class, for temporary foreign workers and recently graduated international students who want to permanently settle and work in Canada

- federal skilled worker class, for workers with the appropriate education, work experience, language skills, and other criteria to help them become economically established

- business immigration class, for experienced investors, entrepreneurs, and self-employed people to own and manage a business

- provincial-nominee class, for individuals nominated by a territory or province (outside of Québec) who can make an immediate contribution to the economy

- Québec-selected skilled worker class, for workers who are chosen by the Government of Québec and want to settle and work in that province (CIC, 2012a)

The Federal Skilled Worker Class

The federal skilled worker class (FSWC) admits the most immigrants of any immigration category. However, according to a program evaluation in 2010, more than 20 percent of FSWC immigrants are not satisfied with their work in Canada, and many FSWC newcomers have trouble succeeding in the workforce. To address these issues, the federal government began tightening the FSWC's eligibility rules; beginning in 2013, immigrants with weak English- or French-language skills, low education levels, or modest work experience will find it more difficult to immigrate to Canada. The new rules also favour younger workers who are likely to work more years and (theoretically) adapt more easily to Canadian society than older workers (CIC, 2012b). Changes in the FSWC rules could potentially reshape Canada's ethnocultural profile; for example, the emphasis on a high level of English proficiency may mean greater numbers of immigrants from Britain, Australia, and the United States, and fewer immigrants from Asia (Suhasini, 2012).

■ **Backgrounder: Canada's Immigration Policy**

1. How might the racist immigration policies of Canada's past influence people's current attitudes toward immigrants?

2. Canada's main priority is to admit immigrants who can benefit the economy. What other criteria, if any, should Canada use when selecting immigrants?

2   THE SETTLEMENT PROCESS

The process of moving from one country to another can be complicated, exciting, and stressful. Moreover, adjusting to the Canadian climate, geography, culture, people, language, and way of doing things, can take considerable time, energy, and patience. These types of adjustments are some of the many tasks of the **settlement process**.

STAGES OF SETTLEMENT

Although the settlement process is unique for everyone, it usually takes several years and involves three stages:

- *Acclimatization* marks the period when newcomers become accustomed to their new country in terms of language, culture, people, and the environment. During this stage, newcomers are likely to feel excited, optimistic, and confident.

- *Adaptation* is a period when newcomers gain confidence in managing their life, and require less assistance from immigration services or other formal sources of help. By this time, newcomers have dealt with many of the disappointments, frustrations, and confusions of living in a new country, and have a more realistic view of their situation.

- *Integration* is achieved when newcomers participate fully in the economic, political, social, and cultural aspects of their new country. Integration is synonymous with social inclusion, a process that is characterized by a sense of belonging, acceptance, and recognition. At this stage, newcomers are likely to have friends, community interests, and employment, and are generally feeling content with their new situation (CIC, 2010a).

Exhibit 13.4 takes a closer look at the types of supports needed by newcomers to Canada at each of these stages.

Successful integration depends largely on Canadians' attitudes toward immigrants. A relatively high public opinion of immigration is likely to encourage a welcoming environment, which supports newcomers in their efforts to find work, housing, social supports, and other important resources. In contrast, a low opinion of immigration can influence people to think

EXHIBIT 13.4

WHAT DO RECENT IMMIGRANTS NEED?

SOCIAL NEEDS	FINANCIAL NEEDS
• social networks • community participation • psychological support • citizenship information and training • advocacy	• income support • health insurance • Canadian bank account and credit rating • rental deposit and other housing costs • education tuition fees

© arabianEye/Getty

TRAINING AND INFORMATION NEEDS	PHYSICAL NEEDS
• financial orientation • language training • employment services • labour market information • job placement or internship • small business training	• housing • household goods (e.g., furniture, appliances) • transportation • educational supplies (for self or dependent child) • employment supports (e.g., tools, uniform)

Source: Adapted from: Robson-Haddow, J. & Ladner, S. (2005). *Asset-based approaches to settlement services in Canada*. Retrieved from http://www.sedi.org/DataRegV2-unified/sedi-Publications/Newcomers%20Policy%20Paper.PDF.

negatively of recent immigrants and exclude them from opportunities and resources. One poll found an even split among Canadians in their views of immigration: 39 percent see immigration as having a positive effect, while another 39 percent believe that immigration is having a negative effect (the negative attitudes relate primarily to the problem of illegal immigration) (Angus Reid, 2012).

The federal government argues that successful integration is a "two-way street," requiring an effort by both newcomers and Canadians to make the necessary adjustments. Canada-born individuals are encouraged to respect the cultural gifts that newcomers bring, to teach newcomers about life in Canada, and to promote the benefits of immigration. In turn, newcomers are urged to adapt to Canadian ways without giving up their cultures and to help Canadians understand the challenges of moving to a new country (CIC, 2010b). According to Dorais (2002), this mutual obligation is critical to a socially cohesive society. Unfortunately, full integration never occurs for many immigrants.

SETTLEMENT PROGRAMS

Canada offers a variety of **settlement programs** to help recent immigrants successfully complete basic settlement tasks, adjust to their new homeland, and, ultimately integrate into Canadian society. These settlement programs are particularly important to immigrants who are finding the settlement process to be stressful or complicated; these immigrants are likely to be dealing with one or more of the following factors:

- They have difficulty communicating in English or French.
- Their foreign professional credentials or work experience are rejected by employers.
- They have little choice but to take low-paying jobs or work for long hours.
- They have limited access to affordable child care.
- They experience racism or discrimination.
- They suffer from loneliness, a sense of isolation, or anxiety (Affiliation of Multicultural Societies and Services Agencies of BC [AMSSA], 2011).

A Modernized Approach to Settlement

Until recently, **settlement service-provider organizations (SSPOs)** have helped recent immigrants settle in Canada through three main programs: the Immigrant

Settlement and Adaptation Program (ISAP), the Language Instruction for Newcomers to Canada (LINC), and the Host Program. Shortly after coming to power in 2006, the Conservative government conducted formal program evaluations on those three programs. Researchers confirmed the benefits of ISAP, LINC, and the Host Program but also found several gaps and inconsistencies in the planning, coordination, and delivery of those services (CIC, 2011b). In an effort to modernize its approach to settlement, Citizenship and Immigration Canada reorganized settlement programs into six activity streams under a broad Settlement Program umbrella:

- *Needs assessment and referral* activities determine a newcomer's eligibility for services and their settlement needs, and refer eligible clients to appropriate programs or services.

- *Support services* provide child-care services, translators, transportation assistance, short-term supportive counselling, and other services.

- *Information and orientation* services offer information on finding work, housing, training, and other areas before, or shortly after, arriving in Canada.

- *Language learning and skills development* services provide training in English and French, and instruction on developing soft skills (for example, conversation etiquette).

- *Labour market participation* activities provide employment services (for example, job search skills, and work placements) and information about workplace culture and customs.

- *Community connections* activities provide opportunities for participating in and contributing to the community (for example, youth mentoring programs and women's support groups) (Smith, 2010).

Compared with previous settlement programming, the CIC's modernized approach puts a greater emphasis on newcomer outcomes (such as language proficiency and employment) and the assessment of newcomers' needs *before* their arrival in Canada. The approach also expects more from service providers in terms of the coordination of settlement programs, collaboration among service providers, the efficient use of resources, and accountability for the provision of high quality programs (CIC, 2009).

Administration and Service Delivery

Although Canada offered settlement programs in 1948 to help war refugees and the families of returning Canadian soldiers, it was not until the 1970s that the federal government began to support settlement services on an ongoing basis. Today, Citizenship and Immigration Canada (CIC) is responsible for settlement policies and services. While CIC funds settlement services, SSPOs deliver most of those services. SSPOs include school boards, postsecondary institutions, municipal governments, businesses, and voluntary agencies. An example of an SSPO is the Ottawa Community Immigrant Services Organization (OCISO, 2007); this agency works with government and other community partners to provide cultural and language programs to recent immigrants, and supports community-based projects that help newcomers settle into the community.

The administrative control of settlement services continues to shift from one level of government to another. Initially, the federal government treated settlement programs as a national responsibility, administered by federal agents. However, in 1991, the Government of Canada signed an agreement with Québec, giving that province the full control of its settlement programs, albeit with federal funding. In subsequent years, other provinces entered similar agreements with the federal government and gained more control over the design, management, and delivery of settlement programs in their jurisdictions. In 2012, the federal government reversed its plan to decentralize immigration services and announced that it would phase out all bilateral agreements with the provinces (except Québec). Settlement programs have once again become a national concern, with the federal government taking the helm of those programs.

Support for Refugees

Immigrants move to another country by choice; in contrast, **refugees** flee their homeland for their own safety or survival. Canada's refugee program aims to save people's lives, protect displaced and persecuted individuals, and help those in need of **resettlement**. Under the UN's Convention Relating to the Status of Refugees (the Geneva Convention) and other international agreements, Canada has a legal obligation to protect legitimate refugees. Canada accepts, on average, about 28000 refugees a year; this represents almost 11 percent of all newcomers to Canada (CIC, 2012c).

To qualify as refugees, people must first meet the criteria for Convention refugees or people in need of protection. For Convention refugees, Canadian officials consider a refugee's claim and decide whether the applicant meets the Refugee and Humanitarian Resettlement Program (for people seeking protection from outside Canada) or the In-Canada Asylum Program (for people making refugee protection claims from within Canada). People in a refugee-like situation who do not meet the criteria of a Convention refugee can apply for protection under Canada's Country of Asylum Class (CIC, 2012d).

In addition to personal protection and safety, and the promise of a permanent home, refugees need many of the same supports as other immigrants. Many refugees also have specific needs resulting from a crisis in their homeland; for example, refugees who are survivors of torture, or have lived in refugee camps for years, may be dealing with serious physical and psychological consequences when they arrive in Canada (Canadian Council for Refugees, 2008). Refugees may access a broad range of support from settlement programs, including life skills workshops, basic healthcare services and, in some cases, income support and help in finding housing. Some organizations also advocate for the rights of refugees (See Exhibit 13.5). Specialized programs exist for refugees as well; the Women at Risk program, for example, gives refuge to women and their dependants who are experiencing violence or other oppressive treatment in their homeland.

In 2012, the enactment of the Protecting Canada's Immigration System Act reformed several aspects of Canada's refugee legislation. Among other things, the Act gives the federal government the power to crack down on people who abuse the refugee system by imposing higher penalties on human smugglers and penalizing refugees who illegally enter Canada. Under the Act, the Government of Canada can detain smuggled men, women, and children without warrant or judicial review. According to the Canadian Council for Refugees (2012), the new legislation contravenes Canada's Charter of Rights and Freedoms and the Geneva Convention, which prohibits imposing penalties on refugees for being in a country illegally. Some organizations—such as UNICEF Canada—point out that the detention process may be particularly hard on the well-being of refugee children and youth, who may suffer anything from separation anxiety to post-traumatic stress disorder. In 2012, the Government of Canada held 289 migrant children—many under the age of ten—in detention centres across Canada ("Detention Centres," 2012).

DISCUSSION QUESTIONS

■ **The Settlement Process**

1. How might settlement programs help immigrants progress through the acclimatization and adaptation stages toward an eventual integration?

2. In the name of national security, Canadian authorities can detain people who enter this country illegally for an indefinite period. Do you believe this is an appropriate way to deal with illegal immigrants? Give reasons for your answer.

EXHIBIT 13.5

This poster promotes the Canadian Council for Refugees' thirtieth anniversary and "30 years of building a home of justice for refugees and immigrants."

3 SETTLEMENT PATTERNS AND ISSUES

In general, immigrant settlement patterns have largely been an urban phenomenon, with almost half of all immigrants settling in Toronto, Montréal, and Vancouver. The heavy influx and concentration of immigrants in these cities has created a number of challenges, especially in terms of urban development and demands on health services, social welfare programs, and schools. Immigration has also contributed to a more culturally and racially diverse environment in which racism has become a serious social problem. This section looks at some of these settlement patterns and issues.

THE DISTRIBUTION OF IMMIGRANTS

Canadian governments have been trying to disperse immigrants more evenly across the country to reduce the strain on resources in large centres and fill labour shortages in smaller towns and cities. To help matters, the federal government now allows the provinces and territories to accept a greater number of immigrants. The Provincial Nominee Program has also helped the regional governments to fast-track skilled workers to fill serious labour gaps; Manitoba, for example, has been able to address its shortage of nurses by sponsoring over 100 registered nurses from the Philippines (CIC, 2010c). Many regions are trying to attract immigrants through elaborate advertising campaigns that promote their rural and smaller centres as desirable places to live, work, and raise a family.

Census data suggests that the various recruitment strategies are starting to pay off for places that normally struggle to attract immigrants. Saskatchewan, for instance, attracted three times as many immigrants from 2006 to 2011 than it did in the previous five years. Prince Edward Island is one of the Atlantic provinces that is enjoying population growth as a result of immigration; that province's population grew eight-fold from 2006 to 2011 (Statistics Canada, 2012k). Many of Canada's sparsely populated or poorer regions consider immigration as a key to their future economic prosperity.

Ethnic Enclaves

One of the trends related to urban immigration is the phenomenon of **ethnic enclaves**. These enclaves are neighbourhoods where at least 30 percent of the population belongs to the same ethnic group (Hou & Picot, 2003). Ethnic enclaves—such as Little Italies or Chinatowns—are known for their unique restaurants, groceries, retail stores, and cultural events (see Exhibit 13.6). The number of ethnic enclaves in Canada has grown over the years, from six in 1981 to more than 250 in 2001 (Merrill Cooper, Guyn Cooper Research Associates, 2008).

Researchers have identified both pros and cons of ethnic enclaves. On the positive side, the residents in concentrated groups can enjoy common interests and customs. Ethnic enclaves can be especially beneficial to immigrant women, many of whom do not speak English or French, and who desire

© Michael Klinec/Alamy

Chinatowns are some of the most colourful and recognizable ethnic enclaves in Canada.

the closeness of family and friends. On the negative side, ethnic enclaves can segregate residents from the mainstream society and, in turn, limit their opportunities to connect with others, learn English or French, find work, or attend school outside the neighbourhood. Studies show that immigrants who work in ethnic enclaves tend to have lower wages than do other Canadian workers (O'Neil & Nursall, 2012). Some analysts view ethnic enclaves as evidence that Canada has failed to achieve a multicultural society in which newcomers have fully integrated into society (Kim, 2012).

One concern about ethnic enclaves is their potential to concentrate recent immigrants, many of whom are poor, into "enclaves of poverty" or "ghettos"—environments that pose particular risks to the health and well-being of children (Omidvar & Richmond, 2003). While ghettos are a common characteristic of large American cities, analysts suggest that Canada's relatively strong social safety net, a general support of multiculturalism, and a more accepting view of immigration may be protective buffers against ghettoization in this country. Indeed, many ethnic enclaves in Canada—including those in Vancouver and Surrey, British Columbia—are thriving middle-class communities where most community members own property and have children who are training to be doctors, lawyers, and other professionals (Sangha, 2012). As the number of foreign-born Canadians grows, it is likely that ethnic enclaves will become more popular as communities where friends and family already live, where they can speak their native language, and where they may find comfort in familiarity.

RACISM AND MARGINALIZATION

Under the UN's International Convention on the Elimination of All Forms of Racial Discrimination, the Canadian Charter of Rights and Freedoms, and the Canadian Multiculturalism Act, Canada has an obligation to eliminate racism in this country. Broadly speaking, there are three forms of **racism**:

- *Individual racism* is evident in people's attitudes, beliefs, and behaviours; examples include bigotry, stereotyping, belittling remarks, name-calling, and **discrimination** based on race.

- *Systemic racism* is organizational in nature and embedded in policies and practices that favour some groups while disadvantaging others because of their race or ethnicity.

- *Cultural racism*, which underlies individual and systemic discrimination, reflects the dominant society's values, and the concept of cultural superiority or inferiority based on racial differences (Roy, 2005–2010).

Contrary to popular myths about Canada, racism is a growing social problem in this country. According to one poll, four in ten Canadians witnessed a racist incident in the previous year, and almost half of all Canadians think that racism is on the rise in this country (Canadian Race Relations Foundation, 2011). Another study found that when compared with Caucasian immigrants, visible-minority immigrants are more than twice as likely to perceive discrimination in the workplace (Preston et al., 2011). Certain immigrant groups are at a particularly high risk of discrimination in Canada including Muslims, Sikhs, and Blacks (Soroka & Roberton, 2012).

Although everyone might experience discrimination from time to time, some groups are more likely to be racialized than others are. **Racialization** is defined here as a "process through which groups come to be designated as different and on that basis subjected to unequal treatment" (University of Guelph, 2007, p. 12). Racialized groups are usually those that another (usually dominant) group considers unequal, abnormal, or less worthy because of their skin colour, religion, language, or other trait. Because the basis of discrimination may be attributes other than race, racialized groups may or may not be visible minorities.

Since the terrorist attacks in the United States in 2001, Islamophobia has frequently been in the media, a product of the racialization of Muslim people and an unfounded fear of Islam. A poll conducted by Leger Marketing (2011) found that, ten years after 9/11, 40 percent of Canadians approved of airport personnel doing extra security checks on persons appearing to be of Muslim background. Canadian politicians do their share to spread the fear of Muslims; in an interview for *CBC*, Prime Minister Stephen Harper (2011) stated that, when speaking of terrorism, "the major threat is still Islamicism."

Racism has serious implications for the integration of newcomers to Canada. Racialized immigrants are likely to be marginalized from mainstream society; excluded from social, political, and economic activities; and prevented from accessing important resources, such as adequate income, housing, and services. Not only is the oppression and marginalization of immigrant groups a social injustice, but it is also contrary to the objectives of immigration—that is, to help newcomers contribute to population growth and fill significant gaps in the labour market.

The elimination of racism and discrimination is a major focus of public policy in Canada, and a challenge for political leaders. Over the years, the federal government has sponsored a number of antiracism campaigns. For example, projects under the Welcoming Communities Initiative—such as campaigns to raise awareness of racism and outreach programs to welcome newcomers—aim to create more inclusive and welcoming communities for recent immigrants, and to strengthen the relationships between newcomers and Canadians (CIC, 2010d). At the provincial or territorial level is a variety of innovative programs to reduce racism. For example, WelcomeBC funds the Neonology program offered by the North Shore Multicultural Society (see Exhibit 13.7).

DISCUSSION QUESTIONS

■ Settlement Patterns and Issues

1. Many communities in Canada are trying to attract immigrants to fill labour shortages and to increase their population (and tax base). If you were moving to Canada, what features might you be seeking in a community? Do you know of any communities that offer those features?

2. What are some of the potential benefits and detriments of high concentrations of immigrants in Canada's largest cities?

3. Racism is a serious problem at many different levels of society. What might colleges and universities (or students) do to help immigrant students feel included, accepted, and respected?

EXHIBIT 13.7

NEONOLOGY: A FUNKY ANTI-RACISM PROGRAM FOR YOUTH

The North Shore Multicultural Society (NSMS) in North Vancouver, British Columbia, launched Neonology in September 2010. Since then, Neonology has become a popular buzzword on the North Shore, and it is common to see youth in the community wearing the fluorescent Neonology t-shirts. The Neonology initiative challenges youth to make their communities more welcoming and inclusive by adopting a new and brighter perspective on diversity.

One thousand youth have attended Neonology workshops in North Shore high schools. During the sessions, students explore diversity and anti-oppression through hands-on activities and open discussion. The project creates a safe space for youth to express their experiences and thoughts on discrimination and privilege. Youth are encouraged to take an active role as change agents in their communities: after learning more about diversity and inclusion during the sessions, 72 percent of youth participants reported an intention to act on the information they had learned. Neonology also delivers workshops for parents and teachers, to engage them as allies in creating welcoming and inclusive communities for immigrant youth.

Among other achievements, the Neonology team has provided in-depth training for youth leaders to develop Neon Clubs (diversity and inclusive community initiatives in schools); and has sponsored a Neonology Forum for front-line youth workers to learn how youth programs can be more welcoming and inclusive.

Neonology is an initiative of the North Shore Welcoming Action Committee, which serves as the advisory body for this program. The NSMS manages the program, and delivers the program in partnership with the North Vancouver and West Vancouver School Districts. Funding for Neonology comes from the Welcoming and Inclusive Communities and Workplaces Initiative, which makes it possible for the NSMS to explore a fresh outlook on diversity.

Source: Adapted from North Shore Welcoming Action Committee. (2010, July). *NSWAC Newsletter*, 1(2), p. 2. Retrieved from http://www.northshorewac.ca/File/NSWACNewsletter_July_2010.pdf.

4 CHALLENGES FOR SELECTED IMMIGRANT GROUPS

Each newcomer to Canada experiences the immigration process differently. Many factors influence those experiences, including age, gender, skills, and the readiness and willingness of the host country to accept newcomers. This section considers some of the challenges of immigrating to Canada for young people, women, and people seeking employment.

CHILDREN AND YOUTH

One in five children in Canada under the age of fifteen was born either in an immigrant family or in another country (New Canadian Children and Youth Study, n.d.). Although most young immigrants are adapting well to life in Canada, many encounter difficulties:

- They cannot speak English or French when they arrive in Canada, which puts them at risk of doing poorly in school or having trouble making friends.

- They experience discrimination or are socially excluded, which may interfere with their ability to engage in school and makes them vulnerable to criminal and deviant behaviour.

- They face identity conflict when trying to fit into the contrasting cultures of their family and their peer group.

- Their family lives in poverty, a factor that puts young people at risk of physical and mental health problems, social isolation, and difficulties concentrating in school (AMSSA, 2012; BC Centre for Safe Schools and Communities, 2012; CIC, 2012e).

A number of studies have explored the relationship between the ethnic or racial identity of young newcomers and their mental health status. Psychological distress among young immigrants is linked to such issues as language difficulties and adjusting to a new school system. Those who experience racism or discrimination tend to have higher than normal levels of stress, depression, low self-esteem, behavioural disorders (such as substance abuse or violence), and other functional problems (Shakya, Khanlou, & Gonsalves, 2010). Young refugees face particular mental health challenges: children who have fled war or abuse in their homeland, or who been separated from their parents, may be under considerable stress when they arrive in Canada. In his study of Canada's boat people, Morton Beiser (1999) found that refugee youth were twice as likely as adults were to suffer from depression; the youth were also at a higher risk of suicide.

A growing body of research on the needs and issues of young immigrants is fuelling the expansion of programs for this group. Citizenship and Immigration Canada funds many of those programs under its settlement services framework. One of the more popular CIC programs is the Settlement Workers in Schools (SWIS) initiative. Under SWIS, settlement workers in public schools orient newcomer students to the school system, assess their needs, and provide information and language translation. Psychological counselling is also available for children and youth experiencing adjustment difficulties. In addition to school-based programs are a wide range of programs offered by organizations, such as the YMCA, Red Cross, and the United Way; those organizations may deliver a specific activity (for example, recreation services) or target their services to young people from a specific region, such as Africa or the Middle East.

Certain programs for young immigrants are in particularly high demand; those programs include mental health counselling, English-as-a-second-language training, and culturally relevant early learning and child-care programs. Also in demand are outreach programs, in which workers connect with young newcomers and help them engage in school and community activities. Moreover, the need is growing for prevention and support programs that target youth at risk of gang behaviour, criminal activity, and dropping out of school (Mitchell, 2005).

IMMIGRANT WOMEN

Approximately one in five women in Canada is foreign born, and more than one-quarter of them belong to a visible minority group. In recent years, most immigrant women have come from Asia and the Middle East, and settled in large urban centres (for example, almost half of Toronto's female population are immigrants) (Chui, 2011).

Immigrant women face a number of challenges when adapting to their new life in Canada. In general, immigrant women

- who cannot speak English or French, or belong to a visible or religious minority, have limited job opportunities and, therefore, tend to be poor, unemployed, or underemployed

- face cultural barriers, discrimination, and racism when trying to access training, jobs, health care, and other essential services

- experience stress and other mental health issues in response to their economic situations, personal isolation, or perceived discrimination (Morris & Sinnott, 2010)

Although women newcomers are at a lower risk of abuse than Canada-born women, they are less likely to report incidents of abuse (Du Mont et al., 2012). Studies show that underreporting is most common among women who do not understand their legal rights or the way the justice system works. In turn, victims who are financially dependent on their husbands (who are usually the abusers) and cannot speak French or English are also unlikely to report abuse (Smith, 2004). According to the 2004 General Social Survey on Victimization, about 5 percent of recent immigrant women experience spousal abuse; however, because of underreporting, the actual rate may be much higher (Statistics Canada, 2006).

With the exception of language training, the service needs of immigrant women are similar to those of Canada-born women; for instance, most women need basic healthcare, and many benefit from such things as employment support. Research has shown that the way in which organizations *deliver services* strongly influences a woman newcomer's *use of services*. Overall, women immigrants are more likely to seek help from agencies that offer culturally sensitive programs—that is, programs that recognize and respect their particular values, beliefs, and norms. In her study of immigrant women in Atlantic Canada, researcher Barbara Cottrell (2008) found that women immigrants are more likely to seek help if the helper is female and speaks the same language. It is also important to women that helpers know something about their culture and are, ideally, from the same country of origin.

Settlement service-provider organizations in Canada have taken various steps to make their operations more culturally sensitive. It is common for SSPOs to employ workers who represent the racial and ethnic diversity of the population they serve and to ensure that front-line staff and office workers receive **cross-cultural training**. In this type of training, participants immerse themselves in a specific ethnocultural community to gain sensitivity to another culture and to develop a better understanding of their own prejudices, stereotypes, and cultural values. Many agencies also regularly review their program standards, policies, and procedures to ensure that they are inclusive of immigrants and ethnic minorities (Luther, 2007). Some agencies—such as Immigrant Women Services Ottawa—tailor all their programs to the needs of immigrant women. Despite the expansion of women-centred programs, the need continues for more culturally appropriate services for immigrant women and for the inclusion of immigrant women in the design, development, and delivery of the services they are likely to use.

IMMIGRANT WORKERS

Employment plays an important role in settlement in a new country and the eventual integration and participation in Canadian society. Aycan and Berry (1996, p. 11) observe that work "provides purpose to life, it defines status and identity, and enables individuals to establish relationships with others in the society. It is especially the latter function that becomes critical for immigrants, because adaptation is facilitated by social interactions. The more one interacts with the groups in the larger society, the faster one acquires skills to manage everyday life."

Until the 1980s, newcomers to Canada could expect that, after the initial settling-in period, they would be able to find a well-paying job (see Exhibit 13.8). In those days, employment rates for immigrants were as high as or higher than that of Canada-born workers, and their earnings were comparable. Since that time, the ability of working-age immigrants to find good jobs has steadily deteriorated. In 2011, 14 percent of immigrants who were in Canada for five years or less were unemployed (compared with 7 percent of Canada-born workers). On average, those immigrants also earned less than Canada-born workers did and had less access to workplace pensions and other benefits (Statistics Canada, 2012j). The problem with finding work is not due to a lack of education; indeed, more than 40 percent of recent immigrants have at least a bachelor's degree, compared with just 17 percent of Canada-born workers (Desjardins & Cornelson, 2011).

EXHIBIT 13.8

From the Sforza Family Collection of the Pier 21 Society

In 1959, when these Italian immigrants arrived at Pier 21 in Halifax, Canada had plenty of jobs to offer newcomers.

Some immigrant job seekers run into problems when trying to get their educational credentials from abroad recognized in Canada. Newcomers also find that not having Canadian work experience hinders employment, as does not being able to speak English or French (Schellenberg & Maheux, 2007). Many of the well-educated immigrants who manage to find work are working as clerks, labourers, taxi drivers, and in other low-skill, low-paying occupations. Reports suggest that discrimination is a real barrier to employment. One study found that employers were three times as likely to invite job applicants with English-sounding names for an interview as applicants with Chinese, Pakistani, or Indian names (Oreopoulos, 2009). In general, visible-minority immigrants—especially from Black or Asian origins—have the most difficulty finding work in Canada (Fellegi, 2006).

For many recent immigrants, moving to Canada has meant living in poverty, being jobless or underemployed, and struggling to meet even the most basic of needs. Not only can difficulties in securing well-paying employment result in a loss of social status and economic benefits, but they can also lead to depression, stress, anxiety, and other mental health issues (Fang & Goldner, 2011). From an economic standpoint, unemployment or underemployment among newcomers means that many talents and skills go underused, and chronic labour shortages in many parts of the country persist.

The federal government has introduced various initiatives over the years to reduce the barriers to economic integration among recent immigrants and to equalize working conditions between newcomers and Canada-born workers. Those initiatives include

- the Federal Skilled Worker Program, which allows immigration officials to select immigrants who are most likely to succeed economically in Canada and match them to jobs in their field

- the Pan-Canadian Framework for the Assessment and Recognition of Foreign Credentials, which is used before an immigrant arrives in Canada to assess his or her foreign-obtained education, work experience, and skills against Canadian professional and trade standards

- the Canadian Immigration Integration Project, which offers seminars abroad on how to find work in Canada or apply for credential recognition online (Kenney, 2012)

Various campaigns encourage businesses to recruit more immigrants. For example, Ranstad Canada (2012) is a recruitment firm in the private sector that promotes the benefits of hiring newcomers to Canada. That company also recognizes the benefits for businesses that diversify their workplaces; those benefits include attracting a wider customer base and gaining recognition as a business that respects cultural differences. In some jurisdictions, such as Québec, the government offers a tax credit to encourage businesses to hire immigrants.

DISCUSSION QUESTIONS

■ **Challenges for Selected Immigrant Groups**

1. Young newcomers to Canada may have trouble fitting in, especially if they struggle with such things as language or poverty. What role might the education, justice, or social welfare systems play in helping children and youth adapt to Canadian life?

2. Women immigrants tend to underreport incidents of domestic violence. How might Canadians help female newcomers get the protection and support they need?

3. Why might immigrants from visible-minority groups have more difficulty landing jobs in Canada than non-visible-minority immigrant job seekers?

5 SOCIAL WORKERS AND SETTLEMENT PRACTICE

Newcomers to Canada—especially those from racialized groups—often struggle with poverty, unemployment, underemployment, and a lack of affordable housing. **Settlement workers** can provide valuable support and advocacy to these groups. Many settlement workers are trained as social workers and approach **settlement practice** from a strengths-based, empowerment perspective. This perspective requires workers to demonstrate certain values (such as respect for the individual and professional accountability), professional ethics (including respect for client confidentiality and avoidance of conflicts of interest), and skills (for example, interviewing, case management, and advocacy) (Canadian Council for Refugees, 2000). Settlement practice also requires a strong grounding in theories and principles relating to the following:

- the settlement process (including the adaptation process, influences on integration, and the effects of settlement on family)

- the immigrant and refugee experience

- multiculturalism and cultural change

- human rights

- global and Canadian influences that shape immigration and settlement

- systems that affect settlement (such as the social welfare, health, education, and justice systems)

To be effective, settlement workers have to be sensitive to racism issues and to the impact that professional helpers can have on clients. Cross-cultural training may assist in this process. A growing number of social workers are also finding that an **anti-oppressive approach** is an effective method of working with immigrant or refugee clients (Sakamoto, 2007). Among other things, this approach aims to break down the social divisions and structural inequalities in society that prevent successful integration. Exhibit 13.9 compares some of

EXHIBIT 13.9

A COMPARATIVE VIEW: TRADITIONAL AND ANTI-OPPRESSIVE APPROACHES

	TRADITIONAL APPROACH	ANTI-OPPRESSIVE APPROACH
SOCIAL WORKER	From Caucasian, middle-class, Anglo-Saxon background; identifies mainly with dominant group	From any background or social group; may have multiple identities (based on race, gender, locality, religion, etc.)
VIEW OF IMMIGRANT SERVICE USER (CLIENT)	"Different" from the worker and mainstream population; in need; dependent	A fellow human being and citizen; peer; competent; independent
GOAL OF IMMIGRANT ACCULTURATION	To conform to dominant society (achieved through education, training, and information)	To understand the pros and cons of acculturation, identify individual needs, and access services to meet those needs
CULTURAL COMPETENCE OF SERVICE PROVIDER	Professional learns about the cultures of minority groups	Worker recognizes the overlapping yet unique identities and experiences of individuals in various social groups
RELATIONSHIP BETWEEN SERVICE PROVIDER AND SERVICE USER	Professional (the expert is the teacher; the client is the student)	Egalitarian (the worker and client are equals, allies, and co-learners in the change process)
FOCUS OF CHANGE EFFORTS	The individual (client must develop skills and behaviours to "fit in" to Canadian society)	Established systems and institutions (society must correct the unequal distribution of power and become more inclusive)

Source: Adapted from Izumi Sakamoto, "A Critical Examination of Immigrant Acculturation: Toward an Anti-Oppressive Social Work Model with Immigrant Adults in a Pluralistic Society," *British Journal of Social Work*, 2007, 37, 515–535, by permission of Oxford University Press.

the components of traditional social work with an anti-oppressive approach to settlement practice.

Workers must be able to accurately assess the needs and preferences of clients from various ethnic and cultural backgrounds. Assessment includes recognizing the value that each client places on tradition. While some individuals might want to maintain their traditional values and customs, others may reject them, preferring instead to assimilate into the dominant culture (Herberg & Herberg, 2001). It is therefore crucial for helpers to develop a clear understanding of the client's cultural values and preferences. Unless they can do this, settlement workers may find it difficult to establish rapport with immigrant clients and keep them engaged in settlement activities.

Studies suggest that social workers need more preparation to be able to serve newcomers effectively. In their survey of social workers in British Columbia, Yan and Chan (2010) found that only 43 percent of workers felt "well prepared" to work with recent immigrants. A study by Cottrell (2008) found that settlement workers want to respond effectively to the cultural backgrounds of their clients yet feel they lack the skills to do so. Settlement workers in this study also reported that their social work or other degree program offered only fragmented segments of cultural competence training that was not entirely relevant to their job.

Relatively few social work education programs focus specifically on how to work effectively with newcomer populations. However, as social work's clientele becomes increasingly multicultural, Canadian institutions are beginning to revise their training programs and professional supports to make them more culturally relevant. For example, the Canadian Association of Social Work Education now requires social work training programs to address multiculturalism in their curriculums. The Canadian Association of Social Workers has addressed diversity, discrimination, cultural values, and related concepts in various documents, including its code of ethics.

DISCUSSION QUESTIONS

■ Social Workers and Settlement Practice

1. How might an anti-oppressive approach help newcomers complete the tasks of the settlement process?
2. What might explain the lack of social work education programs in Canada that focus specifically on working with recent immigrants?

SUMMARY

Introduction

Canada is a country of immigrants, and most recent immigrants are visible minorities. Immigration has many social, cultural, economic, and demographic benefits. Most Canadians are supportive of immigrants; however, many recent immigrants discover that adapting to life in Canada is not as easy as they had expected.

1 Backgrounder: Canada's Immigration Policy

Canada's early immigration policies limited the entrance of non-Caucasian immigrants. After the Second World War, Canada became more accepting of immigrants; even so, immigration policies ensured a predominantly Caucasian society. In the 1960s, immigration policy became more inclusive. By the 1980s, several problems in the immigration system prompted a series of reforms to immigration legislation. Today's immigration system favours the admittance of self-sufficient immigrants who are younger, can contribute to Canada's economy, and have a good grasp of English or French.

2 The Settlement Process

The settlement process involves three stages: acclimatization, adaptation, and integration. Successful integration requires both newcomers and Canadians to make adjustments. A wide range of programs and services are available to recent immigrants to help them adjust to their new way of life; settlement service-provider organizations (SSPOs) deliver those services. Refugees often have serious physical, psychological, and emotional needs when they arrive in Canada and can seek help from settlement and related programs. Recent changes in Canada's laws allow government officials to detain illegal immigrants for indefinite periods.

3 Settlement Patterns and Issues

Most immigrants settle in large urban centres, creating a number of challenges for cities in terms of urban development and service demands. Immigration is also creating a more diverse workforce. Governments are finding ways to disperse immigrants more evenly across the country. Ethnic enclaves have both pros and cons; the biggest concern is their potential to concentrate large numbers of poor immigrants. Racism is a growing social problem in Canada and can interfere with the integration of visible-minority and racialized immigrant groups. Governments have introduced various campaigns over the years to combat racism in Canada.

4 Challenges for Selected Immigrant Groups

Many young immigrants have trouble adapting to Canadian culture, especially if they do not speak English or French. A growing number of programs are available for young newcomers, including those offered in schools. Although women immigrants may have trouble adjusting to their new life in Canada, they are unlikely to seek help unless agencies and services are culturally sensitive; many social agencies are tailoring their approaches accordingly. Working-age immigrants face a number of barriers in the workplace. The federal government has introduced various initiatives to reduce the barriers to economic integration and to equalize working conditions for newcomers.

5 Social Workers and Settlement Practice

In settlement practice, service providers must be personally suited to working with immigrants and refugees; demonstrate certain values, ethics, and skills; and have a relevant knowledge base. Social workers sometimes take cross-cultural training or adopt an anti-oppressive approach to improve their effectiveness with immigrant clients. Relatively few social work education programs focus on serving newcomer populations; however, those programs as well as professional associations are gradually addressing issues related to diversity.

KEY TERMS

For definitions of the key terms, consult the Glossary on page 453 at the end of the book.

14

Social Welfare and People with Disabilities

OBJECTIVES

The inclusion of persons with disabilities is important to the well-being of all society. This chapter will

- introduce the concept and definitions of disability

- examine the prevalence of and issues related to disability

- discuss the evolution of Canada's disability policy agenda

- explore the achievements of and challenges facing people with disabilities in selected life areas

- introduce social work approaches to working with persons with disabilities

INTRODUCTION

> Given the challenges facing our communities, it is our shared responsibility to uncover and mobilize the latent capacity of all citizens. People with disabilities, like every citizen, have both the capacity and the responsibility to strengthen our communities. We must ensure that each community member thrives and contributes. (Philia, 1997)

Disability is a complex, multidimensional issue and is therefore difficult to define. This lack of definition is why social work, health, education, and other disciplines so often take different approaches to disability; why programs for people with disabilities vary in design and delivery; and why disability related programs tend to have different eligibility criteria. The following three theories have nevertheless shaped people's understanding and response to disability, and influenced the design of disability-related programs and services:

- The **impairment perspective** assumes that disability is a biologically based illness, disease, or "problem" that originates in a person's body or mind. This medical model supports the use of interventions intended to rehabilitate people to help them "fit in" and function "normally" in mainstream society.

- Like the impairment perspective, the **functional limitations perspective** supports the notion that disability has a biological base. However, this view also considers the limiting nature of disability (for example, a limited ability to learn or work) and how people perceive and react to those limitations. This perspective tends to emphasize the costs of disability in terms of lost productivity, diminished social role, and other types of disadvantage.

- Since the mid-1990s, the **ecological perspective** has gained popularity over the impairment and functional limitations perspectives. Like its predecessors, the ecological perspective assumes that disability involves a physical condition that has limiting consequences. However, this perspective also recognizes the impact of a person's environment on his or her *experience* of having a disability. The Government of Canada's definition of disability reflects this broader view: "Disability is a complex phenomenon, reflecting an interaction between features of a person's body and mind and features of the society in which they live" (Human Resources and Skills Development Canada [HRSDC], 2012h, p. 2).

The way in which people understand and define disability can influence the way they perceive and treat those who are mentally or physically "different." Efforts at the international level have reinforced the notion that social attitudes toward disability determine the extent to which people with disabilities are included in society. In 2001, the World Health Organization (WHO, 2009) created the *International Classification of Functioning, Disability and Health* (ICF) to shift the world's focus on disability from the medical or biological *cause* of disability to the *impact* of society's response to disability. The ICF normalizes disability, suggesting that everyone's health is limited to some degree, and therefore everyone experiences some level of disability. By reframing disability as a universal human experience, the ICF aims to challenge society's traditionally negative views of disability, eliminate the stigma attached to having a disability, and reduce the discrimination and marginalization of people with disabilities.

In Canada, people with physical or mental disabilities have always been part of Canadian society, but they have not always had the same opportunities as those without a disability. That situation is gradually changing (see Exhibit 14.1). Today, disability is defined not so much by a person's physical or mental impairment as by the ability (or willingness) of society to accept differences between people. This view assumes that it is social attitudes that must change to accept all persons, regardless of ability, as participants in society. To reflect this view, policies and programs are starting to focus more on improving **access** to all opportunities in society for the benefit of

EXHIBIT 14.1

© Muellek/Shutterstock

Today, people with disabilities are active participants in all aspects of society, including sports.

all members of society (Rajan, 2004). This particular approach recognizes that people with or without disabilities have similar goals: "to participate as valued, appreciated equals in the social, economic, political and cultural life of the community," and "to be involved in mutually trusting, appreciative and respectful interpersonal relationships at the family, peer and community levels" (Crawford, 2003, p. 5).

Much of what we know about Canadians with disabilities comes from information gathered by the federal government. Since the 1980s, Statistics Canada has collected a wide range of disability-related information through various surveys, including the Participation and Activity Limitation Survey. In 2012, Statistics Canada (2012l) began collecting data using the Canadian Survey on Disability, which focuses primarily on people's health conditions or limitations and their impact on daily life.

1 DISABILITY IN CANADA

Disabilities affect some segments of the population more than others and vary in their severity, causes, and consequences. How an individual experiences disability depends on many factors, including age, gender, other people's perceptions, and available supports in the community. This section explores the prevalence and types of disabilities in Canada and some of the issues related to disability among young people, Aboriginal peoples, and women.

PREVALENCE AND TYPES OF DISABILITIES

Approximately 14 percent of Canadians have a disability. Seniors have the highest rate of disability of any age group, at 43 percent; this rate is expected to rise as the population ages. Elderly women are more likely than their male counterparts to have a disability; in contrast, girls aged fourteen and younger have a lower rate of disability than boys do.

People often use the term *disability* generically to refer to a broad range of conditions, even though there are many different types of disability, including those related to sensory impairment (such as blindness and deafness), learning difficulties, mental illness, and physical injury. Almost 82 percent of adults with disabilities have multiple disabilities. For example, an elderly person might have difficulty walking (mobility impairment) and have aphasia (a speech impairment) (Statistics Canada, 2007). Exhibit 14.2 illustrates the prevalence of various types of disabilities in Canada.

EXHIBIT 14.2

PREVALENCE OF DISABILITIES IN ADULTS IN CANADA

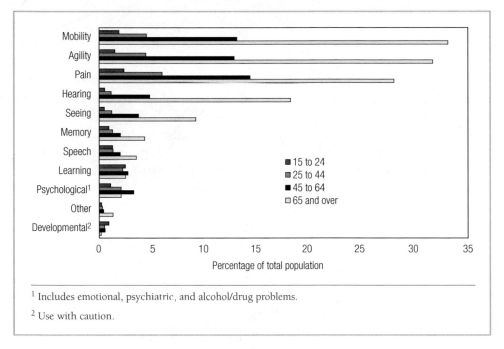

¹ Includes emotional, psychiatric, and alcohol/drug problems.

² Use with caution.

Source: Adapted from Statistics Canada. (2007). *Participation and Activity Limitation Survey 2006: Analytical Report* (Catalogue No. 89-628-XIE).

Among Canadian adults, more than 6 percent have a severe disability. Because a disability may be caused by several factors, its severity can be highly individual. One person with an intellectual disability, for instance, may have no difficulty performing daily tasks of living, whereas another person with the same diagnosis may experience significant functional limitations. Severe disabilities tend to become more common with age and can affect various life areas, such as mobility, independence, the ability to work, income levels, recreation, and emotional well-being. The diversity in needs and abilities of people with the same disability "label" presents a challenge for policymakers when developing social policies and programs for such a wide range of needs (Statistics Canada, 2007).

DISABILITY ISSUES FOR CHILDREN AND YOUTH

About 4 percent of Canadian children have a disability. The most common disabilities among children ages five to fourteen are learning disabilities, chronic health conditions (such as asthma and severe allergies), and communication limitations. Most children with disabilities are likely to have one or more mild to moderate disabilities (Statistics Canada, 2008c).

Children with special needs used to be placed in large institutions, but today, most live at home with their families. Studies reveal the challenges for parents who care for a child with a disability. For example, parents must coordinate their caregiver responsibilities with other commitments, such as work and personal relationships. For most families, it is not the child's disability that poses the greatest challenges but the severity of that disability. When compared with parents of children with mild to moderate disabilities, parents of children with severe disabilities report higher levels of stress and less satisfaction with their own health. Having a child with a severe disability is also likely to affect the parents' income and the ability to work and find child care. About 40 percent of Canadian children with disabilities have severe disabilities (Statistics Canada, 2008c).

A wide range of programs and services aim to help children with disabilities live full and active lives. For example, mainstream public and private schools have come a long way in becoming more inclusive of children with disabilities (see Exhibit 14.3). Most mainstream schools in Canada now offer some level of support for children with disabilities in the form of teacher aides, devices (such as talking books), and services (such as sign language interpreters). Today, eight out of ten children with disabilities attend regular public or private schools (HRSDC, 2009).

Despite progress, children with special needs still face a number of physical and social barriers. In terms of learning, 18 percent of children with disabilities do not receive the technical or human support they need at school; among children with severe disabilities, 37 percent fail to get the support they need (HRSDC, 2010). With regard to accessing community services, some experts suggest that children with disabilities (especially those with severe disabilities) may be discriminated against when trying to access quality healthcare (Canadian Coalition for the Rights of Children, 2009). Evidence also suggests that social and health agency staff lack the training needed to respond effectively to children with various types of disabilities (Bendall, 2008). A study by Kowalchuk and Crompton (2009) revealed several difficulties encountered by children with disabilities who wanted to join in community activities; those children faced such barriers as inadequate transportation systems and sports that could not accommodate a player with physical limitations. Although supports for preschool children with disabilities have improved in recent years, community supports for older children and youth with disabilities tend to be fragmented and uncoordinated (Snowdon, 2012).

EXHIBIT 14.3

Most children with disabilities attend their neighbourhood school and enjoy the same educational opportunities as children without a disability.

DISABILITY AND ABORIGINAL PEOPLES

The disability rate among Aboriginal peoples is almost twice that of non-Aboriginal Canadians. Almost one-third of registered First Nations people has a disability, and many of those disabilities are the result of diabetes (McDonald, 2005). First Nations children are twice as likely as other Canadian children to have a disability. The most common disabling conditions among First Nations children are asthma and allergies (First Nations Regional Longitudinal Health Survey, 2005).

Compared with non-Aboriginal communities, reserves and northern or remote areas of the country have a general scarcity of disability-related programs and services. The lack of those resources tends to exacerbate other disadvantages, such as isolation, poverty, and unemployment. The Government of Canada and First Nations have tried to improve conditions for Aboriginal people with disabilities through various bilateral agreements. One of those agreements created the Assisted Living Program, a program that offers home care, adult foster care, and institutional care for First Nations people with disabilities living on reserve (HRSDC, 2008). Another initiative—the Aboriginal Human Resources Development Strategy—focuses on increasing employment opportunities for Aboriginal people with disabilities. Researchers are beginning to evaluate the quality of these types of programs. For instance, in her analysis of eight federally sponsored programs for First Nations people with disabilities, Raihanna Hirji-Khalfan (2009) found little or no evidence that those programs were effective and, overall, found the programs to be culturally inappropriate for the populations they served.

WOMEN AND DISABILITY

About 15 percent of Canadian women (one in six) live with a disability (Statistics Canada, 2007). Although women tend to suffer from mild rather than severe disabilities, the resultant activity limitations may be enough to hinder day-to-day activities. In particular, cyclical or fluctuating illnesses, such as autoimmune conditions, chronic fatigue syndrome, and depression, together with other illnesses to which women with disabilities are susceptible, can make it difficult for a woman to work (Doe & Kimpson, 1999). Over the last thirty years, employment opportunities have improved for women with disabilities. Nevertheless, most working-age women with disabilities are unemployed or out of the labour market and, among those who work, the average annual income is significantly less than for women without a disability. Many women with disabilities must rely on social assistance benefits; although most of the provinces and territories offer slightly higher rates to people with disabilities, the income gain is rarely enough to cover all disability-related expenses.

Women with disabilities are at a much higher risk of abuse than are women without disabilities; some researchers suggest that as many as two out of five women with disabilities can expect to be sexually or physically abused during their lifetime (McDonald, Wobick, & Graham, 2004). One of the most important influences on the incidence of violence against women with disabilities is the extent to which these women rely on others for their care and security. For instance, many women who are highly dependent on someone else for medical and financial support, housing, or other resources are reluctant to leave an abusive marital relationship, or report an abusive caregiver, for fear of losing that support (Rivers-Moore, 1993).

Most programs and services are designed for the mainstream population yet offer specialized services to women and men with disabilities; those resources include vocational rehabilitation, income security programs, and social housing. In addition, a limited number of programs focus exclusively on the needs of women with a disability; Exhibit 14.4 provides an example of one such program.

EXHIBIT 14.4

EMPOWERING DEAF WOMEN IN CANADA

Comparative studies have found a general lack of services for Deaf women in Canada, which places them behind their peers in other parts of the Western world. To improve that situation, the Canadian Association of the Deaf (CAD) launched a new project called Empowering Deaf Women in Canada. The project set out to facilitate the full inclusion of Deaf women in the political, social, cultural, and economic aspects of society, and to build a strong foundation on which Deaf women could become more active participants in the decision-making process and leaders in Canada's Deaf community.

The objectives of the project were to ensure that Deaf women

- had the tools and supports they needed at the local level to understand their rights and to obtain appropriate services, including those related to violence against women
- worked with the CAD to check that the organization's mandate and strategic plan reflected Deaf women's issues and priorities
- worked with organizations at a grassroots level to identify the key priorities for Deaf women in their communities
- were empowered to work with local organizations to ensure that services were accessible and appropriate to Deaf women's needs

The CAD set up working groups across the country for Deaf women to identify gaps in services and to help develop resources to meet women's needs. Participating women shared information and knowledge related to employment, discrimination, abuse, and healthcare with the Deaf community, including grassroots groups for Deaf women.

Empowering Deaf Women in Canada ran from 2007 to 2010 and received federal funding from the Women's Program, Status of Women Canada.

Source: Adapted from Canadian Association for the Deaf. (2007, June 8). *CAD works to empower deaf women and increase community inclusion.* Retrieved from http://www.cad.ca/news_events_en.php?newsID=15.

DISCUSSION QUESTIONS

■ **Disability in Canada**

1. The impairment, functional limitations, and ecological perspectives of disability have shaped people's understanding and definition of disability. Describe how each theory might influence the way that society treats people with disabilities.

2. Children and youth, Aboriginal peoples, and women face a number of barriers to participation in society because of a disability. What factors other than a disability put these populations at risk of isolation and exclusion from society?

2 CANADA'S DISABILITY POLICY AGENDA

A hundred years ago, society tended to view disability as a social problem, a strain on precious resources, and a threat to the health and well-being of individuals and communities. In turn, disability policy focused on the medical aspects of disability and on strategies to "manage" the behaviour of people with disabilities. Over time, as society learned about disability issues and became more accepting of people with disabilities, public policies began to reflect society's enlightened views. Today, disability policy focuses more on the citizenship of people with disabilities, their contributions to communities, and their right to enjoy the full benefits of society. This section provides an overview of the evolution of disability policy in Canada.

AN ERA OF ISOLATION AND EXCLUSION

The **eugenics** movement at the turn of the twentieth century promoted the view that people with mental or intellectual disabilities were not only inferior to other members of society but were also a danger to themselves and to others. It was common for people with disabilities to live in large hospital-like institutions, where they were educated, trained, and treated by medical staff. Not only did those institutions provide housing and treatment, but they also kept people with disabilities away from mainstream society. Once institutionalized and segregated from society, people with mental or developmental disabilities had little chance of re-entering the community. Sterilization became a widely accepted method for controlling the "menace of the feeble-minded" (MacMurchy, 1932, p. 36) and for preventing mentally "defective" people from "poisoning" the race (Roeher Institute, 1996, p. 4).

From the 1920s to the 1960s, an impairment perspective predominated. In general, people saw disability as an illness or a disease and people with any type of disability as incompetent beings with little or nothing to contribute to society. During this period, governments funded institutions to treat disabilities based on a medical model. Rehabilitation teams—consisting of physicians, psychiatrists, medical social workers, and related health professionals—guided the course of treatment (Status of Disabled Persons Secretariat, 1994).

DEINSTITUTIONALIZATION AND SOCIAL MOVEMENTS

By the mid-twentieth century, Canadians had become critical of the practice of warehousing people with disabilities in large government-funded institutions and of the increasing costs of maintaining those institutions. There was also a general concern that although the institutions promoted the humane treatment of residents, they actually made residents more passive, dependent, and socially excluded; these conditions reduced the likelihood that the resident would ever return to the community. An emerging body of research revealed that community-based services and the administration of therapeutic drugs might be more humane than, and just as effective as, long-term institutionalization in the treatment of disability (Peters, 2003). Moreover, experts on disability issues promoted new and enlightened ways of thinking about people with disabilities. Sociologist Wolf Wolfensberger (1972), for example, argued that if society expected people with developmental disabilities to behave "normally," then society had to allow these individuals to live in normal (non-institutional) settings.

During the 1960s and 1970s, a growing awareness of human rights and long-standing criticisms of institutionalization fostered the **disability rights movement**. This ongoing movement calls for the elimination of barriers to social inclusion and for equal rights and opportunities for people with disabilities. According to special education expert Sally Rogow (2002, p. 1), "At the heart of the disability rights movement is the fact that people with disabilities want to be seen as people first, to be treated as individuals, to have opportunities to participate in and contribute to society. They want to be seen as persons, not cases or categories of disablement, powerless to shape their own lives." These types of yearnings, along with government's desires to reduce the costs of disability-related care and treatment, led to **deinstitutionalization**, a process that moves institutionalized people to community settings and replaces institutional care with community-based programs and services.

Several distinct groups working toward similar ends have driven Canada's deinstitutionalization process. The efforts of those groups have culminated in various social movements, including

- the **community mental health movement**, which advocates for the rights of people with mental illnesses and a non-institutional approach to their care

- the **community living movement**, which focuses on the creation of community-based supports and services for people with intellectual disabilities

- the **independent living movement**, which calls for programs to help people with a disability integrate into the community

These social movements have been instrumental in the large-scale closure of institutions across Canada, the reunification of residents with their families, and, in some cases, the relocation of residents to community-based settings, such as group homes. Despite these sweeping changes, hundreds of Canadians with disabilities still reside in institutions. According to the Canadian Association of Community Living (2012), some provinces and territories have reneged on their promises to close institutions, and at least two jurisdictions are in the process of building new institutions for people with intellectual disabilities.

THE DISABILITY COMMUNITY

While deinstitutionalization moved people out of the institutions, it did not guarantee an easy transition to community living. Indeed, during the early stages of deinstitutionalization, there were few disability-related supports and services, and people with disabilities continued to be isolated and excluded from mainstream activities. In her review of disability discrimination, Yvonne Peters (2003, p. 4) observes: "Because persons with disabilities were relegated to the margins of society, societal norms only reflected characteristics ascribed to 'able-bodiedness.' For example, [buildings were] only constructed for able-bodied persons who could walk, and not for persons who used assistive devices such as wheelchairs." These types of environmental barriers began to break down as parents, extended families, caregivers, people with disabilities, and others advocated for the development of disability-related programs, services, and accommodations. Together, these organizations and individuals make up Canada's **disability community**.

Disability-Related Organizations

In recent decades, Canada has experienced a rapid expansion in the number of disability-related organizations. Individuals with disabilities often run these organizations, which offer programs and services aimed at improving the living conditions of those with disabilities. Disability-related organizations are highly diverse: they may deliver either direct or indirect services, or a combination of both; they may be either national or local in scope; and they may either specialize in a single disability or serve people with any type of disability. Some of the more established voluntary disability-related organizations include

- the Canadian Association for Community Living, a nationwide, nonprofit federation with thirteen provincial and territorial chapters that work on behalf of people with intellectual disabilities

- the Council of Canadians with Disabilities, which advocates at the national level for the equality and inclusion of people with any type of disability

- the Canadian Mental Health Association, which champions the rights and responsibilities of people with mental illness through education, research, advocacy, and services

- Independent Living Canada, which coordinates a network of Independent Living Centres that are open to people with any type of disability, that are controlled by people with disabilities, and that tailor their services to local needs

Parents

Parents of children with special needs have become a force of their own within the disability community. Over the years, parents have championed for their children's right to a fulfilling and stimulating life, for their equal access to mainstream education, and for their full inclusion in social, recreational, cultural, and other community activities. Through their individual and collective efforts, parents have learned how to successfully navigate the maze of bureaucratic systems and make their voices heard. These efforts have resulted in the development of a wide range of supports, programs, and services for families with special needs children.

Parents have also been instrumental in shaping the role of children's advocates. Found in the public and voluntary sectors and at regional and national levels, children's advocates work to protect the rights of children with disabilities and to help families access disability-related services for their children.

THE 1980s: BREAKING DOWN THE BARRIERS

Until the 1980s, Canada focused on providing health, education, and social welfare programs to people with disabilities to help them improve their standard of living and participation in community life. However, many needs—such as the need to use transportation systems and access public buildings—were virtually ignored. Issues related to access gained international attention when the United Nations declared 1981 as the International Year of Disabled Persons, designated an International Day of Disabled Persons, and dedicated the decade 1983 to 1992 as the International Decade of Disabled Persons. These actions also heralded "a global commitment to ensure people with disabilities share equally in the full benefits of citizenship" (Canada, 2005, p. 3).

In 1981, Canada's Parliamentary Special Committee on the Disabled and the Handicapped released *Obstacles*, a report that called attention to a wide range of physical, attitudinal, and other barriers that prevented Canadians with disabilities from accessing community resources and opportunities. *Obstacles* made several recommendations for change, many of which came from people with disabilities and other members of the disability community. In response to the *Obstacles* report, the Government of Canada endorsed a new policy framework that focused on removing environmental barriers to inclusion, changing societal attitudes toward disability, and recognizing the potential of people with disabilities (Canada, 2005).

One year after the release of *Obstacles*, the rights of people with disabilities were included in the Canadian Charter of Rights and Freedoms. By prohibiting discrimination based on physical or mental disability, the Charter became the first national constitution in the world to recognize people with disabilities. This human rights legislation, together with the federal government's new disability policy framework, prompted a flurry of reforms aimed at improving access for people with disabilities. Included in these reforms were changes to the National Building Code of Canada, which made it mandatory for newly constructed public buildings to be barrier free. In addition, a number of telecommunication systems modified their equipment to allow people with speech or hearing impairments to use telephones and other devices more easily. Across Canada, municipalities adapted their public transit systems to make them wheelchair-accessible; cities also installed visual and auditory traffic control signals, widened their sidewalks and gave them curb cuts, and designated parking spaces for people with disabilities. These and other efforts have facilitated the mobility and access of people with disabilities.

In 1983, the Government of Canada designated a Minister Responsible for the Status of Disabled Persons and created a special office on disability. The establishment of a department dedicated to the needs of people with disabilities signalled a shift away from viewing disability solely as a health aspect to seeing disability in the context of citizenship.

Obstacles also inspired a number of developments at the provincial and territorial level. For example, in 1982, New Brunswick created a Premier's Council on the Status of Disabled Persons to collect information on disability issues and priorities, and to share information on disability programs and services. Three years later, New Brunswick became the first province to release an action plan to guide programs and services for persons with disabilities.

THE 1990s: TOWARD FULL CITIZENSHIP

The early 1990s were dominated by efforts to deinstitutionalize people with disabilities and to reintegrate them into communities. In 1991, the Government of Canada introduced the National Strategy for the Integration of Persons with Disabilities, which funded projects across Canada aimed at improving access to transportation, education, housing, employment, and communications for people with disabilities. Following the release of the national strategy were two reports: *Mainstream 1992*, and *Improving Social Security in Canada* (1994). Both reports focused on specific disability-related issues and recommended actions to ensure the full integration of Canadians with disabilities into mainstream society.

By the mid-1990s, the federal government realized the need to address the personal, day-to-day challenges experienced by people living with a disability. The government also recognized the importance of reducing negative attitudes toward disabilities and coordinating the confusing array of disability-related public policies and programs (HRDC, 1999b). To gain headway in these areas, the government appointed a Task Force on Disability Issues. The task force's recommendations would eventually lead to increased federal funding to disability-related organizations and amendments to several pieces of legislation (related to tax, employment, and justice) to improve conditions for people with disabilities.

In 1996, the Federal-Provincial-Territorial Ministers Responsible for Social Services identified Canadians with disabilities as a national priority. Two years later, the first ministers released the document *In Unison: A Canadian Approach to Disability Issues*, which outlined their shared vision and goals for the full citizenship for people with disabilities (Federal-Provincial-Territorial Ministers Responsible for Social Services, 1996). To respond to the changing needs of people with disabilities, *In Unison* proposed a new approach to disability-related programs and services (see Exhibit 14.5). Under the *In Unison* initiative, the achievement of full citizenship would be based on the following building blocks:

- *disability supports* (goods, services, and resources, including technical aids, special equipment, life skills training, and interpreter services)
- *employment* (access to education opportunities and more flexible training programs)
- *income programs* (income security for the unemployed)

EXHIBIT 14.5

IN UNISON: A NEW APPROACH TO DISABILITY ISSUES

OLD . . .	NEW . . .
Recipients	Participants
Passive income support	Active measures to promote employment in addition to providing necessary income support
Dependence	Independence
Government responsibility	Shared responsibility
Labelled as "unemployable"	Identification of work skills
Disincentives to leave income support	Incentives to seek employment and volunteer opportunities
Insufficient employment supports	Opportunities to develop skills and experience
Program-centred approach	Person-centred approach
Insufficient portability of benefits and services	Portable benefits and services
Multiple access requirements	Integrated access requirements

Source: IN UNISON: A Canadian Approach to Disability Issues, SP-113-10-98E, Human Resources and Skills Development Canada, 1998. Reproduced with the permission of the Minister of Public Works and Government Services Canada, 2013.

Following the launch of *In Unison*, the provinces and territories embarked on a broad review of their ministries and departments to see where they could improve the efficiency, effectiveness, and coordination of programs and services for people with disabilities. *In Unison* also sparked a flurry of provincial and territorial strategies to guide the actions needed to create more inclusive environments and to ensure the full citizenship of persons with disabilities.

STEPPING UP THE FOCUS ON ACCESSIBILITY

In 2005, the Standing Committee on Human Resources, Skills Development, Social Development and the Status of Persons with Disabilities (commonly referred to as HUMA) reviewed the federal government's policies and programs relating to persons with disabilities. HUMA's report, *Accessibility for All*, made several recommendations to the Government of Canada to improve the access to programs, services, employment, and other areas for people with disabilities. In response to HUMA's report, the Government of Canada promised to make federal disability-related funding and tax measures more consistent, and to continue improving access to federal buildings, transportation systems, employment practices, and services (Canada, 2005).

In 2006, the federal government promised to "introduce a National Disability Act to promote reasonable access to medical care, medical equipment, education, employment, transportation, and housing for Canadians with disabilities" (Human Resources and Social Development Canada, 2007b). To date, however, there has been no mention of the proposed act in any federal budget. The federal government nevertheless introduced the Enabling Accessibility Fund in 2008 to help the provinces and territories improve access to existing buildings and, in so doing, encourage the participation of people with disabilities in their communities.

Although Canada lacks national standards on accessibility, Ontario has taken the initiative to ensure that standards exist across its own jurisdiction. Since passing the Ontarians with Disabilities Act in 2005, the Government of Ontario (2009) requires businesses and organizations to prevent and remove all barriers to accessibility related to employment, transportation, communication and information, customer service, and, eventually, buildings and outdoor spaces. Ontario is the first jurisdiction in the world to guarantee accessibility through legislation (Bourque, 2012).

Some jurisdictions have developed, or are in the process of developing, a disability policy lens. British Columbia uses its disability lens when creating or evaluating policies and programs, to ensure that they reflect the rights and needs of persons with disabilities. The City of Charlottetown in Prince Edward Island adopted a disability lens in 2011 to guide the development of all city projects, including building and program design.

CONVENTION ON THE RIGHTS OF PERSONS WITH DISABILITIES

In 2006, the United Nations General Assembly adopted the Convention on the Rights of Persons with Disabilities (CRPD) in an effort to advance and protect the rights of people with disabilities. The CRPD encourages a greater public acceptance of people with disabilities and urges governments around the world to do more to facilitate the full participation of this population. Canada ratified the international treaty in 2010; in so doing, Canada promised "to promote, protect and ensure the full and equal enjoyment of all human rights and fundamental freedoms by all persons with disabilities, and to promote respect for their inherent dignity" (United Nations, 2006, p. 3). According to Marie White (2010), of the Council of Canadians with Disabilities, Canada's ratification of the CRPD marks the end of an era when society saw people with disabilities merely as "objects of charity," and in need of medical treatment. Moreover, ratification makes the goal of full citizenship a reality for Canadians with disabilities.

All jurisdictions in Canada must comply with various pieces of human rights legislation (such as the Charter of Rights and Freedoms); however, the CRPD is unique because it specifically focuses on the rights of persons with disabilities. The federal, provincial, and territorial governments are now in the process of bringing their laws, practices, customs, or regulations in line with CRPD standards. See Exhibit 14.6 for a summary of those standards.

DISCUSSION QUESTIONS

■ **Canada's Disability Policy Agenda**

1. People with disabilities and other members of the disability community have come a long way in their struggle for disability rights. Do you believe that society today accepts people with disabilities as full citizens? If not, what more could Canadians do to include people with disabilities?

2. How might the full inclusion of people with disabilities benefit not only those with disabilities but also society in general?

EXHIBIT 14.6

THE UNITED NATIONS CONVENTION ON THE RIGHTS OF PERSONS WITH DISABILITIES: IN BRIEF

Article 1 explains the Convention's main "purpose"—that is, to ensure the full and equal rights and freedoms for people with disabilities.

Article 2 provides "definitions" for certain words used in the Convention (for example, "language" refers to both spoken words and non-spoken languages, such as sign language).

Article 3 lists the Convention's "general principles," including self-determination and free choice; fair treatment and equal access to resources and opportunities; equal right to inclusion in society; respect and acceptance; gender equality; and respect for the abilities of children with disabilities.

Article 4 outlines the "general obligations" of countries to ensure the equal treatment of people with disabilities (such as changing existing laws to make them non-discriminatory).

Article 5 recognizes the right to "equality and non-discrimination," and that all persons are equal before and under the law.

Article 6 refers to "women with disabilities" and their full and equal rights and freedoms.

Article 7 assures that "children with disabilities" have the same rights as other children.

Article 8 refers to "awareness-raising," and the need to combat stereotypes of people with disabilities, educate the public on disability rights, and promote the abilities of people with disabilities.

Article 9 recognizes the importance of equal "accessibility" to public buildings, information, services, and technologies, so that people with disabilities can live independently and participate in society.

Article 10 affirms that human beings have a "right to life," and that countries must make sure that people with disabilities have an equal chance to enjoy their lives.

Article 11 requires countries to protect people with disabilities in "situations of risk and humanitarian emergencies."

Article 12 refers to the right of people with disabilities to have "equal recognition before the law," make their own decisions, own or inherit property, and control their own money.

Article 13 recognizes that people with disabilities have a "right to justice," including the right to fair treatment under the law, and by the courts and police.

Article 14 relates to "liberty and security of the person," and the right of people with disabilities to freedom and security under the law.

Article 15 recognizes the right of people with disabilities to enjoy "freedom from torture or cruel, inhuman or degrading treatment or punishment" (including subjection to medical experiments without the individual's consent).

Continued

Article 16 refers to the right of people with disabilities to enjoy "freedom from exploitation, violence and abuse," to be protected from maltreatment, and to have access to victim services.

Article 17 recognizes that "protecting the integrity of the person" is important, and that people's bodies and minds are their own.

Article 18 refers to the right of people with disabilities to the "liberty of movement and nationality," to move about, visit or leave a country, and to own a passport.

Article 19 relates to "living independently and being included in the community," choosing where to live, who to live with, and having access to supports for independent living.

Article 20 refers to "personal mobility," and having access to the necessary mobility aids, devices, and assistive technologies to get about freely.

Article 21 recognizes people's "freedom of expression and opinion, and access to information," including information in sign language, EasyRead, or Braille.

Article 22 calls attention to the "respect for privacy," and the right of people with disabilities to a private life without unlawful interference.

Article 23 refers to the "respect for home and the family," and the right of people with disabilities to marry, have children, and to form personal relationships, and to have equal access to information related to family planning and parenting.

Article 24 focuses on people's right to "education," the right to attend mainstream schools, and to access supports needed to learn.

Article 25 refers to "health," and the right of people with disabilities to access health services in their own communities, and receive treatment without discrimination.

Article 26 addresses "habilitation and rehabilitation," and government's obligation to ensure that people with disabilities receive the supports they need to live as independently as possible.

Article 27 looks at the right of people with disabilities to "work and employment," including equal pay and being treated the same way as other workers.

Article 28 refers to the right of people with disabilities to an "adequate standard of living and social protection," including adequate food, housing, and proper living conditions.

Article 29 relates to the right of people with disabilities to "participation in political and public life," including the right to vote, run for office, and join political organizations.

Article 30 recognizes the right to "participation in cultural life, recreation, leisure and sport," including the right to access cultural buildings and events, create art, and take part in sports.

Source: Adapted from United Nations General Assembly. (2006). *Convention on the rights of persons with disabilities*. Retrieved from http://www.un.org/disabilities/convention/conventionfull.shtml.

3 ACHIEVEMENTS AND CHALLENGES IN SELECTED LIFE AREAS

Despite the progress of inclusion, people with disabilities continue to face disability-related barriers to obtaining basic necessities. This section discusses the achievements of and remaining challenges for people with disabilities in terms of accessing adequate housing, employment, and income.

HOUSING

Various housing reforms are making independent living a reality for many people with disabilities. These reforms are often the result of bilateral agreements between the federal and provincial or territorial governments, or partnerships between government and nonprofit organizations. Modern developments include the introduction of new housing designs and features to make new homes more accessible and visitable (see Exhibit 14.7). A number of innovations focus on making housing more affordable for low-income people with disabilities; as a result, more specially designed social housing units are available in Canada. In addition, various government programs are available for modifying existing dwelling to make them safer, healthier, and more accessible.

Deinstitutionalization, and the movement toward inclusion, independence, and self-determination, has inspired the creation of various living options for people with a specific disability. For example, the following types of accommodations and supports are available for people with intellectual disabilities living in British Columbia:

- *Group homes* are houses in the community where paid staff provide personal care, prepare meals, and generally help residents with the tasks of daily living.

- *Cluster housing* consists of living units where individuals live independently and yet close to others with an intellectual disability; the cluster is physically separate from the rest of the community.

- *Supported living* tailors services to individual needs and provides those services to individuals living in their own home, an institution, or other type of residence.

- *Semi-independent living services* pay staff to provide weekly support to individuals living alone or with roommates in their own house or apartment.

EXHIBIT 14.7

© Larry Dale Gordon/The Image Bank/Getty Images

Homes can be modified to accommodate the daily living needs of people with disabilities, thereby enhancing independence and self-sufficiency.

- *Family model home or foster care home* is a private residence in which a host family provides care and support for one or more unrelated individuals.
- *Family home or family support* is a home owned or rented by a family member in which the individual lives and receives support from a family member or other helper (Community Living Research Project, 2006).

To be able to engage in community activities and live independently, housing for people with disabilities must be accessible, affordable, suitable, and adequate. However, many Canadians with disabilities live in dwellings that do not meet those criteria. According to the 2010 Federal Disability Report, 5 percent of adults with disabilities need but do not have an accessibility feature in their home, such as an elevator or a visual or audio alarm. Finding affordable and well-maintained housing is a challenge for many low-income people with disabilities. Moreover, almost 14 percent of low-income earning adults with a disability live in dwellings that require major repairs (compared with 9 percent of low-income adults without a disability). Living in a rundown house or apartment makes residents susceptible to health problems, psychological stress, and social isolation (HRSDC, 2010).

Various factors—such as discrimination from landlords, a lack of accessible housing, and limited access to good paying jobs—put people with disabilities at risk of homelessness. Some communities are introducing innovative strategies to reduce the incidence of homelessness among this vulnerable population. Calgary's Kootenay Lodge, for example, provides transitional housing to homeless Aboriginal people with severe disabilities. The lodge is fully accessible, and offers a wide range of supports to meet the specific needs of residents.

WORKING WITH A DISABILITY

In addition to its financial rewards, employment offers a number of health and well-being benefits for people with disabilities, including the opportunity for meaningful social interactions and increased self-esteem and self-confidence. Many working-age Canadians with disabilities are able and willing to work; however, they face a 10 percent rate of unemployment (compared with about 7 percent among populations without disabilities) (HRSDC, 2010). This relatively high rate of unemployment reflects a number of attitudinal and structural barriers in the workplace.

Barriers to Employment

Discrimination continues to be a barrier for many people with disabilities. Despite public awareness campaigns about disability issues, Canadian employers still operate under a variety of myths about disability. According to a study by the Bank of Montreal (2012), many managers overestimate the cost of workplace accommodations (such as technological supports) to meet the needs of workers with disabilities; some employers also assume that a job applicant's disability would prevent him or her from doing the job. This study also found that half of Canadians believe that employers are more likely to hire people who do not have a disability, and six out of ten Canadians believe that a visible disability puts people at a distinct disadvantage of being hired.

A major gap in Canada's disability-related policies is the lack of recognition given to people with a disability who can work only some of the time. This is the case for many people with an **episodic disability**, such as HIV, multiple sclerosis, or a mental disorder, which affects them on a sporadic and often unpredictable basis (Stapleton & Tweddle, 2008). Traditionally, social assistance and employment insurance programs have considered a working-age person to be either totally disabled and unemployable or totally able and employable, with little recognition of anything in between. This has created a situation in which short periods of employment may mean a loss of some or all disability benefits. Thus, some people with a disability may start working but not be able to continue; meanwhile, their benefits have been cut off. To avoid ending up in this situation, some individuals who are able to work only part time do not work at all.

Employment Initiatives and Best Practices

All levels of government in Canada have agreed to help people with disabilities improve their employment prospects and to make appropriate job and workplace accommodations for persons with disabilities. Various partnerships with the federal government allow each province and territory to tailor employment initiatives for people with disabilities, to local needs. Many jurisdictions are basing their initiatives on best practices—that is, methods that have worked for some organizations and can be used or adapted by others. Examples of best practices in helping Canadians with disabilities to find and keep jobs include the following:

- *Effective school-to-work transitions for youth* require interventions—such as literacy training, work preparation, and community work experiences—to prepare young people with disabilities for employment or postsecondary education while they are still in high school. Alberta's Transition Planning Protocol for Youth with Disabilities is an example of a guide for supporting youth through the transition process.

- *Individualized employment supports* acknowledge that each person with a disability has unique needs when it comes to employment and any support given should be specific to a person's disability. An example is the federal Opportunities Fund for Persons with Disabilities program, which provides individualized support and financial assistance to those who can work.

- *Employment First* policies, practices, and strategies support the belief that employment is the desired outcome for people with disabilities and that programs should focus on helping participants reach their full work potential. This approach is gaining popularity at the provincial and territorial level, where social assistance departments are introducing incentives for people with disabilities who are able to work at least part of the time; those incentives include more generous wage exemptions for persons with a disability and permission to cycle in and out of the workforce (as needed) without financial penalty. At the federal level, reforms to the Disability Vocational Rehabilitation Program (under the Canada Pension Plan) ensure a rapid reinstatement of benefits to individuals who try to work but because of a disability have to quit.

With the rising popularity of social economy enterprises (SEEs), innovative employment options are opening up for people with disabilities. Through these enterprises, people who might otherwise be classified by government systems as unemployable because of a disability are gaining skills and earning a living. In their study of seven SEEs in British Columbia, researchers Priest et al. (2008) found that most successful SEEs incorporate two main strategies:

- *Workplace accommodations* include creating flexible schedules with staff, giving employees adequate breaks, and matching job tasks to individual ability and preference.
- *Social supports* include personal and life skills counselling, job coaching, and referrals to community services, such as mental health centres.

Priest and her colleagues found that workers with disabilities generally enjoyed a higher standard of living, greater financial security, improved self-esteem, increased independence, and broader social networks than their unemployed peers did. Exhibit 14.8 profiles a successful social economy enterprise in British Columbia.

THE DISABILITY INCOME SYSTEM

On average, adults with disabilities have lower incomes than those without disabilities. The inability to purchase necessities—such as food, shelter, and clothing—puts people with disabilities at risk of social isolation and physical and mental health problems. Not having enough money can also limit a person's opportunities in life, including access to jobs and higher education (Canadian Labour Congress, 2010).

For people with disabilities who are unable to earn enough to support themselves, income support is available under the **disability income system**. Four categories of income make up this system:

- *Earnings replacement* programs replace income for those who cannot work because of an injury, an illness, or a disability-related

FROM BIRDHOUSES TO BUSINESS

BURNABY, B.C. —What was once a day program at Burnaby Association for Community Inclusion (BACI) is transforming into a lucrative business employing twelve people. Called BC Woodworks, the social enterprise hires people who have a disability or barriers to employment. The business produces high-quality wood products ranging from Adirondack chairs, tables and park benches to wine boxes and gift boxes.

The furniture is made from reclaimed western red cedar and pine-beetle stained wood, turning what some would deem waste into valuable and aesthetically pleasing products. Since it rebranded from the Grape Box in March, the company has been doing a brisk business, filling orders for wineries in the Okanagan and Vancouver community garden boxes and bulletin boards.

While it is rewarding to see the products get picked up, watching BC Woodworks shift to a work environment that provides paid employment for people with disabilities is most meaningful for Kevin Lusignan, BACI's senior manager of social and economic inclusion. He says BC Woodworks underwent a strategic planning session last year, creating a path forward that includes hiring more people and having staff receive regular reviews and opportunities to advance.

"This is a business. We support our staff, but we've raised the bar and there are expectations," he says, adding the profits from the social enterprise enables BACI to rely on less government funding.

Master carpenter Pratap Singh has been with BC Woodworks for more than twenty years. He says the wood shop is demonstrating what is possible for people who have a disability. He remembers starting with BACI when woodworking was still a program. People were making birdhouses and picture frames, but not much else.

Pratap encouraged the organization to invest in new machinery that would enable people to build products that were more complex. They started building tables for a daycare, and picnic tables for BC Hydro.

"It feels good," says Pratap. "They didn't think we could do this. These guys have come a long way."

Source: Adapted from Jensen, Camille (2012). *From birdhouses to business*. This story was written and published by Axiom News on behalf of the Burnaby Association for Community Inclusion.

condition (such as AIDS). This category includes various contributory programs, including Employment Insurance (which has a sickness benefit), the Canada and Quebéc Pension Plans (which have a disability program), and Workers' Compensation (which insures against earnings loss).

- *Income supplement programs* reduce the additional costs of having a disability, such as the cost of a wheelchair. These programs include the Canada Child Tax Benefit, provincial and territorial child tax benefits, and the federal Disability Tax Credit.

- *Income support* programs—such as social assistance—substitute income that people normally obtain through employment, savings, and other sources. Provincial or territorial welfare departments usually deliver these programs.

- *Compensation for loss* is money paid to those who are dealing with the negative effects of a disabling injury or accident. Compensatory programs include automobile insurance, and the Veterans' Disability Pension (Mendelson, Battle, Torjman, & Lightman, 2010).

Although Canada's disability income system supports many people with special needs, it has two main flaws. First, it is a highly confusing system. Different levels of government have introduced the various types of income programs at different times, and each program has its own rules for administering benefits and for assessing eligibility. Adding to the confusion is a lack of coordination and integration of these programs across governments and even within single governments. In short, the disability income system is far from being user friendly (Stapleton & Tweddle, 2008). Second, even when people access an income program, that program does not guarantee benefits sufficient to meet their needs. Many people with disabilities have little choice but to apply for welfare or a disability pension; however, in most jurisdictions, the benefit rates under these programs are below the LICOs, and many fail to recognize the full costs of disability (Council of Canadians with Disabilities, 2011).

In recent years, Canadian governments have tried to improve the long-term financial security of people with disabilities. For example, through the Registered Disability Savings Plan, the federal government matches contributions made by low- to modest-earning families for a member with a disability. Some provinces have made special provisions in their poverty-reduction strategies for people with disabilities. For example, Nova Scotia is steadily increasing welfare benefit rates to improve the quality of life and the participation of welfare recipients with disabilities. Similarly, Ontario is in the process of improving access to buildings, transportation, and other systems so that Ontarians with disabilities can gain opportunities to increase their income.

DISCUSSION QUESTIONS

■ **Achievements and Challenges in Selected Life Areas**

1. People with disabilities are at a high risk of homelessness. What do you think needs to happen to ensure that this population has reasonable access to appropriate housing?

2. Social economy enterprises (SEEs) are potentially good sources of employment for people with disabilities. What SEEs (if any) are operating in your community, and what types of products or services do they provide? Identify the ways SEEs might help or hinder the inclusion of people with disabilities in the community.

3. Criticisms of Canada's disability income system usually centre on two main flaws. Identify these flaws and describe how they might affect the lives of people with special needs.

4 IMPLICATIONS FOR SOCIAL WORK PRACTICE

As part of the transition from institution-based treatment to community-based services, social work practice has gradually shifted from traditional medical models toward social models. Until the 1970s, medical social workers focused primarily on the physical care of people with disabilities in institutional settings. The deinstitutionalization movement required social workers to direct more attention to helping clients adjust to community living through such strategies as sheltered workshops and residential group homes. By the 1990s, the focus of services had shifted again, this time toward helping clients achieve independence in mainstream settings.

In many respects, the evolution of social work practice within the disability community parallels the transition from segregation to mainstreaming (see Exhibit 14.9). The **open house concept** emphasizes the full participation of people with disabilities in school, work, social, and other activities, and their enjoyment of the same rights and privileges as Canadians without disabilities. This section briefly reviews each component of the open house concept as it relates to social work practice.

EXHIBIT 14.9

FROM SEGREGATION TO MAINSTREAMING:
A CONCEPTUAL MODEL

WAREHOUSE	GREENHOUSE	OPEN HOUSE
Caring for	Enabling	Accommodating
Protection	Support	Autonomy/empowerment
Labelled permanently incapacitated	Adaptation of individual	Adaptation of social and physical environment
Deemed incompetent	Recognition of capacity	Rights/responsibilities

Source: IN UNISON: A Canadian Approach to Disability Issues, ISBN: 0-662-2730-6, Human Resources and Skills Development Canada 1998. Reproduced with the permission of the Minister of Public Works and Government Services Canada, 2013.

ACCOMMODATION

Accommodation involves modifying the environment so that people with disabilities can participate in activities that take place in that environment. Social workers might promote accommodation by, for example, helping a client obtain special computer equipment for training or employment. Similarly, social workers can help people with disabilities work with government agencies on making public transportation and other systems more accessible.

AUTONOMY AND EMPOWERMENT

Although social workers do not directly empower others, they can help their clients acquire the knowledge and skills they need to enhance their sense of empowerment. Social workers facilitate many activities that can be personally empowering for people with disabilities, including assertiveness training, life skills training, problem-solving exercises, and peer-leadership training. Workers can also facilitate the empowering process by

- providing adequate information about possible options so that clients can make their own informed choices and decisions

- encouraging clients to express their wishes and exercise their right to self-determination

- acknowledging the capabilities that clients have to manage their own lives
- helping clients advocate for themselves, challenge oppressive labels, and regain control of their lives (Roeher Institute, 1996)

ADAPTATION OF THE SOCIAL AND PHYSICAL ENVIRONMENT

Social workers can help staff in various organizations focus on the problems in their own systems rather than viewing the person with the disability as a "problem to be solved." In addition, social workers can participate in reviews of agency policies, programs, and practices to make them barrier free and therefore more inclusive. Many social workers who serve the disability community find that a community development approach is more effective than traditional counselling approaches: "By promoting community development, the focus is shifted away from individuals and placed on strengthening the capacity of communities to be inclusive" (Panitch, 1998, p. 10).

RIGHTS AND RESPONSIBILITIES

Social workers have long called attention to and demanded changes in policies and programs that inhibit independent living for people with disabilities. In recent years, however, social workers have shifted much of their attention to helping people with disabilities assert their rights and speak out on their own behalf. One of the underlying themes of the disability movement is the demand for "rights, not charity;" social workers can play an important role in helping people with disabilities gain both control of resources and the right to make decisions that affect their own lives.

DISCUSSION QUESTIONS

■ **Implications for Social Work Practice**

1. How might the open house concept be adapted to specific populations, such as children with disabilities or women with disabilities?

2. The concepts of accommodation and adaptation are integral to the open house approach. Describe the difference between *accommodating* and *adapting* an environment for people with disabilities.

3. Why might a community development approach be more effective than traditional counselling when working with people with disabilities?

SUMMARY

Introduction

The impairment, functional limitations, and ecological perspectives shape the way people understand disability. Social attitudes determine the extent to which people with disabilities are included in society. Current definitions of disability focus on society's failure to accept differences between people, rather than on a person's physical or mental impairment. Canadian policies and programs reflect this view, and aim to eliminate barriers to full inclusion and accommodate the diverse needs of all citizens.

1 Disability in Canada

Approximately 14 percent of Canadians have a disability. Seniors have the highest rate of disability of any age group; most adults with disabilities have multiple disabilities. Although supports for young children with disabilities are improving, community supports for older children and youth with disabilities tend to be fragmented and uncoordinated. Aboriginal peoples experience a higher rate of disability than non-Aboriginal Canadians do; there is a general lack of effective programs for Aboriginal people with a disability. Women with disabilities have a high rate of unemployment and are vulnerable to abuse; a relatively small number of specialized programs are available for this population.

2 Canada's Disability Policy Agenda

Changing attitudes and social movements have led to deinstitutionalization and a community-based approach to disability. Various disability-related organizations make up the disability community. The issue of access continues to be a main theme and the focus of many disability-related policies and programs, as does citizenship, equal rights, and community integration. Such reports as *Obstacles* and the In Unison initiative guide efforts to promote full citizenship for people with disabilities. Canada's ratification of the UN's Convention on the Rights of Persons with Disabilities requires Canadian governments to meet the convention standards.

3 Achievements and Challenges in Selected Life Areas

Deinstitutionalization has helped to expand living options and housing designs for people with disabilities. Discrimination is an ongoing barrier to employment for people with disabilities. Employment initiatives and social economy enterprises are enhancing opportunities for people with disabilities. Canadian governments are taking steps to make the disability income system more responsive to the needs of people with disabilities; however, the system continues to be confusing for service users and offers inadequate benefit rates.

4 **Implications for Social Work Practice**

Over the years, social workers and other professional helpers have modified their approaches to working with people with disabilities; the focus today is on helping clients achieve independence in mainstream settings. Practitioners can use an open house approach to help people with disabilities participate fully in society. This approach emphasizes accommodation, autonomy and empowerment, adaptation of the environment, and rights and responsibilities.

KEY TERMS

For definitions of the key terms, consult the Glossary on page 453 at the end of the book.

disability, p. 395
impairment perspective, p. 396
functional limitations perspective, p. 396
ecological perspective, p. 396
access, p. 397
eugenics, p. 404
disability rights movement, p. 405

deinstitutionalization, p. 405
community mental health movement, p. 406
community living movement, p. 406
independent living movement, p. 406
disability community, p. 406

episodic disability, p. 418
disability income system, p. 420
open house concept, p. 422
accommodation, p. 423

APPENDIX A

Historical Highlights

1844   The British government transfers the responsibility for Aboriginal peoples to the Province of Canada.

1857   The passage of the Gradual Civilization Act formalizes Canada's commitment to assimilate Aboriginal peoples into mainstream society.

1869   Canada passes a compulsory enfranchisement law, which deprives Aboriginal women of their Status if they marry a non-Status man.

1876   Canada enacts its first Indian Act.

1879   John A. Macdonald introduces a federally funded and managed system of residential schools for Aboriginal children.

Canada introduces its first immigration law to control the entry of "paupers," criminals, and other "vicious classes" from other countries.

1885   The passage of the Chinese Immigration Act allows the federal government to collect a $50 head tax on immigrants of Chinese origin.

1893   Ontario passes the Act for the Prevention of Cruelty to and Better Protection of Children, the first child welfare law in Canada.

1906   Canada's new Immigration Act restricts entry to immigrants from Asia.

1908   The federal government passes the Juvenile Delinquents Act.

The Annuities Act—precursor of the Old Age Pension Act—becomes law.

1910   The federal government amends the Canadian Immigration Act to keep poor, sick, and "immoral" applicants out of Canada.

1913   This year marks the peak of immigration, as 400 000 immigrants arrive in Canada.

1914 The First World War begins.

Parliament creates the Canadian Patriotic Fund to provide financial assistance to the families of soldiers.

Ontario becomes the first province to enact workers' compensation legislation.

1916 Manitoba introduces the first mothers' allowances in Canada.

1918 The federal government introduces its first child-based tax credit.

The Canadian Mental Health Association is founded.

The Canadian National Institute for the Blind opens.

The First World War ends.

1919 Parliament passes the Soldier Settlement Act.

The Winnipeg General Strike takes place.

The Community Welfare Council in Winnipeg becomes one of Canada's first social action groups.

1920 Parliament passes the Returned Soldiers' Insurance Act.

1923 By this year, about 81 000 Chinese immigrants have paid a head tax, raising $23 million in revenue for Canadian governments.

1926 The Canadian Association of Social Workers is founded.

1927 Parliament passes the Old Age Pension Act.

1929 After being declared "persons" by the Judicial Committee of the British Privy Council, women become eligible for appointment to the Canadian Senate.

1930 The Great Depression begins.

For the first time in Canadian history, the federal government funds unemployment relief in municipalities.

Parliament passes the War Veterans Allowance Act.

1931 The number of Indian residential schools peaks (eighty schools are in operation across Canada).

1932 The Cooperative Commonwealth Federation (CCF) is founded in Calgary.

1935 William Lyon Mackenzie King is sworn in as prime minister (under a Liberal government).

Unemployed men take part in the On to Ottawa Trek in protest of poor work camp conditions and high unemployment.

Parliament passes the Employment and Social Insurance Act (it is repealed in 1937).

1937   The Government of Canada appoints the Royal Commission on Dominion–Provincial Relations (Rowell-Sirois Commission) to study the economy and federal–provincial relations.

1938   The Canadian Association of Social Workers develops a code of ethics.

1939   Parliament passes the Youth Training Act.

The Second World War begins, putting an end to the Great Depression.

The Supreme Court of Canada rules that the term "Indian" in Section 91(24) of the Constitution Act includes Inuit.

1940   Parliament passes the Unemployment Insurance Act.

1942   Britain releases its *Report of the Inter-Departmental Committee on Social Insurance and Allied Services* (also known as the Beveridge Report).

1943   Leonard Marsh releases his *Report on Social Security for Canada* (also known as the Marsh Report).

1944   Parliament passes the Family Allowances Act (the program is implemented in 1945).

Parliament passes the National Housing Act.

The federal government establishes the Department of National Health and Welfare, and the Department of Veterans Affairs.

A scientific approach to aging in Canada begins with the founding of the Gerontologic Research Unit at McGill University in Montréal.

1945   Parliament passes the Veterans Rehabilitation Act.

The Second World War ends.

1946   The federal government establishes the Central Mortgage and Housing Corporation (it is later renamed Canada Mortgage and Housing Corporation).

Parliament passes a new War Veterans Allowance Act.

1947   Canada's first health insurance program begins in Saskatchewan.

The Government of Canada repeals the Chinese Immigration Act, abolishing the ban on Chinese immigrants entering Canada.

1948   Lester Pearson is sworn in as prime minister (under a Liberal government).

The federal government implements settlement and integration programs for immigrants.

Canada endorses the United Nations' Universal Declaration of Human Rights.

1951   Parliament amends the Indian Act, lifting bans on several traditional ceremonies.

Parliament passes the Old Age Assistance Act and the Old Age Security Act.

The federal Blind Persons Act comes into effect.

The University of Toronto offers Canada's first social work doctorate program.

The UN adopts the Convention Related to the Status of Refugees (the Geneva Convention).

1953   Parliament amends the Immigration Act, inviting more immigrants from Caucasian countries.

1954   Parliament passes the Rehabilitation of Disabled Persons Act.

1956   Parliament passes the Unemployment Assistance Act (the federal government begins sharing the cost of provincial social assistance).

1957   John Diefenbaker is sworn in as prime minister (under a Progressive Conservative government).

The federal government introduces registered retirement savings plans (RRSPs).

1958   The Canadian Association for Community Living is founded.

1960   Status Indians gain the right to vote in federal elections.

1961   Parliament passes the Vocational Rehabilitation of Disabled Persons Act.

The *Canadian Bill of Rights* becomes law.

1964   Parliament passes the Youth Allowances Act.

1965   The Canada and Québec Pension Plans are introduced.

1966   The federal government introduces the Canada Assistance Plan and the Guaranteed Income Supplement.

Parliament passes the Medical Care Act.

The University of Windsor offers Canada's first bachelor of social work program.

1967   The Canadian Association of Schools of Social Work is established.

The Government of Canada appoints the Royal Commission on the Status of Women.

Amendments to the Immigration Act eliminate discriminatory criteria for selecting immigrants.

1968   Pierre Trudeau is sworn in as prime minister (under a Liberal government).

The federal government appoints the Senate Committee on Poverty (the Croll Committee).

Canada amends its Divorce Act, making divorce easier to obtain.

1969   The Statement of the Government of Canada on Indian Policy (the "White Paper") is released.

Acts between consenting adults of the same sex are decriminalized.

1970   The federal government publishes *Income Security for Canadians*, reviewing Canada's social security system.

Canada ratifies the United Nations' International Convention on the Elimination of All Forms of Racial Discrimination.

1971   Parliament amends the Unemployment Insurance Act (it eases eligibility rules and provides special benefits).

The Senate Committee on Poverty releases its report *Poverty in Canada*.

Canada introduces a Multicultural Policy (the first of its kind in the world).

The federal government establishes a National Council of Welfare.

Canada's first peer support service—the Mental Patients Society—opens its doors.

1972   The federal government introduces a Child Care Expenses Deduction, providing a tax deduction to families with work-related child-care expenses.

1973   Newfoundland passes the Neglected Adults Welfare Act—the first adult protection legislation in North America.

The federal government launches a social security review with the *Working Paper on Social Security in Canada*.

The Canadian Advisory Council on the Status of Women is established.

The federal Residential Rehabilitation Assistance Program begins.

The federal government triples Family Allowance benefits, indexes the benefits to the cost of living, and makes the benefits taxable.

1974   Manitoba launches Mincome, Canada's first large-scale guaranteed annual income experiment.

The federal government appoints a National Advisory Council on Voluntary Action as a first step to improving Government of Canada–voluntary sector relations.

The federal government launches the Immigration Settlement and Adaptation Program.

1975 This year is the UN's International Year of Women.

1976 The UN's Decade for Women: Equality, Development and Peace begins.

The federal government introduces the Spouse's Allowance.

Parliament passes a new Immigration Act to improve the settlement of newcomers (the Act is implemented in 1978).

Canada ratifies the United Nations' International Covenant on Economic, Cultural, and Social Rights.

1977 The federal government initiates the Established Programs Financing (EPF), which combines funding for healthcare and postsecondary education into one funding formula.

The Canadian Human Rights Act is passed.

Quebéc becomes the first province to forbid discrimination based on sexual orientation.

1978 The federal government establishes a Non-Profit Housing Program.

The Government of Canada introduces the Refundable Child Tax Credit and, for the first time, uses the income tax system to give benefits to families that do not pay income tax.

An amendment to the Immigration Act allows refugees to apply to Canada as immigrants.

1979 This year is the UN's International Year of the Child.

1980 The World Health Organization releases the International Classification of Impairments, Disabilities, and Handicaps (ICIDH).

Parliament establishes the Special Committee on the Disabled and the Handicapped to evaluate programs for persons with disabilities.

The federal government appoints the National Advisory Council on Aging to advise the Minister of Health on issues related to seniors.

1981 This year is the UN's International Year for Disabled Persons.

The Parliamentary Special Committee on the Disabled and the Handicapped releases its *Obstacles* report.

Canada's first food bank opens in Edmonton, Alberta.

The federal government introduces the Language Instruction for Newcomers to Canada program.

Indian and Northern Affairs Canada creates the Community Well-Being (CWB) Index to measure the quality of life of First Nations and Inuit communities.

Canada ratifies the United Nations' Declaration on the Elimination of Violence Against Women.

1982   The Canadian Charter of Rights and Freedoms is entrenched in the Canadian Constitution.

The federal government establishes the National Native Alcohol and Drug Abuse Program.

The federal government creates the National Clearinghouse on Family Violence.

The UN introduces its first International Plan of Action on Ageing in Vienna.

1983   The UN declares 1983 to 1992 as the International Decade of Disabled Persons.

1984   Brian Mulroney is sworn in as prime minister (under a Progressive Conservative government).

Parliament passes the Canada Health Act.

The federal government introduces the Host Program to help refugees resettle (services are extended to immigrants in 1991).

1985   The Royal Commission on the Economic Union and Development Prospects for Canada (Macdonald Commission) releases its final report.

Parliament amends the Indian Act and extends several status and property rights to members of First Nations.

The federal government appoints the Status of Disabled Persons Secretariat to raise awareness of disability issues and support the inclusion of persons with disabilities.

Statistics Canada launches the General Social Survey to gather information and report on social trends and issues every five years.

1986   Statistics Canada completes the first Health and Activity Limitation Survey (HALS).

The federal government launches a five-year Child Sexual Abuse Initiative.

The national Task Force on Child Care recommends a universal system of child care.

1987   The Parliamentary Committee on Human Rights and the Status of Disabled Persons is established.

This year is the UN's International Year of Shelter for the Homeless.

1988   The federal government converts the Refundable Child Tax Credit to the Non-Refundable Child Tax Credit.

The Government of Canada announces Phase I of the Family Violence Initiative.

The Canada–U.S. Free Trade Agreement is ratified.

The federal government launches the Seniors Independence Program.

Parliament passes the Canadian Multiculturalism Act.

The federal government introduces the Women at Risk Program to assist refugee women and their dependants.

1989 The House of Commons resolves to end child poverty by the year 2000 (this goal is never reached).

The federal government introduces clawbacks to family allowance and Old Age Security benefits, eliminating the universal status of these programs.

Ryerson Polytechnical Institute administers the National Survey on Elder Abuse, Canada's first major survey to study elder abuse.

The House of Commons establishes the Standing Committee on Human Rights and the Status of Disabled Persons to support the integration and equality of persons with disabilities.

1990 Parliament amends the Unemployment Insurance Act to shift responsibility for funding from the federal government to employers and employees.

The Standing Senate Committee on Aboriginal Peoples begins its review of parliamentary bills on native issues.

The federal government proposes a Native Agenda to settle land claims, improve living conditions on reserves, and enhance Aboriginal–government relations.

The First Nations Child and Family Services program is created, allowing First Nations to develop their own child welfare services on reserves.

Canada signs the UN Declaration of the Rights of the Child.

1991 The Canada–Quebéc Accord is signed, giving Québec control of its own immigrant settlement programs and language training.

Phase II of the federal Family Violence Initiative is announced.

The federal government appoints the Royal Commission on Aboriginal Peoples.

The First Nations Child and Family Services program begins.

The federal government imposes a funding cap on Canada's wealthiest provinces under the Canada Assistance Plan.

Canada ratifies the United Nations Convention on the Rights of the Child.

Statistics Canada completes the second Health and Activity Limitation Survey.

Canada introduces the National Strategy for the Integration of Persons with Disabilities.

1992   Mainstream 1992 provides a framework for fully integrating people with disabilities into society.

The Government of Canada releases its Action Plan for Children to improve the well-being of children.

The UN introduces a revised International Plan of Action on Ageing in Madrid.

The Federal-Provincial-Territorial Ministers Responsible for Seniors Forum meets for the first time to discuss the needs and issues of Canadian seniors.

The federal government launches the Self-Sufficiency Project to test a new policy that encourages work and independence among welfare recipients.

1993   Jean Chrétien is sworn in as prime minister (under a Liberal government).

This year is the UN's International Year of the World's Indigenous People.

Statistics Canada releases the findings of the Violence Against Women Survey, Canada's first national survey of violence against women.

The federal government replaces Family Allowances with the Canada Child Tax Benefit.

Canada celebrates the first annual National Child Day to commemorate the adoption of the United Nations Declaration of the Rights of the Child (1959) and the United Nations Convention on the Rights of the Child (1989).

The federal government initiates the Ventures in Independence program for seniors.

Parliament amends the Unemployment Insurance Act (and reduces benefits).

The UN begins using the Human Development Index to measure social conditions in member countries.

1994   The North American Free Trade Agreement (NAFTA) comes into effect.

The federal government conducts a general Program Review (the department of Human Resources Development Canada launches its own Social Security Review).

This year is the UN's International Year of the Family.

Health Canada launches its Community Action Programs for Children (CAPC).

Canada conducts the National Longitudinal Survey of Children and Youth.

Statistics Canada introduces the National Population Health Survey.

The federal government launches the Settlement Renewal Initiative to devolve responsibilities for immigrant settlement to the provinces.

1995   The Federal-Provincial-Territorial Council on Social Policy Renewal is formed.

The federal government introduces the New Horizons: Partners in Aging initiative.

The federal government introduces the Inherent Rights Policy as a guide to First Nations self-government.

The UN's International Decade of the World's Indigenous People begins.

Health Canada introduces Aboriginal Head Start programs.

The First Nations and Inuit Child Care Initiative is launched.

Twelve national organizations form a Voluntary Sector Roundtable to address common issues relating to voluntary organizations.

1996   The Federal Task Force on Disability Issues releases its report, *Equal Citizenship for Canadians with Disabilities.*

The *Report of the Royal Commission on Aboriginal Peoples* is released.

The federal government launches the Self-Government Negotiations Funding Support program (for First Nations).

The Canada Health and Social Transfer replaces the Canada Assistance Plan.

The Federal-Provincial-Territorial Ministers Responsible for Seniors agrees on a National Framework on Aging.

The new Employment Insurance Act replaces Unemployment Insurance.

Labour Market Development Agreements between the federal and regional governments come into force.

Canada's child poverty rate reaches an alarming 21 percent.

The Canadian Council on Social Development launches the Urban Poverty Project to consider poverty-reduction initiatives.

The Federal-Provincial-Territorial Council on Social Policy Renewal meets for the first time and identifies young children and people with disabilities as national priorities.

The Employability Assistance for People with Disabilities replaces the Vocational Rehabilitation of Disabled Persons Act.

The federal government closes the last Indian residential school.

1997   Phase III of Canada's Family Violence Initiative begins.

Amendments to the Immigration Act create three categories of immigrant applications: an economic class, a family class, and a refugee class.

The Canadian Race Relations Foundation begins operation, dedicated to the elimination of racism in Canada.

The federal government establishes the Social Cohesion Network to help clarify the meaning of social cohesion and to identify directions for future policy research.

The Federal-Provincial-Territorial Council on Social Policy Renewal agrees to develop a national children's agenda.

Statistics Canada administers the first National Survey of Giving, Volunteering and Participating.

Ontario's Social Assistance Reform Act paves the way for welfare-to-work programs in that province (other jurisdictions soon follow suit).

Québec introduces the first comprehensive family and child policy in Canada.

The federal government launches the Aboriginal Healing Strategy.

The federal and regional governments develop a National Reinvestment Framework to funnel unused social assistance funds into programs for low-income families with children.

The UN's International Decade for the Eradication of Poverty begins.

The federal government introduces the Opportunities Fund for Persons with Disabilities and the Entrepreneurs with Disabilities Program to enable people with disabilities to work.

1998   The federal government launches Gathering Strength: Canada's Aboriginal Action Plan and establishes the Aboriginal Healing Foundation.

The federal government makes a formal apology to Aboriginal peoples in the form of a Statement of Reconciliation.

The federal government introduces the Urban Aboriginal Strategy.

The Canadian Incidence Study of Reported Child Abuse and Neglect becomes the first national study to examine reported child abuse.

The federal government introduces the National Child Benefit (includes the Canada Child Tax Benefit and the National Child Benefit Supplement).

The federal government achieves a balanced budget for the first time in nearly twenty years.

The Canada Pension Plan undergoes drastic changes to make it more sustainable.

Ontario enacts its Social Work and Social Service Work Act.

The Federal-Provincial-Territorial Ministers Responsible for Social Services release the document *In Unison: A Canadian Approach to Disability Issues* to guide the full integration of people with disabilities.

Canada releases its National Action Plan for Food Security to improve the diets of high-risk groups.

The federal government launches the Social Development Partnerships program to promote the inclusion of people with disabilities.

The Canadian Centre for Justice Statistics releases the first annual *Family Violence in Canada: A Statistical Profile*.

The federal government launches the Resettlement Assistance Program to help government-assisted refugees.

The federal government introduces Canada's first caregiver tax credit to individuals providing in-home care of a dependent relative.

1999   This year is the UN's International Year of the Older Person.

Ontario becomes the first province to extend to same-sex couples the same rights as those extended to heterosexual common-law couples.

Members of the Federal-Provincial-Territorial Council on Social Policy Renewal sign the Social Union Framework Agreement (SUFA).

The National Welfare to Work Study reports on the effects of welfare-to-work programs on welfare recipients.

The federal government launches Understanding the Early Years.

The federally funded Aboriginal Human Resources Development Strategy begins.

Phase I of the National Homelessness Initiative begins.

The Panel on Accountability and Governance in the Voluntary Sector releases its report, *Building on Strength: Improving Governance and Accountability in Canada's Voluntary Sector*.

The federal government releases *Future Directions: The Challenges Facing Persons with Disabilities*, a guide to disability policy reform.

The National Improving the Quality of Life of Canadian Seniors Project is launched.

2000   Canada's unemployment rate falls to its lowest level in twenty-five years (6.8 percent).

Phase I of the Voluntary Sector Initiative begins.

The findings of the social services sector human resources study are released in the document *In Critical Demand: Social Work in Canada*.

The federal and regional governments sign the Early Childhood Development Agreement to cost-share early childhood development programs.

The Public Health Agency of Canada establishes four Centres of Excellence for Children's Well-Being as part of the National Children's Agenda.

The federal government launches the nine-year *learn*$ave demonstration project to help low- and modest-income Canadians save for education.

2001 Canada launches its Affordable Housing Program.

An Accord Between the Government of Canada and the Voluntary Sector is released.

This year is the UN's International Year of the Volunteer.

Statistics Canada administers the first Aboriginal Peoples Survey.

The federal government creates the Office of Indian Residential Schools Resolution of Canada to resolve claims related to residential schools.

For the first time in Canadian history, the census collects data on same-sex unions.

Statistics Canada launches the national Longitudinal Survey of Immigrants to Canada.

The World Health Organization introduces its International Classification of Functioning, Disability and Health.

The Canada Volunteerism Initiative is launched to encourage volunteerism.

Statistics Canada replaces the Health and Limitations Survey (HALS) with the Participation and Activity Limitation Survey (PALS).

2002 Phase II of the Voluntary Sector Initiative begins.

Quebéc introduces its National Strategy to Combat Poverty and Social Exclusion, the first government-sponsored poverty reduction plan in Canada.

British Columbia becomes the first province to put a time limit on how long a person can stay on welfare (the province reversed this decision in 2004).

Canada and other nations adopt the UN's A World Fit for Children strategy.

The UN develops its second International Plan of Action on Ageing (also known as the Madrid Plan).

Statistics Canada administers the Survey of First Nations People Living On-Reserve.

The Federal Strategy on Early Childhood Development for First Nations and Other Aboriginal Children is introduced.

The Immigration and Refugee Protection Act comes into force.

The Prime Minister's Caucus Task Force on Urban Issues releases its report, *Canada's Urban Strategy—A Vision for the 21st Century.*

The Standing Senate Committee on Social Affairs, Science and Technology releases its final report (the Kirby Report) on Canada's healthcare system.

The Romanow Commission releases its final report, *Building on Values: The Future of Health Care in Canada.*

The first Canadian Community Health Survey gets underway.

Vibrant Communities is launched as a national multisector collaborative strategy to reduce poverty in Canada.

Experts estimate the overall costs of substance abuse in Canada (in terms of lost productivity, premature death, and burden on services) to be $40 billion.

2003   Paul Martin is sworn in as prime minister (under a Liberal government).

The federal 2003 Budget announces substantial reinvestments in social programs.

Canadian governments agree on a Multilateral Framework on Early Learning and Child Care.

The federal government appoints a Task Force on Active Living and Dignity for Seniors.

The total number of food banks in Canada reaches 639.

Manitoba passes the Child and Family Services Authorities Act, which allows Métis and First Nations to provide child welfare services.

The "10 Percent Rule" comes into effect and restricts advocacy by registered charities under the federal Income Tax Act.

2004   The Canada Social Transfer and the Canada Health Transfer replace the Canada Health and Social Transfer.

The federal government implements the Child Disability Benefit.

The Employment Insurance account reports a surplus of nearly $44 billion.

Canada releases A Canada Fit for Children, a plan to improve conditions for children.

The Community Well-Being Index begins reporting on the socioeconomic conditions of First Nations and Inuit.

The federal government launches the Aboriginal Skills and Employment Training Strategy.

The federal government initiates the Kelowna Accord, an intergovernmental and inter-tribal agreement aimed at improving conditions for Aboriginal peoples.

2005   The federal government introduces the Canada Learning Bond to help modest-income families save for their children's postsecondary education.

The federal government passes a law legalizing same-sex unions.

The UN's Second International Decade of the World's Indigenous People begins.

The Ministers Responsible for Seniors releases the document *Planning for Canada's Aging Population: A Framework*.

The Standing Committee on Human Resources, Skills Development, Social Development and the Status of Persons with Disabilities (HUMA) releases their report, *Accessibility for All*.

Ontario takes the lead and passes the Ontarians with Disabilities Act to establish access standards across the province.

2006   Steven Harper is sworn in as prime minister (under a Conservative government).

The federal government introduces the Universal Child Care Benefit in lieu of a national child-care program.

Prime Minister Stephen Harper apologizes to Chinese-Canadians for the head tax imposed on Chinese immigrants and promises a monetary "gift" to head tax payers (or their widows).

The federal government cancels the Canada Volunteerism Initiative.

The federal government cancels any agreements made with the provinces under the Multilateral Framework on Early Learning and Child Care.

The Government of Canada makes funds available under the Targeted Initiative for Older Workers.

The Special Senate Committee on Aging begins its large-scale review of issues, policies, and programs related to seniors and their care.

The World Health Organization launches its Global Age-Friendly Cities Project in Vancouver.

Statistics Canada administers the Aboriginal Children's Survey as part of the 2006 census.

A Standing Senate Committee on Social Affairs, Science and Technology completes a ground-breaking national study (*Out of the Shadows at Last*) on mental health, mental illness, and addiction.

An international network of practitioners, researchers, academics, and seniors launch the National Initiative for the Care of the Elderly to improve the care of older adults.

2007   The Homelessness Partnering Strategy begins.

The federal government appoints the Mental Health Commission of Canada to study mental health, mental illness, and addiction in Canada.

Human Resources and Social Development Canada establishes the Expert Panel on Older Workers to consider the current and future prospects of older workers.

The federal government hires a Secretary of State for Seniors to advocate for Canadian seniors.

The National Seniors Council replaces the National Advisory Council on Aging (established in 1980).

The federal government announces the Enabling Accessibility Fund to enable the participation in society of people with disabilities.

The federal government announces a Registered Disability Savings Plan, the Canada Disability Savings Grant, and the Canada Disability Savings Bond to help Canadians save for long-term financial security.

The Government of Canada agrees to compensate Aboriginal peoples for their losses incurred from attending residential schools.

The federal government introduces the Enhanced Prevention Focused Approach to provide preventative child welfare services on-reserve.

2008   Canada slides into the deepest economic recession since the Great Depression.

The federal government introduces the Tax-Free Savings Account.

The Standing Senate Committee on Social Affairs, Science and Technology begins to examine social issues in Canada's largest cities.

The House of Commons Standing Committee on Human Resources, Social Development and the Status of Persons with Disabilities (HUMA) begins a feasibility study on a national poverty reduction strategy.

The federal New Horizons for Seniors Program launches an Elder Abuse Awareness Campaign.

The federal Home Adaptations for Seniors' Independence program begins.

A UNICEF study rates Canada the worst of twenty-five countries in providing child-care services.

The federal government scraps the Immigration Settlement and Adaptation Program, the Host Program and the Language Instruction for Newcomers to Canada program, and introduces a "modernized approach" to settlement services.

Prime Minister Harper makes a Statement of Apology to former students of Indian residential schools.

2009 The Canadian Longitudinal Study on Aging begins recruiting subjects.

The Urban Aboriginal Peoples Study begins collecting data.

In January, Ontario loses 71 000 of the 129 000 jobs lost in Canada because of the economic downturn.

The number of welfare recipients in British Columbia reaches more than 32 000 in March—a 47 percent increase since September 2008.

In March, Canada's unemployment rate reaches 8 percent, the highest rate in seven years.

The federal government releases Canada's Economic Action Plan (Budget 2009), a multi-billion dollar strategy to stimulate economic growth during a severe economic recession.

2010 The federal government scraps the mandatory long-form census questionnaire in favour of a voluntary household survey.

The Native Women's Association of Canada estimates that more than 580 Aboriginal women and girls have either gone missing or been murdered in Canada, most within the last thirty years.

The federal government administers the Canada Survey of Giving, Volunteering and Participating.

The passage of the Balanced Refugee Reform Act allows the federal government to increase the number of refugees admitted each year and process refugee claims more quickly.

Canada ratifies the United Nations' Convention on the Rights of Persons with Disabilities.

2011 The federal government administers the first Canadian Survey on Disability (which replaces the Participation and Activity Limitation Survey).

The Occupy social movement begins, bringing worldwide attention to corporate greed and income inequality.

The Canadian Index of Wellbeing releases its first composite report, which shows that economic progress fails to translate into social and economic well-being for many Canadians.

2012 The enhanced federal Family Caregiver Tax Credit comes into effect.

The National Institute for the Care of the Elderly (NICE) launches the National Survey on the Mistreatment of Older Canadians.

The House of Commons increases the age of eligibility for Old Age Security from sixty-five to sixty-seven, beginning in 2023.

The Government of Alberta launches Phase I of the development of a new Social Policy Framework.

Kateri Tekakwitha becomes North America's first Aboriginal saint.

The federal budget introduces the concept of "social finance" as a method of funding social welfare programs by using private sector money.

The federal government eliminates the National Council of Welfare, the primary source of information on poverty and other social issues in Canada since 1971.

Human Resources and Skills Development Canada launches a Call for Concepts for Social Finance as a first step to reshaping social policy in Canada.

The Idle No More social movement begins in protest of the federal Bill C-45.

The Protecting Canada's Immigration System Act passes into law and builds on the reforms to refugee legislation.

The World Economic Forum ranks Canada twenty-first (out of 135 countries) on the Global Gender Gap Index.

UNICEF ranks Canada as having the twenty-fourth worst child poverty rate among thirty-five industrialized countries.

The Broadbent Institute releases *Towards a More Equal Canada: A Report on Canada' Social and Economic Inequality*, to stimulate discussion on income inequality.

2013   Amendments to the Federal Skilled Worker Class restrict older immigrants with weak English or French skills, low education, or modest work experience from immigrating to Canada.

The Federal Court declares Métis and non-Status Indians as "Indians" under the Constitution Act of 1867.

The Conference Board of Canada ranks Canada as the third worst out of seventeen countries in terms of poverty among working-age adults.

The Homelessness Research Network and the Canadian Alliance to end Homelessness release the first extensive study on homelessness in Canada.

A study by the Canadian Centre for Policy Alternatives and Save the Children Canada finds that half of status First Nations children in Canada live in poverty.

APPENDIX

Globalization and Social Welfare

It has been said that arguing against globalization is like arguing against the law of gravity. (UN Secretary-General Kofi Annan, 2002)

GLOBALIZATION: FRIEND OR FOE?

The International Federation of Social Workers (2012b) defines **globalization** as "the process by which all peoples and communities come to experience an increasingly common economic, social and cultural environment. By definition, the process affects everybody throughout the world." Modern-day globalization is the brainchild of several Western nations that came together shortly after the Second World War to develop a new framework for restructuring economic and political relations. To foster global economic development, world leaders created the U.S.-dominated World Bank, the Organisation for Economic Co-operation and Development (OECD), the International Monetary Fund, and eventually, the World Trade Organization. Globalization is synonymous with free trade, unlimited investment, neoliberalism, and the spread of capitalism.

In 1995, at the World Summit for Social Development in Copenhagen, nations from around the world recognized the contradictions of globalization:

Globalization . . . opens new opportunities for sustained economic growth and development of the world economy, particularly in developing countries.

> Globalization also permits countries to share experiences and to learn from one another's achievements and difficulties, and promotes a cross-fertilization of ideals, cultural values and aspirations. At the same time, the rapid processes of change and adjustment have been accompanied by intensified poverty, unemployment and social disintegration. Threats to human well-being, such as environmental risks, have also been globalized. (United Nations, 1995)

The following section briefly describes some of the risks and opportunities associated with globalization.

Economic Dependence and Vulnerability

In a global economy, governments tend to relax their duties and tariffs, and encourage the free flow of imports and exports across borders. The easy flow of investment, labour, goods, and services between countries has made most nations economically dependent on one another. Those close economic ties also make trading partners economically vulnerable; a case in point is the collapse of the mortgage market in the United States in 2008, which affected stock markets around the world and triggered a global economic recession.

Loss of Democracy

National governments have become torn between responding to the needs of their own citizens and the needs of the global community. While becoming less accountable to citizens, governments are becoming more accountable to business (largely **transnational corporations** or TNCs). TNCs control most of the world's trade, and some are reportedly richer than some countries. These corporations have the power to dictate where they do business (usually in countries that offer the least regulation, the most resources, and the biggest tax breaks) and what types of conditions they want to do business under (sometimes at the expense of the environment and human rights). Democracy is threatened when the welfare of citizens becomes secondary to the profits of business (McDonagh, 2002).

A Blending of Cultures

Groups of people with different ethnic backgrounds, religious beliefs, values, and language are interacting more than ever. Closer cultural contacts can lead to a greater understanding of people and subsequently more tolerance for one another. However, greater cultural interactions may also produce more tension and conflict. Overall, globalization has made cultures less distinguishable, more homogenous, and—in particular—more "Americanized."

Global Economy: Global Risks

Globalization promotes technologies, such as the Internet, wireless telephones, TV satellites, and the rapid transmission of information and ideas around the world. The opening of borders also allows for the easy, and often rapid, infiltration of undesirable elements across borders, which can threaten both personal and national security by allowing

- infectious diseases to spread around the world in record time
- terrorists to access countries more easily and operate in and against several nations simultaneously
- transnational corporations to relocate to countries with weak environmental laws, cheaply extract resources, and dump waste into the environment

Globalization is also associated with rising fuel costs, erratic weather caused by global warming, the increase in crops for biofuels, and the ruination of farmlands from an overuse of pesticides and chemical fertilizers, all of which contribute to a global food crisis.

These risks are most likely to affect those who are already vulnerable or marginalized, such as those living in poverty. Floods associated with global warming, for example, tend to have the greatest impact on those who live in substandard housing; when disaster strikes, the rich can board up their homes and leave town, while the poor are left behind to cope with the aftermath.

JOBS AND JOB SECURITY

Between the 1970s and the 1990s, globalization shifted Western nations into a postindustrial era. During that period, Canada underwent significant **labour market restructuring**, which has changed the world of work for Canadians.

Good Jobs, Bad Jobs

Technology has revolutionized the labour market by automating many labour-intensive tasks. While this change has created a demand for highly literate workers with strong computer and other technical skills, it has also created many low-skilled jobs and an increasing disparity between "good" and "bad" jobs.

"Good" jobs are usually full-time, permanent, and well paid, with benefits and opportunities for promotion. These jobs are largely filled by highly skilled, well-educated workers. "Bad" jobs (or "McJobs") tend to be non-unionized, offer poor pay and working conditions, and provide few (if any) benefits and little chance of advancement. Part-time and non-standard jobs—for example, seasonal, casual, and short-term contract positions—are often considered "bad jobs," especially among those wanting to work full time. Between 1976 and 2011, the proportion of Canadian workers in part-time positions rose from about 7 percent to almost 12 percent (Human Resources and Skills Development Canada, 2013c). A large proportion of these workers are older or young adults, recent immigrants, visible minorities, and women, many of which have relatively few skills and education.

Down with Manufacturing, Up with Services

Much of the labour-intensive manufacturing that once took place in Canada is now outsourced to emerging economies, such as China and India. Between 2002 and when a global economic recession hit in 2008, Canada lost 388000 manufacturing jobs. During the 2008–2009 recession, total employment in the manufacturing industry shrank back to 1997 levels. The regions hit hardest were Ontario (with a loss of up to one in five manufacturing jobs) and Québec (which lost one in six manufacturing jobs) (Weir, 2008).

While manufacturing jobs continue to disappear, the number of service jobs keeps growing. In 1961, the service industry employed about half of all Canadian workers; by 2006, about three-quarters of Canadians worked in real estate, healthcare, social welfare, government, and other service sectors (Foreign Affairs and International Trade Canada, 2012). Many service workers, including those in the health sector, are well paid and in high demand. Others, such as retail clerks, cleaners, and food service workers, often work for minimum wage and are more easily replaced; this group includes a high percentage of women (especially visible-minority women).

Income Inequality

Over the last three decades, low-income and middle-class workers have seen their incomes shrink or stagnate. Meanwhile, affluent corporate managers and executives have taken an increasingly larger share of available wealth in the form of salaries, bonuses, and company profits. In the late 1970s, the average CEO earned an income that was 25 times that of the average Canadian; by 2010, that ratio had reached 250 times the average (McQuaig, 2010). Although **income inequality** is rising to some extent in advanced nations, it is occurring at an accelerated rate in Canada. The graph in Exhibit B.1 shows the income share of each quintile of Canadian earners in 2009.

Although many critics blame globalization for rising income inequality, a report by the OECD (2011) reveals that globalization is not the main cause of income disparity. Rather, advances in information, communication, and other technologies have benefited high-skilled workers more than low-skilled workers, leading to a wider spread in labour income. Moreover, the *pressure to globalize*—rather than globalization per se—has led nations (including Canada) to change many of their domestic policies, the effects of which have increased the income gap between rich and poor earners. Those policies relate to such things as

- labour market restructuring, which has increased the number of workers in low-paying part-time and temporary jobs (and subsequently widened the pay gap between low- and high-income earners)

EXHIBIT B.1

INCOME INEQUALITY IN CANADA, 2009

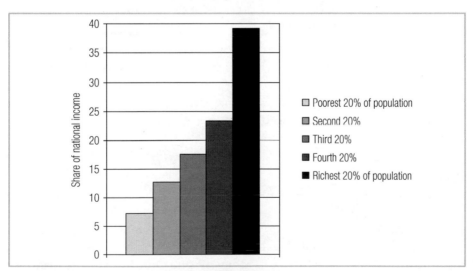

Source: Author-generated chart; data from The Conference Board of Canada. (2013). *Canadian income inequality, Richest group accounts for the largest share of National income, 2009*. Retrieved from http://www. conferenceboard.ca/hcp/hot-topics/caninequality.aspx.

- a decline in government's willingness to redistribute income more equitably across the population through tax benefits and cash transfers targeting the lowest-income earners

THE DIMINISHED ROLE OF SOCIAL WELFARE PROGRAMS

Labour market restructuring has undoubtedly benefited many Canadians. Many others, however, are at an increasingly high risk of job displacement, unemployment, underemployment, debt overload, bankruptcy, and poverty. A growing number of vulnerable or out-of-work people place a heavier demand on income security programs and social services, including emergency shelters and food programs. Unemployment and poverty can create considerable psychological stress, which in turn, can raise the incidence of mental health disorders, suicide, spousal abuse, and child maltreatment—all problems that require a wide range of services.

Although the demand for social welfare programs keeps rising, Canadian governments continue to diminish the capacity of those programs to serve. Neoliberal governments tend to see market solutions to social problems and see jobs as the best form of social security. However, in their eagerness to facilitate globalization and attract foreign investment and trade, neoliberal governments have created a highly competitive labour market with not enough "good" jobs to go around. Many workers end up working for poverty wages in jobs with no benefits and limited opportunities for advancement. Quitting is not always an option since there are fewer resources—such as EI and social assistance—available to fall back on. These workers are virtually trapped in poverty, unable to adequately support themselves or their families. In 2011, almost one-quarter of Canadian workers earned less than $13.33 per hour (Canadian Labour Congress, 2012).

CONCLUSION

Proponents of globalization use the metaphor "a rising tide floats all boats" to promote the notion that everyone will benefit from a healthy economy. The reality is, after several decades of globalization and neoliberal policies, some boats are floating better than others. While globalization has made the rich even richer, the wealth from economic growth has failed to trickle down to the broader population. Numerous reports suggest that global poverty and other social problems have actually worsened since globalization began in earnest after the Second World War.

Globalization is more popular than ever, and trade activity among Canada and other nations continues to grow. Governments expect that the economic growth resulting from trade deals will make Canada a richer country and, ultimately, ensure social well-being and prosperity to all Canadians over the long term. However, a troubling trend is that Canada's living standards continue to fall, and income inequality continues to rise, even in good economic times when work is plentiful and unemployment rates are low.

KEY TERMS

For definitions of the key terms, consult the Glossary on page 453 at the end of the book.

globalization, p. 445

transnational
corporations, p. 446

labour market
restructuring,
p. 447

income inequality,
p. 449

GLOSSARY

The number at the end of the definition refers to the chapter containing the key term.

A

Aboriginal cultural awareness training Education and skill building that helps professional helpers raise their level of cultural sensitivity as it relates to the Aboriginal population. (12; p. 362)

Aboriginal peoples The descendants of the original inhabitants of North America. The Canadian Constitution recognizes three groups of Aboriginal peoples: Indians, Métis, and Inuit. (12; p. 331)

acceptable housing Housing that is adequate (in good repair), suitable (uncrowded), and affordable (costs less than 30 percent of a household's before-tax income). (9; p. 246)

access The ability and right to enter, use, or take advantage of opportunities, services, or resources. (14; p. 397)

accommodation The act of modifying an environment so that a person with a disability can participate in activities that take place in that environment. (14; p. 423)

accountability The demonstration or proof of how resources are used to achieve results; the obligation to account to others; or the obligation to answer to, report or explain, or give reasons for one's actions. (5; p. 132)

active aging Participating in activities throughout the lifespan that maximize social, physical, and mental well-being, and that relate to extended life expectancy and a good quality of life in later years. (11; p. 300)

active labour market policies Government strategies that require able-bodied beneficiaries of public programs to take steps toward entering (or re-entering) the workforce, or that give incentives to beneficiaries who choose work or training in lieu of benefits. (2, 4; pp. 47, 104)

administration An organizational activity that involves developing or interpreting policies and procedures, planning and managing direct service activities, and ensuring that the organization meets its goals and objectives. (6; p. 160)

advocacy Speaking or acting on behalf of another person or group by, for example, disseminating information to influence the opinions of others or calling for changes in laws, regulations, and government policies. (5; p. 140)

age-friendly community A geographic location—such as a city or neighbourhood—that recognizes the capabilities of seniors, responds to their needs, respects their decisions and choices, protects them, and promotes their inclusion. (11; p. 308)

ageism Prejudice and discrimination against a person on the basis of age; usually used in reference to elderly people. (11; p. 302)

agency goal Part of an organization's strategic framework that states the concrete steps the organization plans to take over the long term to achieve its vision and mission. (6; p. 158)

agency volunteers Non-professional helpers who donate their time and skills to an organization without monetary compensation. (7; p. 189)

aging in place The act of growing old in the dwelling of one's choice (which is usually one's home, not an institution). (6, 11; pp. 153, 305)

alternative service delivery A framework to guide government when reorganizing their departments or agencies, coordinating their efforts, and collaborating with private sector agencies in the delivery of public programs. (5; p. 131)

anti-oppressive approaches Forms of social work practice that value egalitarianism, embrace a person-centred philosophy, and focus on empowering oppressed or marginalized groups, and on changing structures in society that create social divisions and inequalities. (8, 9, 13; pp. 221, 263, 391)

asset-based social policies Public policies that help disadvantaged groups or communities achieve financial security and self-sufficiency through the accumulation of human, social, physical, or financial capital. (9; p. 256)

asset tests Financial tests used to determine eligibility for income security programs or social services. Eligibility is based on applicants' tangible assets, such as property, savings, or investments. (1; p. 14)

assimilation A process in which a person or a group of people adopt aspects of a dominant culture; this process may or may not be voluntary. (12; p. 333)

assisted living facilities Supported housing for seniors and people with disabilities that offer private living space and meals, as well as such services as personal care, laundry, and housekeeping. (11; p. 319)

austerity measure An economic policy aimed at reducing government deficits through severe cuts in public spending. (4; p. 96)

B

baby boom generation A segment of the population that was born between 1946 and 1965, a period in which the average number of children born per woman (3.7) reached the highest in Canadian history. Note: the definition of the baby boom period varies between countries. (11; p. 299)

band A group of First Nations people for whom lands have been set apart or whose money is held by the Crown. Many bands prefer to be known as First Nations. (12; p. 334)

best practices Strategies, methods, or approaches that are perceived as working well and would be recommended to others. (6; p. 172)

bill A written proposal for a law or piece of legislation that is submitted for approval by Parliament or the Senate (federal level), or a provincial or territorial legislature. (2; p. 50)

block fund A lump sum of money given by one level of government to a lower government for a specific purpose; the amount of the fund is usually calculated on a per capita basis. (4; p. 99)

brief therapies Therapeutic interventions that aim to achieve specific, measurable, and short-term goals; emphasize the client's present and future (rather than the past); and focus on personal strengths. (8; p. 210)

budget deficits The amounts by which government spending exceeds income. (4; p. 92)

bureaucratic model of organization A framework used to structure organizations, characterized by several divisions or departments, specialization, formalization, departmentalization, a clear chain of command, centralization, and a hierarchical structure. (6; p. 167)

C

capacity The ability, capability, means, or power required to reach specific goals over the long term. (8; p. 207)

capital Various types of wealth that can be applied to improving one's quality of life. Types of capital include human (such as skills and knowledge), social (such as relationships and contacts), physical (such as material goods), natural (such as food and water), and financial (such as income and savings). (1; p. 10)

caregiver strain The negative physical, psychological, financial, or other negative consequence of caring for another person for an extended time. (7; p. 200)

care team A group of professional helpers and non-professional helpers who coordinate their efforts on behalf of clients who have a variety of needs or are connected to several different agencies. (7; p. 179)

categorical A criteria used by government to determine who is or is not eligible for assistance. For example, under the English Poor Laws, governments categorized people in need as being either "deserving" or "undeserving" of public relief. (3; p. 67)

charities Non-profit organizations that have philanthropic goals (e.g., social, educational, or religious). (3; p. 64)

child abuse An act against a child that harms or threatens that child's well-being; those acts include physical or sexual assault, neglect or abandonment, emotional or psychological mistreatment, and witnessing family violence. Also called child maltreatment. (10; p. 287)

child care The act of caring for and supervising a child in a home or a centre. (10; p. 272)

child neglect A type of child abuse characterized by the failure of a caregiver to provide appropriate care, supervision, or protection to a child. (10; p. 287)

child welfare system A government program that provides mandated services to families with children, investigates reports of alleged child abuse, and provides various care options for children in care. (10; p. 290)

children in care Children who come under the protection of a child welfare system and reside either in their own home (under the supervision of a child protection worker) or in alternative care, such as a foster home or kinship care. (10; p. 293)

citizen participation The active involvement of citizens or community members in the planning, development, or administration of policies and programs that affect them. (2; p. 45)

clawbacks The amounts high-income-earning individuals are required to repay of the cash benefits they receive from income security programs. (4; p. 94)

client A consumer, participant, or beneficiary of a social welfare program or service. (1; p. 11)

collaborative governance An approach to leadership and management in which all parties in a working group enjoy an equal status and share power, decision making, and accountability to achieve a common goal. (2, 5; pp. 43, 131)

colonization The encroachment on and subjugation of one group by a more powerful group, usually to exploit the less powerful group's resources; the term is often used in reference to the treatment of Aboriginal peoples by the Government of Canada. (12; p. 343)

commercial sector A subdivision of the private sector in which businesses, corporations, and companies deliver programs and services for a profit. (5; p. 122)

community development A process in which citizens resolve local problems and increase the problem-solving capacity of the community by working with existing systems in the community. (8; p. 225)

community living movement A collective, grassroots effort aimed at helping people with an intellectual disability make a smooth transition from institutional to community-based living. (14; p. 406)

community mental health movement A collective, grassroots effort that advocates for the rights of people with a mental health disorder and the provision of care in non-institutional settings. (14; p. 406)

community needs assessment An evaluation used to determine the need for a particular program or service in a given community. (6; p. 156)

community practice A social work field that focuses on motivating and helping community members to evaluate, plan, and coordinate their efforts to meet local needs; also called developmental social work. (8; p. 232)

community system of care A mix of services and resources that, when offered in a coordinated and integrated fashion, is responsive to the varying levels and changing needs of clients. (6; p. 154)

community-based model A framework used by social agencies to meet community needs, match services to people's needs and preferences, build on local strengths, and offer services in natural (as opposed to institutional) settings. (6; p. 150)

comprehensive community initiative A community-based organized effort that has multiple targets of change and aims to transform communities or neighbourhoods and the living conditions of residents. (8, 9; pp. 226, 261)

congregate housing A type of supportive housing for seniors and people with disabilities that provides a private apartment or room within a larger complex and minimal care (such as the provision of meals). (11; p. 319)

conservatism A political ideology that promotes traditional values, moral (religious) standards, and conformity to the existing social order. (1; p. 18)

contracting-out A process in which the government purchases services from an individual or a group in the private sector while remaining accountable for the delivery of those services. Also known as outsourcing. (5; p. 131)

contributory programs Income security programs that work as savings plans, requiring working individuals to contribute to a fund that then compensates them when they are not working; examples are Employment Insurance and the Canada/Quebec Pension Plans. Formerly called social insurance programs. (1; p. 12)

core funding Income that can be applied to a voluntary social agency's basic or core activities, such as administration, staffing, operational costs, agency promotion, and ongoing programs. (5; p. 137)

core housing need A need produced by housing that is overcrowded, is unaffordable, or requires repair. (9; p. 246)

corporate social responsibility An approach taken by businesses to include the public interest in its corporate decision making, thereby garnering the goodwill of the community. (5; p. 127)

cross-cultural training Education and skill building that helps professional helpers raise their level of cultural sensitivity and improve their effectiveness in working with minority groups. (13; p. 387)

cycle of poverty A set of factors or events that trap people in the negative effects of poverty and perpetuate in a seemingly endless fashion. (9; p. 248)

D

data collection tools Instruments or procedures used to collect quantitative or qualitative information about social conditions and problems. Examples include statistics, surveys, interviews, and focus groups. (2; p. 35)

decentralization The distribution of a central government's functions, authority, or assets among several authorities, such as lower levels of government. (4; p. 95)

deinstitutionalization A process to move institutionalized people into community settings and to replace institutional care with community-based programs and services. (14; p. 405)

depth of poverty A statistic that measures how far a person's income is below a certain threshold or low-income cut-off (LICO). (9; p. 241)

deserving poor A social label used until the mid-twentieth century to identify people who were worthy of public relief because they were sick or aged, had a disability, or were otherwise incapable of supporting themselves. (1; p. 23)

direct relief Government aid given to the poor in the form of cash, vouchers for basic necessities, or essential resources such as food, fuel, and clothing. (3; p. 76)

direct services Assistance delivered through face-to-face interactions, often by front-line workers; examples include personal counselling and therapy groups. (6; p. 155)

disability A physical, mental, or environmental condition that substantially restricts a person's ability to perform tasks that are typical for his or her age. (14; p. 395)

disability community A loosely defined segment of the population comprising people with disabilities, their families, caregivers, advocates, and the organizations that serve them. (14; p. 406)

disability income system A range of federal, provincial, and territorial income security programs for people with disabilities who are unable to earn enough to support themselves. (14; p. 420)

disability rights movement A collective, grassroots, large-scale effort aimed at eliminating socially imposed restrictions on people with disabilities, ensuring their full citizenship, and creating equal access to mainstream resources and opportunities. (14; p. 405)

discrimination The prejudicial or distinguishing (usually negative) treatment of an individual based on his or her membership (or perceived membership) in a certain social group. (13; p. 382)

diversity A concept that embraces the "differentness" of people and cultures. (6; p. 170)

E

ecological perspective A theory that accepts disability as a physical condition with limiting consequences but also recognizes the impact of a person's environment on his or her experience of disability. Also known as the sociopolitical perspective. (14; p. 396)

economic immigrants A category of immigrants within the immigration application process, reserved for skilled workers and business people. (13; p. 371)

elder abuse The maltreatment of an older person within a relationship in which there is an expectation of trust; includes physical, sexual, or emotional abuse; financial exploitation; and neglect. (11; p. 316)

empowerment The process of gaining personal control, authority, or decision-making power over one's affairs by individuals, families, groups, organizations, or communities. (8, 10; pp. 214, 295)

enfranchisement A process that gives the rights of citizenship (including the right to vote) to a person or group. (12; p. 334)

English Poor Laws A series of British parliamentary acts that Elizabeth I enacted during the sixteenth and seventeenth centuries to reduce poverty and begging in England; some colonial governments in Canada adopted certain principles of these laws. (3; p. 67)

environmental scan A method of assessing a community's social and economic conditions that may influence local needs or affect an organization's ability to meet those needs. (6; p. 156)

episodic disability A type of disability that can affect individuals on a sporadic and often unpredictable basis. Examples include HIV, multiple sclerosis, and mental health disorders. (14; p. 418)

ethnic enclaves Neighbourhoods or districts that are distinct from the larger population because of certain cultural, racial, religious, ancestral, or other characteristics, and often populated by immigrant and visible-minority groups. Examples are Chinatown and Little Italy. (13; p. 380)

eugenics The study, belief, or practice of improving the human population by controlled, selective breeding. (14; p. 404)

F

family A group of people composed of a married couple or a common-law couple, with or without children, or of a lone parent living with at least one child. (10; p. 267)

family casework A social work approach that emerged in the 1920s designed to help the entire family unit (or several members of a family). (8; p. 211)

family policy A type of social policy used to guide government initiatives for families with children. Examples include the National Children's Agenda and the Family Violence Initiative. (10; p. 270)

family type A classification of a family based on certain characteristics and membership. Examples include married or common-law couples with children, lone-parent families, families of divorce, and stepfamilies. (10; p. 280)

family violence The abuse of power within a family or in relationships of trust or dependency; family violence includes physical assault, emotional abuse, neglect, sexual assault, financial exploitation, and stalking. (10; p. 285)

feminization of poverty A view of poverty that illustrates the ways women are more likely than men to be poor, regardless of the woman's age, family status, ethnicity, or other characteristic. (9; p. 242)

First Nations people A term that came into vogue in the 1970s to replace the term "Indian." The term includes those that have either Status or non-Status under the Indian Act. (12; p. 331)

fiscalization A process in which government uses the tax system, rather than programs and services, to achieve social goals. (4; p. 108)

flat hierarchical structures Organizational structures that have few levels of management; characteristic of the organic model of organization. (6; p. 168)

food insecurity The state of not having or eating adequate amounts of nutritious food or worrying about not being able to obtain an adequate amount or quality of food. (9; p. 246)

formative evaluation A formal assessment that occurs during a planned change process to determine whether an action plan is working or how the plan might be modified to reach the desired goal. (8; p. 221)

functional limitations perspective A theory that defines disability largely in terms of how it limits a person's functioning, as well as how people with a disability and others perceive and react to those limitations. (14; p. 396)

G

gerontechnology A field that combines knowledge from gerontology and technology to create innovative tools to help seniors with special needs age in place safely and comfortably. (11; p. 319)

gerontology The formal study of aging. (11; p. 301)

globalization The development of an interconnected and interdependent global economy, characterized by free trade, the free flow of capital, and the sharing of innovation and technology. (4, Appendix B; pp. 92, 445)

government-assisted housing A government program that provides full or partial subsidies for housing to low-income individuals and families. Examples include public or social housing, nonprofit housing, cooperative housing, and rent supplements. (9; p. 257)

grassroots approach Activities or projects that are started by citizens rather than by government or professions; considered a bottom-up rather than a top-down approach to social change. (8; p. 225)

guaranteed annual income A concept that suggests that all citizens have the right to a minimum income as the result of either paid work or government subsidies. (3; p. 84)

H

head tax A fixed entry fee charged by the Government of Canada to deter so-called undesirables from immigrating to Canada. (13; p. 368)

healing In Aboriginal theory, the process of restoring balance or harmony to the overall health and well-being of individuals, families, groups, or communities. (12; p. 344)

holistic view Looking at the whole of something rather than just its individual parts; recognition of the interconnectedness between various components of a system. (12; p. 344)

home and community care Programs that provide professional care in a person's home (rather than in a hospital or nursing home) that aim to prevent chronic health problems and help people age in place. (11; p. 320)

homelessness A situation in which an individual or a family lacks appropriate, permanent, or stable housing; lacks the means or ability to acquire appropriate housing; or faces the immediate prospect of losing housing. (9; p. 247)

I

immigrants People who were born in another country, have moved to Canada by choice, and have been granted the legal right to live in this country. (13; p. 366)

immigration rate The number of immigrants per one thousand Canadians in any given year. (13; p. 370)

impairment perspective A theory based on the medical model that defines disability as a biologically based illness or disease that originates in a person's body or mind and that can be cured by specific treatments. (14; p. 396)

inclusion lens A tool or method for analyzing laws, policies, programs, and practices to determine the extent to which people are either included or excluded from social, economic, and other benefits. (2; p. 56)

income inequality The unequal distribution of wealth in capitalist systems, reflected in the disparity in income between the rich and the poor. (1, 4, Appendix B; pp. 24, 114, 449)

income redistribution A strategy based on Keynesian economics that governments use to shift income away from high- and moderate-income earners toward those with lower incomes. (1; p. 25)

income security programs Government-sponsored initiatives that provide financial aid to replace or supplement the incomes of people who are unemployed, elderly, or sick, or have a disability. (1; p. 11)

income tests Financial tests used to determine eligibility for income security programs or social services; eligibility is based on the applicant's income. (1; p. 14)

independent living movement A philosophy and grassroots social movement that uses political organization to promote self-representation for people with disabilities. (14; p. 406)

indexation The mechanism by which government benefits are indexed to inflation by using the Consumer Price Index; programs that are indexed (for example, Old Age Security pension) automatically increase benefits as the cost of living rises. (3; p. 82)

Indians First Nations, Métis, or Inuit who meet the Government of Canada's criteria for Status Indians, non-Status Indians, or Treaty Indians. (12; p. 331)

indicators Statistics or pieces of data that measure or "indicate" the existence of something and show how social or economic conditions manifest themselves in society and change over time. (1, 2; pp. 5, 37)

indirect relief Aid provided through government-funded work projects during the Great Depression, designed to get the unemployed back to work. (3; p. 76)

indirect services Activities in social agencies that do not usually involve personal contact with clients but can influence the type and quality of direct services. Examples include administration, program planning, and program evaluation. (6; p. 155)

individual development accounts Government-sponsored savings accounts designed to help low-income Canadians save money; both individuals and government contribute to the funds. (9; p. 256)

indoor relief A type of public relief provided by colonial governments to people in need, which came in the form of room and board in institutions, such as workhouses and poorhouses. (3; p. 68)

institutional approach The view that social welfare is a primary institution of society (similar to religion, government, and education) and therefore has a normal, legitimate, and necessary function in a civilized, modern society. (1; p. 23)

inter-agency cooperation A management approach in which the members of social agencies cooperate and work together to improve a community's programs and services. (6; p. 173)

interdisciplinary knowledge base A foundation of knowledge that is based on the shared experience and research of people from various professions, vocations, or academic fields. (7; p. 181)

interest groups Organized collectives that support specific causes and try to influence government policy for the benefit of their own members or on behalf of the general public. (2; p. 45)

intra-agency cooperation A management approach used by social agencies to empower workers, clients, and other stakeholders, and to foster an environment of inclusion and participation in the workplace. (6; p. 173)

Inuit An Aboriginal person living in the northern regions of Canada, including Nunavut, the Northwest Territories, and the northern parts of Labrador and Québec. (12; p. 331)

K

Keynesian economics An economic theory that advocates for government intervention in monetary policy and market processes to stimulate and stabilize the economy. (4; p. 92)

L

labour market restructuring Significant changes in employment conditions, industrial relations, the types of work offered, and unionization. (Appendix B; p. 447)

liberalism A political ideology that emphasizes people's rights to individuality, freedom of self-expression, and lifestyle choice. (1; p. 21)

LICOs (low-income cut-offs) A relative measure of low income that identifies the minimum level of income required for a family to purchase food, shelter, and other basics. (9; p. 240)

life-course lens A tool or method for analyzing people's experiences over the life course and how they manage transitions from one life phase to another. (2; p. 57)

logic model A framework that describes the components of a policy or program and the causal relationships between them. (2; p. 54)

lone-parent families Families that are headed by one parent of any marital status, with at least one child living in the same dwelling. (10; p. 280)

longitudinal surveys Statistical surveys that are administered to constant groups of people several times at regular intervals over a relatively long time. (2; p. 35)

M

macro level (of society) The largest, most complex, and established institutions and systems of society, including government, communities, societal norms and values, cultural traditions and customs, and economic processes. (8; p. 207)

mainstream approaches (to helping) Processes of helping people that are based on medical models; the approaches view human disorders as discrete entities that can be treated through medication, psychotherapy, or other Western practices. (12; p. 344)

mandated services Programs or services that must be provided as a matter of federal or provincial or territorial law; an example is child protection services. (2, 5; pp. 53, 125)

mandatory volunteers People who are required to volunteer in order to qualify for another event, such as high school graduation, or to meet the requirements of a court order. (7; p. 191)

marginalized groups Segments of the population that lack power, knowledge, social recognition, respect, and economic resources, and are subsequently excluded or pushed to the margins of society. (1; p. 9)

means test A financial test once used by Canadian governments to determine eligibility for income security programs; eligibility is based on an applicant's income and assets and virtually ignores personal needs. (3; p. 75)

mental health A person's capacity to think, feel, and behave in ways that enhance the quality and enjoyment of life and the skills to deal with life's challenges. (10; p. 274)

mental health disorder A psychological (cognitive or emotional) disorder that is characterized by distress or disability and that interferes with a person's ability to complete the daily tasks of living. (10; p. 275)

Métis A person of mixed European-Aboriginal ancestry who identifies as a Métis and is accepted as a Métis by his or her community or organization. A Métis is distinct from Inuit and First Nations peoples. (12; p. 331)

mezzo level (of society) The segment of society that comprises organizations, social agencies, businesses, clubs, associations, and other formal collectives. (8; p. 207)

micro level (of society) The segment of society that is made up of the smallest units, such as individuals, families, and small groups. (8; p. 207)

mission statement Part of an organization's strategic framework that describes what the organization is, what it does, to whom its efforts will be targeted, and what it intends to achieve. (6; p. 158)

mixed economy of welfare The provision of social welfare programs through various service delivery systems, all of which focus on the provision of well-being and are organized, funded, and managed in their own distinct ways. (5; p. 122)

monetarism An economic theory or practice of stabilizing the economy by controlling the supply of money in circulation. (4; p. 92)

multilevel approach to practice A social work orientation that supports interventions at micro, mezzo, and macro levels of society. (7; p. 181)

multiservice centres Single locations offering a combination of supports, such as healthcare, social services, and legal services. (6; p. 153)

N

National Aboriginal Organizations Formal, organized, and recognized groups of Aboriginal peoples that engage in activities to protect their common interests and rights, publicly promote their causes, and reclaim their ancestral rights. (12; p. 337)

natural helping skills Human abilities or attributes acquired through personal experience rather than formal training, and that other people find helpful. (7; p. 190)

need A necessary condition or requirement of human development that if not met will result in serious physical, psychological, or social harm. (1; p. 7)

needs tests Financial tests used to determine eligibility for income security programs or social services; eligibility is based on an applicant's needs and the income required to meet those needs. (1; p. 14)

neoliberalism A contemporary form of conservatism that promotes small government, fiscal responsibility, and the role of the market in the provision of economic and social well-being. (1, 4; pp. 20, 92)

non-professional helpers People who help others without monetary compensation, including natural helpers, informal helpers, lay helpers, agency volunteers, self-help groups, and family caregivers. (7; p. 178)

non-residential centres Non-institutional social agencies that provide services on a drop-in, appointment, or outreach basis. (6; p. 153)

O

open house concept An idea that recognizes the value of the full participation of people with disabilities in society and their enjoyment of the same rights and privileges as people who do not have a disability. (14; p. 422)

operational framework An internal structure of an organization used as a practical guide to delivering direct services and managing indirect services. (6; p. 155)

organic model of organization A framework used to structure organizations that views organizations as living organisms, capable of adapting to an ever-changing environment. (6; p. 167)

organizational change A change occurring at the mezzo level of society, often involving a significant restructuring of an organization's internal systems, resulting in a fundamental shift in the way the organization operates. (8; p. 215)

outcome evaluation A type of program evaluation that assesses the extent to which an action, an intervention, a policy, or a program has benefited the participants (or target population). (6; p. 162)

outcomes The impacts, desired results, or benefits of an action, an intervention, a policy, or a program. (2; p. 39)

outdoor relief A type of public relief provided by colonial governments to people in need; the relief was in the form of cash and other assistance, given to people living in their own homes. (3; p. 68)

out-of-home care The placement of a child or youth in residential, kinship, community, or foster care by a child welfare authority that has legal custody or guardianship of the child. (10; p. 292)

P

paraprofessionals Formally trained people who are not qualified to practise according to the standards set by a particular profession but can be assigned tasks and functions within that profession; examples include social service workers and community support workers. (7; p. 186)

parens patriae A Latin term meaning "father of the nation"; the term refers to laws that allow the state to use its authority to override parental rights and intervene on behalf of a child. (10; p. 289)

parenting style A set of strategies used by parents to socialize, teach, discipline, and otherwise raise their children. (10; p. 279)

passive labour market policies Government plans of action that do not require beneficiaries of government assistance to give anything in exchange for benefits. (2, 4; pp. 47, 103)

peer counsellors Formally trained yet non-professional helpers who assist others with a similar experience or concern either in a group or on a one-to-one basis. (7; p. 197)

peer support Non-professional help that one person gives to another in an egalitarian and mutually supportive way. Also called mutual aid. (7; p. 194)

permanent resident A person who has lived in Canada for at least two years within a five-year period and has been granted permanent resident status. (13; p. 370)

persistence of poverty A statistic that measures the percentage of people living with low income every year over a six-year period. (9; p. 241)

person-in-environment A social work perspective that recognizes the complexity of interactions between people and their environment, and promotes the notion that people both shape and are shaped by their environment. (7; p. 181)

planned change process A step-by-step scientific, methodical approach used to facilitate change in people, organizations, or other systems. The process involves a target of change, a change agent, a method of change, a beneficiary of change, and a context of change. (8; p. 207)

points system A system to objectively assess the qualifications of people applying for immigration to Canada. (13; p. 370)

policies and procedures A set of documents outlining a fixed set of rules that organizations use to guide their operations. (6; p. 163)

policy community A loosely defined set of individuals, groups, and organizations from both inside and outside government that influence the development of public policy. (2; p. 39)

political ideology A set of beliefs that shape people's views of society, how that society should function, and what should be done to achieve the ideal society. (1; p. 18)

political protests Expressions of objection made by citizens against government, often in the form of strikes, rallies, marches, demonstrations, or occupation aimed at influencing the decisions of those in power. (8; p. 230)

poorhouses Types of institutions or "almshouses" created in colonial times to house and manage the poor and homeless, and to keep them from roaming the streets. (3; p. 68)

population aging A demographic phenomenon characterized by an increasing number of older people in the population. (2, 11; pp. 32, 299)

population dependency ratio A measure showing the number of dependants for every 100 people in the working age population. (11; p. 300)

poverty (1) A state of living characterized by lack, deprivation, and an inability to obtain the basic necessities. (2) A form of social exclusion, in which a person is unable, or is denied the opportunity, to fully engage in society or meet society's expectations. (3) A state of being powerless, voiceless, or dependent on others for resources. (2, 9; pp. 34, 239)

poverty rate A statistic that quantifies the percentage of people living in low income in a geographic area. (9; p. 240)

poverty reduction An organized and formal process that addresses both the symptoms and the causes of poverty. (9; p. 261)

primary prevention Activities usually targeted at large segments of the population to prevent the development of personal or societal problems; activities often focus on education, information giving, or the promotion of certain practices. (6; p. 159)

principle of less eligibility A guideline established under the English Poor Laws, used during colonial times, that required public benefits to be minimal and less than the wage of the lowest-paid workers in a settlement. (3; p. 67)

private sector A non-government component of the economy in which organizations are privately owned and operated; includes both profit-making and nonprofit operations. (5; p. 122)

privatization The transfer of most or all assets, services, or functions from a government to either a nonprofit or a profit-making agency in the private sector. (5; p. 132)

process model A framework used to analyze or evaluate a policy or program, focusing on how the policy or program has been developed or implemented. (2; p. 55)

professional helpers People paid to provide helping services and to bring a recognized knowledge base, training, code of ethics, and relevant experience to their practice; examples include social workers, psychiatrists, and psychologists. (7; p. 178)

professions Vocations based on specialized education that have a code of ethics, the means to regulate and enforce standards of practice among their members, and theoretical bodies of knowledge that guide practice; examples are social work, nursing, and law. (7; p. 184)

program eligibility A set of criteria that when met allows a person to participate in, or potentially benefit from, a publicly sponsored program. (1; p. 13)

program evaluation A process of assessing the usefulness, effectiveness, and efficiency of programs and services. (6; p. 162)

program planning The design and development of programs and services to meet client needs and the community's broader goals. (6; p. 161)

progressive tax system A type of income tax system in which high income earners pay a higher percentage of tax than do low-income earners. (4; p. 92)

progressive universalism An approach to the provision of income security benefits that supplies benefits to all persons who are eligible but gives a larger benefit to those who need it most. This is a contemporary (and European) version of a universal program. (1; p. 16)

project funding A source of short-term money that is earmarked for a certain activity or program. (5; p. 137)

Protestant work ethic A belief that stresses the virtues of thrift, hard work, self-help, and self-discipline, and sees these virtues as a means to material prosperity and personal salvation. (3; p. 66)

provincialized social policy The devolution of a national social welfare policy to the provincial and territorial levels of government, resulting in systems and services that vary across the country. (4; p. 99)

psychosocial approach A therapeutic way of working that recognizes the importance of the relationship and interactions between a person's psychology and his or her environment. (11; p. 311)

public adoption The process of legally assuming responsibility for a child or youth who is in the care of a provincial or territorial child welfare agency. (10; p. 293)

public debt The accumulated amount of government deficits. (4; p. 92)

public policies Plans of action developed by government in response to particular issues or needs; these plans give structure to public programs. (2; p. 30)

public programs Activities or projects that stem from public policies, are funded by taxpayers, are administered by government, and have public benefits. (5; p. 124)

public relief An early form of government aid given to people who were unable to support themselves through work or other means; a precursor to social assistance or welfare. (3; p. 67)

public sector The government component of the economy in which programs and services are funded fully by tax revenues, and government is accountable for those programs or services. (5; p. 122)

public social agencies Government departments or divisions that provide social welfare programs; examples include welfare offices and government-based child protection units. (6; p. 149)

Q

qualitative measures Research methods used to evaluate or estimate the quality, nature, meaning, or other subjective aspect of a person's experiences. (8; p. 221)

quantitative measures Research methods used to count or quantify objective data (such as staff turnover rates or service usage statistics). (8; p. 221)

R

racialization A process of differentiating or categorizing a group of people according to their skin colour, religion, language, or other trait, and subjecting that group to unequal treatment. Because the basis of discrimination may be attributes other than race, racialized groups may or may not be visible minorities. (13; p. 382)

racism Prejudice or discrimination against a person or group based on the belief that race determines certain traits, behaviours, or abilities. (13; p. 382)

recent immigrants People who immigrated to Canada within the past ten years. (13; p. 367)

refugees People who have been forced to flee persecution in their homeland and to take refuge in a foreign country. (13; p. 377)

rent-geared-to-income A component of government-assisted housing in which the government subsidy is based on a tenant's total income. (9; p. 257)

reserves Tracts of land owned by the Government of Canada and set apart for the use and benefit of First Nations peoples; many First Nations have replaced the term "reserves" with "First Nations communities." (12; p. 333)

resettlement The legal process of selecting and transferring a refugee to Canada to live as a permanent resident. (13; p. 377)

residential centres Organizations that provide living quarters, meals, and a range of services to people who require round-the-clock care; originally called institutions. (6; p. 151)

residential schools Boarding schools that offer students both an education and a place to live. In Canada, the term usually refers to a federal educational system that existed from 1883 to 1996, used to assimilate Aboriginal peoples into mainstream society. (12; p. 335)

residential school syndrome A cluster of psychological, social, physical, and other symptoms experienced by Aboriginal peoples who attended residential schools. The syndrome does not apply to non-Aboriginal residential schools. (12; p. 343)

residual approach The view that social welfare programs should be used sparingly and only as a last resort, when help from one's family, church, banks, and other private sources has been exhausted. (1; p. 22)

respite services Programs that give unpaid caregivers a break from their caregiving duties by providing day programs or home support to those needing care. (7; p. 202)

restricted practice activities Tasks that can be carried out only by certain occupational groups or by designated professionals within those groups. (7; p. 185)

retirement income system A range of income security programs available to people in their senior or retirement years. (11; p. 313)

risk factors of poverty Conditions or circumstances that increase people's likelihood of experiencing poverty. (9; p. 242)

S

sandwich generation A segment of the population that has the role of caregiver to both dependent children and aging relatives. (7; p. 199)

scope of practice A defined set of functions and activities that limit the range of what professional helpers can and cannot do in their provision of service. (7; p. 181)

secondary prevention Activities that focus on identifying a social problem in its early stages of development and then controlling or changing the conditions that caused it. Also referred to as early intervention. (6; p. 159)

self-government An arrangement between a government and a group of people that allows the group to govern themselves (usually within the structures of the existing laws). Canadian law allows some Aboriginal groups to live under this type of arrangement. (12; p. 339)

self-help groups Organized yet non-professional networks of individuals who provide mutual aid and share common experiences, situations, problems, and strategies. (7; p. 195)

service silos Divisions, departments, units, or individuals in an organization that function as their own entities, often in isolation from others, and provide services without consideration of how those services affect the rest of the organization. (6; p. 167)

settlement practice A collection of interventions, values, knowledge, and professional ethics adopted by settlement workers and applied to their work with recent immigrants or refugees. (13; p. 390)

settlement process The steps taken by a recent immigrant to become a full-fledged member of a new country or society. The process typically involves three stages: acclimatization, adaptation, and integration. (13; p. 373)

settlement programs Federal initiatives designed to help recent immigrants and refugees quickly become established, self-sufficient, and contributing members of Canadian society. (13; p. 375)

settlement service-provider organizations (SSPOs) Government-funded organizations in the public or private sector that deliver a settlement program. (13; p. 375)

settlement workers Professional helpers who deliver settlement programs or services to recent immigrants or refugees on behalf of government. (13; p. 390)

shelter poverty A situation in which a disproportionate amount of a person's income is spent on rent, leaving little money for other necessities. (9; p. 246)

social action Collective, coordinated, and grassroots efforts that aim to eliminate a social problem, correct an injustice, or meet a human need by influencing those with power (such as politicians) to change certain policies, laws, or procedures, or reform social institutions that are deemed inadequate. (8; p. 229)

social agencies Formally structured organizations in the public and voluntary sectors whose main objective is to meet human needs. (6; p. 148)

social assistance The income security program of last resort that gives cash and subsidized social services to individuals and families who are unable to adequately meet their needs, and who have exhausted all other means of support. Originally known as public relief; commonly known as welfare. (9; p. 253)

social casework A social work approach to practice that involves a scientific, step-by-step method to helping individuals. (8; p. 210)

social citizenship A concept that promotes an equal access to services and minimum levels of health, education, and personal well-being as a right by virtue of being a citizen. (3; p. 71)

social conditions Circumstances that exist for large segments of the population and are not problematic in and of themselves but have the potential to become social issues or social problems. Examples include divorce and high density housing. (2; p. 32)

social connectedness A term used to describe both the quality and the number of connections a person has with other people. (11; p. 313)

social deficit A theory that emphasizes an excess of social and economic liabilities—such as poverty, unmet human potential, and limited opportunities—relative to social and economic assets. (4; p. 105)

social democracy A political ideology that rejects the competitive values of capitalism, individualism, and private enterprise; encourages cooperation among citizens; and supports governments that use their powers to equalize social and economic conditions. (1; p. 21)

social economy A community-based or grassroots sector that is entrepreneurial yet nonprofit in nature, has strong ties to the voluntary sector, and aims to improve conditions for disadvantaged groups. (5; p. 122)

social economy enterprises Organizations within the social economy that are run like businesses, are often staffed by a mix of paid employees and volunteers, produce goods and services for the market, and apply their profits toward the achievement of social or environmental goals. (5; p. 144)

social exclusion The process of blocking an individual's participation in or integration into society; excluded people tend to feel alienated, marginalized, or unaccepted by the mainstream society. (2, 9; pp. 33, 239)

social financing A method of money management that relies on the private rather than the public sector to fund social welfare programs and other public benefit initiatives. (5, p. 138)

social group work A social work approach directed toward a specific small group of people who have compatible needs or lifestyles, are dealing with a common issue, or are working toward similar personal goals. (8; p. 213)

social housing Government-subsidized rental housing aimed at keeping rent at affordable levels for low-income earners. (11; p. 318)

social impact bond A contract between government and private sector organizations whereby a private investor pays the costs of a social initiative and then receives a bonus if the service provider (usually a voluntary agency) achieves certain social outcomes. (5; p. 138)

social inclusion A social goal that is achieved when citizens gain full and equal participation in the economic, social, cultural, and political dimensions of society. (1; p. 26)

social innovation The development and implementation of new ideas, concepts, and strategies to solve social problems. (6; p. 172)

social insurance A government-sponsored forced savings plan that requires working individuals to contribute to a program that then compensates them when they are not working; the claimant's contributions determine the amount of benefits available. Examples include Employment Insurance and the Canada/Quebec Pension Plans. Also called contributory programs. (3; p. 72)

social investment approach A set of strategies that focus on preventing rather than reacting to social problems, fostering social inclusion and participation, and designing social welfare programs in a way that will yield long-term benefits. (1; p. 26)

social isolation A lack of human contact that may lead to physical, psychological, or other difficulties. (11; p. 313)

social issue A social condition that is not problematic but has the potential to become so if not addressed promptly. An example is an aging population. (2; p. 32)

social knowledge A body of information, data, research results, and practice knowledge that is used to understand and address social conditions and social problems. (2; p. 34)

social minimum A reasonable standard of living or quality of life that can be subjectively measured by social norms or objectively measured by the average real gross domestic product (GDP) per person. (1, 3; pp. 11, 80)

social movements Organized, large-scale, collective efforts aimed at achieving identified social goals. Examples include the labour reform movement, the child welfare movement, and the disability rights movement. (3; p. 71)

social planning A model of community change that involves a rational, formal, and technical problem-solving procedure led by expert (professional) planners. (8; p. 228)

social policy A plan or guideline developed and used by government to create, maintain, or change living conditions to make them conducive to people's health and well-being. Examples include social welfare policy, healthcare policy, and education policy. (2; p. 30)

social policymakers Appointed or elected government officials who create the laws, legislation, and policies related to social programs. (2; p. 31)

social problem A condition in society that creates a measurable degree of social hardship, psychological or physical injury, or other negative consequence for a large segment of the population, and that people are concerned about and want changed. (2; p. 32)

social program A government-sponsored initiative consisting of services, benefits, or activities that aim to improve human welfare or meet a social need. Canada's three main social programs are social welfare, healthcare, and postsecondary education. (1; p. 11)

social safety net An informal term that refers to the collection of publicly funded programs designed to protect people from the negative consequences of natural disasters, personal crises, health problems, and other hardships. (1; p. 22)

social security The protection of individuals and families from socially recognized conditions (such as unemployment) that hinder people's ability to meet basic human needs; the protection may come from various sources, including employment and "cradle-to-grave" public programs. (3; p. 79)

social services Non-income and intangible benefits that aim to enhance social functioning and general well-being for individuals, families, and small groups; sometimes called transfers-in-kind because they are given to individuals and families in lieu of cash transfer payments. (1; p. 12)

social service workers People who have been trained—usually at the college level—as generalist social workers and have reached a certain level of competence in basic social work methods, values, and ethics. Also referred to as paraprofessionals or other titles, such as human service workers. (7; p. 186)

social welfare A concept, field, or system that is concerned with individual and collective well-being; that helps people meet their basic social and economic needs; and that prevents, reduces, or alleviates social problems. (1; p. 4)

social welfare policy A type of public policy and social policy that provides the direction for most income security programs and social services. (2; p. 30)

social welfare program A set of projects, activities, or initiatives that aim to enhance the well-being of society and meet a public need. Examples include income security programs, social services, and social research. Programs may or may not have a service component. (1; p. 10)

social work A profession dedicated to helping individuals, groups, and communities strengthen their skills, abilities, and capacity for the purpose of enhancing well-being. (7; p. 180)

social workers People officially recognized by a provincial or territorial social work association or college to practise the profession of social work. (7; p. 180)

spousal abuse A form of family violence committed by one marital or common-law partner against the other; includes physical abuse, sexual assault or exploitation, emotional abuse, criminal harassment or stalking, economic or financial abuse, and spiritual abuse. Spousal abuse may occur in opposite-sex and same-sex couples. (10; p. 285)

stakeholders People, groups, or organizations (including governments) that have a vested interest in a specific issue or organization. (2; p. 39)

stepfamily A family that comprises at least one biological or adopted child of a spouse or common-law partner from a previous union, or has at least one child from a previous union and one or more children in the current union. (10; p. 283)

strategic framework An internal structure used by social agencies to describe their priorities and how they plan to achieve their ultimate goal, mission, and vision. (6; p. 155)

strengths-based approach A social work practice that focuses on the inherent strengths, capabilities, and resources of an individual, a family, a group, or a community; assumes that people can learn and find their own solutions; and respects people's right to self-determination. (10; p. 295)

structural poverty A theory that attributes the incidence of poverty to certain structural flaws in the social, economic, political, or other macro system. (9; p. 252)

structural social work One of the many anti-oppressive social work models that focus on changing the organizations that employ them to improve conditions for clients and staff. (8; p. 221)

summative evaluation A formal assessment that measures the end results of a planned change process. (8; p. 221)

supportive housing A living arrangement for seniors or people with disabilities that offers a private living space combined with a certain level of care; includes congregate housing and assisted living facilities. (11; p. 319)

SWOT analysis An in-depth look at an agency's internal strengths and weaknesses, and its external opportunities and threats. (6; p. 157)

systemic change An approach to organizational change that occurs in all aspects or levels of an organization, usually involving the modification of an agency's policies, procedures, and practices. (8; p. 220)

T

targeted cash transfers Financial benefits that government transfers to individuals whose income or assets fall below a certain threshold. Examples include the Guaranteed Income Supplement, social assistance, and disability pensions. (1; p. 11)

targeted programs Income security programs or social services for specific segments of the population deemed vulnerable, disadvantaged, or at risk of certain social or economic hardships. (1; p. 13)

target population A segment of the population for whom a program or service is intended; often includes people who are identified as being vulnerable, disadvantaged, or at risk of certain hardships. (6; p. 156)

tax relief measures Credits, deductions, and other claims a taxpayer can make on his or her income tax returns that lower the amount of tax that individual has to pay. (1; p. 12)

tertiary prevention Activities that aim to reduce the negative effects of personal or social problems that have become chronic or complex; also known as treatment. (6; p. 159)

traditional approaches (to helping) Aboriginal ways of seeing and intervening in personal and social problems; processes of healing that are shaped by a holistic view of human needs and problems; methods that emphasize the participation of individuals in their own healing process. (12; p. 344)

transnational corporation A multinational company that is registered or operates in more than one country or manages production or delivers services in more than one country. (Appendix B; p. 446)

treaties (Indian) Constitutionally recognized, written agreements between the Government of Canada and Aboriginal groups that outline obligations and benefits for both parties. (12; p. 337)

U

underemployed A term that describes people who are not working as much as they could or want to, or whose skills exceed those required for the job they have. (9; p. 255)

undeserving poor A nineteenth-century social label that referred to able-bodied, unemployed people who were capable of supporting themselves through paid labour and were thus unworthy of government assistance. (1; p. 23)

unemployment rate A statistic that reports on the proportion of the workforce that is not working but is actively looking for and available for work. (9; p. 254)

universal cash transfers Income security programs provided to all persons, regardless of financial status or need, who meet a basic requirement, such as age or residency. One example is the Universal Child Care Benefit. (1; p. 11)

universal programs Government benefits available to all Canadians as a matter of right, regardless of economic status or need. (1; p. 15)

unpaid caregivers Adult relatives, spouses, friends, neighbours, or other informal helpers who provide assistance to dependent people (usually with chronic health conditions or disabilities) without monetary reimbursement. (7; p. 198)

V

value statements Parts of an organization's strategic framework that reflect the organization's core ideology. (6; p. 158)

visible minorities Non-Aboriginal people whose race is not Caucasian. (13; p. 366)

vision statement Part of an organization's strategic framework that describes the organization's image of an ideal community and what the organization intends to achieve. (6; p. 158)

voluntary sector A segment of the private sector comprising non-governmental organizations that fulfill a social purpose and deliver programs on a nonprofit basis. Also called the charitable, independent, or third sector. (5; p. 122)

voluntary social agencies Nonprofit organizations in the private sector that provide one or more social services, often on behalf of government; many of these agencies are registered charities. (5, 6; pp. 127, 149)

W

welfare states Nations whose governments intervene in the workings of the market through income redistribution to correct the problem of income inequality. Sometimes called social welfare states. (1; p. 24)

welfare state retrenchment Actions by government to curb the costs of social welfare programs by reducing or eliminating programs. (4; p. 92)

welfare wall A characteristic of welfare systems that inadvertently makes social assistance more financially attractive than employment. (9; p. 253)

welfare-to-work programs Provincial and territorial government initiatives designed to move welfare recipients off social assistance by making them work or train in exchange for benefits. Sometimes called "workfare." (4; p. 104)

workhouses In colonial times, institutions built with public funds in which able-bodied unemployed people were expected to learn good work habits and pay for their keep through labour. Also known as houses of industry. (3; p. 68)

working poor A portion of the employed population that earns more than half its income from employment and yet does not earn enough to stay out of poverty. (3, 9; pp. 84, 255)

Y

youth engagement approach A method used to reduce risk-taking behaviours among youth by enabling their participation in meaningful and empowering activities. (10; p. 278)

youth policy A plan of action developed by a government in response to an issue or a need related to older children or young adults. Note: the age parameters of youth vary by jurisdiction. (10; p. 276)

REFERENCES

The number in parentheses at the end of the reference refers to the chapter containing the citation.

Abele, F. (2004). *Urgent need, serious opportunity: Towards a new social model for Canada's Aboriginal peoples* (CPRN Social Architecture Papers, Research Report F39, Family Network). Retrieved from http://www.cprn.org/download.cfm?doc=569&file=28340_en.pdf&format=pdf&l=en (12)

Aboriginal Affairs and Northern Development Canada. (2010). *Backgrounder—Update of the Community Well-Being (CWB) Index.* Retrieved from http://www.aadnc-aandc.gc.ca/eng/1100100016582/1100100016583 (12)

Aboriginal Affairs and Northern Development Canada. (2012a). *Fact sheet: Aboriginal self-government.* Retrieved from http://www.aadnc-aandc.gc.ca/eng/1100100016293/1100100016294 (12)

Aboriginal Affairs and Northern Development Canada. (2012b). *Income Assistance Program—Background.* Retrieved from http://www.aadnc-aandc.gc.ca/eng/1334589796211/1334589859785 (12)

Aboriginal Affairs and Northern Development Canada. (2012c). *First Nation Child and Family Services Program—Questions and answers.* Retrieved from http://www.aadnc-aandc.gc.ca/eng/1334326697754/1334326744598 (12)

Aboriginal Affairs and Northern Development Canada. (2012d). *Better outcomes for First Nation Children: Aboriginal Affairs and Northern Development Canada's role as a funder in First Nation child and family services.* Retrieved from http://www.aadnc-aandc.gc.ca/DAM/DAM-INTER-HQ/STAGING/texte-text/cfsd1_1100100035211_eng.pdf (12)

Aboriginal Healing Foundation. (2008). *The Aboriginal Healing Foundation: Summary points of the AHF final report.* Retrieved from http://www.fadg.ca/downloads/rapport-final-eng.pdf (12)

Aboriginal Healing Foundation. (2012). *Funded projects.* Retrieved from http://www.ahf.ca/funded-projects (12)

Abramovitz, M. (2004). Definition and functions of social welfare policy: Setting the stage for social change. In J. Blau & M. Abramovitz (Eds.), *The dynamics of social welfare policy* (pp. 19–55). New York, NY: Oxford University Press. (2)

Adamson, P. (2008). *The child care transition* (Innocenti Report Card 8). Retrieved from UNICEF Innocenti Research Centre website: http://www.unicef-irc.org/publications/pdf/rc8_eng.pdf (10)

Adamson, P. (2012). *Measuring child poverty: New league tables of child poverty in the world's rich countries* (Innocenti Report Card 10). Retrieved from UNICEF Innocenti Research Centre website: http://www.unicef.ca/sites/default/files/imce_uploads/DISCOVER/OUR%20WORK/ADVOCACY/DOMESTIC/POLICY%20ADVOCACY/DOCS/unicefreportcard10-eng.pdf (10)

Adoption Council of Canada. (2012). *Myths and realities.* Retrieved from http://www.adoption.ca/myths-and-realities (10)

Affiliation of Multicultural Societies and Services Agencies of BC. (2011). Family dynamics. *ANCIE Bulletin* (February). Retrieved from http://www.amssa.org/files/CulturesWest/CulturesWestWinter2011-12.pdf (13)

Affiliation of Multicultural Societies and Services Agencies of BC. (2012). Mind busters quiz. *Cultures West, 29*(2), 7. Retrieved from http://www.amssa.org/files/CulturesWest/CulturesWestWinter2011-12.pdf (13)

Ahmed, I. (2006). *On the front lines of Toronto's community service sector: Improving working conditions and ensuring quality services.* Retrieved from Social Planning Toronto webste: http://socialplanningtoronto.org/wp-content/uploads/2009/01/on-the-front-lines_community-sector_july-2006.pdf (5, 7)

Alberta. Ministry of Human Services. (2011). *Income support.* Retrieved from http://humanservices.alberta.ca/financial-support/689.html (9)

Alzheimer Society of Canada. (2012a). *Facts about dementia.* Retrieved from http://www.alzheimer.ca/en/About-dementia/Dementias/What-is-dementia/Facts-about-dementia (11)

Alzheimer Society of Canada. (2012b). *Alzheimer's disease.* Retrieved from http://www.alzheimer.ca/en/About-dementia/Dementias/Alzheimer-s-disease (11)

Ambert, M. A. (2006). *One-parent families: Characteristics, causes, consequences, and issues.* Retrieved from Vanier Institute of the Family website: http://www.vanierinstitute.ca/include/get.php?nodeid=1147 (10)

American Psychological Association. (2012). *Making stepfamilies work.* Retrieved from http://www.apa.org/helpcenter/stepfamily.aspx (10)

Amoroso, J. (2010). From women to children: Reframing child care in Canada. *Queen's Policy Review, 1*(1). Retrieved from http://www.cccabc.bc.ca/res/pdf/From_women_to_children.pdf (10)

Angus Reid. (2012, January 31). *Canadians are divided on the actual effect of immigration.* Retrieved from http://www.angus-reid.com/polls/44322/canadians-are-divided-on-the-actual-effect-of-immigration/ (13)

Annan, K. (2002). *Secretary General, accepting Moscow award, says strength of Russian spirit "is your country's greatest natural asset."* UN Press Release SG/SM/826205/06/2002. Retrieved from http://www.un.org/News/Press/docs/2002/sgsm8262.doc.htm (Appendix B)

Antony, W., Black, E., Frankel, S., Henley, D., Hudson, P., Land, W., . . . Tychonick, R. (2007). *The state of public services in Manitoba, 2007: Privatization: The public service Trojan horse.* Retrieved from Canadian Centre for Policy Alternatives website: http://www.policyalternatives.ca/sites/default/files/uploads/publications/Manitoba_Pubs/2007/State_of_Public_Services_2007.pdf (5)

Armitage, A. (2003). *Social welfare in Canada* (4th ed.). Don Mills, Canada: Oxford University Press. (3)

Ashley, N. (2000). Beyond Maslow: Asset building with people whose basic needs are not met or who are in crisis. *Heliogram, 3*(1). Retrieved from http://www.heliotropeseattle.com/wp-content/files/newsletters/HeliogramSummer2000.pdf (1)

Assembly of First Nations. (2007a). *First Nations child and family services—Questions and answers.* Retrieved from http://64.26.129.156/article.asp?id=3372 (10)

Assembly of First Nations. (2007b). *Sustaining the caregiving cycle: First Nations people and aging: A report from the Assembly of First Nations to the Special Senate Committee on Aging, May 2007.* Retrieved from http://64.26.129.156/misc/SCC.pdf (12)

AuCoin, K. (2005). Children and youth as victims of violent crime. *Juristat, 25*(1). Retrieved from Statistics Canada website: http://www.statcan.gc.ca/pub/85-002-x/85-002-x2005001-eng.pdf (10)

August, R. (2006). Community social services. In *The encyclopedia of Saskatchewan.* Retrieved from Canadian Plains Research Center, University of Regina website: http://esask.uregina.ca/entry/community_social_services.html (5)

Aycan, Z., & Berry, J. W. (1996). Impact of employment-related experiences on immigrants' psychological well-being and adaptation to Canada. *Canadian Journal of Behavioural Science, 28*(3), 240–251. (13)

B.C.–Alberta Social Economy Research Alliance. (n.d.). *What is the social economy?* Retrieved from http://www.socialeconomy-bcalberta.ca/social-economy/ (5)

Baker, L., & Cunningham, A. (2005). *Learning to listen, learning to help: Understanding woman abuse and its effects on children.* Retrieved from Centre for Children and Families in the Justice System website: http://www.lfcc.on.ca/learning_to_listen.pdf (2)

Bank of Montreal. (2012, October 11). *BMO study—Canadians believe people with disabilities are victims of hiring bias.* Retrieved from http://newsroom.bmo.com/press-releases/bmo-study-canadians-believe-people-with-disabilit-tsx-bmo-201210110825216001 (14)

Banting, K. G. (1987). Visions of the welfare state. In S. B. Seward (Ed.), *The future of social welfare systems in Canada and the United Kingdom: Proceedings of a Canada/UK Colloquium, October 17–18, 1986, Ottawa/Meech Lake* (pp. 147–63). Halifax, Canada: Institute for Research on Public Policy. (3)

Battle, K. (2006). *The choice in child care allowance: What you see is not what you get.* Retrieved from Caledon Institute of Social Policy website: http://www.caledoninst.org/Publications/PDF/564ENG.pdf (1)

Battle, K., & Torjman, S. (2001). *The post–welfare state in Canada: Income testing and inclusion.* Retrieved from Caledon Institute of Social Policy website: http://www.caledoninst.org/PDF/894598814.pdf (4)

Battle, K., Torjman, S., & Mendelson, M. (2006). *Finding common ground on child care.* Retrieved from Caledon Institute of Social Policy website: http://www.caledoninst.org/Publications/PDF/572ENG.pdf (4)

BC Centre for Safe Schools and Communities. (2012). *Barriers to successful integration for immigrant youth*. Retrieved from University of the Fraser Valley website: http://www.ufv.ca/media/assets/bc-centres-crim/safe-schools/factsheets/Barriers_Fact_Sheet_English.pdf (13)

Beiser, M. (1999). *Strangers at the gate: The "'boat people's'" first ten years in Canada*. Toronto, Canada: University of Toronto Press. (13)

Beland, D., & Lecours, A. (2008). *Nationalism and social policy: The politics of territorial solidarity*. New York, NY: Oxford University Press. (2)

Bélanger, C. (2006). *Quebec history: Why did Canadian immigration policy change after 1945?* Retrieved from Marianopolis College website: http://faculty.marianopolis.edu/c.belanger/QuebecHistory/readings/Whytheimmogrationpolicychangedafter1945.html (13)

Bellamy, D. (1965). Social welfare in Canada. In *Encyclopedia of social work* (15th ed., pp. 36–48). New York, NY: National Association of Social Workers. (3)

Bellemare, D. (1993). The history of economic insecurity. In *Family security in insecure times* (pp. 57–86). Ottawa, Canada: National Forum on Family Security. (3)

Bendall, L. (2008, May 2). Attitudes towards children with disabilities need improvement, parents say. *CBC News*. Retrieved from http://www.cbc.ca/health/story/2008/05/02/fhealth-specialneeds.html (14)

Bennett, D. (2012). *Vancouver man sues city over ticketing of homeless people*. Retrieved from Pivot Legal Society website: http://www.pivotlegal.org/vancouver_man_sues_city_over_ticketing_of_homeless_people (2)

Bibby, R. (2004–2005). Future families project: A survey of Canadián hopes and dreams. *Transition Magazine, 34*(4), 3–14. Retrieved from http://www.vanierinstitute.ca/include/get.php?nodeid=432 (10)

Blackstock, C., Cross, T., George, J., Brown, I., & Formsma, J. (2006). *Reconciliation in child welfare: Touchstones of hope for indigenous children, youth, and families*. Retrieved from http://www.reconciliationmovement.org/docs/Touchstones_of_Hope.pdf (12)

Blake, R. B. (2009). *From rights to needs: A history of Family Allowances in Canada, 1929–92*. Vancouver, Canada: UBC Press. (3)

Bliss, M. (1975). Preface. In L. Marsh (Ed.), *Report on social security for Canada* (pp. ix–x). Toronto, Canada: University of Toronto Press. (3)

Block, P. (1996). *Stewardship: Choosing service over self interest*. San Francisco, CA: Berrett-Koehler. (8)

Board of Trustees of Michigan State University. (2000). *Best practice briefs, No. 9: 1998–1999*. Retrieved from http://outreach.msu.edu/bpbriefs/issues/brief9.pdf (6)

Bornstein, L., & Bornstein, M. (2009) Parenting styles and child social development. *Canada's Children, 16*(2), 10–14. Retreived from http://www.cwlc.ca/sites/default/files/file/Canada%27s%20Children/CC%20SUMMER%202009.pdf (10)

Bothwell, R., Drummond, I. A., & English, J. (1989). *Canada since 1945: Power, politics, and provincialism* (2nd ed.). Toronto, Canada: University of Toronto Press. (11)

Bourque, C. (2012). *Everyone wins when client service includes accessibility.* Retrieved from Human Resources, University of Ottawa website: http://www.hr.uottawa.ca/hrinfo/2012/03/accessibility.php (14)

Boychuk, G. (2004). *The Canadian social model: The logics of policy development* (CPRN Social Architecture Papers, Research Report F/36: Family Network). Retrieved from Canadian Policy Research Networks website: http://www.cprn.org/documents/26085_en.pdf (1)

Boyer, Y. (2006). *Discussion paper series in Aboriginal health—Legal issues, No. 4: First Nations, Métis, and Inuit women's health.* Retrieved from National Aboriginal Health Organization website: http://www.naho.ca/documents/naho/english/publications/DP_womens_health.pdf (12)

Bradford, N. (2003). *Cities and communities that work: Innovative practices, enabling policies.* Retrieved from http://www.urbancentre.utoronto.ca/pdfs/elibrary/CPRNcitieswork.pdf (8)

Brasfield, C. R. (2001). Residential school syndrome. *BC Medical Journal, 43*(2), 78–81. Retrieved from http://www.bcmj.org/article/residential-school-syndrome (12)

Bredin Institute. (2006). *Cultural diversity in the workplace.* Retrieved September 1, 2008, from http://www.bredin.ab.ca/ImmigrantServices/Employment%20Preparation/Cultural%20Diversity%20in%20the%20Workplace.aspx (6)

Brewster, S., Buckley, M., Cox, P., & Griep, L. (2002, April). *Diversity education research project: A literature review. Retrieved from Alberta Justice and Solicitor General website:* http://justice.alberta.ca/programs_services/humanrights/pubsandresources/Documents/LiteratureReview.pdf (8)

Briggs, A. (1961). The welfare state in historical perspective. *European Journal of Sociology II*(2), 221–258. (1)

British Columbia Schizophrenia Society. (2005). *Family peer support buddy program: Families of persons with a mental illness helping one another. Coordinator's guide.* Retrieved from http://www.bcss.org/wp-content/uploads/2007/06/familysupport-buddycoordinatorsguide.pdf (7)

British Columbia. Provincial Health Services Authority. (2012). *Indigenous cultural competency training.* Retrieved from http://www.culturalcompetency.ca/training (12)

British Columbia. Work Futures. (2011). *BC Work Futures, Community and social service workers (NOC 4212): Employment prospects.* Retrieved from https://www.workbc.ca/Careers/Career-Profiles/Pages/Community-and-Social-Service-Workers-4212-page5.aspx (7)

Broadbent Institute. (2012a). *Towards a more equal Canada.* Retrieved from http://www.broadbentinstitute.ca/sites/default/files/documents/towards_a_more_equal_canada.pdf (4)

Broadbent Institute. (2012b). *Equality project*. Retrieved from http://www.
broadbentinstitute.ca/sites/default/files/documents/equality-project_0.pdf (4)

Broadbent, E. (2001). Ten propositions about equality and democracy. In E.
Broadbent (Ed.), *Democratic equality: What went wrong?* (pp. 3–13). Toronto,
Canada: University of Toronto Press. (3)

Brock, K., Brook, D., Elliott, J., & LaForest, R. (2003). *Globalization and the
voluntary sector in Canada: An exploratory study by the Public Policy Forum
and the Queen's School of Policy Studies*. Retrieved from Public Policy Forum
website: http://www.ppforum.ca/sites/default/files/globalization_voluntary_
sector.pdf (5)

Brodie, J., & Bakker, I. (2007) *Canada's social policy regime and women: An assessment of the last decade*. Retrieved from Status of Women Canada archive
website: http://epe.lac-bac.gc.ca/100/200/301/swc-cfc/canadas_social-e/SW21-
156-2007E.pdf (4)

Brooks, N., & Hwong, T. (2006). *The social benefits and economic costs of taxation:
A comparison of high- and low-tax countries*. Retrieved from Canadian Centre
for Policy Alternatives website: http://www.policyalternatives.ca/sites/default/
files/uploads/publications/National_Office_Pubs/2006/Benefits_and_Costs_of_
Taxation.pdf (4)

Buckland, L., Jackson, A., Roberts, P., & Smith, P. (2001). *Structural and systemic factors
contributing to homelessness in Canada: An analysis of research gaps and proposed
research directions*. Retrieved from http://homeless.samhsa.gov/ResourceFiles/
Structural&Systemic_Fctrs_Contributing_to_Homelessnes.pdf (9)

Buckley, M. (2005, November). *Litigating section 15: The path to substantive equality in
charter adjudication*. Retrieved from http://www.20years.ca/Buckley-Litigating_s_15_
Nov_7_2005-withrevs-2.pdf (2)

Calgary Chamber of Voluntary Organizations. (2006). *Financing voluntary and
nonprofit organizations in Alberta: A report on the Alberta Regional Finance Action
Group*. Retrieved from http://www.calgarycvo.org/sites/default/files/resources/
RegionalFinanceActionGroupSummaryReport2006_0.pdf (5)

Campaign 2000. (2010). *Report card on child and family poverty in Canada,
1989–2010*. Retrieved from http://www.campaign2000.ca/reportCards/national/
2010EnglishC2000NationalReportCard.pdf (9)

Campaign 2000. (2011). *2011 Report card on child and family poverty in Canada*.
Retrieved from http://www.campaign2000.ca/reportCards/national/
2011EnglishRreportCard.pdf (9)

Campbell, C. (2003). *Anti-oppressive social work: Promoting equity and social justice*.
Retrieved from Anti-oppressive Social Work website: http://aosw.socialwork.dal.ca/
whatisaosw.html#principles (9)

Canada Co-operatives Secretariat, Co-operatives Policy and Research Team.
(2010). *Discussion Paper: Towards 2012: Building a conducive environment*

for co-operatives: Policy forum on co-operatives: Discussion paper. Retrieved May 24, 2012, from http://www.coop.gc.ca/COOP/display-afficher. do?id=1284054567395&lang=eng (8)

Canada Mortgage and Housing Corporation. (2012a). *Government assisted housing.* Retrieved from http://cmhc.beyond2020.com/HiCODefinitions_EN.html#_Core_ Housing_Need_Status (9)

Canada Mortgage and Housing Corporation. (2012b). *Housing for older Canadians: The definitive guide to the over 55 market: Volume 1, understanding the market.* Retrieved from http://www.cmhc-schl.gc.ca/odpub/pdf/67514.pdf (11)

Canada Mortgage and Housing Corporation. (2013). *FAQs, Affordable housing.* Retrieved from http://www.cmhc-schl.gc.ca/en/corp/faq/faq_002.cfm#4 (9)

Canada Without Poverty. (2012a). *Human rights and international law.* Retrieved from http://www.cwp-csp.ca/human-rights-and-international-law/ (2)

Canada Without Poverty. (2012b). *About.* Retrieved from http://www.cwp-csp.ca/ about-us (8)

Canada. (2004a). *National homelessness initiative: About the initiative.* Retrieved from Collections Canada website: http://www.collectionscanada.gc.ca/webar-chives/ 20060205140104/http://www21.hrdc-drhc.gc.ca/initiative/index_e. asp (6)

Canada. (2004b). *A Canada fit for children: Canada's plan of action in response to the May 2002 United Nations special session on children.* Retrieved from Government of Canada Publications website: http://publications.gc.ca/collections/Collection/ SD13-4-2004E.pdf (10)

Canada. (2004c). *Speech from the Throne to open the third session of the 37th Parliament of Canada.* Retrieved from http://www.pco-bcp.gc.ca/index.asp?lang=eng&page= information&sub=publications&doc=aarchives/sft-ddt/2004_1-eng.htm (12)

Canada. (2005). *Government response to "Eighth report of the Standing Committee on Human Resources, Skills Development, Social Development and the Status of Persons with Disabilities, Accessibility for All."* Retrieved from Collections Canada website: http://www.collectionscanada.gc.ca/ webarchives/20060126154655/http://www.sdc.gc.ca/en/isp/pub/cpp/ disability/8threport/8threport.pdf (14)

Canada. (2010). *Speech from the Throne.* Retrieved from http://www.speech.gc.ca/ eng/media.asp?id=1388 (5)

Canada. (2011). *National Child Benefit: A unique partnership of the Government of Canada, Provinces and Territories and First Nations.* Retrieved from http:// www.nationalchildbenefit.ca/eng/06/ncb.shtml (10)

Canada. (2012a). *Speaking points for the Honourable Diane Finley to launch the National Call for Concepts for social finance at the 5th annual Social Finance Forum.* Retrieved from http://news.gc.ca/web/article-eng.do?nid=705509 (4)

Canada. (2012b). *Budget 2012: Annex 4: Tax measures: Supplementary information, notices of ways and means motions and draft amendments to various GST/HST regulations.* Retrieved from http://www.budget.gc.ca/2012/plan/anx4-eng.html#OTM2 (5)

Canada. (2013). *Harper government provides continued tax relief in 2013.* Retrieved from http://actionplan.gc.ca/en/news/harper-government-provides-continued-tax-relief (4)

Canada. Department of Finance. (1995). *Budget in brief.* Ottawa, Canada: Author. Retrieved from http://www.fin.gc.ca/budget95/binb/brief.pdf (4)

Canada. Department of Finance. (2000). *Economic statement and budget update: Overview.* Retrieved from http://www.fin.gc.ca/ec2000/pdf/overe.pdf (4)

Canada. Department of Finance. (2003). *Budget 2003: Annex 5: Fiscal performance of Canada's federal-provincial-territorial government sector.* Retrieved from http://fin.gc.ca/budget03/bp/bpa5-eng.asp (4)

Canada. Department of Finance. (2009). *Canada's economic plan.* Retrieved from http://www.budget.gc.ca/2009/pdf/budget-planbugetaire-eng.pdf (4)

Canada. Department of Finance. (2010). *Ensuring the ongoing strength of Canada's retirement income system.* Retrieved from http://www.fin.gc.ca/activty/consult/retirement-eng.asp#background (11)

Canada. Department of Finance. (2011a). *Canada social transfer.* Retrieved from http://www.fin.gc.ca/fedprov/cst-eng.asp (2)

Canada. Department of Finance. (2011b). *Equalization program.* Retrieved from http://www.fin.gc.ca/fedprov/eqp-eng.asp (2)

Canada. Department of Finance. (2011c). *Territorial formula financing.* Retrieved from http://www.fin.gc.ca/fedprov/tff-eng.asp (2)

Canada. Department of Justice. (2006). *Child abuse: A fact sheet from the Department of Justice Canada.* Retrieved from Government of Canada Publications website: http://publications.gc.ca/collections/Collection/J2-295-2002E.pdf (10)

Canada. Department of National Health and Welfare. (1970). *Income security for Canadians* Ottawa, Canada: Queen's Printer. (3)

Canada. Federal-Provincial-Territorial Council of Ministers on Social Policy Renewal. (1999). *A national children's agenda: Developing a shared vision.* Ottawa, Canada: Author. (10)

Canada. Treasury Board Secretariat. (2010). *Results-based management lexicon.* Retrieved from http://www.tbs-sct.gc.ca/cee/pubs/lex-eng.asp (2)

Canadian Association for Retired Persons. (2011). *Age-centred poll report.* Retrieved from http://www.carp.ca/o/pdf/age%20centred%20report.pdf (11)

Canadian Association for Retired Persons. (2012). *Briefing on elder abuse.* Retrieved from http://www.carp.ca/wp-content/uploads/2012/01/Elder-Abuse-Brief-Jan-2012.pdf (11)

Canadian Association of Community Living. (2012). *Close institutions in Canada*. Retrieved from http://www.cacl.ca/action/campaigns/institution-watch (14)

Canadian Association of Paediatric Health Centres, National Infant, Child, and Youth Mental Health Consortium Advisory, and Provincial Centre of Excellence for Child and Youth Mental Health at CHEO. (2010). *Access & wait times in child and youth mental health: A background paper*. Retrieved from http://www.excellenceforchildandyouth.ca/sites/default/files/policy_access_ and_wait_times.pdf (10)

Canadian Association of Social Workers. (1998). *CASW statement on preventive practices and health promotion*. Retrieved February 14, 2009, from http:// www.casw-acts.ca/practice/recpubsart3.html (8)

Canadian Association of Social Workers. (2004). *The impacts of working conditions on social workers and their practice: A CASW review of current literature*. Ottawa, Canada: Author. (7)

Canadian Association of Social Workers. (2005). *Code of ethics*. Retrieved from http://casw-acts.ca/sites/default/files/attachements/CASW_ Code%20of%20Ethics.pdf (7)

Canadian Association of Social Workers. (2008). *Social work scope of practice*. Retrieved from http://www.casw-acts.ca/sites/default/files/attachements/ Scope%20of%20Practice_August_08_E_Final.pdf (7, 8)

Canadian Association of Social Workers and National Association of Social Workers. (2008). *Putting poverty on the election platform: The time to eradicate poverty is now*. Retrieved from http://www.naswdc.org/pressroom/2008/101708.asp (9)

Canadian Auto Workers. (2007). *Unemployment Insurance and labour market deregulation*. Retrieved from http://www.caw.ca/en/about-the-caw-policies-and-papers-unemployment-insurance-and-labour-market-deregulation.htm (4)

Canadian CED Network. (2003). *Human capital development in Canada: Closing the gaps*. Retrieved from http://ccednet-rcdec.ca/files/human%20capital%20 FINAL%20PDF.pdf (4)

Canadian CED Network. (2008, April). Poverty hearings have begun: HUMA Committee of Parliament. *CCEDNet Newsletter: BC/Yukon*. Retrieved from http:// www.ccednet-rcdec.ca/?q=en/node/4916#huma (2)

Canadian Centre for Elder Law. (2010). *World elder abuse awareness day—June 15, 2010*. Retrieved from British Columbia Law Institute website: http://www.bcli.org/ccel/ news/2010/06/world-elder-abuse-awareness-day-june-15-2010 (11)

Canadian Child Welfare Research Portal. (2009). *Frequently asked questions*. Retrieved from http://www.cecw-cepb.ca/faqs#Q11 (12)

Canadian Coalition for the Rights of Children (2009). *Realizing the rights of children with disabilities in Canada: Working Paper*. Retrieved from http://rightsofchildren. ca/wp-content/uploads/children-with-disabilities-research-document.pdf (14)

Canadian Council for Refugees. (2000). *Canadian national settlement service standards framework*. Retrieved from http://ccrweb.ca/standards.PDF (13)

Canadian Council for Refugees. (2008). *State of refugees: An introduction to refugee and immigration issues in Canada*. Retrieved from http://ccrweb.ca/documents/state-of-refugees.pdf (13)

Canadian Council for Refugees. (2012). *Canada rolls back refugee protection: Bill C-31 receives royal assent* [Press release]. Retrieved from http://ccrweb.ca/en/bulletin/12/06/29 (13)

Canadian Economy Online. (2007). *Key economic events, 1944: Family allowance program: Supporting Canadian children*. Retrieved from http://www.canadianeconomy.gc.ca/English/economy/1944family.html (1)

Canadian Feminist Alliance for International Action. (2012). *Disappearances and murders of Aboriginal women and girls in Canada. Submission to the United Nations Committee on the Elimination of Racial Discrimination, January 2012*. Retrieved from http://fafia-afai.org/wp-content/uploads/2011/06/FAFIACERDsubmissionfinalJan252012.pdf (12)

Canadian Healthcare Association. (2012). *Respite care in Canada*. Retrieved from http://www.cha.ca/wp-content/uploads/2012/11/Respite_Care_in_Canada_EN_web.pdf (7)

Canadian Homelessness Research Network. (2012). Canadian definition of homelessness. Retrieved from the Homeless Hub website: http://www.homelesshub.ca/ResourceFiles/CHRNhomelessdefinition-1pager.pdf (9)

Canadian Index of Wellbeing. (2011). *How are Canadians really doing? Highlights: Canadian Index of Wellbeing 1.0*. Retrieved from http://ciw.ca/reports/en/Reports%20and%20FAQs/CIW-HowAreCanadiansReallyDoing-FINAL.pdf (4)

Canadian Index of Wellbeing. (2012). *How are Canadians really doing? The 2012 CIW Report*. Retrieved from University of Waterloo website: https://uwaterloo.ca/canadian-index-wellbeing/sites/ca.canadian-index-wellbeing/files/uploads/files/CIW2012-HowAreCanadiansReallyDoing-23Oct2012_0.pdf (1)

Canadian Institute for Health Information. (2010). *Supporting informal caregivers: The heart of home care*. Retrieved from https://secure.cihi.ca/free_products/Caregiver_Distress_AIB_2010_EN.pdf (7)

Canadian Institute for Health Information. (2011). *Health care in Canada, 2011: A focus on seniors and aging*. Retrieved from https://secure.cihi.ca/free_products/HCIC_2011_seniors_report_en.pdf (11)

Canadian International Development Agency. (2006). *Voluntary sector: Capacity development strategy*. Retrieved from Collections Canada website: http://www.collectionscanada.gc.ca/webarchives/20061031013655/http://www.cida.gc.ca/cidaweb/acdicida.nsf/En/NAT-6127358-FLJ (8)

Canadian Labour Congress. (2010). *International day of persons with disabilities*. Retrieved from http://www.canadianlabour.ca/sites/default/files/dec-3-2010-web-en.pdf (14)

Canadian Labour Congress. (2012). *Canadian economy falling behind in job creation: CLC President comments Statistics Canada report*. Retrieved from http://www.canadianlabour.ca/national/news/canadian-economy-falling-behind-job-creation-clc-president-comments-statistics-canada- (Appendix B)

Canadian Museum of Civilization Corporation. (2002). *The history of Canada's public pensions: 1928–1951: Demanding more*. Retrieved from http://www.civilization.ca/cmc/exhibitions/hist/pensions/1928-1951_e.pdf (3)

Canadian Museum of Civilization Corporation. (2008). *The history of Canada's public pensions: 1867–1914: Old age and poverty*. Retrieved from http://www.civilization.ca/cmc/exhibitions/hist/pensions/1867-1914_e.pdf (3)

Canadian Paediatric Society. (2012). *Caring for kids: Healthy bodies: Your child's mental health*. Retrieved from http://www.caringforkids.cps.ca/handouts/mental_health (10)

Canadian Race Relations Foundation. (2011). *A four country survey of opinion on racism and prejudice in 2010: Canada, the United States, Germany and Spain*. Retrieved from http://www.crr.ca/divers-files/en/survey/racismandprejudice-2010.pdf (13)

Canadian Resource Centre for Victims of Crime. (2006). *Child abuse: How to help victims*. Retrieved from http://www.crcvc.ca/docs/child_abuse.pdf (10)

Cappe, M. (2002). *Leadership forum awards dinner: Remarks by Mr. Mel Cappe to the Arthur Kroeger College of Public Affairs*. Retrieved from Privy Council Office website: http://www.pco-bcp.gc.ca/index.asp?lang=eng&page=clerk-greffier&sub=archives &doc=20020206-eng.htm (5)

Carniol, B. (1990). Social work and the labour movement. In B. Wharf (Ed.), *Social work and social change in Canada* (pp. 114–143). Toronto, Canada: McClelland and Stewart. (3)

Carniol, B. (2005). *Case critical: Social services and social justice in Canada* (5th ed.). Toronto, Canada: Between the Lines. (3)

Carr, R. (1996). *Peer helping: Youth working together; Information for parents, adolescents, and children*. Retrieved from Peer Systems Consulting Group website: http://www.peer.ca/broch.html (7)

Cassidy, H. M. (1943). *Social security and reconstruction in Canada*. Toronto, Canada: Ryerson Press. (3)

Centre for Suicide Prevention. (2011). *Trends in youth suicide*. Retrieved from http://suicideinfo.ca/LinkClick.aspx?fileticket=toImoDM3Bck%3d&tabid=532 (10, 12)

Centre of Excellence for Child Welfare. (2011). *Frequently asked questions*. Retrieved from Canadian Child Welfare Research Portal website: http://cwrp.ca/faqs#Q9 (10)

Centre of Excellence for Youth Engagement. (2012). *Vision*. Retrieved from http://www.engagementcentre.ca/vision.php (10)

Challinor, A. (2011). *Canada's immigration policy: A focus on human capital*. Retrieved from Migration Policy Institute website: http://www.migrationinformation.org/feature/display.cfm?ID=853 (13)

Chandler, M., & Lalonde, C. (2008). Cultural continuity as a protective factor against suicide in First Nations youth. *Horizons, 10*(1). Retrieved from Government of Canada Publications website: http://publications.gc.ca/collections/collection_2008/policyresearch/CP12-1-10-1E.pdf (12)

Chansonneuve, D. (2005). *Reclaiming connections: Understanding residential school trauma among Aboriginal people*. Retrieved from Aboriginal Healing Foundation website: http://www.ahf.ca/downloads/healing-trauma-web-eng.pdf (12)

Chappell, N. (1999). *Volunteering and healthy aging: What we know*. Ottawa, Canada: Volunteer Canada. Retrieved September 18, 2008, from Canadian Forum on Volunteering website: http://volunteer.ca/en/volcan/older-adults/canada_adults_report_printable (7)

Charter Committee on Poverty Issues. (1998). Submissions to the Committee on Economic, Social and Cultural Rights by the Charter Committee on Poverty Issues. Retrieved from Centre for Equality Rights in Accommodation website: http://www.equalityrights.org/ngoun98/ccpi.htm#part1 (4)

Chartrand, L., & McKay, C. (2006). *A review of research and criminal victimization and First Nations, Métis and Inuit peoples, 1990 to 2001*. Retrieved from Department of Justice Canada website: http://www.justice.gc.ca/eng/rp-pr/aj-ja/rr06_vic1/rr06_vic1.pdf (12)

Chinook Multimedia. (2000). *Immigrant voices: 1967–present: Overview*. Retrieved from http://www.canadianhistory.ca/iv/1967-Present/overview2.html (13)

Chrétien says he's sorry for remarks. (1994, April 22). *Calgary Herald*, p. A13. (1)

Christie, N., & Gauvreau, M. (1996). *A full-orbed Christianity: The Protestant churches and social welfare in Canada 1900–1940*. Montreal, Canada: McGill-Queens University Press. (3)

Chui, T. (2011). *Women in Canada: A gender-based statistical report: Immigrant women*. Retrieved from Statistics Canada website: http://www.statcan.gc.ca/pub/89-503-x/2010001/article/11528-eng.pdf (13)

Chui, T., Tran, K., & Maheux, H. (2007). *Immigration in Canada: A portrait of the foreign-born population, 2006 census*. Retrieved from Statistics Canada website: http://www12.statcan.ca/english/census06/analysis/immcit/pdf/97-557- XIE2006001.pdf (13)

Citizenship and Immigration Canada. (1995). *Growing together: A backgrounder on immigration and citizenship: The history of immigration*. Retrieved February 3, 2000, from http://www.cic.gc.ca/english/pub/grow/grow_00e.html (13)

Citizenship and Immigration Canada. (1998). *Building on a strong foundation for the 21st century: New directions for immigration and refugee policy and legislation*. Retrieved from Government of Canada Publications website: http://publications.gc.ca/collections/Collection/Ci51-86-1998E.pdf (13)

Citizenship and Immigration Canada. (2009). *Settlement program implementation of the modernized approach (for external stakeholders)*. Retrieved from OrgWise website: http://www.orgwise.ca/sites/osi.ocasi.org.stage/files/resources/FINAL%20-%20Modernized%20Approach%20-%20SPOs%20-%20ENGLISH%20-%202009-10-23.pdf (13)

Citizenship and Immigration Canada. (2010a). *Adapting to culture shock: Common stages of adapting to culture shock.* Retrieved from http://www.cic.gc.ca/english/newcomers/after-life-shock.asp (13)

Citizenship and Immigration Canada. (2010b). *Evaluation of the Host program.* Retrieved from http://www.cic.gc.ca/english/pdf/research-stats/2010-eval-host-eng.pdf (13)

Citizenship and Immigration Canada. (2010c). *Three more reasons the province of Manitoba is a destination of choice.* Retrieved from http://www.cicnews.com/2010/09/reasons-province-manitoba-destination-choice-09804.html (13)

Citizenship and Immigration Canada. (2010d). *Evaluation of the Welcoming Communities initiative.* Retrieved from http://www.cic.gc.ca/english/pdf/research-stats/ER201103_05E_WCI.pdf (13)

Citizenship and Immigration Canada. (2011a). *Facts and figures, 2010.* Retrieved from http://www.cic.gc.ca/english/pdf/research-stats/facts2010.pdf (13)

Citizenship and Immigration Canada. (2011b). *Evaluation of the Immigrant Settlement and Adaptation Program (ISAP).* Retrieved from http://www.cic.gc.ca/english/pdf/research-stats/evaluation-isap2011.pdf (13)

Citizenship and Immigration Canada. (2012a). *Immigrate to Canada.* Retrieved from http://www.cic.gc.ca/english/immigrate/index.asp (13)

Citizenship and Immigration Canada. (2012b). *New federal skilled worker program prepares immigrants to succeed.* Retrieved from http://www.cicnews.com/2012/09/federal-skilled-worker-program-prepares-immigrants-succeed-091788.html (13)

Citizenship and Immigration Canada. (2012c). *Backgrounder—2013 immigration levels planning: Public and stakeholder consultations.* Retrieved from http://www.cic.gc.ca/english/department/media/backgrounders/2012/2012-07-31.asp (13)

Citizenship and Immigration Canada. (2012d). *Resettlement from outside Canada.* Retrieved from http://www.cic.gc.ca/english/refugees/outside/index.asp (13)

Citizenship and Immigration Canada. (2012e). *Evaluation of the strategic plan for settlement and language training under the Canada-Ontario Immigration Agreement (COIA): 3. Evaluation findings.* Retrieved from http://www.cic.gc.ca/english/resources/evaluation/2012-coia/sec03.asp (13)

City of Ottawa. (2010). *Equity and inclusion lens: A user's guide.* Retrieved from http://ottawa.ca/sites/ottawa.ca/files/attachments/ottpage/eil_user_guide_en.pdf (2)

Cleveland, G., Corter, C., Pelletier, J., Colley, S., Bertrand, J., & Jamieson, J. (2006). *A review of the field of early childhood learning and development in child care, kindergarten and family support programs.* Retrieved from Canadian Council on Learning website: http://www.ccl-cca.ca/pdfs/StateOfField/SFREarlyChildhoodLearning.pdf (10)

Cohen, M. (2012). *Caring for BC's aging population: improving health care for all*. Retrieved from http://www.policyalternatives.ca/sites/default/files/uploads/publications/BC%20Office/2012/07/CCPABC-Caring-BC-Aging-Pop.pdf (11)

Collin, C. (2007). *Poverty reduction in Canada: The federal role*. Retrieved from Library of Parliament website: http://www.parl.gc.ca/content/LOP/ResearchPublications/prb0722-e.pdf (9)

Collin, C. (2008). *Measuring poverty: A challenge for Canada*. Retrieved from Library of Parliament website: http://www.parl.gc.ca/Content/LOP/ResearchPublications/prb0865-e.pdf (9)

Collin, C., & Jensen, H. (2009). *A statistical profile of poverty in Canada*. Retrieved from Library of Parliament website: http://www.parl.gc.ca/Content/LOP/ResearchPublications/prb0917-e.pdf (9)

Commission to Promote Sustainable Child Welfare. (2011). *Aboriginal child welfare in Ontario—A discussion Paper*. Retrieved from http://www.sustainingchildwelfare.ca/assets/Aboriginal-Child-Welfare-in-Ontario-Discussion-Paper-July-2011.pdf (12)

Committee on the Rights of the Child. (2012). *Consideration of reports submitted by States parties under article 44 of the Convention: Concluding observations: Canada*. Retrieved from http://www2.ohchr.org/english/bodies/crc/docs/co/CRC-C-CAN-CO-3-4_en.pdf (10)

Community Living Research Project. (2006). *Residential options for adults with developmental disabilities: Quality and cost outcomes: Literature and initial program review*. Retrieved from Council of Canadians with Disabilities website: http://www.ccdonline.ca/en/socialpolicy/poverty-citizenship/demographic-profile/low-household-income-and-disability (14)

Community Sector Council Newfoundland and Labrador. (2010). *Why involve youth volunteers?* Retrieved from http://communitysector.nl.ca/voluntary-sector-resources/volunteer-management/engaging-young-volunteers/why-involve-youth-voluntee (7)

Community Social Planning Council of Toronto and Family Service Association of Toronto. (2006). *On the front lines of Toronto's community service sector: Improving working conditions and ensuring quality services*. Retrieved from http://www.familyservicetoronto.org/programs/social/FrontLinesCommunitySector2006.pdf (6)

Conceptual Framework Subcommittee of the Residential Services Advisory Committee. (2002). *Working with community to support children, youth and families*. Retrieved from Legislative Assemby of British Columbia website: http://www.llbc.leg.bc.ca/public/pubdocs/bcdocs/354463/bccfd_working_with_comm_2002.pdf (6)

Conference Board of Canada. (2000). *Performance and potential 2000–2001: Seeking "Made in Canada" solutions*. Ottawa, Canada: Author. (2)

Conference Board of Canada. (2013a). *Society*. Retrieved from http://www.conferenceboard.ca/hcp/details/society.aspx (4)

Conference Board of Canada. (2013b). *Working-age poverty*. Retrieved from http://www.conferenceboard.ca/hcp/details/society/working-age-poverty.aspx (4)

Conference Board of Canada. (2013c). *Income inequality*. Retrieved from http://www.conferenceboard.ca/hcp/details/society/income-inequality.aspx (4)

Conference Board of Canada. (2013d). *How Canada performs: Child poverty*. Retrieved from http://www.conferenceboard.ca/hcp/details/society/child-poverty.aspx (9)

Conservative Party of Canada. (2012). *Taxes*. Retrieved from http://www.conservative.ca/?page_id=1416 (4)

Cooper, M., & Bartlett, D. (2008). *Toward a new funding framework and priorities for FCSS Phase I: Overview and Recommendations for Phases II and III: Summary*. Retrieved from http://www.calgary.ca/CSPS/CNS/Documents/fcss/fcss_funding_framework_consultation_paper.pdf (5)

Corak, M. (2013). Inequality from generation to generation: The United States in comparison [Online draft]. In M. Corak (Ed.), *The economics of inequality, poverty, and discrimination in the 21st century* (pp. 107–124). Retrieved from http://milescorak.files.wordpress.com/2012/01/inequality-from-generation-to-generation-the-united-states-in-comparison-v3.pdf (4)

Cottrell, B. (2008). Providing services to immigrant women in Atlantic Canada. *Our Diverse Cities*, 5(Spring), 133–137. Retrieved from http://canada.metropolis.net/pdfs/ODC_spring2008_e.pdf (13)

Council of Canadians with Disabilities. (2011). *Low household income and disability: Income sources, employment and employment discrimination*. Retrieved from Council of Canadians with Disabilities website: http://www.ccdonline.ca/en/socialpolicy/poverty-citizenship/demographic-profile/low-household-income-and-disability (14)

Council of the Federation. (2012). *Premiers announce health care innovation working group*. Retrieved from http://www.councilofthefederation.ca/pdfs/Communique_Task%20Force_Jan_17.pdf (11)

Coyle, G. L. (1959). Some basic assumptions about social group work. In M. Murphy (Ed.), *The social group work method in social work education* (Curriculum Study XI, pp. 91–100). New York, NY: Council on Social Work Education. (8)

Cranswick, K., & Dosman, D. (2008). *Eldercare: What we know today*. Retrieved from http://www.homecareontario.ca/public/docs/publications/family-caregivers/eldercare-what-we-know-today.pdf (7)

Crawford, C. (2003). *Towards a common approach to thinking about and measuring social inclusion: DRAFT?* Roeher Institute. Retrieved from http://www.ccsd.ca/events/inclusion/papers/crawford.pdf (14)

Cross, S. (1985). Professionalism: The occupational hazard of social work, 1920–1960. *The Social Worker, 53*(1), 29–33. (7)

Crossroads Christian Communications. (2013). *Homelessness in Canada*. Retrieved from http://crossroads.ca/missions/canadian/homelessness-in-canada2 (9)

Cunningham, A., & Baker, L. (2007). *Little eyes, little ears: How violence against a mother shapes children as they grow*. Retrieved from Public Health Agency of Canada website: http://www.phac-aspc.gc.ca/ncfv-cnivf/pdfs/fem-2007-LELE_e.pdf (10)

Davies, L., McMullin, J. A., Avison, W. R., & Cassidy, G. L. (2001). *Social policy, gender inequality and poverty*. Retrieved from Government of Canada Publications website: http://publications.gc.ca/collections/Collection/SW21-64-2000E.pdf (1)

Davis, B., & Tarasuk, V. (1994). Hunger in Canada. *Agriculture and Human Values, 11*, 50–57. (9)

Dean, T. (2011). *Is public service delivery obsolete? Why competition between civil servants, corporations and non-profits is good for everyone*. Retrieved from Literary Review of Canada website: http://reviewcanada.ca/essays/2011/09/01/is-public-service-delivery-obsolete/ (5)

Desjardins, D., & Cornelson, K. (2011). *Immigrant labour market outcomes in Canada: The benefits of addressing wage and employment gaps*. Retrieved from Royal Bank of Canada website: http://www.rbc.com/economics/market/pdf/immigration.pdf (13)

Detention centres no place for migrant children, critics argue. (2012). *CBC News*. Retrieved from http://www.cbc.ca/news/canada/story/2012/12/13/detention-children-canada.html (13)

Disraeli, B. (2012). Speech at Edinburgh, 29 October 1867. In A. Jay (Ed.), *The Oxford dictionary of political quotations* (4th ed.). NewYork, NY: Oxford University Press. (8)

District of Nipissing Social Services Admistration Board. (2012). *Ontario works*. Retrieved from http://www.dnssab.on.ca/ow.htm (7)

Dobelstein, A. W. (1978). Introduction: Social resources, human need, and the field of social work. In A. Fink (Ed.), *The field of social work* (7th ed., pp. 3–21). New York, NY: Holt, Rinehart & Winston. (1)

Dobelstein, A. W. (2003). *Social welfare policy and analysis* (3rd ed.). Pacific Grove, CA: Brooks/Cole-Thomson Learning. (1)

Dobie, R. (2006). *Proceedings of the Special Senate Committee on Aging: Issue 1–Evidence*. Retrieved from Parliament of Canada website: http://www.parl.gc.ca/Content/SEN/Committee/391/agei/01evb-e.htm?Language=E&Parl=39&Ses=1&comm_id=600 (11)

Dobrowolsky, A. (2003, September). *Fostering social cohesion: Social investment state/civil society interactionism: New forms of governance in Britain* (Working Paper #9). Paper presented at the Atlantic Provinces Political Studies Association Meeting, St. John's, Newfoundland. Retrieved from http://www.cccg.umontreal.ca/pdf/wp9.pdf (1)

Doe, T., & Kimpson, S. (1999, March). *Enabling income: CPP disability benefits and women with disabilities*. Ottawa, Canada: Status of Women Canada. Retrieved from Government of Canada Publications website: http://publications.gc.ca/collections/Collection/SW21-38-1999E.pdf (14)

Dorais, M. (2002). Immigration and integration through a social cohesion perspective. *Horizons, 5*(2), 4–5. Retrieved from Collections Canada website: http://www.collectionscanada.gc.ca/webarchives/20060211225806/http://www.policyresearch.gc.ca/v5n2_e.pdf (13)

Doré, N., & Le Hénaff, D. (2013). *From tiny tot to toddler: A practical guide for parents from pregnancy to age two.* Retrieved from Institut national de santé publique du Québec website : http://www.inspq.qc.ca/tinytot/sections/TT2013_Guide.pdf (1)

Drover, G. (1983). Beyond the welfare state: Brief to the Royal Commission on the Economic Union and Development Prospects for Canada. *The Social Worker, 51*(4), 141–144. (1)

Du Mont, J., Hyman, I., O'Brien, K., White, M., Odette, F., & Tyyskä, V. (2012). *Research summary, Immigration status and abuse by a former partner.* Retrieved from CERIS—The Ontario Metropolis Centre website: http://www.ceris.metropolis.net/wp-content/uploads/2012/03/Exploring-intimate-partner-abuse.pdf (13)

Dudding, P. (2011). Editorial. *Canada's Children, 18*(1), 4–5. Retrieved from http://www.cwlc.ca/sites/default/files/file/Canada%27s%20Children/CC%20Winter%202011%20%28final%20final%29.pdf (10)

Dudgeon, S. (2010). *Rising tide: The impact of dementia on Canadain society.* Retrieved from the Alzheimer Society of Canada website: http://www.alzheimer.ca/en/Get-involved/Raise-your-voice/~/media/Files/national/Advocacy/ASC_Rising%20Tide_Full%20Report_Eng.ashx (11)

Dujon, G. (2010). *Women and leadership: Towards a gender, race and class analysis.* Retrieved from https://tspace.library.utoronto.ca/bitstream/1807/25646/1/Dujon_Genither_201011_MA_thesis.pdf (8)

Eakin, L. (2007). *We can't afford to do business this way: A study of the administrative burden resulting from funder accountability and compliance practices.* Retrieved from Wellesley Institute website: http://www.wellesleyinstitute.com/files/cant_do_business_this_way_report_web.pdf (5)

Eakin, L., & Richmond, T. (2004). Community service organizations at risk. *The Philanthropist 19*(4), 261–272. Retrieved from http://thephilanthropist.ca/index.php/phil/article/view/40/40 (5)

Echenberg, H., & Jensen, H. (2008). *Defining and enumerating homelessness in Canada* (Publication No. PRB 08-30E). Retrieved from Library of Parliament website: http://www.parl.gc.ca/content/lop/researchpublications/prb0830-e.pdf (9)

Economic Council of Canada. (1968). *Fifth annual review.* Ottawa, Canada: Author. (3)

Edwards, P., & Mawani, A. (2006). *Healthy aging in Canada: A new vision, a vital investment: From evidence to action.* Retrieved from http://www.health.gov.nl.ca/health/publications/vision_rpt_e.pdf (11)

Eichler, M., & Lavigne, M. (2012). Women's movement. In *The Canadian encyclopedia.* Retrieved from http://www.thecanadianencyclopedia.com/articles/womens-movement (3)

Environics Institute. (2010). *Urban Aboriginal peoples study—Main report.* Retrieved from http://uaps.ca/wp-content/uploads/2010/03/UAPS-Main-Report_Dec.pdf (12)

Environics Research Group. (2006). *Canadians' attitudes toward national child care policy.* Prepared for the Child Care Advocacy Association of Canada. Retrieved from http://www.ccaac.ca/pdf/resources/Reports/Public_Opinion_on_Child_Care_Policy.pdf (10)

Epstein, L. (1980). *Helping people: The task-centered approach.* St. Louis, MO: C.V. Mosby. (8)

Esquimaux, C. C. W., & Smolewski, M. (2004). *Historic trauma and Aboriginal healing.* Retrieved from Aboriginal Healing Foundation website: http://www.ahf.ca/downloads/historic-trauma.pdf (12)

Evans, B., & Shields, J. (2006). *Neoliberal restructuring and the third sector: Reshaping governance, civil society and local relations* (Working Paper Series Number 13, July 2000). Retrieved from Ryerson Univeristy Centre for Voluntary Sector Studies website: http://www.ryerson.ca/~cvss/WP13.pdf (5)

Evans, B., Richmond, T., & Shields, J. (2005). Structuring neoliberal governance: The nonprofit sector, emerging new modes of control and the marketisation of service delivery. *Policy & Society 24*(1), 73–97. doi:10.1016/S1449-4035(05) 70050-3 (5, 7)

Family Services of Greater Vancouver. (2013). *Who we are: Mission/value statement.* Retrieved from http://www.fsgv.ca/mainpages/whoweare/missionvaluestatement.html (6)

Fang, M., & Goldner, E. (2011). Transitioning into the Canadian workplace: Challenges of immigrants and its effect on mental health. *Canadian Journal of Humanities and Social Sciences 2*(1), 93–102. Retrieved from http://cjhss.org/_cjhss/pubData/v_2/i_1/20110223-1/20110223-1.pdf (13)

Federal, Provincial, and Territorial Ministers Responsible for Social Services. (2010). *The National Child Benefit: Progress report, 2007.* Retrieved from http://www.nationalchildbenefit.ca/eng/pdf/ncb_progress_report_2007.pdf (10)

Federal-Provincial-Territorial Ministers Responsible for Social Services. (1996). *In Unison: A Canadian approach to disability issues.* Retrieved from Council of Canadians with Disabilities website: http://www.ccdonline.ca/en/socialpolicy/poverty-citizenship/income-security-reform/in-unison (14)

Federation of Canadian Municipalities. (2010). *Mending Canada's frayed social safety net: The role of municipal governments.* Retrieved from http://www.fcm.ca/Documents/reports/Mending_Canadas_Frayed_Social_Safety_Net_The_role_of_municipal_governments_EN.pdf (4, 5, 11)

Federation of Canadian Municipalities. (2012). *No vacancy: Trends in rental housing in Canada.* Retrieved from http://www.fcm.ca/Documents/reports/FCM/No_Vacancy_Trends_in_Rental_Housing_in_Canada_EN.pdf (9)

Federation of Saskatchewan Indian Nations. (1975). Supplement: Our way: Historical review. *Saskatchewan Indian,* (June), 6–8. Retrieved from http://www.sicc.sk.ca/archive/saskindian/a75our06.htm (12)

Federation of Saskatchewan Indian Nations. (1978). History of the Indian Act. *Saskatchewan Indian 8*(3), 4–5. Retrieved from http://www.sicc.sk.ca/archive/saskindian/a78mar04.htm (12)

Fellegi, I. (2006). A multicultural profile of Canada. *Transition Magazine 36*(2), 3–6. Retrieved from http://www.vanierinstitute.ca/include/get.php?nodeid=746&format=download (13)

Ference Weicker & Company. (2009). *Outcome evaluation of the British Columbia Settlement and Adaptation Program (BCSAP): Final report prepared for the Ministry of Advanced Education and Labour*. Retrieved from Provine of British Columbia website: http://www.welcomebc.ca/welcome_bc/media/Media-Gallery/docs/service/programs/settlement_program/pdf/bcsap_-outcome_evaluation_final_report07-08.pdf (6)

Ferrao, V. (2010). *Paid work*. Retrieved from Statistics Canada website: http://www.statcan.gc.ca/pub/89-503-x/2010001/article/11387-eng.pdf (9)

Fildes, R., & Cooper, B. (2003, November). *Preparing for change: Social work in primary health care*. Retrieved from Canadian Association of Social Workers website: http://www.casw-acts.ca/sites/default/files/attachements/Preparing%20for%20Change.%20Social%20Work%20in%20Primary%20Health%20Care%20Report_0.pdf (7)

Financial crisis creating "perfect storm" for charity organizations: Donations declining as need for help rises, say community groups. (2008). *CBC News, November 10, 2008*. Retrieved from http://www.cbc.ca/news/canada/story/2008/11/10/charitable-donations.html?ref=rss (4)

Findlay, P. (1983). Social welfare in Canada: The case for universality. In *Canadian Social Work Review '83* (pp. 17–24). Ottawa, Canada: Canadian Association of Schools of Social Work. (1)

First Nations Regional Longitudinal Health Survey. (2005, November 15). *First Nations health survey reveals the "good, the bad, the ugly" about life in First Nations in Canada* [news release]. Retrieved February 23, 2009, from http://www.rhs-ers.ca/english/pdf/press_releases/rhs_press_release-nov15-2005-childrens_health.pdf (14)

Fischer, J. (1978). *Effective casework practice: An eclectic approach*. New York, NY: McGraw-Hill. (8)

Fontaine, P. (2005, November 23). *Assembly of First Nations National Chief applauds historic reconciliation and compensation agreement as a major victory for residential school survivors*. Retrieved March 12, 2009, from Assembly of First Nations website: http://www.afn.ca/article.asp?id=1935 (12)

Food Banks Canada. (2012). *Hungercount, 2012*. Retrieved from http://www.foodbankscanada.ca/getmedia/3b946e67-fbe2-490e-90dc-4a313dfb97e5/HungerCount2012.pdf.aspx (9)

Foreign Affairs and International Trade Canada. (2012). *Trade in services: Canada and trade in services*. Retrieved from http://www.international.gc.ca/trade-agreements-accords-commerciaux/services/canada-ts.aspx?view=d (Appendix B)

Fort Garry Women's Resource Centre. (2012). *About us*. Retrieved from http://www.fgwrc.ca/about (6)

Foucault, M. (1965). *Madness and civilization*. London, England: Random House. (12)

Fowler, K. (2008). *Children in care in Newfoundland and Labrador: A review of issues and trends with recommendations for programs and services*. Retrieved from http://www.gov.nl.ca/cyfs/publications/childcare/InCareReport.pdf (10)

Frank, F., & Smith, A. (1999). *The community development handbook: A tool to build community capacity*. Retrieved from Government of Canada Publications website: http://publications.gc.ca/collections/Collection/MP33-13-1999E.pdf (8)

Fredette, C. (2012). *Leadership diversity in the nonprofit sector: Baby steps, big strides, and bold stances*. Retrieved from http://diversecitytoronto.ca/wp-content/uploads/DiverseCity-Counts-Report-Final.pdf (6)

Freeman, J., King, M., & Pickett, W. (2011). *The health of Canada's young people: A mental health focus*. Retrieved from Public Health Agency of Canada website: http://www.phac-aspc.gc.ca/hp-ps/dca-dea/publications/hbsc-mental-mentale/assets/pdf/hbsc-mental-mentale-eng.pdf (10)

Fuchs, S. E. (2004, March 9). *Organizational change in the Internet era*. Retrieved from IBM webiste: http://www.ibm.com/developerworks/rational/library/3770.html (8)

Gaetz, S., Donaldson, J., Richter, T., & Gulliver, T. (2013). *The state of homelessness in Canada 2013*. Toronto: Canadian Homelessness Research Network Press. Retrieved from the Homeless Hub website: http://www.homelesshub.ca/ResourceFiles/SOHC2103.pdf (9)

Galabuzi, G. E., & Labonte, R. (2002, November). *Social inclusion as a determinant of health*. Paper presented at the Social Determinants of Health Across the Life-Span Conference, Toronto. Retrieved from http://action.web.ca/home/narcc/attach/Social%20Inclusion%20as%20a%20Determinant%20of%20Health%20-%20Galabuzi%202003%5B1%5D.pdf (2)

Galper, J. H. (1975). *The politics of social services*. Englewood Cliffs, NJ: Prentice-Hall. (1)

Gardner, B. (2011). *Comprehensive community initiatives: The promise of realist evaluation*. Retrieved from http://www.wellesleyinstitute.com/wp-content/uploads/2011/07/Q-and-A-on-Evaluating-Community-Impact.pdf (8)

George, V., & Wilding, P. (1985). *Ideology and social welfare*. New York, NY: Routledge. (1)

Goar, C. (2011, December 15). Harper's unlikely social breakthrough. *Toronto Star*. Retrieved from http://www.thestar.com/opinion/editorialopinion/article/1102957--goar-harper-s-unlikely-social-breakthrough (7)

Goss Gilroy. (2004). *Doing what works: Barriers to participation in the labour market: Labour market development strategy: Background report #4*. Retrieved from Newfoundland and Labrador Department of Advanced Education and Skills website: http://www.aes.gov.nl.ca/publications/lmd/doing_what_works_background_report4.pdf (9)

Goss Gilroy. (2008). *Evaluation of the JobsNow Pilot: Final report.* Retrieved from Ontario Ministry of Community and Social Services website: http://www.mcss.gov.on.ca/documents/en/mcss/social/publications/ JobsNowDraftEvaluationReportWeb.pdf (5)

Gough, P. (2006). *Manitoba's child welfare system.* Retrieved from Centre of Excellence for Child Welfare website: http://cwrp.ca/sites/default/files/publications/en/ ManitobaChildWelfareSystem34E.pdf (12)

Gough, P., Shlonsky, A., & Dudding, P. (2009). An overview of the child welfare systems in Canada. *International Journal on Child Health and Human Development, 2*(3), 357–372. Retrieved from http://www.cwlc.ca/sites/default/files/file/resources/ Overview_of_the_CW_Systems_in_Canada_Nov_09.pdf (10)

Gravelle, M., Baird, K., & Green, I. (2008). *Collaborative governance and changing federal roles: A PPF and PRI joint roundtable outcomes report.* Retrieved from Public Policy Forum website: http://www.ppforum.ca/sites/default/files/ PRI_PPF_roundtable_en_0.pdf (2)

Gray, G. (1990). Social policy by stealth. *Policy Options,* March, 17–29. (4)

Greenwood, J. (2005). Whither welfare? *Canadian Journal of Public Health, 96*(1), 9–10. Retrieved from http://journal.cpha.ca/index.php/cjph/article/view/599/599 (4)

Guest, D. (1980). *The emergence of social security in Canada.* Vancouver, Canada: University of British Columbia Press. (3)

Guest, D. (1997). *The emergence of social security in Canada* (3rd ed.). Vancouver, Canada: University of British Columbia Press. (3)

Guest, D. (2012). Social security. In *The Canadian encyclopedia.* Retrieved from http://www.thecanadianencyclopedia.com/articles/social-security. (3)

Hall, C. (2007). *Social work practice in community development.* Retrieved from Canadian Association of Social Workers website: http://www.casw-acts.ca/en/ social-work-practice-community-development (8)

Hall, M. H., Andrukow, A., Barr, C., Brock, K., deWit, M., Embuldeniya, D., . . . Vaillancourt, Y. (2003). *The capacity to serve: A qualitative study of the challenges facing Canada's nonprofit and voluntary organizations.* Retrieved from Imagine Canada Sector Source website: http://sectorsource.ca/sites/default/files/resources/ files/capacity_to_serve_english.pdf (6)

Hall, M. H., Phillips, S. D., Meillat, C., & Pickering, D. (2003). *Assessing performance: Evaluation practices and perspectives in Canada's voluntary sector.* Retrieved from Imagine Canada website: http://www.imaginecanada.ca/files/www/en/library/ vserp/vserp_report.pdf (6)

Hall, M., de Wit, M., Lasby, D., McIver, D., Evers, T., Johnston, C., . . . Murray, V. (2005). *Cornerstones of community: Highlights of the National Survey of Nonprofit and Voluntary Organizations: 2003 revised.* Retrieved from Imagine Canada website: http://library.imaginecanada.ca/files/nonprofitscan/en/nsnvo/nsnvo_report_ english.pdf (5)

Halseth, G., & Booth, A. (1998). *Paper #2: Community participation in the new forest economy: Discussion paper on concepts: Community development.* Retrieved from British Columbia Forest, Lands and Natural Resource Operations website: http://www.for.gov.bc.ca/hfd/library/documents/bib95182.pdf (8)

Handel, G. (1982). *Social welfare in Western society.* New York, NY: Random House. (1)

Hanson, E. (2009). *Indigenous foundations, government policy, the Indian Act.* Retrieved from First Nations Studies Program at UBC website: http://indigenousfoundations. arts.ubc.ca/home/government-policy/the-indian-act.html (12)

Hanvey, L. (2002). *Middle childhood: Building on the early years: A discussion paper.* Retrieved from National Children's Alliance website: http://www. nationalchildrensalliance.com/nca/pubs/2002/hanvey.pdf (10)

Hareven, T. K. (1969, April). An ambiguous alliance: Some aspects of American influences on Canadian social welfare. *Social History: A Canadian Review, 3,* 82–98. (1)

Harper, S. (2011). Transcript of Peter Mansbridge's interview with PM Stephen Harper: 9/11, 10 years later. *CBC News,* September 8. Retrieved from http://www.cbc.ca/ news/politics/story/2011/09/08/pol-harper-mansbridge-transcript.html (13)

Hart, L., & Jamieson, W. (2001). *Woman abuse: Overview paper.* Retrieved from Public Health Agency of Canada website: http://www.phac-aspc.gc.ca/ncfv-cnivf/ publications/femviof-eng.php (10)

Hay, D. (2008). *Investing in youth: Evidence from policy, practice and research.* Retrieved February 24, 2009, from Policy Research Initiative website: http:// www.policyresearch.gc.ca/page.asp?pagenm=rp_iy_bkg (10)

Hay, D. I. (2009). *Poverty reduction policies and programs in Canada.* Retrieved from Canadian Council on Social Development website: http://www.ccsd.ca/SDR2009/ Reports/Canada_Report_FINAL.pdf (2, 9)

Health Canada. (2006). *First Nations & Inuit health: Suicide prevention.* Retrieved from http://www.hc-sc.gc.ca/fniah-spnia/promotion/suicide/index-eng.php (10)

Health Canada. (2012). *First Nations and Inuit health: Indian residential schools.* Retrieved from http://www.hc-sc.gc.ca/fniah-spnia/services/indiresident/index-eng.php (12)

HeartWood. (2012). *What we do: For youth.* Retrieved from http://www.heartwood.ns.ca/ foryouth.html (10)

Heclo, H. (1981). Toward a new welfare state? In P. Flora & A. J. Heidenheimer (Eds.), *The development of welfare states in Europe and America* (pp. 383–406). New Brunswick, NJ: Transaction Books. (3)

Henslin, J. M. (2003). *Social problems* (6th ed.). Upper Saddle River, NJ: Prentice Hall. (2)

Herberg, C., & Herberg, E. N. (2001). Canada's ethno-racial diversity: Policies and programs in Canadian social welfare. In J. C. Turner & F. J. Turner (Eds.), *Canadian social welfare* (4th ed., pp. 167–179). Toronto, Canada: Pearson Education. (13)

Herd, D., Mitchell, A., & Lightman, E. (2005). Rituals of degradation: Administration as policy in the Ontario Works programme. *Social Policy and Administration, 39*(1), 65–79. Retrieved from http://www.socialwork.utoronto.ca/Assets/Social%2BWork% 2BDigital%2BAssets/SANE/Rituals%2Bof%2BDegradation.pdf (6)

Hick, S. (2004). *Social work in Canada: Understanding income security: An introduction; glossary: Gerontological social work.* Toronto, Canada: Thompson Educational Publishing. Retrieved February 28, 2009, from http://www.socialpolicy.ca/swc/book_g.htm (11)

Hirji-Khalfan, R (2009). *Federal supports for Aboriginal people with disabilities.* Retrieved from https://pi.library.yorku.ca/ojs/index.php/cdd/article/viewFile/23386/21577 (14)

Hiscott, R. (2002). *Trends: Longer hours, more stress: The way we work.* Retrieved from CBC News website: http://www.cbc.ca/news/work/nomore9to5/234.html (6)

Hollander, M. J., Liu, G., & Chappell, N. L. (2009). Who cares and how much? The imputed economic contribution to the Canadian healthcare system of middle-aged and older unpaid caregivers providing care to the elderly. *Healthcare Quarterly, 12*(2), 42–49. Retrieved from http://www.longwoods.com/product/download/code/20660 (7)

Horn, M. (1984). *The great depression of the 1930s in Canada* (Historical Booklet No. 39). Ottawa, Canada: Canadian Historical Association. (3)

Hou, F., & Picot, G. (2003, July). *Visible minority neighbourhood enclaves and labour market outcomes of immigrants.* Retrieved from Statistics Canada website: http://www.statcan.gc.ca/pub/11f0019m/11f0019m2003204-eng.pdf (13)

Howlett, D. (1992). The arithmetic, chemistry, and art of coalition projects. *Action Canada Dossier, 37*(May/June), 7–9. (3)

HR Council for the Voluntary and Non-profit Sector. (2008). *Toward a labour force strategy for Canada's voluntary & non-profit sector.* Retrieved from http://hrcouncil.ca/about/documents/LFS_R2_ES_web_000.pdf (6)

Hrab, R. (2004, January). *Private delivery of public services: Public private partnerships and contracting-out* (Research Paper #21). Retrieved from http://www.law-lib.utoronto.ca/investing/reports/rp21.pdf (5)

Huebner, F. (1999). *A guide for the development of policies and procedures in Ontario's community literacy agencies.* Barrie, Canada: Community Literacy of Ontario. Retrieved from National Adult Literacy Database: http://www.nald.ca/library/research/development-vol1/policies/guide1/devpol-1.pdf (6)

Hulchanski, J. D. (2005). *Rethinking Canada's housing affordability challenge.* Retrieved from http://www.urbancentre.utoronto.ca/pdfs/elibrary/Hulchanski-Housing-Affd-pap.pdf (9)

Human Resources and Skills Development Canada. (2008). *Advancing the inclusion of people with disabilities 2008: Federal disability report.* Retrieved from http://biac-aclc.ca/pdf/fdr_2008.pdf (14)

Human Resources and Skills Development Canada. (2009). *2009 Federal disability report: The Government of Canada's annual report on disability issues*. Retrieved from http://www.hrsdc.gc.ca/eng/disability_issues/reports/fdr/2009/fdr_2009.pdf (14)

Human Resources and Skills Development Canada. (2010). *2010 Federal disability report: The Government of Canada's annual report on disability issues*. Retrieved from http://www.hrsdc.gc.ca/eng/disability_issues/reports/fdr/2010/fdr_2010.pdf (14)

Human Resources and Skills Development Canada. (2012a). *Indicators of Well-being in Canada*. Retrieved from http://www4.hrsdc.gc.ca/c.4nt.2nt@-eng.jsp?cid=14 (1)

Human Resources and Skills Development Canada. (2012b). *4212, Social and community service workers*. Retrieved from http://www5.hrsdc.gc.ca/NOC/English/NOC/ 2011/Profile.aspx?val=4&val1=4212 (7)

Human Resources and Skills Development Canada. (2012c). *Indicators of well-being in Canada: Financial security—Low income incidence*. Retrieved from http://www4.hrsdc.gc.ca/.3ndic.1t.4r@-eng.jsp?iid=23 (9)

Human Resources and Skills Development Canada. (2012d). *Indicators of well-being in Canada: Financial security—Low income persistence*. Retrieved from http://www4.hrsdc.gc.ca/.3ndic.1t.4r@-eng.jsp?iid=83 (9)

Human Resources and Skills Development Canada. (2012e). *2011 Federal disability report: Seniors with disabilities in Canada: Section 2: Health*. Retrieved from http://www.hrsdc.gc.ca/eng/disability/arc/federal_report2011/pdf/fdr_2011.pdf (11)

Human Resources and Skills Development Canada. (2012f). *Indicators of well-being in Canada: Canadians in context: Population size and growth*. Retrieved from http://www4.hrsdc.gc.ca/.3ndic.1t.4r@-eng.jsp?iid=35 (11)

Human Resources and Skills Development Canada. (2012g). *Indicators of well-being in Canada: Canadians in context: Aging population*. Retrieved from http://www4.hrsdc.gc.ca/.3ndic.1t.4r@-eng.jsp?iid=33 (11)

Human Resources and Skills Development Canada. (2012h). *Federal disability reference guide*. Retrieved from http://www.hrsdc.gc.ca/eng/disability/arc/reference_guide.pdf (14)

Human Resources and Skills Development Canada. (2013a). *National call for concepts, social finance*. Retrieved from http://www.hrsdc.gc.ca/eng/consultations/socialfinance/index.shtml (4)

Human Resources and Skills Development Canada. (2013b). *Housing: Homeless shelters and beds*. Retrieved from http://www4.hrsdc.gc.ca/.3ndic.1t.4r@-eng.jsp?iid=44. (9)

Human Resources and Skills Development Canada. (2013c). *Indicators of well-being in Canada: Work—employment rate*. Retrieved from http://www4.hrsdc.gc.ca/.3ndic.1t.4r@-eng.jsp?iid=13 (Appendix B)

Human Resources and Social Development Canada. (2005). *Social economy: Questions and answers*. Retrieved January 11, 2009, from http://www.hrsdc.gc.ca/eng/cs/comm/sd/social_economy.shtml (5)

Human Resources and Social Development Canada. (2007a). *2007–2008 Estimates: A report on plans and priorities.* Retrieved from http://www.tbs-sct.gc.ca/rpp/2007-2008/hrsdc-rhdsc/hrsdc-rhdsc-eng.pdf (10)

Human Resources and Social Development Canada. (2007b). *2006 Federal report: Advancing the inclusion of people with disabilities.* Retrieved from http://www.cndd.ca/assets/research%20documents/Canadian%20Government/Advancing%20Inclusion%20Persons%20with%20Disabilities%20-%20Can%20Govt%202006.pdf (14)

Human Resources Council for the Voluntary & Non-Profit Sector. (2008). *Toward a labour force strategy for Canada's voluntary & non-profit sector: Report #2.* Retrieved from http://hrcouncil.ca/about/documents/LFS_R2_web_001.pdf (7)

Human Resources Development Canada. (1994a). *Improving social security in Canada: A discussion paper.* Retrieved from http://www.canadiansocialresearch.net/ssrdiscussionpaper.htm (1)

Human Resources Development Canada. (1994b). *Improving social security in Canada: Reforming the Canada Assistance Plan: A supplementary paper.* Hull-Ottawa, Canada: Minister of Supply and Services Canada. (3)

Human Resources Development Canada. (1994c). *Improving social security in Canada: A discussion paper.* Retrieved from http://www.canadiansocialresearch.net/ssrdiscussionpaper.htm#context (4)

Human Resources Development Canada. (1995). *The need for change.* Retrieved June 7, 2000, from http://www.hrdc-drch.gc.ca/hrdc/initiatv/eilaunch/newsrele/95792e.html (4)

Human Resources Development Canada. (1999a, October). *Investing in children: Ideas for action.* Report from the National Research Conference, Ottawa. Retrieved from http://www.peelearlyyears.com/pdf/Investing%20in%20Children-Ideas%20for%20Action,%20Canada.pdf (10)

Human Resources Development Canada. (1999b). *Future directions: The challenges facing persons with disabilities.* Retrieved from Collections Canada website: http://www.collectionscanada.gc.ca/webarchives/20060216185526/http://www1.servicecanada.gc.ca/en/cs/sp/sdc/socpol/publications/reports/1999-000046/1999-000046.pdf (14)

Hunte, B. (2009). *Peer counselling: A draft training manual for peer support providers.* Retrieved from Caribbean HIV&AIDS Alliance website: http://caribbeanhivaidsalliance.org/uploaded/pdf/Manual%20-%20Peer%20Counselling%20for%20Peer%20Support%20Providers.pdf (7)

Hylton, J.H. (2002). *Appendix C: Aboriginal health and healing: A review of best practices.* A background paper prepared for the Regina Qu'Appelle Health Region, Working Together Towards Excellence Project. Retrieved from Regina Qu'Appelle Health Region website: http://www.rqhealth.ca/programs/aboriginal/pdf_files/appendix_c.pdf (12)

Ilcan, S., & Basok, T. (2004). Community government: Voluntary agencies, social justice, and the responsibilization of citizens. *Citizenship Studies 8*(2), 129–144. doi:10.1080/1362102042000214714 (5)

Imagine Canada. (2006). *A portrait of social services organizations in Canada.* Retrieved from http://library.imaginecanada.ca/files/nonprofitscan/en/synthesis/s-s_executives.pdf (5)

Indian and Northern Affairs Canada. (1990). *The Canadian Indian.* Hull-Ottawa, Canada: Minister of Supply and Services Canada. (12)

Indian and Northern Affairs Canada. (2007). *Evaluation of the Income Assistance Program: Audit and Evaluation Sector: Indian and Northern Affairs Canada: Project 07/06.* Retrieved from (Statistics Canada, 2008a (12)

Indian and Northern Affairs Canada. (2009). *Final report—Evaluation of community-based healing initiatives supported through the Aboriginal Healing Foundation.* Retrieved from Aboriginal Healting Foundation website: http://www.ahf.ca/downloads/inac-evaluation.pdf (12)

Indian and Northern Affairs Canada. (2010). *First Nation and Inuit community well-being: Describing historical trends (1981–2006).* Aboriginal Affairs and Northern Development Canada website: Retrieved from http://www.aadnc-aandc.gc.ca/DAM/DAM-INTER-HQ/STAGING/texte-text/cwbdck_1100100016601_eng.pdf (12)

Innovation Network. (2005). *Logic model workbook.* Retrieved from http://www.innonet.org/client_docs/File/logic_model_workbook.pdf (2)

Institute on Governance. (2008). *Governance basics: What is governance? Where governance fits.* Retrieved September 16, 2008, from http://www.iog.ca/boardgovernance/ html/gov_whe.html (6)

Institute on Governance. (2011). *Basic role of the board.* Retrieved March 3, 2012, from http://iog.ca/en/knowledge-areas/board-organizational-governance/basic-role-of-board (6)

International Federation of Social Workers. (2012a). *Definition of social work.* Retrieved from http://ifsw.org/resources/definition-of-social-work/ (7)

International Federation of Social Workers. (2012b). *Policies: Globalisation and the environment.* Retrieved from http://ifsw.org/policies/globalisation-and-the-environment/ (1, Appendix B)

Ismael, J. S. (Ed.). (1985). Introduction. In *Canadian social welfare policy: Federal and provincial dimensions* (pp. xi–xv). Kingston, Canada: McGill-Queen's University Press. (1)

Ismael, S. (2006). *Child poverty and the Canadian welfare state: From entitlement to charity.* Edmonton, Canada: University of Alberta Press. (1)

Ivanova, I. (2011, July). *The cost of poverty in BC.* Retrieved from http://www.policyalternatives.ca/sites/default/files/uploads/publications/BC%20Office/2011/07/CCPA_BC_cost_of_poverty_full_report.pdf (9)

Jackson, A. (2004). *Asset-based social policies: A new idea whose time has come?* Retrieved from Caledon Institute of Social Policy website: http://www.caledoninst.org/Publications/PDF/452ENG.pdf (9)

Jaco, R. M., & Pierce, B. D. (2005). Social agencies and human service organizations. In J. C. Turner & F. J. Turner (Eds.), *Canadian social welfare* (5th ed., pp. 225–241). Toronto, Canada: Pearson. (6)

Jamieson, W., & Gomes, L. (2010). *The family violence initiative performance report for April 2004 to March 2008.* Retrieved from Public Health Agency of Canada website: http://www.phac-aspc.gc.ca/ncfv-cnivf/sources/fv/fv-perf-rprt-2008/assets/pdf/fvi-perf-rprt-eng.pdf (10)

Jansen, I., & Murphy, J. (2009). *Residential long-term care in Canada: Our vision for better seniors' care.* Retrieved from the Canadian Union of Public Employees website http://cupe.ca/updir/CUPE-long-term-care-seniors-care-vision.pdf (11)

Janzen, C., & Harris, O. (1997). *Family treatment in social work practice* (3rd ed.). Itasca, IL: F.E. Peacock. (8)

Jeffrey, K. (2008, February). *Youth policy: What works and what doesn't: A report of United Way Toronto.* Retrieved from United Way Toronto website: http://www.unitedwaytoronto.com/downloads/whatWeDo/reports/YouthPolicy-WhatWorks-fullreport.pdf (10)

Jenson, J. (2004). *Catching up to reality: Building the case for a new social model* (CPRN Social Architecture Papers, Research Report F35, Family Network). Retrieved from Canadian Policy Research Networks website: http://www.cprn.org/documents/26067_en.pdf (5)

Jewell, L. (2005). Mental health and community counselling, and private practice. In P. Hayduk, L. Jewell, & S. Konrad (Eds.), *An introduction to counselling in Canada.* Retrieved from Centre for Psychology, Athabasca University website: http://psych.athabascau.ca/html/Resources/Psych388/CanadianSupplement/Chapter14/00_intro.shtml (1)

Jiwani, I. (2000). *Globalization at the level of the nation-state: The case of Canada's third sector.* Retrieved from http://www.ucalgary.ca/innovations/files/innovations/Inv2000-4.pdf (5, 7)

Johnson, H. (2006). *Measuring violence against women: Statistical trends 2006.* Ottawa, Canada: Minister of Industry. Retrieved from http://ywcacanada.ca/data/research_docs/00000043.pdf (10)

Johnson, L. C., McClelland, R. W., & Austin, C. D. (2000). *Social work practice: A generalist approach* (Cdn. ed.). Scarborough, Canada: Prentice-Hall Canada. (7, 8)

Johnston, P. (1983). *Native children and the child welfare system.* Toronto, Canada: Canadian Council on Social Development in association with James Lorimer and Company. (12)

Jolivet, K. (2011). The psychological iImpact of divorce on children: What is a family lawyer to do? *American Journal of Family Law, 25*(4), 175–183. (10)

Jones, C., Clark, L., Grusec, J., Hart, R., Plickert, G., & Tepperman, L. (2002, March). *Poverty, social capital, parenting and child outcomes in Canada: Final report* (Catalogue #SP-557-01-03E). Retrieved from Government of Canada Publications website: http://publications.gc.ca/collections/Collection/RH63-1-557-01-03E.pdf (9)

Kashefi, M. (2009, November). Job satisfaction and/or job stress: The psychological consequences of working in "high performance work organizations." *Current sociology 57*(6), 809–828. Retrieved from http://www.choixdecarriere.com/pdf/6573/2010/Kashefi2009.pdf (6)

Katz, S. (2012). Old is not what it used to be. *Showcase* (Spring), 1–2. Retrieved from Trent University website: http://www.trentu.ca/showcase/documents/ShowcaseSpring2012.pdf (11)

Keefe, J. (2011). *Supporting caregivers and caregiving in an aging Canada: IRPP study #23*. Retrieved from Institute for Research on Public Policy website: http://www.irpp.org/pubs/IRPPstudy/IRPP_Study_no23.pdf (7)

Kelly, M. (2012). *Divorce cases in civil court, 2010/2011* (Catalogue No. 85-002-X). Retrieved from Statistics Canada website: http://www.statcan.gc.ca/pub/85-002-x/2012001/article/11634-eng.pdf (10)

Kenney, J. (2012). *Speaking notes for The Honourable Jason Kenney, P.C., M.P. Minister of Citizenship, Immigration and Multiculturalism. At the National Metropolis Conference, Toronto, March 1, 2012.* Retrieved from Citizen and Immigration Canada website: http://www.cic.gc.ca/english/DEPARTMENT/media/speeches/2012/2012-03-01.asp (13)

Kent, T. (2011). *The social democracy of Canadian federalism*. Retrieved from Broadbent Institute website: http://www.broadbentinstitute.ca/sites/default/files/documents/social-democracy-canadian-federalism.pdf (1)

Kerr, D., & Michalski, J. (2007). Family structure and children's hyperactivity problems: A longitudinal analysis. *Canadian Journal of Sociology, 32*(1), 85–112. (10)

Kim, S. (2012). *Is living in an ethnic enclave so bad?* Retrieved from http://canadianimmigrant.ca/community/is-living-in-an-ethnic-enclave-really-so-bad (13)

Kirmayer, G., Brass, M., & Tait, C. L. (2000). The mental health of Aboriginal peoples: Transformations of identity and community. *Canadian Journal of Psychiatry, 45*(7), 607–616. Retrieved from https://ww1.cpa-apc.org/Publications/Archives/CJP/2000/Sep/InReview.asp (12)

Kowalchuk, K., & Crompton, S. (2009). *Social participation of children with disabilities*. Retrieved from Statistics Canada website: http://www.statcan.gc.ca/pub/11-008-x/2009002/article/11021-eng.pdf (14)

Kutcher, S., & McLuckie, A., for the Child and Youth Advisory Committee, Mental Health Commission of Canada. (2010). *Evergreen: A child and youth mental health framework for Canada*. Calgary, Canada: Mental Health Commission of Canada. Retrieved from http://www.mentalhealthcommission.ca/English/system/files/private/document/C%2526Y_Evergreen_Framework_ENG_0.pdf (10)

Lalonde, M. (1973). *Working paper on social security in Canada*. Ottawa, Canada: Department of National Health and Welfare. (3)

Lankin, F., & Sheikh, M. (2012). *Brighter prospects: Transforming social assistance in Ontario. A Report to the Minister of Community and Social Services*. Retrieved from http://www.socialassistancereview.ca/uploads/File/COMM_Report_FinalH-t-Eng.pdf (6)

LaRocque, E. (1994, March). Violence in Aboriginal communities. Reprinted from *The path to healing: Royal Commissions on Aboriginal Peoples*. Retrieved from Government of Canada Publications website: http://publications.gc.ca/collections/Collection/H72-21-100-1994E.pdf (12)

Lasby, D., & Barr, C. (2010). *Sector Monitor, 1*(1). Retrieved from http://www.imaginecanada.ca/files/www/en/sectormonitor/sectormonitor_vol1_no1_2010.pdf (5)

Laucius, J. (2011, May 31). Stepfamilies create big challenges. *Nanaimo Daily News*. Retrieved from http://www2.canada.com/nanaimodailynews/story.html?id=2641215d-b3f6-49ba-a309-1e464882376d&p=1 (10)

Laurie, N. (2008). *The cost of poverty*. Retrieved from http://metcalffoundation.com/wp-content/uploads/2011/05/cost-of-poverty.pdf (9)

Lautenschlager, J. (1992). *Volunteering: A traditional Canadian value*. Ottawa, Canada: Voluntary Action Program, Canadian Heritage. Retrieved from http://www.nald.ca/library/research/heritage/compartne/pdfdocs/tradval.pdf (3)

LeBlanc, R. (1996). *Romeo LeBlanc, Speech: February 23, 1996: Presentation of the 1996 Native Role Models*. Retrieved from http://archive.gg.ca/media/doc.asp?lang=e&DocID=140 (12)

Lecomte, R. (2005). Distinguishing features of social work education in Canada. In J. C. Turner & F. J. Turner (Eds.), *Canadian social welfare* (5th ed., pp. 465–471). Toronto, Canada: Pearson. (7)

Leger Marketing. (2011). *A decade after Sept 11, 2001*. Retrieved October 23, 2012, from http://www.legermarketing.com/documents/SPCLM/119122ENG.pdf (13)

Leiby, J. (1977). Social welfare: History of basic ideas. In *Encyclopedia of social work* (17th ed., pp. 1512–1529, Vol. 2). Washington, DC: National Association of Social Workers. (1)

Lenihan, D. (2012). *Rescuing policy: The case for public engagement*. Retrieved from Canada's Public Policy Forum website: http://issuu.com/ppforumca/docs/rescuing-policy?mode=window&backgroundColor=%23222222 (2)

LeRoy, S., & Clemens, J. (2003, September 25). *Ending welfare as we know it: Lessons from Canada* (Brief Analysis No. 457). Retrieved from National Center for Policy Analysis website: http://www.ncpa.org/pdfs/ba457.pdf (4)

Liberal Party of Canada. (1997). *Securing our future together: Preparing Canada for the 21st century*. Ottawa, Canada: Author. Retrieved Legislative Assembly of British Columbia website: http://www.llbc.leg.bc.ca/public/pubdocs/docs/289598/securing_our_future_together%20.pdf (5)

Lipman, E., & Boyle. M. (2008). *Linking poverty and mental health: A lifespan view.* Retrieved from Ontario Centre of Excellence for Child and Youth Mental Health website: http://www.excellenceforchildandyouth.ca/sites/default/files/position_poverty.pdf (10)

Lipman, E., & Offord, D. (1994). Disadvantaged children. In *Guide to Clinical Preventive Health Care* (pp. 355–368). Retrieved from Public Health Agency of Canada website: http://www.phac-aspc.gc.ca/publicat/clinic-clinique/pdf/s2c32e.pdf (9)

Loewen, G. (2009). *A compendium of poverty reduction strategies and frameworks.* Retrieved from Tamarack Community website: http://tamarackcommunity.ca/downloads/vc/Poverty_Reduction_GL_042209.pdf (9)

Luther, R. (2007). Access and equity in Ottawa: A snapshot of social service issues, institutional responses and remaining challenges regarding culture, race and language. *Our Diverse Cities, Fall*(4), 39–43. Retrieved from Metropolis Canada website: http://canada.metropolis.net/pdfs/ODC%20Ontario%20Eng.pdf (13)

Lutherwood. (2012). *Woodlands.* Retrieved from http://www.lutherwood.ca/mentalhealth/services/woodlands-residential (10)

Macdonald, D. & Wilson, D. (2013, June). *Poverty or prosperity: Indigenous children in Canada.* Retrieved from the Canadian Centre for Policy Alternatives website: http://www.policyalternatives.ca/sites/default/files/uploads/publications/National%20Office/2013/06/Poverty_or_Prosperity_Indigenous_Children.pdf (9)

MacKinnon, M. P. (2004). *Citizens' values and the Canadian social architecture: Evidence from the citizens' dialogue on Canada's future* (CPRN Social Architecture Papers, Research Report F42, Family Network). Retrieved from Canadian Policy Research Networks website: http://cprn.org/documents/29860_en.pdf (2)

MacMurchy, H. (1932). *Sterilization? Birth control?* Toronto, Canada: Macmillan. (14)

Mailloux, L., Horak, H., & Godin, C. (2002). *Motivation at the margins: Gender issues in the Canadian voluntary sector.* Retrieved from Voluntary Sector Initiative website: http://www.vsi-isbc.org/eng/knowledge/pdf/reports_motivation.pdf (7)

Maioni, A. (2004). New century, new risks: The Marsh Report and the post-war welfare state in Canada. *Policy Options, 25*(7), 20–23. Retrieved from the Institute for Research on Public Policy website: http://www.irpp.org/po/archive/aug04/maioni.pdf (3)

Makarenko, J. (2008, June 2). *The Indian Act: Historical overview.* Retrieved from http://www.mapleleafweb.com/features/the-indian-act-historical-overview (12)

Manitoba. Aboriginal Justice Implementation Commission. (1999). Chapter 13: Aboriginal Women. In *Report of the Aboriginal Justice Inquiry of Manitoba, Aboriginal Justice Implementation Commission.* Retrieved from http://www.ajic.mb.ca/volumel/chapter13.html#5 (12)

Marsh, L. (1950). The welfare state: Is it a threat to Canada? In *Proceedings on the Canadian Conference on Social Work, 1950* (pp. 34–44). Ottawa, Canada: Canadian Conference on Social Work. (3)

Marsh, L. (1975). *Report on social security for Canada.* Toronto, Canada: University of Toronto Press. (3)

Martel, L., & Ménard, F. (2012). *Census in brief: Generations in Canada: Age and sex: 2011 census.* Retrieved from Statistics Canada website: http://www12.statcan.gc.ca/census-recensement/2011/as-sa/98-311-x/98-311-x2011003_2-eng.pdf (11)

Martin, S. A. (1985). *An essential grace: Funding Canada's health care, education, welfare, religion and culture.* Toronto, Canada: McClelland and Stewart. (3)

Matthews, D. (2004). *Review of employment assistance programs in Ontario Works & Ontario Disability Support Program. Report to The Honourable Sandra Pupatello, Minister of Community & Social Services.* Retrieved from http://www.mcss.gov.on.ca/documents/en/mcss/social/publications/EmploymentAssistanceProgram_Matthews_engl.pdf (6)

Maxwell, J. (2006, September). *Strategies for social justice: Place, people and policy.* Retrieved from Community Foundations of Canada website: http://www.cfc-fcc.ca/documents/pf_4_Maxwell_Strategies.pdf (1)

Mayo, S. (2010). *Women and poverty in Hamilton.* Retrieved from Social Planning and Research Council of Hamilton website: http://www.sprc.hamilton.on.ca/wp-content/uploads/2010/05/Women-and-Poverty-in-Hamilton-May-2010.pdf (9)

McCaskill, D., Fitzmaurice, K., & Cidro, J. (2011). *Toronto Aboriginal research project: Final report.* Retrieved from http://abdc.bc.ca/uploads/file/09%20Harvest/TARP-FinalReport-Oct%202011.pdf (12)

McDaniel S., & Bernard, P. (2011). Life course as a policy lens: Challenges and opportunities [Abstract]. *Canadian Public Policy, 37,* 1–13. Abstract retrieved from http://www.synergiescanada.org/journals/utp/120328/m677255hn88r/eh76x64v37234q64 (2)

McDonagh, A. (2002, October). *Globalization.* Retrieved January 11, 2009, from Workers' Educational Association of Canada website: http://www.weacanada.ca/files/articles/25.pdf (Appendix B)

McDonald, G. (2009). Evaluation as control. In J. C. Turner & F. J. Turner (Eds.), *Canadian social welfare* (6th ed., pp. 418–425). Toronto, Canada: Pearson. (6)

McDonald, L. (2010). *National initiative for the care of the elderly: Knowledge transfer in the field of aging.* Retrieved from http://theconference.ca/index.php/topic-pages/ageing/35-ageing/571-nice-knowledge-transfer-in-the-field-of-aging (11)

McDonald, R. A. (2005, October 21). *Comparative resource analysis of support services for First Nations people with disabilities.* Retrieved from Katenies Research and Management Services website: http://64.26.129.156/cmslib/general/fndp.pdf (14)

McDonald, S., Wobick, A., & Graham, J. (2004). *Bill C-46 Records applications Post-Mills: A caselaw review.* Retrieved from Department of Justice website: http://www.justice.gc.ca/eng/pi/rs/rep-rap/2006/rr06_vic2/rr06_vic2.pdf (14)

McGill University, School of Social Work, Greater Victoria Survey Committee. (1931). *Problems in family welfare: Relief and child development.* Montreal, Canada: Author. (8)

McGilly, F. (1998). *An introduction to Canada's public social services: Understanding income and health programs* (2nd ed.). Don Mills, Canada: Oxford University Press. (3)

McGregor, M., & Ronald, L. (2011). *Residential long-term care for Canadian seniors: Nonprofit, for-profit or does it matter?* Retrieved from Institute for Research on Public Policy website: http://www.irpp.org/pubs/irppstudy/2011/irpp_study_no1.pdf (11)

McIntyre, L. (2003). Food security: More than a determinant of health. *Policy Options, 24*(3), 46–51. Retrieved from http://www.irpp.org/po/archive/mar03/mcintyre.pdf (9)

McKenzie, B., & Morrissette, V. (2003). Social work practice with Canadians of Aboriginal background: Guidelines for respectful social work. In A. Al Krenawi & J. Graham (Eds.), *Multicultural social work in Canada* (pp. 251–282). Don Mills, Canada: Oxford University Press. (12)

McLachlin, B. (2008). *The law's response to an aging population: Remarks of the Right Honourable Beverley McLachlin, P.C., Chief Justice of Canada.* Retrieved from http://www.cnpea.ca/Ottawa%20Presentations%202008_files/Cheif%20Justice%27s%20speech%20final.pdf (11)

McMahon, M. O. (1994). *Advanced generalist practice with an international perspective.* Englewood Cliffs, NJ: Prentice Hall. (7)

McQuaig, L. (1995). *Shooting the hippo: Death by deficit and other Canadian myths.* Toronto, Canada: Penguin. (4)

McQuaig, L. (2010, December 28). *Canada discovers trickle-up economics.* Retrieved from *Star.com.* http://www.thestar.com/opinion/columns/article/911829--canada-discovers-trickle-up-economics (Appendix B)

Meekis, D. (2013). *Press release.* Retrieved from Idle No More webiste: http://idlenomore.ca/index.php/about-us/press-releases/item/83-press-release-january-10-2013-for-immediate-release (8)

Mehra, N. (2012, August 29). *Falling behind: Ontario's backslide into widening inequality, growing poverty and cuts to social programs.* Retrieved from Ontario Common Front website: http://pathwaytopotential.ca/wp-content/uploads/2011/01/falling-behind.pdf (4)

Meinhard, A., & Foster, M. (2002). *Responses of Canada's voluntary organizations to shifts in social policy: A provincial perspective.* Working paper prepared for the Centre for Voluntary Sector Studies ISTR Conference (Vol. III), Cape Town. Retrieved from http://www.ryerson.ca/~cvss/WP19.pdf (3)

Mendelson, M., & Battle, K. (2011, December). *Fixing the hole in EI: Temporary income assistance for the unemployed.* Retrieved from The Caledon Institute of Social Policy website: http://www.caledoninst.org/Publications/PDF/967ENG.pdf (1)

Mendelson, M., Battle, K., Torjman, S., & Lightman, E. (2010). *A basic income plan for Canadians with severe disabilities.* Retrieved from http://www.caledoninst.org/Publications/PDF/906ENG.pdf (14)

Merrill Cooper, Guyn Cooper Research Associates. (2008). *Overcoming barriers to the positive development and engagement of ethno-racial minority youth in Canada.* Completed for Canadian Heritage, Alberta Division. Retrieved from Immigrant

Sector Council of Calgary website: http://www.isccalgary.ca/carestrategy/documents/Overcomingbarrierstodevelopmentandengagement2008.pdf (13)

Michaud, S., Cotton, C., & Bishop, K. (2004, February). *Exploration of methodological issues in the development of the market basket measure of low income for Human Resources Development Canada.* Retrieved from Statistics Canada website: http://www.statcan.gc.ca/pub/75f0002m/75f0002m2004001-eng.pdf (9)

Mihorean, K. (2005). Trends in self-reported spousal violence. In K. AuCoin (Ed.), *Family violence in Canada: A statistical profile, 2005* (pp. 13–32). Ottawa, Canada: Statistics Canada. Retrieved from Government of Canada Publications website: http://publications.gc.ca/Collection/Statcan/85-224-X/85-224-XIE2006000.pdf (10)

Milan, A. (2000). One hundred years of families. *Canadian Social Trends* (Spring), 2–12. (10)

Milan, A. (2011). *Migration: International, 2009.* Retrieved from Statistics Canada website: http://www.statcan.gc.ca/pub/91-209-x/2011001/article/11526-eng.pdf (13)

Milan, A., & Bohnert, N. (2012). *Census in brief—Fifty years of families in Canada: 1961 to 2011: Families, households and marital status, 2011 census of population.* Retrieved from Statistics Canada website: http://www12.statcan.gc.ca/census-recensement/2011/as-sa/98-312-x/98-312-x2011003_1-eng.pdf (10)

Milan, A., & Vézina, M. (2011). *Senior women.* Retrieved from Statistics Canada website: http://www.statcan.gc.ca/pub/89-503-x/2010001/article/11441-eng.pdf (11)

Mitchell, B. (2005). *Canada's growing visible minority population: Generational challenges, opportunities and federal policy considerations* (Discussion paper commissioned by The Multicultural Program, Dept. of Canadian Heritage, Gatineau, Quebec, pp. 51–62). Retrieved from Collections Canada website: http://www.collectionscanada.gc.ca/webarchives/20060118063615/http://www.canadianheritage.gc.ca/multi/canada2017/7_e.cfm (13)

Montgomery, J. E. (1977). The housing patterns of older people. In R. A. Kalish (Ed.), *The later years* (pp. 253–261). Belmont, CA: Wadsworth Publishing. (11)

Mood Disorders Society of Canada. (2009). *Quick facts: Mental illness and addiction in Canada* (3rd ed.). Retrieved from http://www.mooddisorderscanada.ca/documents/Media%20Room/Quick%20Facts%203rd%20Edition%20Eng%20Nov%2012%2009.pdf (11)

Mook, J., Quarter, L., & Richmond, B. (2007). *What counts: Social accounting for nonprofits and cooperatives* (2nd ed.). London, England: Sigel Press. (5)

Morel, S. (2002). *The insertion model or the workfare model? The transformation of social assistance within Quebec and Canada.* Retrieved from Government of Canada Publications website: http://publications.gc.ca/collections/Collection/SW21-95-2002E.pdf (1, 3)

Morley, J. (2005). *Issue paper II, The Convention on the Rights of the Child: A framework for public policy in British Columbia.* Retrieved from Public Health Association of BC website: http://www.phabc.org/pdf/CYO_Issue_Paper_2.pdf (6)

Morris, M., & Gonsalves, T. (2012). *Women and poverty, third edition.* Retrieved from Canadian Research Institute for the Advancement of Women website: http://criaw-icref.ca/WomenAndPoverty (12)

Morris, M., & Sinnott, J. (2010). *Immigrant and refugee women, fact sheet.* Retrieved from Canadian Research Institute for the Advancement of Women website: http://www.criaw-icref.ca/ImmigrantandRefugeeWomen (13)

Moscovitch, A., & Drover, G. (1987). Social expenditures and the welfare state: The Canadian experience in historical perspective. In A. Moscovitch & J. Albert (Eds.), *The benevolent state: The growth of welfare in Canada* (pp. 13–43). Toronto, Canada: Garamond Press. (3)

Muegge, J., & Ross, N. (1996, November). *Volunteers: The heart of community organizations.* Retrieved from Ontario Ministry of Agriculture and Food website: http://www.omafra.gov.on.ca/english/rural/facts/96-017.htm (7)

Mulcahy, M., & Trocmé, N. (2010). *Children and Youth in out-of-home care in Canada* (CECW Information 2010, #78E) Retrieved from http://www.cecw-cepb.ca/sites/default/files/publications/en/ChildrenInCare78E.pdf (10)

Mullaly, R. (1997). *Structural social work.* Toronto, Canada: Oxford University Press. (8)

Mussell, B., Cardiff, K., & White, J. (2004). *The mental health and well-being of Aboriginal children and youth: Guidance for new approaches and services* (Vol. 1, report 9). Retrieved from http://www.fsin.com/healthandsocial/childportal/images/Mental%20health%20needs%20of%20Aboriginal%20Children%20and%20Youth.pdf (12)

MyHealthAlberta. (2011). *Child abuse and neglect: Symptoms.* Retrieved from https://myhealth.alberta.ca/health/pages/conditions.aspx?hwid=tm4865&#tm4882 (10)

National Aboriginal Health Organization. (2011). *Inuit child welfare and family support.* Retrieved from http://www.naho.ca/documents/it/2011_Inuit_Child_Welfare_Family_Support.pdf (10)

National Anti-Poverty Organization. (2003). *Submission to the Standing Committee on Finance pre-budget consultations—Sharing the wealth: Economic prosperity and rebuilding Canada's social safety net.* Ottawa, Canada: Author. (4)

National Association of Friendship Centres. (2012). *Home.* Retrieved from http://www.nafc.ca (12)

National Collaborating Centre for Aboriginal Health. (2009–2010). *Child welfare services in Canada: Aboriginal & mainstream.* Retrieved from http://www.nccah-ccnsa.ca/docs/fact%20sheets/child%20and%20youth/NCCAH-fs-ChildWelServCDA-2EN.pdf (12)

National Council of Welfare. (1995). *The 1995 budget and block funding.* Ottawa, Canada: Author. (4)

National Council of Welfare. (2003). *Recommendations on the creation of the Canada social transfer: Presentation to the Liberal Caucus Social Policy Committee.* Retrieved August 27, 2008, from http://www.ncwcnbes.net/documents/publicstatements/Archives/2003_NCWPresentationtoSocialPolicyCommittee_cstENG.pdf (4)

National Council of Welfare. (2010). *Welfare incomes 2009.* Retrieved from Government of Canada Publications website: http://publications.gc.ca/collections/collection_2011/cnb-ncw/HS51-1-2009-eng.pdf (1)

National Council of Welfare. (2011). *The dollars and cents of solving poverty.* Retrieved from http://www.sixthestate.net/docs/welfare/dollarsandsense.pdf (9)

National Food Security Assembly. (2006). Affordable housing, income/wages and food security, sustainable livelihoods. In E. Desjardins & S. Govindaraj (Eds.), *Proceedings of the Third National Food Assemby.* Retrieved from http://www.ryerson.ca/content/dam/foodsecurity/publications/books_reports/ASSEMBLY_PROCEEDINGS.pdf (9)

National Seniors Council. (2007). *Report of the National Seniors Council on elder abuse.* Retrieved from http://www.seniorscouncil.gc.ca/eng/research_publications/elder_abuse/2007/hs4_38/page05.shtml (11)

National Seniors Council. (2009). *Report of the National Seniors Council on low income among seniors.* Retrieved from http://www.seniorscouncil.gc.ca/eng/research_publications/low_income/2009/hs1_9/hs1_9.pdf (11)

National Seniors Council. (2011). *Report on the labour force participation of seniors and near seniors, and intergenerational relations.* Retrieved from http://www.seniorscouncil.gc.ca/eng/research_publications/labour_force/labour_force_participation.pdf (11)

Native Women's Association of Canada. (2010). *What their stories tell us: Research findings from the Sisters In Spirit initiative.* Retrieved from http://www.uregina.ca/resolve/PDFs/NWAC%20Report.pdf (12)

NDP seen as most in touch with seniors, survey suggests. (2012, June 27). CBC News and Nanos Research. Retrieved from CBC News website: http://www.cbc.ca/news/politics/story/2012/06/27/pol-pnp-nanos-survey-parties.html (11)

New Canadian Children and Youth Study. (n.d.). *About NCCYS.* Retrieved from http://www.nccys.com (13)

Nova Scotia. (2006). *Nova Scotia's new minister of volunteerism.* Retrieved from http://gov.ns.ca/news/details.asp?id=20060511007 (7)

Novick, M. (2007). *Summoned to stewardship: Make poverty reduction a collective legacy.* Retrieved from Campaign 2000 website: http://www.campaign2000.ca/resources/papers/SummonedToStewardship.pdf (4)

O'Donnell, V., & Wallace, S. (2011). *Women in Canada: A gender-based statistical report: First Nations.* Retrieved from Statistics Canada website: http://www.statcan.gc.ca/pub/89-503-x/2010001/article/11442-eng.pdf (12)

O'Neil, P., & Nursall, K. (2012). Working in ethnic enclaves limits newcomers' opportunities: Report. *Vancouver Sun.* Retrieved October 18, 2012, from http://www.vancouversun.com/Working+ethnic+enclaves+limits+newcomers+opportunities+Report/6770509/story.html (13)

Oderkirk, J. (1996). Government sponsored income security programs for seniors: Canada and Quebec pension plans. *Canadian Social Trends, 40*(Spring), 8–15. (3)

Office of the Auditor General of Canada. (2006). *Report of the auditor general of canada to the House of Commons: An overview of the federal government's expenditure management system.* Retrieved from http://www.oag-bvg.gc.ca/internet/docs/20061100ce.pdf (1, 4)

Offord Centre for Child Studies. (2012). *Oppositional defiant disorder and conduct disorder.* Retrieved from http://www.knowledge.offordcentre.com/behaviour-and-mental-health-problems/odd-and-cd (10)

Olasky, M. (1992). *The tragedy of American compassion.* Washington, DC: Regnery Publishing. (3)

Omidvar, R., & Richmond, T. (2003). *Immigrant settlement and social inclusion in Canada.* Retrieved from CERIS–The Ontario Metropolis Centre website http://www.ceris.metropolis.net/wp-content/uploads/pdf/research_publication/policy_matters/pm16.pdf (10, 13)

Ontario Healthy Communities Coalition. (2004). *Inclusive community organizations: A tool kit: II An organizational change strategy.* Retrieved from http://www.ohcc-ccso.ca/en/webfm_send/181 (8)

Ontario. (2009). *Accessibility for Ontarians with Disabilities Act, 2005: S.O. 2005, chapter 11.* Retrieved from http://www.e-laws.gov.on.ca/html/statutes/english/elaws_statutes_05a11_e.htm (14)

Ontario. Ministry of Community and Social Services. (2013). *Ontario disability support program—4.1: Income support directives.* Retrieved from http://www.mcss.gov.on.ca/en/mcss/programs/social/directives/directives/ODSPDirectives/income_support/4_1_ODSP_ISDirectives.aspx (9)

OPP Human Resources Bureau. (2006). *The impact of stress on officers and the OPP response.* Retrieved from http://www.attorneygeneral.jus.gov.on.ca/inquiries/ipperwash/policy_part/projects/pdf/Tab9_TheImpactofStressonOfficersandtheOPPResponse.pdf (7)

Oreopoulos, P. (2009). *Why do skilled immigrants struggle in the labor market? A field experiment with six thousand résumés.* Retrieved from Hire Immigrants Ottawa website: http://www.hireimmigrantsottawa.ca/downloads/WhyDoSkilledImmigrantsStruggleintheLaborMarket.pdf (13)

Organisation for Economic Co-operation and Development. (2005). *Combating poverty and social exclusion through work, policy brief.* Retrieved from http://www.oecd.org/els/soc/34598300.pdf (4)

Organisation for Economic Co-operation and Development. (2009). *Canada, Country highlights, Doing better for children.* Retrieved from http://www.oecd.org/dataoecd/21/3/43590221.pdf (10)

Organisation for Economic Co-operation and Development. (2011). *Divided we stand: Why inequality keeps rising.* Retrieved from http://www.oecd.org/social/soc/49170768.pdf (4, Appendix B)

Ornstein, M., & Stevenson, H. (2003). *Politics and ideology in Canada: Elite and public opinion in the transformation of a welfare state.* Kingston, Canada: McGill-Queen's University Press. (2)

Osborne, J. E. (1986). The evolution of the Canada Assistance Plan (CAP). In *Task Force on Program Review, Service to the public: Canada assistance plan, June 10, 1985* (pp. 57–92). Ottawa, Canada: Minister of Supply & Services Canada. Retrieved from http://www.canadiansocialresearch.net/capjack.htm (3)

Ottawa Community Immigrant Services Organization. (2012). *Mission statement.* Retrieved from http://ociso.org/En/index.php/about-us/mission-statement (13)

Overton, J. (1991). Dissenting opinions. *Perception, 15*(1), 17–21. (2)

Panitch, M. (1998). Forty years on! Lessons from our history. *Entourage, 11*(4), 9–16. (14)

Pape, B. (1990). *Self-help/mutual aid* (Canadian Mental Health Association, Social Action Series). Retrieved June 8, 2004, from www.cmha.ca/english/sas/selfhelp.htm (7)

Park, J. (2011). *Retirement, health and employment among those 55 plus.* Retrieved from Statistics Canada website: http://www.statcan.gc.ca/pub/75-001-x/2011001/pdf/11402-eng.pdf (11)

Parrott, L., Buchanan, J., & Williams, D. (2006) Volunteers, families and children in need: An evaluation of family friends. *Child & Family Social Work, 11*(2), 147–155. Retrieved from http://epubs.glyndwr.ac.uk/cgi/viewcontent.cgi?article=1016&context=siru (7)

Patterson, S. L., Memmott, J. L., Brennan, E. M., & Germain, C. B. (1992). Patterns of natural helping in rural areas: Implications for social work research. *Social Work Research and Abstracts, 28*(3), 22–28. (7)

Peters, J. (2010). *Walk the walk and talk the talk: A summary of some peer support activities in IIMHL countries.* Retrieved from International Initiative for Mental Health Leaders website: http://www.iimhl.com/IIMHLUpdates/20110404.pdf (7)

Peters, Y. (2003). *Federally sentenced women with mental disabilities: A dark corner in Canadian human rights: Part 1–Overview of disability discrimination.* Ottawa, Canada: DisAbled Women's Action Network (DAWN) Canada. Retrieved from http://www.elizabethfry.ca/submissn/dawn/dawn.pdf (14)

Phelan, M. L. (2012, August 1). *Attawapiskat First Nation v. Canada.* Retrieved from Federal Court Decisions website: http://decisions.fct-cf.gc.ca/en/2012/2012fc948/2012fc948.html (12)

Philia. (1997). *A short history of Philia: Enabling communities: Report to the J. W. McConnell Family Foundation.* Retrieved February 23, 2009, from http://www.philia.ca/cms_en/page1292.cfm (14)

Phillips, S. D. (2001). SUFA and citizen engagement: Fake or genuine masterpiece? *Policy Matters 2*(7). Retrieved from Institute for Research on Public Policy website: http://www.irpp.org/pm/archive/pmvol2no7.pdf (2)

Policy Horizons Canada. (2011). *Re-defining progress: The well-being objective.* Retrieved from http://www.horizons.gc.ca/doclib/2011-0095-eng.pdf (1)

Policy Research Initiative. (2005). *What we need to know about the social economy: A guide for policy research.* Retrieved from http://www.envision.ca/pdf/SocialEconomy/ResearchGuide.pdf (5)

Preece, M. (2003). When lone parents marry: The challenge of stepfamily relationships. *Transition Magazine, 33*(4), 7–10. Retrieved from Vanier Institute of the Family website: http://www.vanierinstitute.ca/include/get.php?nodeid=756 (10)

Preston, V., Chua, J., Phan, M., Park, S., Kelly, P., & Lemoine, M. (2011). *What are immigrants' experiences of discrimination in the workplace?* (TIEDI Analytical Report 21). Retrieved from Toronto Immigrant Employment Data Initiative website: http://www.yorku.ca/tiedi/doc/AnalyticalReport21.pdf (13)

Priest, A., Cohen, M., Goldberg, M., Istvanffy, N., Stainton, T., Wasik, A., & Woods, K. M. (2008). *Removing barriers to work: Flexible employment options for people with disabilities in BC: Summary.* Retrieved from Canadian Centre for Policy Alternatives website: http://www.policyalternatives.ca/sites/default/files/uploads/publications/BC_Office_Pubs/bc_2008/bc_removing_barriers_summary.pdf (14)

Prince, M. (2008, March). *The evolution of social policy in Canada and the expression of Canada in social policy.* Remarks to The Elder College, Malaspina University College Speaker Series, Nanaimo Campus. Retrieved from University of Victoria website: http://web.uvic.ca/spp/people/faculty/documents/nanaimoelders.pdf (2)

Privy Council Office. (1999). *The voluntary sector: Society's vital third pillar.* Retrieved February 17, 2004, from http://www.pco-bcp.gc.ca/volunteer/backgrounder3_e.htm (5)

Pross, P. (1995). Pressure groups: talking chameleons. In M. S. Whittington & G. Williams (Eds.), *Canadian politics in the 1990s* (2nd ed., pp. 252–227). Toronto, Canada: Nelson Canada. (2)

Public Health Agency of Canada. (2009). *Woman abuse—Overview paper.* Retrieved from http://www.phac-aspc.gc.ca/ncfv-cnivf/publications/femviof-eng.php (2)

Public Health Agency of Canada. (2010a). *Canadian incidence study of reported child abuse and neglect, 2008: Major findings.* Retrieved from http://www.phac-aspc.gc.ca/cm-vee/csca-ecve/2008/assets/pdf/cis-2008_report_eng.pdf (10)

Public Health Agency of Canada. (2010b). *The chief public health officer's report on the state of public health in Canada, 2010: Growing older—Adding life to years.* Retrieved from http://www.phac-aspc.gc.ca/cphorsphc-respcacsp/2010/fr-rc/pdf/cpho_report_2010_e.pdf (11)

Public Health Agency of Canada. (2011). *Nobody's perfect.* Retrieved from http://www.phac-aspc.gc.ca/hp-ps/dca-dea/parent/nobody-personne/index-eng.php (1)

Public Health Agency of Canada. (2012). *Mental health promotion: Promoting mental health means promoting the best of ourselves.* Retrieved from http://www.phac-aspc.gc.ca/mh-sm/mhp-psm/index-eng.php (10)

Public Safety and Emergency Preparedness Canada. (2003). *Cost-benefit analysis of a community healing process* (Research Summary: Corrections Research and Development. Vol. 8, No. 6). Retrieved from http://www.publicsafety.gc.ca/res/cor/sum/_fl/cprs200311-eng.pdf (12)

Public Service Alliance of Canada. (2008). *PSAC statement on National Aboriginal Peoples' Day: June 21, 2008: Making Aboriginal poverty history.* Retrieved from http://www.psac-afpc.com/what/humanrights/june21factsheet1-e.shtml (12)

Quarter, J. (1992). *Canada's social economy: Co-operatives, non-profits, and other community enterprises.* Toronto, Canada: James Lorimer. (5)

Québec. (2009). *2009–2010 Budget: Status report on Québec's family policy.* Retrieved from http://www.budget.finances.gouv.qc.ca/Budget/2009-2010/en/documents/pdf/FamilyPolicy.pdf (10)

Rajan, D. (2004). *Violence against women with disabilities.* Ottawa, Canada: National Clearinghouse on Family Violence. Retrieved from Government of Canada Publications website: http://publications.gc.ca/collections/Collection/H72-22-9-2004E.pdf (14)

Ranstad Canada. (2012). *Workforce diversity: The fresh face of employment in Canada.* Retrieved from http://www.randstad.ca/downloads/Workforce_Diversity_stf.en.pdf (13)

Raphael, D. (2011). *Poverty in Canada: Implications for health and quality of life.* Retrieved from http://www.phabc.org/userfiles/file/PovertyinCanada_Front%20Pages.pdf (9)

Reed, P. B., & Howe, V. J. (2000). *Voluntary organizations in Ontario in the 1990s.* Retrieved from Statistics Canada website: http://dsp-psd.pwgsc.gc.ca/Collection/Statcan/75F0048M/75F0048MIE2002002.pdf (8)

Regional Geriatric Program of Toronto. (2012). *The aging and homelessness Project.* Retrieved from http://rgp.toronto.on.ca/aging_and_homelessness_project (11)

Rektor, L. (2002, September). *Advocacy: The sound of citizens' voices: A position paper from the advocacy working group.* Retrieved from Voluntary Sector Initiative website: http://www.vsi-isbc.org/eng/policy/pdf/position_paper.pdf (5)

Research Alliance for Canadian Homelessness, Housing and Health. (2010). *Housing vulnerability and health: Canada's hidden emergency.* Retrieved from Homeless Hub website: http://www.homelesshub.ca/ResourceFiles/HousingVulnerabilityHealth-REACH3-Nov2010.pdf (9)

Research on Aging, Policies, and Practice. (2010). *Gender differences in family/friend caregiving in Canada.* Retrieved from University of Alberta website: http://www.rapp.ualberta.ca/en/Publications/~/media/rapp/Publications/Documents/Characteristics_of_caregivers_2010Dec_final.pdf (7)

Research on Aging, Policies, and Practice. (2011). *Employment consequences of family/friend caregiving in Canada.* Retrieved from University of Alberta website: http://www.rapp.ualberta.ca/en/Publications/~/media/rapp/Publications/Documents/2011EmploymentConsequencesFFCaregiving.pdf (7)

Residential schools: A history of residential schools in Canada. (2010). *CBC News*. Retrieved from http://www.cbc.ca/canada/story/2008/05/16/f-faqs-residential-schools.html (12)

Rice, B., & Snyder, A. (2008). Reconciliation in the context of a settler society: Healing the legacy of colonialism in Canada. In M. B. Castellano, L. Archibald, & M. DeGagné (Eds.), *From truth to reconciliation: Transforming the legacy of residential schools* (pp. 43–63). Retrieved from Aboriginal Healing Foundation website: http://www.ahf.ca/downloads/from-truth-to-reconciliation-transforming-the-legacy-of-residential-schools.pdf (12)

Rice, J. J., & Prince, M. J. (2000). *Changing politics of Canadian social policy*. Toronto, Canada: University of Toronto Press. (3, 4, 5)

Richmond, T., & Shields, J. (2003, June). *NGO restructuring: Constraints and consequences*. Presentation to the 11th Biennial Social Welfare Policy Conference, University of Ottawa, June. Retrieved from Ontario Council of Agencies Serving Immigrants website: http://www.ocasi.org/downloads/NGO_Restructuring.pdf (5)

Rittel, H., & Webber, M. (1973). Dilemmas in a general theory of planning. *Policy Sciences, 4,* 155–169. Retrieved from http://www.uctc.net/mwebber/Rittel+Webber+Dilemmas+General_Theory_of_Planning.pdf (5)

Rivers-Moore, B. (1993). *Family violence against women with disabilities*. Ottawa, Canada: Dawn Canada for National Clearinghouse on Family Violence. Retrieved from Government of Canada Publications website: http://publications.gc.ca/collections/Collection/H72-22-9-1993E.pdf (14)

Roeher Institute. (1996). *Disability, community, and society: Exploring the links*. North York, Canada: Author. (14)

Rogers, F. (2001, August 27). Mister Rogers takes off the cardigan. Robert Bianco, *USA Today*. Retrieved from http://www.usatoday.com/life/television/2001-08-22-rogers.htm (7)

Rogers, R. E., & Fong, J. Y. (2000). *Organizational assessment: Diagnosis and intervention*. Amherst, MA: Human Resource Development Press. (8)

Rogow, S. M. (2002, May). *The disability rights movement: The Canadian experience*. Paper presented at the International Conference on Autism, Kamloops, B.C. Retrieved from International Special Education website: http://www.internationalsped.com/magazines_articles/The%20Disability%20Rights%20Movement%20Ed.1.pdf (14)

Rondeau, G. (2001, October). *Challenges that confront social work education in Canada: Canadian social work forum 2001*. Paper presented at the National Social Work Forum conference, Montreal. Retrieved from Canadian Association of Deans and Directors of Schools of Social Work website: http://www.caddssw-acddess.org/CHALLENGES%20THAT%20CONFRONT%20SOCIAL%20WORK.pdf (7)

Rosenfeld, M. (2009). *Nontraditional families and childhood progress through school*. Retrieved from Stanford University website: http://www.stanford.edu/dept/soc/people/mrosenfeld/documents/Rosenfeld_Nontraditional_Families_Children.pdf (10)

Ross, D. P. (1987). Income security. In S. A. Yelaja (Ed.), *Canadian social policy* (Rev. ed., pp. 27–46). Waterloo, Canada: Wilfrid Laurier University Press. (3)

Ross, D. P. (1995). Who will speak for Canada's children? *Perception, 19*(2), 2–3. Retrieved from http://www.ccsd.ca/perception/192/speak.html (4)

Ross, D. P., Roberts, P. A., & Scott, K. (1998). *Variations in child development outcomes among children living in lone-parent families.* Retrieved from Collections Canada website: http://www.collectionscanada.gc.ca/webarchives/20061029083308/http://www1.servicecanada.gc.ca/en/cs/sp/sdc/pkrf/publications/research/1998-001325/1998-001325.pdf (10)

Roy, J. (2005–2010). *Acknowledging racism.* Retrieved from Canadian Race Relations Foundation website: http://www.crr.ca/en/library-a-clearinghouse/publications-a-resources/31/220-acknowledging-racism (13)

Royal Canadian Mounted Police. (2012a). *The effects of family violence on children.* Retrieved from http://www.rcmp-grc.gc.ca/cp-pc/pdfs/vio-chil-enfa-eng.pdf (10)

Royal Canadian Mounted Police. (2012b). *Elder abuse.* Retrieved from http://www.rcmp-grc.gc.ca/ccaps-spcca/elder-aine-eng.htm (11)

Royal Commission on Aboriginal Peoples. (1996). Conclusions. In *Report of the Royal Commission on Aboriginal peoples: Looking forward, looking back.* Retrieved from Collections Canada website: http://www.collectionscanada.gc.ca/webarchives/20071213042737/http://www.ainc-inac.gc.ca/ch/rcap/sg/cg13_e.pdf (12)

Royal Commission on the Status of Women of Canada. (1977). Chapter 6. *Report of the Royal Commission on the Status of Women of Canada.* Retrieved from http://www.acswcccf.nb.ca/media/acsw/files/english/Chapter%206%20Poverty.doc (9)

Russell, B. (1952). *The impact of science on society.* London, England: George Allen and Unwin. (6)

Saewyc, E., Bingham, B., Brunanski, D., Smith, A., Hunt, S., Northcott, M., & the McCreary Centre Society. (2008). *Moving upstream: Aboriginal marginalized and street-involved youth in B.C.* Retrieved from http://www.mcs.bc.ca/pdf/Moving_Upstream_Websmall.pdf (12)

Saint-Martin, D. (2004). *Coordinating interdependence: Governance and social policy redesign in Britain, the European Union and Canada* (CPRN Social Architecture Papers, Research Report F41, Family Network). Retrieved from Canadian Policy Research Networks website: http://www.cprn.org/documents/29040_en.pdf (2)

Sakamoto, I. (2007). A critical examination of immigrant acculturation: Toward an anti-oppressive social work model with immigrant adults in a pluralistic society. *British Journal of Social Work, 37*, 515–535. doi:10.1093/bjsw/bcm024 (13)

Sangha, A. (2012). What to do about ethnic enclaves in Canada? *Straight.com.* Retrieved from http://www.straight.com/article-679251/vancouver/alex-sangha-what-do-about-ethnic-enclaves-canada (13)

Sauber, R. (1983). *The human services delivery system.* New York, NY: Columbia University. (5)

Saunders, R. (2004). *Passion and commitment under stress: Human resource issues in Canada's non-profit sector: A synthesis report* (CPRN Research Series on Human Resources in the Non-Profit Sector No. 5). Retrieved from Canadian Policy Research Networks website: http://www.cprn.org/documents/25808_en.pdf (5, 7)

Schellenberg, G., & Maheux, H. (2007, April). Immigrants' perspectives on their first four years in Canada: Highlights from three waves of the Longitudinal Survey of Immigrants to Canada. *Canadian Social Trends* (Special Edition), 2–34. Retrieved from Statistics Canada website: http://www.statcan.gc.ca/pub/11-008-x/2007000/pdf/9627-eng.pdf (13)

Scott, B. (2004). *Establishing professional social work in Vancouver and at the University of British Columbia.* Retrieved February 14, 2009, from UBC Library website: http://toby.library.ubc.ca/webpage/webpage.cfm?id=97 (8)

Scott, K. (2003a). Chapter 2: Financial capacity and sources of funding. In *Funding matters: The impact of Canada's new funding regime on nonprofit and voluntary organizations.* Retrieved from Canadian Council on Social Development website: http://www.ccsd.ca/pubs/2003/fm/chapter2.pdf (5)

Scott, K. (2003b). Chapter 5: How funding trends are affecting nonprofit and voluntary organizations. *Funding matters: The impact of Canada's new funding regime on nonprofit and voluntary organizations.* Retrieved from Canadian Council on Social Development website: http://www.ccsd.ca/pubs/2003/fm/chapter5.pdf (5, 8)

Scott, K. (2008). *The economic well-being of children in Canada, the United States, and Mexico.* Retrieved from Canadian Council on Social Development website: http://www.ccsd.ca/pubs/2008/cina/TriEcono_English.pdf (10)

SEED Winnipeg. (n.d.). *Individual development account program.* Retrieved from http://seedwinnipeg.ca/programs/detail/individual-development-account (9)

Service Canada. (2012a). *Social workers.* Retrieved from http://www.servicecanada.gc.ca/eng/qc/job_futures/statistics/4152.shtml (7)

Service Canada. (2012b). *Questions and answers regarding the changes to the Old Age Security Act.* Retrieved from http://www.servicecanada.gc.ca/eng/isp/oas/changes/faq.shtml#s4 (11)

Service Canada. (n.d.). *Canada Pension Plan/Old Age Security, quarterly report—Monthly amounts and related figures, type of benefit from January to March 2012.* Retrieved from http://www.servicecanada.gc.ca/eng/isp/statistics/rates/pdf/janmar12.pdf (1)

Shakya, Y, Khanlou, N., & Gonsalves, T. (2010). Determinants of mental health for newcomer youth: Policy and service implications. *Canadian Issues,* (Summer), 98–102. Retrieved from http://canada.metropolis.net/pdfs/immi_health/Immigrant%20Mental%20Health%20-%20pgs98-102.pdf (13)

Shangreaux, C., & Blackstock, C. (2004). *Staying at home: Examining the implications of least disruptive measures in First Nations child and family service agencies.* Retrieved from http://www.fncfcs.com/sites/default/files/docs/Staying_at_Home.pdf (10)

Shapiro, J. (2003). *Action planning toolkit: Developing a financing strategy.* Retrieved from CIVICUS website: https://www.civicus.org/new/media/Developing%20a%20Financing%20Strategy.pdf (6)

Shields, J. (2003, January). *No safe haven: Markets, welfare, and migrants* (CERIS Working Paper No. 22). Retrieved from Joint Centre of Excellence for Research on Immigration and Settlement—Toronto website: http://www.ceris.metropolis.net/Virtual%20Library/Demographics/wkpp22_shields.pdf (5)

Single Parent Association of Newfoundland. (2012). *Home.* Retrieved from http://www.envision.ca/webs/span/ (10)

Sinha, M. (2012). *Family violence in Canada: A statistical profile, 2010.* Retrieved from Statistics Canada website: http://www.statcan.gc.ca/pub/85-002-x/2012001/article/11643-eng.pdf (10)

Smith, A. (2010). CIC's modernized approach to settlement programming: A brief description. *International Settlement Canada, 23*(3), 1–4. Retrieved from http://www3.carleton.ca/cimss/inscan-e/v23_3e.pdf (13)

Smith, C., Van Wert, M., Ma, J., & Fallon, B. (2012). *OIS-2008: Rates of out-of-home placement in substantiated maltreatment investigations.* Retrieved from http://www.cwrp.ca/infosheets/ois-2008-rates-out-home-placement-in-investigations (10)

Smith, E. (2004). *Nowhere to turn? Responding to partner violence against immigrant and visible minority women.* Retrieved from Canadian Council for Refugees website: http://ccrweb.ca/files/nowhere_to_turn.pdf (13)

Smith, J., & McKitrick, A. (2010). *Current conceptualizations of the social economy in the Canadian context.* Retrieved from Canadian Social Economy Hub website: http://socialeconomyhub.ca/sites/socialeconomyhub.ca/files/DefinitionPaper.pdf (5)

Smith, M. (2004). Interest groups and social movements. In M. Whittington & G. Williams (Eds.), *Canadian politics in the 21st century* (6th ed., pp. 213–30). Toronto, Canada: Nelson Thomson Canada. (3)

Snowdon, A. (2012, January 19). *Strengthening communities for Canadian children with disabilities: Discussion document.* Retrieved from http://sandboxproject.ca/wp-content/uploads/2012/01/SandboxProjectDiscussionDocument.pdf (14)

Social and Enterprise Development Innovations. (2003). *Asset-building guide.* Retrieved from http://www.sedi.org/DataRegV2-unified/sedi-Publications/AB%20Guide%20-%202003.pdf (9)

Social Planning and Research Council of BC. (2008). *Dawson Creek social plan: Final report.* Retrieved from http://www.dawsoncreek.ca/wordpress/wp-content/uploads/2011/10/DawsonCreekSocialPlanFinalReport-Sept182008.pdf (8)

Social Research and Demonstration Corporation. (2005). Whither welfare? *Learning what works, 5*(1), 6–9. Retrieved from http://www.srdc.org/uploads/volume_5_number_1-en.pdf (4, 9)

Social service staff work 60-hour weeks to make up for employee shortage. (2007, September 30). *The Edmonton Journal*. Retrieved from http://www.canada.com/edmontonjournal/story.html?id=1331bf6c-9ab0-4101-8f3a-c83b0d87b08e (7)

Soroka, S., & Roberton, S. (2012, March). *A literature review of public opinion research on Canadian attitudes towards multiculturalism and immigration, 2006–2009*. Retrieved from Citizen and Immigration Canada website: http://www.cic.gc.ca/english/pdf/research-stats/2012-por-multi-imm-eng.pdf (13)

Special Senate Committee on Aging. (2007). *First interim report: Embracing the challenge of aging*. Retrieved from Parliament of Canada website: http://www.parl.gc.ca/Content/SEN/Committee/391/agei/rep/repintfeb07-e.pdf (11)

Special Senate Committee on Aging. (2008). *Second interim report: Issues and options for an aging population*. Retrieved from Parliament of Canada website: http://www.parl.gc.ca/Content/SEN/Committee/392/agei/rep/repfinmar08-e.pdf (11)

Special Senate Committee on Aging. (2009). *Final report on Canada's aging population: Seizing the opportunity*. Retrieved from Parliament of Canada website: http://www.parl.gc.ca/Content/SEN/Committee/402/agei/rep/AgingFinalReport-e.pdf (7, 11)

Special Senate Committee on Poverty. (1971). *Report of the Special Senate Committee on Poverty: Poverty in Canada*. Ottawa, Canada: Government of Canada. (4)

Spicker, P. (2012). *An introduction to social policy: The politics of welfare*. Retrieved from Robert Gordon University Aberdeen website: http://www2.rgu.ac.uk/publicpolicy/introduction/contents.htm (1)

Stahl, J., & Hill, C. (2008). A comparison of four methods for assessing natural helping ability. *Journal of Community Psychology, 36*(3), 289–298. (7)

Standing Committee on the Status of Women. (2011a). *Interim report, call into the night: An overview of violence against Aboriginal women*. 40th Parliament, 3rd session. Retrieved from Parliament of Canada website: http://www.parl.gc.ca/content/hoc/Committee/403/FEWO/Reports/RP5056509/feworp14/feworp14-e.pdf (12)

Standing Committee on the Status of Women. (2011b). *Parliamentary committee races against election clock to table an urgent interim report on violence against Aboriginal women*. Retrieved from Parliament of Canada website: http://www.parl.gc.ca/HousePublications/Publication.aspx?DocId=5069740&Language=E&Mode=1&Parl=40&Ses=3 (12)

Standing Senate Committee on Human Rights. (2007). *Children: The silenced citizens report: Executive summary*. Retrieved from Parliament of Canada website: http://www.parl.gc.ca/Content/SEN/Committee/391/huma/press/26apr07-e.htm (10)

Standing Senate Committee on Social Affairs, Science and Technology. (2006a). *Out of the shadows at last: Transforming mental health, mental illness and addiction services in Canada. Part 1*. Retrieved from Parliament of Canada website: http://www.parl.gc.ca/Content/SEN/Committee/391/soci/rep/pdf/rep02may06part1-e.pdf (6, 7)

Standing Senate Committee on Social Affairs, Science and Technology. (2006b). *Out of the shadows at last: Transforming mental health, mental illness and addiction services in Canada. Part V: Federal leadership.* Retrieved from Parliament of Canada website: http://www.parl.gc.ca/Content/SEN/Committee/391/SOCI/rep/pdf/rep02may06part2-e.pdf (12)

Stapleton, J., & Tweddle, A. (2008, August). *Navigating the maze: Improving coordination and integration of disability income and employment policies and programs for people living with HIV/AIDS: A discussion paper.* Retrieved from http://www.hivandrehab.ca/EN/episodic_disabilities/documents/NavigatingtheMazeFinal.pdf (14)

Stasiulis, D., & Abu-Laban, Y. (2004). Unequal relations and the struggle for equality: Race and ethnicity in Canadian politics. In M. Whittington & G. Williams (Eds.), *Canadian politics in the 21st century* (6th ed., pp. 371–397). Scarborough, Canada: Thomson Nelson. (13)

Statistics Canada. (2003, January). *2001 census: Analysis series: Canada's ethnocultural portrait: The changing mosaic.* Retrieved from http://www12.statcan.gc.ca/english/census01/products/analytic/companion/etoimm/pdf/96F0030XIE2001008.pdf (13)

Statistics Canada. (2005, December 13). Study: Divorce and the mental health of children. *The Daily,* p. 6. Retrieved from http://www.statcan.gc.ca/daily-quotidien/051213/dq051213-eng.pdf (10)

Statistics Canada. (2006). *Measuring violence against women: Statistical trends, 2006.* Retrieved from http://www.statcan.gc.ca/pub/85-570-x/85-570-x2006001-eng.pdf (13)

Statistics Canada. (2007). *Participation and Activity Limitation Survey 2006: Analytical report.* Retrieved from http://www.statcan.gc.ca/pub/89-628-x/89-628-x2007002-eng.pdf (14)

Statistics Canada. (2008a). *Aboriginal peoples in Canada in 2006: Inuit, Métis and First Nations, 2006 census: Aboriginal peoples, 2006 census: Census year 2006.* Retrieved from http://www12.statcan.ca/english/census06/analysis/aboriginal/pdf/97-558-XIE2006001.pdf (12)

Statistics Canada. (2008b). *Canadian demographics at a glance.* Retrieved from http://www.statcan.gc.ca/pub/91-003-x/91-003-x2007001-eng.pdf (13)

Statistics Canada. (2008c). *Participation and Activity Limitation Survey 2006: Families of children with disabilities in Canada.* Retrieved from http://www.statcan.gc.ca/pub/89-628-x/89-628-x2008009-eng.pdf (14)

Statistics Canada. (2010a). *Household food insecurity, 2007–2008.* Retrieved from http://www.statcan.gc.ca/pub/82-625-x/2010001/article/11162-eng.htm (9)

Statistics Canada. (2010b). Minimum wage. *Perspectives on labour and income: Minimum Wage.* Retrieved from http://www.statcan.gc.ca/pub/75-001-x/topics-sujets/pdf/topics-sujets/minimumwage-salaireminimum-2009-eng.pdf (9)

Statistics Canada. (2010c, December 16). Women in Canada: Economic well-being, 2008. *The Daily.* Retrieved from http://www.statcan.gc.ca/daily-quotidien/101216/dq101216c-eng.htm (9)

Statistics Canada. (2010d). *Projected population, by projection scenario, sex and age group as of July 1, Canada, provinces and territories, Table 052-0005*. Retrieved from http://www5.statcan.gc.ca/cansim/a26?lang=eng&retrLang=eng&id=0520005&paSer=&pattern=&stByVal=1&p1=1&p2=37&tabMode=dataTable&csid= (11)

Statistics Canada. (2010e). *Healthy people, healthy places: Dependency ratio*. Retrieved from http://www.statcan.gc.ca/pub/82-229-x/2009001/demo/dep-eng.htm (11)

Statistics Canada. (2010f, March 9). Study, Projections of the diversity of the Canadian population: 2006–2031. *They Daily*. Retrieved from http://www.statcan.gc.ca/daily-quotidien/100309/dq100309a-eng.htm (13)

Statistics Canada. (2011a). *Residential care facilities 2009/2010*. Retrieved from http://www.statcan.gc.ca/pub/83-237-x/83-237-x2012001-eng.pdf (6)

Statistics Canada. (2011b). *Family violence in Canada: A statistical profile*. Retrievd from http://www.statcan.gc.ca/pub/85-224-x/85-224-x2010000-eng.pdf (10)

Statistics Canada. (2011c). *Residential care facilities, 2009/2010*. Retrieved from http://www.statcan.gc.ca/pub/83-237-x/83-237-x2012001-eng.pdf (11)

Statistics Canada. (2012a). *Caring Canadians, involved Canadians: Tables report, 2010* (Catalogue no. 89-649-X). Retrieved from http://www.statcan.gc.ca/pub/89-649-x/89-649-x2011001-eng.pdf (7)

Statistics Canada. (2012b). *Persons in low income after tax (in percent, 2006 to 2010)*. Retrieved from http://www.statcan.gc.ca/tables-tableaux/sum-som/l01/cst01/famil19a-eng.htm?sdi=low%20income (9)

Statistics Canada. (2012c). Chapter 14: Families, households and housing. In *Canada year book 2012* (pp. 198–209). Retrieved from http://www.statcan.gc.ca/pub/11-402-x/2012000/pdf/families-familles-eng.pdf (9)

Statistics Canada. (2012d, May 29). 2011 Census: Age and sex. *The Daily*. Retrieved from http://www.statcan.gc.ca/daily-quotidien/120529/dq120529-eng.pdf (10)

Statistics Canada. (2012e). *Family income, by family type (lone-parent families) 2006–2010*. Retrieved from http://www.statcan.gc.ca/tables-tableaux/sum-som/l01/cst01/famil106b-eng.htm (10)

Statistics Canada. (2012f, May 22). Family violence in Canada: A statistical profile, 2010. *The Daily*,p. 2–4. Retrieved from http://www.statcan.gc.ca/daily-quotidien/120522/dq120522-eng.pdf (10)

Statistics Canada. (2012g). *Summary table: Life expectancy at birth, by sex, by province*. Retrieved from http://www.statcan.gc.ca/tables-tableaux/sum-som/l01/cst01/health26-eng.htm (11)

Statistics Canada. (2012h). *Caring Canadians, involved Canadians: Tables report, 2010*. Retrieved from http://www.statcan.gc.ca/pub/89-649-x/89-649-x2011001-eng.pdf (11)

Statistics Canada. (2012i). *Labour force characteristics by immigrant status, by detailed age group, 2011*. Retrieved from http://www.statcan.gc.ca/tables-tableaux/sum-som/l01/cst01/labor91a-eng.htm (13)

Statistics Canada. (2012j). *Labour force survey estimates (LFS), by immigrant status, age group, Canada, regions, provinces and Montreal, Toronto, Vancouver census metropolitan areas: Table 282-0102*. Retrieved from http://www5.statcan.gc.ca/cansim/pick-choisir?lang=eng&p2=33&id=2820102 (13)

Statistics Canada. (2012k). *The Canadian population in 2011: Population counts and growth: Population and dwelling counts, 2011 census*. Retrieved from http://www12.statcan.gc.ca/census-recensement/2011/as-sa/98-310-x/98-310-x2011001-eng.pdf (13)

Statistics Canada. (2012l). *Canadian survey on disability: Topics covered in the survey*. Retrieved from http://www.statcan.gc.ca/survey-enquete/household-menages/3251a-eng.htm (14)

Status of Disabled Persons Secretariat. (1994). *Disability policy and programs in Canada: A brief overview*. Ottawa, Canada: Human Resources Development Canada. (14)

Step Families Canada. (2012, April 13). *How does remarraige affect children?* Retrieved from http://stepfamiliescanada.blogspot.ca (10)

Stephenson, M., Rondeau, G., Michaud, J. C., & Fiddler, S. (2000). *In critical demand: Social work in Canada* (Vol. 1: Final report prepared for the Social Work Sector Steering Committee). Retrieved from Canadian Association of Social Workers website: http://casw-acts.ca/sites/default/files/attachements/In%20Critical%20Demand%20Social%20Work%20in%20Canada%20Volume%201%20pages%201-24%20.pdf (7)

Stewart, J. (2002). *Speaking notes for the Honourable Jane Stewart, Minister of Human Resources Development Canada, to the International Social Security Association, Vancouver, BC*. Retrieved December 27, 2008, from http://www.hrsdc.gc.ca/eng/cs/comm/speeches/hrdc/2002/020910_e.shtml (2)

Strong-Boag, V. (1979). Wages for housework: Mothers' allowances and the beginnings of social security in Canada. *Journal of Canadian Studies, 14*(1), 24–34. (3)

Struthers, J. (1983). *No fault of their own: Unemployment and the Canadian welfare state, 1914–1941*. Toronto, Canada: University of Toronto Press. (3)

Suhasini, G. (2012). *New policies could change the demographics of Canada*. Retrieved from http://canadianimmigrant.ca/immigrate/new-policies-could-change-the-demographics-of-canada (13)

Taft, K. (2010, May). *Follow the money. Where is Alberta's wealth actually going? A profile of key public and private sector economic trends in Alberta from 1989 to 2008*. Retrieved from http://saveourfinearts.ca/wp-content/uploads/2012/01/Follow-the-Money-Where-is-Albertas-Wealth-Actually-Going.pdf (2)

Tamarack. (2012). *Community engagement: Poverty reduction*. Retrieved from http://tamarackcommunity.ca/g3s3_3.html (9)

Taylor, G. (1969). *The problem of poverty, 1660–1834*. Wimbledon, England: Longmans. (3)

Teeple, G. (2000). *Globalization and the decline of social reform: Into the twenty-first century*. Aurora, Canada: Garamond Press. (1)

Thomas, A., & Skage, S. (1998). Overview of perspectives on family literacy: Research and practice. In A. Thomas (Ed.), *Family literacy in Canada: Profiles of effective practices* (pp. 5–24). Welland, Canada: Soleil Publishing. (6)

Thompson, A. H., Howard, A. W., & Jin, Y. (2001). A social problem index for Canada. *Canadian Journal of Psychiatry, 46,* 45–51. Retrieved from http://ww1.cpa-apc.org:8080/Publications/Archives/CJP/2001/Feb/Original.asp (2)

Thompson, D. (2010). *What is a food charter and why should Sault Ste Marie want one?* Retrieved from Algoma Food Network website: http://algomafoodnetwork.wordpress.com/2010/01/09/what-is-a-food-charter-and-why-should-sault-ste-marie-want-one/ (9)

Thorburn, H. G. (2012). Pressure group. In *The Canadian encyclopedia.* Retrieved from http://www.thecanadianencyclopedia.com/articles/pressure-group (2)

Thursz, D. (1977). Social Action. In J. B. Turner (Ed.), *Encyclopedia of Social Work* (17th ed., vol. 2, pp. 1274–1280). Washington, DC: National Association of Social Workers. (8)

Tobin, S. (2005). *Ageing and employment policies: Canada 2005: Executive summary.* Retrieved from Organisation for Economic Co-operation and Development website: http://www.oecd.org/employment/employmentpoliciesand-data/35386591.pdf (11)

Torjman, S. (2005). *What is policy?* Ottawa, Canada: Caledon Institute of Social Policy. Retrieved from http://www.caledoninst.org/Publications/PDF/544ENG.pdf (2)

Toronto Community and Neighbourhood Services. (2004). *Cracks in the foundation: Community agency survey 2003: A study of Toronto's community-based human service sector: Final report.* Retrieved from http://neighbourhoodcentres.ca/reportspub/Cracks-in-the-foundation-Feb-04.pdf (6)

Townsend, P. (1993). *The international analysis of poverty.* Hemel Hempstead, England: Harvester Wheatsheaf. (9)

Treasury Board of Canada Secretariat. (2002). *Policy on alternative service delivery.* Retrieved from http://www.tbs-sct.gc.ca/pubs_pol/opepubs/tb_b4/asd-dmps01-eng.asp (5)

Treasury Board of Canada Secretariat. (2006, September). *Backgrounder: Effective spending.* Retrieved from Collections Canada website: http://www.collectionscanada.gc.ca/webarchives/20061129210730/http://www.tbs-sct.gc.ca/media/nr-cp/2006/0925_e.asp (7)

Treasury Board of Canada Secretariat. (2008). *Guide on strategic planning: Tips and advice for IM or IT strategic plans* (Final Draft–Version 1.0). Retrieved from http://www.uquebec.ca/observgo/fichiers/89111_b.pdf (6)

Trocméi, N., MacLaurin, B., Fallon, B., Shlonsky, A., Mulcahy, M., & Esposito, T. (2009). *National child welfare outcomes indicator matrix.* Retrieved from McGill University website: http://www.mcgill.ca/files/crcf/NOM_09Final.pdf (10)

Truth and Reconciliation Commission of Canada. (2012). *Truth and Reconciliation Commission of Canada interim report.* Retrieved from Attendance Marketing website: http://www.attendancemarketing.com/~attmk/TRC_jd/Interim_report_English_electronic_copy.pdf (12)

Turcotte, M., & Schellenberg, G. (2007). *A portrait of seniors in Canada.* Retrieved from Statistics Canada website: http://www.statcan.gc.ca/pub/89-519-x/89-519-x2006001-eng.pdf (11)

Turner, A., & Findlay, L. (2012). Informal caregiving for seniors: Health matters. *Health Reports* 23(3) (Catalogue no. 82-003-XPE). Retrieved from Statistics Canada website: http://www.statcan.gc.ca/pub/82-003-x/2012003/article/11694-eng.pdf (7)

Turner, A., Crompton, S., & Langlois, S. (2013). *Aboriginal Peoples in Canada: First Nations People, Métis and Inuit.* Retrieved from Statistics Canada website: http://www12.statcan.gc.ca/nhs-enm/2011/as-sa/99-011-x/99-011-x2011001-eng.pdf (7)

UNICEF. (2007). *Child poverty in perspective: An overview of child well-being in rich countries* (Innocenti Report Card 7). Florence: Italy: UNICEF Innocenti Research Centre. Retrieved from http://www.unicef-irc.org/publications/pdf/rc7_eng.pdf (10)

UNICEF. (2012). *Measuring child poverty: New league tables of child poverty in the world's rich countries* (Innocenti Report Card 10). Florence: UNICEF Innocenti Research Centre. Retrieved from http://www.unicef-irc.org/publications/pdf/rc10_eng.pdf (9)

United Nations Economic and Social Council: Committee on Economic, Social and Cultural Rights. (2001). *Substantive issues arising in the implementation of the international covenant on social, economic, and cultural rights: Poverty and the international covenant on social, economic, and cultural rights: Twenty-fifth session, Geneva, Agenda item 5.* Retieved from http://www2.ohchr.org/english/bodies/cescr/docs/statements/E.C.12.2001.10Poverty-2001.pdf (2)

United Nations Office of the United Nations High Commissioner for Human Rights. (2006). *Convention on the rights of persons with disabilities.* Retrieved from http://www.un.org/disabilities/convention/conventionfull.shtml (14)

United Nations. (1993). *Declaration on the elimination of violence against women* (General Assembly resolution 48/104). Retrieved from http://www.unhchr.ch/huridocda/huridoca.nsf/(symbol)/a.res.48.104.en (2)

United Nations. (1995). *World summit for social development, Copenhagen 1995: Copenhagen Declaration on Social Development: Part A: Current social situation and reasons for convening the Summit.* Retrieved from http://www.un.org/esa/socdev/wssd/text-version/agreements/decparta.htm (Appendix B)

University of British Columbia. (2011). *Canada unprepared for an aging population.* Retrieved from https://news.ok.ubc.ca/2011/02/23/canada-unprepared-for-an-aging-population/ (11)

University of British Columbia. (2012a). *New poll shows Canadians want to make family a priority.* Retrieved from http://www.publicaffairs.ubc.ca/2012/02/07/new-poll-shows-canadians-want-to-make-family-a-priority/ (10)

University of British Columbia. (2012b). *Preventing dementia: New research by VCH and UBC shows the trajectory of cognitive decline can be altered in seniors at risk for dementia.* Retrieved from http://www.publicaffairs.ubc.ca/2012/04/23/preventing-dementia-new-research-by-vch-and-ubc-shows-the-trajectory-of-cognitive-decline-can-be-altered-in-seniors-at-risk-for-dementia/ (11)

University of Guelph, Human Rights & Equity Office. (2007). *Understanding racialization: Creating a racially equitable university.* Retrieved from http://www.uoguelph.ca/hre/hr/docs/UnderstandingRacialization.pdf (13)

Uppal, S., & LaRochelle-Côté, S. (2012). *Factors associated with voting.* Retrieved from Statistics Canada website: http://www.statcan.gc.ca/pub/75-001-x/2012001/article/11629-eng.pdf (11)

Urban Native Youth Association. (2003). Urban Native Youth Association, Submission. As cited in Standing Senate Committee on Aboriginal Peoples, *Urban aboriginal youth: An action plan for change: Final report: October 2003.* Retrieved from Parliament of Canada website: http://www.parl.gc.ca/Content/SEN/Committee/372/ABOR/24app-e.pdf (12)

Vancouver Coastal Health. (2012). *Home and community care: Caregiver support.* Retrieved from http://caregivers.vch.ca (7)

Vézina, M. (2012). *2011 general social survey: Overview of families in Canada—Being a parent in a stepfamily: A profile.* Retrieved from Statistics Canada website: http://www.statcan.gc.ca/pub/89-650-x/89-650-x2012002-eng.pdf (10)

Vézina, M., & Crompton, S. (2012). Volunteering in Canada. *Canadian Social Trends, 93,* 37–55. Retrieved from Statistics Canada website: http://www.statcan.gc.ca/pub/11-008-x/2012001/article/11638-eng.pdf (7)

Victims of Violence. (2011). *Research: Child physical abuse.* Retrieved August 2, 2012, from http://www.victimsofviolence.on.ca/rev2/index.php?option=com_content&task=view&id=328&Itemid=18 (10)

Victorian Order of Nurses (2011). *VON Canada's submission to the Honourable Blaine Higgs, Minister of Finance in preparation for the 2011–12 New Brunswick budget.* Retrieved from http://www.von.ca/en/resources/pdf/Pre-Budget_NB_03Feb11.pdf (7)

Vital Signs. (2013a). *Gap between rich and poor: Elderly (65 years of age and older) poverty rate.* Retrieved from http://www.vitalsignscanada.ca/en/research-90-gap-between-rich-and-poor-elderly-65-years (9)

Vital Signs. (2013b). *Housing: Percentage of households spending 30% or more of income on housing.* Retrieved from http://www.vitalsignscanada.ca/en/research-87-housing-percentage-of-households-spending (9)

Volpe, R., Cox, S., Goddard, L., & Tilleczek, K. (1997). *Children's rights in Canada: A review of provincial policies.* Retrieved from http://fcis.oise.utoronto.ca/~rvolpe/rights.html (10)

Voluntary Sector Initiative. (2002). *A code of good practice on policy dialogue: Building on an accord between the Government of Canada and the voluntary sector.* Retrieved from http://www.vsi-isbc.org/eng/policy/pdf/codes_policy.pdf (5)

Voluntary Sector Steering Group. (2002, Autumn). *Building a stronger voluntary sector: How the VSI is making a difference: Voluntary Sector Steering Group Report to the Voluntary Sector in Canada.* Retrieved from Voluntary Sector Initiative website: http://www.vsi-isbc.org/eng/about/pdf/building.pdf (5)

Volunteer Canada. (2006a). *The Canadian code for volunteer involvement.* Retrieved from http://volunteer.ca/content/canadian-code-volunteer-involvement-2012-edition (7)

Volunteer Canada. (2006b). *Volunteering and mandatory community service: Choice— incentive—coercion—obligation: Implications for volunteer program management.* Retrieved from http://volunteer.ca/content/volunteering-and-mandatory-community-service-exploring-theme (7)

Volunteer Canada. (2008). *Canada Volunteerism Initiative (CVI): Overview.* Retrieved September 18, 2008, from http://volunteer.ca/en/about/programming/pastprojects/cvi (7)

Volunteer Canada. (2010). *Bridging the gap: Enriching the volunteer experience to build a better future for our communities: Findings of a pan-Canadian research study: Full Report.* Retrieved from http://volunteer.ca/content/bridging-gap-report (7)

Voyer, J. P. (2005). A life-course approach to social policy. In *Exploring new approaches to social policy: Synthesis report* (pp. 4–7). Retrieved from Government of Canada Publications website: http://publications.gc.ca/collections/Collection/PH4-20-2005E.pdf (2)

Wallace, B., & Richards, T. (2008). *The rise and fall of welfare time limits in British Columbia.* Retrieved from Vancouver Island Public Interest Research Group website: http://www.vipirg.ca/wp-content/uploads/2011/08/welfare_time_limits_june_08.pdf (4)

Watson-Wright, W. (2001). *The role of evidence in the development of national policies to enhance children's well-being: A Canadian case story (1990–2001).* Retrieved January 26, 2009, from http://209.85.173.132/search?q=cache:aVLmENDVs4gJ:www.phac-aspc.gc.ca/ph-sp/implement/news_iuhpe-eng.ppt+%22policy+making+is+a%22&hl=en&ct=clnk&cd=10&gl=ca (2)

Weir, E. (2008). *Ontario's manufacturing crisis.* Retrieved from the Progressive Economics Forum website: http://www.progressive-economics.ca/2008/12/11/ontario-manufacturing-crisis/ (Appendix B)

Westhues, A. (2002). Social policy practice. In F. J. Turner (Ed.), *Social work practice: A Canadian perspective* (2nd ed., pp. 315–329). Toronto, Canada: Prentice Hall. (2)

Westhues, A. (2005). *Social work education in Canada: Inching toward the progressive.* Retrieved from http://rabida.uhu.es/dspace/bitstream/handle/10272/246/b15179825.pdf?sequence=1 (7)

Wharf, B. (2007) Introduction: People, politics, and child welfare. In L. T. Foster & B. Wharf, *People, politics, and child welfare in British Columbia* (pp. 1–9). Retrieved from http://www.ubcpress.ca/books/pdf/chapters/2007/PeoplePoliticsandChildWelfare.pdf (1)

White, D. (2003). *The rising profile of services and partnerships: What implications for analysing welfare state dynamics?* International Sociological Association Research Committee 19 on Poverty, Social Welfare and Social Policy. Retrieved August 25, 2008, from http://individual.utoronto.ca/RC19_2003/pdf/White_The_Rising_Profile_of_Services_and_Partnerships.pdf (5)

White, M. (2010). *Canada ratifies UN Convention on the Rights of Persons with Disabilities.* Retrieved from Foreign Affairs and International Trade Canada website: http://www.international.gc.ca/media/aff/news-communiques/2010/99.aspx?view=d (14)

Wilensky, H., & Lebeaux, C. (1965). *Industrial society and social welfare.* New York, NY: The Free Press. (1)

Wilkinson, R., & Pickett, K. (2010). *The spirit level: Why more equal societies almost always do better.* New York, NY: Bloomsbury Press. (4)

Will Dunning. (2009). *The Dunning report: Dimensions of core housing need in Canada* (2nd ed.). Retrieved from Co-operative Housing Federation of Canada website: http://www.chfcanada.coop/eng/pdf/DunningReport2009EnWeb.pdf (11)

Williams, A. P., Challis, D., Deber, R., Watkins, J., Kuluski, K., Lum, J. M., & Daub, D. (2009). Balancing institutional and community-based care: Why some older persons can age successfully at home while others require residential long-term care. *Healthcare Quarterly, 12*(2), 95–105. Retrieved from http://www.longwoods.com/content/20694 (6)

Williams, C. (2010). *Economic well-being.* Retrieved from Statistics Canada website: http://www.statcan.gc.ca/pub/89-503-x/2010001/article/11388-eng.pdf (9)

Willms, J.D. (2007). *Vulnerable children.* Retrieved from Investing in Children website: http://www.investinginchildren.on.ca/Communications/articles/vulnerable%20children.htm (10)

Wilson, D., & Macdonald, D. (2010). *The income gap between Aboriginal peoples and the rest of Canada.* Retrieved from Canadian Centre for Policy Alternatives website: http://www.policyalternatives.ca/sites/default/files/uploads/publications/reports/docs/Aboriginal%20Income%20Gap.pdf (12)

Wolfensberger, W. (1972). *The principle of normalization in human services.* Toronto, Canada: National Institute on Mental Retardation. (14)

World Health Organization. (2007). *Global age-friendly cities: A guide.* Retrieved from http://www.who.int/ageing/publications/Global_age_friendly_cities_Guide_English.pdf (11)

World Health Organization. (2009). *International classification of functioning, disability and health (ICF).* Retrieved from http://www.who.int/classifications/icf/en/ (14)

World Health Organization. (2012). *Ageing and life course: Elder abuse.* Retrieved from http://www.who.int/ageing/projects/elder_abuse/en/ (11)

Yalnizyan, A. (1994). Securing society: Creating Canadian social policy. In A. Yalnizyan, T. R. Ide, & A. J. Cordell (Eds.), *Shifting time: Social policy and the future of work* (pp. 17–71). Toronto, Canada: Between the Lines. (3)

Yan, M., & Chan, S. (2010). Are social workers ready to work with newcomers? *Canadian Social Work, 12*(2), 16–23. Retrieved from http://integration-net.ca:81/infocentre/2011/002e.pdf (7, 13)

York Region Violence Against Women Coordinating Committee. (2006). *York region woman abuse protocol: Best practice guidelines.* Retrieved from http://www.yrvawcc.ca/site/PDFs/VAW_Protocol_Master.pdf (2)

Zastrow, C. (2010). *Introduction to social work and social welfare: Empowering people* (10th ed.). Belmont, CA: Brooks/Cole. (8, 11)

Zelenev, S. (2008). *Preventing abuse of older persons: Progress in implementing the Madrid international plan of action on ageing.* Retrieved from Canadian Network for Prevention of Elder Abuse website: http://www.cnpea.ca/frequently_asked_questions_files/Zelenev%20final%20v.%20full%20text.pdf (11)

INDEX

Note: **Bold** page numbers refer to defined terms.

Knowledge
    preparing for change and building,
      216–17
    social work, 180–81
Knowledge-based economy, 223

Labour market restructuring, **447**, 450
Labour movement, 71–72
Labour strikes, 230
Laissez-faire, 20
Language Instruction for Newcomers to
    Canada (LINC), 376
Legislation (legislative process), 50–52
Lenihan, Don, 44
Less eligibility, principle of, **67**
Level of need or functioning, 303
Liberal government, budget surpluses,
    106
Liberalism, **21–22**
Liberal Party, 18 service sectors and, 122
Liberals, 95
Liberal Task Force on Seniors, 326
Life-course lens, **57**
Life events indicators, 5
Life expectancy, increased, 299
LINKages Society of Alberta, 314
Logic model, **54–55**
London (Ontario), as Global Age-
    Friendly Community, 308
Lone-parent families, **280–81**
Longitudinal surveys, **35**
Low-income cut-offs (LICOs), 239–41,
    240
Low-income measure (LIM), 239–40

Macdonald Commission (Royal
    Commission on the Economic
    Union and Development
    Prospects for Canada), 93
Macro level, change at (community
    change), **207**, 222–32
    community development model,
      224–26
    community practice, 232
    models of, 223–31

    social action model, 224, 229–31
    social planning model, 224, 228–29
Macro level of practice, 181
Mainstream 1992 (report), 409
Mainstream approaches to helping
    Aboriginal peoples, **344**
Management level of an agency, 160
Mandated services, **53**, 125
Mandatory volunteers (voluntolds),
    191–92
Manitoba, 75, 87, 135, 256, 361, 380
    Civil Service Commission, 219
Manitoba Society of Seniors, 325
Manufacturing jobs, 448
Marginalized groups, **9**
Market-based associations, 144
Market basket measure (MBM), 240
Marsh, Leonard, 79–81
Marsh Report (*Report on Social Security
    for Canada*), 79–81
Martin, Paul, 96, 340
Maslow, Abraham, 7, 8
Means test, **75**
Mental health, **274**
    of children and youth, 274–76
    of seniors, 311–12
Mental Health Commission of Canada,
    276, 277
Mental health disorder, **274**
Mental Patients Society, 195
Method of change, 207
Métis, **331**. *See also* Aboriginal
    peoples
Mezzo level of practice, 181
Mezzo level of society, change at, **207**,
    215–22
    building knowledge, 216–17
    committing to, 217–18
    developing a vision, 216
    evaluating change, 220–21
    identifying the need for change,
      215–16
    implementing, 218
    individual change, 218–20
    preparing for, 216–18